Israel

a travel survival kit

Neil Tilbury

Israel – a travel survival kit

2nd edition

Published by
Lonely Planet Publications
Head Office: PO Box 617, Hawthorn, Vic 3122, Australia
Branches: PO Box 2001A, Berkeley, CA 94702, USA and London, UK

Printed by
Colorcraft Ltd, Hong Kong

Photographs by
Richard Everist (RE)
Neil Tilbury (NT)
Tony Wheeler (TW)

Front cover: Gulf of Eilat, Borodulin, The Image Bank
Back cover: Jerusalem's Old City from the Mount of Olives, Neil Tilbury

First Published
August 1989

This Edition
November 1992

National Library of Australia Cataloguing in Publication Data

Tilbury, Neil.
  Israel – a travel survival kit.

  2nd ed.
  Includes index.
  ISBN 0 86442 128 1.

  1. Israel – Guidebooks. I. Title. (Series: Lonely Planet travel survival kit).

915.6940454

text & maps © Lonely Planet 1992
photos © photographers as indicated 1992

Neil Tilbury

Neil Tilbury was born in Portsmouth, England, where he studied hotel management. Moving up to London, he spent a few years working in the hotel and wine trades before travelling to the USA via Europe, the Middle East, Asia and Australia. One of the countries that he visited was Israel, and he returned there to write this guide. On completion of the first edition, he went to India to update Lonely Planet's *Kashmir, Ladakh & Zanskar – a travel survival kit*. Neil now lives in New York, where he also works for EastQuest, a travel company specialising in Asia.

Acknowledgements

Extra special thanks again to Ilan Levy for his invaluable help, to David Shapiro and family for terrific hospitality and input, and to Micha Herzberg.

In New York, thanks to Christopher Ross Leong for technical assistance and Jet Toy for the alarm clocks.

A personal thanks to all those readers who took the time to write having picked up the first edition. In particular, the following readers' comments were especially constructive and helpful: Simon & Lorraine Flack, Cathy Keenan, Natalie & Jonathan Lourie, Kristin Miller, John Phillips, Petra Poorter, Richard Rebhun, Benny Shanon, R L Stern (Mrs), David Strasburg, Judith Weil, and a mother (no name but you mention a daughter Lisa).

Special thanks to all involved at Lonely Planet for their hard work in putting this edition together and getting it out to the bookshops.

From the Publisher

Jeff Williams edited this 2nd edition, and was assisted in the early stages by Jenny Missen. It was carefully proofed by Miriam Cannell and Sandra Smythe was responsible for updating the maps, layout, cover design and many of the illustrations.

Thanks also to Margaret Jung and Valerie Tellini for their illustrations.

Warning & Request

Things change – prices go up, schedules change, good places go bad and bad places go bankrupt – nothing stays the same. So if you find things better or worse, recently opened or long since closed, please write and tell us and help make the next edition better.

Your letters will be used to help update future editions and, where possible, important changes will also be included in a Stop Press section in reprints.

We greatly appreciate all information that is sent to us by travellers. Back at Lonely Planet we employ a hard-working readers' letters team to sort through the many letters we receive. The best ones will be rewarded with a free copy of the next edition or another Lonely Planet guide if you prefer. We give away lots of books, but, unfortunately, not every letter/postcard receives one.

Thanks

Thanks must go to the travellers who used the 1st edition of this book and wrote to Lonely Planet with information, comments and suggestions:

H Abraham (AUS), Sharon & Arnon Amid (Isr), Sister Anna (Isr), Olle Backland (NL), Mordechai Beliuco (Isr), Diane Brown (UK), Joss Buchanan (UK), Adrian Bunting (UK), Elliot Cohen (Isr), Danny Connolly, Yigal Dayan (Isr), Rudy Devriendt (Isr), Angela Dykes (USA), Randall Edwards (USA), Simon & Lorraine Flack (UK), Andrew Florides (UK), Duncan Forbes (UK), J Andrew Garratt (USA), Merav Gilai, Craig Grodman (USA), Catlin Hankey (UK), Derek Hill (UK), Shuichi Kanazawa (J), Frances Katzengold (Isr), Cathy Keenan (UK), Ruthli Kemmerer (USA), David Khavia (Isr), T Kristal (Isr), Patrick Lenz (CH), Dora Levi-Boutelje (NL), Ronald Levy (Isr), Joseph Levy (Isr), Natalie & Jonathan Lourie (Isr), Bruce Mackie (AUS), Anne McClaran, Mickey Mestet (Isr), Dov Midalia (AUS), Kristin Miller (USA), Chris Morey (UK), John Phillips (UK), Petra Poorter (Isr), Richard Rebhun (USA), Ingrid Remijn (NL), Brett Robson (AUS), Charlie Savenor (USA), Mario Sbordone (USA), Anne Schmalisch (D), Benny Shanon (Isr), Lee Sharrocks (UK), Ilana Shoket (Isr), Louis B Silk (USA), Susan Spigelman (USA), Ellen Steinberg (USA), R L Stern (UK), David Strasburg (Isr), H Tillis (UK), Ineke Von Bronswijk (NL), Micki Vosko (C), Judith Weil (Isr), Aeleen Wiltshire (NZ), and a mother (no name given but a daughter Lisa is mentioned)

Contents

Map Legend

BOUNDARIES

.... International Boundary
.... Internal Boundary
.... National Park or Reserve
.... The Equator
.... The Tropics

SYMBOLS

◉ NEW DELHI .... National Capital
● BOMBAY .... Provincial or State Capital
● Pune .... Major Town
• Barsi .... Minor Town
■ .... Places to Stay
▼ .... Places to Eat
≜ .... Post Office
✈ .... Airport
i .... Tourist Information
● .... Bus Station or Terminal
66 .... Highway Route Number
♜♱♰ ...... Mosque, Church, Cathedral
∴ .... Temple or Ruin
✛ .... Hospital
※ .... Lookout
Å .... Camping Area
⊓ .... Picnic Area
⌂ .... Hut or Chalet
▲ .... Mountain or Hill
.... Railway Station
.... Road Bridge
.... Railway Bridge
.... Road Tunnel
.... Railway Tunnel
.... Escarpment or Cliff
.... Pass
.... Ancient or Historic Wall

ROUTES

.... Major Road or Highway
.... Unsealed Major Road
.... Sealed Road
..... Unsealed Road or Track
.... City Street
.... Railway
.... Subway
.... Walking Track
.... Ferry Route
.... Cable Car or Chair Lift

HYDROGRAPHIC FEATURES

.... River or Creek
.... Intermittent Stream
.... Lake, Intermittent Lake
.... Coast Line
.... Spring
.... Waterfall
.... Swamp
.... Salt Lake or Reef
.... Glacier

OTHER FEATURES

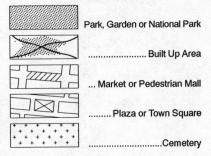

Park, Garden or National Park
.... Built Up Area
... Market or Pedestrian Mall
.... Plaza or Town Square
.... Cemetery

Note: not all symbols displayed above appear in this book

Introduction

One of the golden rules for successful travelling is to avoid discussing religion and politics. In Israel, however, they collide inseparably, both with each other and with virtually everything else. This is the Holy Land, and this is Palestine. Trying not to preach, condemn or promote, the broad aim of this guide is to encourage you to go and see Israel for yourself, by providing an honest and accurate account of what you will find here.

Variety and interest are two of the main ingredients required of a country to justify a visit, and Israel has to be one of the most diverse and fascinating places in the world. A land of incredible contrasts, it offers a wealth of changing landscapes, different climates, culture, history and, of course, religion. What makes Israel even more remarkable is its tiny size, perhaps best appreciated by comparing it to the US state of New Jersey or to Belgium, which are both slightly larger, or to Tasmania, which is over twice as large. Despite being so small, Israel contains almost every type of geographical terrain: mountains, sub-tropical valleys, fertile farmland, and deserts, with a richly varied flora & fauna that makes it a paradise for nature lovers.

Israel is the Jewish Promised Land, this is where the Prophet Mohammed stopped on his Night Journey and ascended to Heaven, and this is the land of Jesus. Jewish, Muslim and Christian pilgrims are drawn here by the conviction that 'this is where it happened'. These conflicting beliefs, combined with Israel's strategic location, have made this one of the most hotly disputed areas in the world. Major wars have raged here throughout the centuries: the Israelites and Canaanites, the Jews and Romans, the Muslims and Crusaders, the Turks and British, and now the Israelis and the Palestinians.

In its PR campaigns, Israel's Ministry of Tourism does an excellent job of emphasising the sandy beaches, ancient cities and biblical sites, with no mention of the real-life

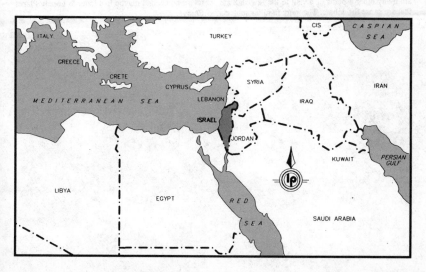

situation. As a result, many people enjoy themselves here without really considering local politics. Most of you, however, will realise that this is not simply a beautiful country full of friendly English-speaking people everywhere you go. Whilst the Palestine problem is tragically real and should not be minimised or ignored, it should also not deter you from making a visit here. I have tried to illustrate the various sensitivities of the locals to enable you to avoid any major problems.

With so much to see and do, Israel means different things to different people. Read on to discover what you can make of it all.

Matters of Opinion – Footnote

Few places inspire such strongly held and opposing points of view as Israel. This was perfectly illustrated by two readers' letters that arrived in the mail the very same day.

'Congratulations on producing the most accurate, readable, practical and finely detailed guide book I have used in 20 years' said one. The other wrote 'I'm thinking how I can best use your book *Israel – a travel survival kit*. I decided I can either give it to the Museum of the Potential Holocaust in Jerusalem or I can burn it'.

In addition to the merits of this publication, there are many other aspects of a visit to the Jewish State that are cause for debate. The more familiar subjects include the acceptability of the terms Israel, Palestine, and Occupied Territories; the justification of violence to pursue a political agenda; the route taken by Jesus to the site of His crucifixion and the location of His tomb; deciding whether a critical comment is balanced or anti-Semitic/anti-Arab; the credibility of either Israeli or Palestinian-sponsored peace plans; the relative safety of Arab areas like Jerusalem's Old City and Hebron; the Middle East policies of the USA and other Western nations; and the question of civil rights.

Rarely mentioned in print but frequently discussed by travellers are such matters as comparing the hospitality received from Israelis versus Palestinians; the number of archaeological sites, places of worship and museums you can visit before saying 'enough already!'; the validity of Israel's claims to have made the desert bloom; the effectiveness of the intifada's general strikes; the question of bias in the presentation of history in local museums; the role of the Christian hierarchy in Israeli politics and its administration of the holy sites; the cost, variety and quality of eating out here; the level of rudeness experienced in Israel as compared to elsewhere; whether or not Masada is worth the price of admission and a ticket for the cablecar ride; the necessity for some of those countless questions you face from airport security and their response to certain answers you give them when trying to board a plane to/from Ben-Gurion Airport; and the desire to return for another visit.

These are just some of the subjects you may well find yourself dealing with 'on the road', on your return home, and maybe in a letter to Lonely Planet. Enjoy!

Facts about the Country

HISTORY

The human history of the land known today as Israel, or Palestine, goes back over 500,000 years. Due to its geographical position between Africa and Asia and on the edge of Europe, several nations have continuously moved back and forth across it, making that history somewhat complicated. Going back so far in time, getting the exact year is a matter of dispute, let alone agreeing on who descended from whom in sufficient numbers to justify today's hereditary claims. Hopefully, this outline will give you a basic picture of the land's history and encourage you to find out more for yourself. One further source of information readily available is the Bible and I have included some of the main references.

Stone Age (600,000-4000 BC)

This period is dated by part of a human skeleton found in Palestine. Then, the population lived by the numerous rivers and lakes, and while Europe suffered the Ice Age, wet and dry ages occurred here. Nomads began to settle and develop new ways of life, with animal domestication and the cultivation of crops, from which evolved new skills and social organisations.

Notable remains of the Stone Age can be seen in En Avdat (in the Negev), Tel es-Sultan (Jericho) and Wadi Khareitun (near Bethlehem).

Copper & Bronze Ages (4000-1200 BC)

Villages had begun to replace temporary camps, and these earliest settlements were usually near springs, due to the drier climate caused by the recession of the ice caps. The urban environment played a large part in the development of copper and bronze-making skills, but compared to other areas nearby, evolution was slow.

In Egypt and Mesopotamia, empires had grown while what was to become known as Canaan was still a disjointed land.

In about 1800 BC when Abraham led a group of nomads, the Israelites, from Mesopotamia into the mountains of Canaan, the Egyptians had already held the coastal plain for several centuries. The Israelites stayed until famine forced them to move to Egypt. They remained there until around 1250 BC when Moses led the exodus. The Bible's Old Testament Books of Genesis, Exodus, Leviticus and Deuteronomy include the story of Abraham, the move to Egypt, and the exodus.

Moses failed to make it to the Promised Land but, led by Joshua, the rest of the Israelites did. It is almost certain that they did not conquer the whole land, but only took most of the mountains from the Canaanites, while the Philistines from Crete took the coastal plain. The Old Testament Book of Joshua relates to this, and the Books of Judges and Ruth deal with the social state of the land and foreign invasion attempts.

Notable remains of the Bronze Age can be seen in Arad, Jerusalem (City of David) and Megiddo. The Palestinian Arabs believe that their ancestry derives from an assimilation of the Canaanite tribes, which came from the Arab Peninsula around 3500 BC, with the Philistines.

Iron Age (1200-586 BC)

The Philistines and the Canaanites developed the use of iron and eventually controlled more of the land. This forced the Israelites to change from their loose tribal system to a centralised monarchy. Their first king was Saul (circa 1023-1004 BC), whose capital was Gev'a.

His adopted son and successor, David (circa 1004-965 BC), conquered Jerusalem, making it his capital and installing there the Ark of the Covenant, a chest believed to contain the stone tablets on which the Ten Commandments were written. The Old Testament Book of Samuel deals with Saul and David.

Israel (Including the Occupied Territories)

0   25   50 km

King Solomon (circa 965-928 BC) built on his father's success and is noted for his literary skills. He is believed to have written the Books of Proverbs, Ecclesiastes and the Song of Songs. Solomon's reign is often referred to as Israel's Golden Era. In approximately 950 BC the First Temple was built in Jerusalem.

After Solomon's death the kingdom split in two, becoming Israel and Judah. Around 721 BC, Assyria (today Kurdistan in northern Iraq) invaded and conquered Israel and its people were scattered, becoming the Ten Lost Tribes. Judah was conquered by Babylonia about 586 BC and Jerusalem, with the First Temple, was destroyed. The Old Testament Book of Ezekiel deals with these events. Notable remains of the Iron Age can be seen in Beersheba, Jerusalem (City of David, Jewish Quarter, Kidron Valley) and Megiddo.

Persian Period (538-322 BC)

The people of Judah were exiled to Babylonia but were permitted to return to their homeland in 538 BC by Cyrus, King of Persia, who had conquered Babylonia the year before. In a spiritual revival, Jerusalem and the Temple were rebuilt. The Old Testament Book of Zachariah deals with visions of Jerusalem's reconstruction, while the Books of Esther and Ezra deal with the Jews' exile and their deliverance, and Ezra and Nehemiah deal with the reconstruction of Jerusalem and the Temple.

Hellenistic & Hasmonean Periods (332-63 BC)

The end of the Persian Empire came in 331 BC with Alexander the Great's legendary successes. When he died about eight years later, his short-lived empire was carved up by his generals. Ptolemy and Seleucus fought each other over Palestine and eventually the Seleucids took control, uniting it with the north in 200 BC.

Since the Exile, the High Priest had assumed many of the duties previously undertaken by the king. The Seleucids needed to control this office to ensure their dominance, but the extent of their influence on religion sparked off a revolt led by the three Maccabaean brothers in 167 BC. The fight, initially for religious freedom, became a bid for political independence.

The Maccabees started the Hasmonean dynasty, which extended Jewish dominance to the whole of Palestine, the Golan, and the east bank of Jordan – another Golden Era, which is perhaps comparable to David's and Solomon's empire. Notable remains of the Hellenistic Period can be seen in Jerusalem (Citadel, City of David, St Anne's) and Nablus.

Roman Period (63 BC-324 AD)

Palestine became a Roman province because internal strife had reduced its effectiveness as a buffer against the Romans' enemies, but Herod the Great was given autonomy due to his commitment to the Roman Empire and his proven authority. The Romans took control around 6 AD, as after Herod's death his sons proved to be less able rulers.

Jesus of Nazareth's ministry (circa 27-30 AD) was the notable factor in an intense religious and political upheaval which led to the First Revolt about 66 AD. After a prolonged siege of Jerusalem in 70 AD, the Roman General Titus breached the city wall and destroyed the Temple. The Temple's destruction made sacrificial worship impossible, and a new theory was developed: that the scattered Jewish community could only be held together by adherence to a common law. Rabbi Yohanan Ben Zakkai re-established the supreme legislative judicial body, the Sanhedrin, at Yavne; and elsewhere, for example in Tiberias, centres of learning sprang up. Over the next several centuries, the Talmud was recorded – the vast body of the Oral Law relating to all aspects of Jewish life. Following the Temple's destruction, many Jews were sold into slavery or exiled abroad. Their descendants became the Diaspora, the Jewish communities dispersed worldwide.

Jerusalem remained central, but the Emperor Hadrian decided to destroy it completely as it was a focus of renewed

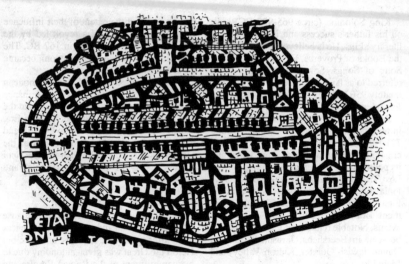

Madaba map from Byzantine Period

nationalist aspirations. This provoked the Second Revolt (132-135 AD), led by Bar Kochba. He ruled briefly, but the Romans eventually defeated him and Aelia Capitolina was built on the now levelled ruins of Jerusalem. Jews were barred from the new city and moved north to Galilee and the Golan.

Notable remains of the Roman Period can be seen in Beit She'arim, Caesarea, Gamla, Hebron, Herodian (near Bethlehem), Jerusalem (Citadel, Damascus Gate, Ecce Homo Arch, St Anne's, Temple Mount), Katzrin, Mamshit (Negev), Masada, Qumran and Solomon's Pools (between Bethlehem and Hebron).

Byzantine Period (324-640 AD)
This period marked the transfer of the Roman Empire's capital from Rome to Byzantium, renamed Constantinople in 330 AD. More importantly, in 331 AD Emperor Constantine, a recent convert, legalised Christianity and encouraged its development. Due to his policies and the subsequent consecration of sites associated with Christ's

life by the churches, interest in the Holy Places was massive. Pilgrims were attracted to the Holy Land and their arrival stimulated a wide range of developments, such as the building of numerous churches and monasteries, and urban expansion. Jerusalem, for example, grew to the size it had been under Herod the Great.

Theological controversy dominated this period, but there were two serious violent episodes: the Samaritan revolt in 529 AD and the Persian invasion in 614 AD, which resulted in the sacking of Jerusalem.

Notable remains of the Byzantine Period can be observed in Avdat, Bethlehem, Capernaum and Hammat Gader, Jerusalem (Bethany, Dominus Flevit, Holy Sepulchre, St Anne's, Haram esh-Sharif), Latrun, Mar Saba (near Bethlehem), Mamshit and Mount Gerizim.

Early Arab Period (640-1099 AD)
The new faith of Islam, preached by Mohammed (570-632 AD), inspired the Arab invasion which ended with the surrender of Jerusalem in 638 AD. The city became a

centre of pilgrimage due to its holy status for Christians under the Umayyad, Abbasid and Fatamid dynasties. In 1009 churches were destroyed in a wave of brutal persecution under Caliph Hakim. In 1071 Jerusalem was captured by the Seljuk Turks, who refused to co-operate with the continuing stream of Christian pilgrims. The dispute resulted in Pope Urban II's call in 1095 for a crusade to liberate the Holy Places.

Notable remains of the Arab Period can be seen in Jerusalem (the Dome of the Rock and excavations around the Haram esh-Sharif) and Jericho.

Crusader Period (1099-1291)

Although the more flexible Fatamids managed to retake Jerusalem in early 1099, the Crusaders were already on their way and determined to rid the Holy Land of Islam. They occupied Jerusalem on 15 June 1099 and massacred all the Muslim inhabitants. Episodes of such Christian fanaticism are thought by many to have been a major cause of the inflexibility of Islam. Jewish inhabitants were also massacred on a large scale by the Crusaders.

The reign of the first Crusader king, Baldwin I (1100-1118), saw the introduction of the feudal system. This gave Palestine its most effective administration so far, taking advantage of the alms flowing in from Europe.

In 1187 Saladin (Salah ed-Din) defeated the Crusaders at the Horns of Hattin. Richard I (the Lionheart) of England led the unsuccessful Third Crusade in 1188. The Fourth to Eighth Crusades followed but recovered only some of the former territories. The end of the Crusades came with the fall of Akko in 1291 to the Bahri Mamelukes. They had already toppled Saladin's Ayyubid dynasty.

Notable remains of the Crusader period can be seen in Abu Gosh, Akko, Belvoir, Caesarea, Hebron, Jerusalem (Bethany, Cathedral of St James, Holy Sepulchre, St Anne's, Virgin's Tomb), Latrun and Nimrod.

Mameluke Period (1250-1517)

Palestine became a backwater due to the Mamelukes being preoccupied with a power struggle in Egypt and their defence of Syria against Mongol attacks. Jerusalem attracted pilgrims and scholars, and also renewed Jewish settlement. In 1492 Jews were expelled from Spain and some refugees arrived in Palestine.

Notable remains of the Mameluke Period can be seen in Jerusalem (Citadel, Haram esh-Sharif and the Muslim Quarter).

Ottoman Period (1517-1918)

Sultan Salim I led the Ottoman Turks to victory against the Mamelukes in 1517. They had taken Constantinople in 1453 and Egypt joined Palestine to extend their empire into Africa. Their second sultan, Suleiman the Magnificent, is credited with the rebuilding of Jerusalem's city walls.

These two effective administrators were followed by apparently less worthy leaders, who were mostly occupied by the task of containing power struggles with Egyptian pashas. Again Palestine was relegated in terms of priority, and was under the control of pashas best remembered for their corrupt and violent brand of officialdom.

The country languished and local chieftains and Bedouin took advantage of the lack of law and order, carving out independent domains. Jews and Christians, particularly in Galilee, were subjected to harsh treatment. Despite this, the end of the 17th century saw an increase in Jewish immigration, due to persecution in the Diaspora. This continued slowly through the 18th century, with centres of Hasidism being set up in Safed and Tiberias by Jews from Poland and Lithuania.

The Ottoman Empire was showing signs of weakness, and the Jews, Europe and the US all took note and jockeyed for position in the years to come – and they are still at it. In 1838 the first regular British consulate was opened in Jerusalem and became a defender of Jewish and Druze elements in Syria and Palestine. Evangelistic activities, ostensibly involving the custody of the holy shrines, often looked suspiciously like the manoeuvring of international politics. The Suez Canal, opened in 1869, speeded the rebirth of the area as a strategic crossroads. While the leading nations of the world were eyeing Palestine, so were some of the dispersed Jews, and Jewish nationalism was being revived.

Contact between the Jews in Palestine and the Diaspora had continued over the centuries, with the hope that some day all Jews would be able to meet in the Holy Land – a major part of their religious observance.

In 1839, in London, the Jewish philanthropist Sir Moses Montefiore had proposed the establishment of a Jewish state, and he won some support from influential Christians in Europe. This perhaps set the stage for the eventual founding of political Zionism and the modern State of Israel.

Zionism & Arab Nationalism

The name Zionism is derived from the word Zion, the traditional synonym for Jerusalem and Israel.

In Palestine, the revival of Jewish nationalism began in 1878 with the founding of Petah Tiqwa, the first Jewish colony, by a group of native Jews from Jerusalem. The arrival of refugees in 1882 from the Russian pogroms (anti-Jewish riots and killings) and others from Rumania and Yemen expanded the movement. Many were members of the Love of Zion movement. They tended to join existing agricultural villages, or established new ones such as Rishon le Zion, Zichron Ya'acov and Rosh Pinna. The new arrivals were later termed the First Aliyah (Ascent to the Land).

In 1894, Austrian journalist Theodor Herzl published *The Jewish State*, a book outlining his idea that the only solution to Jewish persecution would be a Jewish state in Palestine. In 1897 the World Zionist Organisation (WZO) was founded at the First Zionist Conference, convened by Herzl in Basle, Switzerland.

In 1901 the Jewish National Fund (JNF) was founded to purchase land in Palestine for the Zionists. In its formative years, much of the JNF's work was land reclamation and reafforestation. Once a land covered in

forest, Palestine had been gradually stripped of most of its trees by successive rulers over the centuries. When the Zionists arrived in Palestine, much of the land was, in their opinion, suffering from neglect and exploitation. This is strongly disputed by critics who say that the Zionists exaggerated the conditions in Palestine to win support for their cause.

In 1903 came Britain's rejected offer to the WZO to found the Jewish state in Uganda. Also rejected were sites in Argentina, Cyprus and the Congo. With the swift formation of the WZO and the JNF came a well-organised programme to arrange the return of the Jews to Palestine. In 1904 came the Second Aliyah, mainly Jews escaping pogroms in Russia and Poland. Degania, the first kibbutz, was founded on the shore of the Sea of Galilee in 1909. Tel Aviv, the first modern Jewish city, was established north of Jaffa the same year.

During WW I, Britain and the Allies sought support from the Arabs and Jews to topple the Ottoman Empire. The future of Palestine was a most sensitive subject because of its spiritual and strategic significance.

In 1916 a secret British-French agreement provided for the recognition of an independent Arab state or a confederation of Arab states, but with an international administration for Palestine to be decided after discussions with the other Allies and the Sherif of Mecca. The latter acted as the Arabs' representative, even though most were not under his political authority. This was due to his spiritual status as keeper of Islam's most holy cities. He led the Arab revolt against the Turks and the British Government assured him of their support in his plans for Arab independence.

This assurance came principally through the McMahon Letters (Sir Henry McMahon being the British High Commissioner in Egypt). The British later claimed that Palestine was excluded from such plans by virtue of subsequent discussions, but the Sherif strongly disagreed.

This difference of views over the exact

meaning of the British Government communications was the first of many which are a major factor in the Palestine 'problem'.

While the British and French Governments said one thing to the Arabs and did another, the WZO made it clear that they were aiming for the creation of a Jewish state in Palestine. They pressed the British Government for support, inspiring the Balfour Declaration in 1917. A statement of policy by the Foreign Secretary in a letter to Lord Rothschild, it was directed at the WZO, stated that the British Government:

...viewed with favour the establishment of a national home for the Jewish people, and will use their best endeavours to facilitate the achievement of this object, it being clearly understood that nothing shall be done which may prejudice the civil and religious rights of existing non-Jewish communities in Palestine or the rights and political status enjoyed by Jews in any other country.

So ambiguous is the Balfour Declaration that both Jews and Arabs have used it to back their claims. Zionists say that it shows British support for the Jewish state. Arabs say that the civil and religious rights of existing non-Jewish communities have definitely been prejudiced by the establishment of Israel, and that, anyway, the establishment of a national home for the Jewish people never implied the sovereign state that Zionists had always envisaged.

Despite the propaganda value that both Zionists and Arabs place on British Government statements, many would say that as Britain had no sovereign rights over Palestine, such statements should never have been made in the first place.

British Mandate (1919-1948)

British policy over Palestine was far from consistent. Basically, the British Government needed both Arab and Jewish support in WW I. It had its eye on the Arab oilfields but did not appear to know how far its support of the Arabs should go. This led to attempts to appease both parties, and today's considerable confusion.

Shortly after the Balfour Declaration came the Allied victory in WW I. The British now ruled Palestine under the Mandate system. The League of Nations, a forerunner of the United Nations, devised the system to place certain territories under the 'tutelage...of advanced nations' until such time as those same 'advanced nations' decided that the territories were ready for political self-determination.

In 1919, a Jewish delegation to the Peace Conference in Paris was led by Dr Chaim Weizmann. He met with Emir Feisal and they reached an agreement, of sorts, recognising the aspirations of both Arabs and Jews in Palestine. Zionists often refer to it as an important stage of the negotiations, but to the Arabs, the agreement had always been conditional on their independence and so never stood a chance unless that was granted.

While the Allies were dividing up the spoils of their victory in WW I, the Third Aliyah began. Between 1919 and 1928 the Jewish population of Palestine almost tripled. The first wave (till 1923) was spearheaded by young members of the Hehalutz (Pioneer) movement from Russia and Poland who joined the men of the Second Aliyah to form the Histradrut, the General Federation of Jewish Labour, and the Haganah, the illegal Jewish resistance army.

The Fourth Aliyah (1924-28) brought Jews from a mainly different social background: middle-class shopkeepers and artisans, mostly from Poland where economic restrictions were being applied.

In 1921 Feisal's brother, Emir Abdullah, invaded an area east of the Jordan River that was covered by the British Mandate, and was recognised as its ruler by the League of Nations. It was renamed Transjordan, later to become the Hashemite Kingdom of Jordan after independence in 1946.

While trying to appease the WZO, representing the Jews, the British authorities in Palestine dealt with Haj Amin, Mufti of Jerusalem and head of the Supreme Muslim Council, representing the Arabs.

He enjoys a reputation probably second only to Adolf Hitler for his personal and political integrity and performance. He was jailed for instigating attacks on Jews praying at the Western Wall in Jerusalem, but was later released. He then started a programme of terror and intimidation against his Arab political opponents as well as continuing his campaign of hatred and violence against the Jews. His rise to power in Palestine is said to have been a turning point in the course of Jewish-Arab relations. He is also credited with formulating the Arab's uncompromising hostility to the Jewish state, which perhaps led to the poor public relations image from which the Arabs now suffer.

Arab acts of violence against the Jews began in earnest in 1920. The British authorities were regularly accused by the Jews of doing little to stop them. The Jews retaliated: the Haganah fortified Jewish communities and counterattacked.

The increase in this violence seemed to be a major reason behind the British Government's restrictions on Jewish immigration. There were also fears of an unappeased Arab world backing Germany in the by now imminent WW II.

In 1929 the Jewish community of Hebron was massacred by Arab extremists, the height of the violence so far. The Irgun Zvai Leumi, a Jewish underground organisation, was founded by extreme right-wing Zionists, led by Ze'ev Jabotinsky and his assistant Menachem Begin.

Due to Nazi persecution of European Jews, the Fifth Aliyah in 1933 was of the highest importance to the events in Palestine. The largest number of Jews so far made their way to Palestine, refugees from the Holocaust. It triggered off more Arab attacks against the Jewish community. The British authorities eventually arrested the extremist Arab leaders but the Mufti escaped, joining Hitler in Berlin.

Amazingly perhaps, in the face of constant harassment from the British, Jews decided to join British forces and fight against Germany in WW II as they had in WW I. They felt that the need to halt the Holocaust overruled the struggle for a Jewish state, which was therefore partially abandoned.

Not totally, though. In 1942, a conference of American Zionists adopted the Biltmore Program, thus paving the way for greater involvement of the USA in the Palestine 'problem'. This demanded unlimited Jewish immigration into Palestine and the establishment of a Jewish state. The Zionists correctly forecast that after WW II, Britain's role in world affairs would be greatly reduced and that the USA would become the West's major power.

As the extent of the Holocaust was realised, the Jews in Palestine embarked on a national rescue effort, although they felt hampered by the Allies', and particularly Britain's, lack of enthusiasm for their cause.

The British did not want Jews flooding into Palestine and exacerbating the already tense racial situation. Their policy was to stop immigration, thus creating the ironic situation of concentration camp refugees being turned away from Palestine by the British who had helped liberate them. This resulted in Aliyah Bet, the Jews' illegal immigration programme.

Critics claim that there were other areas of the world that the refugees could and should have gone to which did not have the powderkeg environment of Palestine. The USA is mentioned as a country which had plenty of room for refugees, yet only allowed limited numbers to immigrate, while condemning the British authorities for not letting enough into Palestine.

In addition to the programme of Aliyah Bet, the Palestinian Jews determined to rid the country of British rule using a programme of terrorism. The Haganah and the independent Irgun and Lohamei Herut Israel all engaged in violent acts, including bomb attacks and kidnappings.

In one infamous incident the Irgun, led by Menachem Begin, hanged two British Army sergeants in retaliation for Jews being executed by the authorities for terrorist activities.

It has been argued that today's ferocious criticism of Arab terrorism by Israelis is somewhat hypocritical after they engaged in military tactics against the British that involved civilian casualties.

Partition & the End of the British Mandate

In 1947 the UN voted to partition Palestine into an Arab state and a Jewish state with an internationalised Jerusalem. Partition was first mooted in 1937 when a British Government White Paper had proposed such a plan. It had been rejected by both the WZO and the Arabs. The Macdonald White Paper announced the British Government's decision to rescind the partition plan, including the comment that the Balfour Declaration 'could not have intended that Palestine be converted into a Jewish state against the will

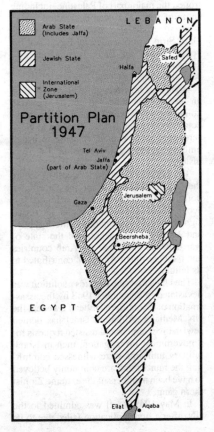

Partition Plan 1947

Arab State (Includes Jaffa)

Jewish State

International Zone (Jerusalem)

of the Arab population of the country'. The White Paper also announced that Palestine would become independent in 1949 as a unified state in which both Jews and Arabs would share in government.

After this, the Zionists really started to build political support in the USA and launched their terrorist programme against the British. Eventually the situation, with its complexities seemingly impossible to solve, caused Britain to prepare for the termination of its Mandate and to hand Palestine and its problems over to the UN. With WW II over, Palestine was the only area where British forces were still engaged in armed combat. On 18 February 1947 the British Government made the following announcement:

His Majesty's Government have...been faced with an irreconcilable conflict of principles. There are in Palestine about 200,000 Arabs and 600,000 Jews. For the Jews, the essential point of principle is the creation of a sovereign Jewish State. For the Arabs, the essential point of principle is to resist to the last the establishment of Jewish sovereignty in any part of Palestine.

...It is in these circumstances that we have decided that we are unable to accept the scheme put forward either by the Arabs or by the Jews, or to impose ourselves a solution of our own. We have, therefore, reached the conclusion that the only course now open to us is to submit the problem to the judgement of the United Nations.

The British had called for a special session of the UN General Assembly to deal with Palestine's future. The Arab delegation's first step was to unsuccessfully request the termination of the Mandate and the declaration of Palestine's independence.

The UN Special Committee on Palestine (UNSCOP) visited the area. It also visited refugee camps in Germany and Austria, which critics claim was unnecessary, as the plight of European Jewry was a subject of world concern and not a facet of the Palestine issue. There have been accusations of Zionist propaganda during these visits, using concentration camp survivors primed to demand refuge in Palestine. UNSCOP fell back on the earlier British plan for partition and created more controversy by the way it divided the area between the Jews and Arabs.

Understandably, debate on the UNSCOP report was intense and lengthy.

Eventually, the partition of Palestine was approved on 29 November 1947. The Partition Resolution included several elaborate safeguards for the rights of minorities, and the 'existing rights' of the area's various religions were safeguarded, and free access to the Holy Places was guaranteed. The Arab countries, which had opposed the proposal while pressing the Palestinian Arabs' case, declared that they would not be bound by it. The Zionists accepted it.

Violence in Palestine had risen while the UN debated the partition programme. As a result, Britain decided to terminate the Mandate and withdraw on 15 August 1948, several months in advance of the date anticipated in the UN proposal. No replacement forces were made available to enforce order, due to a decision that the UN's planned special armed militia could not be put into play in the deteriorating security situation.

The Zionist armed forces were now being organised to be on the offensive, not only to establish control in the areas allotted to the Jewish State but to extend it into the areas designated for an Arab state. This was due to expectations, based on expert intelligence work as well as loud rhetoric, that the Arab countries were planning to wipe out all attempts to establish the Jewish state.

In the months leading up to the British withdrawal, the Zionist and Arab forces clashed constantly. There are accounts of both sides benefiting from British arms, ammunition and even personnel, most of them undoubtedly true.

During these months many Arabs left Palestine and controversy surrounds the reasons for their abrupt departure. Zionists claim that they left because of instructions from Arab leaders that they should temporarily vacate the area to allow Arab forces to 'rid Palestine of the Jews' and establish an independent Arab Palestine. The Arabs argue that the refugees fled Jewish military atrocities.

War of Independence (1948)

On 15 May 1948 the last of the occupying British forces departed, ending the Mandate. On the previous day, David Ben-Gurion, the Jewish state's first prime minister, had proclaimed Israel an independent state. Immediately, violence from both sides mounted. Troops from Egypt, Jordan, Lebanon, Syria, Iraq and Saudi Arabia had already been infiltrating the area and the first Arab-Israeli war had started. On 26 May 1948 the Israel Defence Force (IDF) was established, its first soldiers drawn from the various paramilitary units created during the Mandate.

By the end of May 1949, a UN-sponsored ceasefire came into effect. Israeli forces controlled the major part of Palestine, including some of what had been designated for an Arab state and also West Jerusalem. The Gaza Strip was occupied by Egypt and the rest, including East Jerusalem and Jerusalem's Old City, was occupied by Jordan, not then a UN member.

Israel was now recognised by the UN as an independent state, but not by the Arab countries and several others. Even more countries disputed Israel's decision to name Jerusalem as its capital, refusing to install embassies there and choosing Tel Aviv instead.

The UN continued in its quest to secure the 'inalienable rights' of the Palestinian people. However, Israel's alleged fait accompli of expansion beyond its preassigned borders, together with the Egyptian and Jordanian occupation and the state of war between Israel and the Arab countries and the Palestinian Arabs, all contributed to its failure.

The UN's first step towards a solution was devastated in September 1948 by the assassination of Count Bernadotte of Sweden, the UN Mediator. Although Israel has denied Jewish involvement and resisted requests for a government investigation, men in Israeli military uniforms were witnessed committing the murder and are commonly believed to have been members of the extreme Zionist Stern gang.

In May 1949 Israel was admitted to the UN, after a first application failed due to its non-compliance with UN resolutions. Israel has since been subjected to continued criticism for its lack of observation of UN resolutions and principles, most of which it has vigorously argued against.

Since 1950 the issue of the Palestinian Arabs' rights has been treated as a 'refugee problem', mainly by the UN Relief & Works Agency in Palestine (UNRWA). In 1967 over half the Palestinian Arabs belonging to areas in Israel or under Israeli occupation were refugees in the West Bank, Gaza Strip or neighbouring Arab countries.

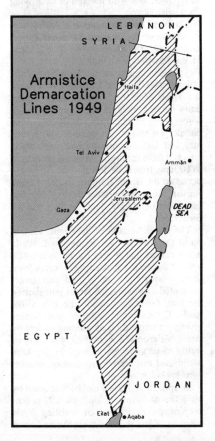

Israel's Initial Development

The Zionists now set about attracting increased Jewish immigration to Israel and planning the rapid development of their new national home. The 1950 Law of Return granted citizenship to every Jewish person requesting it. The Nationality Law (1952) allowed non-Jews to claim citizenship. By the end of 1951 the Jewish population had grown by over 750,000, with over half of them refugees from Muslim Arab countries, fleeing threatened or actual persecution.

Controversy surrounds the treatment of many of these new arrivals from the Arab countries. Many complained about discrimination by European Jews; that they were given the worst jobs or were forcibly sent to the less appealing areas of the country.

Pioneering the generally barren and inhospitable areas became a vital priority for the new country and this saw the development of *kibbutzim* (collective farms) and *moshavim* (co-operative farms). In a very short time the Jews managed to develop the infrastructure of a nation.

The massive aliyah of the initial three years after Israel's independence slowed considerably after 1952. By that time most of the Jews who had wanted to immigrate, and were able to, had done so. Then followed a new wave of immigrants, due to political events elsewhere. In 1955, aliyah from Morocco and Tunisia was encouraged as a result of the rise in local Arab nationalism. The influx of Russian Jews into Poland caused political pressure and an increase in aliyah from there. The Hungarian uprising of 1956 caused many Jews to flee across the border into Austria, and 8680 of them made their way to Israel. After the Sinai War that year, at least 14,000 Egyptian Jews crossed the desert.

Sinai (Suez) War (1956)

The chain of events which led to the next major war in the area varies considerably according to whose version you listen to. The Israelis claim that their actions were an outcome of the Arab policy to destroy the Jewish State, citing terrorist raids launched from the Egyptian-occupied Gaza Strip, the closure of the Suez Canal and the blockade of the Tiran Straits by Egypt which stopped Israeli shipping in those areas. Israeli forces struck back by occupying the Sinai Peninsula and the Gaza Strip.

What the Israelis consistently fail to include in their accounts of the dispute is their involvement with Britain and France, which caused the USA to lead world opinion in strong condemnation of their tactics in what became known as the 'Suez Crisis'. Britain and France, angered by the Egyptian nationalisation of the Suez Canal, which they part-owned, planned an airborne invasion of Egypt, whilst the Israelis moved overland into the Sinai and Gaza. After initial success, the refusal of the USA to bail out Britain, suffering from monetary problems due to the expense of the military operation, caused the withdrawal of British and French troops.

Some critics claim that Israel has always created pretexts for invading Arab territory and that the Suez War was yet another example. According to them, Israel planned to 'set up' Egypt so that it would enter and then lose a war. They point to an unprovoked Israeli raid on the Egyptian forces at Gaza. The argument continues that when Nasser later angered Britain and France with his nationalisation of the Suez Canal, Israel saw an opportunity to go into battle; although Nasser had, on that occasion, done nothing against the Israelis.

Israel eventually withdrew from its occupying positions in Egyptian territory after considerable pressure from the UN, the USA and the USSR. There was criticism of these powers for failing to require Egypt to renounce its intention to continue its state of war with Israel. Instead Egypt soon closed the Suez Canal and returned to the Gaza Strip, contrary to prior assurances that it would not.

More Jewish Immigration

Between 1961 and 1964 a steady flow of Jewish immigrants from Eastern Europe and North Africa arrived, totalling over 215,000. However, when Algeria became independent in 1962, the vast majority of its Jews chose to settle in France, with only 7700 making their way to Israel. In all, almost 700,000 of the new arrivals were refugees from anti-Jewish violence in the Arab world. Zionists argue that this is a group of people conveniently forgotten by the Arabs, who complain about the Arab refugee problem created by Israel.

The Six Day War (1967)

The Six Day War came after a period of relative calm, during which, according to Israel, the Arab countries rebuilt their military power, still with the aim of destroying the Jewish State.

There had been an increase in Arab terrorist attacks on Israel from Syria and Egypt, and in anti-Israeli speeches by Arab leaders, in the previous two years. By June 1967, Egypt again blockaded the Tiran Straits and ordered the UN peace-keeping forces out of the Sinai. With the Egyptian Army apparently moving towards Israel, the Israeli air force attacked and crippled its Egyptian counterpart still on the ground. Jordan then attacked Israel from the east, and Syria attacked from the north. After the six days, 5 to 10 June, Israel had defeated the Arabs and occupied the Golan Heights, the West Bank region, including East Jerusalem and Jerusalem's Old City, the Gaza Strip and the Sinai Desert.

The Israeli version of the events leading up to the Six Day War is disputed. While Israel claims that it was forced to retaliate against the mass attack of Arab forces from three countries, it is argued that Israel attempted to provoke the Arabs into starting the war, failed, and made the first strike itself. Critics claim that, despite Nasser giving the impression of wanting to destroy Israel, his speeches were merely his way of trying to improve his prestige in the Arab world, and that Israeli provocation encouraged his behaviour.

In April 1967, Nasser had been accused by his allies of hiding behind the UN peace-keeping forces instead of assisting Syria when Israel had shot down six Syrian fighter

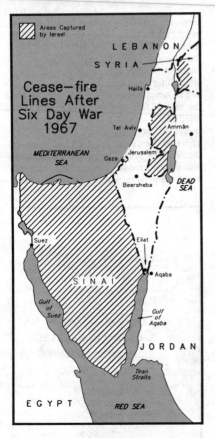

Areas Captured by Israel

LEBANON

SYRIA

Cease—fire
Lines After
Six Day War
1967

Haifa

Tel Aviv

Amman

MEDITERRANEAN
SEA

Gaza

Jerusalem

Beersheba

DEAD
SEA

Suez

Eilat

SINAI

Aqaba

Gulf
of
Suez

Gulf
of
Aqaba

JORDAN

Tiran
Straits

EGYPT

RED SEA

were actually in defensive positions, while Israeli troops were in an offensive order of battle. The Israeli forces were apparently more powerful by a big margin, due mainly to Nasser's army being involved in a five-year-old war in Yemen. According to this argument, it is hardly likely that he would have invaded Israel without waiting to have all his troops available. Finally, it was the Israelis who attacked first, according to them in defence, but according to critics, as part of an overall plan to increase the size of the Jewish state.

The most important outcome of the war was the reunification of Jerusalem. After the 1949 Armistice, Jordan had maintained control there and refused access to the Holy Sites to all Israelis – Jews, Muslims and Christians (at Christmas and Easter, Christians were allowed access). Now Bethlehem, Hebron and Jericho, once virtually inaccessible from Israel, were just a short drive away. This really opened up the country's tourism industry, with Israel becoming a synonym for the Holy Land. The capture of the Golan Heights allowed the development of Tiberias and the Sea of Galilee as a major tourist attraction.

Israel has often claimed that after the Six Day War it wanted to negotiate a peaceful settlement involving the return of the Occupied Territories. The Arab countries' stand, that there would be no peace, no negotiations and no recognition of Israel, is given as the reason for the failure of such a policy. Israel's critics say that the Jewish state has always wanted to expand its borders and never honestly accepted the UN's 1947 borders. These arguments are based largely on constant Zionist references to the area that is now Jordan as being a part of Eretz Israel, the ancient land of Israel, and therefore rightfully being a part of the modern Jewish state.

The Six Day War brought the second great Palestinian Arab exodus as almost 500,000 left their homes, leaving 1,200,000 under Israeli control. Those in the West Bank and the Gaza Strip came under Israeli military occupation. The remaining 1,500,000 Palestinians were now refugees, many for the

planes in Syrian air-space. This provoked Nasser into ordering the UN out, and again closing the Tiran Straits to Israeli shipping. It is argued that the Israelis deliberately created this situation, and that the fuss they made about the closure of the Straits was a calculated exaggeration, as very little Israeli shipping used the area. Egypt had closed the area to Israeli shipping not to cause a major inconvenience, that was impossible, but as a gesture to appease Syria.

The argument concludes that these Israeli tactics failed to provoke Nasser into invading, and that Egyptian troops in the Sinai second time after fleeing first in the 1948 war. They often found themselves unwelcome in foreign countries, in particular the Arab states, and UNRWA has been looking after most of them ever since. The Arab states have been reluctant to permit the mass immigration of refugees from Palestine because, it is argued, they don't want the campaign for a Palestinian Arab state to fizzle out as it probably would if the refugees were to leave the area.

The Six Day War seems to have been a turning point for both the development of Israel and the struggle by the Palestinian Arabs for their rights. As a result of the Israeli victory, aliyah was no longer just a homecoming for persecuted Jews. Between 1967 and 1972 large numbers of Jews arrived from Western Europe, North and South America and the British Commonwealth, largely a result of the 'pull' of Israel rather than the 'push' of anti-Jewish persecution – there was an upsurge in confidence that the Jewish state was here to stay and succeed.

The War of Attrition (1969-70) & the Yom Kippur War (1973)

The War of Attrition lasted 16 months from spring 1969 and was caused by Egyptian shelling attacks across the Suez Canal ceasefire line. Israel responded with its air force. There were also clashes with Jordan and a general increase in Arab terrorist activity. Eventually the UN and the USA managed to secure a new ceasefire agreement.

Although Israeli intelligence was aware of Arab plans to launch a major offensive, the timing of the Yom Kippur War took Israel and the world by surprise. It almost resulted in the defeat of the Jewish state, although Israel has called it one of its greatest military victories. In 1973, Egypt and Syria launched simultaneous attacks on the holiest day of the Jewish calendar – Yom Kippur, the Day of Atonement (see Holidays & Festivals in the Facts for the Visitor chapter). With most of the unprepared IDF's civilian reserves and many of its regulars off-duty and in the synagogues praying, the first three days of the war almost brought an Arab victory.

However, the IDF was soon fully mobilised and it took the offensive by the third day, first on the Syrian front and later in the Suez Canal area. The fighting stopped on 24 October, 18 days after it had started, with a UN call for a ceasefire.

The heavy losses sustained by Israel and the loss of face caused by its highly-rated intelligence service's failure to foresee the timing of the Arab attack had a sobering effect on the euphoria which had followed the Six Day War. The people's confidence was affected and the Labour Party, in power since independence, was severely criticised,

Territory held by Israel during the Six Day War until the Syrian attack on 6 Oct 1973

Syrian territory held by Israel at the cease-fire of 24 Oct 1973

Israeli–Syrian Demarcation Line 1949-1967

Israeli–Syrian Cease–fire Lines

LEBANON

Sidon

Damascus

Hasbaya

Mazraat Beit Jann

Sassa

Qiryat Shemona

Khan Erenbe

Jeba

Safed

Khushniye

Rosh Pinna

Rafid

Ramat Magshimim

Tiberias

Yarmuk

ISRAEL

SYRIA

JORDAN

Irbid

with the result that Prime Minister Golda Meir eventually resigned.

Search for Peace

One of the effects of the shock of the Yom Kippur War was a more urgent desire for peace. Dr Henry Kissinger, the US Secretary of State, became a familiar figure with his 'shuttle diplomacy'. However, it took him until May 1974 to negotiate an agreement between Israel and Syria, after the earlier UN Middle East Peace Conference in Geneva concluded an agreement between Israel and Egypt.

On 21 June 1977, the new Israeli Prime Minister, Menachem Begin of the Likud Party, called for the leaders of Jordan, Syria and Egypt to meet him to end the dispute. Critics were sceptical of Begin's sincerity, claiming that he was merely appeasing the voters who had just elected him and that his subsequent actions, including the encouragement of West Bank settlement, the Taba dispute and the question of the Gaza Strip and the West Bank in general, show that Israel was not so willing to negotiate.

President Sadat of Egypt accepted Begin's challenge and after both had broadcast messages to each other's respective populations, Sadat visited Israel on 19 November 1977. The importance of his visit cannot be overstated – a top Arab leader, who had previously denied the Jewish state's right to exist, was now flying there to negotiate peace. Begin reciprocated with a visit to Egypt. During the following 16 months of negotiations the USA, led by President Carter, played an active role. On 26 March 1979, the historic Egypt-Israel Peace Treaty was signed by Sadat and Begin.

Unfortunately, the results of the treaty have not lived up to expectations. Israel and Egypt's relationship has become known as the 'Cold Peace' and it appears that in their haste to produce the treaty, its authors neglected to include all the necessary elements to produce a genuinely peaceful solution – not that this was necessarily possible. However, Israel and Egypt are at peace, whatever its temperature, and the security situation on the Israel-Egypt border has never been so quiet. President Sadat was assassinated by Arab extremists because of his involvement in the treaty, and his successor, President Mubarak, has taken a less flamboyant course. He has tried to appease both Arab nationalists and Egypt's Western allies. Meanwhile, it is now possible for travellers to visit Israel from Egypt, and vice versa – something which once would have been unheard of.

Operation Peace for Galilee (1982)

The IDF invaded Lebanon in June 1982, the Israeli Government feeling it necessary to destroy PLO bases along Israel's northern borders because of constant terrorist incursions and heavy artillery and rocket attacks against Israel. Critics of the Israeli response point to the remarks allegedly made by David Ben-Gurion, Israel's first prime minister, and Moshe Dayan, Defence Minister in the 1960s and 1970s, that it was important for Israel to create a Christian state in Lebanon, by force if necessary.

Critics claim that Israel was violating international law and Lebanese sovereignty. For the first time, thousands of Israelis demonstrated against the military actions of their government. Prime Minister Begin resigned while controversy raged. He gave no reason for his resignation, but it was thought to be mainly due to guilt over his decision which had cost so many Israeli lives. Those in favour of Operation Peace for Galilee point to the great reduction in terrorist activity in the area as a direct result, and argue that international law guarantees a country the right to enter foreign soil to remove an armed threat which the host country cannot control. Largely successful in driving out the PLO, if not in destroying it, Israel has now mostly withdrawn from Lebanon. However, Palestinians have continued making terrorist strikes across the border and the IDF and Israeli air force are regularly in action in south Lebanon.

The PLO

The Palestine Liberation Organisation

(PLO), first formed in 1964, adopted a new Covenant in 1968. Basically, it committed all Palestinians to fight for their rights because the international community had failed to secure their natural, as well as promised, right to an independent state. This Covenant described Israel as an illegal state, and demanded the 'total liberation of Palestine'.

This led to Israel's refusal to have any dealings with the PLO. Groups under the PLO umbrella continually resorted to violence to focus world attention on the plight of the Palestinians, but it is strongly argued that such tactics did little to benefit the Palestinians themselves. The PLO justified the violence by quoting the UN General Assembly's affirmation of 'the legitimacy of the people's struggle for liberation from...foreign domination and alien subjugation by all available means including armed struggle'.

Despite worldwide condemnation of PLO-sponsored terrorism, the international community generally recognised, to a degree, the Palestinian cause – although it never became a high priority in the international political arena. In 1969 a UN General Assembly resolution recognised 'that the problem of the Palestine Arab refugees has arisen from the denial of their inalienable rights'.

As far as Israel and the USA were concerned, the PLO was an evil organisation not deserving of official recognition. At the same time, the PLO had been admitted into the UN where it received support from several countries. This resulted in resolutions being passed in its favour, and at Israel's expense. One of the most notable of these equated Zionism with racism (it was revoked in 1991). The PLO also established offices in major cities, just like any leading political organisation.

In 1974, the Palestinian National Council, the body which elects the leaders of the PLO, reportedly decided that their previous policy was not working, and resolved to settle for a Palestinian state in the West Bank and the Gaza Strip. This would exist alongside, and not in place of, Israel. It was also decided to

achieve this goal through diplomacy, not force. The PLO therefore claimed to have accepted since 1974 the existence of Israel behind its pre-1967 borders, and blamed the Israelis and their supporters for suppressing news of this policy. They claimed that the policy was ignored by the Israelis who stepped up their efforts to paint the PLO as a collection of terrorists that could not be trusted.

Certainly this was a common image of the PLO in the wake of acts of terrorism during the 1960s and 1970s, such as attacks on innocent airline passengers, and the hijacking of a Mediterranean cruise ship and the murder of a disabled Jewish passenger. The PLO claimed that such acts were committed by splinter groups of extremists that they had disowned and had no control over. They always fell short, however, of specifically condemning such incidents.

Jewish Settlers

Despite the UN Security Council condemning Israeli settlements in the Occupied Territories, the 1970s and 1980s saw the Likud Government actively encouraging Jewish settlers in the West Bank. The original settlers believe that the occupied territories are an integral part of what rightfully constitutes Israel, regardless of any UN partition and various resolutions. They base their argument on biblical references and also on the military value of the area.

Today

Sparked by a traffic incident in Gaza on 8 December 1987, when Palestinians were believed to have been deliberately killed by a Jewish motorist, the *intifada*, or popular uprising, began in the Occupied Territories. It came at a time when, even in the Arab political arena, the Palestine problem had been relegated to an issue of relatively little importance. However, this policy of non cooperation and active, often violent protest, resulted in a heightening of tensions, the deaths of many Arab protesters, and a great deal of unfavourable publicity for the Israelis due to their heavy handed response to the uprising. Most importantly, it brought the Palestinian cause back to the centre stage of world politics.

In late 1988, with world opinion swinging behind him, Yassar Arafat announced that the PLO was willing to forgo the use of terrorism, that it recognised Israel's right to exist, and that it accepted UN resolutions 242 and 338. This was a vital breakthrough, as it was these concessions that the US had demanded before it would deal with the PLO. After a few anxious days, some incredulity, and requests to rephrase the announcement, the US announced that talks with the PLO would begin. The Israeli Government was dismayed. It claimed that the US had given in to their deadly enemy, and vowed that Israel would never deal with the PLO. In 1990, after its leadership failed to condemn an unsuccessful Palestinian terrorist raid on Tel Aviv beach, the US broke off relations with the PLO.

Meanwhile, Jewish settlements continue to expand in the West Bank, adding to the complexities of the situation. It is interesting to note that an increasing number of the Jews now living in the West Bank are not motivated by religious or political fervour. Rather, they are attracted by the cheaper housing available in the region. With the 'green line' marking the West Bank border being rapidly developed, many Israelis simply do not know where the border really is and are actually unaware that they live in the Occupied Territories.

In January 1991, after US President George Bush responded to Iraq's invasion of Kuwait with Operation Desert Storm, it was feared that Saddam Hussein would try to bring Israel into the war in an effort to break the international coalition. Under heavy pressure from the White House, the IDF stayed put despite Iraqi Scud missile attacks. With the exception of Jordan, all the Arab states continued to support Desert Storm. Who knows what what have happened if Israel had retaliated against Iraq.

After some forty years of a being on a war footing, this was the first time when the vast majority of Israeli men were at home with the women and children when the air raid sirens sounded. Normally, they would have been called up to bolster the full-time ranks of the IDF. With the threat of Iraqi chemical warfare, gas masks were issued to every man, woman and child in the country – Arabs and Jews. It would seem that the effect on Israeli men of experiencing the fear of their families and friends first hand made a lot of them a lot less casual and gung-ho about war. It caused psychological problems for many, with therapists reporting record numbers of cases of this syndrome. As far as the effect this had on the general Israeli point of view of waging war, many appear to have become more determined to negotiate for peace. However, I met some Israelis who felt that the Palestinians' open support for Iraq showed that the concept of peace for Israel was only for the foolish.

Although the exact number of fatalities, wounded and damage caused by Iraqi's missiles will probably never be revealed, both Israelis and Palestinians were killed and wounded, and property was destroyed. In Ramat Gan, a Tel Aviv suburb, one Scud attack levelled a sizeable chunk of housing and was left as an example of what had happened. Visiting dignitaries and tour groups were brought to inspect it, for political and fund raising purposes.

On a lighter note, the circumstances resulting from the Gulf War inspired wry humour and some comical scenes. A common remark about the German-made gas masks was that 'the order reached us 40 years too late'. Throughout the country, Israelis hosted 'End of the World' theme parties in response to the horrors of the war. Most people in the country at the time have a story to tell relating to what happened to them or to someone they know when the sirens sounded. Many have photo albums with snapshots of families, babies, lovers, even pets, all wearing their gas masks.

In the years preceding the collapse of the former Soviet Union, restrictions on Jewish emigration to Israel were relaxed with thousands making their way to the Jewish State. Although it was something that Israel had long wanted to happen, the sudden flood of immigrants created major problems with chronic shortages of housing, schools, and large-scale unemployment. Under employment is a problem, too, as many immigrants are highly qualified professionals.

A high proportion of the Soviet Jews who came to Israel at this time were musicians. A common Israeli joke was that if a Soviet Jew was not carrying a violin case upon arrival at Ben-Gurion Airport, then he must be a pianist. Certainly you cannot walk more than a few blocks in most Israeli cities and towns today without hearing a street musician fresh from the former Soviet Union.

In October, 1991, US Secretary of State George Baker managed to achieve a breakthrough by bringing together Prime Minister Shamir of Israel with representatives of Syria, Lebanon, Jordan, Egypt and, most importantly, with a Palestinian delegation for three days of face to face meetings in Madrid, Spain. Despite there being no realistic signs of an end to the conflict, the intifada and these subsequent initiatives were the start of the most significant turning points in the region since Sadat's 1977 visit to Jerusalem.

In July 1992, the Labour Party was returned to power after some 15 years dominated by Likud rule. With Yitzhak Rabin as leader, they won a relatively decisive victory (by Israeli standards) based largely on the philosophy that it was time to approach the peace talks in a more conciliatory manner than that practised by Likud.

GEOGRAPHY

Israel and the Occupied Territories have a total area of 27,817 sq km. Part of the Asian continent, its western border is the Mediterranean Sea, to the north it is bounded by Lebanon and Syria, to the east by Jordan and to the south by the Red Sea (with views of Saudi Arabia) and Egypt. These current borders are according to the Israel-Lebanon 1949 armistice line, the Israel-Syria disengagement line following the 1973 Yom Kippur War, and the Israel-Egypt boundary agreed to in the 1979 Camp David peace treaty. The task of defining the borders of Israel is impossible without upsetting someone. The described area includes the Occupied Territories, namely the West Bank and the Gaza Strip.

Coastal Plain

A narrow, sandy shoreline, bordered by a stretch of fertile farmland (up to 40 km wide), runs from Rosh Hanikra in the north to the Israel-Egypt border in the south.

Mountain Ranges

A series of ranges runs north to south. The mountains of the Golan Heights and Galilee stretch southward until cut off by the Jezreel Valley. South of here are the ranges and hilly areas of Samaria and Judea in the West Bank, and the Negev. Israel's highest mountain (2766 metres) is Mount Hermon, in the Golan Heights.

Valleys

The 'Rift Valley', part of the great Syrian-African Rift and the longest valley in the world, runs the length of the country, and includes several distinct areas. The Hula Valley, between the mountains of the Golan Heights and Galilee, was once swampland, but is now a rich agricultural area with nature reserves. The Jezreel Valley, between the mountains of Galilee and Samaria, is an agricultural area. The Jordan Valley runs between the mountains of Judea and Samaria in the west, and the mountains of Gilead and Moab in Jordan to the east. The northern part is an agricultural area, but the southern part is arid with limited agriculture. The Arava, a long, arid valley running from the Dead Sea to the Red Sea, is being developed for intensive agriculture.

Arid Regions

The Judean Desert, between Jerusalem and the Dead Sea in the West Bank, is barren but beautiful. In the south, the Negev comprises flatlands of loess, a fine deposit of wind-blown dust and limestone, and leads the world in desert agriculture. It is the largest

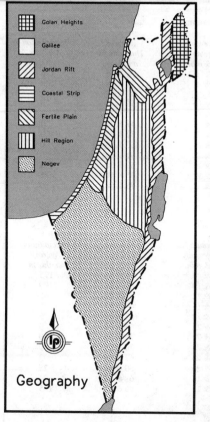

Golan Heights

Galilee

Jordan Rift

Coastal Strip

Fertile Plain

Hill Region

Negev

Geography

magnesium – and the unique water is renowned for its healing qualities. Throughout the coastal plain, rivers flow from the mountains to the Mediterranean Sea. The most important are the Yarkon near Tel Aviv and the Qishon in the Haifa area.

CLIMATE

Climatic conditions vary considerably from region to region. In general, Israel's climate is temperate, with two seasons: winter – cold and rainy – and summer – hot and dry. Rainfall is mainly limited to between November and April, and can vary from over 1000 mm a year on Mount Hermon in the north to less than 100 mm in Eilat in the south. Most rain falls between December and February. The wettest area is Upper Galilee on the heights between Metulla and Safed. The driest areas are the southern Negev and the Arava Valley, between the Dead Sea and the Gulf of Eilat. The winter can be relatively severe, often catching travellers with inadequate clothing. Even in the summer months a warm sweater is needed in many places, as the evening temperatures drop considerably from the daytime high.

The hottest areas are those below sea level: the Jordan Valley, the shores of the Sea of Galilee, the Valley of Beit She'an, the shore of the Dead Sea and the Arava Valley. During the spring and autumn, periodic strong winds increase the temperature. Called the *hamsin* (Arabic for 50), these easterly winds were thought to blow for 50 days each year – thankfully they don't.

The widespread use of solar energy means that for much of the winter in the Jerusalem area and parts of the north there is a distinct lack of hot water and heating in some accommodations, especially at the budget end. The lack of sun in these areas means that returning to the hostel in the early afternoon in the hope of getting a hot shower can become part of the routine.

The climatic variations from region to region are part of what makes Israel so fascinating. For example, in Jerusalem during the winter months it is generally cold and wet, but you can escape for the day by taking

unspoilt area in Israel, yet is regularly left out of travellers' schedules.

Rivers & Lakes

The Jordan River flows from sources in northern Galilee southward to the Dead Sea. The Sea of Galilee, at the foot of the Golan Heights, is an important source of water and since the Golan Heights were annexed by the Israeli Government it has become a major tourist attraction. The Dead Sea, in the Jordan Valley, is the lowest area on earth at 386 metres below sea level. It is the country's major source of minerals – potash, bromide,

Jerusalem

Month	Temperature °F Average daily max & min	Temperature °C Average daily max & min	Relative Humidity % am & pm	Precipitation Average monthly mm
Jan	55 & 41	13 & 5	77 & 66	132
Feb	56 & 42	13 & 6	74 & 58	132
Mar	65 & 46	18 & 8	61 & 57	64
Apr	73 & 50	23 & 10	56 & 42	28
May	81 & 57	27 & 14	47 & 33	3
Jun	85 & 60	29 & 16	48 & 32	0
Jul	87 & 63	31 & 17	52 & 35	0
Aug	87 & 64	31 & 18	58 & 36	0
Sep	85 & 62	29 & 17	61 & 36	0
Oct	81 & 59	27 & 15	60 & 36	13
Nov	70 & 53	21 & 12	65 & 50	71
Dec	59 & 45	15 & 7	73 & 60	86

Haifa

Month	Temperature °F Average daily max & min	Temperature °C Average daily max & min	Relative Humidity % am & pm	Precipitation Average monthly mm
Jan	65 & 49	18 & 9	66 & 56	175
Feb	67 & 50	19 & 10	65 & 56	109
Mar	71 & 53	22 & 12	62 & 56	41
Apr	77 & 58	25 & 14	60 & 57	25
May	83 & 65	28 & 18	62 & 59	5
Jun	85 & 71	29 & 22	67 & 66	0
Jul	88 & 75	31 & 24	70 & 68	0
Aug	90 & 76	32 & 24	70 & 69	0
Sep	88 & 74	31 & 23	67 & 66	3
Oct	85 & 68	29 & 20	60 & 66	25
Nov	78 & 60	26 & 16	61 & 56	94
Dec	68 & 53	20 & 12	66 & 56	185

Eilat

Month	Temperature °F Average daily max & min	Temperature °C Average daily max & min	Relative Humidity % am & pm	Precipitation Average monthly mm
Jan	70 & 50	21 & 10	60 & 39	0
Feb	73 & 52	23 & 11	62 & 40	8
Mar	79 & 57	26 & 14	56 & 38	8
Apr	87 & 64	31 & 18	46 & 30	5
May	96 & 62	36 & 17	41 & 28	0
Jun	101 & 75	38 & 24	38 & 20	0
Jul	103 & 79	39 & 26	36 & 13	0
Aug	104 & 79	40 & 26	40 & 24	0
Sep	99 & 77	37 & 25	52 & 27	0
Oct	92 & 70	33 & 21	55 & 34	0
Nov	82 & 61	28 & 16	56 & 38	0
Dec	74 & 53	23 & 12	58 & 42	8

the bus down (literally) to Jericho or the Dead Sea, both less than an hour's ride away. After waking up in Jerusalem with the temperature at 10°C, you can change into shorts and T-shirts beside the Dead Sea in 23°C sunshine.

Water & Irrigation

The availability of water in Israel is a major concern because of the uneven distribution of rainfall and periodic droughts. Israel leads the world in the field of irrigation, and many countries send personnel there to learn how to develop arid regions. Archaeological discoveries in the Negev and elsewhere reveal that 2000 years ago civilisations in the region used a variety of systems involving the collection and storage of rainwater.

The Jordan River, including the Sea of Galilee, is Israel's main water resource. All of the country's freshwater sources are joined in an integrated national grid. This system has increased the amount of irrigated farmland from 300 sq km in 1948 to over 1600 sq km today. New irrigation techniques have led to increased agricultural output, with savings of up to 50% in water use, and programmes for cloud seeding, desalinating sea water and recycling sewage water have been in operation for several years.

Travellers will notice the drip-irrigation system all over the country. It is used to water virtually everything from crops in the field to the plants and shrubs in town centres. Lengths of hose pipe with holes cut at set distances wind their way along the ground that needs water. Time switches, often computer linked, regulate the water flow. In arid areas, water is mixed with chemical fertiliser to ensure efficient results.

FLORA & FAUNA

Due to its position at the junction of three natural zones, Israel enjoys a wealth of plant and animal life, including 2500 plant types (150 of which are found only here), 430 bird species, and 70 mammal, 80 reptile and eight amphibia species. There are nearly 300 nature reserves, covering almost 1600 sq km.

Some of these are major attractions for travellers and are covered in detail in relevant chapters.

Deuteronomy 8:8 describes the ancient land of Israel, with its wheat, barley, vines, fig trees, pomegranates, olive trees, and dates. These 'seven species' still flourish today, but they are just part of the country's wide range. Biblical, Roman and Crusader writings mention the now-vanished forests in the north of the country, and the Jewish National Fund's tree-planting programmes have set out to restore the county's tree population with millions of new trees.

Highlighting the range of Israel's flora and climate are wintry apple trees, Mediterranean vineyards and desert date palms, all within a few km of each other. Israel's oldest trees are believed to be in the olive groves of the Garden of Gethsemane and may have lived since the time of the Second Temple (500 BC to 70 AD).

Spring is a lovely time of year in Israel, but climatic differences mean that parts of the Israeli countryside blossom at different times. In the north, March and April see wild tulips, irises, lilies and hyacinths. In the south, the desert blooms as early as February. The Negev has lion's leaf, dandelions, groundsels and wild tulips, and in the wadies the white broom and purple irises grow.

Like its flora, Israel's fauna is varied. The leopard, hyaena, polecat, wolf, jackal, coney, porcupine, antelope, ostrich, wild boar and many reptiles can be found if you know where to look. The emblem of the Nature Reserves Authority is the ibex, a wild goat, which can be seen in the desert mountain areas where there is water. Less visible, but perhaps more interesting for its zoological classification as a relative of the elephant, is the hyrax, a sort of rock guinea pig.

Israel's skies teem with birds. Some, such as storks and swallows, rest en route to other climes; coots and ducks spend the winter; African species, such as the turtle dove, prefer the summer. As it is for certain plants and animals, Israel is the northern limit for many southern bird species, and the southern limit for many northern ones. This makes it the world's second largest flyway (after South America) for migratory birds.

Society for the Protection of Nature in Israel

One of Israel's more endearing success stories is the Society for the Protection of Nature in Israel (SPNI), founded in 1953 to safeguard the country's natural assets. Broadly stated, the aims of the SPNI are to conserve landscapes and relics of the past, to protect plant and animal life, and to protect and improve the quality of the environment. Its emblem is the Gilboa iris, indigenous to northern Israel.

For the traveller, awareness of the SPNI can be invaluable. The organisation's touring department, Israel Nature Trails, operates a wide range of guided tours of the many natural beauty spots in the country. Varying from a few hours to several days, and graded according to the 'hiking difficulty' involved, these tours start in Tel Aviv and Jerusalem.

Even if your budget rules out a guided tour, the SPNI can be very helpful. Most of its staff are extremely knowledgeable about the country and if you fancy some wilderness wandering then they are a good source of accurate information. Unfortunately, the 30-odd years of its existence have allowed the SPNI to develop a bureaucracy of its own. This has resulted in the main offices being staffed by a significant number of people who seem to have lost touch with the aims of the organisation. They tend to discourage travellers who wish to explore Israel without taking a tour, and are often reluctant to part with information.

Where the SPNI staff are most enthusiastic and helpful is in the 26 Field Study & Conservation centres dotted around Israel. These FSC centres are a key part of the SPNI's grass-roots programme of environmental education and practical nature conservation. Their role is education, conservation and research and data-gathering. They are situated in the different geographical regions of the country and provide hostel accommodation and study facilities (six do not provide accommodation).

Each FSC centre focuses on its immediate geographical area and it is the knowledge and the total involvement with their region of the resident field instructors that provides the backbone of the organisation. Once they are convinced that you are interested in seeing the real country – the varied natural beauty that is everywhere if you know where to look – they will shed the gruff Israeli exterior, open up and be extremely helpful.

Most of the SPNI's range of marvellous publications are only available in Hebrew, and plans to translate them have been suspended due to budget restrictions. It is certainly a good idea to browse through their *Israel Nature Tours* brochure to see what is offered, if only to use the information for independent hikes. Also look out for their free quarterly *Discover Israel with Israelis* brochure. The SPNI's head office and bookstore (☎ (03) 5374425, 375063/267) is in Tel Aviv, near the central bus station at 4 Hashfela St, Tel Aviv 6618. The Jerusalem office and bookstore (☎ (02) 222357, 244605) is at 13 Heleni Hamalka St, PO Box 930, Jerusalem 91008. There are other SPNI offices in various towns.

GOVERNMENT

Israel is a secular, parliamentary and democratic republic, headed by a president. The president's powers are basically formal and he is responsible to the Knesset.

The government, headed by the prime minister, is the main policy-making body. The Knesset is Israel's parliament, a single-chambered house of 120 members (MKs). All MKs are protected by the Act of Immunity from persecution or arrest for anything they say or do in the course of their parliamentary duties. This has resulted in several controversial incidents as certain extremist members have taken advantage of the law and entered the Haram esh-Sharif area in Jerusalem, where access is forbidden to Jews. Proceedings in the Knesset can get rather high-spirited, with MKs constantly losing their tempers; so much so that fighting is not unknown.

Political Parties

The oldest of Israel's political parties are older than the state, having been founded during the British Mandate. Despite the quadrupling of the population between 1948 and 1970, the established parties remain dominant, with new ethnic or communal groupings unable to gain substantial representation. All cabinets have been based on coalitions, and all of these had Mapai (the Labour Party) holding the central position until 1977, when a Likud (conservative/liberal) government took office. Arab electors have shown limited support for the Knesset parties, mainly voting for individual members of the Communist and Mapai parties.

Some smaller parties representing religious, ideological and special-interest groups have loyal, if limited, support among voters. Perhaps the most controversial party is Neturei Karta, a group of about a thousand ultra-orthodox Jews based in Jerusalem's Mea She'arim district. The party's name is Hebrew-Aramaic and means 'Watchmen of the Town'. They loudly refuse to recognise the State of Israel and have even shown active support for the Palestinians, on the grounds that Judaism and Zionism (that is, political power held by Jews) are diametrically opposed. These Jews prefer to speak Yiddish, not Hebrew, and do not use Israeli currency, pay taxes or use hospitals, state schools or any other social services.

The Israeli Flag & National Emblem

The design of Israel's flag is the same as that of the Zionist flag first used officially at the First Zionist Congress, held in Basle, Switzerland, in 1897. It is based on the *tallit* (prayer shawl) with the addition of the Star of David. Israel's official emblem is the *menorah*, the ancient symbol of the Jewish people. The first description of the menorah is in the Book of Exodus, 25: 31-37 and 40. Two olive branches representing a hope for peace are included on either side of the menorah, joined by the word 'Israel' in Hebrew at the bottom.

ISRAEL DEFENCE FORCE (IDF)

Due to the Palestine 'problem', and with the surrounding countries (except Egypt) still basically at war with Israel, security is the major consideration of the Jewish state. Military personnel are a constant presence, and wherever you go you will see soldiers armed with automatic rifles and machine-guns. Virtually everyone gets used to this, and to many they are a reassuring sight. Saying, 'Excuse me, could you move your gun, please?' to the young soldier sitting next to you on the bus soon becomes an acceptable part of travelling in Israel.

Established in May 1948, the IDF has developed into one of the most highly respected armies in the world. It is also one of the scruffiest, and its lack of sartorial elegance illustrates its egalitarian approach and minimalisation of the formal and ceremonial aspects of military life. Unlike most standing armies, it is a citizen's army based on the compulsory reserve and career service of the majority of the population. Compulsory service is three years for men, two for unmarried women. Each soldier is assigned to a reserve unit upon completion of compulsory service. Men up to age 55 serve about 30 days each year, which can be increased in times of emergency. Single women are liable to reserve service up to age 34, although in practice they are exempted at around age 25. Career military service is open to any man or woman having completed compulsory service and meeting current IDF needs.

Understandably, Arabs are not required to serve, although a small number have chosen to do so. The Druze in Galilee are highly valued soldiers, although their Golan counterparts still support Syrian claims to that territory.

The IDF has managed to organise itself around the multiplicity of the Jewish faith. For example, it is not practical to establish synagogues in every military base suited to the various communities present. As a result, a uniform type of synagogue has emerged. Rules for the observance of Shabbat have to take into account the need for the armed forces to be on a state of permanent alert against attack, and leave is so timed that no soldier needs to travel on Shabbat. A unified prayer book tells the soldier what he must do in every eventuality according to Jewish Law. This includes the exemption of those near enemy lines from the injunction to listen to the *shofar* (ram's horn trumpet) on religious occasions if there is a danger of the enemy hearing it. Also, if during Yom Kippur a soldier feels that hunger is affecting his fighting capacity, he must break his fast. On Hanukkah, soldiers without candles or suitable oil are allowed to light the menorah with rifle-lubricating oil.

UNRWA

As a result of the Arab-Jewish conflict during the establishment of the State of Israel in 1948, nearly 750,000 Arabs became refugees. They headed for Arab-held areas, mostly in eastern Palestine or in what is now best known as the occupied West Bank. Many headed for the Gaza Strip, subsequently administered by Egypt, but under Israeli occupation since 1967. Other refugees went to Jordan, Lebanon or Syria. A few went further afield, mainly to the Gulf countries, Europe, Scandinavia, the USA and Australia. In 1950, when hopes for an early return of the refugees to their homes faded, the UN set up the United Nations Relief & Works Agency for Palestine Refugees. UNRWA's present task is to assist needy Palestine refugees with education, relief and health services.

As a result of the natural increases in population, there are now over 2,000,000 refugees with UNRWA. This excludes all those Palestinians who became refugees in or around 1948 but who did not register for assistance with UNRWA as they were not in need. In Israel and the Occupied Territories the number of UNRWA-assisted refugees is approximately 800,000, but the number is constantly changing.

Refugee Camps

Today there are 61 UNRWA camps (West Bank 20, Gaza Strip eight, Jordan 10, Lebanon 13 and Syria 10). In and around these camps, UNRWA provides services for those refugees registered with them, although a minority do not actually live in camps themselves. UNRWA maintains services in the camps, but they are not extra-territorial areas under UN jurisdiction – they are administered by their host country, which holds all legislative and police powers. Nor are they normally closed areas, and the inhabitants are theoretically free to move in and out of them. These movements are often strictly limited by the host government, and Israel is no exception.

Despite the significant presence of these refugee camps in the Occupied Territories, many visitors to Israel are unaware of their existence. The squalor of the camps is a stark contrast to the relatively affluent conditions often only a few km away. To keep the Palestine issue alive, the Arab countries opposing Israel's right to exist have continually refused to allow the Palestine refugees to integrate with them. Israel, too, has refused to accept responsibility for their future.

A visit to the refugee camps is both possible and recommended, although it should only be done by arrangement with UNRWA. They are not tourist attractions and unaccompanied visitors may be given a hostile reception. Hardly surprisingly, the refugee camps have become a hotbed of anti-Israel and anti-Jewish feeling, and terrorist activities are often organised from here. At the same time, non-Jewish visitors are normally welcome and receive extremely warm hospitality if they present themselves correctly and sensitively. Your visit will be seen as a welcomed opportunity by Palestinians to put across their case, so rarely heard by visitors to Israel. To arrange such a visit, contact the UNRWA offices in East Jerusalem or Gaza (see the Jerusalem and Occupied Territories chapters).

Political Bias in UNRWA

Just as most of what you read and hear courtesy of the Israeli tourist information industry is understandably biased in favour of the State of Israel, so UNRWA and its presentation of its work is biased towards the Palestinian viewpoint. Most of UNRWA's local staff are Palestinians and the UN itself has been accused of bias because of its regular support for the Palestinian argument at the expense of Israel and the Zionists.

ECONOMY

Recent years have seen a roller coaster effect in the country's finances. For years Israel suffered from extremely high inflation and the currency was changed from lirot to shekels to new shekels in the struggle to control its devaluation. After a series of severe cuts in the government budget and food subsidies, followed by a freeze on prices, wages and taxes (inspired by Mrs Thatcher's monetarist policies in Britain), the Israeli Government eventually managed to reduce the inflation rate from over 500% to around 20%. Then, however, the programme was relaxed and inflation shot back up to 300%. Major labour strikes followed, and another freeze was implemented. This worked until the intifada robbed Israel of its second largest market, the Palestinians. In addition to the US$1 billion they used to spend on Israeli goods, tourism revenue has declined dramatically and Israel has spent over US$150 million trying to quell the intifada. On top of all that, the massive flood of Jewish immigrants from the Soviet Union has meant more funds needed for housing and schools and higher unemployment.

The years since independence have seen big changes in the emphasis of the country's economy, particularly during the last two decades. Investment has now moved from consumer industries to the large-scale production of chemicals, plastics, metalware, electronic equipment and computers. The kibbutzim now earn almost half their income from industrial output. Israel is now a world leader in various fields, including medical electronics, agrotechnology, computer hardware and software, fine chemicals, solar energy, diamond cutting and polishing, and weapons.

Priority is given to research and development for both industry and agriculture. This has resulted in success in such diverse areas as lasers, executive jets, computerised printing techniques and the genetic cross-breeding of plants and livestock. Israel meets most of its food requirements through domestic production, and agricultural exports more than pay for the necessary imports.

Israel has built on its status as the Holy Land by developing the country as a major tourist attraction. In 1985, nearly 1,500,000 tourists visited Israel, most from the USA. However, the intifada has caused a drop in the number of arrivals, and the Gulf War caused even more potential tourists to stay away. Again, the number of arrivals is increasing now.

Some Problems

Despite obvious determination, scientific and technical knowledge, and research and development programmes, the country still has to deal with the ever-increasing costs of its defence system. Without the massive financial support of the USA, it is hard to see anything but the total collapse of the Israeli economy. Defence costs aside, the lack of natural resources and the water supply problem have also taken their toll. The massive influx of Soviet immigrants in recent years only adds to the problem.

The subject of the economic development of the Arab sectors in Israel and the Occupied Territories is another area for dispute. A common Zionist argument is that, due to Jewish efforts, the Arabs have enjoyed economic growth, beneficial social change, and a constant rise in their standard of living. Israel's democratic system, compulsory education and the weakening of tribal and patriarchal authority have resulted in wider choices for education, employment and lifestyle. Zionists also point to the benefits of the modern technology which has been implemented since independence.

The Palestinians, meanwhile, talk about the Zionist art of rewriting history. They claim that prior to mass Jewish immigration the Palestinians were not living in the desolate, neglected country that is often described. In the second half of the 19th century, they argue, Palestinian agriculture was expanding and the area was an important exporter of agricultural products. Palestinians believe that the sudden increase in the population, caused by Zionism, created the need for higher output and used up the natural supply of water, which until then had apparently been more than adequate for the local population. Another argument is that until the Zionists received international funding they were struggling to survive in Palestine. If the Zionists need superior equipment and massive subsidies to live off the land, how can they condemn the local population who succeeded on their own – ask the Palestinians.

With regard to employment, Palestinians point to high under-employment and unemployment among the Arab population today. They say that this has resulted from their having to move away from areas of likely employment, and from discrimination, making only the unskilled jobs unwanted by Jews available to them.

Felafel & the Tax Collectors

It has been said that tax evasion in Israel is more than a way of life, and I can believe it. While researching this book I was often the cause for alarm as I entered restaurants and bars, sat down, ordered, and promptly brought out my pen and note-pad. Many a guilty proprietor mistook me for a tax inspector.

Another example is the common or garden felafel. You will notice that the person serving will cut into the pitta to make a pocket for the felafel and salad. In the old days they used to do it much quicker by simply cutting off the top of the bread. They stopped doing that because tax inspectors began to count the discarded pieces of pitta, comparing their number with the receipts.

Diamonds

Belgian Jews began Israel's diamond industry in 1939. Since those early days, and despite occasional decline, the industry has grown. In 1985 Israel emerged as the world's leading producer of cut diamonds and over 12,000 diamond cutters were in employment.

In the early 1980s, a worldwide recession in the diamond trade led to fragmentation and restructuring of the industry here into more than 1000 small units. Before then, it had been dominated by a relatively small number of firms with large workforces.

An interesting feature of the Israel Diamond Exchange in Tel Aviv is the Harry Openheimer Diamond Museum. This gives a well-presented introduction to the diamond trade and is proving popular with visitors.

POPULATION & PEOPLE

Israel and the Occupied Territories have a population approaching 6,000,000. This includes over 3,500,000 Jews. Nearly 1,500,000 people, virtually all Arabs, live in the Occupied Territories – the West Bank and the Gaza Strip. These figures are increasing, with both the Jews and the Arabs seemingly intent on out-numbering each other. Who has the higher birth rate depends upon whom you listen to. Judging by the worried noises made by the Jewish political leaders, though, it would appear that the 'average Israeli' of today has swung towards a more materialistic lifestyle, making a large family less popular. The Arabs, meanwhile, appear to be staying with tradition and large families are still the norm. In recent years, the Jewish population has been bolstered by the mass immigration of Soviet Jews.

Jews represent about 83% of the population, Muslims 13%, Christians 2.4% and Druze 1.6%. In this guide I have generally used the terms 'Arab' and 'Palestinian' for the local Arabs, and 'Jew' and 'Israeli' for the local Jews.

Despite presenting an image to the world of the happy Jewish state having to fight non-Jews to survive, your visit to Israel will show you that many of its Jews are also busy fighting each other. 'Two Jews equals three opinions' is an accurate cliché. With all the different cultures and temperaments which exist in Israel, the country constantly faces internal strife.

Jews

Between 1948 and 1952 the Jewish population more than doubled due to immigration of Holocaust survivors and Jews from Arab countries. Israeli Jews are a mixed group of people with different cultures and lifestyles, despite being united in history and religion. The political and religious differences between the various communities developed over the centuries as a result of their worldwide dispersion. This has created major problems in Israeli society.

Ashkenazi 'Germany' in classic Hebrew is Ashkenaz, and these Jews originate from Central and Eastern Europe, mainly Germany and its neighbouring countries. They are also descendants of Ashkenazim who emigrated to North and South America, South Africa and Australia. Some of them still use Yiddish as their common language. This is a combination of Hebrew and medieval German, written in Hebrew characters.

Sephardi 'Spain' in Hebrew is Sephard and these Jews are descendants of those expelled from Spain and Portugal in the 15th century (although a few did arrive in Palestine from Spain earlier). After the Spanish Expulsion, many of those exiled came to Palestine, while others went to various European and Mediterranean countries, and to the New World. The Spanish Jews spoke Ladino, still in use amongst older Sephardim today. This is a mixture of Hebrew and Spanish, written in Hebrew characters. The majority of the Jews in Palestine until the 19th century were Sephardim.

Ma'aravim Loosely referred to as Sephardi, these Jews originate from Morocco, Algeria and Tunisia. These countries are to the west of Palestine and their Hebrew name means 'westerners'. Their language was a North African dialect of Arabic.

Oriental Also referred to as Sephardi, these Jews originate from various Muslim and Arabic-speaking countries. Most of them arrived in Israel relatively recently. The Yemenites come from Yemen, 'Teiman' in Hebrew, and are called Teimanim. Large-scale immigration of Yemenite Jews came soon after independence, when a massive air lift called 'Operation Magic Carpet' brought virtually all the community to Israel. The Iraqi Jews, suffering persecution after Iraq's army was defeated in the 1948 war with Israel, immigrated en masse. The Kurds are also from Iraq – Kurdistan, which is in northern Iraq (ancient Assyria). Kurds first came to Palestine at the turn of the century. The Persians are from what is now Iran. Amongst them are a small group, the Mash-hadim, who originated in Mashed, a holy city near Russia's border with Afghanistan. They were forced to convert to Islam in the 19th century but observed the Jewish faith in secret. There are also Afghans, Bucharians (from Bokhara in the Soviet Union) and Cochins, from Cochin in India.

Ethiopians Airlifted to Israel from their famine-struck country in two massive operations in 1985 and 1991, these Jews should no longer be referred to as *falashas*, meaning strangers, a term now thought to be offensive. Many Jews, especially Ashkenazim, have found it hard to accept that these Black people are really Jewish. Arguments raged about their Jewishness and whether they should go through a religious conversion ceremony, including a ritual bath. There is also concern about the cultural differences between them and their more Westernised neighbours. Critics also say that the Ethiopian Jews have been given poor housing in undesirable areas and are generally treated badly compared with other immigrants.

Ashkenazi Versus Sephardi This is a problem which was a feature of the Jewish race even before Israel's creation. The early Zionist pioneers and illegal immigrants were Ashkenazim. They administered the setting up of the Jewish state and later organised the mass immigration of the Sephardim from the Arab countries. The physical and cultural differences between the two groups were the cause of considerable ill-feeling, which continues to this day. Less educated, lacking good Hebrew and not as wealthy as their fellow Jews, the Sephardim claim that they were treated as second-class citizens.

Today, charges of police brutality against Sephardim suspects and the lack of Sephardim politicians are amongst the arguments for this. The controversy over the status of the Ethiopian Jews showed that being Jewish is not always enough to be acceptable to the authorities, who are predominantly Ashkenazim.

Religious Versus Secular The vast majority of Israeli Jews are not religious. Many of them follow a kosher diet, celebrate the religious holidays and have their sons circumcised, but they normally do so for traditional not religious reasons. However, a tiny religious minority wields a great deal of influence in the life of all Israeli Jews. The religious courts have exclusive jurisdiction of several areas including marriage, education, Shabbat observance, Kashrut and the question of 'Who is a Jew?' This means that Jews may only marry by the traditional ceremony, officiated by a Chief Rabbinate-approved rabbi. Rabbinical courts have exclusive jurisdiction of all matrimonial cases, including alimony and the support of children. Some people get around the law by having a civil marriage abroad. Cyprus, for geographical reasons, is the popular choice.

Shabbat observance enforced by the religious Jews results in public transport and most places of entertainment closing down – just when most people are not working and want to go out and enjoy themselves. The kosher laws are followed in many establishments by law, but more and more Jews are moving away from this diet.

Perhaps the biggest controversy is deciding how to define Jewish nationality. The religious authorities constantly refuse to recognise as Jews those converted by Reform rabbis. They also question the Jewish status of the Ethiopians and the Black Hebrews.

In 1986 a particularly violent episode of the religious *vs* secular Jews conflict took place. Ultra-orthodox Jews, protesting at swimwear advertisements featuring scantily-dressed models, proceeded to set fire to bus-shelters where they were displayed. In apparent retaliation, a synagogue was set alight by a group of secular Jews.

Violent clashes have occurred outside cinemas which screen films on Friday evenings. Religious Jews regularly stone passing cars on Shabbat, angry at those who disregard the Shabbat laws that forbid driving.

Zionists Versus Left-Wingers An attempt to list the various opposing Jewish political viewpoints currently prevailing in Israel is a lengthy task. There are major disagreements on virtually every issue. Probably the subject of defining Israel's borders and what policies should be pursued to achieve them is the major cause of disharmony. The wide range of Jewish-held views on this is often surprising and perhaps indicates why so little has been achieved in this area. Views range from expelling every Arab from Israel and the Occupied Territories, to giving the Palestinians autonomy in their own land.

Arabs & Palestinians
Around 60% of the Arab population live in the Occupied Territories. Over 80% are Sunni Muslims, the remainder are Christians. Their common language is a Syrian dialect of Arabic.

Much controversy surrounds the origins of the Palestinians and this subject is at the heart of the Palestine 'problem'. A common Israeli view is that they are descended from the Arabs who invaded Palestine in the 7th century. Another is that most of them are descendants of immigrants from neighbouring countries who came to Palestine at the turn of the 19th century. Palestinians claim that their ancestry goes back beyond that and that they are a 'cumulative stock' of the many races that have lived in Palestine. This includes not just those Arab invaders, but the Canaanites who had lived here before the Jews first arrived, and the Philistines who arrived from the island of Crete circa 1200 BC.

Nearly 10% of the Arabs are Bedouins. These are tribes of traditionally nomadic people and they are Muslims. They are still mainly concentrated in the Negev, continuing to live in tents and breeding sheep, goats and camels. The Israeli Government has encouraged them to settle permanently and many have, mainly in Galilee.

Christians
Most Christians in Israel are Arabs. The remainder mainly consist of Armenians, foreign clergymen, monks, nuns and those working for Christian organisations.

The Druze
Nearly 10% of the non-Jewish population belong to this mysterious religious sect. They live in a few villages in Galilee and on Mount Carmel. When the Israeli Government annexed the Golan Heights the Druze villages there became part of the country. These Druze are generally unhappy with being considered Israeli and have remained fiercely supportive of Syrian claims to the area. However, the other Druze in Israel are renowned for their loyalty to the Jewish state. From either side of the political fence, the Druze will be among the friendliest people travellers will meet in Israel.

Small Communities
Baha'is The world centre of the Baha'i faith is in Haifa, and most of the followers in Israel live locally. Some are descended from the Baha'i leaders who were exiled to the Ottoman Empire in 1863 from Persia.

Samaritans Believed to be the smallest ethnic group in the world, there are about 600 Samaritans living in Nablus and Holon, south of Tel Aviv.

Black Hebrews This community has attracted controversy ever since the first Hebrews arrived in 1969. They number around 1200, with most of them living in Dimona. Their claim to be the most authentic descendants of the Jews exiled from Israel 4000 years ago is strongly disputed, and they have been refused Israeli citizenship.

Largely ignored by the authorities, the Black Hebrews are one of the understated fascinations of Israel today. This is due not only to their claims of Jewishness, but also to their communal lifestyle which incorporates such elements as a unique tofu-dominated vegetarian diet, colourful clothing, and the practice of polygamy.

Circassians An independent group in the Muslim community, numbering some 4000; they originated in the Caucasian Mountains of Russia, immigrating to Palestine in the 1890s. Mostly loyal to the State of Israel, the community is concentrated in two villages in Galilee.

Karaites A Jewish sect of about 15,000 members centred in Ramla, Ashdod and Beersheba. They reject rabbinical traditions and rulings, and have their own religious courts. After independence, the community had been reduced to only one family. They were living in the Jewish Quarter of Jerusalem's Old City, but were forced to move when it fell to Jordan in the 1948 war. Shortly afterwards, Karaites from Egypt settled in the country and they founded the new colonies.

ARTS
Popular Music
The Israeli popular music scene was such that success in the awful Eurovision Song Contest was considered a major achievement. It seemed that jingoistic, bland folk, and bouncy, insipid pop styles were all that you heard, inspired by the nation's pioneering image and the 1960s hippy movement. Things have improved, though, and there is now an interesting diversity to reflect Israeli society. As with other aspects of Israeli life, the army has made its mark here. Until the 1970s, talented musicians doing their army service produced variety shows for the armed forces. Nearly all of the established artists in Israel older than 25 made their start in this way. The IDF's Chief of Staff in the 1970s disbanded the entertainment unit but in the last few years it has been reformed and the process has begun again.

For Israel musicians, the biggest problems

are the small home market and the struggle to penetrate abroad, where there is little demand for their Hebrew material (translation into English is often impractical). In addition to standard Western-style 'middle of the road' music, you can hear:

Oriental Known as 'bus station music' because its popularity sprang from pirate cassettes sold in the markets around Tel Aviv's central bus station. This style was popular for years amongst Jews from the Arab countries who used to buy the cassettes in large numbers (one cassette apparently sold half a million copies). The music caught on with soldiers who took it home, and now some of the most successful artists are from this section of the business.

Underground/New Wave Several groups are now producing this style of music. The Penguin in Tel Aviv is probably the best venue to see them.

Jazz This has a hard-core following and there are some live venues, mainly in Tel Aviv. The quality of the performances does vary but is often excellent.

Hasidic Rock Hasidic Jews have developed an interesting blend of musical styles well worth listening to. Hasidic rock is usually described as a combination of East European gypsy music with American bluegrass. Often performed at festivals, it can be enjoyed more regularly in Jerusalem.

International Artists With the political situation as it is, Israel has not been a regular feature on world tours by the big names. Prior to the intifada this was slowly changing, but now the country has reverted to being a cultural backwater on the international tour scene. The major venues include HaYarkon Park and the Mann Auditorium in Tel Aviv, Sultan's Pool in Jerusalem and the Roman amphitheatre at Caesarea.

Classical Music
Israel is long associated with excellence in classical music. This really started in the 1930s when Jewish musicians, including the best of Europe's composers, performers and teachers, fled to Palestine to escape Nazism. The Israel Philharmonic Orchestra and violinist Yitzhac Perlman are world-renowned, and there are many other musicians and groups worthy of note. The major orchestras and groups perform regularly, mainly by subscription, from October to July – visitors will not always find it easy to get tickets to these concerts. The most important venues are the Mann Auditorium in Tel Aviv and Jerusalem's Binyanei Ha-Oomah. Cultural centres elsewhere regularly host classical concerts, and the historic settings of Caesarea's Roman amphitheatre and Akko's Crusader castle are often used.

In 1986 the Nuyha/El-Hakawati Theatre in East Jerusalem produced the first-known Arabic operetta. Their music department teaches the use of traditional Arab instruments and incorporates a recording studio.

Cinema
Due largely to its diverse geography, Israel has had some success in developing a film production industry. Israeli cinema has enjoyed limited international critical acclaim with films such as *Runaway Train* and *Othello*, as well as commercial success with lower quality productions that have kept such questionable talents as Chuck Norris fed and watered. The *Missing in Action* series was part of a massive output by Cannon, who have since gone out of business.

Film-making in what is now Israel can be traced back to the beginning of the century, when Edison camera operators came to Jerusalem to shoot footage of the local inhabitants. A series of British and Hollywood productions filmed in Israel in the 1950s and early 1960s, such as *Exodus* and *Cast a Giant Shadow* provided a training ground for technicians and directors. The 1964 production *Shabtei* is said to have signalled the emergence of Israel's own film industry. Since that time, the staple diet of Israeli cinema has been the *bourekas* film. The name derives from a pastry, and is given to low-budget comedies using stereotyped characters lifted from Israel's diverse population. This has usually meant an emotional, lazy and vulgar Sephardi competing with a snobbish, humourless and dull Ashkenazi.

Alternatives to the bourekas films are those by the Kayitz film-makers, who produce more serious films, often on subjects that are typically Israeli: the early Zionist pioneers, illegal immigration, the wars, espionage, etc. Critically acclaimed titles include *Beyond the Walls*, *The Tale of the Lamb*, *Avanti Poppoli*, *The Last Summer* and *Real Time*.

There is currently no domestic Palestinian film industry, but there are some Palestinian film-makers working outside Israel. In particular, Michel Kleifi's *Wedding In Galilee* and *Fertile Memory* enjoyed critical acclaim here and abroad.

As with so many industries in Israel, the small home market presents a problem, and security concerns make distributors abroad reluctant to book Israeli films.

Although the intifada has greatly reduced the number of films being made here, many travellers subsidise their stay in Israel by working as film extras. Note that the pay is low, but you are fed well and it can be fun (see Work in the Facts for the Visitor chapter).

ARCHITECTURE
An Historical Legacy
Palestine's successive invaders have left a range of architectural styles.

Roman Sites such as Herodian, Masada, Hammat Gader, Caesarea, Sebastiya and the renovated Citadel in Jerusalem's Old City attest to the Romans' centuries of rule. Herod the Great's reign saw a great deal of building activity.

Crusader Examples of the Crusaders' European-style castles and fortresses include the subterranean city at Akko, the fortress at Nimrod (with later additions by the Muslims), Monfort Castle in the north, Belvoir fortress in the Jordan Valley and

various additions in Jerusalem's Old City such as the Church of the Holy Sepulchre.

Muslim Undoubtedly the country's most impressive remains, these are dominated by minarets, domes and arches. Classic examples include mosques such as Jerusalem's Dome of the Rock and Akko's El-Jazzar, excavations around Jerusalem's Haram esh-Sharif, Hisham's Palace in Jericho, Tokan Castle in Nablus, and the older buildings in Hebron's market place.

Mameluke With more ornamentation in the stone facades, this style is distinct from the earlier Muslim period. Jerusalem's Old City has the best examples anywhere – do not miss the Muslim Quarter and the Haram esh-Sharif.

Ottoman The lengthy rule of the Ottoman Empire was marked in Palestine by a lack of productive activity, and the architectural field was no exception. However, a marvellous example of what they were capable of is Suleiman's city wall in Jerusalem. Akko also features notable examples of Ottoman artistry.

Israeli Architecture
To have even a basic understanding of contemporary Israeli architecture, three facts are worth knowing:

1 Judaism prohibits the use of an image, sculpture or any other visual aid for religious practice.

2 The 2000 years of the Diaspora left the Jewish people with no architectural background, as they either tried to integrate into their local culture, or kept to themselves discreetly. Even when Jews started to renew settlement in Palestine in the 19th century, they used a mixture of architectural styles from the various parts of the world they had just left.

3 The modern history of Israel has been from the very beginning an extremely hard struggle against enormous odds, and aesthetic considerations in building design are rated low.

Israeli architecture could be said to have begun in the 19th century, when new settlers combined the styles of their European backgrounds with Middle Eastern influences. Examples of this can be found in Jerusalem, in the rectangle marked by Prophet (Hanavi'im) St, Ethiopia St, Harav Shemu'el Salant St and B'nai B'rith St, and in particular the Swedish Theological Institute there. Mostly, though, this architecture tended to be simple, modest and far from noteworthy.

The establishment of new neighbourhoods outside the old cities began with the construction of Mishkenot Sha'ananim, followed by Yemin Moshe in Jerusalem in 1858. They were built at the initiative of Sir Moses Montefiore and designed by an English architect, William Edmond Smith. Marked by a windmill designed to be a working model but rendered useless by the lack of sufficient wind, the complex has recently been restored and is one of the city's most exclusive residential areas.

The architecture of the early 20th century was influenced by the 'International' style, which considers the location of a building to be irrelevant to its design, and the socialist vision of a planned society. These combined with the Zionist ideal of a new society free from the sicknesses of the old Europe left behind by the new immigrants. Ahuzat Bait, a neighbourhood on the outskirts of old Jaffa, built in 1909 to the pattern of a European garden city, is the earliest example of these influences.

The Bezalel School of Art was founded in Jerusalem to foster a Hebrew style derived from biblical and Islamic images. Bialik House, built in Tel Aviv in 1924, is one of the finest examples of the Neo-Eastern style. Although planned in the traditional European way, the flat, unembellished facades, a staircase emphasised by the dome tower and the wooden pergolas at the balconies, give the building its Neo-Eastern image. Recently restored, it is on Bialik St, in one of the city's more attractive neighbourhoods.

During the Mandate period, the British tried to restore local tradition by studying the informal patterning of Arab building styles in villages. The main post office in Jaffa Rd, Jerusalem, (1930s) was designed in a manner similar to many Islamic and English Gothic buildings, and the Rockefeller Museum (1920s) in East Jerusalem is modelled after Islamic palaces. The Scottish St Andrew's Hospice in Jerusalem (1927) shows the architect's interest in Armenian monastery styles.

Examples of the International style of the 1930s include Weizmann House in Rehovot (1936), and Hadassah Hospital (1936-39) and the Shocken Library (1936) in Jerusalem. Socialist Zionism inspired the architecture and building styles of the day. Methods of mass production and the adaptation of building blocks to the land division system were used by contractors. Unfortunately, the end result was usually dreary residential development projects.

Another major influence on the Jewish architects was the Bauhaus School from Germany, and Tel Aviv has the best examples of this style anywhere in the world.

On Frishmann St is the Shikun Ovdim, the best known example of the workers' neighbourhood; in it the architect Arieh Sharan created comfortable and minimalist housing. Bauhaus styles can be found all over Tel Aviv, but for the purer examples look in the area around Allenby and King George Sts.

Architecture Since Independence

Israel's independence brought massive waves of immigrants, and much more housing was required. The centralisation of construction work under a single authority resulted in identical housing projects throughout the country.

The architecture looked bureaucratic, with minimum attention paid appearance and comfort, and an emphasis on low cost and speed of construction.

Without considering basic physical and demographic factors, about 20 new towns were built. This resulted in communities with severe economic and social problems. Major segments of the many neighbourhoods built in those years did not survive the 1970s without the need for rehabilitation.

These early plans were costly failures. The

majority of the population is still concentrated in the three big cities and massive residential construction work continues around Jerusalem and Tel Aviv. Beersheba, Negev's 'capital', was planned in the 1950s, with anonymous blocks built in a park. This park is nothing but arid land, as the planned greenery never grew satisfactorily.

Due mainly to the rejuvenating effects of Israel's victory in the Six Day War, prosperity came to the country and the need to economise on building costs was no longer a major consideration. A need to break away from the 1950s image of low standards was felt, along with a wish to create a new, positive architecture. Many projects were undertaken in this period, and as a result many inexperienced architects were employed. You can see their hideous creations in many central vantage points.

A rare bright point from this period is the Israel Museum in Jerusalem, which integrates a modern building with a type of mountainous topography. The imagery is loosely based on terraced Arab villages while the forms and construction are rooted in European modernism.

While much of modern Israeli architecture is ugly, you can find attractive buildings if you know where to look. In Tel Aviv, the IBM Israel building (corner of Weizmann St and King Saul Blvd) and the adjacent Asia House, and the Wolffson Engineering Building at Tel Aviv University are the centre of much attention. The striking Faculty of Social Studies at Beersheba University was designed for protection from the barren Negev Desert.

Jerusalem's Architecture

Jerusalem is like nowhere else on earth. Local Arab construction was the basis for architectural development at the turn of the century here. Later Jewish and Christian dwellings resembled the typical Arab Mediterranean styles. Houses were generally built around a large courtyard, often with surrounding walls. Check out the Sheikh Jarrah neighbourhood for great examples of the traditional styles. Between Jerusalem and

Bethlehem, along Hebron Rd, there are some wonderful examples of Arab housing.

Jerusalem's Christian architecture, strongly influenced by Europe, is monumental, though sometimes disappointing. The many elaborate churches certainly had an enormous impact on the local styles which had previously been dominated by narrow lanes and simple single and two-storey buildings with small domes and narrow windows. The Catholics initially tended to concentrate outside the Jaffa Gate area, and their buildings were constructed in styles reminiscent of the Florentine Renaissance or the later Baroque. The classic example is the renovated Notre Dame complex opposite New Gate.

The Russian Orthodox churches command their settings, both looking out on and being seen from the Old City. The Russian Compound and the Church of Mary Magdalene on the Mount of Olives are monumental in the Byzantine style.

Many Jewish settlers wanted to be self-sufficient and not dependent on charitable funds (the primary support of the Jewish population). This had an effect on the establishment of the new neighbourhoods in Jerusalem outside the Old City. Jewish building design of this period was greatly affected by archaeological research. A Swiss missionary and amateur archaeologist, Conrad Schick, designed many buildings in Jerusalem, including Mea She'arim and the beautiful Tabor House, now the Swedish Theological Institute.

Further examples of the city's outstanding buildings include the YMCA building at 26 King David St. It is an elegant and imaginative, modern building, which also manages to combine elements of Moorish, Romanesque and Oriental styles. Opposite the YMCA is the King David Hotel, which was intended to be one of the world's great hotels. The exterior is somewhat overshadowed by the YMCA but the interior has touches of Assyrian, Hittite and Phoenician styles. The Sherover Jerusalem Theatre was designed to appear as if it had grown naturally out of the hill on which it stands, merging with the connecting terraces to create one entire piece.

Architects who design buildings for Jerusalem are under immense pressure to try to integrate their structures with the city's traditional aura. Four distinctive elements are featured: the dome, the arch, cantilevered features and the use of stone. The last is enforced by law and goes back to the time of British rule.

In Jerusalem recently, renewal has been the order of the day, particularly in the Jewish Quarter of the Old City. Mostly destroyed by the Jordanians after the 1948 War of Independence, the reunification of Jerusalem after the Six Day War has seen construction here on a massive scale. Planning principles included making use of traditional building techniques and preserving the existing texture of buildings and narrow alleyways; allowing only pedestrian traffic in the local alleyways and using electric vehicles for public services and deliveries; grouping buildings around communal courtyards, using stepped sections which allow air and light to enter lower floors and using roofs as terraces; and incorporating archaeological findings into the new buildings, eg the Cardo. Damascus Gate, the Old City's most ornate, is one of the renovation programme's great successes. Sultan's Pool, below the Old City to the west, is now an open-air amphitheatre and one of the country's top concert venues.

FASHION

Israel has a busy fashion industry, not without its problems, but managing to achieve impressive export sales. Swimwear is the country's most successful clothing export.

It shouldn't take long for you to notice that many Israeli Jews are extremely fashion conscious. Teenage *sabras* (Israel-born Jews) in particular can be seen parading the streets, beaches and discos, glancing at every surface in the hope of a reflection in which to check their outfits and hairstyles. The older generation of Jews are much less fashion conscious, often wearing styles reminiscent of their native countries. Arab men wear a mixture of traditional and contemporary styles, the younger generation turning more towards Western fashions. Arab women generally wear traditional clothes, although most do not cover their faces.

Despite the hot climate, the East European furriers and leather craftspersons have managed to continue their business and Israel produces quality goods with lower than average prices.

Newe Tzedek, in Tel Aviv, is the centre of the country's fashion trade, crammed with workshops and showrooms. Designer boutiques are centred on the city's Yirmiyahu St. A textile and fashion centre has been established in Tel Aviv to provide a meeting place for buyers, manufacturers, suppliers and other interested parties.

CULTURE
The Kibbutz

A kibbutz is a community of people who live together on the basis of shared ownership of the means of production, shared consumption and no direct connection between work and remuneration. Each family has its own apartment but all meals are taken together in a communal dining hall. Kibbutzim vary in size, from up to 100 members to as many as 2000. Most consist of between 300 to 800 members. Originally agricultural settlements, almost every kibbutz today has at least one factory, and some have three or four.

Each kibbutz is an independent legal, social and economic entity. It is run by the general assembly, made up of all the members. This meets once a week, usually on Saturday evening. Some large kibbutzim call general assembly meetings less frequently and use a council of 30 to 40 members for intermediate decisions. The kibbutz secretary is the highest official.

In 1927, the cultivated area of kibbutzim was less than 50 sq km, of which less than 2½ sq km were under irrigation. By 1981 the cultivated area had grown to over 1500 sq km, with half under irrigation. The efficiency of kibbutz agriculture is much talked about, both in Israel and abroad, and it is calculated that by the year 2000 the kibbutzim will supply over half of all the country's agricultural produce. However, the reality is that many kibbutzim are not faring so well and owe millions after years of extravagant spending and poor planning.

There are currently 273 kibbutzim in the kibbutz movement, which is divided into several organisations along political and ideological lines. The largest component is the Labour Party-affiliated United Kibbutz Movement, with 168 kibbutzim, popularly known by its abbreviated Hebrew name Takam. The next largest is the Kibbutz Artzi, with 85 kibbutzim. It is associated with the worldwide Hashomer Hatzair Youth Movement and the left-wing Mapam and has a more strict Marxist ideology. In third place numerically are the 17 religious kibbutzim of Po'el Hamizrachi, better known as Kibbutz Dati. There are also two kibbutzim belonging to the ultra-orthodox Po'el Agudat Israel, and one belonging to Ha'ihud hahaqla'i.

History The kibbutz movement started in Russia at the turn of the century and was inspired by Marx, Engels and, later, the Russian Revolution. Before coming to Palestine the would-be kibbutzniks got together in camps to establish a system. The early kibbutzim were strictly secular and committed to the ideal of a return to the land.

Kibbutz Degania, founded in 1910 beside the Jordan River and close to the Sea of Galilee, was the first. The early kibbutz members had to cope with extremely harsh conditions with virtually no money. Galilee at that time was dominated by malarial swamps, not the trees you see now, and kibbutz life was nowhere near as organised as it is today. Right from the start there was a continuing debate about the right direction for these new communes. Some members wanted to stay as small, primarily agricultural and self-sufficient units, while others wanted to grow, include industry and integrate into a national political and economic organisation. These strong differences of opinion remain today.

The arrival in the 1930s of refugees from Nazism interrupted the debate, as the kibbutzim became absorption centres. As the Zionist leaders drew up plans for a Jewish state amidst rumours of a British partition plan for Palestine, the need to expand Jewish settlement in the country was recognised. The Negev was seen as an important area and dozens of new kibbutzim were established in remote areas. The violent reaction of the local Arabs to these new Jewish settlements inspired the formation of the Palmach, a commando-style strike force and a forerunner of the IDF.

To this day, a disproportionately large number of personnel in the officer corps, air force and commando units are kibbutz members. Similarly, this intense involvement in preparing the way for the State of Israel brought widespread participation in politics, and a disproportionately large number of Knesset members and ministers are kibbutz members.

The establishment of Israel meant transferring many responsibilities from the kibbutzim to the new government. Eventually, the progress made by the kibbutzim in agriculture led them to move into industry with the spare labour that this progress had created. By 1984, kibbutz agriculture formed 40% of the national production. Since the 1960s the 'kibbutz industrial revolution' has caused many major changes in lifestyles and economic activities. Several kibbutzim now earn most of their incomes from industry, not agriculture.

Like farmers in other countries today, members of the kibbutzim face hard times. More and more of their younger generation are moving away, but the biggest problem is debt. Somewhere in the region of US$4 billion is said to be owed collectively.

Kibbutz Members (Kibbutzniks) Kibbutz members surprisingly represent less than 3% of Israel's population, although in rural areas they often form a third of the local inhabitants. Most of the early kibbutz members were from Eastern and Central Europe, but today the vast majority are Israeli-born – to a greater degree than the Israeli population as a whole. Most of the arrivals over the years have come from Europe, the Americas, South Africa and Australia.

The kibbutz population is generally younger than the rest of the Jewish population, as kibbutz families have more children than others, and there is a greater absorption of young people from outside. The ratio of applicants to places available on kibbutzim varies enormously. This places the movement in a dilemma, having to decide whether to increase its growth rate by building more housing and absorbing more outsiders, which could cause financial problems, or by relying on reproduction.

The traditional family, two parents and their children, is a passing phenomenon in kibbutzim. By the time a kibbutz is 50 years old, multi-generational families are well established. Children grow up alongside grandparents and other senior relatives, not just their own parents. These complex multigenerational links are a key factor in guaranteeing communal solidarity and continuity. Close to 90% of kibbutz members live in communities that have reached at least their third generation and in which this multi-generational family style is typical.

Education & Culture The kibbutzim have their own educational system within the framework of the national Ministry of Education, ranging from kindergarten to university level. All children born the same year are raised and educated together from the babies' house to the end of high school. Most also go on to higher education. It used to be that all children slept in separate children's quarters from their parents, but there has been a move towards having children up to high school age sleep with their parents.

Two large adult education centres have been established to cater for a wide range of the kibbutz movement's needs. A third centre specialises in economics, management, technology and agriculture.

It appears that the kibbutz way of life, free from most of the everyday worries about prices and income, encourages the creative energies of kibbutzniks, as the kibbutz movement's cultural productivity is impressive. This includes two orchestras, two internationally known choral groups, a dance group, a theatre group, hundreds of authors, poets, singers, composers and musicians, about 600 recognised artists and sculptors, and more recently a growing number of writers, producers, directors, camera-operators and technicians specialising in video films for television. There are four nationally distributed literary journals as well as other periodicals, including literary works, published by the movement. It owns two of Israel's leading publishing houses and is involved in a third. There are two central art galleries in the Tel Aviv area for kibbutz artists, and another four in kibbutzim. More than 70 museums have been established in kibbutzim, often specialising in the archaeology of the local area where members have taken part in excavations.

The Moshav

The moshav is a cooperative village, featuring aspects of both private and collective farming. Families have their own homes, children live with their parents, and these families have individual plots of land and budgets. Capital items such as machinery are owned by the moshav, which also markets the produce and buys supplies collectively to get a better price. Approximately 5% of Israel's population live on moshavim.

The moshav movement began in 1921, as a blending of the ideals of the kibbutz movement with those of earlier, failed attempts at Jewish settler farming. The five principles of the moshav movement are:

1 The land belongs to the nation, not to the individual.

2 Mutual aid – members help one another, especially in developing years and when someone is sick. Today what is more important is teaming up to secure a better deal with banks and credit companies as a collective.

3 You work by yourself. This principle was followed for the first 25 years or so, but mass immigration changed all that. Most newcomers had no real farming

experience and could not fit into the collective or the kibbutz system. Large numbers of the new immigrants had little choice in where they were sent, and the new country needed to develop the land, so they became farmers. The B'nai HaMoshavim (Sons of the Moshavim) organisation was set up as a result.

This group of agricultural experts trained and led the newcomers but their systems did not aspire to the original moshav ideals, working well as farms but not as collectives. They often employ Arabs and foreign volunteers as cheap labour to work the land whilst they work elsewhere.

4 A collective system for selling.

5 Land and water is shared equally by the members.

Today there are over 400 moshavim in Israel. About 20 of these are collective moshavim, with some aspects similar to a kibbutz. There is no private land and no communal dining room; members have their own living quarters but all the production and income belongs to the community with profits equally divided.

As in the kibbutz movement, there has been an increase, though less dramatic, in industrial activity in the moshavim as agriculture has proved to be an insufficient means of support.

The moshavim do not organise their own schools, or have as much of a community-based lifestyle as the kibbutzim do.

Sports

Israel follows a variety of sports, with soccer, followed by basketball, as the most popular. Israel Television regularly broadcasts matches from England and an Israeli fan's knowledge of the English game will often put his English counterpart to shame.

Sports centres are common, and the generous climate with the coastlines and Sea of Galilee encourage sporting activity. Swimming, windsurfing, sailing and water skiing are all popular.

The most noticeable sport is *matkot*, Israel's beach tennis. On any beach popular with Israelis you will frequently notice this game being played – usually very well, very loudly, and very dangerously for anyone having to cross the unmarked court to get to and from the sea.

Israel stages the 'Jewish Olympics', the Maccabiah Games. Held every four years since 1932, the games attract Jewish athletes from around the world.

Betting

Israel has a national lottery and football pools, and the number of kiosks around the place show the 'sport's' popularity. Chaim Bermont, one of the country's better writers, once observed that the Israeli Jews' attitude to betting sums up their attitude to life in general: 'When they place a bet they don't hope to win; they expect to win'.

RELIGION

The religious status of this area is unique. Jews have lived here, in varying numbers, since the time of the Old Testament; Christianity began here 2000 years ago; and Muslims revere Jerusalem as their third holiest site. In addition to the 'Big Three' monotheistic faiths, Israel is today the world centre of the Baha'i faith; the home of the Samaritans, probably the world's smallest ethnic group; and has attracted the Black Hebrews from their exile in the USA and around the world.

Judaism

Israel is the Jewish state and, as such, Judaism is the country's dominant faith. Many of the country's Jews spend most of their lives studying their faith, so don't expect to find all your questions answered in this book.

According to high Jewish doctrine, Jews are in the world to be witnesses to the claim that there is one God with whom humans can have contact: God has chosen them to act as messengers, whose task it is to pass on these details to the rest of the world. What God has said is written in the Torah, the first five books of the Old Testament. The Torah contains God's revelation to the Jews via their leader, Moses, over 3000 years ago. It contains 613 commandments, interpretations of which cover fundamental issues such as avoiding idolatry, murder and sexual abuse, and apparent trivialities such as never eating cheeseburgers, and not driving a car or making toast on Saturday.

Judaism is an extremely complex faith, and the Torah is only the foundation of Jewish sacred literature. There are also the prophetic, historical and 'poetical' books that constitute the rest of the Old Testament. The prophetic books rank second only to the Torah in Judaism, with Isaiah the most important. It is said that without these ancient prophets Judaism would have remained a mere tribal religion and would have been forgotten long ago. Isaiah, and also Jeremiah and Amos, stressed that God was not just for the Jews but for everyone, and that the Jews were his Priests. This point had been touched upon in the Torah but it only came to the fore in the prophetic period.

The defeat of the Jewish state and the destruction of the Second Temple around 70 AD was a major setback to the Jews. These events were believed to show either that it was no use believing in God, or that he had to be thought of in a broader sense than before. The Jews chose the latter and many believe that this is why they have survived.

Another major written part of the Jewish faith is the Talmud, which includes the Mishnah. This great collection of writings was completed during the early centuries of the Christian era. About 2000 authors contributed towards the 63 books. The Talmud contains rabbinical interpretations of the scriptures and commentaries. Virtually every aspect of life is touched upon and it is this work that many spend a lifetime studying. In days gone by, some scholars in Eastern Europe were said to know it all by heart.

The Talmud is not the last word in Judaism. Rabbinical rulings over the years have had to be made, and they have often been the cause of much controversy. Topical areas subjected to rabbinical rulings include the use of special Shabbat elevators and the complexities of dealing with Shabbat hours when flying across the International Date Line.

The primary Jewish tradition is based upon the Torah, God's commandments. Terms such as 'doctrine', 'creed', and 'theology' are now used in Judaism but they are new to it. Jewish ethics teach that people should be good citizens and act justly towards each other. The non-Jew is referred to in the original revelation to Moses, with the injunction that the Jews should behave well to the stranger in their midst. Judaism supposedly abhors violence, murder and war, but also rejects the Christian policy of 'turning the other cheek'. To Jews, killing is acceptable in self-defence.

Judaism's complexity is largely due to various individual interpretations of the Torah, and the other Jewish Written Laws. Although Judaism is non-denominational, with the same basic prayer book and identical weekly readings in use throughout the world, there have been changes in its practice and perception since the early 19th century. In Israel today, there are three main trends:

Orthodox Maintaining strict adherence to the Jewish code of life, *halacha*, this form embraces both the Written and the Oral Law.

Conservative Advocates adherence to halacha, while believing that it should be adapted to the requirements of modern life. This trend is also known as Traditional or Mesorati Judaism.

Reform Even more leeway in the adaptation of halacha is allowed, with emphasis on the

Menorah

ethical aspects of Judaism and the right of the individual to choose a religious way from among the precepts of halacha.

Appearances Identifying these modern trends is often made simpler by remembering the basic dress styles of the different Jewish groups.

The most religious, pious or ultra-orthodox Jews are the Hasidim, a sect of Jews who follow a mystical interpretation and approach to Judaism. They originated in the late 17th century in Eastern Europe, led by the Rabbi Baal Shem Tov. They are also the most visible Jews with their black hats (on Shabbat often replaced by grand fur hats), long black coats, tieless white shirts, beards and cropped hair with *payot* (side curls). Their appearance is often a source of amusement to others but it has a special meaning to them. The Hasidic clothes are derived from the aristocracy of late medieval Poland and they wear them, regardless of the season, for two main reasons: humility, to remind them that they are less than God and to rid themselves of feelings such as vanity; and mourning, for the Temple which will be rebuilt for the return of the Messiah. The Hasidic haircut is based on the Torah's command: 'You shall not round off the hair on your temples or mar the edges of your beard' (Leviticus 19:27). Therefore, the ultra-orthodox keep their heads cropped – except for the payot – and they grow a beard.

Some Orthodox Jews grow beards and payot but do not go to such lengths as the Hasidim. These Jews will keep their hair short, trim their beards and wear more standard styles of dark suits and hats. Other Orthodox Jews are not so noticeable by their appearance, but still strictly follow the Jewish Law.

The most common sign of a religious Jew is the *yarmulka*, or *kippah* (skullcap). There is no universally recognised size for yarmulkas and you will see various styles, colours and materials used. Many interpret the covering of the head as a sign of modesty before God and an acknowledgement of his supremacy. Nowadays, covering the head is a matter of debate between those who feel it is obligatory, eg the Hasidim and other Orthodox Jews, those who consider it necessary only for prayers and services, and those who are totally opposed to it. Some religious Jews wear a yarmulka in bed, but most do not!

Childhood & the Home By Jewish Law (Genesis 17:9-14) a boy should be circumcised on the eighth day after birth. Today, this is often performed for purely medical reasons, but the more traditional, though not necessarily religious, Jews treat it as an important ceremony with family and friends witnessing the occasion. At circumcision a boy is given a religious name by which he will be later 'called up' to the Torah. An injunction states that a boy should start his religious study from the age of three. Traditionally, boys receive such an education whilst girls primarily learn how to run a home according to Jewish law. Times have changed and it is the area of the women's role that involves many of today's controversies and differences. Nowadays, most children are educated more or less alike.

Many of the major acts of Jewish worship are carried out in the home, with the parents performing a priestly role. This has a considerable effect on the child and even if in later life he/she has ceased to practise the religion, an affection for some of its aspects is often retained. The Jewish home is believed to be a main reason for Judaism's survival during the centuries of persecution.

When he reaches the age of 13, a Jewish boy becomes *bar mitzvah*. Basically, this means that he is subject to Jewish law and therefore, for religious purposes, he is an adult. On the Shabbat after his 13th birthday he reads from the Torah in the synagogue for the first time. This involves about a year's preparation and is often an emotional and noisy occasion with older relatives making their presence felt. Witnessing a bar mitzvah at the Western Wall can be one of the highlights of a visit to Jerusalem. Nowadays there is also a *bat mitzvah* ceremony for Jewish girls.

Food According to Judaism, every meal is a religious rite, as it must be *kosher*, that is, prepared in accordance with God's commandments. In the Reform tradition, the dietary laws may be treated literally or not observed at all. One attitude is that they originate from primitive taboos and are not to be regarded as God's enduring word. Some Reform Jews abstain from foods positively forbidden in the Torah but ignore the detailed rabbinical instructions that control a kosher kitchen.

Shabbat The most important meal of the week in most Jewish homes is Friday night's dinner, at the start of Shabbat. In Judaism, the 'day' begins when the sun sets. Before Shabbat starts, the house is cleaned and the dinner table is set with the best crockery and table linen. Traditionally, religious fathers and sons go to the synagogue while the women prepare the meal. On his return the father blesses the children and recites from the Old Testament. To religious Jews, Shabbat is a joyful day and a time to appreciate what they have been too busy to notice during the week. No work of any kind may be carried out on Shabbat, unless it is necessary to save life.

The Orthodox maintain a particularly meticulous code which forbids writing, handling of money, and the operation of machinery of any kind. Jewish communities tend to be concentrated because religious Jews need to be within walking distance of the synagogue, as driving, using public transport and even walking too far are forbidden on Shabbat. One theory to explain the worldwide trend towards greater orthodoxy is that today's working conditions have made Shabbat observance a lot easier.

Sex & Marriage In sexual matters, Judaism has been said to advocate moderation, but to distrust total abstention. In the past such Jewish sects as the Essenes have advocated celibacy but they were very much the exception.

Mainstream Jewish teaching places great value on married and family life. A number of rabbinical authorities say that a man should not remain unmarried beyond the age of 18. Divorce under Jewish law is relatively easy, but is regarded as a failure and a tragedy in what is a central part of Judaism. Tradition says that the altar of the Temple weeps when a Jewish divorce occurs.

Orthodox Judaism is generally wary of contraception. It believes that Jews should have large families in obedience of God's command to procreate, and also to preserve Judaism, which loses large numbers every generation due to mixed marriages. If having children endangers the mother's health, contraception will be considered, as sex is considered a central part of a marriage. Abortion also is normally permitted only if there is danger to the mother's life.

Death & the Afterlife Basically, Jewish teaching says that at death the body returns to God. Traditionally, the funeral takes place within 24 hours of death, to allow mourners to quickly face the reality of the death; to conform with the interpretation of the Bible which says that the body should return to its natural course of decomposition as soon as possible; and to show respect for the deceased, as it is considered a humiliation to the dead to be unburied.

Maintaining a burial society and a cemetery to ensure that there is no distinction between the funerals of the rich and the poor is one of the highest priorities of a Jewish community. There is no cremation in traditional Judaism, because Jews believe in a physical resurrection on the Day of Judgement. Many Jews are bitterly opposed to autopsies for this reason. It is a Jewish gesture of mourning that a man rips his clothes. This puts the mark of his broken heart on his clothing and can also provide an outlet for the anguish and emotion that a mourner feels. Today this is usually expressed by a symbolic tearing of a lapel. There is no prayer for the dead, as such, but *kaddish*, a prayer that praises God, is recited on their behalf. It is the special duty of a son of the deceased to recite kaddish.

You will notice that visitors to Jewish

graves place stones rather than flowers on the grave, because this is a more permanent way of showing that a visit has been made, and also involves the mourner in the act of burying the deceased, thus helping to return him to God.

Synagogues, Rabbis & Prayers The word 'synagogue' means 'meeting place'. The synagogue is not only a place for prayer. The studying of religious texts by young and old, the meetings of the Community Council and the Rabbinical Court have taken place there. Once, there would be a bakery for the special unleavened bread *(matzah)* baked once a year for Pesah, and probably a ritual bath *(mikvah)*. In medieval times an annexe of the synagogue may have been used as a hostel for travellers. These days, although prayer and study are the main values which the synagogue fosters, many other community activities take place there, such as groups for youngsters, young wives and senior citizens. The head must be covered at all times in a synagogue.

Synagogues have been built in a large variety of architectural styles. As a result, it is quite often possible not to realise that there is a synagogue behind you in certain places, despite the frequent external use of Jewish symbols such as the menorah (seven-branched candelabra) and the Star of David.

The focal point of the interior of a synagogue, normally set in the eastern wall, is a cupboard containing one or more copies of the Torah (and sometimes the Prophets and Writings). These are written in Hebrew on parchment, by a scribe with a quill pen, and kept as a scroll on two rollers. Writing such a scroll (the Sefer Torah) takes over a year and because of their holiness they are treasured and revered possessions. The cupboard is known as the Holy Ark (Aron Hakodesh) and is covered by a curtain (Parochet). A light is kept burning continually in front of the Ark, in remembrance of the continual light in the Temple and as a mark of respect to the holiness of the Scrolls.

Often, above the Holy Ark, are representations of the two tablets of stone on which were written the Ten Commandments. These usually show the first two words, in Hebrew, of each commandment. There are often illustrations of the Western Wall and Rachel's Tomb on the synagogue's walls. In the centre of the synagogue is the reading-desk, normally on a raised platform (Bimah). This is sometimes at the eastern end of the synagogue in front of the Ark. On Shabbat and festivals, readings from the Torah are made from here. During the year, all the five books are read. All over the world, Jews read the same portions each week. Services can be led from here or from a small lectern standing on the floor in front of the Ark.

Sermons are delivered from the pulpit and are a relatively recent addition to the service. As in the Temple, the sexes are seated separately, often with a gallery for the women. Traditional Judaism regards this separation during worship seriously, mainly for reasons of modesty. Basically the men feel that the women's presence would distract them from their prayer.

Services are led by a Ba'al Tephilah, who leads the communally sung or chanted prayers. Services are not necessarily led by the rabbi. He is a religious leader and teacher, employed by his congregation, and his main task is to interpret Jewish teachings to his congregation. Any male over the age of 13 can act as prayer-leader. In Orthodox Judaism, there are still remains of the old hereditary priesthood that officiated until the destruction of the Second Temple, 2000 years ago. Any man named Cohen is likely to be a member of the old priesthood; not that the proof of such descent is available. Today a cohen has the right to bestow certain blessings, but the loss of the Temple deprived the cohenim of their function and religious leadership passed entirely to the rabbis.

Jews should pray three times a day, in the morning, afternoon and evening, with certain additional prayers to be said on Shabbat and holidays. Wherever possible, religious Jews try to form a group of public prayer. In the Orthodox tradition, this consists of a minimum of 10 men (over the age of 13) and is called a *minyan*. There is an old saying that 10 cobblers make a minyan but nine rabbis do not. Services may be held anywhere and Jews frequently arrange informal meetings for daily services at places of work, in the home and student centres, etc.

The apparent lack of decorum in synagogue services often surprises first-time visitors. People talk to each other and go in and out of the synagogue, and children are often playing there. Jewish worship is very diverse by nature and this is all allowed during certain parts of the service.

Non-Jews & Conversion A question often asked of a stranger in the street by Jews in Israel is 'Are you Jewish?'. It is never meant to offend, although it often does when the questioner walks away if the answer is negative. Normally the questioner wants to know if the other person is Jewish in order to invite them to a synagogue, Shabbat dinner or just to engage in Judaic discussion.

Jews should believe that everybody has a responsibility to be humane, moral and generally good. A clear rabbinical teaching deals with what a non-Jew must do to be saved. It includes abstaining from idolatry, blasphemy, murder, theft and incest, acting justly and not eating meat that has been cut from a living animal. Providing non-Jews comply with these Seven Laws to the Sons of Noah, they do not need to comply with the complexity of the rules given specially to the Jews. Jews are encouraged to share their view of morality but some have said that persecution over the centuries has led them to shy away from this responsibility.

Jews are traditionally horror-struck with the idea of one of them marrying a non-Jew, or following another religion. Likewise, they do not encourage conversion to Judaism. They feel that the future of the Jewish people can only be ensured by the continuity of Jewish families, and that a Jew marrying a non-Jew means the end of the line. Another common feeling is that being Jewish is very much a family experience requiring the contribution of both parents.

Conversion to Judaism is usually a slow, hard process, but it does take place. The Orthodox view is that wanting to marry a Jew is not sufficient reason for wanting to become a Jew. To them, evidence of independent religious motivation is necessary. Reform Judaism is more open and, particularly if the prospective convert does not practise another faith, marriage is often considered a sufficient reason for conversion.

Mezuzah The Torah (in Deuteronomy 6:4-9 and 11:13-21) has inspired Jews to attach a *mezuzah* to the entrances of homes, public buildings, synagogues and to the room inside.

The mezuzah is a container of wood, metal, plastic, stone, ceramic or even paper containing a parchment with the afore-mentioned references from the Torah lettered on the front and the Hebrew word Shaddai (Almighty) lettered on the back. Usually the container has a hole through which the word Shaddai can be seen, or the Hebrew letter *shin* displayed on its front.

The mezuzah may date to the period of the Jews' slavery in Egypt, as Egyptians placed a sacred document on the entrance of their houses. The word 'mezuzah' means 'doorpost' and there is some disagreement over the significance of the custom. Some people believe it protects their house, others that it protects the occupants from sinning. Another theory is that it is a reminder that worldly affairs are unimportant when compared to God. It is a common custom for Jews to kiss their fingers after touching the mezuzah as they enter and leave.

Tallit Married Orthodox men, and Jewish Conservative and Reform males past the age of bar mitzvah, wear the tallit (prayer shawl). On each of the four corners of the tallit are the *tzitzit* – symbolic tassles as directed by the Torah (Numbers 15:37-41). While the regular tallit is specifically for prayer, the Torah's instruction is to wear a garment with tzitzit all day. Therefore, traditional Jews wear the smaller tallit katan all day, and the larger tallit just for prayers. Despite the Torah's clear instructions about using blue cord in the tassles, most Jews use white cord.

I was told that the shade of blue required came from a dye acquired from an animal which ceased to be available. The Black Hebrews and the Karaites both use blue thread in their tzitzits, though. Tying the tzitzit involves symbolic methods, as does the wrapping of the individual in the tallit. Verses from Psalms (104:1-2) are read and kabbalistic meditations follow.

Tefillin You will notice at the Western Wall, and perhaps in some of the bus stations, Jewish males wrapping a leather strap around their arm and wearing a small box strapped to their head. This is *tefillin*, the result of the Jews' interpretation of instructions in the Torah (Exodus 13:1-10, 13:11-16; Deuteronomy 6:4-9, 11:13-21).

Tefillin are composed of two main parts which are worn every weekday morning during the Morning Service, Shaharit. *Tefillin shel yad* is the strap wrapped around the arm and hand; and *Tefillin shel rosh* is the small box placed on the head. Both parts include a box, called a *bayit* (plural *batim*). Shel yad has one compartment and shel rosh has four separate compartments, placed tightly together. The shel rosh also has the Hebrew letter shin on two sides. This is seen by some as an allusion to the Ten Commandments and the patriarchs.

Enclosed in each bayit is each of the stipulated portions of the Torah, written on parchment, tightly rolled and tied with animal hair. For the shel yad, they are written on one long piece of parchment; for the shel rosh each quote is written on a separate piece and put in a separate compartment. *Giddin*, threads made from the fibres of a kosher animal's hip muscle tissue, are used to sew the bayit shut.

The shel yad binds the arm, therefore the body; the shel rosh binds the mind. The tefillin, then, binds the whole person, mind, heart and body, together to worship God. It also reminds Jews that the mind, heart and body are to be used for good and not evil. The tefillin are a memorial to the exodus of the Jews from Egypt, a sign of where they have been, who they are and where they are

heading – the permanent duty of God's service. Traditionally only men wear tefillin, but some women do. They are not worn on Shabbat or holidays.

Other Jewish Sects

Black Hebrews This group, mainly former Black Americans, believe that they are Jews, descended from the original tribe of Judah. They claim that their ancestors went into exile in Africa, and were eventually taken as slaves to the USA, the Caribbean islands and England. They do not believe that all Black people are Jews. There has long been a recognised (although not by everyone) Black Jewish community in the USA and Africa, but the Hebrew's claims have been the cause of considerable controversy since they first arrived in Israel in 1969. Both the Israeli Government and the Religious Courts have refused to recognise them as Jews.

The community was founded in Chicago in the early 1960s by Ben-Ami Carter. One of their many controversial theories is that all the biblical characters, including Abraham, Solomon, and Jesus, were Black. This is based on such Bible references as Daniel 7:9; the Song of Solomon 1:5; 4:1; and Revelations 2:18. Their most important belief is that they are descended from the original Hebrew Israelites and have now been called by God to return to the Promised Land. Rather than travel directly to Israel, the Hebrews, led by Carter, first went to Liberia to experience the wilderness in preparation for the Promised Land. There the community developed their principles of a vegetarian diet, and abstinence from smoking, alcohol (except their own wine) and pharmaceutical drugs, and complete isolation from the corrupting influences of the world. They learned the Hebrew language and took up wearing African clothing styles, with the women covered from head to toe and the men growing beards and wearing wool hats. Men were surnamed Ben Israel (Son of Israel) and the women Bat Israel (Daughter of Israel).

In 1967, one of the community arrived in Israel to spy out the land for Carter, rather like spies had for Moses. In 1969 four other Hebrews arrived, posing as tourists. Joining the first arrival they were given accommodation and work in Arad, then a new development town encouraging people to live there.

Later that year more community members, mainly women and children, arrived and for the first time made their citizenship claims, under the Law of Return. The government was not at all keen on the idea, but the new arrivals were given temporary visas and accommodation in nearby Dimona while their claims were investigated.

Initially the Hebrews were popular with the locals, but that was all to change. A few months later, in 1970, another group arrived, claiming to be the fathers and husbands of those living in Dimona. Ben-Ami Carter was amongst this group. By now, the authorities had decided that the Hebrews were not Jews, but, apparently reluctant to break up the families, admitted the newcomers as tourists with no housing privileges. In the following years more Hebrews arrived, mostly posing as tourists rather than returning Jews. Most were now in Dimona, with others in Arad and Mitzpe Ramon, another Negev development town desperate for residents.

In 1972, the Government decided that no more Hebrews were to be allowed into Israel, but gave no guidelines on how to distinguish members of the community from legitimate Black tourists. This allowed Hebrews to avoid the ban by simply posing as tourists and pilgrims, and led to international controversy with lengthy interrogations and considerable harassment for many Blacks entering Israel. At the end of 1972, the Supreme Court ruled that the Hebrews were not Jews and upheld the government's right to deport them. However, it also suggested that those already in the country should be permitted to stay.

Meanwhile, locals, in Dimona in particular, complained about the overcrowded conditions and excessive noise created by the Hebrews' presence. Eventually, the Hebrew community was given a former absorption-centre complex originally designed as temporary accommodation for newly-arrived immigrants, and this is where most of the 1200 or so Hebrews live today.

Another reason for the controversy over the Hebrews has been the statements reportedly made by Ben-Ami Carter and other leaders. He strenuously denies much of what he has been quoted as saying over the years, accusing the media of discrimination. He has been quoted as declaring that the 'White' Jews had stolen the language, history and culture of his community, who are the 'real' Jews, and that he will eventually rule over Israel. His status as leader of the community is indisputable, but whether he is 'dictator', 'con-man', 'prophet' or the 'Prince of Peace' (all of which he has been called) is less clear.

You will see members of the Hebrew community, mainly in Tel Aviv but also in other areas, selling their home-made jewellery and other craftwork. There is also the Eternity Restaurant in Tel Aviv featuring their unique tofu-dominated vegetarian food. They welcome visits to the community's home in Dimona, in order to show people their lifestyle and discuss their claims.

Messianic Jews This small group of Jews differ from the majority in that they accept Jesus Christ as the Son of God and all that he has said as written in the New Testament. They have formed their own denomination within the Christian Church, as they still have major differences with some interpretations of the teachings of Jesus Christ in relation to their understanding of the Old Testament and the status of the Jewish people.

Samaritans According to the Samaritans' fullest version of their history, the Chronicle II, they are directly descended from the Joseph tribes, Ephraim and Manasseh. Until the 17th century they possessed a high priesthood descending directly from Aaron through Eleazar and Phinehas. They claim to have lived continuously in the area and are also believed to be the world's smallest ethnic group. Prior to the publication of

Chronicle II, the most widely available and decisive source of the history of the Samaritans was the Biblical account in II Kings 17.

The Samaritan priesthood dominates life in the community. These men are the sole interpreters of the law and the calendar, which is a vital part of their faith as it governs the observation of their festivals. Unlike the Jews, who have the Bible and the Talmud, the Samaritans have a faith whose beliefs are relatively simple to outline. After Moses, Joshua is the only prophet to be held in high esteem. It could be said that the Samaritan doctrine is that anything not covered in the Five Books of Moses cannot be regarded as valid. They regard the Ten Commandments as nine, adding a 10th of their own stipulating the sanctity of Mount Gerizim.

The Samaritan way of life results from an interpretation of biblical laws which is usually stricter than that of the most ultra-orthodox Jews. They observe Shabbat in similar style to the Jews, and also have the same circumcision rules. During their menstrual period, women are obliged to remain separated from their families for seven days, and the men must look after their families. After giving birth, a woman is considered to be unclean. If the child is a son, the period is 40 days, for a daughter, it is 80 days. The Samaritan bar mitzvah is dependent upon the individual's education and ability, not age. Marriage is the reason for more celebration than any other Samaritan ceremony. The bridegroom's family proclaims a week of celebration, starting the Shabbat before the wedding, which takes place on the fourth day. Intermarriage with the Jewish community is permitted only after the High Priest is convinced that the convert will be suitable for observing the Samaritan traditions. Divorce is rare. The Samaritans bury their dead in their cemetery on Mount Gerizim.

Over the years, the Samaritans have been greatly affected by the political turmoil in the area. During the beginning of the British Mandate the Samaritan community separated, with about half of them moving away from Nablus to Holon near Jaffa.

After Israel's independence the Samaritan communities became split between Israel and Jordan. The Six Day War reunited the two communities.

Karaites The name of this small sect means 'people of the Scriptures' but could also be interpreted as 'propagandists'. Their main characteristic is the recognition of the Scriptures as the only source of religious law, and they reject rabbinical tradition and the Oral Laws. Their name was not applied until the 9th century and the sect appears to have been formed due to a variety of factors, including the amalgamation of several rebel trends in Babylonian-Persian Jewry; the tremendous religious, political and economic fermentation in the entire East due to the Arab conquests; and social and economic grievances of the poorer classes of Jewry.

In principle, the Bible is the Karaites' sole source of creed and law, but apart from its fundamental stand on the Oral Law, Karaite creed does not differ in its essentials from that of Rabbinical Judaism.

Islam

The Arabic word Islam means voluntary surrender to the will of Allah (God) and obedience to his commands. Muslims prefer to use the Arabic word Allah whatever their nationality. Some Muslims interpret 'Islam' as meaning peace, believing that observing total obedience to Allah is the only way to achieve peace. A Muslim is a person who accepts the Islamic way of life and practises it. The three fundamental Islamic beliefs are: Tawhid, oneness of Allah; Risalah, prophethood; and Akhirah, life after death.

Tawhid This is the most important Islamic belief. It implies that everything in earth originates from Allah, who is the 'one and only Creator'. He is also the 'Sustainer and the sole Source of Guidance'. This belief governs all aspects of a Muslim's life. Islam views human life as a compact whole and rejects any compartmentalisation. As there is only one 'Creator and Source of Guidance', there is no scope for any partnership. Allah is neither born 'nor is anyone born of him –

he has no son or daughter'. Humans are 'his' subjects. In Islam, he is 'Allah, the One'.

Tawhid brings a total change to a believer's life. It means worship of Allah, who is 'always watching', and encourages working for this supremacy in all areas of everyday life. The purpose of life is to please Allah.

Risalah It is believed that Allah gives guidance (Hidayah) on how to live, and Risalah is his channel of communication – the prophets and messengers. The chain began with Adam, and includes Noah, Abraham, Ishmael, Isaac, Lot, Jacob, Joseph, Moses, Jesus and lastly Mohammed. The message brought by each of them is believed to be the same. They all urged the people of their time to obey and worship Allah alone and no-one else. It was necessary to send prophets at different times to bring back straying people from deviations to the 'Right Course' (Siratul Mustaqim).

Allah also sent books of guidance with these prophets. The Koran (Qur'an) which was revealed to Mohammed, is the last of these.

Akhirah This means life after death and this belief has a far-reaching impact on the life of the believer, who is accountable to Allah on the Day of Judgement. Belief in Akhirah implies that all actions will be judged by Allah in the life hereafter. People who obey him throughout their lives will be rewarded with a permanent place in Paradise. Evildoers will be sent to Hell. Angels are believed to be recording everyone's actions and believers should always bear in mind that Allah is watching.

Five Basic Duties of Islam These are known as the pillars of Islam, and should be performed regularly and correctly with an awareness of their relevance to practical life. This brings the Muslim's life into line with Allah's wishes. It also enables the believer to fit neatly into the system of Islam which aims at the establishment of truth and the complete eradication of untruth.

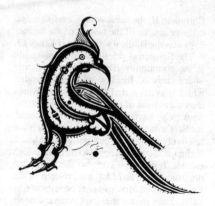

Muslim Iconography – 'In the name of God the Compassionate and the Merciful'

Ash-Shahadah The first and most fundamental of the five basic duties, is to pronounce the first declaration of faith, the *Kalimah* or *La ilaha lah Muhammadur rasalul lah* (There is no God except Allah, and Mohammed is Allah's messenger).

Salah These are compulsory prayers, offered five times a day, either individually or in congregation. They are considered to be the practical demonstration of faith and to keep believers in constant touch with their Creator. This makes them conscious of the basic duty to work for the establishment of a true order in society and to remove untruth, evil and the indecent. Salah should induce qualities of self-discipline, steadfastness and obedience to the truth, making Muslims honest and courageous. The five daily prayers are:

Fajr (dawn prayer)
Zuhr (after midday prayer)
Asr (late afternoon prayer)
Maghrib (after sunset prayer)
Isha (night prayer)

Zakah This welfare contribution is a compulsory payment from a Muslim's annual savings. The rate of payment is 2½% on cash, jewellery and precious metals, with another rate for animals and agricultural produce. It is neither a charity donation nor a tax. Charity is optional and taxes can be used for any governmental purpose. Zakah is an act of worship and it is one of the Islamic economy's fundamental principles, designed to develop an equitable society where everyone has a right to contribute and share.

Sawm From dawn to sunset every day during Ramadan, the ninth month of the Islamic calendar, Muslims should refrain from eating, drinking, smoking and sexual relations. It is a means of achieving self control, designed to raise a person's moral and spiritual standards above selfishness, laxity and other vices. Sawm is an annual training programme to refresh Muslims' determination to fulfil their obligation to Allah. Muslims usually spend more time praying than usual during Ramadan. You will also notice that they stay up later at night, too, in order to eat and socialise.

Haj This pilgrimage to the 'House' of Allah is obligatory at least once in the life of all Muslims who can afford to undertake it. It is a journey to Al-Ka'bah in Mecca, Saudi Arabia, where the prophet Mohammed was born.

Haj symbolises the unity and equality of mankind and is the annual assembly of the Muslim community *(ummah)*. It also stands as the peak of Muslims' obligatory duties because it should lay bare to them that they belong to no-one but Allah. You will often see a brightly coloured sign proudly displayed on the house of a Muslim who has made such a pilgrimage. An illustration of Al-Ka'bah in Mecca is a central theme of the sign.

The Koran This is the sacred book of the Muslims and was sent to Mohammed through the angel Gabriel (Jibrail). It is believed to be the word of Allah. It consists of 114 *suras* (chapters) and 6236 verses.

Muslims usually learn to read it and some memorise it by heart.

The Koran has remained completely unchanged over the past 1400 years. Its teachings, principles, doctrines and directions deal with all areas of this life and the life after death. The Koran's theme basically consists of the three fundamental ideas of Tawhid, Risalah and Akhirah. Muslims believe that success in this life and in life after death depends on obedience to the Koran's teachings.

Mohammed Allah's last messenger was born in 571 AD. Mohammed first received revelations from Allah when he was 40. At that time, the people in Mecca worshipped idols and Mohammed introduced them to Islam with mixed results. He continued to preach Allah's message, gradually increasing the number of followers. Both he and they suffered persecution from the idolators, and in 622 he moved to Medina where he won acceptance as leader and eventually established the first Islamic state. The Islamic calendar begins from the day of the prophet's migration to Medina.

Within two decades most of the Arab world had been converted to Islam. They spread the faith successfully, their methods often violently ruthless. The various Arab conquerors seemed to interpret Islam in a manner matched by the Crusaders' version of Christianity. Muslims today vary considerably in their interpretation of their faith. Their common belief is that its ideology is capable of solving present-day human problems and is, in fact, the only hope for this world – if practised faithfully.

The Sunni At an early stage Islam suffered a major split that remains to this day. The third Caliph, successor to Mohammed, was murdered and followed by Ali, the prophet's son-in-law, in 656. Ali was assassinated in 661 by the Governor of Syria, who set himself up as Caliph in preference to Ali's descendants.

Most Muslims today are Sunnites, followers of the succession of the Caliph, while the others are Shias or Shi'ites who follow the descendants of Ali.

Sunni is the practice of the prophet Mohammed. The practice is outlined in the Hadith, a collection of Mohammed's sayings and actions, and those actions done with his approval. You need to know the Hadith, recorded by the prophet's companions after his death, in order to understand and interpret the Koran.

Islam & the Holy Land In Islam, there are three holy places in the world: the Ka'bah in Mecca; the Mosque of Mohammed in Medina; and the Temple Mount, or Haram esh-Sharif, in Jerusalem – in that order of status. According to Ezekiel 5:5 and 38:12 the Temple Mount is the centre of the world, and Muslim scientists found corroboration for this view in their calculations that the area is in the centre of the fourth climatic zone, the central region north of the equator. However, it is the Koran's description of Mohammed's Night Journey (Sura 17) that has elevated Jerusalem's position. It tells of Mohammed, who was sleeping by the Ka'bah, being taken to the Temple Mount in Jerusalem by a Buraq, a winged creature. From there they rose to heaven, on the way meeting good and evil powers. In heaven they saw Abraham, Moses and Jesus, with whom Mohammed prayed as their leader. Until 624 AD, Muslims prayed in the direction of Jerusalem. It was then decided to face Mecca.

Jerusalem also has a special place in Muslim mysticism. Various traditions relate to the city and inspired Muslims to live in Palestine, especially in Jerusalem's vicinity. It is believed that the Crusades fostered the development of Arab literature in the area. Much of this was important for Islam and later became the principal stimulus for Muslim pilgrimages to the holy places in Jerusalem.

Sex, Marriage & Family Life Marriage is the basis of family life in Islam. Marriages are generally arranged by parents with the couple's consent. The wedding ceremony is a simple service but is surrounded by much celebration and attended by family and many friends. Islam strictly forbids the free mixing of the sexes after puberty. This means all socialising, not just pre-marital sex. Extra-marital sex is also a sin and, according to Muslims, there is no sexual discrimination in Islam. Muslims believe that the husband and wife are equal partners in the family, playing their role in respective fields. Divorce is permitted but is regarded as the most abominable of legal acts. Polygamy is illegal under Israeli law, but this does not affect Muslims in the Occupied Territories – most Muslims there are monogamous anyway.

Diet Islam is not as complex as Judaism when it comes to food and drink, but Muslims are supposed to observe some regulations. They are only allowed to eat animals that are slaughtered in the prescribed manner, and not pigs, carnivorous animals, or the blood of any animal. All alcohol is prohibited.

Dress Simplicity and modesty are encouraged. Muslims are required to cover their bodies properly and decently. Men must be covered from navel to knees, and must not wear pure silk or gold. Women must cover the whole body except the face and hands. Strict Muslims insist that women cover their face when going out and when meeting strangers, although in Israel this is not often enforced. A woman's outfit must not arouse a man's base feelings, so skin-tight, transparent or revealing styles are out. Women's clothes for men and vice versa are not allowed, and neither is symbolic dress of other religions.

Non-Muslims should be aware of these dress codes and, out of respect, adhere to them when in predominantly Muslim areas. Doing so will make their presence much more welcome, and therefore much more enjoyable. Men should appreciate that wandering around Muslim areas in shorts causes offence, especially in Nablus, Hebron and Gaza.

Social Manners Islam teaches decency, humility and good manners. Muslims traditionally greet one another with the words 'as-salamu 'alaikum' (peace be to you), and the reply is 'wa'alaikumus salam' (peace be on you, too). The most valued virtues are keeping promises, honesty, justice, fair play, helping the poor and needy, respect for parents, teachers and elders, love for children, and good relations with neighbours. Islam condemns enmity, back-biting, slander, blasphemy, ridicule, rudeness and arrogance.

Mosques The word 'mosque' comes from the Arabic word *mesjid*, meaning a place of adoration. Most mosques have domes and minarets, making them easy to recognise. Inside, facing the holy city of Mecca, is the *mihrab* (or prayer niche), normally a round recess or alcove covered by an arch. This directs the congregation towards Mecca to honour Mohammed's birth place. The *mimbar* (pulpit) is usually nearby. The *imam* (preacher) gives the Friday sermon from here. The *khatib* is a low, railed wooden platform where the khatib, or reader, sits to recite the Koran to worshippers sitting all around. Outside, or near the doorway, is a water tank for washing the hands, face, and feet before prayers. Prayers are said barefooted and traditionally with the head covered. There is no seating in mosques; you kneel, sit or even lie flat on the floor. Women are normally expected to pray at home, but some of the larger mosques have facilities for them.

There are no professional priests attached to a mosque. The imam who gives the weekly sermon normally has a regular full-time job. The *muezzin* is the man who cries the call to prayer five times every day from the minaret. He has been largely replaced by taped recordings, hence the familiar tone, wherever you are, of what is often an unrequested wake-up call.

Not all mosques welcome non-Muslims. Sometimes a sign saying 'For Prayers Only' or similar can be seen. Do not presume that you are welcome to enter a mosque, but ask. You must always remove your shoes and in some cases leave any bags and cameras outside. I've yet to learn of a case where such items were stolen.

Christianity
The organisation of the Christian faith in Israel is often a cause of mystery and concern to Western pilgrims and non-Christians alike. Certain churches enjoy the advantage of having been established here before others. As a result, the relative standing of churches elsewhere in the world is often irrelevant here. The Greek Orthodox Church, for example, owns more than half of the Church of the Holy Sepulchre (the supposed site of the crucifixion, burial and resurrection of Jesus Christ) and more of the Church of the Nativity in Bethlehem than any other religious body. Its patriarchate has seniority in the Christian hierarchy of Israel, despite the fact that this church constitutes only a fraction of the world's Christian population and is geographically confined mainly to Greece and the Slavic countries. The Armenian Church, established in Palestine in the 5th century, has a world congregation of only 6,000,000 but owns a third of Jerusalem's holy sites. Obscure in

Entrance to Tomb of the Virgin

the church councils of the world, the Copts and Assyrians are highly visible in Israel.

Meanwhile, the Roman Catholic Church owns only 17% of Jerusalem's holy sites. A relative newcomer, it only established itself here during the Crusades. The Protestants have even less authority, and are restricted to singing their Christmas carols in the Church of the Nativity's courtyard because they do not own any part of the building.

All this is a result of the intense rivalry between the factions of the Christian world. Thought to have erupted in the 11th century when the Eastern (Greek Orthodox) and the Latin (Roman Catholic) churches had a major row, there has since been an ongoing struggle to exclude each other from the holy places, with the smaller churches also claiming rights.

After the defeat of the Crusaders in the 12th century, the Muslims claimed ownership of all the holy places, and sold the rights of worship to interested parties. Over the years the poorer churches were forced out. In 1757 the Turkish authorities drew up the rights of possession in nine of the most important shrines. Known as the 'status quo', it is still applicable today. While it may outline the official position, it has not ended the bitter disputes over who should have what.

Orthodox Church The Greek Orthodox Church is the oldest ecclesiastical body in Israel, and is probably the closest successor to the original Judaeo-Christian community of St James. A Greek-speaking Christian community emerged in Jerusalem in the mid-2nd century, gaining importance during the rule of Constantine when most of the holy sites were discovered. Byzantine times saw the church prosper, but it decayed under the Arabs. During the later Middle Ages the Orthodox Church languished, recovering under the Turks, but at the beginning of the 20th century it only numbered a few thousand. Today it has become the linchpin in the often bitter rivalry between the various churches in Israel.

The Orthodox Church community is Arabic-speaking, and led by an almost exclusively Greek-speaking hierarchy. The Orthodox patriarchate of Jerusalem is the only autonomous church in the country, with all the others being dependent to various degrees on a head office abroad.

Israel is also the home of two Russian Orthodox missions. Both in Jerusalem, one represents the Moscow patriarchate, the other the Russian Church Abroad, and each claims to be the legitimate successor of the 19th century Russian Government's mission. The Moscow mission is in possession of the green-domed cathedral in Jerusalem's Russian Compound and other churches in Jaffa, Nazareth, Tiberias and Haifa. The Church Abroad is in charge of the photogenic onion-domed Church of St Mary of Magdalene in Gethsemane, on the Mount of Olives. Being out of communion with the patriarch of Moscow, the Church Abroad is not recognised by the Orthodox patriarch of Jerusalem. The Moscow patriarchate's Jerusalem churches have been assumed to be bases for Soviet intelligence and espionage. The violent death of a Russian nun in the early 1980s was the talk of the town.

The Romanian Orthodox patriarch is also represented by a church and small community in Jerusalem.

Armenian Many travellers might not even know where Armenia is (part of the former USSR), let alone that it is represented by one of the Holy Land's more powerful Christian communities. By the 7th century it had 72 monasteries in Palestine, and under the Arabs and Crusaders the number increased. Much of Mount Zion in Jerusalem is the property of the Armenian Church, and has been since the 10th century.

The beauty of the area is largely due to the Armenian buildings, constructed during the existence of the Armenian Kingdom of Cilicia. All but six of their monasteries were lost in power struggles, mainly with the Greek Orthodox. However, they managed to maintain their rights in the major holy sites.

During the Mandate, the Armenians formed a prosperous community of some

5000 with their own churches, schools and culture. Due to emigration they number only about 2500 today.

The Armenian patriarchate, also based in Jerusalem, shares the churches of the Holy Sepulchre and the Nativity with the Orthodox and Latin patriarchates. This complex system of sharing has often been the cause of violent clashes between rival members of these Christian sects.

Syrian Orthodox & Copts The Syrians have had a bishop in Jerusalem since 1140, the Copts since 1236. Also called the Jacobites, the Syrian Orthodox are headed by an archbishop whose residence is the monastery of St Mark, in Jerusalem. The Copts, from Egypt, have a monastery upstairs at the back of the Church of the Holy Sepulchre. Both these groups celebrate Christmas at the Armenian altars in the Church of the Nativity, but otherwise they use their own small chapels in the Church of the Holy Sepulchre.

Ethiopian From the Middle Ages until the 16th century, the Ethiopians owned chapels and altars in various holy places. Today they are confined to a ramshackle monastery on the roof of the Church of the Holy Sepulchre in Jerusalem, where they also have the chapel of St Helena, as well as a lovely church and monastery in West Jerusalem and a chapel near the Jordan River.

Catholic The Latin patriarchate of Jerusalem was established by the Crusaders in 1099, ceased to exist in 1291 and was re-established in 1847-48.

The Latin community includes over 45 religious orders and congregations. There are around 30 female communities and several hundred houses.

Most Catholic religious groups were established here over the last 130 years, except the Franciscans, who for more than 500 years were the sole body in charge of Catholic interests in Palestine and the Middle East. It was the Franciscans who regained and maintained rights of worship and possession in the major holy places,

established programmes for their restoration, catered for the huge numbers of pilgrims and ministered to the small Catholic communities that sprang up around their monasteries and convents.

Uniate These are the Oriental churches in communion with Rome, and they are represented in Israel by relatively small communities. The largest comprises the Melkites, who are mostly in Akko and Galilee. The next in size are the Maronites, mostly near the Lebanese border. The Chaldeans and the Syrian and Armenian Catholics are far fewer in number.

All the Uniate patriarchs are based in Arab countries and the churches in Israel are controlled by patriarchal vicars as their representatives. The Uniate churches do not have any rights in the principal Holy Places.

Protestant Anglican and Prussian Lutherans arrived in Palestine 160 years ago. Missionary work among Jews and Muslims was one of their aims, but the Greek Orthodox Church was the source of most converts. The British Mandate was a particularly prosperous period of development for the Anglican church here, but by 1948 most of its English-speaking congregation had left the country.

Today, the Evangelical Episcopal Church is primarily Arab-speaking, and the Anglican Archbishop in Jerusalem presides over a synod made up of Egyptian, Libyan, Sudanese, Iranian and Jordanian bishops.

The Israeli Government recognised the church as a separate religious community in 1970. The Anglicans have no rights in the Church of the Holy Sepulchre, but an arrangement with the Greek Orthodox Church allows them to occasionally celebrate mass in the nearby Chapel of St Abraham. The Anglican cathedral in Israel is St George's in East Jerusalem.

The German Lutherans established schools, hospices and hospitals in Palestine, including the Hospice of the Order of St John in Jerusalem and the Augusta Victoria Hospice (now a hospital) on Mount Scopus.

Despite the considerable setbacks as a result of the German involvement in the two world wars, the Lutherans have re-established themselves as the Evangelical Lutheran Church.

There are some non-German Lutheran institutions in Israel. They include the Swedish Theological Institute and the Finnish Missionary School in Jerusalem, the Swedish school and hospital in Bethlehem, and the Scandinavian Seamen's churches in Haifa and Ashdod. There are also several minor Protestant groups representing reformed Christianity. These include Presbyterians, Baptists, Pentecostalists, Quakers and Adventists.

Mormon The Church of Jesus Christ of Latter-day Saints, is perhaps better known as the Mormon Church. Its members are often misunderstood and unrecognised as Christians. Mormons basically accept Christian beliefs but think that Christianity went astray soon after the death of Jesus Christ. The lost authority was restored to Joseph Smith, the church's founder, to whom was revealed the Book of Mormon. The Book of Mormon is a supplement to, not a replacement for, the Bible, and was produced to give a deeper appreciation and understanding of God's truths as revealed in the Bible.

The Mormon church was caught up in controversy when, in 1984, permission was given to the Brigham Young University, which it ran, to build a school on 2½ hectares near the Hebrew University campus on Jerusalem's Mount Scopus. Loud and often vicious protests were heard from Jews over what they perceived as a threat to Judaism from Mormon missionary work. Hasidic Jews led the demonstrations and some wealthy American Jews offered to pay the Mormons several million dollars just to cancel their plans, in addition to buying their land. Despite this, the school project went ahead and stands today.

The episode has highlighted the touchy subject of whether Israel regards itself as a secular state or a Jewish theocracy which attacks minority religions. Israeli politicians were genuinely exasperated by the religious conflict, although not necessarily for the right reasons. They felt that the religious Jews were wrong to harass the Mormons because the Mormons have been among Israel's strongest supporters in the USA. It was also argued that Jews could hardly plead for the freedom of Jewish education and lifestyles in the USSR whilst in Israel Christians were being suppressed.

Christian Zionism & the International Christian Embassy In 1980, when the Israeli Government confirmed that Jerusalem was to remain the capital of the Jewish state, 13 countries closed their embassies in the city in protest at the decision, transferring them to Tel Aviv. These events inspired a group of Christians already living in Israel to open and operate the International Christian Embassy Jerusalem (ICEJ) in the Holy City. They felt that Israel had been unfairly abandoned by the world.

Inspired by Isaiah 40:1, the Embassy's goals are to show concern for the Jewish people, especially for Israel; to remind and encourage Christians to pray for Jerusalem and Israel; to provide an information centre for Christians where they can learn about current events; to begin or assist projects in Israel for the well-being of all, regardless of race, ethnic background or religion; and to be a reconciling influence between Arabs and Jews. The ICEJ does not claim to represent all Christians. It is an embassy in as much as it represents a nation of Christian Zionists who interpret the Bible (eg Romans II) as requiring support for the Jewish people and the modern state of Israel. In fact, one of its beliefs is that Israel's borders should rightly include the area which is now Jordan. Christian Zionists consider Islam's claim of Jerusalem as its third holiest site to be highly questionable. They argue that Muslims believe in the holiness of Jerusalem chiefly because Jews and Christians do and that in practice the city has religious significance to Islam only when it is threatened or occupied by non-Muslims. The ICEJ maintains that the Koran assures Muslims that the Jews would always be smitten and abased and could never rule over them (Sura II: The Cow verse 61). Therefore, Jerusalem's importance to the Islamic world is not that it is the site of Mohammed's flight to heaven but that its possession by Muslims symbolises the triumph over Judaism and Christianity. They also claim that many of the Islamic stories and legends about Jerusalem originally came from Jewish converts.

The creation of the ICEJ was an immense and welcome surprise to most Jews and, in Israel in particular, it was welcomed with emotional gratitude.

The Druze

With its name derived from al-Darazi, one of the group's founders, the Druze religion has its roots in Ismailism, a religio-political movement in the 10th century. A similarly classified group themselves, the Druze are a difficult people to understand due to the nature of their faith, which they call Din al-Tawhid.

It includes a belief in one supreme God operating in the world through a system of cosmic principles, periodic human manifestations of this God, and esoteric interpretations of the revealed religions whose prophets (eg Moses, Jesus and Mohammed) were the bearers of esoteric truth only.

The inner meaning of these prophets' missions was secretly told to a select group of Druze by an incarnation of Jethro, Moses' father-in-law. The traditional site of his grave, near Hittim, in Galilee, is a place of pilgrimage for the Druze. They have few ceremonies or rituals, and only a small number of them are actually told what the faith is all about. Despite their roots in a form of Islam, the Druze are not Muslims.

Speaking Arabic and with similar lifestyles to the Arabs, the Druze have remained a separate community by their effective prohibition of intermarriage, the non-admission of converts, a long history of armed conflict with the many rulers and rival groups over

the years and a strong sense of group solidarity. They are renowned for their hospitality to visitors.

Baha'ism

A world religion which has established its centre in Haifa, it is named after its founder Baha'u'llah (The Splendour of God). Baha'ism developed out of the Bahi, a Muslim mystical movement founded in Persia in 1844. It teaches that religious truth is progressive, not final; that the human race is educated by God through a series of prophets who have appeared throughout history and will always appear to guide the destinies of mankind. These have already included Moses, Zoroaster, Buddha, Jesus Christ, Mohammed and also Baha'u'llah. They apparently give the world the same fundamental teachings but reveal laws and principles designed to suit the requirements of the age in which they appear.

The aims and purposes of Baha'ism include upholding God's unity; recognising the unity of his prophets; teaching the sodality of all people, regardless of culture or race; urging either the creation or selection of an auxiliary international language; and declaring that the purpose of religion is to promote peace and friendship.

The inspiration for the Bahi faith, Sayyid Ali Mohammed, was born in Shiraz, Persia, circa 1820. Accused of heresy, he was arrested and shot in 1850 for his proclamation that he was the Bab, the Gate to the knowledge of divine truth. His body was secretly buried by his followers in Teheran. They suffered persecution and fled to Baghdad, from where the leaders were later exiled to Cyprus (1863).

Mirza Husayn Ali, the stepbrother of the Bahi's successor, proclaimed himself to be the new Bab under the name of Baha'u'llah. He was then exiled again, to Adrianople (1864) and later to Akko, which he reached in 1868, accompanied by about 70 of his family followers. He turned the faith into a universalist ethical religion and in 1899 he organised the transfer of Ali Mohammed's body to Akko from Teheran. The Baha'u'llah died in 1892 and his tomb near Akko has become a shrine and, for the Baha'is, the holiest place in the world.

Abbas Effendi became the leader of the faith under the name of Abd al-Baha (the Servant of Baha). He transferred his residence to Haifa and visited North Africa, Europe and the USA to spread Baha'ism. He also arranged for the Bab's body to be interred in a shrine in Haifa on Mount Carmel. He died in 1921 and was interred in the same shrine.

Baha'ism has since developed worldwide. One of the largest Baha'i communities is in Iran, where they suffer harsh persecution. Membership of the faith is expanding rapidly in India (now with the largest Baha'i community), Africa, South-East Asia, the Pacific region and amongst the South American Indians.

LANGUAGE

Israel's national language is Hebrew, followed by Arabic. English is widely spoken; there will nearly always be someone nearby who understands it. Most of the important road and street signs are in all three languages. With Jews arriving in Israel from around the world, many other languages are commonly understood. French, German and Yiddish are the main ones, but also Spanish and Russian.

Most Arabs are fluent in Hebrew and English as well as Arabic. Many also speak other European languages, and hearing Arab shopkeepers switching languages as they haggle with tourists is quite impressive.

Surprisingly overlooked by the vast majority of Israel guides, museums and Israelis themselves, is the history of the national language. Hebrew is the language of the Bible. During the centuries of the Diaspora, Jews spoke the local language but continued to use Hebrew for prayer and religious study. With the rise of political Zionism in Europe in the mid-19th century, there was a growing awareness and appreciation of the ancient language. This resulted in more prose and poetry being written in Hebrew for a growing readership.

Eliezer Ben Yehuda, who arrived in Palestine from Lithuania in 1881, pioneered the everyday use of Hebrew and the coining of new Hebrew words necessary for modern life and times.

One of his major achievements was the compilation of the first Hebrew dictionary. Ben Yehuda had the vision to revive and develop Hebrew (spoken by the Jews in ancient times) for a Jewish state that would otherwise have no common language. His eldest child was the first in the modern world to have Hebrew as his mother tongue. A minority of ultra-orthodox Jews bitterly opposed Ben Yehuda's work, believing that Hebrew should not be used as an everyday language. Even today there are a few who only use Hebrew on religious occasions.

The modern language contains elements of some European languages and you will hear many English words, taken where the Bible had no similar concept.

Although it is perfectly possible to survive your stay without uttering a word of Hebrew, it is always useful and polite to know a few words and phrases. Especially useful might be 'Shabbat Shalom' – the traditional Shabbat greeting.

Written from right to left, Hebrew has 22 characters. The 'ch' sound is a more guttural version of the German 'ch' sound, and is a noticeable characteristic of the language.

א	ב	ג	ג׳	ד	ה	ו
A	B	G	J	D	H	V

ז	ח	ט	י	כ(ך)	כ׳(ך׳)	ל
Z	H	T	Yi	K	Kh	L

מ(ם)	נ(ן)	ס	ע	פ	פ׳(ף׳)
M	N	S	'A	P	F

צ(ץ)	ק	ר	ש	שׁ	ת
Ts	Q	R	Sh	S	T

Hebrew Alphabet

Hebrew
Useful Words

hello	sha-LOM
goodbye	sha-LOM
good morning	BO-ker tov
good evening	erev tov
goodnight	lie-la tov
see you later	le-HIT-rah-OTT
thank you	to-DAH
please	be-va-ka-SHA
you are welcome	al low da-VAAR
I don't speak Hebrew	AH-NEE lo m'dah-BEHR ee-VREET
do you speak English?	ah-TAH m'dah-BEHR ang-LEET?
money	KES-sef
bank	bank
yes	ken
no	loh
excuse me	slee-CHA
wait	REG-gah
what	mah
when	mah-tiee
where is	AY-fo
right (correct)	na-CHON

Days & Time

Sunday	YOM ree-SHON
Monday	YOM shay-NEE
Tuesday	YOM shlee-SHEE
Wednesday	YOM reh-vee-EE
Thursday	YOM cha-mee SHEE
Friday	YOM shee-SHEE
Saturday	sha-BAT
What is the time?	MA ha-sha-AH?
minute	da-KAH
hour	sha-AH
seven o'clock	ha-sha-AH SHEV-vah
day	yom
week	sha-voo-ah
month	CHO-desh
year	sha-NAH

Getting Around (Transport)

station	ta-cha-na
airport	sde t'uFAH
Which bus goes to...?	EH-seh auto-boos no-SAY-ah le...?
stop here	ah-TSOR kahn
railway	rah-KEH-vet
bus	auto-boos
near	ka-ROV

Food & Accommodation

to eat	le-eh-CHOL
to drink	lish-toth
food	OCHEL
water	my-im
restaurant	MISS-ah-DAH
breakfast	ah-roo-CHAT BO-ker
lunch	ah-roo-CHAT-ha-RYE-in
dinner	ah-roo-CHAT erev
menu	taf-REET
egg	bay-TSA
vegetables	YEH-rah-KOHT
bread	LECH-hem
butter	chem-AH
cheese	g'VEE-nah
milk	cha-LAV
ice cream	glee-DAH
fruit	pay-ROTE
wine	YAH-yin
bill	CHESH-bon
hotel	meh-LON
room	che-der
toilet	bait key SAY, no-chi YOOT

Post Office & Shopping

post office	dough-are
letter	mich-tav
stamps	boolim
envelopes	ma-ata-FOTH
postcard	gloo-yah
telegram	miv-rock
airmail	dough-are ah-veer
how much is it?	KA-mah zeh oh-LEH?
pharmacy	bait mer-kah-CHAT
shop	cha-NOOT
shampoo	ha-fee-FAH
expensive	ya-KAR
cheap	zol

Numbers

1	eh-HAD
2	SHTA-yim
3	sha-LOSH
4	AR-bah
5	cha-MAYSH
6	shaysh
7	SHEV-vah
8	sh-MO-neh
9	TAY-shah
10	ESS-er
11	eh-HAD-ess-RAY
12	shtaym-ess-RAY
20	ess-REEM
21	ess-REEM v'eh-HAD
30	shlo-SHEEM
50	v'ah-CHAT
100	MAY-ah
200	mah-tah-YEEM
300	shlosh may-OAT
500	cha-MAYSH may-OAT
1000	Elef
3000	shlosh-ET elef-EEM
5000	cha-maysh-ET elef-EEM

Arabic

Learning the characters for the Arab numerals is useful, as much of your shopping will be done in Arab markets. Also, any attempts, however unsuccessful, to speak their language will especially endear you to the Arabs. Note that Arabic numerals are read left to right, unlike the language, which is read right to left.

Useful Words

hello	a-halan, mahr-haba
goodbye	salaam aleicham, ma-ah-salameh
good morning	sabah-al-kheir
good evening	masa'al-kheir
please	min fadlach
thank you	shoo-khran
you're welcome	afwan
do you speak English?	tech-kee Ingleesi?
yes	ay-wah
no	la
where	feen
right	yemine
left	she-mal
straight	doo-ree
pardon?	sa-mech-nee?
how much is this?	ah-desh hadah?
tea	schai
coffee	kah-wah

Numbers

0	٠	sifr
1	١	wa-had
2	٢	tinen
3	٣	talatay
4	٤	arbaha
5	٥	chamseh
6	٦	sitteh
7	٧	sabah
8	٨	tamanyeh
9	٩	taisah
10	١٠	ahsharah

Facts for the Visitor

VISAS & EMBASSIES

A tourist visa is not required to visit Israel. On arrival, tourists are normally allowed a three-month visit, although visitors entering through the land borders with Egypt and Jordan are often only allowed a month's stay. Israeli immigration officials will give you a duplicate entry permit to fill in. The second copy will be returned to you, and you need to keep this until you leave the country. Try not to lose it, or you will face a long delay in the already lengthy departure procedure. If you look 'undesirable', or are obviously looking for illegal employment, immigration officials may question the purpose of your visit and ask to see evidence of a return flight/ferry ticket, and financial support. If unimpressed, they may only allow you a shorter stay, say one month. Travellers returning to Israel after visiting Egypt have often been given only a month by Taba and Rafah immigration officials.

Visa Offices

If, after your initial three-month stay, you want more time, you need to apply for a visa. You do this at an office of the Ministry of the Interior. Israel's bureaucracy can be infuriating because of the attitude and performance of the civil servants. Along with the Egged bus information-desk staff who don't like people who ask questions about the buses, the bus drivers who accelerate as they see you running for the bus, and the many Arab men who are strangely affected by non-Arab women, they are about the most unpleasant side of Israel.

The process of applying for an extension of your visit involves an early start to beat the long queues, and proof that you can support yourself without needing to work illegally. Most offices open at 8 am and the queue is usually depressingly long by then. Convincing the civil servants that you should be allowed to stay can be very hard or very easy and they extend visas for varying amounts of time; sometimes one month, sometimes as much as six months, but usually for three months. The process costs about US$25 and one passport-sized photo is required. There is no fee for citizens of Belgium, Luxembourg or the Netherlands.

The Jerusalem office should be avoided – it is extremely busy with the longest queues. Except in Eilat and Tel Aviv, the offices elsewhere tend not to see too many tourists asking for visa extensions. This can mean either that they won't have a clue about the procedure and refuse to deal with you, or that they are really friendly and pleased to have something different to stamp, sign and shuffle from desk to desk.

Office are normally open from 8 am to noon, and are closed on Friday and Saturday. On Monday and Wednesday they often open between 2 and 3 pm. The 55-sheqel question is: 'What happens if you try to leave Israel after overstaying the initial three-month period without getting the visa?' I was told that fines are the order of the day, so it hardly seems worth the hassle of avoiding the procedure. By the way, it's OK to leave applying for your extension for a couple of weeks or so after the initial three months, so don't bother to rush to a main town if you are wandering in the wilderness somewhere when your three months are up. Offices are at:

Afulla
    2 HaRav Levin St (☎ (065) 23890)
Akko
    2 Ha'Agara St (☎ (04) 911103)
Ashkelon
    Nafati Centre (☎ (051) 24246)
Beersheba
    Ramban St (☎ (057) 30460)
Eilat
    Municipality Building – open Sunday 5 to 7 pm; Monday to Thursday 9 am to noon; closed Friday and Saturday (☎ (059) 72133/6)
Hadera
    73 Weizmann St (☎ (063) 24795)

Haifa
    11 Hassan Shuqri (☎ (04) 667781)
Holon
    11 Jabotinsky St (☎ (03) 984181)
Jerusalem
    1 Shlomzion St (☎ (02) 228211)
Nazareth Illit
    Qiryat Memshala (☎ (065) 70510)
Netanya
    14 Remez St (☎ (053) 22153)
Petah Tiqwa
    40 Bar Kochba St (☎ (03) 911906)
Rehovot
    74 Herzl St (☎ (08) 25577)
Ramat Gan
    2 Bialik St (☎ (03) 719375)
Safed
    Municipality, Jerusalem St (☎ (067) 31424)
Tel Aviv
    Jaffa Shalom Tower (☎ (03) 651941, 657758)
Tiberias
    23 Ze'evy El Hadof (☎ (067) 91724)

In theory, (03) 916547 is the number for an information service for general inquiries, but their usual answer is that you should go to the nearest Ministry of the Interior office. Normally a kibbutz or moshav will arrange for the visas of its foreign volunteers as a matter of course, and if you are a valued worker you should be able to get lengthy extensions.

The maximum period a foreigner is allowed to stay in Israel varies according to which official you ask. It can be one week if they don't like the look of you, or several years if they do. Usually, one year is the most you can stay without pulling strings.

Israel is, of course, the venue for that popular traditional Middle Eastern game: the Passport Shuffle. This involves using the same passport to visit as many 'hostile' Arab countries as possible after a visit to Israel. This game was devised because the countries which have refused to recognise Israel also refuse to allow any nationalities to cross their borders if they have previously entered Israel. As a result, the Israeli immigration officials will, if you politely ask them, only stamp the entry permit and not your actual passport. Remember two things, though, before you pack your kaffiyeh and head for the Gulf. If you stay in Israel longer than the initial three month period, when you extend your stay at a Ministry of the Interior office your passport is automatically stamped, and no buts. If entering Israel from Egypt (the only Arab country that recognises the Jewish state and therefore not a problem) or vice versa, do not bother trying to have your passport saved from the stamp of Israel. It will be obvious by the Egyptian border stamp in your passport that you have entered Israel.

If you are heading for Jordan from Israel things get a little complicated, but far from impossible (see the Getting There & Away chapter for details).

Israeli Consulates & Embassies

Most consulates and embassies are in Tel Aviv – see that chapter for addresses. These are Israel's diplomatic offices overseas:

Australia
    Embassy, 6 Turrana Ave, Yarralumla, Canberra, ACT 2600 (☎ (062) 73 1309)
    Consulate, Westfield Towers, 300 William St, Sydney, NSW 2011 (☎ (02) 358 5077)
Canada
    Embassy, 40 Laurier Ave West, Suite 601, Ottawa, Ontario, KIR 7T3 (☎ (613) 237 6450)
Great Britain
    Embassy, 2 Palace Green, London W8 4QB (☎ (01) 937 6450)
Hong Kong
    Consulate, 1121 Princess Building, Chater Rd, Hong Kong (☎ (01) 937 8050)
Netherlands
    Embassy, 47 Buitenhoff, The Hague (☎ (070) 64 7850)
Singapore
    Embassy, Faber House, 7th Floor, 236G Orchard Rd, Singapore 9 (☎ 253 0996)
Thailand
    Embassy, 31 Soi Lung Suan, Ploenchit Rd, Bangkok (☎ 252 6181)
USA
    Embassy, 3514 International Drive NW, Washington DC 20008 (☎ (202) 364 5500)

This list is subject to change. Check in the country you are in to see if Israel is represented.

DOCUMENTS

The only officially required document for

travellers in Israel is a valid passport. An International Youth Hostels Association (IYHA) card and the International Student Identity Card (ISIC) can be useful. IYHA membership will save you money at their hostels throughout the country. Although not usually the best value when competing against local privately-owned hostels, they are the only budget accommodation available in some popular areas, such as the Dead Sea, Mitzpe Ramon and Tabgha.

The ISIC entitles the holder to a 10% discount on Israel's Egged buses, 20% off fares on Israel State Railways, and discounts at many museums and archaeological sites. Even if signs make no mention of student discounts, produce your card and ask. Student fares offered by airlines and ferry companies are usually the same as those offered to anyone under 26 years of age. If you are combining your visit to Israel with one to Egypt, all the more reason to obtain an ISIC card. Egypt offers better discounts than anywhere else for card holders.

An International Driving Permit is not normally required to hire a car in Israel.

MONEY

The best place to change your money is the Arab moneychangers, mainly in Jerusalem's Old City and East Jerusalem. Legalised by the government, they are left over from the years of Jordanian control, and are popular with Israelis as well as travellers. Another good place to change money can be the hostel you are staying in.

Most Israelis, Jews and Arabs will talk in terms of US dollars, not sheqelim. This derives from the days when the Israeli currency constantly devalued, and adopting the US dollar was a reliable way to deal with that situation. Moneychangers and banks will change most foreign currencies or travellers' cheques, with British sterling and the DM often the most popular after the US dollar. It is always worth asking the dollar price when you are quoted a price in sheqelim – it often works out cheaper. Cash is best but small denominations of travellers' cheques will

usually do. Prices in this book are quoted in US dollars.

Banking hours vary from place to place so check in advance. There will usually be someone willing to change your money wherever you are, but it may be at an unfavourable rate.

Payments made in foreign currency are free of the 15% Value Added Tax (VAT). Purchases like ferry and airline tickets and accommodation at IYHA hostels can be made cheaper by paying in foreign currency. You can also get VAT refunds on your departure by presenting receipts of purchases made with foreign currency at a bank. In most private hostels, there is no difference between payment made in local and foreign currency – but it is prudent to check.

Credit cards are very popular in Israel, although most low-cost establishments do not accept them. You can use Visa Card, American Express, Diner's Club, or Master-Card/Mastercharge cards to obtain more funds, depending on your credit status back home.

If you are unfortunate enough to run out of money in Israel, the quickest way to have some transferred from home seems to be through Barclays Discount Bank. Provided that you ensure the Israeli bank sends the speediest message possible to your bank, and that they, in turn, are responsive, your money should be with you in three days. If you are in Tel Aviv, you should receive your money sooner as all transfers go to the main branches before being sent around the country as required. If you are too far away to reach Tel Aviv, have the local bank telephone Tel Aviv after two days. Once the money has arrived there, it can be issued to you locally.

American Express, Citicorp, Visa Card, Bank of America, Thomas Cook and Barclays are among the more widely recognised travellers' cheques in Israel. Always ensure that you have a record of your cheque numbers and their value kept separately in case of theft or loss. Also remember to carry your passport for ID purposes when you want to cash your travellers' cheques.

At the end of your stay you can convert your sheqelim at the airport or at the port in Haifa. You are allowed to reconvert up to US$100 in sheqels without bank receipts. If you are leaving the country to cross into Egypt and Jordan by road, you can convert your sheqelim at a regular bank (there are exchange facilities at both border crossings but they have proved unreliable in the past).

Currency

The new sheqel (NIS) is divided into 100 agorot. There are coins of 1, 5 and 10 agorot, half and 1 new sheqel and notes of 5, 10 and 50 new sheqelim. The change to the new sheqel in 1985 came with other changes in monetary policies in a plan to reduce inflation. It appears to have at least partially succeeded, as the inflation rate has dropped from 500% to around 20%.

Exchange Rates

A$1	=	1.83NIS
US$1	=	2.46NIS
STG£1	=	4.71NIS
SwFr1	=	1.85NIS
C$1	=	2.08NIS
DM1	=	1.65NIS
FFr1	=	0.49NIS

Costs

Many budget travellers have labelled Israel as an expensive place to visit. Certainly, compared to Egypt, Syria, Greece or Turkey you will find yourself spending more here. However, those arriving from Australia, NZ, the UK, the USA and most European countries should find prices compare favourably. Some prices will be higher, some lower. Of course, it is virtually impossible to say what travelling around Israel will cost you. Two people travelling at exactly the same standard can spend vastly different amounts if one travels faster than the other or cannot cook. A week lying on Tel Aviv beach will cost considerably less than a week touring the Galilee region, and living off food purchased in markets and supermarkets will save a packet compared to eating out.

From top to bottom of the accommodation scale – if you stay in luxury hotels and eat out, you can spend a great deal. There are luxury hotels and expensive restaurants aplenty at international prices. For a decent mid-priced hotel room, look at around US$40 to US$60 a single/double. You can eat out for US$10 to US$20 per person. At the other extreme, sleeping in dorms costs about US$8, shopping in markets and supermarkets to cook for yourself saves a packet, and you can survive on less than US$20 a day. It totally depends on what you are looking for.

Tipping

I am told that once no-one tipped in Israel. Today in the more expensive tourist spots, a 10 to 15% tip is the norm. Unfortunately, it is frequently undeserved. Whoever serves you at your streetside café table will also expect a similar-sized tip. In the more modest places, small change is normally the most that is required.

Tipping is a sore point for many budget travellers. Basically I feel that it is wrong to go to a restaurant or bar where tipping is standard procedure and expect to receive the service without paying a tip. Whether we agree with it or not, most wait/bar staff are paid a low rate, calculated with the expectation of tips. The total price at the foot of a bill is not necessarily the final amount due unless it states that service has been included. If it hasn't, and whoever served you did it right, they are entitled to a tip.

Note that taxi drivers in Israel do not expect to be tipped. This is usually just as well: too often, they are rude, unhelpful and quick to overcharge.

Consumer Taxes

Israel charges VAT on most goods, but tourists in Israel are entitled to a refund of VAT on most items purchased with foreign currency in a shop registered with the Ministry of Tourism (identifiable by an official sign). Nothing in life is free, and this is certainly the case here, with a lot of red tape involved

in getting your 15% back from the Israeli Government.

The net figure on one invoice must be at least US$50, with the exception of electrical appliances, cameras, films, photographic accessories and computers. Be sure to get a discount of at least 5% on the displayed price and a copy of the invoice showing the VAT amount paid in both Israeli sheqelim and US dollars. The purchases need to be wrapped in a sealed plastic bag, of which at least one side must be transparent with the original invoice displayed inside the bag so that it can be read without opening the bag. The bag needs to remain sealed for the duration of your time in Israel.

If leaving from Ben-Gurion Airport or Haifa Port, go to the Bank Leumi counter in the departure lounge and present your sealed bag. The bank will stamp the invoice, identify the goods and refund in US dollars the VAT paid (less a commission). At other departure points, customs officials do the honours but the refund will be mailed to your home address.

WHEN TO GO

Israel's climate is not so extreme that there is a specific time to make a point of avoiding. You need to balance personal flexibility regarding travel times with any preferences for the seasonal variations that affect flight and accommodation prices, as well as the climate. Another factor, perhaps unique to Israel, is to remember those religious holidays that cause the country to fill up with pilgrims, prices to double and public transport to grind to a halt.

Most would agree that spring is the nicest time to visit. During Passover and Easter, though, you pay high-season prices for flights and hotels, and have to contend with the disruption of public transport.

For sun worshippers, the summer months provide the best weather; for others, Israel is too hot at this time and high-season prices can again make it prohibitive.

The autumn climate is similar to spring, but you can run into several Jewish holidays that make it almost as tricky to get around as Passover.

Note that many sites of interest are closed for days at a time during these holiday periods. The winter months see the heaviest rainfall and very cold weather in many areas, although Eilat is popular at this time.

WHAT TO BRING

The usual traveller's rule applies – bring as little as possible, but without having to buy too many things in Israel. Clothes and toiletries in particular can be expensive. The one thing most travellers fail to realise is how chilly Israel can be in the winter and that even summer evenings in many areas are cool enough to need a sweater. A sleeping bag is only necessary if you're going to be constantly roughing it. Hostels usually provide sheets and blankets. Also necessary are a sun hat, sunglasses, a water canteen, comfortable walking shoes (worn in but not worn out) and clothes suitable for the hot climate and for visiting religious sites. Remember that most religious sites are not open to anyone dressed immodestly. Men and women must cover their legs, shoulders, necklines and arms to the elbow. In synagogues and most other Jewish holy sites, all heads must be covered.

Several things cost more in Israel than you'd like them to: toiletries, tampons, suntan lotion, film and batteries, for example.

A small daypack is indispensable. Most travellers still opt for the backpack to carry their gear. An alternative is a large, soft but strong zip bag with a wide shoulder strap and hand grips. Not great if making several short trips or for lengthy travelling but perhaps more socially acceptable. My ideal choice is a combination of the two – the travel pack. This is a backpack with a flap which zips over the shoulder straps to turn it into a soft bag. This looks more presentable and is less prone to damage than a backpack.

TOURIST OFFICES

The Israel Government Tourist Offices (IGTO) are numerous both around the world and in Israel. However, obtaining information about Israel is not achieved by staggering out of the nearest IGTO with a great pile of the latest glossy productions, as they are full of political propaganda. You need to read about the country's history, past and present, ensuring that the authors are not all from the same side of the political barbed-wire fence.

Local Tourist Offices

Akko
    Tourist Centre, El-Jazzar St (☎ (04) 9117464, 910251)
Allenby Bridge (☎ (02) 922531)
Arad
    Commercial Centre (☎ (057) 958144)
Ashkelon
    Commercial Centre, Afridar (☎ (051) 32412)
Bat Yam
    Municipality Information Office, Derekh Ben-Gurion 43 (☎ (03) 589766)
Beersheba
    Rehov Nordau (☎ (057) 36001/2/3)
Ben-Gurion Airport (☎ (03) 9711485/6/7)
Bethlehem
    Manger Square (☎ (02) 742591)
Eilat
    Khan Ariel Centre (☎ (059) 34353)
Haifa
    Town: 20 Rehov Herzl (☎ (04) 643616, 666521/2)
    Port: Shed No 12 (on ship's arrival) (☎ (04) 663988)
Jerusalem
    New City: 24 King George St (☎ (02) 241281/2)
    Old City: Jaffa Gate (☎ (02) 282295/6)
Nahariya
    Municipality Building, Sederot Ga'aton (☎ (04) 929800)
Nazareth
    Casa Nova St (☎ (06) 573003, 570555)
Netanya
    Kikar Ha'Atzmaut (☎ (053) 27286)
Rafah
    Israel-Egypt Transit Point (☎ (051) 37999)
Rosh Hanikra
    (☎ (04) 927802)
Safed
    27 Jerusalem St (☎ (06) 930633, 920666)
Tel Aviv
    5 Shalom Aleichem St (☎ (03) 660259/61)
Tiberias
    relocating at time of going to press
    (☎ (06) 720992, 722089)

The performance of these offices varies considerably; some are friendly, but others suffer from the Israeli bureaucratic disease, especially the Jerusalem New City office.

In Bethlehem, for instance, there really is a regular bus to Herodian, the popular archaeological site; in fact a bus has always operated that route, no matter what they may tell you to the contrary.

The IGTO has an excellent selection of free maps, although those for Akko, Beersheba, and Naharya are not accurate or complete. Also worth picking up are current editions of the free tourist magazines *Hello Israel* and local versions in major cities such as *This Week in Jerusalem*.

Overseas Offices

Austria
    Postfach 77, Vienna (☎ (0222) 529399)
Canada
    180 Bloor St West, Toronto (☎ (416) 9643784)
Denmark
    Vesterbrogade 6C, Copenhagen (☎ 129680, 119679)
Egypt
    6 Ibn el Malek, Cairo (☎ 726000)
France
    14 Rue de la Paix, Paris (☎ (4261) 0197, 0367)
Great Britain
    18 Great Marlborough St, London WIV IAF (☎ (071) 4343561)
Italy
    Via Podjora 12B, Milan (☎ (02) 5463021)
Japan
    Kojimachi Sanbancho Mansion No 406-921, Sanbancho, Chiyoda-ku, Tokyo (☎ 2389081/2)
Netherlands
    Wijde Kapelsteeg 2, Amsterdam (☎ (020) 249325)
Spain
    Gran Via 69, Madrid (☎ (1) 2484443)
Sweden
    Sveavagen 28-30, Stockholm (☎ (08) 213386/7)
Switzerland
    Bintheschergasse 12, Zurich (☎ (01) 2112344/5)
USA
    5 South Wabash Ave, Chicago IL 60603 (☎ (312) 7824306)
    4151 Southwest Freeway, Houston TX 77027 (☎ (713) 8509341)
    6380 Wilshire Blvd, LA CA 90048 (☎ (213) 6587462)
    420 Lincoln Rd Building, Lincoln Rd, Miami Beach FL 33139 (☎ (305) 6736862)
    Empire State Building, 19th Floor, 350 5th Ave, New York NY 10118 (☎ (212) 5600650)
West Germany
    Westend Str 4, Frankfurt (☎ (069) 720157)
    Fontenay 1D, Hamburg (☎ (040) 454655)

USEFUL ORGANISATIONS

Christian Information Centre

The Christian Information Centre (☎ (02) 287647) is near Jaffa Gate in Jerusalem's Old City. This is the best source of information in Israel regarding the Christian community, holy sites, etc. Obviously the title subject is their speciality, but they are knowledgeable in other areas, too.

Alternative Information Centre

This centre (☎ (02) 241159; fax 253151) is at 14 Koresh St, PO Box 24278, Jerusalem, and is a joint Israeli-Palestinian project that provides information concerning developments in Palestinian society, the intifada and Israeli society's response to them. Specifically geared to assisting visiting journalists, the AIC will also help individual travellers interested in learning more about local politics. They publish two periodicals, the weekly *The Other Front* and the monthly *News From Within*.

Palestinian Human Rights Information Centre (PHRIC)

The PHRIC (☎ (02) 287076/7; fax 28707) is at 12 Masa'udi St, Top Floor, PO Box 20479, East Jerusalem. Part of the Arab Studies Society, the PHRIC publishes the monthly *Human Rights Update* summarising human rights violations committed by the Israeli army and Jewish settlers in the Occupied Territories, along with research reports on human rights issues. They also provide guidance to travellers.

Volunteer Tourist Service

In operation for over 20 years, the VTS has assisted hundreds of thousands of tourists visiting Israel. Completely voluntary, the organisation's aim is to provide assistance to visitors with problems, answer queries, and trace lost relatives and friends. They can also arrange a visit to an Israeli home for coffee and a chat, matching up the visitor's profession or hobby with that of the host. The volunteers are to be found at Ben-Gurion Airport from noon to 8 pm and in the lobbies of major hotels from 6 to 8.30 pm except

Friday and Jewish holidays. The VTS offices are:

Eilat
    14 Zofit St (☎ (059) 72344)
Haifa
    1 Ahad Ha'am St (☎ (04) 671645)
Jerusalem
    Jaffa Gate (☎ (02) 288140)
Nahariya
    18 Sokolov St (☎ (04) 920135)
Tel Aviv (head office)
    7 Mendele St (☎ (03) 222459, 226520)
Tiberias
    (☎ (06) 795072)

Meet the Israeli

The Ministry of Tourism has come up with a scheme, 'Meet the Israeli', to enable more visitors to meet Israelis at home and thus learn more about them and their lifestyle. You inquire at one of the tourist offices and they will arrange for you to have tea or coffee with an Israeli family. It usually takes a few days to find a convenient time for both you and your hosts. If you want, it is often possible to arrange a meeting with someone from a similar profession to yours, or with similar interests. (In Jerusalem, inquire at the New City office at 24 King George V St, not at the Old City office.)

BUSINESS HOURS & HOLIDAYS

Israel's business hours vary a lot due to the different religions practised. Israel being the Jewish state, Shabbat closes most shops, offices and places of entertainment on Friday afternoon and Saturday. Some reopen on Saturday evening after sundown. At the same time, the vast majority of public transport grinds to a halt. Haifa, where the religious party is unable to do anything about it, and the areas served by the Arab bus services, are the main exceptions. Muslim-owned businesses close on Friday, although many stay open until midday. Christian-owned businesses close on Sunday.

Normal shopping hours are Monday to Thursday 8 am to 1 pm and 4 to 7 pm; and Friday 8 am to 2 pm. Banking hours do vary but generally they are Sunday to Tuesday

and Thursday, 8.30 am to 12.30 pm and 4 to 5.30 pm; Wednesday, Friday and eves of holy days, 8.30 am to noon. In Nazareth, banks are open Friday and Saturday morning but are closed on Sunday. Post offices are generally open 8.30 am to 12.30 pm and 3.30 to 6 pm, except on Wednesday (8 am to 2 pm) and Friday (8 am to 1 pm); closed Saturday and holidays. In main cities and towns they may be open longer.

The effect that religious holidays have on business hours often takes travellers by surprise. It causes a lot of wasted time hanging around until the banks and shops open or the buses start running again. You need to remember to stock up on food in advance, too. Check for any holidays being celebrated during your time in Israel and be prepared.

The most important day to be aware of is the Jewish Shabbat, starting every Friday at sunset and lasting until sunset on Saturday. It causes most of the country's facilities to come to a grinding halt. If you are not an observant Jew, ensure that on Friday you arrive somewhere where you can spend Shabbat doing something that is not affected by the lack of transport, shops, banks and eating places. With a lot of careful planning it is possible to get the most out of every day in Israel.

Festivals & Holidays

January
    Epiphany
    Christmas Day, Orthodox (7th)
    Christmas Day, Armenian (19th)
January-February
    15th of Shevat
February
    Day of Appreciation & Love, Black Hebrew
February-March
    Purim
March
    Annunciation
March-April-May
    Pesah
    Ramadan
    Idul Fitr
    Easter
    Mimouna
    Holocaust Day
April
    Holocaust Day, Armenian (24th)

April-May
Independence Day
May
Lag B'Omer
New World Passover, Black Hebrew
Ascension
Pentecost
May-June
Shavuot
June
Sisters' Day, Black Hebrew
June-July
Fast of 17th of Tammuz
July-August
Fast of 9th of Av
15th of Av
August
Idul Adha
Brothers' Day, Black Hebrew
Dormition
Youth Day, Black Hebrew
September
New Year's Hejira
Prince of Peace Music Festival, Black Hebrew
September-October
Rosh Ha-Shanah
Yom Kippur
October
Sukkot
Simhat Torah
November-December
Quintessence Night, Black Hebrew
Birthday of the Prophet Mohammed
December
Christmas Day (25th)
December-January
Hanukkah

CULTURAL EVENTS
Jewish

The Jewish festivals and celebrations understandably dominate the Israeli scene. Although the religious purposes of these festivals are intended only for the Jews, they have a meaning for everyone and have been adopted as national holidays by the mainly secular Jewish population. The festivals are supposed to remind Jews of their duty to God and to non-Jews, and play an important part in the building of the Kingdom of God where all people recognise God as the Father and love each other.

The Jewish calendar is complex. Based on a lunar year, it has 12 months which, now named, were initially just numbered. They are: Nisan, Iyyar, Sivan, Tammuz, Av, Elul, Tishri, Heshvan, Kislev, Tevet, Shevat and Adar. Nisan is the first month of the year, although the New Year, marked by Rosh Ha-Shanah, occurs in Tishri, the seventh month (usually around September/October). Rosh Ha-Shanah actually marks the world's creation, a different celebration from the first month of the year. The Jewish lunar year has 354 days, so a leap month called Adar II is added seven times in a 19-year cycle to keep the discrepancy with the solar year to a minimum.

Rosh HaShanah Read Leviticus 23:24, Numbers 29:1 and Nehemiah 8:2-3. Rosh Ha-Shanah is one of the two days of the Jewish calendar known as Days of Judgement or Days of Awe. The other is Yom Kippur. On these days, Jews are called upon to account to God. Purely religious in character, they are mainly celebrated in the synagogue.

As for all Jewish holidays, prayer services begin the eve of the holiday and in the case of Rosh HaShanah continue for two days. A special feature during the prayers is the blowing of the shofar, to remind Jews to obey God's command.

Characteristic foods eaten on Rosh Ha-Shanah include pomegranates, over which the blessing of the first fruits of the New Year is recited; apples dipped in honey or other honeyed foods to augur a sweet year; and tongue or fish heads to mark the 'head of the year', a direct translation of Rosh HaShanah.

Yom Kippur Read Leviticus 16:30-31, 23:27-28, 31-32, and Numbers 29:7. Known as the Day of Atonement, it occurs on the 10th of Tishri and ends the 10 days of penitence which begin on New Year's Day. For the observant, Yom Kippur means 25 hours of complete abstinence from food, drink, sex, cosmetics (including soap and toothpaste) and animal products. The time is spent in prayer and contemplation and sins are confessed. It is the only Jewish holiday that is equivalent to Shabbat in sanctity.

This is the day where virtually everything

under Jewish control comes to a stop. Children play in the empty roads, and there is no TV or radio – everything is closed for the day.

Sukkot & Simhat Torah Read Exodus 34:22, Numbers 28:26, Leviticus 23:34 and 36 and Deuteronomy 16:9-10 and 13. The Feast of Tabernacles and Rejoicing in the Law are celebrated in the month of Tishri (15 to 23). The Festival of Sukkot has both religious and cultural significance. Most Jews, religious or not, erect home-made sukkot (shelters) to remind them of the Israelites living in the wilderness after the exodus. The sukkot can be seen on the balconies of apartments and houses, in gardens and even in hotels and restaurants. The major requirement is that the roof is made only of leafy branches to enable the sky to be seen. The agricultural significance is symbolised by the 'four species' used – the palm branch, the myrtle, the willow and the citron or *etrog*. Special blessings are recited on each of these items during the holiday.

The eighth day of the Feast of Tabernacles is Simhat Torah, Rejoicing in the Law. The cycle of reading the Torah in the synagogues has just been completed and another is immediately begun, after the scrolls have been carried around the congregation in seven encirclements *(hakafot)* accompanied by singing and dancing. In Jerusalem it is great to see the *yeshiva* (religious school) students dancing towards the Western Wall carrying the Torah Scrolls. It has become the custom to hold public 'Second Hakafot' programmes on the night following Simat Torah. These are held in parks and squares with music and dancing. Check the IGTO for information.

Hanukkah Read 1 Maccabees 4:52-59, Talmud B, Shabbat 2lb from the Talmud. They tell of the eight days, starting with the 25th day of Kislev, when there is neither mourning nor fasting. Also known as the Festival of Lights, Hanukkah celebrates the triumphant Maccabaean revolt. Its symbol is the menorah, and one of its candles is lit each night. A nice part about Hanukkah is that it has inspired a tradition of eating jam (jelly) doughnuts for a week.

The 15th of Shevat (Tu B'Shevat) The Mishnah dedicated this as the New Year for Trees and it is customary to eat fruit and nuts, in particular the carob fruit. Since independence, the day has been observed as a time for tree-planting.

Purim Read the Book of Esther. Celebrated on the 14th day of Adar, Purim, the Feast of Lots, recalls the story about hunger for power, and the hatred born of the Jews' refusal to assimilate and their unwillingness to compromise religious principle by bowing before the secular authority. Despite such a serious, if highly relevant, theme, the holiday has a carnival atmosphere and can be great fun to participate in. Fancy dress is the order of the day. During the day the streets and buses are filled with proud parents taking Superman, Madonna, Michael Jackson and Rambo to and from school and the shops, while in the evening French tarts, fairies, gangsters, etc are to be seen.

Israel is a nation of nondrinkers, and Purim is their chance to make up for it. Jews are traditionally required to get so drunk that they cannot distinguish between the words 'bless Mordechai' and 'curse Haman'. The most popular of the Purim foods are Haman's Ears, Oznei Haman, a fried, three-cornered pastry filled with apricots or other fruits and covered in poppy seeds.

Pesah Read Exodus 12:17-18, 12:24, 26-27, 34:18. This, the Feast of Passover, is celebrated throughout the Jewish world during the month of Nisan. It recalls and relives the events in the history of the Jews in Egypt and their exodus, led by Moses. Lasting a full week, Pesah results in most of the Jewish stores (including foodstores and markets) being closed or opened for limited hours. Public transport is affected and stops on the first and last days of the festival, no regular bread is made by Jewish bakers, and the country's only brewery stops production.

The holiday commences with the Seder meal on the eve of the festival. During this first meal, the story of the Passover is read. Special foods are served or avoided. For example, Ashkenazim exclude rice, while Sephardim make a point of including it. Matzah (unleavened bread) is the principal ingredient for all Pesah dishes, as it is forbidden to eat, and even to keep, leavened products in Jewish households at this time. Jerusalem is a good place to see the priests' blessings at the Western Wall during the mornings of the intermediate days of Pesah. Hundreds of white-clad priests participate.

The Samaritans celebrate their version of Pesah on Mount Gerizim near Nablus. To them this is the authentic Mount Sinai as well as the site of Abraham's sacrifice of his son, Isaac. Here they sacrifice a lamb, watched by a crowd of onlookers, as they have done for over 2500 years.

Holocaust Day (Yom Ha-Sho'ah) The 27th day of Nisan was set aside in 1951 as a day of mourning for the Holocaust victims. The occasion also serves as a reminder of the potential for similar evils to recur. Throughout Israel on this day, sirens blast to begin a period of respectful silence. It is an effective symbol, with traffic stopping, drivers and passengers getting out of their vehicles to stand to attention. On the beaches, in shops, offices, and factories and on the kibbutzim and in the streets, everything stops. Quite an experience.

Mimouna This festival takes place the day after the last day of Pesah and has been celebrated by the North African Jewish communities for generations. In the last few years it has been reinstated to become a popular fixture on the Israeli calendar. Mimouna's exact origins are unknown. One theory is that it is an Arabisation of the Hebrew word *emunah*, meaning faith or belief, in the coming of the Messiah and the redemption of the Jews. Certainly the theme of Mimouna is confidence in God and

patience in awaiting the Messiah. It is a marvellous chance for you to experience Israeli hospitality, which traditionally excels itself on this occasion. All over the country North African Jews organise street parties and open-house celebrations. Foreigners – Jews and non-Jews alike – are warmly invited to join in. Check the IGTO for the local arrangements wherever you are. The festival has always symbolised friendship and brotherhood – try not to miss it.

Independence Day (Yom Ha'Atzmaut) On the fifth day of Iyyar (14 May) 1948 Israel became an independent state and since then the day has been celebrated by Jews worldwide. In Israel this is done with parades, concerts, picnics and fireworks all over the country.

Lag B'Omer This is a particularly joyous occasion for the Hasidim who, to many people's surprise, do know how to laugh, sing, dance and have a good time. It takes place on the 18th day of Iyyar and comes after 33 days of mourning. A special day of celebration for all Jews, it is interpreted as a rite of spring or as the day when a plague was lifted in Jewish history. Outings and bonfires are a feature of the proceedings.

Thousands of Hasidim pour into Meiron, up near Safed in Galilee. There is a parade ending in torchlight with singing and dancing along the way. On arrival at Meiron, candles are burned on the tomb of Rabbi Shamon and a giant bonfire is lit. Some of the Hasidim throw their clothes onto the fire and the festivities go on all night. In the morning, three-year-old boys are given their first haircuts, and the hair is thrown onto the fire.

What's it all about? For over 1700 years the site has been holy to religious Jews. When the Romans conquered Jerusalem in the second century, the Jews fled to the area around Meiron. One of them, Shimon Bar Yochai, continued to defy the Romans and was forced to hide permanently in a cave in Peqi'in nearby. There he supposedly wrote the Book of Splendour, the bible of the Kabbalists (mystic Jews).

The enthusiastic pilgrimage serves partly to recall the teachings of the Torah and celebrate it as a gift from God. The act of cutting young boys' hair and throwing it on the fire is called Halaka (Arabic for 'shaving'). This is a variation of the ancient Israelite practice, based on Deuteronomy 18:4, of offering the first fleece of a sheep to the priest.

Shavuot Read Exodus 34:22, Numbers 28:26 and Deuteronomy 16:9-10. This is the Jewish celebration of Pentecost, the Feast of Weeks. A happy harvest event, it occurs on the sixth day of Sivan and can be a particular highlight on kibbutzim and moshavim. It is often marked by plays; people dress in white clothes and eat dairy foods. In the time of the Temple, the first crop of the year would be taken there and destroyed with fire.

Fast of 17th of Tammuz This day marks the Roman destruction of Jerusalem's city walls and observant Jews fast during the daylight hours.

Fast of Ninth of Av (Tishah be-Av) This day is set aside to remember the destruction of the First and Second Temples. If you are in Jerusalem, check out the packed Western Wall.

15th of Av This is the Day of Love and, according to the Mishnah, the happiest day of the year. Tradition states that the woodcutters used to return to Jerusalem after working in the fields and girls, dressed in white, would be waiting for a proposal of marriage.

Black Hebrews
Down in Dimona, you are welcome to join in the community's various celebrations during the year.

Day of Appreciation & Love On this day, around the end of February, the Hebrews set aside the time specifically to show love to one another and to exchange gifts. They celebrate in style with their own music and

singers, they all dress up in fancy clothes and there's plenty to eat, especially in the way of sweets and cakes. They also enjoy their own wine.

New World Passover During May the Hebrews celebrate the second exodus from a land of captivity, when they left the USA to return to Africa. This occasion lasts for two days. On the first day they go for a picnic and have a sports event called the Rockameera (Merry) Games. On the second day the children perform a presentation for the adults.

Sisters' Day On this occasion in June, the women of the community display their creations in the way of fine clothes, handicrafts and vegetarian food. They perform plays and organise forums, which the men attend while also taking care of the housework and minding the children for the day.

Brothers' Day The following week, the men show what they can do. Some great jewellery, shoes and clothes are made by them.

Youth Day At the end of August the kids take over and put on a show.

Prince of Peace Music Festival Here the Hebrews celebrate with music. They play a variety of soul, jazz/funk and gospel styles, much of which they write themselves.

Quintessence Night This is an evening, in November or December, for the family to be together. Candlelight and music help create an atmosphere of love and unity, and together families praise God.

Muslim
The Muslim festivals are observed with some solemnity, although there are occasions of joy and happiness. The pleasure of Allah is the cornerstone of all Islamic activity and there is no concept of a festival for pleasure's own sake. Apparently the happiest occasion of a Muslim's life is to see the sovereignty of Allah established in his land. Islamic festivals are observed according to

the Islamic Calendar which is based on 12 lunar months.

Birth of the Prophet Mohammed's birthday and a day of thanks and praise to Allah.

Lailatul Miraj This remembers the night Mohammed ascended to heaven from the Temple Mount in Jerusalem.

Ramadan For non-Muslim visitors, the major effect of this month-long dawn-to-sunset fast is that the less commercial Muslim Arab areas are very quiet, with businesses closed. After dark, though, things liven up everywhere and the Arabs seem to be up all hours.

Idul Fitr This day is observed at the end of Ramadan. Muslims express their joy at the end of their fast by offering a congregational prayer, preferably in an open field. They should express their gratitude to Allah for enabling them to observe the fast, thus preparing them for life as a Muslim. Special dishes are prepared and it is customary to visit relatives and friends, to go out for a day trip and to give presents to children. Everyone eats a great deal.

Idul Adha Idul Adha begins on the 10th of Dulil Hijja, its most important day, and continues until the 12th day of the month. It commemorates the occasion when Allah asked Abraham to sacrifice his son, Ishmael. A lamb was sacrificed instead of the boy after Abraham had shown his readiness to obey Allah. Today Muslims offer congregational prayer on the day and follow it with a sacrifice mainly of sheep, but also goats, and cows. The meat of the sacrificed animal is given to needy people and to older relatives. Clothes and money are sometimes given, too.

New Year's Hejira This day recalls the migration of the prophet Mohammed from Mecca to Medina. This is the time for Muslims to make the haj, the pilgrimage to Mecca.

Christian
Many visitors with a Christian background will find the festivals celebrated very differently from the way they are used to. This is largely due to the domination of the Orthodox Churches, and also to the fact that Christianity is very much in third place in the religious stakes here. Christmas Day, for example (ignoring the fact that it is celebrated on three separate occasions by the various denominations) is just another day for most people. Even in Jerusalem there are no highly visible signs of the great event, such as decorated trees or street lights. Simply being here is the key for most of the pilgrims.

Christmas Day Apart from 25 December, Christmas is celebrated on 7 January by the Orthodox and on 19 January by the Armenians. The place to go is Bethlehem for the midnight mass on Christmas Eve (24 December). Due to the popularity of the service, space inside the Church of the Nativity is reserved for observant Catholics. Outside in Manger Square there is a large crowd watching a Protestant choir concert with participants from around the world. The actual Midnight Mass is shown on a large video screen affixed to the police station in the square and is also broadcast around the world. It can be an extremely cold night, so do wrap up.

During the day on Christmas Eve there is a traditional procession from Jerusalem's Old City to Bethlehem. Admission into the Midnight Mass service on Christmas Eve is by ticket only. These are free and can be applied for at the Terra Sancta office in the Christian Information Centre, Old City, Jerusalem. Extra buses are arranged to cater to the crowds travelling between Jerusalem and Bethlehem. These buses run irregularly all night. Since the intifada, though, these Christmas celebrations in Bethlehem have effectively been cancelled.

Easter Celebrated first by the Roman Catholics and the Protestants and then about two weeks later by the Orthodox Church. The

Church of the Holy Sepulchre and the Via Dolorosa are the centre of events for both occasions. The Orthodox celebrations are responsible for Jerusalem's Old City being packed out with pilgrims, mainly black-clad senior citizens from Greece and Cyprus. These devout Christians are extremely keen to celebrate Easter in Jerusalem and can be seen wandering around carrying their fold-up stools, used when waiting for hours to ensure a good spot for the services, some of which are outside. Note that the same pilgrims fill many of the cheap hostels in the Old City for the weeks of Easter celebration.

Celebration of the Baptism of Jesus Christ The traditional site where John the Baptist baptised Jesus Christ is on the west bank of the Jordan River, a few km from Jericho. The area has long been off-limits for security reasons and a baptism site further up river was provided near the Sea of Galilee at Kibbutz Degania. However, the Roman Catholics have recently been able to organise a special celebration at the revered site in October. Contact the Christian Information Centre in Jerusalem for details, including transport arrangements.

Armenian Holocaust Day Every year on 24 April the Armenians commemorate their overlooked tragedy with a parade and service in Jerusalem's Old City.

Needless to say, all the other Christian festivals are celebrated in the country, with Jerusalem's Old City, crammed as it is with churches and chapels of all sizes and denominations, the centre of activity.

POST & TELECOMMUNICATIONS
Post, Telegrams, Telexes & Faxes
Letters posted in Israel can take longer than two weeks to reach North America and Australia; only a little less to Europe. Most locals carry mail for each other when they leave the country, but you should think twice about doing so yourself unless you are very confident about the person who has given you the

mail. It wouldn't be much fun to travel with a package that started ticking at 30,000 feet.

Poste restante seems to work quite well. As in some other countries, do not rely solely on the word of the clerk that the letter you are expecting has not arrived. Check under all your names, and if necessary ask to check for yourself. Remember that American Express offices will receive mail for card holders.

Telegram services are available in post offices, or telephone 171. In main post offices a 24 hour service is provided, although you will often find yourself having to wake up the person on duty during the night. The system of queuing has been introduced to some Israeli post offices, but to most of the locals it's a whole new ball-game. Be firm and repel all pushers-in.

To send a fax or telex, telephone ☎ (02) 244737, operating 24 hours daily. Alternatively, you can go to a main post office or Bezeq office (see Telephone below). Israeli businesses have fallen in love with the fax as much as anywhere else, and I have included fax numbers for hotels and useful organisations wherever possible.

Telephone

Public telephones do not take coins, but tokens. These are called *asimonim* and are available from machines, post offices, some hotel reception desks and street kiosks. Make sure that you stock up with them if you expect to be making any calls. For a local call, one asimon lasts for an unlimited period; long-distance calls (ie requiring an area code) can use up a lot, depending on the distance, duration and time of day. Whatever, just keep dropping your asimonim into the phone and any that are unused are returned when the call is finished. It's easy enough to sell unused asimonim when you leave Israel, so don't worry about having too many – worry about running out halfway through a call!

Public phones are regularly out of order – either not working at all or swallowing asimonim without connecting you. You can often dial even a local call and after the first two or three digits the number will be engaged. When you do get through the lines are frequently bad – a typical street scene in Israel is not complete without somebody screaming down a public telephone.

The demand for asimonim has created an industry staffed by those people Israel tends not to talk about – the Jewish tramps. They can often be seen propping up a wall in the central bus stations, ankle-deep in asimonim. Buying from them saves having to queue behind a bus-load of Israelis at the nearest kiosk. It will hardly improve your Hebrew, though.

To phone abroad from Israel, public telephones can only be used for collect calls.

Note, it is not possible to call collect to either West Germany or Austria from any telephone. For collect calls elsewhere, either dial the international operator on 188 or, better still, dial ☎ (03 (if outside Tel Aviv-Jaffa) 633881 or 622881/2. These numbers are frequently busy so you need to be patient and keep trying. The rumour that there is only one international operator for the whole country is denied by the post office.

To dial direct abroad you need a private phone, otherwise go to a main post office or Bezeq office. Bezeq is a part private, part state-owned telecommunications company providing international phone and fax services. They are currently in Tel Aviv, Jerusalem, Eilat, Tiberias and Netanya, and soon to be established elsewhere as the post office will eventually cease to be responsible for telecommunications. You make most international calls by direct dialling, then pay for the units used. Note that only Israeli currency is accepted – no travellers' cheques, credit cards or US dollars. These facilities for international calls are not open in the evenings or during Shabbat and Jewish holidays.

Here are the area codes that you are most likely to use:

Place	Code	Place	Code
Afulla	06	Masada	057
Airport (Ben-Gurion)	03	Mitzpe Ramon	057
Akko	04	Nahariya	04
Arad	057	Nazareth	065
Ashdod	055	Netanya	053
Ashkelon	051	Negev Area (most)	057
Beersheba	057	Qiryat Shimona	06
Bethlehem	02	Ramla	08
Dead Sea Region	057	Rehovot	054
Dimona	057	Rishon le Zion	03
Eilat	059	Safed	06
Ein Gedi	057	Tel Aviv-Jaffa	03
Gaza	051	Tiberias	06
Hadera	063	Bethlehem	02
Haifa	04	Hebron	02
Herzlia	052	Jericho	02
Jerusalem	02	Nablus	053
Katzrin	06	Ramallah	02

Useful Telephone Numbers

Information 144 – this requires one asimon (which is returned after the call). The line is usually busy and a recorded message will often ask you (in Hebrew) to hold until an operator can answer your call. Unfortunately the local telephone directories are mainly printed in Hebrew.

Police 100
First Aid/Ambulance 101
Fire Service 102
Airport Information (03) 9712484 (24-hour service); (03) 381111 (arrivals only – taped message)

Public telephones in Israel are often to be found in an area noisy enough to make it impossible to hear yourself speak, let alone the poor unfortunate on the other end of the crackly line. An example is Jerusalem central bus station. Here the public telephones have been installed right next to the spot where every arriving bus screams to a halt.

TIME

Israel's adoption of Daylight Saving Time in summer has caused controversy and confusion. It will probably continue to do so in a country where people love to argue. Israel is basically two hours ahead of GMT, eight hours behind Australian Eastern Standard Time, and seven hours ahead of American Eastern Standard Time.

ELECTRICITY

This is 220 volts, 50 cycles, alternating current. Wall plugs are the round, two-prong type; bring an adaptor if required, it's cheaper than buying one in Israel.

LAUNDRY

Virtually all hostels allow you to do your own laundry on the premises and that's what most travellers do. Otherwise there are coin-operated laundromats in many Israeli towns.

WEIGHTS & MEASURES

Israel uses the metric system. There is a standard conversion table at the back of this guide.

BOOKS

Reading is a popular pastime here: the 'average Israeli' supposedly reads 10 books a year. Every spring, Hebrew Book Week is celebrated throughout the country with open-air markets. Bookshops are plentiful,

with a great many dealing in second-hand books. Steimatzky's is the largest chain of bookstores. Found everywhere, they are one of the best places for that popular travellers' pastime – glancing at the foreign newspapers and magazines.

With so many keen readers and such a tumultuous history, Israel is the subject of more books than most countries. A list of relevant books for someone visiting Israel could easily become a book in its own right.

Politics

The ever-popular subject. Here are some titles, covering a variety of viewpoints, to give you verbal ammunition (and perhaps other ailments) for the discussions to come.

Abu Nidal – A Gun for Hire (Random House, NY, 1992), by Patrick Seale, is an exploration of PLO claims that Israeli intelligence has penetrated Nidal's organisation to assassinate Palestinian moderates.

Arab and Jew: Wounded Spirits in a Promised Land (Times Books, NY, 1986), by David K Shipler, is a Pulitzer Prize winner and a must for anyone with an interest in the subject. The observations of the realities of Israel today are spot-on and all visitors will benefit from reading his book.

The Gun and the Olive Branch: The Roots of Violence in the Middle East (Futura, London), by David Hirst (from the *Guardian*), is an historical survey of the region.

In the Land of Israel (Chatto & Windus, Hogarth Press, London; Harcourt Brace Jovanovitch, San Diego, 1983) is written by Amos Oz, a leading Israeli writer. He has travelled the country, discussing politics with those he met from all sections of the population.

They Must Go by Rabbi Meir Kahane (Groset & Dunlap, NY, 1981). The controversial Brooklyn-born Kahane, assassinated in 1991, led Israel's Koch political party, which advocates, amongst other things, the expulsion of all the Arabs from Israel and the Occupied Territories.

From Time Immemorial (Harper & Row, NY, 1984), by Joan Peters, is championed by Zionists for its conclusion that Israel's Arabs arrived more recently than is often claimed, so reducing the argument for Palestinian rights.

This Land is Our Land (Zed Press, London, 1983), by Metzer, Orth & Sterzing, is a study of the West Bank dispute.

My Friend the Enemy (Lawrence Hill, Westport CT, 1986) is by Uri Avnery, a left-wing radical, a millionaire author, publisher, and former Knesset member. He visited the PLO's Yasser Arafat at the height of the war in Lebanon (to which he was opposed). This book is his account of why he went and how it went.

Jews & American Politics (Doubleday, NY, 1974) by Stephen D Isaacs takes a look at the USA's political and financial support of Israel.

They Dare to Speak Out (Lawrence Hill, Westport CT, 1985) by Paul Findley, a former US Congressman, studies the pro-Israel lobby in America.

Biographies

Tongue of the Prophets – The Life Story of Eliezer Ben Yehuda (Doubleday, NY, 1952), by Robert St John, is about the man who revived the Hebrew language.

Herzl (Holt, Reinhart & Winston, NY, 1975), by Amos Elon, is about the founder of political Zionism.

The Revolt – the Story of the Irgun (Nash, NY, 1977), Menachem Begin.

The Labyrinth of Exile – A Life of Theodor Herzl (Farar, Strauss & Giroux, NY, 1989), Ernst Pawel, is more balanced than the average biography of modern Zionism's founder.

Ben-Gurion: Prophet of Fire (Simon & Schuster, NY, 1983), Dan Kurzman, is about Israel's first Prime Minister.

My Life (Weidenfield & Nicholson, London, 1975), Golda Meir.

Arafat: Terrorist or Peacemaker? (Sidgwick & Jackson, London, 1984), Alan Hart, has some thought-provoking conclusions.

Arafat: In the Eyes of the Beholder (Prime Publishing, NY, 1990), by Janet & John Wallach, was written after the PLO leader

renounced terrorism and recognised Israel's right to exist.

Our Man in Damascus: Elie Cohen (Crown, NY, 1969), by Eli Ben-Hanan, is a fascinating account of Israel's most celebrated spy.

Israel's Secret Wars: A History of Israel's Intelligence Services (Grove Weidenfield, NY, 1991), by Ian Black & Benny Morris, is a well-documented analysis of the country's three spy services, and includes their failures as well as successes.

Travel

The Innocents Abroad (American Publishing Co., Hartford, CT, 1871), by Mark Twain, is still one of the best books dealing with the tourist experience in the Holy Land.

Cook's Travellers Handbook: Palestine and Syria (London, 1929) is an early travel guide, with some great tips and information for its time.

The Folklore of the Holy Land (London, 1907), Canon J E Hanauer, is still partly relevant after all these years, and a fascinating read.

Enemy in the Promised Land – An Egyptian Woman's Journey into Israel (Shocken Books, NY, 1986) is by Sana Hasan, who three years before Sadat, visited the Jewish State. Her interesting account is full of observations and experiences that illustrate the real Israel.

Jerusalem

Most visitors are captivated by this city. To get to know it better, the following books are well worth reading:

O Jerusalem (Simon & Schuster, NY, 1972), by Larry Collins & Dominique Lapierre, is the most popular book with travellers in Israel, as it provides a balanced look at the 1948 War of Independence and the birth of the modern State of Israel.

Jerusalem – Problems & Prospects (Praeger, NY, 1980), edited by Joel L Kaemer, includes such chapters as 'Israeli policy in East Jerusalem' and 'The Christian Establishment in Jerusalem'.

For Jerusalem – a Life (Random House,

NY, 1978), by Teddy Kollek (with his son Amos), provides an insight into the administration of the Holy City as seen through the eyes of its colourful mayor.

Footloose in Jerusalem (Crown, New York, 1981), by Sarah Fox Kaminker, is a popular guide outlining several detailed walks in the Old and New Cities.

Religion
This is My God. The Jewish Way of Life (Simon & Schuster, New York, 1959), Herman Wouk.

Wanderings: Chaim Potok's History of the Jews (Knopf, New York, 1978).

In the Steps of the Master (Dodd, Mead, New York, 1979), by H V Morton, is a guide to the land of Jesus.

The Orthodox Church (Penguin, London/New York, 1975), Timothy Ware.

Islam: Beliefs & Teachings (Muslim Education Trust, London, 1982), Ghulam Sawar.

The Druzes in Israel (Magnes Press, Jerusalem, 1979), Gabriel Ben-Don.

Archaeology
The Holy Land (Oxford University Press, London/New York, 1986), Jerome Murphy-O'Conner, is simply the best archaeological guide; concise and interesting, with some deft touches of humour.

Fiction
To be enjoyed, not believed, these are probably the two most popular of the countless titles with an Israeli theme.

The Source (Random House, New York, 1965), James A Michener, and *Exodus* (Doubleday, New York, 1958), Leon Uris.

MAPS
Another area of controversy: maps are forbidden by Israeli law to show the 'green line' (the West Bank border), and the Gaza Strip and Golan Heights borders. Instead, these areas are included within Israel's national borders. Except for those pro-Palestinians wishing to be politically correct, awareness of these disputes will still allow most travellers to use these maps to get around. The most detailed maps are in Hebrew, and readily available from the SPNI stores in Jerusalem and Tel Aviv. For most of you, these are superfluous and the *Israel Touring Map* (Scale 1:400,000), available free from IGTOs, will suffice. For those planning a more extensive independent tour, get *Bazak's* (Scale 1:250,000). Available at Steimatzky's for about US$6, it divides the country in two with a northern and a southern sheet, printed back to back, and includes most minor roads and tracks. This will be enough to get virtually anywhere you are permitted to go. If there are places beyond those illustrated here, chances are you are advised not to go without a guide eg in the desert or the Golan.

MEDIA
Newspapers & Magazines
Unless you read Hebrew or Arabic, your appreciation of Israel's extensive press will be limited. The *Jerusalem Post* is the only Jewish English-language daily (available every day except Saturday). You may find the limited subject matter of the Israeli press tedious. Who is a Jew?, the holocaust, the Jewish birth rate, the lack of Zionism, US political and financial support of Israel – these are the kind of subjects often discussed in its pages. The *Post* should be read regularly, though, as it does give an insight into the Jewish population that would otherwise be hard to achieve in a short space of time.

For decent articles and photography, look for *Eretz*, a quarterly magazine. The monthly *Israel Scene* covers the community, politics, industry and the arts, together with a bit of gossip. It is light and usually well-written, especially Chaim Bermont's witty column.

In addition to the publications listed under information, the Palestinian press features an English-language weekly *Al-Fajr*. You will normally only find this sold in East Jerusalem, Jerusalem's Old City and towns in the Occupied Territories. Rhetorical in style, it provides an alternative picture to the official Israeli presentation of the Palestine problem.

Radio & TV

One of the most popular radio stations is the army service (96FM, 1000AM). It offers a wide variety of programmes, and due to the involvement of virtually the entire Jewish population with the IDF, there is a wide audience. Kol Israel has four stations: Station A (540AM) broadcasts educational, discussion, and current affairs programmes. From 7 pm it broadcasts in 18 languages for Jews from all over the world now in Israel. Station B (650AM) has easy listening, recipes, phone-ins, and so on. Station C (94FM) was recently introduced to compete with the army station. It plays mainly popular music for a younger audience. The Voice of Music (88FM) is the classical music station.

Very popular with travellers as well as Israelis is the Voice of Peace (100FM, 1540AM). Broadcasting 24 hours from a ship anchored off the coast of Tel Aviv, often in English, this station plays an excellent selection of popular music virtually nonstop. Its founder, Abie J Nathan, is a well-known peace campaigner and has led many colourful campaigns to further the cause. The Voice of Peace broadcasts do not reach beyond Haifa to the north and Beersheba to the south. In Jerusalem, a good alternative is Radio Jordan's broadcasts in English (99FM). Their schedule includes the British pop charts, and classic BBC radio comedies.

Listening to the news is a necessity of life for Israelis and news programmes in various languages can be heard frequently. On the Jewish buses the radio, if not already on, will be turned on loudly for the news. Check current schedules for news broadcasts in English.

Israel has two television stations, and over 25% of the population now has cable (32 channels). People also tune to Jordan Television, and in the north to Syrian Television and Middle East Television (a Christian station administered by North Americans).

FILM & PHOTOGRAPHY

Most types of film are available in Israel but you can buy it cheaper elsewhere. The quality of processing is not particularly good.

Photography in Israel presents no special problems. In strong sunlight, reflections can become glaring and a polarising filter is useful. Be careful when taking photographs to avoid military installations, although photographing soldiers elsewhere does not seem to cause problems. In general, people are not keen on you pointing your lens at them, particularly Hasidic Jews and Arab women. As travel posters and postcards show, however, it is possible to wander right up to the Western Wall and snap away (but not during Shabbat or a Jewish holiday). I am still amazed that photography is permitted in most of the holy sites; unless a sign says that you can't, you can.

When it comes to photography, the best time of the year to visit Israel is between November and April. This avoids the highest temperatures, which create a misty haze in such places as the Sea of Galilee, Jericho and the Dead Sea region – some of the best photographic locations.

HEALTH

Travel health depends on your pre-departure preparations, your day-to-day health care while travelling, and how you handle any medical problem or emergency that does develop. Israel presents no major health hazards for the visitor; the most you can normally expect to face are over exposure to the sun and sea and an upset stomach.

Travel Health Guides

There are a number of books on travel health, few of which are really necessary for a trip to Israel. The following may be worth a look, though:

Travellers' Health, Dr Richard Dawood, Oxford University Press. Comprehensive, easy to read and authoritative, and also highly recommended, although it's rather large to lug around.

Travel with Children, Maureen Wheeler, Lonely Planet Publications. Includes basic advice on travel health for younger children.

Pre-Departure Preparations

Health Insurance A travel insurance policy to cover theft, loss and medical problems is a wise idea. There are a wide variety of policies and your travel agent will have recommendations. The international student travel policies handled by STA or other student travel organisations are usually good value. Some policies offer lower and higher medical expenses options but the higher one is chiefly for countries like the USA which have extremely high medical costs. Check the small print:

1 Some policies specifically exclude 'dangerous activities' which can include scuba diving, motorcycling, even trekking. If such activities are on your agenda you don't want that sort of policy.
2 You may prefer a policy which pays doctors or hospitals direct rather than you having to pay on the spot and claim later. If you have to claim later make sure you keep all documentation. Some policies ask you to call back (reverse charges) to a centre in your home country where an immediate assessment of your problem is made.
3 Check if the policy covers ambulances or an emergency flight home. If you have to stretch out, you will need two seats and somebody has to pay for them!

Medical Kit A small, straightforward medical kit is a wise thing to carry. A possible kit list includes:

1 Aspirin or Panadol – for pain or fever.
2 Antihistamine (such as Benadryl) – useful as a decongestant for colds, allergies, to ease the itch from insect bites or stings or to help prevent motion sickness.
3 Antibiotics – useful if you're travelling well off the beaten track, but they must be prescribed and you should carry the prescription with you.
4 Kaolin preparation (Pepto-Bismol), Imodium or Lomotil – for stomach upsets.
5 Rehydration mixture – for treatment of severe diarrhoea, this is particularly important if travelling with children.
6 Antiseptic, mercurochrome and antibiotic powder or similar 'dry' spray – for cuts and grazes.
7 Calamine lotion – to ease irritation from bites or stings.
8 Bandages and Band-aids – for minor injuries.

9 Scissors, tweezers and a thermometer (note that mercury thermometers are prohibited by airlines).
10 Insect repellent, sunscreen, suntan lotion, chap stick and water purification tablets.

Ideally, antibiotics should be administered only under medical supervision and should never be taken indiscriminately. Overuse of antibiotics can weaken your body's ability to deal with infections naturally and can reduce the drug's efficacy on a future occasion. Take only the recommended dose at the prescribed intervals and continue using the antibiotic for the prescribed period, even if the illness seems to be cured earlier. Antibiotics are quite specific to the infections they can treat, stop immediately if there are any serious reactions and don't use it at all if you are unsure if you have the correct one.

In Israel, if a medicine is available at all it will generally be available over the counter and the price will either be comparable to what it costs in the West or higher.

Health Preparations Make sure you're healthy before you start travelling. If you are embarking on a long trip make sure your teeth are OK; in Israel, dental costs are prohibitive if not covered by insurance.

If you wear glasses, take a spare pair and your prescription. Losing your glasses can be very costly here.

If you require a particular medication take an adequate supply, as it may not be available when you need it. Take the prescription, with the generic rather than the brand name (which may not be locally available), as it will make getting replacements easier. It's a wise idea to have the prescription with you to show you legally use the medication – it's surprising how often over-the-counter drugs from one place are illegal without a prescription or even banned in another.

Immunisations Vaccinations provide protection against diseases you might meet along the way. Unless you are coming from an infected area, no immunisations are needed for Israel – yellow fever and cholera are the two most likely requirements. Nevertheless, all vaccinations should be recorded on an International Health Certificate, which is available from your physician or government health department.

Plan ahead for getting any vaccinations: some of them require an initial shot followed by a booster, while some vaccinations should not be given together. Most travellers from Western countries will have been immunised against various diseases during childhood but your doctor may still recommend booster shots against measles or polio, diseases still prevalent in many developing countries that you may plan to visit in conjunction with Israel. The period of protection offered by vaccinations differs widely and some are contraindicated if you are pregnant.

Basic Rules

As in the West, care in what you eat and drink is the only real health rule in Israel. You should not feel it necessary to dwell on this as a serious threat to your well-being as you might in other parts of the Middle East. Stomach upsets are the most likely travel health problem for travellers here, but the majority of these upsets will be relatively minor. Don't become paranoid, trying the local food is part of the experience of travel after all.

Water In Israel, the old 'don't drink the water' rule does not apply. However, with more and more Westerners choosing to drink bottled water at home, many of you will feel more secure doing the same here. Reputable brands of bottled water or soft drinks are of the highest quality, if expensive.

Food As at home in the West, only the basic health standards need to be applied when eating in Israel. Salads and fruit should be washed with clean water where possible; ice cream is perfectly safe and often of excellent quality; thoroughly cooked food is safest, but even if it has been left to cool or if it has been reheated it should be fine. As you would anywhere, take great care with shellfish or fish and avoid undercooked meat. Thanks to the kosher laws, dairy products are also very safe and very good.

Nutrition If your food is poor or limited in availability, if you're travelling hard and fast and therefore missing meals, or if you simply lose your appetite, you can soon start to lose weight and place your health at risk.

Make sure your diet is well balanced. Eggs, tofu, beans, lentils and nuts are all safe ways to get protein. All fruit in Israel, not just those you can peel, is always safe and a good source of vitamins. Try to eat plenty of grains (rice) and bread.

Remember, that although food is generally safer if it is cooked well, overcooked food loses much of its nutritional value. If your diet isn't well balanced or if your food intake is insufficient, it's a good idea to take vitamin and iron pills.

When it gets hot, especially in Israel's desert areas, make sure you drink enough – don't rely on feeling thirsty to indicate when you should drink. Not needing to urinate or very dark yellow urine is a danger sign. Always carry a water bottle with you on long trips. Excessive sweating can lead to loss of salt and therefore muscle cramping. Salt tablets are not a good idea as a preventative, but if you aren't getting much salt in your diet, adding salt to your food can help.

Everyday Health A normal body temperature is 98.6°F or 37°C; more than 2°C higher is a 'high' fever. A normal adult pulse rate is 60 to 80 per minute (children 80 to 100, babies 100 to 140). You should know how to take a temperature and a pulse rate. As a general rule the pulse increases about 20 beats per minute for each °C rise in fever.

Respiration (breathing) rate is also an indicator of illness. Count the number of breaths per minute: between 12 and 20 is normal for adults and older children (up to 30 for younger children, 40 for babies). People with a high fever or serious respiratory illness (like pneumonia) breathe more quickly than normal. More than 40 shallow breaths a minute usually means pneumonia. Many health problems can be avoided by taking care of yourself. Wash your hands frequently – it's quite easy to contaminate your own food. Avoid climatic extremes: keep out of the sun when it's hot, dress warmly when it's cold. Avoid potential diseases by dressing sensibly. You can get worm infections through walking barefoot or (in Eilat) dangerous coral cuts by walking over coral without shoes. You can avoid insect bites by covering bare skin when insects are around, by screening windows or beds or by using insect repellents. Seek local advice: if you're told the water is unsafe due to jellyfish, don't go in. In situations where there is no information, discretion is the better part of valour.

Medical Problems & Treatment
Potential medical problems can be broken down into several areas. First there are the climatic and geographical considerations – problems caused by extremes of temperature, altitude or motion. Then there are diseases and illnesses caused by insanitation, insect bites or stings, and animal or human contact. Simple cuts, bites or scratches can also cause problems.

Self-diagnosis and treatment can be risky, so wherever possible seek qualified help. Although we do give treatment dosages in this section, they are for emergency use only. Medical advice should be sought before the administration of any drugs.

An embassy or consulate can usually recommend a good place to go for such advice, but so can most hostel managers. If you can afford it, Israel offers some of the best medical facilities in the world. This is when that medical insurance really comes in useful!

Climatic & Geographical Considerations
Sunburn In Israel, and not just in the desert, you can get sunburnt surprisingly quickly. Despite all the talk of its health benefits, you can get burned in the Dead Sea region. Use a sunscreen and take extra care to cover areas which don't normally see sun – eg, your feet.

A hat provides added protection, and you should also use zinc cream or some other barrier cream for your nose and lips.

Calamine lotion is good for mild sunburn.

Prickly Heat Prickly heat is an itchy rash caused by excessive perspiration trapped under the skin. It usually strikes people who have just arrived in a hot climate and whose pores have not yet opened sufficiently to cope with greater sweating. Keeping cool but bathing often, using a mild talcum powder or even resorting to air-conditioning may help until you acclimatise.

Heat Exhaustion Dehydration or salt deficiency can cause heat exhaustion. Take time to acclimatise to high temperatures and make sure you get sufficient liquids. Salt deficiency is characterised by fatigue, lethargy, headaches, giddiness and muscle cramps and in this case salt tablets may help. Vomiting or diarrhoea can deplete your liquid and salt levels.

Anhydrotic heat exhaustion, caused by an inability to sweat, is quite rare. Unlike the other forms of heat exhaustion it is likely to strike people who have been in a hot climate for some time, rather than newcomers.

Heat Stroke This serious, sometimes fatal, condition can occur if the body's heat-regulating mechanism breaks down and the body temperature rises to dangerous levels. Long, continuous periods of exposure to high temperatures can leave you vulnerable to heat stroke. You should avoid excessive alcohol or strenuous activity if temperatures are high.

The symptoms are feeling unwell, not sweating very much or at all and a high body temperature (39°C to 41°C). Where sweating has ceased the skin becomes flushed and red. Severe, throbbing headaches and lack of coordination will also occur, and the sufferer may be confused or aggressive. Eventually the victim will become delirious or convulse. Hospitalisation is essential, but meanwhile get patients out of the sun, remove their clothing, cover them with a wet sheet or towel and then fan continually.

Fungal Infections Hot weather fungal infections are most likely to occur on the scalp, between the toes or fingers (athlete's foot), in the groin (jock itch or crotch rot) and on the body (ringworm). You get ringworm (which is a fungal infection, not a worm) from infected animals or by walking on damp areas, like shower floors.

To prevent fungal infections wear loose, comfortable clothes, avoid artificial fibres, wash frequently and dry carefully. If you do get an infection, wash the infected area daily with a disinfectant or medicated soap and water, and rinse and dry well. Apply an anti-fungal powder like the widely available Tinaderm. Try to expose the infected area to air or sunlight as much as possible and wash all towels and underwear in hot water as well as changing them often.

Cold Too much cold is just as dangerous as too much heat, particularly if it leads to hypothermia. If you are hiking, say in the Galilee or the Golan, be prepared. Catching most visitors by suprise, you should be prepared for cold, wet or windy conditions in many parts of Israel, even if you're just out walking.

Hypothermia occurs when the body loses heat faster than it can produce it and the core temperature of the body falls. It is surprisingly easy to progress from very cold to dangerously cold due to a combination of wind, wet clothing, fatigue and hunger, even if the air temperature is above freezing. It is best to dress in layers; silk, wool and some of the new artificial fibres are all good insulating materials. A hat is important, as a lot of heat is lost through the head. A strong, waterproof outer layer is essential, as keeping dry is vital. Carry basic supplies, including food containing simple sugars to generate heat quickly and lots of fluid to drink.

Symptoms of hypothermia are exhaustion, numb skin (particularly toes and fingers), shivering, slurred speech, irrational or violent behaviour, lethargy, stumbling, dizzy spells, muscle cramps and violent bursts of energy. Irrationality may take the form of sufferers claiming they are warm and trying to take off their clothes.

To treat hypothermia, first get the patient out of the wind and/or rain, remove their clothing if its wet and replace it with dry, warm clothing. Give them hot liquids – not alcohol – and some high-kilojoule, easily digestible food. This should be enough for the early stages of hypothermia, but if it has gone further it may be necessary to place victims in warm sleeping bags and get in with them. Do not rub patients, place them near a fire or remove their wet clothes in the wind. If possible, place a sufferer in a warm (not hot) bath.

Motion Sickness Eating lightly before and during a trip will reduce the chances of motion sickness. If you are prone to motion sickness try to find a place that minimises disturbance – near the wing on aircraft, close to midships on boats, near the centre on buses. Fresh air usually helps, reading or cigarette smoke doesn't. Commercial anti-motion-sickness preparations, which can cause drowsiness, have to be taken before the trip commences; when you're feeling sick it's too late. Ginger is a natural preventative and is available in capsule form.

Diseases of Insanitation

Diarrhoea A change of water, food or climate can all cause the runs; diarrhoea caused by contaminated food or water is more serious. Despite all your precautions you may still have a bout of mild travellers' diarrhoea, but a few rushed toilet trips with no other symptoms is not indicative of a serious problem. Moderate diarrhoea, involving half-a-dozen loose movements in a day, is more of a nuisance.

Dehydration is the main danger with any diarrhoea, particularly for children, so fluid replenishment is the number one treatment. Weak black tea (readily available in Israel!) with a little sugar, soda water, or soft drinks allowed to go flat and diluted 50% with water are all good.

With severe diarrhoea a rehydrating solution is necessary to replace minerals and salts. You should stick to a bland diet as you recover.

Lomotil or Imodium can be used to bring relief from the symptoms, although they do not actually cure the problem. Only use these drugs if absolutely necessary – eg, if you travel. For children Imodium is preferable, but do not use these drugs if the patient has a high fever or is severely dehydrated.

Antibiotics can be very useful in treating severe diarrhoea especially if it is accompanied by nausea, vomiting, stomach cramps or mild fever. Ampicillin, a broad spectrum penicillin, is usually recommended. Two capsules of 250 mg each taken four times a day is the recommended dose for an adult. Children aged between eight and 12 years should have half the adult dose; younger children should have half a capsule four times a day.

Note, that if the patient is allergic to penicillin ampicillin should not be administered.

Three days of treatment should be sufficient and an improvement should occur within 24 hours.

Diseases Spread by People & Animals

Tetanus This potentially fatal disease is found in undeveloped tropical areas. It is difficult to treat but is preventable with immunisation. Tetanus occurs when a wound becomes infected by a germ which lives in the faeces of animals or people, so clean all cuts, punctures or animal bites. Tetanus is known as lockjaw, and the first symptom may be discomfort in swallowing, or stiffening of the jaw and neck; this is followed by painful convulsions of the jaw and whole body.

Rabies Rabies is caused by a bite or scratch by an infected animal. Dogs are a noted carrier. Although not currently a problem in Israel, any bite, scratch or even lick from a mammal should be cleaned immediately and thoroughly. Scrub with soap and running water, and even clean with an alcohol solution. If there is any possibility that the animal is infected medical help should be sought immediately. Even if the animal is not rabid,

all bites should be treated seriously as they can become infected or can result in tetanus. A rabies vaccination is now available and should be considered if you are in a high-risk category – eg, if you intend to work with animals.

Meningococcal Meningitis Sub-Saharan Africa is considered the 'meningitis belt' and the meningitis season falls at the time most people would be attempting the overland trip across the Sahara – the northern winter before the rains come. Other areas which have recurring epidemics include Egypt's Nile Valley, often combined with a visit to Israel.

This very serious disease attacks the brain and can be fatal. A scattered, blotchy rash, fever, severe headache, sensitivity to light and neck stiffness which prevents forward bending of the head are the first symptoms. Death can occur within a few hours, so immediate treatment is important.

Treatment is large doses of penicillin given intravenously, or, if that is not possible, intramuscularly (ie, in the buttocks). Vaccination offers good protection for over a year, but you should also check for reports of current epidemics.

Diptheria Diptheria can be a skin infection or a more dangerous throat infection. It is spread by contaminated dust contacting the skin or by the inhalation of infected cough or sneeze droplets. Frequent washing and keeping the skin dry will help prevent skin infection. A vaccination is available to prevent the throat infection.

Sexually Transmitted Diseases Sexual contact with an infected sexual partner spreads these diseases. While abstinence is the only 100% preventative, using condoms is also effective. Gonorrhoea and syphilis are the most common of these diseases; sores, blisters or rashes around the genitals, discharges or pain when urinating are common symptoms. Symptoms may be less marked or not observed at all in women. Syphilis symptoms eventually disappear completely but the disease continues and can cause severe problems in later years. The treatment of gonorrhoea and syphilis is by antibiotics.

There are numerous other sexually transmitted diseases, for most of which effective treatment is available. However, there is no cure for herpes and there is also currently no cure for AIDS. Like everywhere else, the latter threatens to become more widespread in Israel and is rarely discussed. Using condoms is the most effective preventative.

AIDS can be spread through infected blood transfusions; most developing countries cannot afford to screen blood for transfusions. It can also be spread by dirty needles – vaccinations, acupuncture and tattooing can potentially be as dangerous as intravenous drug use if the equipment is not clean. If you do need an injection it may be a good idea, if only for your peace of mind, to buy a new syringe from a pharmacy and ask the doctor to use it.

Cuts, Bites & Stings

Cuts & Scratches Skin punctures can easily become infected in hot climates and may be difficult to heal. Treat any cut with an antiseptic solution and mercurochrome. Where possible avoid bandages and Band-aids, which can keep wounds wet. Coral cuts are notoriously slow to heal, as the coral injects a weak venom into the wound. Avoid coral cuts by wearing shoes when walking on reefs, and clean any cut thoroughly.

Bites & Stings Bee and wasp stings are usually painful rather than dangerous. Calamine lotion will give relief or ice packs will reduce the pain and swelling.

In Eilat, there are various fish and other sea creatures which can sting or bite dangerously; local advice is the best suggestion.

Snakes & Scorpions To minimise your chances of being bitten always wear boots, socks and long trousers when walking through undergrowth where snakes may be present, and keep your eyes peeled in the desert where scorpions make their home. Don't put your hands into holes and crevices,

be careful when collecting firewood, and look carefully before you sit down!

Snake and scorpion bites do not cause instantaneous death and antivenenes are usually available. Keep the victim calm and still, wrap the bitten limb tightly, as you would for a sprained ankle, and then attach a splint to immobilise it. Then seek medical help; for snake bites, try to keep the dead snake for identification. Don't attempt to catch the snake if there is even a remote possibility of being bitten again. Tourniquets and sucking out the poison are now comprehensively discredited.

Jellyfish Local advice is the best way of avoiding contact with these sea creatures with their stinging tentacles. Dousing in vinegar will de-activate any stingers which have not 'fired'. Calamine lotion, antihistamines and analgesics may reduce the reaction and relieve the pain.

Bedbugs & Lice Bedbugs live in various places, but particularly in dirty mattresses and bedding. Spots of blood on bedclothes or on the wall around the bed can be read as a suggestion to find another hotel. Bedbugs leave itchy bites in neat rows. Calamine lotion may help.

All lice cause itching and discomfort. They make themselves at home in your hair (head lice), your clothing (body lice) or in your pubic hair (crabs). You catch lice through direct contact with infected people or by sharing combs, clothing and the like. Powder or shampoo treatment will kill the lice and infected clothing should then be washed in very hot water.

Women's Health

Gynaecological Problems Poor diet, lowered resistance due to the use of antibiotics for stomach upsets and even contraceptive pills can lead to vaginal infections when travelling in hot climates. Keeping the genital area clean, and wearing skirts or loose-fitting trousers and cotton underwear will help to prevent infections.

Yeast infections, characterised by a rash,

itch and discharge, can be treated with a vinegar or even lemon-juice douche or with yoghurt. Nystatin suppositories are the usual medical prescription. Trichomonas is a more serious infection; symptoms are a discharge and a burning sensation when urinating. Male sexual partners must also be treated, and if a vinegar-water douche is not effective medical attention should be sought. Flagyl is the prescribed drug.

Pregnancy Most miscarriages occur during the first three months of pregnancy, so this is the most risky time to travel. The last three months should also be spent within reasonable distance of good medical care, as quite serious problems can develop at this time. Pregnant women should avoid all unnecessary medication, but vaccinations and malarial prophylactics should still be taken where possible. Additional care should be taken to prevent illness and particular attention should be paid to diet and nutrition.

WOMEN TRAVELLERS
In Israel, sexual harassment is a perennial problem for women travellers. The majority of problems will arise with Arab males, but Israeli men are not known for their gentlemanly conduct towards women either, and women will also be constantly bothered by them. Verbal and physical abuse can be a threat to your enjoyment of the country unless you observe certain guidelines.

Often the Islamic way of life is blamed for for causing the average Arab male, from boy to old man, to behave badly toward female travellers. However, many other males in Israel often have similar habits. The solo male traveller usually experiences wonderful hospitality from all groups, but if accompanied by a woman for only a short time, he soon appreciates the problems she has to face. Israeli men tend to fall into the 'Mediterranean male' cliché.

On many occasions you will get the impression that a non-Arab woman is subjected to sexual harassment whatever she looks like and no matter however discreetly she conducts herself. One way to deal with

it is to emulate the dress and behaviour of the local Arab women as much as possible when in the Occupied Territories or other Arab areas. Basically this means not wearing tight-fitting or revealing outer garments, and ensuring that legs, arms, shoulders and neckline are covered. The single act of wearing a bra will avoid countless unwelcome confrontations, and a hat or headscarf is also a good idea.

Normally, it is best to totally ignore the predictable and constant come-ons. Even the most negative and impolite of responses from you may end up encouraging your would-be companion, who may not understand your verbal or visual snub. A forceful slap or kick in the right place has proved an effective deterrent. Avoid general conversation, keep to short, sharp but polite sentences when necessary, and don't stop when you are approached or shouted at. Never hitchhike alone or with only female companions.

Some women readers wrote to say that a better way to deal with these problems is to confront male aggressors. They had shamed aggressors into leaving them alone by screaming 'are you a Muslim?'or simply 'Muslim! Muslim!' at them. Most Muslims are proud of their faith, and when they realised that their actions were being associated with Islam they stopped.

By giving such advice, I don't want to paint a picture of Israel as a place unsafe for women. It is not, and thousands of women travellers thoroughly enjoy their visit. Common sense and an awareness of the local culture will be the key to a good visit.

DANGERS & ANNOYANCES
Safety
Israel is not nearly as dangerous a place to visit as the headlines might have you assume. Israel's well-developed preoccupation with security has undoubtedly played a major part in making the country as safe as it is. However, there has been a noticeable increase in the tensions here in recent years, and it would be foolish to blindly believe the Israeli tourist information literature stating

that you are safe, or even safer than elsewhere, when in Israel.

For instance, when you try to plan a visit to certain Arab areas, you are discouraged from going. Unless determined to visit the Occupied Territories, visitors will find themselves being steered around the country to avoid such places as Hebron, Ramallah, Gaza, and even Bethlehem and Jericho.

Violence in Israel has almost exclusively involved the local population, but the occasional foreigner has been affected. There have been isolated incidents recently where tourists were attacked, and even killed. It has not been proved whether they were targeted as tourists by their assailants, and in at least some cases they simply happened to be in the wrong place at the wrong time. Some foreigners have been targeted in the past, because they were Jewish or, as has been the case in Jerusalem, because they have annoyed locals with their claims to be the Messiah.

Tourists are strongly recommended against driving through areas of the Occupied Territories because of the frequency of stonings by local Arabs and the risk of serious injury. (My Eldan hire car was stoned in Bethany.)

This does not mean that you should avoid these areas completely. Travelling on Arab buses and taxis does allow you to visit in relative safety. With the political climate subject to change, certain areas can be too dangerous to visit at certain times, regardless of how you get there. You need to keep abreast of current events and check before travelling in the Occupied Territories. Note that the average Israeli, especially those working in the tourist information industry, will discourage you from going to the Occupied Territories at the best of times.

The general Palestinian attitude towards tourists seems mixed. Traditionally, Arabs in the country have warmly welcomed foreign tourists, especially in the Occupied Territories. Some see such visits as good for business, others as an ideal opportunity to put across their version of life in the Jewish state, or under occupation. Arabs are rightly renowned for their generous hospitality, and this still seems to be the prevailing attitude.

With the intifada, though, there is a growing feeling that, as a major source of income for the Jewish state, tourism should be discouraged. Hence the stoning of tourists' rental cars and the hostile reception given visitors in some areas. Mostly, though, you will be well received, especially if you go out of your way to meet and talk with the locals.

Jews of any nationality would be right to feel insecure in most Arab areas. As in many countries, Americans of any religion should be extremely sensitive and diplomatic to ensure an enjoyable visit, due to their government's foreign policy. Canadians should just display their maple leaf as they always do!

Again, always keep up to date with the current situation, and be aware of events that could affect your movements.

Theft

This does not seem to be any more of a problem in Israel than anywhere else – nor any less. Like elsewhere in today's world, crime is on the increase, and in Israel's urban areas the rarely discussed drug problem has had an effect. The standard precautionary measures should be taken. Always keep valuables with you or locked in a safe – never leave them in your room or in a car or bus. Use a money belt, a pouch under your clothes, a leather wallet attached to your belt, or extra internal pockets in your clothing. Keep a record of your passport, credit card and travellers' cheque numbers separately in case tragedy occurs. It won't cure problems, but it will make them easier to bear.

Travelling on Egged's inter-city buses, you generally stow large bags in the luggage hold. This is a virtually trouble-free system, but keep valuables with you just in case. Crowded tourist spots and markets are an obvious hunting ground for pickpockets, so take extra care.

Beware of your fellow travellers. Unhappily there are more than a few backpackers who make their money go further by helping themselves to other people's. Sleeping on the beach, especially in Eilat, Tel Aviv and Haifa, is taking the risk that you will lose

something worth more than the sheqelim saved by not paying for accommodation. Some things which are stolen are replaceable, albeit at a cost. Some things are not, like used film and addresses. Treat them as the valuables they are. Finally, a good travel insurance policy helps. Devote some time to shopping around – don't take the easy way out and listen to your bank or travel agent. You can save money on the policy this way, and give yourself more coverage.

Drugs

Although more widely available than ever before, the possession of drugs in Israel is a serious offence, often punished by a spell in prison and deportation. Purchasing drugs here is a risky business, as suppliers and police informers can be one and the same. Bringing drugs in and out of the country yourself is foolhardy – the thoroughness of Israeli security searches is much talked about amongst travellers. Carrying packages for strangers is just asking for trouble.

WORK

Many people automatically associate a visit to Israel with a spell as a kibbutz or moshav volunteer. Certainly each year sees thousands of young people from all over the world descending on the Holy Land for the experience. In reality, life as a kibbutz or moshav volunteer is often clouded by inaccurate images presented by recruitment organisations, many of which (especially those dealing with moshavim), seem to be motivated more by making a fast buck than developing the flow of milk and honey. Also, former volunteers often forget the realities of hard and/or boring work, indifferent and/or unfriendly kibbutzniks and moshavniks and other negative factors, and only talk about the more enjoyable aspects of a volunteer's life.

This results in many people arriving as volunteers and being disappointed with what they find. Before committing yourself to a volunteer programme you should study carefully what it actually involves. When it comes down to discussing which kibbutzim or moshavim are the 'best', it is difficult to recommend individual sites. Location and the type of work carried out are often less important factors than the volunteers you work with, the kibbutzniks you work for and your relationships with them. What might be a fantastic place for one volunteer may well be a living hell for another.

Kibbutz Volunteers

The kibbutz movement has changed considerably from the early days and one of those changes is the system of volunteers itself. To be accepted as a kibbutz volunteer you need to be 18 to 32, in good physical and mental health, and you will be expected to work hard at whatever job is assigned to you eight hours a day, six days a week for a minimum of one month.

Every kibbutz has agriculture as its main activity but most now have some form of light industry too. Volunteers nowadays find themselves working on production lines in factories as well as picking fruit. Another possibility is working in the services, that is the dining room, kitchen or laundry. Working with the kibbutz children is not so common because of the language barrier.

Volunteers are accommodated in separate quarters from the kibbutzniks, usually two or four to a room. The conditions in these quarters do vary and some are extremely pleasant. Most, however, are old and/or have been poorly treated over the years by a succession of bored, frustrated and drunk volunteers.

In effect, volunteers work for their keep. The kibbutz provides the basic needs – meals, accommodation, basic toilet requisites, stationery, postage stamps, cigarettes and a small personal allowance (about US$50 per month). The facilities of the kibbutz are more or less available for volunteers to enjoy. These normally include a swimming pool and a variety of other sports facilities, a library and a cinema. The best parts of kibbutz volunteering can be the kibbutz-organised trips. These are part of the deal for volunteers and the kibbutz takes them to interesting sites around the country,

often including places that most visitors would not get to see.

One of the kibbutzniks has the job of volunteer leader, and he/she is basically in charge of the volunteers, organising their work schedules, days off and leisure activities, and dealing with any problems that arise.

There is often considerable friction between volunteers and their host communities. The volunteers are there for a variety of reasons, many of which do not endear themselves to the locals. Some have come for a 'working holiday' but dislike the fact that the emphasis is more on the work aspect. Many volunteers have to start work as early as 3.30 am. Six eight-hour working days a week can be demanding, especially on those who have never done such constant manual work before or who came out to Israel expecting to be able to spend more time lying in the sun as opposed to labouring under it. However, it is boredom, rather than exhaustion, which becomes a common characteristic of the working day.

Another preconceived idea about kibbutz volunteering is that it enables you to see Israel. It doesn't. With only one day off a week plus three more per month, you will need to be on a kibbutz for several months before you get to see a significant amount of the country. Being in the countryside, kibbutzim do not make ideal tour bases, anyway. The allowance is often insufficient to pay for the drinks and extra food that are normally required on kibbutz, much less the transport, food and accommodation that has to be paid for if you leave the kibbutz on days off.

A small number of volunteers are attracted by the socialist ideals of the movement and they too are often disappointed by what they find. Many volunteers are here because the alternative that they face is either poorly paid work back home, or no job at all. The vast majority of volunteers are teenagers experiencing their first time away from their own country, if not from home.

No doubt the large number of young people, unsupervised for perhaps the first time, with access to alcohol and the opposite sex, and isolated from other diversions, are the main factors contributing to the volunteers' unofficial battlecry of 'hedonism rules OK'.

This is how volunteers are seen by most of the kibbutzniks, and with volunteers arriving and leaving constantly there is little motivation for the kibbutzniks to open up and be super-friendly. A volunteer usually has to prove his/her efficiency at work over a period of months rather than days or weeks to win them over. Those volunteers who are fully committed may still have problems because many of them form close relationships with kibbutzniks. The threat of intermarriage and the possibility of the couple leaving the kibbutz are enough to upset most kibbutz members.

Most volunteers do enjoy their time on kibbutzim, but would agree that it turned out to be a lot different than they had expected. Their reasons for enjoying it would probably convince kibbutzniks that they are right to be cautious about welcoming volunteers with open arms. Some kibbutzim have scrapped the volunteer programme, and there has been talk of it being scrapped everywhere. This would be highly unlikely, if only because volunteers tend to be responsible for the more unpleasant menial tasks which would not appeal to a lot of kibbutzniks these days.

There are basically four ways to go about becoming a volunteer. The first two involve contacting a kibbutz representative office in your own country. You can either join a group of about 15 people or travel as an individual. The groups fly out to Israel together, are met at Ben-Gurion Airport and taken directly to the kibbutz. They normally stay on the kibbutz for three months and will have had an opportunity to meet one another and hear about their kibbutz before flying out.

If you travel as an individual you do not have to arrive on a preset date like the group, but within a month of your allocation. You are then given instructions on how to reach the Tel Aviv Kibbutz Office and a letter of introduction guaranteeing you a place. As an individual you are not met at the airport in Israel and you will not necessarily get a place on a kibbutz immediately; you may have to wait more than a day or two. You also have to pay for your own accommodation, food and travel expenses whilst waiting in Tel Aviv for placement. Try not to arrive in Israel on a Friday, Saturday or just before a Jewish festival to avoid having to wait for the kibbutz office to open.

A basic registration fee is charged (about US$50). You will usually find that the price charged by the kibbutz representatives for the airfare to Israel is more than you would pay if you shopped around yourself. If you choose to join a group you have no option but to fly with them, but as an individual you can register and then make your own travel arrangements. To find out more, contact your nearest kibbutz representative's office:

Australia
  Habonim, 1 Sinclair St, Elsternwick, Victoria 3185
Belgium
  Bureau de Volontaires, 68 Ave Ducpetiaux, 1060 Bruxelles (☎ (02) 538 1050)
Canada
  Kibbutz Aliya Desk, 1000 Finch Ave West, Downsview, Ontario MSJ 2E7
France
  Agence Juive, Kibbutz Desk, 17 Rue Fortuny, Paris 17
Holland
  Volunteers Desk, John Veermeerstr 22, Amsterdam
New Zealand
  Wellington Jewish Community Centre, PO Box 27-156, Wellington 1
UK
  Kibbutz Representatives, 1A Accommodation Rd, London NW11 (☎ (071) 458 9235
  Project 67, 10 Hatton Garden, London EC1N 8AH (☎ (071) 831 7626)
  Kibbutz Representatives, Harold House, Dunbabin Rd, Liverpool (☎ (051) 722 5671)
  Kibbutz Representatives, 11 Upper Park Rd, Salford, Manchester M7 0HY (☎ (061) 795 9447)
  Kibbutz Representatives, 43 Queen's Square, Glasgow S1 (☎ (041) 423 7379)
USA
  Kibbutz Aliya Desk, 27 West 20th St, NY, 10011 (☎ (212) 255 1338)

You can make your own way to the kibbutz offices in Tel Aviv to apply there in person for a place. The movement is not at all keen on prospective volunteers doing this as they prefer to have everything pre-arranged. However, as only a few people do it this way there is a good chance of your application being successful, if time-consuming. This is dependent not only on there actually being a space for you, but on your being able to convince the kibbutz officials that you are not going to live up to the poor image that the volunteers suffer from amongst kibbutzniks. If you are British, your chances of being accepted this way are virtually non-existent due to the large number of young Brits proving to be unable to work, rest and play. Applicants from Australia and New Zealand should have no problem as they enjoy a good reputation. There are three offices in Tel Aviv to apply to:

United Kibbutz Movement & Kibbutz Artzi
   (☎ (03) 65 1710), 124 HaYarkon St
Project 67 (☎ (03) 523 0140) 78 Ben Yehuda St –
   enter at 18 Mapu St and go down to the basement
Kibbutz Dati (☎ (03) 25 7231), 7 Dubnov St – only
   Jews are accepted here, with some religious
   observance required

You may have to wait a few days before an opening comes up, even if you are accepted. On the other hand, it is not unusual for kibbutz representatives abroad to be telling applicants that there are no places, while in Israel the kibbutzim are literally crying out for volunteers.

The final way to become a volunteer is to apply directly to an individual kibbutz. This is not normally possible but can be done, for example if there is a desperate need for volunteers due to a crop harvest. It's also possible if you have a friend who is a volunteer already and can pull a few strings with the volunteer leader.

Moshav Volunteers

Moshav volunteers need to be aged 18 to 35 and be prepared to stay on a moshav for at least five weeks. A moshav volunteer is normally assigned to an individual farmer, although some do work for more than one, according to their needs. Most volunteers are provided with separate accommodation, usually shared with other volunteers and of comparable quality with kibbutz volunteers' quarters. A few live with the moshavniks. Most volunteers provide their own meals, rather than eating with their farmer and his family. They are paid US$260 per month for an eight-hour day, six-day working week. Overtime is often available although complaints about farmers not paying for overtime and worked days-off are not uncommon. If food is provided, the volunteers' pay is approximately halved.

A fair number of volunteers soon leave a moshav, finding the work too hard and underpaid. Those who do stick it out often look back fondly at their time spent down on the farm, despite the conditions.

The major differences between being a volunteer on a moshav as opposed to kibbutz are that the work is generally much harder and you can have more of a chance to save some money (although it is not easy for most volunteers), to do more interesting and less menial tasks (not always possible though) or to be alone, if that is what you want. Relations between volunteers and moshavniks are just as strained as those on kibbutzim. Most moshav volunteers seem to be attracted by the potential, or the urgent need, to earn some money, and many are unaware of the sometimes harsh conditions that they are letting themselves in for and the difficulties involved in saving money here. The isolation of farming communities and the lack of social activities again contribute to the pressure on volunteers to spend the small amount of money earned on drink.

There are three ways to join a moshav as a volunteer. In some countries there are moshav representatives who make arrangements for individuals. It makes sense, however, for prospective volunteers to make their own way to Tel Aviv, often saving the best part of US$100 on what a moshav representative would charge for their services and the airfare. The official moshav main office (☎ (03) 258473) is downstairs at 13

Leonardo de Vinci St. From Tel Aviv central bus station take bus No 70 on the opposite side of Petah Tiqwa St. It's open Sunday to Thursday, 9 am to noon. You can also try Project 67 (see kibbutz section) or Meira's, a private volunteer office at 103 Ben Yehuda St, Tel Aviv (☎ (03) 5237369, 5238073). Each volunteer has to take out a health insurance policy which includes coverage for hospitalisation. There are usually more volunteers needed than are available, so as long as you present yourself as hard-working, punctual and well-behaved, you should have no problems and probably find work in a day or two.

The shortage of moshav volunteers is sometimes so bad that farmers will feel forced to go to Haifa port and offer jobs to young people as they disembark from the ferries from Greece. The other way to become a volunteer is to go direct to a moshav and ask an individual farmer. This will not endear you to the volunteers' offices in Tel Aviv and you may end up regretting not having them on your side if you have any problems.

Other Volunteer Projects

Work Camps Less publicised than kibbutz volunteering, Palestinian work camps are operated by universities and other organisations in Israel and the Occupied Territories. Their purpose is basically to promote solidarity with the Palestinian community, provide an opportunity for foreigners to meet Palestinians and also to assist the locals in community projects like road maintenance, rubbish collecting, painting, decorating and other odd jobs.

The work camps are mostly held during July and August. Volunteers pay their own travel expenses, a $50 registration fee and spending money. Accommodation and some meals are provided, either with a family or in a school or tented camp. The work can be mundane, but for the politically motivated it is a very popular way to do something constructive and rewarding. If you want to participate, it is best to write both directly to the work camps and to the following

UK/USA organisations as early as possible for the current schedules.

In Israel
Al Hadaf, PO Box 169, Um el Fahm 30010 (☎ (06) 311956; fax 312915)

Al Nahdah Centre, PO Box 52, Taibeh 40400 (☎ (052) 993035, fax 993018)

Arab Association for Human Rights, PO Box 215, 34/604 Mary's Well St, Nazareth 16100 (☎ (06) 561923; fax 564934)

Association for the Support and Defense of Bedouin Rights in Israel, PO Box 5212, 37 Hativat HaNegev St, Beersheba (☎ (057) 31687)

Committee of Arab Affairs in Jaffa/League of Jaffa Arabs, PO Box 41087, 73 Yefet St, Jaffa (☎ (03) 812290)

Golan Heights Academic Association, Majdal Shams, 12438, Golan Heights (☎ (06) 982995/959, 983360)

In the UK
Friends of Beir Zeit University (FOBZU), 21 Collingham Rd, London SW5 0NU (☎ (071) 3738414)

Medical Aid for Palestinians, 29 Enford St, London W1H 1DG (☎ (071) 7237766

United Nations Associated International Service (UNAIS), 3 Whitehall Crt, London SW1 (☎ (071) 9300679)

Witness For Palestine, 20 Dartmouth Park Hill, London NW5 1HL (☎ (071) 2637187)

World University Service, *(WUS)* 20 Compton Terrace, London N1 2UN (☎ (071) 2266747)

In the USA
Volunteers for Peace, 43 Tiffany Rd, Belmont, VT 05730 (☎ (802) 2592759)

Medical & Social Work The organisations listed under work camps can also help with inquiries regarding other volunteer and salaried projects such as teaching, nursing and counselling.

Christian hospitals in Jerusalem and Nazareth in particular use volunteer nurses. These can be trained and qualified people or those willing to assist in feeding patients. In Jerusalem inquire at St Louis' French Hospital, next door to Notre Dame outside the Old City's New Gate; and in Nazareth to the EMS, French and Italian hospitals. In Gaza, the Ahli Arab Hospital (☎ (051) 863014) often requires experienced volunteer nurses. Inquire in person or write in advance to The

Director, Ahli Arab Hospital, PO Box 72, Palestine Square, Gaza.

For Jews there are the many Jewish charities all over the country. These include projects in the renovation of buildings and neighbourhoods as well as hospitals, helping the elderly, and childcare.

SPNI Volunteers The Society for the Protection of Nature in Israel's Field Study Centres (FSCs) sometimes take volunteers. You work about six hours a day, five days a week in return for food, accommodation and a small allowance. It is probably best to inquire at the individual FSCs even if the SPNI office staff tell you that there are no vacancies. You will have to convince the staff at the FSC that you are suitable; that you are conscientious, and likely to remain for at least a couple of months. There is normally only one volunteer required at a time by a FSC, if any, and duties would include cleaning, gardening and any odd jobs.

Volunteers for Israel During the dark days of Operation Peace for Galilee, this programme was launched to place volunteers in non-combat support jobs in the IDF. The idea is to give more reserve soldiers time off to attend to family and business matters. The 23-day programme involves very menial duties in kitchens, stores – even polishing boots! Volunteers are issued with military fatigues and housed on a base but are not armed. Your air ticket to/from Israel is partially subsidised by the programme if you stick it out, and you are allowed free time to travel (after your work is done) before flying home. Contact the nearest IGTO or write to Volunteers for Israel (☎ (212) 6084848), 40 Worth St, NY, 10013.

Working Holidays
Many travellers find themselves wanting to work in Israel but many more find themselves having to, after running out of money. Indeed a sense of desperation would seem to be required to want to work here, due to the generally appalling rates of pay and the many cases of employers exploiting foreign

labour. This is partly because most of the work undertaken by travellers is illegal. Israel is not a good place to make money to continue your travelling. It can be done, but it involves a lot of very low-paid work.

As anywhere else, the catering industry employs the largest number of illegal workers. The gradual increase in the custom of tipping has meant that restaurant waiting work in the right place can be relatively well paid. To get such work simply ask around cafés and restaurants. The larger, higher quality hotels/restaurants tend not to employ foreigners. Everywhere else, though, it seems that illegal labour is relied upon to keep premises and dishes clean.

Eilat, being tourist-oriented, has the most job openings, and is also a good place to get a more strenuous job such as labourer on building sites and road crews. Hang out in the Peace Café (see Eilat in the Negev chapter) from about 5 am, when foremen arrive looking for casual workers. If you oversleep, inquire at the various building sites (mainly to the south). Again, the pay is as low as the temperature is high and Eilat's employers generally have a worse reputation than the sharks in the adjacent Red Sea!

In Tel Aviv the job situation fluctuates. Ask around at the various hostels; Gordons Hostel and The Home are often good sources.

The best-paid job for travellers that I came across was egg collecting on Shabbat for observant Jews. This marvellous position paid about the same for one day's work as most jobs pay for a week. Finding such jobs is not easy. Check the *Jerusalem Post* (Friday's edition is the best for jobs) and also the noticeboards in hostels and Jerusalem and Tel Aviv universities.

Other paid jobs in Israel include working in laundromats, just go in and ask; au pairing, via advertisements in the *Post* and agencies in Tel Aviv; and portering and catering work in hospitals – inquire at individual hospitals. Doing odd jobs in the hostels is popular as accommodation, food and often a small allowance is provided. Ask around. Tel Aviv, Jerusalem and Eilat are the best places to look, but Tiberias is often overlooked and hostels there are often in need of staff.

The intifada has meant fewer films being made in Israel, but a popular way for travellers to pay their way, or just to have the experience regardless of their financial status, has been to work as film extras when there is a project in production. The casting agency, Studio 91 (☎ (03) 220225), 91 Dizengoff St, Tel Aviv happily employs travellers to work as extras and crew.

Archaeological Digs Definitely not for gold-diggers, most archaeological digs require that you pay to work. In January of each year the Israel Department of Antiquities and Museums, part of the Ministry of Education and Culture, publishes a list of the archaeological excavations of the coming year. You can ask for it at the Rockefeller Museum. General enquiries regarding excavations in Israel can be made to Israel Department of Antiquities & Museums, Rockefeller Museum (☎ (02) 278603), PO Box 586, Jerusalem 91004. In the USA, contact the Archaeological Institute of America (☎ (617) 3539361), 627 Commonwealth Ave, Boston, MA 02216.

The busy archaeological season is May to September when universities are not in session and the weather is hot and dry. No previous excavating experience is usually necessary but volunteers should be prepared to participate for a minimum of one or two weeks, depending on the individual dig. A fee for food and accommodation (varying from sleeping bags in a field to three-star hotels) is required. Some expeditions do provide volunteers with an allowance for food, accommodation and/or travel expenses within Israel. Tourist offices, particularly the Jerusalem Old City branch, sometimes have notices displayed requesting volunteers for a dig, so remember to check there.

For those interested in trying archaeology a day at a time, consider the Dig for a Day programme. Operating July and August, this involves a three-hour excavation, seminars and a tour. It costs about US$20. Contact Archaeological Seminars (☎ (02) 273515), PO Box 14002, Jaffa Gate, 34 Habad St, Jerusalem 91140.

ACTIVITIES

In addition to the numerous historical and religious sights and places of natural beauty to be seen throughout the country, Israel offers some special interest activities for the visitor.

Cultural

Meeting the locals and the experiences that result are usually an important factor of any trip. In Israel, there are some organised formats to help the visitor make direct contact with both Israelis and Palestinians, and to experience something of life in this part of the world. Like virtually everything else in Israel, 'cultural' is intertwined with 'political' and all parties involved will be sure to put across their version of life here.

Kibbutz & Moshav Volunteering The most popular way to visit Israel is to spend at least a few weeks on the farm.

Work Camps A little known alternative to the kibbutzim are the Palestinian work camps.

Meet the Israeli Arranged through tourist offices and the Volunteer Tourist Service, this scheme sets up meetings for tourists with locals in their homes.

Outdoors

The natural beauty of Israel is even more appreciated by experiencing some of these outdoor activities. In addition to those specific places mentioned, the SPNI offices in Tel Aviv and Jerusalem are the best sources for more information on where to go:

Hiking With its changing landscapes, Israel offers a wealth of superb hiking opportunities, both leisurely and more strenuous. The regional chapters feature some of the more rewarding routes.

Birdwatching Eilat's International Bird-watching Centre is the best site to appreciate this and to find out about other locations. For more information, see Flora & Fauna in Facts about the Country and the Eilat section in the Negev chapter. Israel is the world's second largest bird migratory flyway, after South America.

Desert Tours The Judean and Negev deserts are now being developed for tourism (see the Tours section in the Getting Around chapter). In addition to these organised trips, there are also trails designed for independent hikes (see the Negev, Dead Sea and Occupied Territories chapters). Note that venturing into any desert on your own involves serious risks, so take all the recommended safety precautions before setting out.

Watersports
With the Red and Mediterranean seas and the Sea of Galilee, there are ample opportunities to enjoy the pleasures of swimming, windsurfing and sailing. Scuba diving, as elsewhere in the world, is increasingly popular. Eilat is the Israeli scuba centre, with superior sites nearby in the Sinai Desert (now a part of Egypt). The Dead Sea provides its unique floating experience.

Spas
With the 'Rift Valley' running the length of the country, Israel features some great natural spas. These offer hot sulphur springs and mud with health-giving qualities. Check the facilities at the Dead Sea, Tiberias and nearby Hammat Gader.

Archaeology
With its wealth of ancient history, Israel offers unparalleled opportunities for visiting archaeological sites. See the Working Holidays section earlier in this chapter for details on digs. Specific sites are covered throughout the regional chapters.

National Parks Green Card
The National Parks Authority maintains 37 of the country's top historical sites. Those of you planning to visit enough of these should save some money and purchase a 'Green Card'. Valid for 14 days from the date of the first visit and non-transferable, it costs about US$14 per person and allows the holder to visit all of these sites. With an entrance fee of about US$3 per site, this can be a good buy.

The card can only be purchased from the National Parks Authority head office (☎ (03) 252281), 4 Rav Aluf Maklef St, Tel Aviv, or from the following sites: Masada, Tel Jericho, Herodion, Caesarea and Megiddo.

This a complete list of the National Parks Authority sites at the time of writing:

Nimrod Castle	Avdat
Bar'am	Hurshat Tal
Achziv	Tel Hazor
Korazim	Yeh'iam Fortress
Hammat Tiberias	Kursi
Beit She'an	Belvoir
Beit Alpha	Sachne
Megiddo	Ma'ayon Harod
Mount Carmel	Beit She'arim
Sebastiya	Caesarea
Aqua Bella	Afek
Old City Ramparts,	Castel
Jerusalem	Herodion
Tel Jericho	Jericho Synagogue
Hisham's Palace,	Qumran
Jericho	Beit Guvrin
Masada	Yad Mordechai
Ashkelon	Tel Arad
Eshkol	Shivta
Mamshit	En Avdat
Ben-Gurion's Grave	

Courses
Some of the Israeli universities operate overseas student programmes in various subjects, including Hebrew, Arabic and Middle East studies. It is not always necessary to speak Hebrew to enrol, although you will often need to study the language as part of the curriculum. Contact the nearest tourist office in your home country for information.

St George's College (☎ (02) 894704/5; fax 894703), PO Box 19018, 20 Nablus Rd, Jerusalem, describes itself as a centre for fieldwork, study and reflection in the Holy Land, allowing you to study the bible in its appropriate geographical setting. Teaching appreciation of local history and archaeology and introducing local communities of all faiths, it offers courses that include bible study and field trips throughout the Holy Land and to the Sinai. Lasting from 16 days (US$1500) to three (US$1720), four (US$2250) and 10 weeks (US$5100), subjects include The Bible and the Holy Land Today, Palestine of Jesus, and The Bible and its Setting. Food and board are included.

Scuba-diving courses are popular with visitors to Israel (see the Eilat section in the Negev chapter).

Language Study After a few weeks in Israel, it is not uncommon for travellers to find that they want to learn Hebrew or Arabic. Although some will gain a basic understanding of the languages through their day-to-day existence, learning it properly (especially reading and writing) will only be achieved through study. Unfortunately, finding a place to learn Hebrew in Israel is neither cheap nor easy, and to learn Arabic can be even harder.

Most *ulpanim* (language schools) cater for new Jewish immigrants and do not seem to encourage non-Jews. You will have to look around to find a place. Jerusalem is a good area because the municipality seems to run a slightly cheaper programme of classes. Contact the Ulpan Office, Division of Adult Education (☎ (02) 224156), 11 Beit Ha'am, Bezalel St, Jerusalem 94591.

The Ulpan Akiva Netanya (☎ (053) 52312/3), PO Box 6086, Netanya 42160, is an international school for Jews and non-Jews and has various programmes for learning Hebrew and Arabic. Fees for the 24-day programme are US$1875, including tuition, cultural activities, accommodation and meals. Courses of eight, 12 and 16 to 20 weeks are also available for varying fees. Kibbutz Ulpan is a 4½ or six-month programme for those who want to learn Hebrew and experience kibbutz life. Students spend half the day at work, and the other half studying, six days a week. Contact your nearest kibbutz office or the Kibbutz Aliya Desk (☎ (212) 2551338), 27 West 20th St, New York, NY 10011, USA.

HIGHLIGHTS
Beaches

With the freshwater Sea of Galilee (actually a lake) and the Red-Dead-Med combination, Israel offers plenty of scope for beach life, and much of it is unique. The Galilee was the main area of Jesus' ministry and, in particular, where he gave the Sermon on the Mount and walked on the water.

Nowhere in the world can compare to the Dead Sea, and a visit to Israel is incomplete without the obligatory float. Most people head for the beach at Ein Gedi but En Boqeq has sand, is cleaner and has the added attraction of those salt crystals that resemble icebergs from a distance.

Because of its offensive architecture, most of Eilat's publicity photographs are taken underwater. The beautiful colours of the coral and tropical fish here combine with clear water and sand to make it a special place.

On the Mediterranean coast, Tel Aviv beach on a hot August Shabbat is packed solid. The beach here is right in the centre of things and is a major attraction. Elsewhere Herzlia, Netanya and Haifa lead the beach parade.

Sea of Galilee, page 335
En Boqeq, Dead Sea, page 384
Coral Beach, Eilat, page 406
Tel Aviv, page 230
Sydney Ali Beach, Herzlia, page 257
Netanya, page 268
Carmel Beach, Haifa, page 277

Natural Beauty Spots

Try to see the world's largest crater, Maktesh Ramon, which offers an eerie, coloured lunar landscape with its various rock formations; the Dead Sea region, bordered by the Judean Desert and Jordan's Moab mountains; the Sea of Galilee, surrounded by rolling hills and rich in the history of the New Testament; the war-torn Golan with its outstanding views across the multicoloured patchwork of fields in the Hula Valley; the Negev Desert with its many hidden treasures such as En Avdat and the Valley of Zin; and the Judean Desert, including such marvellous hikes as the Wadi Qelt and a visit to Mar Saba. There is much more; these are just some of the highlights.

Makteṡh Ramon, Mitzpe Ramon, page 401
Dead Sea Region, page 368
Sea of Galilee, page 334
Golan, page 353
Negev Desert, page 386
Judean Desert, page 421

Springs & Waterfalls Israel has a wonderful selection of beauty spots featuring water, some of which are in the desert, others in milder climes. You can be in a desert landscape and see a trail of trees following a wadi (a dry river bed). Empty for much of the year, a sudden rainfall can cause a flash flood and a raging torrent of muddy water. In the Golan Heights, one of the three main sources of the Jordan River is Banyas. Just below, a waterfall crashes down and is a popular attraction for Israelis and tourists.

One of my favourite spots in the country is En Avdat in the Negev, between Beersheba and Mitzpe Ramon. Here you can go on an awe-inspiring walk through a stunning canyon, involving some easy but slightly energetic climbing. On the way along the wadi you see various pools of spring water, ibex (the desert animal) and trees in the middle of the desert. A waterfall (in season) finishes off the show.

Sachne, or Gan HaShlosha, south of Golan, is a beautiful park featuring a natural pool and waterfalls of warm but refreshing crystalline water. It dates back to Roman times and has managed to survive without too much commercialisation.

In the Dead Sea area, two of the lesser-known attractions involve freshwater, not the famous mineral-rich salty variety. The more popular of the two, Ein Gedi, is a natural oasis in the Judean Desert. It features two pretty waterfalls, providing a refreshing change from the heat of the area and its salty competitor across the road. Ein Feshka, a little to the north along the Dead Sea's shore, is a series of pools filled by springs.

Hopefully, the hottest water that most of

you will end up in can be found back in Galilee at Hammat Gader. In the valley of the Yarmuk River, this combination of natural hot sulphur springs with Roman ruins and a crocodile park is a successful tourist attraction.

A visit to Hezekiah's Tunnel, just outside Jerusalem's Old City, is a great way to cool down on a hot day. It was built to secretly bring the city's supply of water from the natural Gihon spring nearby, thus avoiding the danger of the enemy tampering with it. It is now possible to slosh through the tunnel with the water coming up to your knees, or higher.

En Avdat, Negev, page 397
Banyas, Golan, page 362
Sachne (Gan HaShlosha), Galilee, page 320
Ein Gedi, Dead Sea, page 375
Ein Feshka, Dead Sea, page 374
Hammat Gader, Galilee, page 340
Hezekiah's Tunnel, Jerusalem, page 180

Archaeological Sites
Archaeology is an extremely popular subject with the Israelis, as well as many of the country's visitors. The inspiration for this is the rich supply of excavations, a fascination with the renowned past, the busy schedule of digging and the extensive press coverage given to new discoveries.

Jericho is arguably the world's oldest town, and the 9000-year-old remains of Tel Jericho are one of the many archaeological highlights you can visit in Israel. The City of David, outside Jerusalem's Old City, is the site of the Jebusite city conquered by King David circa 997 BC. Remains dating from Herod the Great (37-4 BC) include Caesarea, which features a Roman amphitheatre and a Crusader port; Herodian, a palace complex; Sebastiya, including a lesser known amphitheatre and what was the showpiece of the Holy Land; and Masada, the last Jewish stronghold against the Romans, spectacularly situated on the flat summit of a mountain overlooking the Dead Sea. In the Negev, between Beersheba and Mitzpe Ramon, is Avdat, the site of the Nabateans' most impressive desert city. North of the Sea of Galilee is Gamla, site of another siege by the Romans of a Jewish city. Impressive Roman and Byzantine remains, including a well-preserved Roman amphitheatre, are the attraction at Beit She'an.

Museums

Israelis thrive on their history and reference to it was necessary to argue for the Jewish state. This should be borne in mind when you visit museums and read the understandably biased accounts of various events. Regardless of your views on the accuracy of Israeli museums and their accounts of events, there can be no disputing their presentational quality.

The Israel Museum in Jerusalem is the home of the Dead Sea Scrolls, and also houses a wide range of exhibits covering archaeology and art. The Rockefeller Museum in East Jerusalem is the original purpose-built archaeological centre of the country.

On the outskirts of Jerusalem's rapidly expanding New City is Yad Vashem, the leading Israeli Holocaust museum. The importance of this museum to the Jews cannot be overemphasised. The Diaspora Museum in Tel Aviv tells of the Jews' dispersion around the world and features several striking presentations of Jewish history. The nearby Ha'Aretz Museum is an extensive complex consisting of eight different museums, such as the popular Glass Museum, Ceramics Museum, Lasky Planetarium and the Museum of Ethnography & Folklore. The Tel Aviv Museum is for art lovers and includes Impressionist work by Renoir and Monet, as well as more recent pieces by Roualt, Matisse and Picasso.

The Diamond Museum in the Israel Diamond Exchange complex in Ramat Gan, north of Tel Aviv, tells you virtually everything you wanted to know about the precious stones, except how to afford them.

Holy Cities

The ultimate holy city has to be Jerusalem; no other city in the world enjoys such status. It is revered by the three major monotheistic faiths of Judaism, Islam and Christianity. The Jews also regard Hebron, Safed and Tiberias as holy. The four Jewish holy cities have been compared to the four elements: Jerusalem representing fire (the Temple sacrifices); Hebron – earth (Abraham purchased the land and the patriarchs are buried here); Tiberias – water (the city is on the lakeside); and Safed – air (being the highest city in the country and the most spiritual as a centre of biblical and talmudic study). Hebron is also holy to the Muslims, due to the patriarchs being buried there.

Bethlehem, the traditional birthplace of Jesus, is holy to Christians, and also to the Jews, being the location of Rachel's Tomb. Nazareth is the traditional site of the Annunciation, where the angel Gabriel informed Mary that she had been chosen to mother the Son of God. Jesus is also believed to have lived here as a child. Haifa is the world centre of the Baha'i faith, and the Baha'i Shrine is one of the country's most attractive buildings. Mount Gerizim, overlooking Nablus, is the holy centre for the Samaritans.

Haifa, page 272
Nablus, page 449

Synagogues

Visiting a synagogue in the Jewish state is a logical and popular thing to do for Jews, but many non-Jews do not seem to want to, or feel able to. They are, however, more than welcome to visit synagogues and doing so would undoubtedly lead to more understanding of the Jewish faith.

Jerusalem is the site of the Great Synagogue, part of the Heichal Shlomo complex, the seat of the Chief Rabbinate of Israel and the Supreme Religious Centre. In the Old City down the road, the Jewish Quarter features reconstructed synagogues of much importance: the Hurva, the Ramban and the Four Sephardic synagogues. One of the highlights of a visit to the Mount Scopus Campus of the Hebrew University in Jerusalem is the spectacular new Hecht Synagogue. Its architecture aside, there is that wonderful view down towards the Old City.

In Safed's synagogue quarter (Qiryat Batei Haknesset) you can visit some of the country's more beautiful synagogues. These include the Caro, Ha'Ari, Alsheik and Abuhav synagogues. In occupied Hebron, one of the most important Jewish holy sites is the synagogue in the Tomb of the Patriarchs, the only synagogue in a mosque.

Great Synagogue, Jerusalem, page 191
Hurva Synagogue, Jerusalem, page 159
Ramban Synagogue, Jerusalem, page 159
Four Sephardic Synagogues, Jerusalem, page 162
Hecht Synagogue, Jerusalem, page 184
Caro Synagogue, Safed, page 348
Ha'Ari Ashkenazi Synagogue, Safed, page 348
Alsheikh Synagogue, Safed, page 348
Abuhav Synagogue, Safed, page 348
Tomb of the Patriarchs, Hebron, page 443

Mosques

Dominating the skyline to such an extent that the gold Dome of the Rock has become the Jewish state's most recognisable landmark, mosques are an integral part of the country's heritage. The Haram esh-Sharif (Temple Mount) is the site of the two most important:

El-Aqsa, Israel's largest, and the Dome of the Rock. The Tomb of the Patriarchs in Hebron is now a mosque and a synagogue, and is one of the few places where Arabs and Jews pray together, albeit with extreme reluctance.

In Akko, the green-domed El-Jazzar Mosque is one of the largest in Israel. Gaza has the El Jamia El Kbur (the Great Mosque), originally a church built by Queen Helena and later used by the Crusaders. In the interesting streets of Nablus' Old City is the Kabir Mosque, with its beautiful arch. Revered by Muslims as the grave of the prophet Moses, the fascinating Nebi Musa is set in a spectacular location overlooking the Judean Desert.

Dome of the Rock, Jerusalem, page 155
El-Aqsa Mosque, Jerusalem, page 153
Tomb of the Patriarchs, Hebron, page 443
El-Jazzar Mosque, Akko, page 298
Great Mosque, Gaza, page 460
Kabir Mosque, Nablus, page 452
Nebi Musa, page 420

Churches

Many of the churches which mark the key Christian sites in Israel are a source of disappointment to pilgrims. This is mainly due to the annoying presence of souvenir salesmen and Holy Land church politics, with the domination of the Orthodox churches over the Roman Catholic and Protestant churches and the fierce rivalry between them. Nevertheless, a trip to Israel is, for many, inconceivable without at least visiting two churches: the Church of the Nativity, in Bethlehem, traditional site of Jesus' birth; and the Church of the Holy Sepulchre in Jerusalem, the traditional but disputed site of Jesus' crucifixion, burial and resurrection. Other important churches include those on the Mount of Olives, the most popular of which is the Church of All Nations in the garden of Gethsemane.

Often overlooked in Jerusalem is the beautifully situated Church of St Peter in Gallicantu, on the eastern slope of Mount Zion. Also on Mount Zion is the Church of the Dormition, the recently renovated interior of which contrasts nicely with the dominating exterior, a popular landmark. Of

Jerusalem's many churches, the Crusaders' St Anne's is perhaps the overall favourite when status is disregarded. Its superb acoustics, stark interior and crypt, along with the excavations of the Bethesda pools combine to delight most visitors.

Moving to Galilee, the Church of the Mount of the Beatitudes combines biblical relevance of the highest degree with attractive architecture, surrounded by beautiful scenery. The Basilica of the Transfiguration on Mount Tabor, perhaps my favourite, is often left out of a busy traveller's itinerary.

Nazareth's Basilica of the Annunciation is a church which most either love or hate for its bold but controversial architecture. The interesting collection of murals from around the world is enchanting, though.

Monasteries

Visiting a monastery in Israel can be, perhaps surprisingly, one of the highlights of your visit. Many are in dramatic locations and feature stunning architecture. The prime examples of these are at Mar Saba in the Judean Desert, St George's in the Wadi Qelt, and the Monastery of Temptation in Jericho. All three are in desert climes, with hearty walks and/or climbs for those who wish to reach them. Check the current security situation before setting off for Mar Saba, though.

In Abu Gosh, between Jerusalem and Tel Aviv, the Crusader-built monastery is a place where men only can experience the monastic life. The monasteries at Latrun and Cremisan, noteworthy for their wines, are also in beautiful locations.

St Elijah's Monastery at Mukhraqa marks the traditional site of Elijah's biblical victory over the 450 priests of Ba'al. On the eastern side of Mount Carmel, it has incredible views across Galilee and on that proverbial clear day you can see for miles.

Markets

The best Oriental market is in Jerusalem's Old City. It has the best of everything in the country; history, range of products and atmosphere. In Jerusalem's New City, the Jewish market at Mahane Yehuda offers the best prices for fruit and vegetables and has an atmosphere all of its own.

You will hear and read a lot about how wonderful the Thursday morning Bedouin market is in Beersheba – but not from me. I think it is a real letdown. Instead of waking up early on Thursday, do yourself a favour and enjoy a lie-in. Then get up bright and early on a Friday morning in Jerusalem. There, the Arab sheep market outside the Old City, east of Herod's Gate, has more tradition and general photogenic hubbub than you could expect (and without the commercialisation of Beersheba).

The markets of Hebron and Nablus, centres of violent resistance to Israeli occupation by local Arabs, are the most authentic in the country. In Tel Aviv, the Carmel Market is a humid version of Mahane Yehuda. With the Oriental Jewish majority it is also noisier. Along the coast a little, the Jaffa flea market can be a good place to discover a variety of antiques and more recent bric-a-brac. Finally, Akko's small bazaar, underneath those green domes and minarets, is popular with visitors.

SUGGESTED ITINERARIES

To help plan your trip, here are suggested itineraries for a one-week and two-week visit. The places listed at each stop cannot all be seen within these time frames; you will need to decide your personal priorities.

One Week

Jerusalem (three to four nights): Old City (one to three days); Mount of Olives (½ day); Mea She'arim & Mahane Yehuda Market (a few hours to ½ day for both); Israel & Islamic Art museums (½ day for both to one day for each); and Yad Vashem (½ day to one day).
Sidetrips: Jericho, Bethlehem and Hebron (½ day to one day for each).

Dead Sea Region (sidetrip or one night): Ein Gedi (½ day to one day); and Masada (½ day)

Tiberias (one to two nights): Tabgha and Capernaeum (½ day for both).
Sidetrip: Golan (one day).
En route: Safed, Nazareth, Beit She'an, Haifa, and Caesarea (½ day for each).

Tel Aviv (one night): Diaspora Museum, beaches, Jaffa, (½ day to one day for each); Nahal Binyamin (a few hours); and City/Jaffa nightlife.

Two Weeks

Jerusalem (four to six nights): Old City (one to three days); Mount of Olives (½ day to one day); Mea She'arim & Mahane Yehuda Market (a few hours to ½ day for both); Israel & Islamic Art museums (½ day for both to one day for each); and Yad Vashem (½ day to one day).
Sidetrips: Wadi Qelt hike, Jericho, Bethlehem and Hebron (½ day to one day for each).

Dead Sea Region (one to two nights):

Qumran (½ day); Ein Gedi (½ day to one day); and Masada (½ day).

Eilat (two to three nights): Coral Beach (½ day to two days); and nightlife. If visiting the Sinai, or not interested in beaches/nightlife, consider skipping Eilat to spend more time elsewhere.
En route: Hai-Bar Arava Wildlife Park (½ day).

Mitzpe Ramon (two to three nights): Visitors' Centre (½ day); crater hike (½ day to one day); and a stay at Sukkah in the Desert.
Sidetrips: Avdat, En Avdat, and Sde Boker (a few hours to ½ day for each)
En route: Beersheba (a few hours to one day).

Tiberias (two to four nights): Sea of Galilee: Tabgha and Capernaeum.
Sidetrips: Safed (½ day to one day); Beit She'an (a few hours to one day); and Golan (one day).
En route: Safed (½ day to one day) and Beit She'an (a few hours to one day).

Qiryat Shimona/Tel Hai (one to two nights): Hula Valley for hikes and inner tube rafting; Katzrin, Metulla (½ day to one day for each); and Nimrod Castle (½ day).
En route (or as sidetrips from Tiberias): Nazareth and Safed (½ day to one day for each).

Safed (one night): Old City.

Haifa (one to two nights): Baha'i Shrine and museums (½ day to one day for both); and beaches.
Sidetrips: Akko, Druze villages (½ day to one day for each).
En route: Caesarea (½ day).

Tel Aviv (two to three nights): Diaspora, Tel Aviv & Land of Israel museums, beaches, Jaffa (½ day to one day for each); Nahal Binyamin (a few hours); and City/Jaffa nightlife.
Sidetrips: Rehovot (½ day to one day).

ACCOMMODATION

Israel has a wide range of accommodation with plenty of scope for both the big spenders and the budget travellers. Before you convert your money into sheqelim, remember that by paying in foreign currency you avoid the 15% VAT. Costs rise sharply in the high season, although the drop in visitors since the intifada means that bargains can often be struck at other times. Israeli hotels are graded from five stars down. Prices normally include an Israeli breakfast, except for budget accommodation.

Wherever you stay, hot water and heating can be a problem, especially in the winter. Solar heaters are usually the main energy source, and hotel/hostel owners are often reluctant to boost a low supply of hot water with electricity.

In many places, it pays to stand up for yourself in order to get a better price and better service. Israelis and Palestinians alike are often guilty of providing gruff service while charging a rate that should include at least a hint of a smile and some enthusiasm. Whether or not there's much to smile about here, people are not going to stay long in a place unless they feel welcome.

Camping

All over the country there are camping areas equipped with all the amenities but charging substantially more than most hostels. Still, there are plenty of opportunities to pitch your tent for free, just ensure that your chosen spot is not off-limits for security reasons. Camping seems to be tolerated on most public beaches. Notable exceptions include the Dead Sea shore, the Mediterranean coast north of Nahariya and in the Gaza Strip. Do be careful – theft is very common on beaches, especially in Eilat, Tel Aviv and Haifa.

Hostels

Israel has 31 IYHA hostels. In the Dead Sea region and Mitzpe Ramon they are the sole budget accommodation choice, but elsewhere privately-owned hostels usually offer better value and service. Also, most IYHA hostels insist that you take breakfast, instead of allowing you to provide your own at a fraction of the cost. Nonmembers are allowed to use IYHA hostels at a slightly higher price.

You can use a YHA card from your own country or buy one from the Israel Youth Hostels Association (☎ (02) 252706), 3 Rehov Dorot Rishonim, Jerusalem 91009. Card holders save 10% on accommodation and food, so estimate how many times you would use the IYHA hostels when deciding to join. At the time of writing, the IYHA hostels in Haifa, Akko, Rosh Hanikra, Safed, Rosh Pinna and Qiryat Anavim are closed to members as they are being used to house Jewish immigrants from Ethiopia and the former USSR.

Kibbutz Guesthouses

The kibbutzim have had to search for alternatives to agriculture for income, and in recent years they have been developing the guesthouse concept. Originally designed for fellow Israelis as a rustic escape from city life, they are now more up-market and attract overseas visitors, too. They mainly fit into the middle price range and have good facilities such as swimming pools or beaches, renowned restaurants and special activities for guests. Mostly located in the countryside, they can be inconvenient for travellers relying heavily on public transport. However, for those with a car they can be a great alternative to hotels, especially in the Dead Sea area, Galilee and the Golan. The Kibbutz Hotels Central Office (☎ (03) 5246161), 90 Ben Yehuda St, POB 3193, Tel Aviv 6130, publishes a booklet listing all their hotels, restaurants and campsites with prices, amenities and a map (also available at IGTOs).

Christian Hospices

Various Christian denominations have accommodation in the vicinity of their religious sites. They are often the best value in the low to moderate price range, with cleanliness seemingly the top priority. You do not need to be a Christian to stay in most of these hospices, but you must be prepared to abide by the rules, which usually involve a strict curfew and an early start in the morning. Some hospices, however, are extremely informal and are more like regular guesthouses or hotels. A significant number of their guests are Jewish!

Luxury Hotels

There are luxury hotels in the major cities and resorts and more are planned. Hilton and Sheraton lead the international brigade, and the Israeli company Dan has several top-rated properties. Except during the high season, prices for these hotels compare favourably with those in other parts of the world. The level of service provided in Israel's top hotels, however, is generally lower than elsewhere. Catering to a predominantly Jewish clientele, these properties invariably feature such facilities as kosher kitchens, synagogues and Shabbat elevators and clocks.

Moderate Hotels

Modestly priced hotels are found throughout the country and their quality varies considerably. Prices in this category range from about US$45 to US$80 per night for a double room. Generally, Israeli hotels are on the dull side, featuring cheap and nasty modern architecture with miniature rooms. Arab hotels tend to be older, more solid buildings with larger rooms.

Bed & Breakfast

In many popular tourist areas you will find accommodation in private homes. In some places they form the bulk of moderately-priced rooms. They can be found by inquiring at the local tourist office, looking for signs posted in the street or in some places by simply hanging out at the bus station with your bags. Israel Bed & Breakfast Ltd (☎ (02) 817001), PO Box 24119, Jerusalem, Israel 91240, is a new agency which can arrange rooms and breakfast in homes throughout Israel. Daily rates range from US$20 to US$30 per person in double occupancy and US$35 to US$60 in single occupancy.

Renting an Apartment

If you plan a lengthy stay, this can be a comfortable way to save money on hotel and even hostel accommodation. Israel Bed & Breakfast Ltd (address above) and Homtel (☎ (03) 289141/2, 289503), 33 Dizendoff St, Tel Aviv, Israel, both offer private apartments and villas throughout the country. (See also Jerusalem, Tel Aviv and Eilat chapters.)

FOOD

Despite loud and constant claims that Israel has an incredible variety of international cuisine due to its worldwide immigration, you'll find much of the food expensive and disappointing. However, good food can be found.

Budget travellers will find that eating out on a regular basis will ruin them financially. Luckily, most hostels have a communal kitchen for guests, and so you shop in the street markets, grocery shops and supermarkets, choose from the good range of quality vegetables and fruit, and cook for yourself. Among the best places to eat out cheaply are the Egged self-service restaurants in the main bus stations. Basic food here costs about US$5 for a filling dish. The restaurants are open for breakfast and lunch and usually close late in the afternoon. In places where there is a sizable Arab population, there are always places to buy a filling cheap meal.

On the fast-food scene, there are hamburgers and pizzas, but felafel is more common. The popular hamburgers are those found in the Burger Ranch chain, and MacDavid's. Pizza is also very popular in Israel, but generally it is of poor quality. The best type does not imitate the style of other countries and is made by Arabs.

Although both Jews and Arabs in Israel love to sit in cafés drinking tea and coffee, people mainly eat at home with their families. However, more and more Israelis are eating out in restaurants and drinking in bars.

Kashrut & Kosher

Kashrut is the noun derived from the adjective 'kosher' which, roughly translated, means 'ritually acceptable'.

Genesis (1:29) permits all fruit and vegetables, and 'clean' animals (7:2). Basically, animals that chew the cud and which have wholly cloven hooves are clean (Leviticus 11; Deuteronomy 14). According to the Mishnah, clean birds must have a crop, a gizzard which can be easily peeled off and an extra talon. All birds of prey are forbidden. Today, those birds which are considered 'traditional' are permitted. This allows for variations according to different Jews' interpretations. Pheasant, for example, is considered clean in some communities and not others. In Israel, turkey is definitely considered clean. It is on menus everywhere, often uncredited in kebabs and schnitzels in the hope that it will be thought of as lamb or veal. The Talmud directs that fertilised eggs are forbidden, as are any with a spot of blood.

Only fish that have at least one fin and easily removable scales are clean. Honey is allowed despite the bee's status as a forbidden insect. The Mishnah regards it as 'transferred nectar'.

The laws of kashrut stipulate that the slaughter must be carried out by a licensed *shohet*. After slaughtering, he must examine the animal for defects which would make it unclean. These might be perforated organ walls, split pipes, missing limbs, missing or defective organs, torn walls or membrane covers of organs, a poisonous substance introduced into the body when mauled by another animal, shattering by a fall, and broken or fractured bones. The animal is suspended head down to allow as much blood as possible to drain out. Leviticus (7:26-27 & 17:10-14) prohibits the consumption of blood and any which does not drain out is removed by salting the meat or roasting it over an open flame.

It is forbidden to eat certain parts of clean animals, including the sciatic nerve (except on a bird), the fat attached to an animal's stomach and intestines, and the abdominal fat of oxen, sheep and goats (unless covered by flesh). The rule that the meat of an animal must not be boiled in the milk of its mother is interpreted by Orthodox Jews to mean that they cannot cook or eat meat and milk (including all dairy products) together. In order to ensure that this rule was never disobeyed unknowingly, the rabbis ruled that the separation of milk and meat must be as complete as possible. This has meant that separate utensils, dishes and cutlery must be used for dairy foods and meat. They must be stored separately and washed in separate sinks or bowls, using separate dishcloths for washing and drying. Strict observance of the Talmud means waiting for up to six hours between eating milk and meat dishes. This interval varies depending on the community.

Foods which are neither milk nor meat are known as *parve* or *pareve* and should be prepared with separate utensils. Once prepared they may be used together with milk or meat. Items for sale which have been accepted as parve by the rabbinate are certified on the label to ensure that mistakes can be avoided. Kosher restaurants serve either meat or dairy products, and they will not serve cheeseburgers, a cream sauce with chicken, or tea with milk in a meat restaurant.

Kosher laws greatly affect the process of winemaking. Most notably, only Orthodox Jews are permitted to touch the selected grapes and wine during production. Only when bottled and sealed can a secular or non-Jew handle the product.

Theories explaining the kosher laws include hygienic, sanitary, aesthetic, folkloric, ethical and psychological viewpoints. Reform Judaism does not insist on the observance of kashrut, and this major disagreement amongst religious Jews highlights the complexities of Judaism.

General

Due to the kosher laws and the high price of meat, the Israeli diet includes large amounts of dairy products and vegetables.

Meals commonly include salad (often tomato and cucumber), *hummus* (a paste from chick peas and olive oil) and *tehina* (a thinner paste from sesame seeds and olive oil), often combined with eggplant to make *baba ghanoush*. These vary in quality from place to place and, with hummus in particular, there is much discussion over who makes the best. Served spread out over a plate with pitta bread and pickles, or in a pitta sandwich, these salads are one of the cheapest meals to enjoy in a café/restaurant, and if you eat enough bread (which is often free), you will be full.

The most popular fast food has to be the felafel, and by the time they leave Israel budget travellers unable to cook for themselves will have had an overdose of this item. Felafel is ground chick peas blended with herbs and spices and normally shaped into a ball before deep frying in oil. It is most commonly served with an assortment of salads in pitta bread with tehina sauce topping it.

Even more than hummus, felafel inspires patrons of certain establishments to argue about whose is the best. The secret would seem to be the blend of herbs and spices (sounds like a commercial for fried chicken), the frequency with which the oil in the deep fryer is changed, whether or not any addition of breadcrumbs is noticeable and the quality of the salads and tehina. Some felafel stalls allow you to help yourself to as much salad and tehina as you like.

The most popular way to eat meat would seem to be *shwarma*, also known elsewhere as *doner kebab*. Originating in Turkey, it is traditionally lamb sliced from a revolving vertical spit. In Israel, unfortunately, it is usually turkey made to taste like lamb. This is eaten along with salad and pitta or in a pitta sandwich like felafel.

Now, all of these items are popular with Jews and Arabs alike, and it is an indication of the intense friction between them that you might well hear a member of one community claim that it is their food and not the others'.

Oriental & Eastern European

Jewish food in Israel can be divided into two categories: Oriental (or Sephardim) and Eastern European (or Ashkenazi).

Oriental food was brought to Israel by the Jews from the Arab countries and is very similar to the food eaten by the Arabs. In addition to salads, felafel and shwarma, one of the most common types of Oriental food is meat cooked 'on the fire'. *Shishlik* is chunks of meat, while *kebabs* are minced meat, both on a skewer. Lamb, beef and chicken are the most popular meats used this way. Offal is also used, and restaurants serving turkey's testicles, cow's udder, spleen, heart, kidneys and the like are increasingly popular and inexpensive.

One of the tastiest aspects of Oriental cooking is the art of stuffing vegetables and meat with rice, nuts, meat, spices and other goodies. Soups are usually made from meat stock and have a hot, spicy flavour. Bourekas are flaky pastry filled with either cheese, potato or spinach, and eaten as a snack.

Eastern European food is characterised by the familiar Viennese schnitzel, Hungarian goulash, and gefilte fish. Most Israelis I have met denied enjoying the latter. Basically, it consists of ball-shaped pieces of fish heads and tails and is served chilled. Romanian restaurants, among Israel's best, are particularly good for steaks and liver. Goulash soup can be very tasty and is often a meal in itself. Stews and casseroles appear frequently on East European menus, and the Jewish favourite, chicken soup, must not be forgotten.

Blintzes, which for the uninitiated are a type of pancake, are, on the whole, disappointing.

On Shabbat, most secular Jews join the religious and follow the traditional rule of no cooking. For many, this will mean eating *cholent*, a heavy stew prepared before sunset on Friday.

Palestinian

Most of the best hummus is made by Arabs, and before the intifada, Jews were among their best customers. Good places for this are the cheap sit-down Arab restaurants that only serve hummus, *foul* (pronounced 'fool' – beans) and, as an accompaniment, felafel. Hummus is often served with *snobar* (roasted pine kernels). Others may also serve shwarma and shishlik and a variety of Palestinian dishes. These could include *mansaf*, rice with small pieces of lamb, nuts, lemon juice and the herbs which give this cuisine its character. This dish is a speciality of Jericho and Hebron.

Specifically from the Jerusalem area is *makluki*, an upside-down dish of rice, lamb, eggplant and other vegetables. From Nablus and the north comes *musakan*, chicken cooked on the fire with olive oil, onions and *sumak*, a red-coloured lemony spice, served on pitta bread. *Melok* is a soup made from greens. Chicken and vegetables are stuffed with *mahsi*, rice, meat, almonds and snobar. *Kubbe* is minced spiced lamb or beef stuffed in a case of *burghul* (cracked wheat) and deep fried. It's also available in Oriental Jewish and Armenian establishments. Sometimes you will find kebabs served in a tehina sauce, or vegetables stuffed with meat, rice, nuts, herbs and spices.

In the more up-market places, *mazza*, a selection of starters, is a speciality. These include hummus, brain salad, eggplant purée, stuffed vine leaves, olives and pickles. It can be a meal in itself.

Fish
Kosher laws forbid the use of shellfish, and Israeli law protects lobsters in particular. Shrimps are not protected and can often be found. Lobster is occasionally imported. Squid or calamari is popular, and the popular fresh fish are red mullet, red snapper, groper and sole. St Peter fish, indigenous to the Sea of Galilee, are now farmed commercially.

Vegetarian Food
The Black Hebrews' (see Religion in the Facts about the Country chapter) Eternity Restaurant in Tel Aviv should not be missed. They produce and serve their own tofu dishes, with convincing versions of such meat dishes as shwarma and hot dogs, and a variety of cheeses, yoghurts, ice cream and shakes. They use no animal products whatsoever, meat or dairy, and they are inexpensive.

Elsewhere, there are a number of Jewish vegetarian restaurants that are recommended. Due to the kosher laws, there are numerous dairy restaurants where meat is not served.

Dairy & Eggs
Milk is packaged either in plastic bags (homogenised) or cartons (sterilised, long life). Cheeses sold by weight (as opposed to the less expensive pre-packed variety) include feta, from sheep's milk; Bulgarian, with a salty, vinegary taste; zefat, white, round, half salty, also made with pepper or onion or garlic; labana, a dry Arab cheese from sheep's milk, sometimes sold in oil to preserve it and also made yoghurt style; Turkish cashcavel, dry and strong, made from sheep's milk, and Balkanic yoghurt, creamy and a bit sour. The Israelis also make good versions of mozzarella, roquefort, boursin and cream cheese.

Eggs in Israel are usually terrible. The yolks are pale and the flavour is so subtle it almost isn't there. It sounds corny, but the best eggs are Arab! This is because they are free-range, while the Jewish farmers have battery hens fed on a strict diet.

Breads
Israel has a delicious selection of breads, both Jewish and Arabic. Many travellers make the mistake of assuming that the cheapest is *pitta*, the small, flat, round loaves produced by Arabs and Oriental Jews. If you are counting every agorot, then buying the subsidised Jewish standard white loaves from grocery stores and supermarkets will cost you about half the price. *Hallah*, a softer style of bread, is baked for Shabbat. Jewish bakeries produce sweet breads, too. Glazed with sugar syrup, filled with currants or chocolate, they vary in quality but can be great. Matza is the unleavened bread eaten by Jews during Passover.

Jewish Oriental bakeries produce similar breads to the Arabs. Iraqi pitta is very thin and resembles a large pancake. Arabs mainly bake pitta, and it can be thickly covered with sesame seeds or have the top sprinkled with *zarta* or *dogga*, a mixture of herbs (mainly oregano) and spices – it's served separately with pitta and bagels, which you dip into the mixture after dipping them in olive oil.

Bagels are very popular. Originally from Eastern Europe, Israeli bagels are different from most others, being crisper and drier. In Tel Aviv a softer style is produced, sprinkled with sesame seeds. A traditional way to end a night out is to visit the bagel factory and pick up a hot bagel or two. Arab bagels are similar but larger. In East Jerusalem and the Old City they are sold from carts everywhere. A variation of the Arab bagel is *ka'ak*, a ring of bread covered with sesame seeds and eaten with *za'atar* (ground thyme), hard boiled eggs, cheese or felafel.

Snacks
Israel features a wide range of nuts, seeds and pulses. Peanuts, pistachios, almonds, sunflower and melon seeds, and chickpeas are popular with Jews and Arabs alike. Everywhere you go you'll see people crunching away. You will be amazed by the way the locals can pop a fistful of seeds into their mouth, crunch, spit out the shells and chew the seeds – often talking and driving simultaneously. Pickles are also popular: olives, peppers and cucumbers.

Desserts & Sweets
One of the edible highlights in Israel are the Arab sweets or pastries. Usually soaked in honey and full of sugar, they cannot be good for you, but who cares? *Baklava (burma)*, toasted shredded wheat, stuffed with pistachios or hazelnuts and soaked in honey; the crumpet-like *katayeef* and *kanafe*, a contrast of cheese, wheat, sugar and honey, are the most common. A special Arab sweet treat is *moutabak*, which is cheese inside super flaky pastry covered in sugar syrup.

Palestinians are proud of their sweets and while Nablus is recognised as the top producer, with kanafe its speciality, Gaza claims to be the best. Jerusalem's Old City, though, is the place to try moutabak. *Halvah*, a kind of nougat made from sesame seeds, is popular. An original version of Turkish Delight is available, mainly in Nablus.

The Jews also have a sweet tooth and you will never be short of somewhere to dive into cream cakes and pastries. Due to the kosher laws, many of the bakers unfortunately use synthetic cream. Biscuits seem to be part of the staple diet – they are produced in large numbers by Jewish and Arab bakers.

Ice Cream
A combination of influences from the Diaspora have made Israel's ice-cream industry a busy one. From the USA, the ecologically sound Ben & Jerry's and Carmel have several branches. In Tel Aviv, Manalito's is made by Argentinian Jews and Gelateia Artegianale produces top-quality Italian ices. Very popular with travellers are the Eternity Restaurant's vegetable ice creams, made from calcium-rich soya bean milk. There are also some Israeli ice-cream makers attracting an enthusiastic following, such as Jaffa's Dr Leck and Tel Aviv's Glida Beer Sheva. Frozen yoghurt has recently become very popular with Israelis and you will see it sold all over the place.

Fruit
With its varied climate, Israel is able to produce a wide range of fruits, including oranges, apples, mangoes, guava, melons, persimmons, pomegranates, figs, dates and avocado pears. They are available at reasonable prices in the street markets and supermarkets. Israel has long been known for its vineyards, and grapes in season are very affordable.

'Sabra' is the nickname for Israeli-born Jews, derived from the cactus fruit imported to Palestine from Mexico a few centuries ago. It looks like a hand-grenade and is the inspiration for the description of Israeli Jews as tough and prickly on the outside, soft and sweet on the inside. Sold on the streets everywhere when in season, it's an acquired taste. The seeds give the locals another chance to use their unsurpassed spitting skills.

Other Cuisines
Israel has a growing number of restaurants featuring international cuisines, including

Chinese, South-East Asian, French, Italian, Indian and Mexican.

Worthy of special note is the Panorama Restaurant in Tel Aviv's Astor Hotel, featuring Israeli nouvelle cuisine.

Breakfast

The Israeli breakfast, traditionally salad-based, is usually made out to be something pretty special. Tourist brochures feature photographs of buffet tables laden with what is described as 'huge selections of fresh fruits, salads and cheeses, eggs cooked various ways, yoghurt, herring, smoked salmon and endless varieties of freshly baked bread and rolls'. In reality, most Israeli breakfasts often fail to live up to such an enthusiastic description and consist of a somewhat less exciting selection.

DRINKS
Nonalcoholic Drinks

Tea and coffee are Israel's most popular beverages. A lover of strong tea, I find the local Jewish blends extremely weak and use two tea bags per cup. The Arabs, meanwhile, are the best tea-makers anywhere. The Arabs usually serve tea in a glass, black, very sweet (tell them if you don't want sugar before it's too late) and often with *na'ana* (mint) or *maramia* (sage), which is supposedly good for the stomach. Jews serve tea black, with lemon, milk or non-dairy creamer to satisfy the kosher laws. Vegetarian restaurants and some others usually have a range of herbal teas.

'Coffee' here can mean Turkish coffee, with 'Nescafé' or 'nes' the terms sometimes used for instant coffee. Espresso and cappuccino are increasingly available in Jewish establishments, and the quality is improving with time. Arabs and Oriental Jews often serve Turkish coffee with *hehl* (cardamon). Street cafés are as popular as they are in Europe. Sitting, slurping and staring at the interesting variety of people going by is a national pastime.

Soft drinks in Israel are expensive. Save a small fortune by buying one-litre and two-litre bottles at supermarkets and grocery stores. Freshly squeezed fruit juices are widely available. Israel markets its own mineral water, produced in the Golan. The best tap water for drinking is in Safed and Rosh Pinna. Most travellers have no problems with drinking the water, although in Eilat, if anywhere, you might be careful.

Tamar hindi (tamarind juice), *asir tamar* (date juice) and *asir loz* (almond juice) are traditional Palestinian drinks. Very sweet, you'll see the former sold in the Damascus Gate area of East Jerusalem by Arabs with a giant silver 'coffee pot' on their backs, wearing a belt carrying glasses in which to serve it. Although an impressive sight, the drink tastes better, or cleaner at least, from the nearby cafés. The milky-coloured drink also sold there is made from carob. Another local favourite, served hot in the winter, cold in the summer, is *sahlab*. It is made up of sahlab powder (like tapioca), milk, coconut, sugar, raisins, chopped nuts, rosewater and a glacé cherry garnish.

Alcohol

Beer The National Brewery Ltd controls 98% of the beer market. Starting from the bottom, price-wise, Nesher (3.8 or 4.2% alcohol) is often overlooked by travellers as it is not served in most bars or cafés and seems to be disappearing from the market. It is considerably cheaper than other products, which improves its flavour no end. Do not mistake the brown-labelled Nesher beer for the blue-labelled Nesher Malt, a dark, sweet, beer-based beverage with less than 1% alcohol. Goldstar (4.7%) is the most popular beer with travellers, both bottled and draught. Maccabee (4.9%) is the Israeli favourite, considered up-market and the only beer exported.

Wine & Spirits Although you will see several shelves in supermarkets and grocery shops lined with bottles of wine and spirits, Israelis do not drink very much. There has been an increase in consumption among younger Israelis, but for most Jews here, wine is only drunk on holy days such as Shabbat and during Passover, and spirits are hardly touched at all. The Arab population also tends to abstain, due to the Muslim laws. However, vines and wines have existed in Israel since 3000 BC, making it one of the world's oldest wine-producing areas. The symbol of the Ministry of Tourism, as well as of Carmel, Israel's largest wine company, depicts the two men sent by Moses to spy out the land of Canaan who carried back a bunch of grapes slung on a pole between them (Numbers 13).

The modern wine industry began in the late 19th century, when Jews from Eastern Europe made their way to Palestine. Some settled in Rishon le Zion and suffered considerable hardship in their attempts at farming. The hunger, thirst and disease that followed had not been expected in the Promised Land. Faced with defeat, they sent an emissary back to Europe to raise money. Baron Edmond de Rothschild, of the French wine family, later known as the 'Benefactor', agreed to help. He sent wine experts and business consultants to Rishon le Zion to develop the land. This aid was not limited to the immediate area, and after the experts surveyed the country and met other Zionist pioneers, more vineyards were developed along the coast and another winery was built at Zichron Ya'acov. In 1906, both wineries were signed over to the farmers, establishing the Societé Cooperative Vigneronne des Grandes Caves.

That co-operative is today the Carmel wine company. Originally, the co-operative's aim was to produce kosher wines for Jews worldwide, so sweet wines were developed. Soon after independence, it was decided to develop kosher table wine for a wider market. Progress has been very slow, but internationally competitive wines have been produced and improvements continue to be made.

Monfort is the second most popular wine label in Israel. Based in Netanya and named after the Crusader castle in the north, this winery specialised in spirits during the Mandate. It uses the respected Stock label for its range of spirits and vermouths under an agreement with the Italian company.

In the mid-1970s, the first vines were planted in the Golan Heights. The development there of vineyards and a winery by a co-operative of kibbutzim and moshavim took the industry by storm. Under the Yarden and Gamla labels, these wines have been by far the best Israel has produced.

The other notable wine producers in the country are Christian monks. The Trappist monastery at Latrun, between Tel Aviv and Jerusalem, was founded in 1890. Winemaking started there in 1899 when the French founders decided upon manual work as a means of support. Near Bethlehem is the Cremisan Monastery, whose inexpensive white wine is good value. Here the Italian Salesian monks have been making wine since 1885. Their main markets are Israel and Jordan. Note that these two monasteries use the term Holy Land, not Israel, on their labels. They also both produce vermouths and fortified wines.

Although the quality of the wines and spirits in Israel can be exaggerated, the fierce competition has generally kept prices low. In the US$4 to US$6 price range, you have a fair choice of enjoyable wines.

Arak and brandy are the best-selling Israeli spirits. *Arak* is a word of Arab origin and covers many different spirits. It is distilled from various fermented bases such as rice, palm sap, yams and dates. Ramallah is reputedly the best arak in Israel. Normally only available in Jaffa, its label is written in Arabic and it comes in a square-shaped bottle á la Johhny Walker Scotch whisky. Good Israeli brandies are Stock, Carmel's 777 and Carmei-Zion's Grand 41.

Israeli spirits are very cheap, about US$6, and well worth taking across with you on a trip to Egypt to sell on the black market. Whisky and vodka (Gold brand) are popular there.

Vermouths and fortified wines, mainly sherry and port, are also produced locally. Other than the Stock range, their dusty state on shop shelves is more than justified. More successful are some of the Israeli liqueurs, especially Carmei-Zion's Hallelujah, a sort of Jewish Grand Marnier.

ENTERTAINMENT
With a much more liberal society than its Middle East neighbours, Israel offers a variety of entertainment sources that should interest the traveller.

Under a general heading of 'nightlife', you can find an increasing number of bars in most towns, along with different versions of discos and live music venues. These are generally as Western as you would find in the West. For more traditional nightlife, Jerusalem, Tel Aviv and Beersheba, in particular, feature venues where Israeli folk dancing and traditional live music from the Diaspora are regularly performed. Classical music concerts, usually of an excellent standard, are frequently staged throughout the country.

Cinema is very popular with Israelis, although the box office is suffering with the advent of video and cable television (see the Arts section in this chapter). Israel has a pretty active theatre and dance scene, but as in many places today it faces an increasing struggle for funds and an audience. Most performances are in Hebrew.

For sports fans, Israel's small population and political isolation reduces the choice of spectator sports to soccer, basketball, the occasional tennis tournament and the Maccabiah Games (see Sports section in the Facts about the Country chapter).

Arab entertainment sources are limited to music from the neighbouring Arab nations, most notably Egypt, and a small theatre in East Jerusalem (see the Jerusalem chapter). Home grown entertainment has been curtailed by the intifada. With most local artists vocal in their support of the uprising, live performances are rare. An invitation to a wedding is your best way of getting to see a performance of some wonderful music, song and dance.

THINGS TO BUY
Israel is full of shops stocked with tacky souvenirs for gullible tourists. To find bargains and quality items you will need time to shop around and patience to haggle. Bargaining is not always the fun it is made out to be. Mostly limited to Arab markets, it can be time-consuming, frustrating and, in general, an unwelcome hassle. The golden rules are: don't start bargaining with a shopkeeper unless you are really interested in buying; have a good idea of the item's value both locally and back home; and don't be intimidated. Easier said than done. Do not use large notes or travellers' cheques, as getting change can be a problem.

Basically, the bargaining game is played like this: the shopkeeper usually attracts your attention and gives you a price three to 10 times above the realistic going rate. If you are genuinely interested you pull a face showing disgust or amusement at his quote, and state your offer, saying 'Take it or leave it'. Traditionally, this should be below the amount you are willing to pay. Whatever, stick to your guns and do not be bullied or cajoled into paying too much. Turning away from a bargaining session can often cut a price in half. A good idea is to observe the shopkeepers at work. Note how they flirt with young ladies, or bully them and the older tourists. They can also act respectfully towards potential customers.

Traditionally, Arab shopkeepers sell something cheaper early in the day, as a quick first sale means good business later. However, this line is often used to persuade customers to pay more, thinking that they are getting a bargain.

Not all your shopping needs to be done in markets. Some of Israel's best buys are luxury items from regular stores and galleries. It's worth remembering that some stores give a special discount if you pay in foreign currency. Check prices elsewhere all the same as, even without a discount, they may be cheaper.

Sandals
Most travellers seem to feel that they have to buy a pair of sandals, with Jerusalem's Old City being the obvious place. If you are passing through Greece at some point on this trip, buy your sandals there – the Old City Arabs do. Jewish shoe shops offer better quality but they are more expensive.

T-Shirts

Buy T-shirts from the Arabs in Jerusalem's Old City. Popular designs include the Voice of Peace, names in Hebrew and Arabic, 'Don't worry America, Israel is Right Behind You' and pro-Palestinian slogans written in Arabic with the tree symbol of Palestine. You can pay double elsewhere for similar shirts.

Ceramics

Some good quality ceramics in modern and traditional styles are available. Tiles and plates seem to be very popular – the Armenians are recognised as the leading makers of these. The best selection, again, is in Jerusalem's Old City, and also in Akko and Jaffa. Pottery in general is widespread, and the quality varies. Hebron stands out as a place where you can see the potters at work.

Copper & Brassware

They're difficult to transport, but great-looking items are to be had if you have done your homework on the prices back home. Oriental coffee pots, trays and little cups, *nargilas* (hubble-bubble pipes), and various ornaments are widely available. Do shop around, and check the Jaffa flea market, Jerusalem's Old City and Mea She'arim, Nazareth and Akko in particular.

Woodwork

Olive wood is the popular material and souvenirs for all budgets are made. Most popular are crucifixes, camels, worry beads and carvings of biblical scenes and characters. Olive woodcarvings are available everywhere.

Glassware

Loud claims are made about this industry in Israel but little I saw inspired me. Hebron is the recognised leader in the field, and buying there should save money.

Canework & Basketware

Gaza produces the best canework and it's sold all over the country; usually furniture, but also decorative pieces, baskets and trays. Basketware materials include rushes and raffia and are coloured with different interwoven shades.

Fashion – leather & furs

Leather and furs are of high quality but not cheap – just cheaper than in most other places, especially as tourists get 35% off. Begged Or (Hebrew for 'leatherware'), which uses Italian and Israeli leather, is the leading house, with stores in several places. Others include D R Jordan in Tel Aviv's Dizengoff Centre, and Ginette in Ha Yarkon St (corner of Yirmiyahu St), Tel Aviv. For furs, check out Scharf's Furs' showroom in Talpiot, Jerusalem.

The fashion scene is centred in Tel Aviv, with Newe Tzedek being a hotbed of textile workshops and showrooms. Explore this area and also Yirmiyahu St, home to the top designer boutiques.

Tel Aviv beach is full of sabra poseurs, many of whom will be (almost) wearing Israeli design swimwear, one of the country's more successful exports. Gottex is the leading name, with Gideon Oberson producing some of the most daring designs. You may find the prices for Israeli swimwear cheaper back home. If buying clothes in a sale, check garments thoroughly. Damaged goods are often sold on the sly and there is no legal comeback.

A popular fashion accessory worldwide, but often unrecognised by those wearing it, is the *kaffiyeh* (Arab headscarf). The black design is traditionally associated with Palestine, the red with Jordan. Other items of traditional Arab clothing can be found in the Arab markets.

Jewellery

This can range from the cheap but fashionable street variety to gold and diamonds. The Black Hebrews' handmade jewellery is some of the best and cheapest available. Jerusalem's Ben Yehuda St and Tel Aviv's Dizengoff St are the busiest street-selling zones. Yemenite jewellery is a delicate style of intricately joined metals. Heavier, massive and more roughly executed is Bedouin, Arab and Druze jewellery. Amber is one of the more commonly used stones. Religious jewellery is obviously popular.

More up-market items, incorporating gold, silver and precious stones, are widely available. Knowledge of this field is essential to avoid paying too much. Do not rely on the honesty of the vendor wherever you are shopping.

THINGS TO SELL

Goods such as cassette/radios (the 'ghetto-blaster' type with detachable speakers is popular), personal stereos and cameras can be sold for a healthy profit. Sony is the most popular hi-fi make, and quality camera lenses and flashes like Vivitar are admired. Other electrical goods will not normally fetch a good price, especially in Tel Aviv and Haifa where most of the black-market trade seems to operate.

I met some travellers who had arrived from Greece and Turkey with wool and leather clothing which sold like hot cakes. You will hear many fellow travellers and locals say that you can no longer succeed at the selling game. It is not true, but you must know who to sell to and where. Do not accept low offers from entrepreneurs who want to sell your gear to someone else. Check local shop prices and sell your items at a lower but profitable rate.

Getting There & Away

You have the choice of land, sea and air when travelling to Israel, but this is complicated by the delicate political situation if you want to include other Middle Eastern countries on your itinerary.

AIR

Airfares to Israel vary considerably according to season. July to September and Jewish holidays in particular mean much higher prices. Note that it is often difficult to get a flight out of Israel in a hurry, so think carefully before getting there on a one-way ticket.

To/From the USA & Canada

New York offers the widest choice of carriers, but you can also fly from Los Angeles, Chicago, Miami, Atlanta and Toronto. Many North American travellers prefer to fly nonstop with El Al for security reasons. El Al also flies via London, Manchester or Paris. Tower Air flies nonstop and via Paris for less than El Al. Delta started flying to Ben-Gurion in 1991 to join TWA as the other US carrier with scheduled departures. All of these airlines have special promotions from time to time. The Belgian carrier Sabena is often good value with an overnight in Brussels. Cheaper fares are around US$700 return to Ben-Gurion from New York. Consult the cheap flight advertisements in Sunday newspapers and do not rely on your local travel agent for the lowest price available.

Another choice is to fly via Eastern Europe. The journey time is longer than a direct flight, and their reputation for awful service and delays is pretty much deserved, but the low fares offered by Tarom (Rumanian Airlines), Hungarian and Czechoslovak Airlines can be tempting options, nonetheless.

To/From the UK & Europe

A number of charter flights to Israel from the UK continue to offer the best deals at around £220 for a 12-month open return. This can come down to as little as £180 for a one to four-week return. A one-way charter ticket averages about £110. It is worth shopping around London and Manchester's cheap flight specialists for current offers. STA Travel (☎ (071) 5811022) at 74 Old Brompton Rd, London SW7, is regularly amongst the cheapest, as are the various Earls Court Rd cheap ticket specialists. Check out the ads in the *Jewish Chronicle*, *Time Out*, *City Limits*, the *Times* and the Sunday newspapers.

Most European countries also have charter flights to Israel with considerable savings on scheduled fares: West Germany, France, Belgium, the Netherlands and Scandinavia in particular. Prices are slightly higher than those from the UK.

The inexpensive option to fly via Eastern Europe is also available to North Europeans (see To/From the USA & Canada).

To/From Australia & New Zealand

There are no direct flights between Australia/New Zealand and Israel. One option is to buy a Round-the-World (RTW) ticket with, say Qantas or British Airways (about A$2700), with a side trip to Israel. Check to see if buying a more specific ticket to Israel via London, Paris, Athens or Rome is cheaper. If you are flexible with time, you can be better off flying to London or Athens and looking for a cheap ticket for the next leg once you arrive there. Again, don't believe the first travel agent's version of the best deal – shop around.

To/From Egypt

There are El Al and Air Sinai flights available between Israel and Egypt, which will save you having an Egypt-Israel border stamp in your passport, at a cost of around US$130 one way.

Cheap Tickets in Israel

Despite the long queues, the Israel Student Travel Association (ISSTA) offices do not always offer very competitive fares. The following agencies seem to be amongst the cheapest:

Airtour Ltd, 32 Ben Yehuda St, Tel Aviv (☎ (03) 295361)
Galilee Tours, 42 Ben Yehuda St, Tel Aviv (☎ (03) 546633) and Centre 1, 43 Yirmiyahu St, near the central bus station, Jerusalem (☎ (02) 383460)
GSTS, 57 Ben Yehuda St, Tel Aviv (☎ (03) 222261); they also have a good selection of Lonely Planet guides
Mona Tours, 25 Bograshov St (off Ben Yehuda St), Tel Aviv (☎ (03) 290071, 202310, 203210)

Airport Transport

The country's main international air terminal is Ben-Gurion Airport at Lod, 18 km east of Tel Aviv and 50 km from Jerusalem. Most travellers head for either Tel Aviv or Jerusalem on arrival. There is a regular flow of buses to both cities, as well as to Haifa and Beersheba.

Eilat Airport is used for an increasing number of charter flights, and is centrally located within walking distance of the town centre, many hotels and the hostel area, and a short taxi ride from everything.

On arrival at Ben-Gurion Airport, once through immigration and with your luggage, you come outside the arrival terminal to where people are waiting for family, friends, clients, etc. Ahead are the car rental offices, to their right and the rear is the taxi station. A large sign here lists taxi fares to various destinations throughout the country. The only *sherut* (shared taxi) service is to Jerusalem. For all other destinations you have regular or special taxis. To your left from the arrivals area are the Egged bus company's office and bus stops. United Tours buses to Jerusalem and Tel Aviv leave from nearby.

Bus The two main destinations are Tel Aviv and Jerusalem:

Tel Aviv United Tours bus No 222 to Tel Aviv (US$4) departs hourly and stops at the following points: the Panorama Hotel on Herbert Samuel Esplanade (a 15-minute walk from the Old Jaffa Hostel), via Hatayashim Rd; the central railway station; Weizmann St (for the YHA hostel); and three stops on HaYarkon St – corner of Nordau Blvd, corner of Arlosoroff St (for the Greenhouse and Back Pack hostels and the Hilton, Marina and Shalom hotels), and near the Diplomat Hotel (also for the Plaza, Ramada, Sheraton, Basel and City hotels, and the Gordon Hostel).

This provides just about the most convenient way to get to central Tel Aviv. Alternatively, Egged buses take you to the city's central bus station (20 minutes) where you take a city bus to get to your ultimate destination (see Getting Around in the Tel Aviv chapter).

Jerusalem United Tours bus No 111 to Jerusalem (US$6) departs hourly and stops at the following middle-range and top-end hotels in the New City: Ramada Renaissance, Sonesta, Hilton, Sheraton Plaza, Tirat Bat-Sheva, Jerusalem Tower (also for the Jerusalem Inn and King George hostels), King David and the YMCA, Moriah, Laromme and the Mount Zion Hotel (also for St Andrew's Scottish Hospice).

None of these stops are very convenient for the Old City or East Jerusalem, especially if you're carrying heavy luggage and need to look for a place to stay. If this is you, take an Egged bus to Jerusalem's central bus station (30 minutes), then take an Egged city bus to wherever you want to go (see Getting Around in the Jerusalem chapter).

Other Destinations Egged also has buses departing from Ben-Gurion Airport for Beersheba and Haifa.

Sheruts (Shared Taxis) The only airport service is Nesher Tours & Megdal Taxi to Jerusalem. They will take each of the seven passengers right to the door of their hotel/hostel anywhere within the Jerusalem city limits (good value at US$10, any time of the day or night).

Taxis For all other destinations, regular taxis are available. To protect arrivals from the rip-off tactics of Israel's taxi drivers, the authorities have posted most fares on a massive sign. Check this carefully before you're hustled into a cab.

There are two rates: daytime is applicable from 5.30 am to 9 pm, night-time from 9.01 pm to 5.29 am. Sample fares: Tel Aviv US$15 (night-time US$18), Haifa US$60 (US$73), Netanya US$26 (US$32) and Jerusalem US$30 (US$38).

LAND

Egypt is the only country that has an open land border with Israel, while you can cross to/from Jordan by telling a few white lies and using the right words. Israel's borders with Lebanon and Syria are effectively closed to tourists. The best overland routing depends on your overall itinerary, such as how you get to/from the Middle East in the first place.

Basically, travellers planning to combine Israel with Egypt and Jordan are better off either going to Jordan first, making a round-trip visit to Israel, then taking the ferry from Aqaba to the Egyptian Sinai, or vice versa. To avoid backtracking, an alternative would be to start in Jordan, cross into Israel and continue into Egypt from the Jewish state.

To/From Egypt

Once impossible, travel between Israel and Egypt is now a thriving part of the tourist scene. For those who have the time, combining a visit to both countries is extremely popular.

In Israel, tour operators provide coach services, mainly from Tel Aviv but also from Jerusalem and Eilat, to Cairo nonstop, with tours of the Sinai Desert, Cairo and the rest of the country. One-way/return bus tickets to Cairo are about US$25/40 from either place, with tour options that include sightseeing and hotel accommodation. Check the tour operators listed below and the *Jerusalem Post* for current prices and schedules. To save money, you can use local transport and cross the border on your own, then take an Egyptian bus or taxi into the Sinai or on to Cairo.

The tour buses mostly cross the border at Rafah in the Gaza Strip. If planning an independent crossing, you are better off crossing at Taba, near Eilat, as it has more frequent public transport than Rafah. A tourist visa is required to enter Egypt. These can be processed in the Egyptian Embassy in Tel Aviv or the consulate in Eilat. The visa is not required for visits to the Sinai only; a Sinai permit is processed at the border.

Tel Aviv to Egypt For this connection try:

Egged/Nizza Tours 15 Frishmann St (☎ (03) 231502, 213725)
Galilee Tours 42 Ben Yehuda St (☎ (03) 5466622, 291310)
Mazada Tours 141 Ibn Gevirol St (☎ (03) 5463075);
Neot HaKikar 78 Ben Yehuda St (☎ (03) 225151/3);
United Tours 113 HaYarkon St (☎ (03) 7543412, 5271028)

Jerusalem to Egypt For this connection try:

Galilee Tours, Centre 1, 43 Yirmiyahu St, near the central bus station (☎ (02) 383460)
Mazada Tours 20 Shlomzion HaMalka St (☎ (02) 225433)
Neot HaKikar, 36 Keren Hayesod St (☎ (02) 699385)

Eilat to Egypt Galilee Tours (☎ (059) 74720) King Solomon Promenade. To do it yourself, take local bus No 15 from Eilat to the Taba border, then take a local Egyptian bus or taxi to your next stop. There are two daily buses to Cairo (nine hours), via Nuweiba and St Catherine's Monastery in the Sinai, and two other daily buses to the Sinai's Sharm el Sheikh via Nuweiba and Dahab. Shared taxis also operate the same routes, taking about five hours to reach Cairo.

Rafah to Egypt Egged has an infrequent bus service to Rafah from Tel Aviv and Ashkelon. Alternatively, you can take an early morning or late afternoon service taxi from Damascus Gate, East Jerusalem or Jaffa. Once across the border, take a local bus or service taxi. With fewer people going this way, there is less chance of filling the seven-seat Mercedes, which invariably means a higher fare.

Egypt to Israel Either make your own way via public bus/taxi across the Sinai, or take a direct coach from Cairo to Tel Aviv or Jerusalem via Taba or Rafah. In Cairo, contact:

Eastern Delta Transportation Co, Abassiya Station (☎ 839589, 824773)
Isis Travel, 48 Giza St (☎ 3484821, 3487761)
Travco 13 Sharia Mahmoud Azmy, near the Cairo Marriott (☎ 3420488)

Egyptian Tourist Visas Single-entry tourist visas, valid for one month, cost about US$25 but must be paid for in Israeli currency. Nationals of Cyprus, Finland, Norway, Sweden, the USA, the CIS, Germany and Yugoslavia only pay about US$15. Mutiple-entry visas cost about US$40. One photo is required. Visas are processed the same day (hand in applications, passports and photo in the morning, then pick up that afternoon), except for Israelis, who need to wait 15 days.

In Tel Aviv The Egyptian Embassy (☎ (03) 224152; for visa information 464151) is at 54 Basel St, just off Ibn Gevirol St. An easy way to get there is to take Dan bus No 5 and get off by the police station on Dizengoff St. Walk east along Basel St, the embassy is near the end on the right (look for the Egyptian flag).

It's open Sunday to Thursday 9 to 11 am for visa applications, closed Friday and Saturday. Return between 2 and 3 pm the same day for collection. The offices closes at 11 am regardless of any queue of applicants, so it's best to arrive as early as possible as there can be a long line of hopefuls.

In Eilat The Egyptian Consulate (☎ (059) 76882) is at 68 Ha'Efroni St in a residential area. From the central bus station, head west (uphill) on HaTemarim Blvd, turn south (left) on Eilot St, turn west (right) on Yotam Rd, cross this dual-carriageway, turn south (first left) on Ha'Efroni St and it's at the bottom of the hill on the left (look for the flag).

The consulate is open Sunday to Thursday 9 am to 12 pm, closed Friday and Saturday; return between 1 and 2 pm the same day for collection.

To/From Jordan

It is possible to enter Israel from Jordan, and vice versa, but you need to be very diplomatic since the legal status of the West Bank depends on whether you are talking to Jordanian or Israeli officialdom. According to the Israelis the West Bank is part of Israel, according to the Jordanians it is occupied territory. The Jordanians will allow you to enter from the Occupied West Bank, but not from Israel. Therefore, you will not be allowed to enter Jordan if you have an Israeli stamp in your passport, visas issued in Israel, entry or exit stamps from the Israeli/Egyptian border (the Egyptians always enter these in your passport), or Israeli currency.

The crossing point between Israel/Occupied West Bank and Jordan is a bridge, the Allenby Bridge to the Israelis, the King Hussein Bridge to the Jordanians. It's an international border according to the Israelis, but not to the Jordanians. It's open for tourists Sunday to Thursday from 8 am to 1 pm, and on Friday and holidays eves from 8 to 11 am – allow plenty of time to cross. On Saturdays, and Israeli and Jordanian holidays the bridge is closed. Note that the slightest political disturbance on either side can cause the bridge to close without notice for days on end.

You may find it impossible to change money at the bridge, so if you're heading to Jordan bring Jordanian dinars with you (readily available in the West Bank and Jerusalem). This is not such a problem crossing into the West Bank, as Jordanian dinars are accepted by many Palestinians.

Absolutely no photography is allowed in this extremely sensitive area. Jordanian buses are the only vehicles allowed to take passengers across the bridge – it's not possible to walk, hitch or take a private vehicle across.

Israel to Jordan You must have a Jordanian visa, best obtained at a Jordanian embassy or consulate but also issued at the Jordan-Syria border and in Aqaba. Visas are not issued at the Allenby/King Hussein Bridge nor anywhere in Israel.

The quickest way to get to the bridge is to take a service taxi from East Jerusalem (about US$10). Abdo Taxi & Travel Services (☎ (02) 283281, 286292) on the corner of Suleiman and HaNevi'im Sts (behind the Faisal Hostel) in East Jerusalem, specialise in the 40-minute drive.

You can save money travelling via Jericho by bus or service taxi. From Jerusalem to Jericho catch Arab bus No 28 (US$1) from the East Jerusalem Arab bus station, or Egged bus Nos 961 and 963 (US$1.50) from the central bus station in Jaffa Rd. Service taxis leave from the rank on the corner of HaNevi'im and Suleiman Sts (US$3).

From Jericho to the bridge transfer to another service taxi or, if you can find one at a suitable hour, squeeze onto a Shakeen bus. Service taxis leave from the main square by the 'Jericho Municipality' sign. Be sure that you choose a driver who is licensed to take you right up to the bridge or you may be dropped off short with little chance of making it in time. Some readers experienced delays with drivers demanding extra payment if the taxi was not full. They stood, or rather sat, firm and eventually reached the bridge for the same fare.

The Shakeen Bus Company's service from Hebron passes through Jerusalem and Jericho on its way to the bridge. It is difficult to know when it will arrive at any of these points, so give yourself plenty of time. From Hebron the fare is US$4.50, Jerusalem US$3.50 and Jericho US$1.50.

At the bridge there is an inspection of luggage and cameras, and a Jordanian bus takes you to the other side (JD1.5). Here you get a Jordanian permit which may have to be produced on departure or for security checks. Service taxis and JETT buses run to Amman.

An East Jerusalem travel agency has been highly recommended by travellers for their assistance in arranging crossings into Jordan (and also Syria) for those already in Israel without the required visas. Guiding Star Ltd is located at 4 Al Hariri St, East Jerusalem (☎ (02) 273150, after hours 322919; fax 273147). For US$60 they can arrange a permit allowing you to cross from the West Bank into Jordan. You need a valid passport that is free of Israeli stamps; allow two weeks processing. They also book daily tours to Jordan from Jerusalem. Including accommodations, breakfast, roundtrip transfers from the West Bank-Jordan border to Amman, and Petra, Jerash and Amman sightseeing, a three/five night package costs US$220/520 (three-star hotel), US$265/620 (four-star) or US$295/700 (five-star), per person, twin share. Single and triple rates are available. Visa fees, Amman departure tax and tips are not included, and there is a supplement for Christmas and Easter dates.

Jordan to Israel Entering Israel from Jordan presents few problems unless you are attempting to return to Israel having entered Jordan via the Allenby/King Hussein Bridge. This is technically impossible and if you don't make it you'll have to fly from Amman or cross into Egypt.

Since the West Bank is not a part of Israel (according to the Jordanians) you require a Jordanian-issued West Bank permit to enter it. This is available from the Ministry of the Interior in Amman. The issuing process normally involves some form-filling and takes three working days, but as they don't keep your passport you can use this time for more travel in Jordan.

The application form asks your religion, and it's a good idea to have one (perhaps not Judaism). You are also asked where you arrived. If you say you entered at the King Hussein Bridge you are, in Jordanian eyes, saying that you consider this to be an international border – and you won't get a permit. Try writing 'Jerusalem', or nothing at all. If the official sees the permit you received when you crossed the bridge into Jordan, your chances will plummet. Good luck!

The permit allows you a one-month stay on the West Bank. Of course once you are across the bridge you are in Israel, as far as the Israeli authorities are concerned, and are free to travel anywhere in the country. You can return to Jordan within the month so long as your Jordanian visa is still valid and your passport doesn't have an Israeli stamp in it.

From Amman, service taxis and JETT buses run to the bridge. Buses go to the Israeli check-point but taxis drop you at the foreigners' terminal from where a bus crosses to the Israeli side. A tax of JD2.5 has to be paid to enter Israel. Note that you cannot bring any food items into Israel.

SEA
To/From Greece
Thousands of travellers arrive in Israel via the ferry service from Piraeus, near Athens. The Piraeus-Haifa run usually involves a stopover in Rhodes, sometimes in Crete instead, with all ferries stopping at Limassol in Cyprus. The cheapest tickets are US$65 (US$54 students and those under 26) for deck, US$75 (US$62) for a pullman seat and from US$125 (US$100) per person in a four-berth cabin. These prices are for one-way voyages in the low season. In the high season, prices go up by about 20%. Varying slightly between the different shipping companies, the high season is basically from July to the end of September. A port tax of US$12 is added for each stopover made by each

passenger en route. For return voyages, 20% reductions are made (not from the student and under-26 prices).

The Piraeus-Haifa run takes about 58 hours, so take plenty of food and drink, if not money, for the voyage. Also, avoid sitting/sleeping downwind of the ship's funnel when up on deck; I met several soot-covered travellers disembarking at Haifa! There are two major ferry companies:

Stability Line, 11 Sachtouri St, Piraeus (☎ (01) 4132392); their Israeli agent is Jacob Caspi, 76 Ha'Atzmaut St, Haifa (☎ (04) 674449)

Afroessa Lines, 1 Harilaou Tricoupi St, Piraeus (☎ (01) 4183777); their Israeli agent is Mano Passenger Lines, 39/41 HaMeginim St, Haifa (☎ (04) 351631); 60 Ben Yehuda St, Tel Aviv (☎ (03) 282121/2/3)

To/From Turkey
Take a ferry to Rhodes from Kusadisi and then board a Haifa-bound ferry from there (from about US$50 for deck class).

LEAVING ISRAEL
Israel's departure tax is around US$12, and is charged when you purchase your ticket. Flights to/from Eilat are not subject to departure tax. (Israeli citizens are slugged about US$50 to US$75 each time they leave their country.)

Getting Around

AIR

Arkia, Israel's domestic airline (which has now extended its operations to include charters to/from abroad) operates scheduled flights between Jerusalem, Tel Aviv, Haifa, Rosh Pinna and Eilat.

Prices are not really competitive with the alternative forms of public transport on the ground. You can inquire about current Arkia prices and schedules at IGTOs around the world and in Israel, as well as at the following Arkia offices:

Eilat
    Shalom Centre (☎ (059) 76102/3)
    Downtown Airport (☎ (059) 73142/4)
Haifa
    84 Ha'Atzmaut St (☎ (04) 643371)
Jerusalem
    Klal Centre, 97 Jaffa Rd (☎ (02) 225888)
Netanya
    11 Ha'Atzmaut Square (☎ (03) 340734)
Rosh Pinna
    Airport (☎ (06) 935301)
Tel Aviv
    11 Frishmann St (☎ (03) 6992222)

BUS

Israel's small size and its excellent road system have combined to make bus travel the choice of public transport to be developed.

Israel's bus network is dominated by Egged, the second largest bus company in the world, after Greyhound and ahead of London Transport. Egged is a cooperative, with about 6000 members and 3500 salaried employees. Together they operate about 4000 buses on over 3000 scheduled routes, as well as numerous special trips. Dan provides urban services in the Dan region: Tel Aviv and the immediate surrounding area. At the time of writing, there are plans for Egged and Dan to merge.

Egged

The Egged network has a fascinating history. When the Zionist settlements were springing up in isolated areas, mainly in Galilee, a system of cooperative transport evolved to provide the vital link between them. Highways were nonexistent, and the bus carried not only passengers, but also newspapers, mail, food and general supplies. The early Jewish bus driver's job is seriously compared to that of stagecoach drivers in the Wild West of America, and they often had one hand on the wheel and the other on a concealed gun. Perhaps this explains the common habit of today's Jewish bus driver to have just one hand on the wheel even during the most awkward manoeuvres – except that these days his other hand is busy counting his change, reorganising his various tickets, adjusting the radio to catch the latest news broadcast or popping sunflower seeds into his mouth. The pioneer days gave Jewish bus drivers a reputation of bravery and dedication and they still enjoy a status in the community above that of their peers in other countries.

Egged was formed in 1933 when four earlier cooperatives merged. The name Egged means 'linked together' and was proposed by the Jewish national poet H N Bialik to express the close bond between the new cooperative members.

A unique aspect of Egged is its national security role. Especially in the Negev region, you will often get the impression that Egged buses are glorified troop carriers, as you constantly have to wake up a dozing platoon to move their assortment of weapons and kit bags in order for you to get a seat. In fact, Egged's National Security Officer coordinates with the IDF to ensure that there is sufficient transport on busy routes, especially on Friday, Saturday evening after Shabbat, Sunday and before/after Jewish holidays, to enable soldiers to get to and from their bases. Often they appear to only just make it. In times of war, Egged assists the IDF by acting as a back-up fleet transporting personnel and equipment.

Egged Information Call this number from anywhere in the country for information on schedules, tickets and prices: 1770-225555 (no area code is necessary to connect).

Arab Buses

In Nazareth, East Jerusalem and the Occupied Territories, around 30 small Arab companies provide bus services. More and more, the Jewish buses tend to be of the highest quality: air-conditioned, clean, fast and modern; whilst the Arab buses, although improving, are comparatively rut, dirty, painfully slow climbing the hilly areas where they mainly operate, and a bit on the old side. However, from their central stations in East Jerusalem to such destinations as the Mount of Olives, Bethlehem, Jericho, Hebron, Ramallah and Nablus, they are often more convenient and cheaper to use than Egged, and always safer.

Costs

Due to massive cuts in Government subsidies, Israel's bus system is not as cheap as it used to be, but with mostly short distances involved your travel budget should not be too large. Your longest journey is likely to be the run between Eilat and Jerusalem (four hours) or Tel Aviv (five hours), costing about US$12. ISIC holders are entitled to a discount of about 10% on inter-urban fares.

Israbus Passes Like most unlimited travel passes, their value is totally dependent on the amount of travelling done. They are valid for all Egged buses, which means all buses except those in the Tel Aviv area and the Arab network. You can be pretty certain of saving money if you get the 30-day Israbus pass, or if you plan inter-urban trips virtually every day of a seven to 21-day period. This is not so uncommon amongst visitors to Israel and, especially if you end up using the urban buses as well, the Israbus pass certainly becomes good value.

Buying tickets is not too much of a problem – apart from the lack of smiling faces from Egged staff locked into their ticket booths and the struggle by locals to understand the rules of queuing. Being an Israbus pass holder does save you most of those minor hassles and it entitles you to discounts on certain tours, car rentals, and at some restaurants and museums.

Israbus pass rates are:

Days	Cost US$	US$ per day
7	59	8.43
14	95	6.79
21	115	5.48
30	129	4.30

The Israbus pass can be purchased at any of these Egged Tours Offices:

Afulla
    Central Bus Station (☎ (06) 523444, 591234/6)
Ashdod
    Central Bus Station (☎ (08) 523444, 591234/6)
Ashkelon
    Central Bus Station (☎ (051) 750654, 750221)
Beersheba
    Central Bus Station (☎ (057) 74341/5, 75262)
Ben-Gurion Airport (☎ (03) 9711070/9)
Eilat
    Central Bus Station (☎ (059) 73148/9)
Hadera
    Central Bus Station (☎ (063) 37722/6)
Haifa
    4 Nordau St (☎ (04) 643131/2)
    Central Bus Station (☎ (04) 549486)
Holon
    47 Shenkar St (☎ (03) 882797, 883385)
Jerusalem
    Reservations Centre, 224 Jaffa Rd
    (☎ (02) 304422)
    44A Jaffa Rd (Zion Square) (☎ (02) 253454, 254198)

Central Bus Station, 224 Jaffa Rd
(☎ (02) 304868, 534596)
Terminal opposite Jaffa Gate (☎ (02) 248144, 247783)

Nahariya
Central Bus Station (☎ (04) 922656)

Netanya
28 Herzl St (☎ (053) 28333, 338881)

Rehovot
Central Bus Station (☎ (08) 452520/4)

Safed
Central Bus Station (☎ (06) 921122)

Tel Aviv
(Head Office) 15 Frishmann St (☎ (03) 5271212)
59 Ben Yehuda St (☎ (03) 5271212)
Kikkar Namir (Atarim Square) (☎ (03) 5271818)
Central Bus Station (☎ (03) 375588)

Tiberias
Central Bus Station (☎ (06) 791080, 720474)

Multi-Fare Discount Passes These are available on Egged and Dan urban buses and cost about US$20. Each card is valid for a calendar month (it is sold from the 27th of the preceding month until the 5th of the month in question) and allows a set number of single rides at a 25% saving. Another attraction is that the pass can be shared between as many people as there are rides on it, so you and anyone else with you can use it.

These passes are not valid for inter-urban rides, only for routes within a city/town. You should calculate whether you are likely to benefit from using one, particularly a Dan pass which is basically valid only for Tel Aviv-Jaffa, Herzlia, Rehovot, Rishon le Zion and Ramla.

Return Tickets Purchasing a return inter-urban ticket can often save a considerable amount, and with the small travelling distances involved many travellers will find that it is often preferable to base themselves in one place and take a bus to visit other areas, avoiding constant packing, unpacking and searching for accommodation.

Another advantage of return tickets is that there are no time limits. For example, you could buy a Tel Aviv-Beersheba return and from Beersheba wander around the Negev region at your will, later returning from Beersheba to Tel Aviv. The deal for a Tel Aviv-Jerusalem return is particularly good value and the two major cities are only about 50 minutes apart with a virtually constant flow of express buses.

Operating Hours & Frequency of Services

Overall, Israel's bus service is very good and the vast majority of locals, as well as travellers, use it. This does mean that buses fill up, especially in the rush hours which are mainly from 7 to 8 am and 4 to 6 pm Monday to Thursday, and most of Saturday evening and Sunday, as a result of the Shabbat shut-down. Egged and Dan buses operate from about 5.30 am to about 10.30 pm; major routes go on until midnight. On Friday and the eve of Jewish holidays buses run only until 3 or 4 pm. On Saturday these buses don't run at all until sunset, or a little earlier. Some Jewish buses in Haifa and Akko (but not all of them) and the Arab buses operate every day as normal. Arab buses stop earlier, usually 6 or 7 pm.

On busy inter-urban routes, mainly to and from Jerusalem, Tel Aviv and Haifa, the buses run almost continually throughout the day. The only areas apparently lacking in a frequent bus service, although perhaps it is because there seems to be so many elsewhere, are the Dead Sea region and the Golan. The latter I can understand because of the lack of population, but the Dead Sea is such a popular destination. Yet you usually have to contend with a huge and, even by Israeli standards, impatient crowd of prospective passengers at the Jerusalem central bus station waiting for a trip down to a swim, and waiting for a bus to leave the Dead Sea region can be a lengthy exercise.

TRAIN

The small passenger network of the Israel State Railways (IRS) is even cheaper than the buses but, due to the location of most of the stations away from city and town centres, it is less convenient. For ISIC holders, rail travel is even better value, with a 20% discount being offered. Another advantage of the train network is that it passes through

IRS Network

Betzet

Nahariya
Akko

Haifa
Qiryat Motzkin

Tel Hanan

Atlit

Zichron Ya'acov
Binyamina
Remez Junction
Hadera Ma'arau
Hadera

Netanya

Tel Aviv North
Tel Aviv South
Lod
Ramla
Na'an
Ashdod

Ashkelon

Qiryat Gat

Gaza

Beersheba

Dimona
Mamshit

Nahal Zin

Ein Hatzeva

SEA OF
GALILEE

Jerusalem

DEAD
SEA

Sodom

Eilat

++++++++ Existing Lines

HHHHH Lines Planned
or Under
Construction

some delightfully scenic countryside, particularly the Tel Aviv to Jerusalem route, although the bus service is a lot faster.

The passenger service is limited in scope, with about three million passengers per year. The main line is Haifa-Tel Aviv Central (North), used primarily by commuters. Some trains continue to Nahariya and there is a daily train running in each direction between Haifa and Jerusalem. Despite problems with outdated equipment, the level of service and comfort is generally acceptable.

TAXI
Sherut/Service Taxi

In Israel, taking a taxi does not normally mean splurging on your own chauffeur-driven vehicle. Like its Middle Eastern neighbours, Israel is the land of the shared taxi. Most commonly called the sherut, the Arabs call it the service taxi, or taxi service.

These are one and the same, operating on a fixed route at a fixed price which can vary from a regular weekday rate to higher rates for the late hours, Shabbat and holidays. Except for innocent airport arrivals, there is little scope for rip-off merchants with this system. Sheruts/service taxis are usually stretch-Mercedes seating up to seven passengers and you simply pay the same as everyone else.

If you are uncertain about the fare, just ask locals, your fellow passengers, or check with the nearest tourist office. Regular rates are normally about 20% more than the bus, but are sometimes on a par.

Most sheruts travel between towns and cities from recognised taxi ranks. They simply drive off when they are full. This can sometimes involve waiting for six other people but you will be surprised how popular the system is, and long delays are rare. Also, what often appears to be an empty vehicle will rapidly fill up and zoom off when you climb in. The locals tend not to sit inside and wait, but stand around outside instead. You can get out anywhere along the way but you pay the same fare regardless. After dropping off a passenger the sherut then picks up replacement passengers wherever possible.

Top: Dome of the Rock (TW)
Left: Mount Zion, Jerusalem (RE)
Right: Orthodox Jews contemplate layers of history at the Citadel, Jerusalem (RE)

Top: Palestinian shoe shine, Old City, Jerusalem (NT)
Left: Palestinian selling tamar hindi, Damascus Gate, Jerusalem (NT)
Right: Resident of Mea She'arim, Jerusalem (NT)

It is interesting to witness the use of hand signals by both drivers and prospective passengers at the roadside to indicate the number of spaces available or required.

Most notably in Tel Aviv, but also in Jerusalem on Shabbat, some sheruts operate at the same price and on the same route as the local bus service, picking up/dropping off passengers as requested. On Shabbat, sheruts provide the only transport on certain major inter-city routes whilst Egged is off the road. Check what services are available to avoid being a victim of the Shabbat shut-down.

In the Occupied Territories, where the Egged service is limited to Jewish settlements rather than to general towns and places of interest, the service taxis save hours of travelling time compared to the local Arab buses.

Special Taxis

Throughout Israel, drivers of 'special' (ie non-shared) taxis have a terrible reputation with tourists and locals alike for overcharging, unhelpfulness and being impolite. The usual 'my meter doesn't work' or 'for you, friend, special price' tricks are popular. Be sure that the meter is used or risk paying too much.

These highwaymen of the Middle East are so notorious at ripping off passengers that even the luxury King David Hotel in Jerusalem has official fares posted up in its lobby to protect guests. Tourist offices can also advise how much to pay.

CAR

Good roads, beautiful scenery and short distances make Israel a great place to hire a car. Also, in places like the Golan and the Negev, the buses do not cover so much ground and having your own vehicle can help you to really see the area. If you are on a tight budget, a few people sharing a car can be an economically viable way to see specific areas, if not the whole country.

Except for Tel Aviv, Jerusalem, and the rush hours in other major cities and on commuter routes, traffic is pretty light. With overland entry to Israel so limited, bringing your own vehicle makes little sense.

Although it can be exaggerated and should not stop you from getting behind the wheel yourself, Israel's death and injury rate due to

Distances Between Major Cities & Towns (km)

	Beersheba	Eilat	Haifa	Jerusalem	Tel Aviv	Tiberias
Akko	227	474	23	177	118	56
Ashdod	90	333	136	72	41	176
Ashkelon	67	306	151	75	56	197
Beersheba		243	208	83	113	236
Ben-Gurion	98	341	112	50	18	152
Bethlehem	76	319	168	10	73	169
Eilat	243		451	312	356	403
Ein Gedi	106	232	210	78	153	179
Gaza	44	288	172	128	77	212
Haifa	208	451		158	95	70
Hebron	48	291	195	37	100	186
Jericho	117	287	148	35	98	118
Jerusalem	83	312	159		63	159
Masada	64	216	261	109	169	183
Netanya	145	388	63	95	32	103
Ramallah	98	341	140	15	75	150
Tel Aviv	113	356	95	63		132
Tiberias	236	403	70	159	132	

motoring accidents is tragically high. Careless driving can be witnessed everywhere, so be extra cautious.

Since the intifada, hire cars are often stoned in certain areas of the Occupied Territories, and you are advised not to drive in those places. Check with the car company and other travellers about places to avoid. Despite these conditions, having your own car in Israel is the desirable way to travel if your budget allows it.

Road Rules

In Israel you drive on the right-hand side of the road. Seat belts should be worn at all times by front seat occupants. The speed limit is 50 km/h (31 mph) in built up areas and 90 km/h (56 mph) elsewhere unless stated, but this is typically ignored. There seems to be a lack of regulatory road signs, but virtually all major cities, towns and places of interest are signposted in English.

Parking With a rapid increase in private car ownership, parking is a major problem in urban centres. Especially in Tel Aviv, but in most places, street parking is strictly regulated. To avoid a ticket or having your car towed, be sure to follow the rules.

Generally, there is no free street parking in most city or town centres; parking cards need to be purchased from the post office or street kiosks. Each parking card has five hours' worth of street parking, and costs about US$5. With a parking card affixed to the car's front window, you can park where the kerb is marked by blue and white stripes. You cannot legally park anywhere else.

Between 7 am and 5 pm, you can only park here for one hour. Between 5 and 10 pm you can park for longer, with a set of displayed parking cards indicating the number of hours parked. Overnight parking on the blue and white stripes is unregulated. If you need to park for a longer period during the day, use a public car park.

Car Rental

Local car-hire firms generally offer lower rates than the international companies like Avis, Budget and Hertz. Eldan, in particular, stands out with good rates and offices nationwide. If you are planning to drive throughout the country, it can be a good idea to use a company that has a few offices in case you need a replacement car. Note that you are not allowed to take hired vehicles into the Sinai.

Prices do vary dramatically and shopping around is recommended. Check the *Jerusalem Post* and the free tourist magazines like *This Week in Israel* for special promotions. Based on three days' rental, look at around US$55 to US$75 per day for a Fiat Uno or similar, with air-conditioning, insurance and unlimited mileage. July and August rates are substantially higher than the rest of the year. Be wary of initial quotes – check if insurance and unlimited mileage are included, and if there is a minimum rental period. Petrol costs around US$0.80 a litre (less in tax-free Eilat).

Most car-rental companies require that drivers be over 23 years old and have a clean, valid driver's licence (an International Driving Permit is not necessary for most nationalities). Some of the suggested companies follow:

Beersheba
    Avis, Hebron Rd (☎ (057) 71777)
    Budget, 1 Ha'Atzmaut St (☎ (057) 76681)
    Eldan, Desert Inn (☎ (057) 430344)
    Europcar, 1 Hebron Rd (☎ (057) 75353; fax 34606)
    Hertz, 5A Ben Zvi St, near the central bus station (☎ (057) 73878)
Ben-Gurion Airport
    Budget, (☎ (03) 9711504/5)
    Eldan, (☎ (03) 9721027/8)
    Europcar, (☎ (03) 9721097; fax 9711386)
    Hertz, (☎ (03) 9711165/6)
Eilat
    Budget, Etzion Hotel, HaTamarim Blvd (☎ (059) 74124/6)
    Eldan, Ha'Arava Rd, near the airport (☎ (059) 74027)
    Europcar, Shalom Centre (☎ (059) 74014; fax 74028)
    Hertz, HaTamarin Blvd (☎ (059) 76682,75050)
Haifa
    Budget, 118 Ha'Atzmaut Rd (☎ (04) 538558)
    Eldan, Carmel (☎ (04) 375303), Checkpost (☎ (04) 410910)

Europcar, 100 Jaffa St (☎ (04) 534587; fax 534303)
Hertz, Sonol Gas Station, 90 Ha'Atzmaut St (☎ (04) 523239, 539786/8)

Jerusalem
Budget, 14 King David St (☎ (02) 248991)
Eldan, King David Hotel (☎ (02) 251111) Hilton Hotels (☎ (02) 513030)
Europcar, 8 King David St (☎ (02) 248464; fax 248801)
Hertz, 18 King David St (☎ (02) 231351/226334)
Hyatt Hotel (☎ (02) 815069)

Nahariya
Budget, 31 HaGa'aton Blvd (☎ (04) 929252)

Netanya
Avis, 1 Ussishkin St (☎ (053) 31619)
Budget, 2 Gad Machnes St (☎ (053) 330618)
Eldan, 12 Ha'Atzmaut Square (☎ (053) 616982)
Europcar, 2 Gad Machnes St (☎ (053) 62126; fax 6211181)
Hertz, 8 Ha'Atzmaut Square (☎ (053) 28890)

Tel Aviv
Avis, (☎ (03) 384242)
Budget, 99 HaYarkon St (☎ (03) 227741), Dan Panorama (☎ (03) 5190136/7)
Eldan, 40 Hamasger St (☎ (03) 5371130), 112 HaYarkon St (☎ (03) 5271166/8)
Europcar, 75 HaYarkon St (☎ (03) 662866; fax 662867)
Hagar, 8 Yona Hanavi St, corner of HaYarkon St (☎ (03) 661031), 41 HaYarkon St (☎ (03) 223496, 244750)
Hertz, 144 HaYarkon St (☎ (03) 22332)

Tiberias
Budget, 9 Elhadiff St (☎ (06) 723496, 720864)
Eldan, (☎ (06) 791822)
Europcar, Elhadiff St (☎ (06) 722777; fax 723868)
Hertz, Jordan River Hotel (☎ (06) 721804, 723939)

An often overlooked alternative to the Jewish-owned companies are two Palestinian operations. In addition to any political attractions of giving them your business, their cars are considered 'protected' in East Jerusalem and other Arab areas, including the West Bank, and should be spared the hostility and stones that can be targeted towards Jewish cars with yellow plates.

Note that these vehicles can be driven throughout Israel, although you will undoubtedly attract some unfriendly stares from Israelis as you cruise around the country. Rates can be competitive, especially for a week or more and if you bargain.

Orabi, Jerusalem St, El-Bireh, near Ramallah (☎ (02) 953521 (24 hours), 955601; fax 953521). Their cars have blue Palestinian plates.

Petra, Main St, East Jerusalem (☎ (02) 820716; fax 822668). Their cars have yellow plates, but with the Arabic company insignia they should be safer than Jewish-owned vehicles.

BICYCLE

To consider a cycle tour of Israel, you must bear in mind the hot climate in much of the country most of the year, the frequent rainfall in certain areas at certain times, the innumerable steep hills to be negotiated (cycling from the Dead Sea up to Jerusalem is not something I am rushing to do) and, ultimately, the fact that most drivers fail to recognise your status as a road user and will not give you room as they overtake, usually tooting loudly as they pass in either direction – a very annoying habit. Despite all this, there are a few cyclists to be seen pedalling around the Holy Land.

Hiring a bicycle locally for a few hours is not common, but Jericho, Tiberias and Eilat are places where it can be done; it's a great way to get around.

HITCHING

Hitchhiking was once a common way for locals and travellers to get around. Hitching is still possible, but not as easy as it used to be. This is probably due to the increased tensions since the intifada and, preceding that, an increase in non-political incidents where hitchhikers were abducted and killed.

Women should not hitchhike without male company. You will no doubt hear Israelis say that it is unsafe for anyone to accept lifts from Arabs, and more specifically from those cars with blue registration plates (the symbol of cars owned by residents of the Occupied Territories). A large number of Arabs live within Israel's borders and so drive cars with the standard yellow registration plates that Jews use, so telling who is who is not so easy.

As you travel around Israel you will notice what seems to be a large percentage of the army hitchhiking to and from their bases. Israelis are actively encouraged to give lifts to soldiers, so bear in mind that if you are hitchhiking you will be last in line for a lift if there are any IDF uniforms to be seen. Note that female soldiers are now forbidden to hitchhike because of the potential danger.

Finally, remember that sticking out your thumb is not the locally accepted way to advertise to drivers that you are hitchhiking. Here it means something more basic and impolite, although most locals recognise the foreigner's intentions. The local signal is to point to the road with your index finger.

TOURS

With the centuries-old tradition of pilgrimage to the Holy Land, organised tours are big business in Israel. The Ministry of Tourism ensures that prices are in line with itineraries and that the transport is up to scratch. Tours can vary between a few hours, one day, and over a week of organised sightseeing.

Egged Tours is the largest tourist carrier and they have offices in most towns (see the list under Bus in this chapter). Numerous

smaller companies compete for the remainder of the market. For details of available tours contact any tourist office or travel agent.

You will continually come across these tours in progress, and will benefit from listening in on a tour guide. Here is yet another area of controversy. Not the problem of freeloaders listening to a guide that someone else has paid for, but the law that only permits tour guides who are licensed by the Ministry of Tourism.

Major exceptions to this rule are the various Christian clergymen who lead hundreds of thousands of pilgrims around Israel. The churches maintain that their own guides are the best for their needs and that banning them would reduce the number of pilgrims. Rather than lose the good business that the Christians provide, the authorities upset the local guides by allowing the priests, vicars and monks to continue.

On the subject of tours and controversies, the Israeli guides are extremely knowledgeable about the country, its history and geography – it is often astounding how much they can tell you.

However, not all of what you hear can be taken at face value. They are an important part of Israel's unofficial public relations department, and they can offer an often

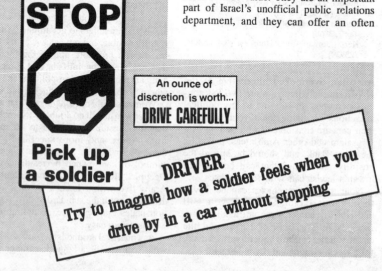

extremely biased version of the country's political status.

More and more private hostels are getting in on the tour business, with inexpensive trips geared to the traveller. It often makes sense to take these tours as they show you places that can involve more time and money getting there independently. In Jerusalem, for example, walking tours of the Old City and day trips to Jericho and the Wadi Qelt, the Dead Sea region and refugee camps are widely available.

Another development in the tour business are the 'soft adventure' tours to the Dead Sea region and the Judean and Negev deserts. Various operators offer trips that generally include a variation of 4WD excursions, hikes, rappeling and, in the Negev, camel safaris and a Bedouin cultural experience (a traditional meal and/or an overnight in a Bedouin tent). Specific information is given in the relevant chapters. Also, don't forget the SPNI's organised tours which specialise in taking you 'off the beaten track'. Even if your budget does not allow such tours, at least read their brochures and go independently to the more accessible destinations.

Hiring an independent guide locally, either for the day or for a few hours, can be good value. The official guides' standard of knowledge and languages is generally high, but do not get talked into hiring an unofficial guide unless they have been recommended by someone whose opinion you can trust.

Jerusalem

(Population: 524,500)

Jerusalem is the highly disputed capital of Israel and perhaps the most fascinating city in the world, as well as one of the most beautiful. It is also surely the holiest city of all – so many people have attached so much importance to Jerusalem, for so many different and conflicting reasons for so many years. In Hebrew it is called 'Yerushalayim' (City of Peace), in Arabic 'El Khudz' (the Holy).

Jerusalem can be divided into three parts: the walled Old City, East Jerusalem, and the New City which rapidly continues to grow around both. The Old City is the main attraction for everyone: the religious, the historian and the more casual visitor. Within its walls you will find the holiest Jewish site: the Western Wall, part of the Temple; the third-holiest Muslim site: the Haram esh-Sharif (Temple Mount), from where Mohammed rose to heaven; and the holy Christian sites of the trial of Jesus, His crucifixion, burial and resurrection. East Jerusalem, along with the Old City, was under Jordanian control until 1967. The Old City also has the Arab markets, and in East Jerusalem you could be in any modern-day Arab town. The New City is cleaner, more modern and less exotic. However, here you will find some of Israel's leading museums, the Knesset building, and most of the city's Jewish restaurants, cafés and nightlife.

History

Jerusalem's oldest part lies on the Ophel ridge between the Kidron Valley to the east and the Tyropoeon Valley to the west, and south from the Temple Mount. A small Jebusite city was mentioned in Egyptian texts of the 20th century BC, and in 997 BC the Israelite King David conquered it. By bringing to Jerusalem the Ark of the Covenant he made the city his capital. Under King Solomon, David's son, the city's boundaries extended to include the present-day Temple Mount/Haram esh-Sharif with the construction of the Temple in 950 BC. After Solomon's death in 933 BC, the city became the capital of Judah as the 12 tribes of Israel divided. In 586 BC Jerusalem fell to Nebuchadnezer, the King of Babylon, and the city, including the First Temple, was destroyed. The people of Jerusalem were exiled to Babylonia until 583 BC when the King of Persia, Cyrus, allowed them to return. The Second Temple was constructed around 520 BC and around 445 BC the city walls were rebuilt under the leadership of Nehemiah, Governor of Judah.

The next notable stage in Jerusalem's history came with Alexander the Great's conquest of the city in 331 BC. After his death eight years later, the Seleucids eventually took over until the Maccabaean revolt 30 years later. This launched the Hasmonean Dynasty who resanctified the Temple in 164 BC after it had been desecrated by the Seleucids. Jerusalem was conquered by the Romans led by General Pompey around 63 BC. In 37 BC they installed Herod the Great to rule what they called the Kingdom of Judea. The Romans resumed direct control after Herod's death, unimpressed with his son's performance, and the city was administered by a procurator. Pontius Pilate, best known for ordering the crucifixion of Jesus around 30 AD, was the fifth procurator.

About 36 years later came the First Revolt by the Jews against the Romans, but after four years of conflict the Roman General Titus triumphed. With the Second Temple destroyed and Jerusalem burnt, many Jews became slaves or exiles: it was the beginning of the Diaspora. Jerusalem continued as the capital but Emperor Hadrian decided to destroy it completely in 132 AD due to the threat of renewed Jewish national aspirations. This provoked the unsuccessful Second Revolt led by Bar Kochba, after which Jews were forbidden to enter Aelia

Capitolina, the new city built on the ruins of Jerusalem. The Aelia Capitolina is the basis for today's Old City. In 331 AD Christianity was legalised by the Roman Emperor Constantine, and his mother visited the Holy Land in search of the Christian holy places. This sparked off the building of basilicas and churches, and the city quickly grew to the size it had been under Herod the Great. Meanwhile, the Roman Empire's capital moved from Rome to Constantinople, formerly Byzantium.

The Byzantine Empire was defeated by the Persians who conquered Jerusalem in 614, led by the Caliph Omar. In 688 the Dome of the Rock was constructed on the site of the destroyed Temple. Under the early Islamic leaders, Jerusalem was a protected centre of pilgrimage for Jews and Christians as well as Muslims, but this came to an end in the 10th century. Under Caliph Hakim, non-Muslims were cruelly persecuted and churches and synagogues were destroyed, finally provoking the Crusades 90 years later.

The Crusaders took Jerusalem in 1099 from the Fatamids who had only just regained control from the Seljuks. After almost 90 years the Latin kingdom was defeated by Saladin in 1187. During that time the area had benefited from its most effective administration so far. Under Saladin, Muslims and Jews were allowed to resettle in the city. From the 13th to the 16th centuries the Mamelukes constructed a number of outstanding buildings dedicated to religious study.

Although a Muslim academic centre, Jerusalem became a relative backwater. In 1517 the Ottoman Turks defeated the Mamelukes to add Palestine to their large empire and although they, too, are remembered for their lack of efficiency in local administration, their initial impact on the city is still much admired today. The impressive Old City walls that you see now were built by their second sultan, Suleiman the Magnificent. After Suleiman, Jerusalem's rulers allowed the city, like the rest of the country, to decline. Buildings and streets were not maintained, and corruption amongst the authorities was rife.

As a result of the Turkish sultan's 1856 Edict of Toleration for all religions, Jews and Christians were again able to settle in the city. In the 1860s, inspired and largely financed by an English Jew, Sir Moses Montefiore, Jewish settlement outside the city walls began. As Jewish immigration rapidly increased, these settlements developed into what is now the New City.

After WW I Jerusalem, which had been captured by General Allenby's forces from the Turks, became the administrative capital of the British Mandate. In these times of fervent Arab and Jewish nationalism, the city became a hotbed of political tensions. Jerusalem was always the most sought-after area of the country for both the Arabs and the Jews, and the city was the stage for much terrorism and more open warfare.

After the British withdrew from Palestine, the UN became responsible for supervising the situation. Its subsequent partition plan was accepted by the Jews, but rejected by the Arabs. Jerusalem was to be internationalised, surrounded by independent Arab and Jewish states. In the 1948 War of Independence the Jordanians took the Old City and East Jerusalem, while the Jews held the New City. Patches of no-man's land separated them and the new State of Israel declared its part of Jerusalem as its capital.

For 19 years it was a divided city and Mandelbaum Gate became the official crossing point between East Jerusalem and the New City for the few who were permitted to move between them. The 1967 Six Day War saw the reunification of the whole of Jerusalem, and the Israelis began a massive programme of restoration, refurbishment and landscaping.

Controversy continues to surround the status of Jerusalem, and most countries maintain their embassies in Tel Aviv. According to Palestinians and other opponents of Israel, the Jewish State has no right to declare the city its capital and you would be unwise to underestimate the strength of this sentiment. There is a sincere resentment

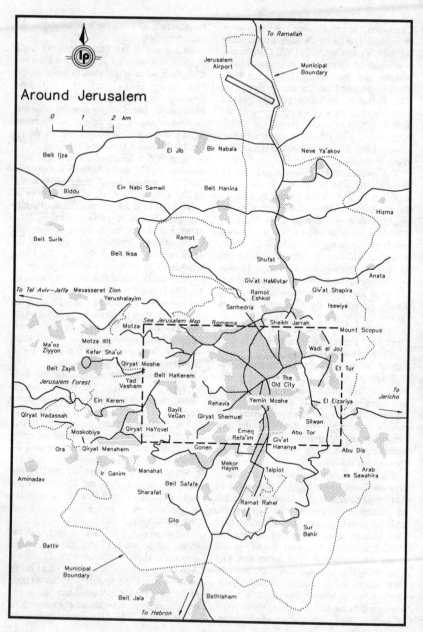

Around Jerusalem

among local Arabs of what Israel has done and continues to do, regardless of the many cosmetic changes made. The Israelis, meanwhile, are determined to keep all of Jerusalem as their capital regardless of any such opposition.

Orientation

Finding your way around Jerusalem can be confusing at first. Just remember the three basic areas, Old, East and New, and concentrate on each of them separately, rather than trying to take in the whole sprawling and bewildering mass.

Old City Definitely the main attraction and easily defined, the Old City contains 20,000 people within one sq km, behind solid and recently renovated walls. Seven gates give access to the fascinating narrow streets within. Jaffa Gate, at the end of Jaffa Rd, is the main entrance from the New City, while Damascus Gate does the job from East Jerusalem. These are two very important Old City landmarks: Haram esh-Sharif/Temple Mount, the site of the First and Second Temples, now dominated by the Dome of the Rock and El-Aqsa mosques and the Western Wall; and the Church of the Holy Sepulchre, marking the site of Jesus' crucifixion, burial and resurrection. There are numerous other religious and historical sites in the Old City, plus the popular market. Some of Jerusalem's best cheap hostels and eating places are here.

East Jerusalem This area is a compact Arab district of businesses, shops, travel agencies, moneychangers, hotels and restaurants. It is easy to find your way around when you remember that the two main streets, Nablus Rd and Salah ed-Din St, form a triangle with Suleiman St which runs alongside the northern wall of the Old City. East Jerusalem's cheap hostels and eating places are on a par with those of the Old City, and their quality and value for money make up for the lack of attractive surroundings. This district is also important to travellers because of the two Arab bus stations and the service-taxi rank.

Also in East Jerusalem are the Rockefeller Museum with its archaeological exhibits; Solomon's Quarries; the Garden Tomb, considered a possible site of Jesus' crucifixion, burial and resurrection; the Tomb of the Kings; and the Tourjeman Post Museum – a reminder of the days when this was a divided city.

New City This area is sometimes referred to as West Jerusalem, but it is no longer an accurate term due to the area's rapid expansion in virtually all directions. It is the government and commercial district and where most travellers first arrive. Your initial contact with the city is most likely to be the central bus station situated towards the northern end of Jaffa Rd, one of the New City's main streets. The city centre is basically the area in and around the triangle formed by Jaffa Rd, King George V St and Ben Yehuda St (which is linked to Jaffa Rd by Zion Square).

Most of the middle and top-end hotels and eating places are in this central area, along with the most popular cafés and bars. Others are nearer the Old City. Mahane Yehuda, the New City's cheap market, is just to the west of the central area. Moving further away from the centre to the west are the Knesset building, the Israel Museum, Yad Vashem (the Jewish State's major Holocaust memorial), and the Hadassah Medical Centre.

Other Districts Not easily slotted into the Old, East and New categories are the Mount of Olives, Mount Scopus and the Jehoshaphat and Kidron valleys which lie to the east and south of the Old City and East Jerusalem. On the Mount of Olives is the Garden of Gethsemane, the world's largest Jewish cemetery and, according to the Bible, the site of Jesus' ascension to heaven. To the north, Mount Scopus is dominated by the modern campus of the Hebrew University, adjacent to the Hadassah Hospital and the

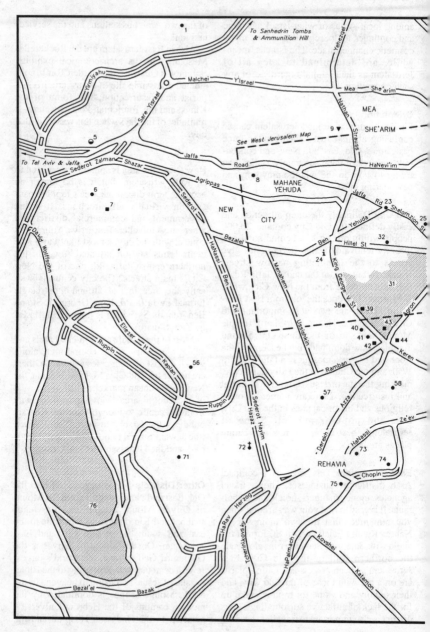

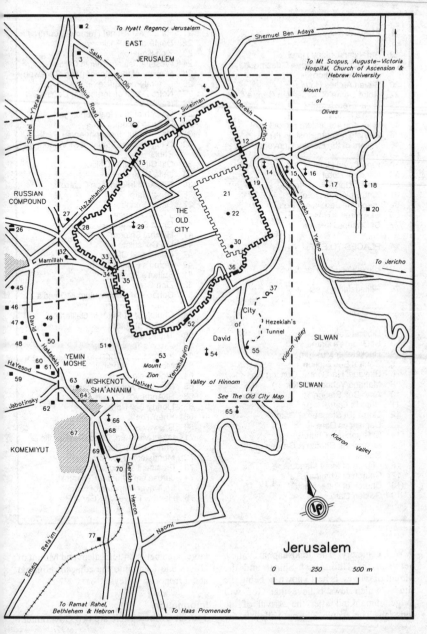

■ PLACES TO STAY

2	American Colony Hotel
3	St George's Cathedral Guesthouse
7	Jerusalem Hilton
20	Seven Arches Hotel
27	Notre Dame of Jerusalem Centre
39	Hotel Eretz Israel
42	King's Hotel
43	Sheraton Jerusalem Plaza Hotel
44	Bernstein Youth Hostel - IYHA
46	Sisters of the Rosary Convent
48	YMCA
50	King David Hotel
59	Windmill Hotel
60	Moriah Jerusalem Hotel
61	King Solomon Hotel
62	Laromme Jerusalem Hotel
66	St Andrew's Hospice
77	St Charles Hospice

▼ PLACES TO EAT

9	Bakery on Peri Hadash St
63	Cinemateque
70	Philadelphia West

OTHER

1	Biblical Zoo
3	St George's Cathedral
4	Rockefeller Museum
5	Central Bus Station
6	Binyanei Ha-Oomah Concert Hall
8	Mahane Yehuda Market
10	Arab Bus Station
11	Herod's Gate
12	Lion's (St Stephen's) Gate
13	Damascus Gate
14	St Stephen's Church
15	All Nations Church & Garden of Gethsemane
16	Church of Mary Magdalene
17	Church of Dominus Flevit
18	Church of Pater Noster
19	Golden Gate

21	Haram esh-Sharif (Temple Mount)
22	Dome of the Rock
23	Zion Square
24	West Jerusalem Tourist Office
25	Ministry of the Interior (Visa Renewal)
26	Central Post Office
27	Notre Dame of Jerusalem Centre
28	New Gate
29	Church of the Holy Sepulchre
30	El-Aqsa Mosque
31	Ha'Atzmaut (Independence) Park
32	Daughters of Charity of St Vincent de Paul
33	Old City Tourist Office
34	Jaffa Gate
35	Christian Information Centre
36	Dung Gate
37	Gihon Spring
38	Jewish Agency
40	Great Synagogue
41	Heichal Shlomo
45	US Consulate
47	Car Rental Offices
49	Herod's Family Tomb
51	Sultan's Pool
52	Zion Gate
53	Cenacle of Coenaculum & David's Tomb
54	Church of St Peter in Gallicantu
55	Pool of Shiloah
56	The Knesset
57	Jason's Tomb
58	International Christian Embassy
63	Montefiore Windmill
64	Bloomfield Garden
65	Monastery of St Onuphrius
66	St Andrew's Church
67	Liberty Bell Park
68	Khan Theatre
69	Railway Station
71	Israel Museum, Dead Sea Scrolls & Shrine of the Book
72	Monastery of the Cross
73	President's Official Residence
74	Jerusalem Sherover Theatre
75	LA Mayer Museum of Islamic Art
76	Hebrew University (Giv'at Ram)

WW I cemetery. The Jehoshaphat Valley, between the Haram esh-Sharif and the Mount of Olives, is best known as being the site at which Jews believe that God will judge humankind after the arrival of the Messiah. The scenic Kidron Valley is the larger area between Jerusalem and Mount of Olives and leads into the adjacent Hinnom and Tyropoeon valleys.

Information
Tourist Offices There are two Government

tourist information offices in Jerusalem. The head office (☎ 241281/2) is in the New City at 24 King George V St, and the Old City office (☎ 282295/6) is located just inside Jaffa Gate on the left as you enter. Both are open Sunday to Thursday 8.30 am to 5 pm, Friday 8.30 am to 2 pm, and are closed on Saturday.

The Municipal Information Office (☎ 228844) at 17 Jaffa Rd is not so well known and therefore less busy. The staff are not always too knowledgeable, but they try. It's open Sunday to Thursday 8 am to 12.30 pm, Friday 8 am to noon, and is closed on Saturday.

The Christian Information Centre (☎ 287647) is at al-Khattab Square, Old City, just inside from Jaffa Gate and to the right. They are very knowledgeable on their specialised subject and have a good selection of books. You apply here for a ticket (if you are a practising Catholic) for the Christmas Eve Midnight Mass in Bethlehem's Church of the Nativity. The centre is open Monday to Friday from 8.30 am to 12.30 pm and 3 to 6 pm (in winter until 5.30 pm), Saturday 8.30 am to 12.30 pm, and is closed on Sunday.

The Jewish Student Information Centre is at PO Box 18163, 5 Bet El St, Jerusalem 91180 (☎ 288338; 24-hour answer service 512131; extension 1792). The Jewish Quarter, Old City location (adjacent to the Hurva Synagogue) provides a lounge with refreshments, a library, evening activities, assistance with accommodation, Shabbat dinners and free tours, as well as general information for the Jewish visitor.

Post Offices The main post office and poste restante (☎ 244745) is at 23 Jaffa Rd. The main section is open Sunday to Thursday 7 am to 7 pm, Friday 7 am to noon, and is closed on Saturday. The parcel office is on the west side of the building, down the steps from Jaffa Rd, and is open Sunday to Thursday 8.30 am to 1.30 pm, Friday 8.30 am to noon, and is closed on Saturday. Poste restante closes at noon on Fridays. After hours you can send letters, telegrams and telexes from the information desk here.

During the night you'll need patience to wake up somebody, and chances are they will not speak English.

For telegrams go around to Koresh St at the rear; open Sunday to Thursday 6 am to 10 pm, Friday 6 am to 3.30 pm, and closed on Saturday. Cheaper but slower is the LT (letter telegram).

There are several branches, including one in al-Khattab Square inside Jaffa Gate in the Old City, just up from the Christian Information Centre, across from the police station; and in the Jewish Quarter, east of Batei Mahseh Square. Both are open Sunday, Monday, Tuesday and Thursday 8 am to 12.30 pm, 3.30 to 6 pm, Wednesday 8 to 1.30 pm, Friday 8 am to noon, and are closed on Saturday.

East Jerusalem's main post office is at the corner of Salah ed-Din and Suleiman Sts. It's open Sunday and Thursday 8.30 am to 2.30 pm and 4 to 6.30 pm, Monday, Wednesday and Friday 8.30 am to 12.30 pm, Tuesday 8.30 am to 2.30 pm and is closed on Saturday.

In the New City, there is a branch just off Ben Yehuda St at 6 Shamai St. It's open Sunday to Thursday 7.45 am to 2 pm, Friday 7.45 am to noon, and is closed Saturday.

International Telephones The Bezeq office is behind the main post office in Koresh St. You can use them from Sunday to Thursday 8 am to 8.45 pm, Friday 8 am to 1.45 pm, but they're closed on Saturday.

Banks & Moneychangers If you want the best deal when changing money, go to the legal moneychangers in the Old City and East Jerusalem. The two just inside Damascus Gate seem to give a better price than anywhere else. The moneychanger just inside the Petra Hostel near Jaffa Gate seems to be open when the others are closed. Other moneychangers can be found on David St, the Old City's main market street going east from Jaffa Gate, and on Salah-ed Din Street in East Jerusalem.

You will find banks on Jaffa Rd in the New City, mainly around Zion Square. Most are open Sunday to Tuesday and Thursday, 8.30 am to 12.30 pm and 4 to 5.30 pm, Wednesday and Friday 8.30 am to noon, and are closed Saturday.

The American Express office (☎ 222211) is at Meditrad Ltd, 27 King George V St, on the corner of Hillel St, opposite the New City tourist office. They will replace lost/stolen travellers' cheques, receive mail, etc; they're open Sunday to Thursday 9 am to 5 pm, but are closed Friday and Saturday.

Police Dial 100. The sensitivities involved in the policing of the Arab sections of Jerusalem do not help to make a problem-free system. Arab police seem to be responsible for basic duties in East Jerusalem and the Old City; their station is in al-Khattab Square, an old Turkish building inside Jaffa Gate and to the right. Only go there regarding incidents within the Old City walls.

For any other problems (and the Old City boys in blue will probably refer you there anyway), go to the central police station in the Russian Compound, between Jaffa Rd and HaNevi'im St in the New City. The green domes of the Russian Cathedral are a good landmark. The Lost & Found Office here deals with items lost and found in any section of the city. It's open Sunday, Tuesday and Thursday 7.30 am to 4 pm, Monday and Wednesday 7.30 am to 2 pm, Friday 9.30 am to 12.30 pm, but closes Saturday.

Consulates Although most countries maintain embassies in Tel Aviv for political reasons, many are represented in Jerusalem by consulates. They may refer you to the embassy, depending on your requirements.

Austria
    8 Hovevei Zion, New City (☎ 631291)
Belgium
    5 Bibah St, Sheikh Jarrah, East Jerusalem (☎ 828263)
Denmark
    5 Bnei Brit St, New City (☎ 228083)
France
    6 Emile Botta St, New City (☎ 231451);
    and Sheikh Jarrah, East Jerusalem (☎ 282387)

Greece
    31 Rahel Immenu, New City (☎ 633003);
    and Sheikh Jarrah, East Jerusalem (☎ 283316)
International Christian Embassy Jerusalem
    10 Brenner St, New City (☎ 669823, 699389).
Italy
    16 November St, New City (☎ 631236);
    and Sheikh Jarrah, East Jerusalem (☎ 282138)
Spain
    53 Ramban St, New City (☎ 633473)
Sweden
    58 Nablus Rd, East Jerusalem (☎ 828117)
UK
    19 Nashashibi St, Sheikh Jarrah, East Jerusalem (☎ 828281)
USA
    18 Agron St, New City (☎ 234271);and
    27 Nablus Rd, East Jerusalem (☎ 282231)

SPNI This office is at 13 Heleni HaMalka St (☎ 222357/244605). The society's head office is in what was originally a pilgrims' hospice built by the Russian Church in the 19th century. The office is open Sunday, Monday, Wednesday 9 am to 3.45 pm, Tuesday 9 am to 4.45 pm, Thursday 9 am to 5.45 pm and Friday 9 am to 12.30 pm.

Student Travel ISSTA (☎ 225258) is at 5 Eliasmar St, New City, across Jaffa Rd from Zion Square. The office is open Sunday to Tuesday and Thursday 8.30 am to 1 pm and 3 to 6 pm, Wednesday and Friday 9 am to 12.30 pm, but is closed on Saturday.

Bookshops & Libraries Steimatzsky's carry many English-language books, magazines and newspapers. In the New City they are at 39 Jaffa Rd just east of Zion Square, and 9 King George V St, east side; in the Old City they have a shop on the Cardo.

Yalkut (☎ 222786) sell second-hand books. They are at 1 Heleni HaMalka St and open Sunday to Thursday 8 am to 7 pm, Friday 8 am to 1.30 pm, but are closed on Saturday.

Also in the New City, Sefer VeSefel is upstairs at 2 Ya'Avetz St (the alley linking Jaffa Rd with Hillel St). They have a useful selection of new and used books in various languages, and a café.

The Bookstop, at 6 Yosef Du Nawas St

(off Jaffa Rd, east of Zion Square), New City, has new and used books and magazines. It's open Sunday, Monday, Wednesday and Thursday 9 am to 7 pm, Tuesday and Friday 9 am to 1.30 pm, and is closed Saturday.

In the Old City, The Bookshelf at the southern end of Hayehudim St, parallel to Habad St, above the Cardo in the Jewish Quarter, has used books. In East Jerusalem, the Universal Library Bookstore on Salah ed-Din St has a wide selection and, in particular, deals with Middle East politics and religion.

The fascinating surroundings often inspire visitors to read up on the city's history. You can find many relevant books in the British Council libraries: 31 Nablus Rd, East Jerusalem (just after the East Jerusalem YMCA) and 3 Ethiopia St, off HaNevi'im St; they are open Monday to Friday 9.30 am to 6 pm and Saturday 9.30 am to 1 pm. Both stock English newspapers and magazines as well.

Swimming Pools Some of the luxury hotels have pools but for residents only. There are several public pools in the New City. The YMCA (☎ 227111) at 26 King David St has a small indoor pool which is open to non-members at differing times. It is, however, dependent on a confusing schedule of sessions for men only, children only, members only and anybody only. The Beit Taylor pool (☎ 414362) in Qiryat Yovel is open daily 9 am to 5 pm (Egged bus Nos 18 or 24).

The Jerusalem Swimming Pool (☎ 63 2092) on Emek Refaim St is open daily 8 am to 5 pm (Egged bus Nos 4 or 18). The last two charge US$1.80 Sunday to Friday but US$4.20 on Saturday. Kibbutz Ramat Rahel (☎ 702555), just two km from the city, charges US$6 for nonresidents to use its popular pool.

Other For camera repairs, try Kerenor (☎ 240674) at 5 Ben Yehuda St, New City.

There are a number of laundromats in the New City. Superclean Rehavia is at 26 Ussishkin St – get there on Egged bus No 19 from the city centre. Superclean Geulah, 1

Ezer Yoldot St, is the closest to East Jerusalem and the Old City. In the Mea She'arim district you walk west from the intersection of Mea She'arim and Strauss Sts and it's the first alley on the left.

Bakah Washmatic is at 35 Emek Refaim St, south of the centre. Take Egged bus Nos 4, 14 or 18, get off at the Emek Refaim post office and it's a half block further down and across the street.

Camping equipment can be bought or rented from Orha (☎ 226665), at 22 Nahalat Shiva, in the alley off 27 Yoel Salomon St. Two-person tents cost around US$15 per week, a snorkel and mask US$8 per week.

The Jerusalem Syndrome

Each year dozens of foreign visitors to Jerusalem simply go mad, overwhelmed by the impact of the Holy City's historical and religious heritage.

Most of them touch down at Ben-Gurion Airport with a mental history of their own. The belief that they are a biblical character, anything from the Messiah to the Devil, or that they have the solution to world peace and should reveal all right here, is the basis for what has become known as the Jerusalem Syndrome. About a quarter of those cases on file, though, had no previous psychiatric record.

Located on the outskirts of West Jerusalem, the government psychiatric hospital Kefar Shaul receives most of these cases. These include the Canadian Jew who, claiming to be Samson, decided to prove his ID by smashing through the wall of his room to escape. An elderly American Christian woman attending a religious college here believed she was the Virgin Mary. She went to Bethlehem to look for the baby Jesus and invited anyone who would listen to His birthday party. In perhaps the most serious case, an Australian Christian man set fire to El-Aqsa Mosque, causing considerable damage. He believed that he had to clear the Temple Mount of such non-Christian buildings to prepare for the Messiah.

The most recent case to make the headlines was in spring 1992 when an American Christian man went into a violent rage in the Church of the Holy Sepulchre. Before the security guards were able to subdue him, he had smashed lamps and icons and torn down the cross at the 12th Station, the traditional site of the crucifixion of Jesus.

The Jerusalem Syndrome is nothing new. In the 1930s, an English Christian woman was certain that Christ's Second Coming was imminent and would regularly climb Mount Scopus to welcome Him back to earth with a cup of tea.

Christian syndrome cases tend to break down at such traditional sites as the Mount of Olives, the Via

Dolorosa or the Garden Tomb, and identify with such characters as Jesus or the Virgin Mary, with John the Baptist apparently the most popular. In addition to Samson, Jewish cases involve Moses, King David, and other prophets and Old Testament characters. They normally proclaim themselves at the Western Wall, David's Tomb, and at the Jewish cemetery on the Mount of Olives. Muslim cases are not discussed much, probably due to security concerns.

As with everything else in Israel, opinions vary on what causes the syndrome. Some say that these people arrive in Jerusalem hoping to find peace, calm and to get away from their troubles back home. Instead, all they find is the conflict and tension and their minds snap. Others see these cases as people who come anticipating that the Holy City will somehow affect them or fulfil their spiritual needs, and they simply lose control. Although their ages and backgrounds vary, there is a trend of the syndrome affecting unmarried 20 to 30 year old Christians and Jews from North America and Western Europe who grew up in religious homes. Men seem to outnumber women two to one.

Treatment of the Jerusalem Syndrome cases tends to take the form of observation until the patient is deemed well enough to be flown home. In most cases, this takes a week or so. Doctors at Kefar Shaul have found it virtually pointless trying to persuade them that they are not who they claim to be. The hospital cites the example of two patients, both claiming to be the Messiah. Put together, each accused the other of being the imposter.

Old City

The Old City is divided into five areas – the Armenian Quarter, the Christian Quarter, the Muslim Quarter, the Jewish Quarter and the Haram esh-Sharif/Temple Mount – which in practical terms are not always so easy to define. Regardless of the current political status of Jerusalem, the Old City remains predominantly Arab.

Three of the four quarters of the Old City were never strictly defined districts or ghettos, and their boundaries changed with population shifts. The exception is the Armenian Quarter, which has remained within its boundaries. Controversy rages in particular over the status of the Muslim Quarter and the Jewish Quarter. This is due to Jews purchasing property in the Muslim Quarter to escape the overcrowded Jewish Quarter, a move

which started in the 1830s. They seem to have peacefully co-existed with the locals there for over 100 years until the Arab riots of 1936-39 forced them to leave.

Today there exists a minority Jewish movement, 'Ateret Cohanim', whose aim is to encourage an understanding of the historical and geographical importance of these former Jewish properties in the Muslim Quarter, and to return them to Jewish ownership and occupation. They argue that Jews were forcibly driven out of their homes which were taken over by Arab 'squatters'. They claim that the Muslim Quarter was only given this title by the British in 1936 and that those buildings previously occupied by Jews should be returned to Jews.

Critics point to the far larger number of Arabs who lost their homes as a result of Jewish aggression in the establishment of the State of Israel. For more information about the Jewish argument and details about their free guided tours of the area, contact Ateret Cohanim (☎ 895101).

The intifada has inspired regular strike days when Arab establishments remain closed for an entire day or only open in the morning. Check the current strike schedule to avoid finding the Old City inactive rather than in action.

WALLS & GATES

The current walls are the legacy of Suleiman the Magnificent. Built between 1537-42, they have since been renovated. The north wall was built first, followed by the east and west sides. The completion of the south wall is believed to have been delayed due to a dispute over whether or not Mount Zion should be included within the walled city. The authorities were not prepared to foot the considerable bill for extending the wall for the sake of including the Cenacle, containing the Room of the Last Supper, and insisted that the Franciscans pay for it. They had no money and so the wall excluded Mount Zion. Suleiman was said to have been angry enough to have the architects beheaded, showing perhaps that he intended his walls to honour and protect all of the city's prominent holy places.

There were six new gates in his walls and there are similarities in their style despite alterations to three of them. Jaffa, Damascus and Zion Gates still have their indirect entrances. This L-shape was designed to break the momentum of an attacking charge on horseback. Try to make a point of entering/leaving the Old City from all of the seven accessible gates during your stay in Jerusalem to be able to see as much as possible. Given official names originally, the gates' current names vary according to language and religion.

Ramparts Walk

One of the best ways to see the Old City and also its surroundings is to stroll around the ramparts. Up here you will benefit from views across the city's rooftops to East and New Jerusalem and the surrounding hills to see aspects that pass unnoticed from street level. Be careful – despite additional paving and guardrails, the stone can be slippery underfoot. Women should not go unaccompanied, due to the frequency of sexual assaults and thefts. Due to religious and security considerations, the walls around Haram esh-Sharif/Temple Mount are strictly out of bounds and are not part of the Ramparts Walk.

The walk is divided into sections: Jaffa Gate-Damascus Gate, the Citadel-Zion Gate and Zion Gate-Dung Gate. On my last visit, the Damascus Gate-St Stephen's Gate section was closed for security reasons due to tensions stemming from the intifada. Opening hours are Saturday to Thursday 9 am to 4 pm, and Friday and holiday eves 9 am to 2 pm. The Citadel-Zion Gate section is open until 9.30 pm Sunday to Thursday. Tickets cost US$1.40 (students US$0.65) and are valid for four admissions over two days (three at the weekend), allowing you to do the walk gradually. Note that tickets cannot be purchased on Saturday.

Finding the ramparts walk is not always easy. At Jaffa Gate access is up the stairs on the left as you enter the Old City. The Citadel

stairway is outside Jaffa Gate. Zion Gate's is in the gate itself, but Damascus Gate can be the most confusing. You must enter through the ancient carriage-way to the east (left) from the amphitheatre-styled plaza outside and underneath the gate, which is reached by following the steps from the west (right). At Lion's/St Stephen's Gate the stairway, if open, joins the walk just before it stops north of the Temple Mount/Haram esh-Sharif.

Jaffa Gate

Restored courtesy of South African Jewry, this was the start of the old road to Jaffa, when it was Jerusalem's port, and was the main route for traffic to and from the city. The Arabic name for the gate is its original one, Bab el-Khalil (Gate of the Friend). This refers to the holy city Hebron (El-Khalil in Arabic), named after Abraham 'the Friend of God'. In Hebrew it is Sha'ar Yafo. There used to be a wall between the gate and the Citadel but it was pulled down and the moat was filled in by the Turkish Sultan Abdul Hamid in 1898 to permit Kaiser Wilhelm II and his party to ride into the city. Just inside the gate behind a wrought-iron fence are two graves believed to be those of the architects beheaded by Suleiman for leaving Mount Zion outside the walls.

The Citadel – Tower of David

The Citadel's minaret and towers dominate

The Citadel

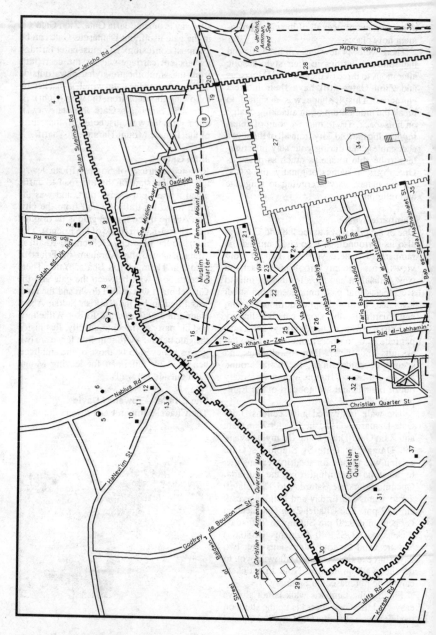

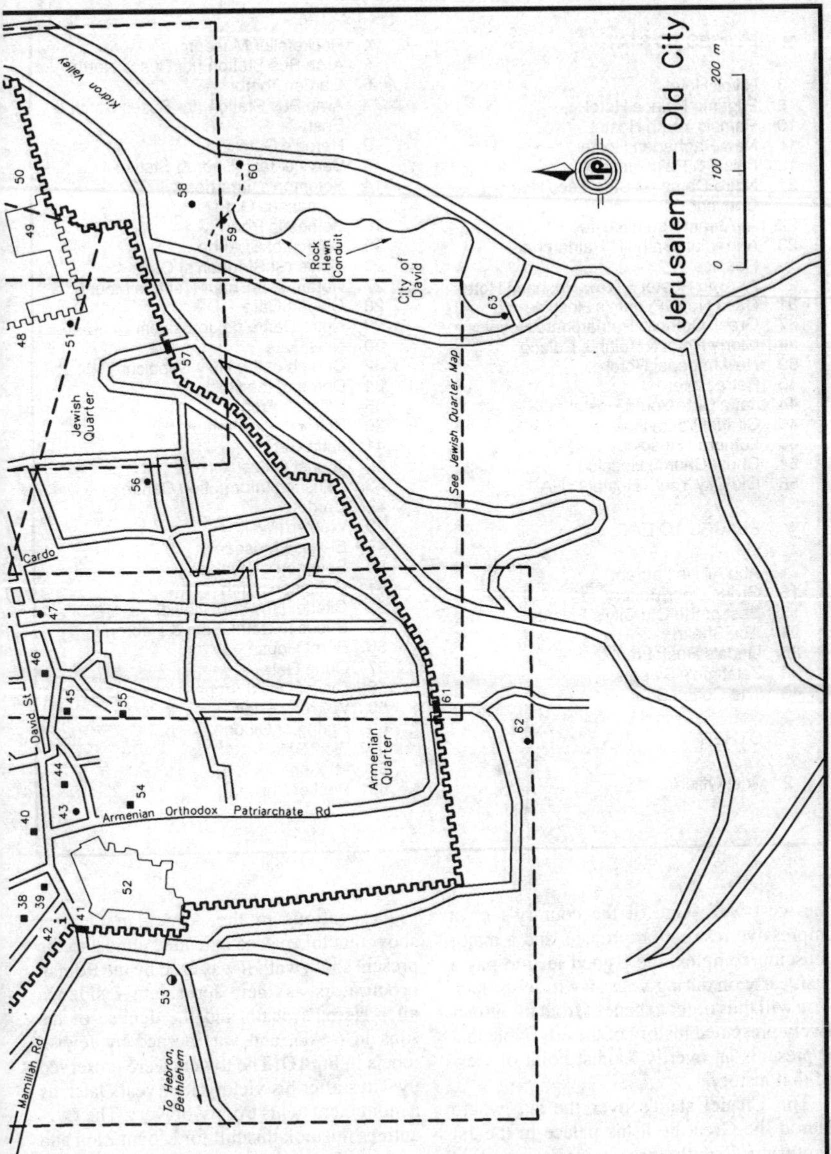
Jerusalem – Old City
0
100
200 m
Kidron Valley
Rock Hewn Conduit
City of David
See Jewish Quarter Map
Jewish Quarter
Armenian Quarter
Cardo
David St
Armenian Orthodox Patriarchate Rd
Mamillah Rd
To Hebron, Bethlehem
38
39
40
41
42
43
44
45
46
47
48
49
50
51
52
53
54
55
56
57
58
59
60
61
62
63

■ PLACES TO STAY

3	Rivoli Hotel
8	Pilgrims Palace Hotel
10	Ramsis Youth Hostel
11	New Raghadan Hostel
12	Faisal & Palm Hostels
21	Notre Dame de Sion Ecco Homo Convent
22	Al-Ahram Youth Hostel
23	Armenian Catholic Patriarchate Hospice
25	Al-Arab Hostel & New Hashami Hotel
31	Casa Nova Pilgrim's Hospice
37	Greek Catholic Patriarchate Hospice
38	Gloria Hotel & Knights Palace
39	New Imperial Hotel
40	Petra Hotel
44	Jaffa Gate Youth Hostel
45	Citadel Youth Hostel
46	Lutheran Hospice
54	Christ Church Hospice
55	Old City Youth Hostel-IYHA

▼ PLACES TO EAT

1	Abu Ali Restaurant
16	Green Door Bakery
17	Best of the Old City's Felafel
24	Abu Shukri
26	Linda's Restaurant
33	Zalatimo's Sweets
43	The Coffee Shop

OTHER

2	Post Office

4	Rockefeller Museum
5	Arab Bus Station (for Buses North)
6	Garden Tomb
7	Arab Bus Station (for Buses South & East)
9	Herod's Gate
13	Service-Taxi (Sherut) Station
14	Solomon's Quarries
15	Damascus Gate
18	Bethesda Pool
19	Church of St Anne
20	Lion's (St Stephen's) Gate
27	Haram esh-Sharif (Temple Mount)
28	Golden Gate
29	Notre Dame de Jerusalem
30	New Gate
32	Church of the Holy Sepulchre
34	Dome of the Rock
35	Wilsons Arch
36	Kidron Valley Tombs
41	Jaffa Gate
42	Tourist Office
43	Christian Information Centre
47	Cardo
48	Western Wall
49	El-Aqsa Mosque
50	Solomon's Stables
51	Robinsons Arch
52	Citadel (Tower of David)
53	Buses to Bethlehem & Hebron
56	Burnt House
57	Dung Gate
58	City of David Archaeological Garden
59	Warrens Shaft
60	Spring of Gihon
61	Zion Gate
62	Mt Zion
63	Pool of Shiloah

the west wall. One of the country's most impressive restoration projects and a major museum complex, it's a good idea to pay a visit early on during your stay in Jerusalem. You will thus order to benefit from the attractively presented history of the city. Note that it presents an overtly Zionist point of view of that history.

The Citadel stands over the site where Herod the Great built his palace in the 1st century BC with three towers named in memory of his friend, Hippicus, his brother Phasael and his wife, Mariamne.

Excavations in the Armenian Quarter show that this palace extended almost to the present south wall. It was used by the Roman procurators as their Jerusalem residence after Herod's death and the demise of his sons in 6 AD, and was burned by Jewish rebels in 66 AD. The towers were preserved by Titus after his victory four years later, as a monument to his troops' bravery. The Byzantines mistook this hill for Mount Zion and presumed that this was David's palace – hence the name David's Tower for the one previously named Phasael. The complex was then fully incorporated into the city walls but its status during the next few centuries is uncertain.

The Crusader kings of Jerusalem used it as their residence from 1128, followed by Saladin in 1187 when he took the city. The fortress took on its present form in 1310 under the Mameluke Sultan Malik an-Nasir. The Crusader walls were retained but the old city wall which had divided the interior was levelled. The outer gateway, stone bridge and western terrace were added by Suleiman the Magnificent between 1531 and 1538. The prominent minaret was added in 1655.

Museum of the History of Jerusalem The complex includes this popular museum, which uses computerised graphics, holograms and videos as well as regular models and dioramas to portray the city's history. An impressive model of the city, made in 1873, a multi-screen film show and the Museum of Modern Religious Dress, with small figures wearing examples of Jerusalem's various cultural, religious and ethnic groups, are among the attractions.

The entrance to the Citadel is just inside Jaffa Gate, around to the right as you enter the Old City, and it is open Sunday to Thursday 10 am to 5 pm, and Friday, Saturday and holidays 10 am to 4 pm. Admission is US$4.80 (students US$4).

It seems that every important historical site feels a need to put on a sound & light show. The Citadel joins the club with a production of questionable quality. However good you think the show is, you are liable to shiver all the way through it if you don't wrap up warmly – Jerusalem evenings are often surprisingly cold, even in the summer months. The show is presented in various languages, from April to October, Saturday to Thursday evenings.

Damascus Gate
The most attractive gate and, except on strike days, the most crowded. Its Arabic name is Bab el-Amud (Gate of the Column), after the column erected by the Roman Emperor

Hadrian nearby. The Christians called it Damascus Gate as it marked the start of the road to Syria's capital. The Hebrew name is Sha'ar Shechem (Nablus Gate), as the same road passed the Jewish capital of Samaria. This is the only gate that has been excavated and the whole area has been refurbished. By the entrance to the ramparts walk is the Roman Square excavation, open daily from 9 am to 5 pm for a mere US$0.35.

A copy of the Madaba map is displayed. Found in Madaba, Jordan, it depicts Jerusalem in the Byzantine period, and it has been of great help to archaeologists. The museum's plaza is original, but the missing column is represented by a hologram.

Herod's Gate
In Hebrew Sha'ar HaPerahim, its Arabic name is Bab ez-Zahra (the Flowered Gate). The present name came about when 16th and 17th-century pilgrims believed a Mameluke house, now within the Franciscan Monastery of the Flagellation, to be Herod Antipas' palace. It was here that the Crusaders first established themselves in the Old City on 15 July 1099.

Lion's/St Stephen's Gate
Although Suleiman called it Bab el-Ghor (the Jordan Gate), the name never stuck and it became known as St Stephen's Gate after the fall of the Crusaders in 1187, in reference to the first Christian martyr who was stoned nearby. Initially, the Christians called the present Damascus Gate by this name, but the Arabs would only let Christian pilgrims leave the city by the gate facing the Mount of Olives, so the name was moved.

The Hebrew name, Sha'ar HaPerahim (Lion's Gate), refers to the heraldic emblems of the Mameluke Sultan Baybars, reused by Suleiman. Legend has it that they represent the lions which would have eaten Suleiman's father if he had implemented his plan to level the city. The British removed the original back wall to allow cars to enter what leads into the Via Dolorosa, the Way of the Cross.

Dung Gate

Its Hebrew name is Sha'ar HaAshpot and theories about its current name include one that it resulted from the debris from the various occasions when the city was destroyed, and another that the area above the wall around the gate was the local rubbish dump. Its Arabic name is Bab el-Magharbeh (the Gate of the Moors) because North African immigrants lived nearby in the 16th century. The gate was widened by the Jordanians during their occupation of the city (1948-67) to allow cars to enter. Notice the small Ottoman arch showing how the original gate was smaller.

Zion Gate

In Hebrew Sha'ar Ziyyon, this became known in Arabic as Bab Kharet el-Yahud (Gate of the Jewish Quarter) in late medieval times. Today the many bullet marks are signs of the fierce fighting that took place in the area during the 1948 War of Independence.

New Gate

In Hebrew Sha'ar HeHadash and Arabic Bab al-Jadid, this is the most recent gate, opened in 1887 by Sultan Abdul Hamid to improve access to the Old City from the new settlements developing outside the north wall.

Golden Gate

Uncertainty surrounds this sealed entrance to the Temple Mount. The Mishnah mentions

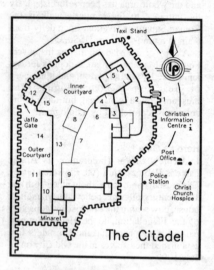

The Citadel

1   A plaque by the ornamental outer gate commemorates General Allenby accepting the surrender of Jerusalem from the Ottoman Governor in 1917.
2   Leading to the entrance, the 16th-century stone bridge to the barbican spans the moat, now partially filled in.
3   The angled main gate is Mameluke.
4   You enter the courtyard via this 14th-century hexagonal room.
5   Climb the outside stairs to the Phasael Tower's roof to get a great view of the excavations below and of the whole Old City and its surroundings.
6   These walls were built to hold the rubble Herod used to create the esplanade on which he built his palace.
7   The 2nd-century BC Hasmonaean wall held the network walls to the west and had two towers.
8   This tower's orientation was altered in the Middle Ages.
9   However, this tower's original masonry is still visible.
10 Mameluke mosque.
11 A Crusader gate was here and a wall led to the middle of the north-western tower.
12 This tower's exclusively medieval foundations make it impossible to identify it with the Herodian towers, Hippicus or Mariamne.
13 The Mamelukes moved this west wall inwards.
14 Suleiman the Magnificent built the outer wall...
15 ...and this gate

the Temple's eastern gate and there are Herodian elements in the present structure. Some believe it to be where Ezekiel 44:1-3 claims the Messiah will enter the city. The gate was probably sealed by the Muslims in the 7th century to deny access to the Haram esh-Sharif to non-Muslims. It was known as the Beautiful Gate, but the Greek word for beautiful, *horain*, was confused with the Latin word for golden, *aurea*.

A popular theory explaining why the gate was sealed is that the Muslims did it to prevent the Jewish Messiah from entering the Haram. It is said that the Muslim cemetery was put here because they believe that the Jewish Messiah will be a Cohen, and they are not allowed to enter cemeteries. The Jews, however, believe that their Messiah will be a descendant of King David and will, therefore, be able to cross the cemetery

MARKETS

The Old City's markets dominate the narrow streets and are one of its major attractions. The two most direct access points to the market areas are via Jaffa Gate from the New City and through Damascus Gate from East Jerusalem.

From Jaffa Gate, the main street going straight ahead and down is David St. This first section is the most touristy market area. The street continues right up to the Haram, becoming Bab el-Silsila St along the way. Various streets branch northwards from David St. The first is Christian Quarter Rd, full of the regular souvenir shops but with an emphasis on religious items in the immediate vicinity of the Church of the Holy Sepulchre. South-east of the traditional site of Calvary is the **Muristan Market**, which is usually less crowded than the other markets and specialises in leather goods, clothes and carpets. The Christian Quarter has several quiet backstreets with shops selling Christian literature and icons.

Descending along David St you come to the food markets. The huge rooms on the left, with some fruit and vegetable stalls inside, date from the Second Crusade. Heading

north just past here is a narrow trio of streets, the third of which soon turns west into the second. This area is the most crowded centre of the markets, with a combination of intrigued tourists and locals shopping for everyday items such as food and hardware. The first street is lined with that stomach-churning spectacle, the Oriental butchers and is named Suq el-Lahhamin (the **Butchers' Market**). The next street is Suq el-Attarin and the clothes market here is known as Suq el-Hauratjat (**Gentlemen's Market**).

Continuing along David St you follow a bend where it becomes Bab el-Silsila St (Gate of the Chain St) and end up at the Haram esh-Sharif. Turning south where David St ends brings you into the Jewish Quarter and a swift change in the surroundings. The old, dark, narrow streets are replaced by newly restored, bright and generally cleaner streets.

Dominating the Jewish Quarter's market is the reconstructed **Cardo**, which has not pleased everyone with its new look as an up-market mall complete with expensive

Tamar hindi vendor, Jerusalem

jewellers, furriers, leatherware and boutiques. From David St, one entrance takes
you directly into the Cardo, another takes
you up some steps to Habad St west of
(before) the Cardo and HaYehudim St slopes
up east of (behind) it.

At Damascus Gate you will often find a
market outside the Old City in the piazza.
Once you have made your way through the
gate, you are in a wide sloping street,
crowded with people and vendors selling a
variety of food, hardware and toys, but rarely
souvenirs. The shops are mainly cafés or sell
luggage and electrical goods.

Down the slope are two main streets
branching south-east (left) and south-west
(right). To your left is El-Wad Rd, lined with
vast showrooms of brass items such as coffee
pots and trays; sweet shops, vegetable stalls
and an egg stall amongst the souvenirs. The
road leads directly to the Western Wall, along
the way crossing the Via Dolorosa. The
section of the Via Dolorosa heading uphill to
the west (right) is crowded with Christian
pilgrims, tour groups and shoppers battling
for the right of way. Souvenir shops line the
route, with ceramics the speciality.

Back at Damascus Gate, the road branching south-west (right) is Suq Khan ez-Zeit St
and is busier than El-Wad Rd as the locals
flock to do their regular shopping. Fruit,
vegetables, sweets, hardware and oriental
spice and nut shops with their full sacks
prominently displayed, dominate this market
area. This road runs all the way to the bottom
of David St, crossing the Via Dolorosa and
passing the Dabbaga Rd turn-off for the
Church of the Holy Sepulchre and the
Muristan Market.

At this junction is one end of the butchers'
street, Suq el-Lahhamin. To the east (left) of
the main junction is a very photogenic Arab
café, usually full of locals wearing kaffiyeh
and smoking hubble-bubble pipes.

This section of Suq Khan ez-Zeit St is
dominated by confectionery shops (which
specialise in halvah), cafés and a fruit juice
bar. Khan ez-Zeit means Inn of the Olive Oil,
but its numerous eating places and their
strong odours of questionable quality

inspired the Crusaders to call it Rue de
Malcuisinat or Bad Cookery Street.

HARAM ESH-SHARIF/TEMPLE MOUNT

Dominating the whole country, not just the
Old City, this beautiful, vast and holiest of
esplanades is something of a contrast to the
noise and congestion of the surrounding
narrow streets. Holy to Jews, Muslims and
Christians, the area is considered to be
Mount Moriah, the site of Abraham's sacrifice (Genesis 22:2-19). The word 'moriah' is
derived from the Hebrew word *mora* (awe)
and can also be derived from the Hebrew
word *orah* (light), and some believe that
when the world was created and God said
'Let there be light', the light first shone over
this area. 'Moriah' is also interpreted as 'my
guide is God'.

The Old Testament later tells of David's
desire to build a house for God (2 Samuel
7:1-17), his purchase of the threshing floor
of Arounah (2 Samuel 24:18-25), construction of the Temple of Solomon (1 Kings 5 &
6), its dedication (1 Kings 8), the prophet
Isaiah's vision in the Temple (Isaiah 6:1-8),
God's threats regarding the sins of people
(Jeremiah 7:1-15), Ezekiel's vision on idolatry (Ezekiel 8), the destruction of the
Temple by Nebuchadnezer (II Kings 25), the
vision of the future Temple (Ezekiel 40 & 44)
and its reconstruction and dedication (Ezra
4).

The New Testament mentions the Temple
in its coverage of the birth of John the Baptist
(Luke 1:5-25), Jesus' presentation in the
Temple (Luke 2:22-28) and his parents
finding him there (Luke 2:40-42), the
Devil's temptation of Jesus (Luke 4:9-12),
Jesus throwing the traders from the Temple
(Matthew 21:12-17), Jesus meeting with the
man he had cured at Bethzatha (John 5:14),
Jesus teaching in the Temple (John 7:14-53),
his invitation to those who had not sinned to
throw the first stone (John 8:2-11), Jesus
saying that the sheep hear his voice (John
10:22-39), the Jewish leaders' 'plot' against
Jesus (John 11:45-53); the widow's mite
(Mark 12:41-44), the prophecy of the

Temple's ruin (Matthew 24:1-25), the return of the 30 silver coins by Judas (Matthew 27:2-10) and the Temple's veil torn in two (Matthew 27:52).

The Haram is a walled area within the Old City walls, and there are eight access gates plus the sealed Golden Gate. Although you can leave the compound by any of them, non-Muslims are only allowed to enter through two: Moors' Gate, the gate just south of the Western Wall; and Chain Gate, at the eastern end of Bab el-Silsila Rd (HaShashelet Rd). Observant Jews do not visit the Haram because the original Holy of Holies was out of bounds to all Jews except the High Priests on Yom Kippur. As no-one knows the exact location of the Holy of Holies, the Chief Rabbinate has ruled that the entire Temple Mount is out of bounds. Some rabbis disagree, saying that Jews need only avoid the vicinity of the Dome of the Rock and that the rest of the Haram, including El-Aqsa Mosque, can be visited.

Entrance to the Haram itself is free, but to visit the two mosques (highly recommended) and the museum, tickets must be purchased. Visiting hours are slightly confusing as they are based around Muslim prayer schedules, which depend on the lunar calendar.

Basically, the Haram is open Saturday to Thursday (closed Friday) 8 am to 3 pm, although those inside by then are allowed to stay until 4 pm. During prayers (approximately 11.30 am to 12.30 pm winter and 12.30 to 1.30 pm summer), the museum shuts and entry to the mosques is for Muslims only. Note also that during the month of Ramadan the area is only open from 8 to 11 am.

You are not allowed to enter the Haram unless suitably dressed, and although long robes are usually available for those with bare legs and arms, you should dress appropriately out of respect. All bags are searched on entry to the Haram and once inside you should proceed quietly in one of the holiest of holy places. There are patrols of plain-clothed Muslim guards, uniformed Arab police and IDF soldiers, and couples will be loudly accosted if they so much as hold hands.

In addition, certain unmarked areas are strictly off-limits and if you stray, even unintentionally, you will be lectured and perhaps even arrested. Stay away from the sides of the El-Aqsa Mosque, the Solomon's stables corner and the garden on the east side.

Tickets for the mosques and the museum are sold from two kiosks. The main one is between El-Aqsa Mosque and the museum – the kiosk by Chain Gate is not always open. Tickets for admission to both mosques and the museum are US$3.60 (students US$2.40). Note that in addition to having to remove your footwear to enter the mosques, all bags and cameras must be left outside, too. You might want to leave bags and cameras with the museum security desk.

Islamic Museum

Personally, I find this collection of Islamic designs quite interesting, but many seem to disagree. However, admission is included in the price of your ticket to the mosques, so you might as well take a look. Exhibits include architectural pieces from various mosques, weaponry, textiles, ceramics, manuscripts, glassware and coins.

El-Aqsa Mosque

For the best effect, it is better to visit El-Aqsa Mosque before you visit the spectacular Dome of the Rock. Believed by some to have originally been the 6th-century Crusader Church of St Mary converted into a mosque, it is known to Jews as Midrash Shlomo (School of King Solomon). Muslims maintain that it was built in the 10th century to confirm that Jerusalem is the 'furthest sanctuary' from where Mohammed began his Night Journey. Now the country's largest mosque, it is used as the main prayer mosque in preference to the Dome of the Rock.

The columns, ceiling, carpets and stained glass windows dominate the mosque's interior. The large glacial marble columns, donated by Mussolini, and the ceiling's paint job, courtesy of Egypt's King Farouk, were

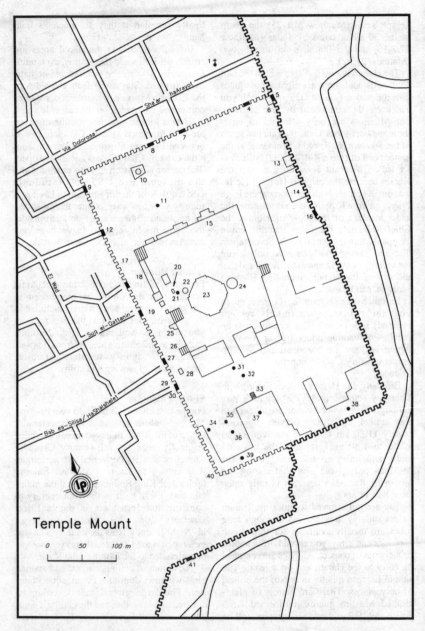

Sha'ar haArayot

Via Dolorosa

El Wad

Suq el-Qattanin

Bab es-Silsila / HaShalshelet

Temple Mount

0   50   100 m

1 Church of St Anne's
2 Lions Gate (St Stephen's Gate)
3 Tourist Entrance
4 El-Asbat Gate
5 Gate of the Tribes
6 Herodian Tower
7 Remission Gate
8 King Faisal's Gate
9 Gate of the Bani Ghanim
10 Throne of Jesus
11 Herodian Pavement of Temple
     Courtyard
12 Prison Gate
13 Solomon's Throne
14 Muslim Cemetery
15 The Scales
16 Golden Gate
17 Small or Hidden Wall
18 Iron Gate
19 Gate of the Cotton Merchants
20 Dome of the Ascension
21 Tickets
22 Dome of the Prophet
23 Dome of the Rock
24 Dome of the Chain
25 Meddressa Sultaniyya
26 Medressa Shrafiya
27 Chain Gate
28 Fountain of Sultan Qaytbay
29 Wilsons Arch
30 Tourist Entrance/Moors' Gate
31 Olive Tree of the Prophet
32 El-Kas (The Cup)
33 Steps to Ancient Aqsa
34 Islamic Museum
35 Tickets
36 Dome of Joseph
37 El-Aqsa Mosque
38 Solomon's Stables
39 Women's Mosque
40 Robinson's Arch
41 Dung Gate

on high' to restore the Jewish Temple (see
The Jerusalem Syndrome earlier).

Solomon's Stables

Turn right as you leave El-Aqsa Mosque, to
see this south-eastern corner which is
believed to be the site of the Temple's pinna-
cle where Jesus was tempted by the Devil
(Matthew 4:5). However, this is one of the
off-limits areas, so stay away. A stairway
leads down to a large underground area
which has nothing to do with Solomon.
Twelve rows of pillars support the esplanade
above, and Muslim fears of Jewish terrorist
attacks on the area (attempts have been
made) are the cause of their sensitivity.
Access is said to be possible to the diplomatic among you, keen enough to persuade
an official of the Supreme Muslim Council
to send someone with a key. The council
office is near the Ribat Ala ed-Din el-Basir
building in Tariq Bab en-Nazir (Tariq Bab
el-Habs) street in the Mameluke area.

Dome of the Rock

Head past El-Kas Pool, where Muslims wash
before prayers, and up the steps towards the
Dome of the Rock. Also known as the
Mosque of Omar, it was built between 688-
691 by the Ommayad Khalif Abdul Malik
ibn Marwan. Popular Arab tradition suggests
that its purpose was to commemorate
Mohammed's ascension to heaven but this is
contradicted by the more recent Dome of the
Ascension (Qubbat el-Miraj) nearby. A more
cynical theory suggests that it was built to
overshadow the Christian churches in the
vicinity which were attracting Arab converts
impressed by such images of power.

The mosque's design is based on mathe-
matical dimensions related to the centre
circle drawn around the rock inside. It com-
pares with the Mausoleum of Diocletian in
Split, Yugoslavia, built in 303, and in principle with 6th-century churches in Syria.

Inside the mosque is the sacred rock upon
which Abraham prepared to sacrifice his son,
Isaac, and from which Mohammed began his
Night Journey.

the result of the 1938-42 restoration programme. Nothing much remains from the
original construction which was twice
destroyed by earthquakes in its first 60 years.
Saladin provided the mihrab decoration in
1187 along with what was a magnificent
carved wood pulpit.

The latter was destroyed in a fire in 1969
which was started by an Australian Christian
fanatic who acted in the name of a 'call from

Dome of the Rock

In one corner there is supposed to be his footprint and nearby is a box containing what are believed to be hairs from his beard. The interior of the dome is masterfully covered in gold-dominated mosaics, produced by Syrian Christians. Crosses on some of the columns in the centre circle were borrowed from churches. The carved ceilings on either side of the octagon are a 13th-century addition, and the Mameluke star is the dominant motif.

The cave under the rock is called Bir el-Arwah (Well of Souls) with the voices of the dead supposedly combining with the sounds of the lower rivers of paradise as they plunge into eternity. Tradition has it that the rock marks the world's centre. After the mosque was completed, El-Malek had an inscription made, saying that he had built it and giving the date. Two hundred years later the Abbasid Caliph al-Mamun named the inscription to claim credit for the construction but neglected to alter the original date.

Suleiman the Magnificent had what remained of the original mosaics removed, replacing them with his own tiles. The external mosaics were renewed in 1963. The prominent dome was originally gold, but this was eventually melted down to pay the caliph's debts. At the time of writing, the convincing aluminium bronze alloy is being replaced with a new copper base gilded with gold leaf.

The attractive arcades at the top of the eight stairways leading to the Dome of the Rock's esplanade are called *maurazin* (scales) in Arabic. This is based on the belief that on the Last Day the scales of judgement will be suspended here to weigh the hearts of people against truth. The two on the south side are the oldest (10th century) and the newest is 15th century.

Dome of the Chain

This is the smaller version of the Dome of the Rock, in the exact centre of the Haram. Mystery surrounds the reason for its construction. A popular theory is that it was a trial-run for the real thing; another is that it was the Haram's treasury. Its name comes from the legend that Solomon hung a chain from the dome and those who swore falsely whilst holding it were struck by lightning. This perhaps confirms the treasury theory, with superstitious fear a good security system.

Mameluke Buildings

Make a point of strolling around the northern section of the Haram to admire the facades on the north and west sides. Mainly religious schools, these buildings feature some delightfully ornate stonework. The gates too, especially the Gate of the Cotton Merchants, deserve a closer inspection.

The Fountain of Sultan Qaytbay is another of the city's beautiful structures overshadowed by more illustrious neighbours. Adjacent to the Dome of the Rock, it was built by Egyptians in 1482 as a charitable act to please Allah. Interestingly its construction was supervised by a Christian master builder.

WESTERN WALL

The Western Wall (known in Hebrew as Kotel Hama'aravi or just the Kotel) is often referred to by non-Jews as the Wailing Wall because the Jews have traditionally come here to mourn the Temple's destruction. It is part of the retaining wall built by Herod the Great in 20 BC to support the Temple's esplanade. Look closely and you will see the different styles of bricks in the wall. The top ones are those added by Byzantines and Muslims after the Romans had pushed out parts of the wall that projected above the inside floor level.

The original Herodian stones can be identified by their carved frames. In the south corner of the women's section smaller stones were used to fill in one of the original Temple entrances.

The wall can be reached by foot from Dung Gate, the Jewish Quarter, or via the Arab markets on El-Wad Rd or Bab el-Silsila St. Egged bus No 1 runs from the central bus station to Dung Gate. Access to the wall is open to all, Jewish or not. It is open 24 hours with every access route marked by a security checkpoint.

All men must cover their heads; complimentary cardboard yarmulkas are provided, and women may borrow shawls and leg coverings if required. Men, however, can wear shorts. Photography is permitted except during Shabbat and Jewish festivals when it's strictly banned in the whole area, as is smoking.

The wall should be visited at different times of the day and the week to really experience its status. On Monday and Thursday mornings, bar mitzvahs are held here and can be fascinating to watch.

The wall is divided into two areas, the northern section for men, the small southern section for women. When I asked why the men had that particular end of the wall, I was told that it was chosen by them because it received more shade from the hot sun! Day and night you will always see Hasidic Jews in their distinctive black clothes bobbing to and fro as they pray. This motion, is made in time with the prayers and becomes reflex action for most praying Jews. You will see the cracks in the wall crammed with bits of paper containing prayers – an old tradition.

To celebrate the arrival of Shabbat there is always a large crowd on Friday at sunset and students from the nearby Yeshiva HaKotel shuffle down to the wall to dance and sing. During Shabbat and the Jewish festivals the wall is a major attraction for worshippers.

Make a point of visiting the area at night, when the floodlit Dome of the Rock looms quietly behind the wall. The piazza is often the site for youth and military parades, although in keeping with the country's minimalised style of formality they are not usually very spectacular to watch.

Wilsons Arch

Situated to the north of the men's prayer section, this arch (now inside a room) carries the Street of the Chain to the Temple across the Tyropoeon (Cheesemaker's) Valley. It was once used by priests on their way to the Temple. Look down the two illuminated shafts to get an idea of the wall's original height. Possibly Hasmonean (150-40 BC) but at least Herodian, the room's function is unknown. Women are not permitted into the room, and the site is often closed to men too. Officially it is open Sunday, Tuesday and Wednesday 8.30 am to 3 pm, Monday and Thursday 12.30 to 3 pm, and Friday 8.30 am to noon, and it's closed on Saturday.

Hasidic Jews praying at the Western Wall

Robinsons Arch

Named after an American scholar, Edward Robinson, this is at the southern end of the wall. It was the entrance to the passageway whereby the royal party had access from the Upper City to the Temple. Ruins of shops and stalls that supported the bridge are below the arch.

JEWISH QUARTER

In the south-east sector, the Jewish Quarter stands out from the rest of the Old City because of its continuing large-scale restoration programme. This work commenced almost immediately after the reunification of

Jerusalem in 1967 and it is one of the most successful building projects in the country.

There are few historic monuments above ground level due to the mass destruction by the Jordanians between 1948-67 but several archaeological discoveries have been made. These tell of Jewish settlement beginning in the First Temple Period (around 1000-586 BC), continuing right through to the British Mandate (1918-48).

These historical sites are used by Jews to highlight the continuity (and, therefore, the legitimacy) of the Jewish presence.

Prior to 1948, the Jewish Quarter had become a congested slum due to the growth of the Jewish population and unsatisfactory building practices. As a result of this, large numbers began to move to the Muslim Quarter and later outside the Old City altogether. During the British Mandate the local population began to decrease and by 1948 only about 2000 Jews remained. With the Jordanian capture of the Old City they were all evacuated.

Rooftop Promenade

One of the most interesting ways to see the Old City is to climb the metal stairway on the corner of Habad St and St Mark's Rd. This takes you up onto the rooftops of the David St and surrounding markets and gives you a unique angle on the sights and sounds of the Old City.

You can see the Haram esh-Sharif and the Mount of Olives to the east; East Jerusalem and Mount Scopus to the north-east; while the Lutheran Church of the Redeemer's tall white tower and the domes of the Church of the Holy Sepulchre dominate the view to the north. Check out the ventilation ducts through which you can hear and see the markets below you. Visit both in the daytime and at night. In the clear moonlight, the Old City buildings are unforgettable.

The Cardo

Dominating the entrances to the Quarter from the David St access points, this is the reconstructed main street of Roman and Byzantine Jerusalem – the Cardo Maximus. Shown on the 6th-century Madaba map of the Old City, a copy of which is displayed here, the Cardo is dominated today by fancy stores, lacklustre modern-day versions of what must have been a colourful market place in its heyday. Remains of the city walls from the days of the First and Second Temples, part of the Byzantine main street, and remains of the Crusader market can be seen. The original street was bounded on the west by the heavy wall, on the east by a row of pillars and flanked by seven-metre-wide porticos.

One Last Day Located in the Cardo, this exhibition of photographs by John Phillips

was taken the day the Jewish Quarter fell to the Jordanians in 1948. It's open from Sunday to Thursday 9 am to 5 pm, Friday 9 am to 1 pm, and admission is US$0.75.

Wide Wall

At the western end of Tiferet Y'Israel Rd and to the north on Plugat HaKotel Rd is the Wide Wall, remains of King Hezekiah's wide stone wall built around 701 BC. Its purpose was to protect the city from the Ashurites, against whom he had rebelled.

Israelite Tower

On Shonei HaLakhot St, on the corner of Plugat HaKotel St, is the tower of the northern wall gate from the Babylonian siege and destruction of the First Temple in 586 BC. Hamonean remains are also displayed.

It's open from Sunday to Thursday 9 am to 5 pm, Friday 9 am to 1 pm, and admission is US$2.20 (this is combined with the Burnt House and Wohl Archaeological Museum).

Rachel Ben-Zvi Centre

Across from the Israelite Tower, this institute (☎ 286288) teaches and researches the history of Jewish communities. The attraction for visitors is a scale model of Jerusalem in the First Temple period. It shows the archaeological findings from the period of King David and his followers, the temple and city life at that time. One of the model's interesting features is its portrayal of the city's constructed water systems. Other exhibits include an audiovisual history of the city from 1000 BC to 586 BC.

It's open Sunday to Thursday 9 am to 4 pm, Friday by appointment, but is closed Saturday; admission is US$2.

Hurva & Ramban Synagogues

Dominated by the minaret of Sidi Umar Mosque and the symbolically restored arch of the Hurva (Hurba) Synagogue, both of these synagogues rest on the ruins of the Crusader Church of St Martin. The Hurva Synagogue, its additions and the group of buildings east of it were the centre of Jerusalem's Ashkenazi community from the

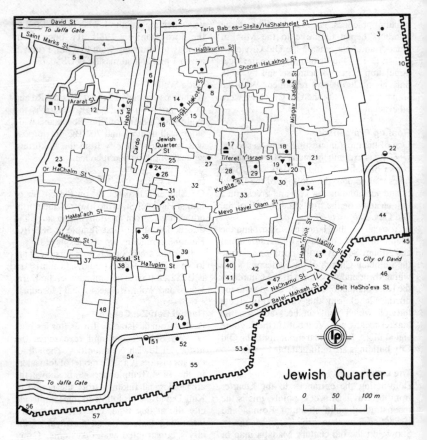

Jewish Quarter

0   50   100 m

15th century until the start of the 20th century. Hurva means ruins and was the name given to the surrounding courtyard which, in 1721, was razed by Muslims who were owed a considerable amount by the Jews who lived and worshipped here and were unable to pay up. During the next 90 years the Ashkenazi community continued to live in the vicinity but without their own synagogue, leaving the ruins as they were.

The Hurva Synagogue itself was dedicated in 1864 but was destroyed by the Jordanians in 1948. Restoration work went little further than rebuilding the main arch,

which may be left as it is rather than completely rebuilding the structure.

The Ramban Synagogue is named after Rabbi Moshe Ben Nahman. Ramban is an acronym for his name and he is also known as Nachmanides. One of the great Jewish sages, he immigrated to Palestine from Spain in 1267 and played a prominent role in the return of the Jews to the city after they had fled the approaching Mongols. Believed to have originally been on Mount Zion, the synagogue was moved to its present site around 1400. A letter written by the Ramban to his family describing the miserable state of the Jewish community on his arrival from Spain is displayed here.

The minaret was constructed in the 15th century by the mother of one of the community's members who had converted to Islam after quarrelling with his neighbours. In the 16th century Jews were forbidden to pray here and the synagogue became a work-shop. During the British Mandate it became a store and a cheesery. Today it is again used as a synagogue and is open for morning and evening prayers.

War of Independence Memorial
Adjacent to the Hurva and Ramban syn-agogues, this memorial is to those Jews who fell in the battle for the quarter in the 1948 War of Independence.

It includes an illuminated map showing the stages of the fighting, and an audiovisual presentation covering the quarter's history from the First Temple Period up to the present day.

Old Yishuv Court Museum
This museum (☎ 284636) at 6 Or HaChaim St is set up as a house, with each room showing an aspect of Jewish life in the quarter before the destruction of 1948.

It's open Sunday to Thursday 9 am to 2 pm; admission is US$2.20 (students US$1.60).

Jerusalem – a Multi-Media Presentation

At 1 Jewish Quarter St, near the parking lot, a 35-minute audiovisual history of the city (aimed at Jewish visitors) is screened. Times (in English) are 11 am, 2 and 5 pm, Sunday to Thursday; admission is US$3.20.

Sephardic Synagogues

These synagogues were constructed by the Sephardic community at the end of the 16th century. They were built below ground level because a law at that time said synagogues could not be taller than neighbouring buildings. Looted and then used as a sheep pen by the Jordanians, they have been restored using the remains of Italian synagogues damaged during WW II. They are still used for morning and evening services.

They are open Sunday to Thursday 9.30 am to 4 pm, Friday 9.30 am to 12.30 pm; admission is US$1.30 (students US$0.65).

Shelter Houses – Batei Mahseh Square

This was the quarter's largest square at one time and in the 19th century the site of an independent Jewish neighbourhood. The Shelter Houses were built to provide housing for the poor. During the last fortnight of the battle for the quarter in May 1948, hundreds of Jews sheltered in the basements of these buildings as the Jewish military headquarters was nearby. The area's most notable building is known as Rothschild Building A. Built in 1871 it was funded by a contribution from Baron Wolf Rothschild of Frankfurt.

Tiferet Y'Israel Synagogue

Dedicated in 1872, this is the 'twin brother' of the Hurva Synagogue, and its tall structure, capped by a dome, was one of the quarter's best-known landmarks until its destruction by the Jordanians in 1948. Its name means 'the Glory of Israel' and it was the largest Hasidic centre in the Old City.

Burnt House

Next to the Quarter Café, this is the reconstruction of a luxurious house in what was the Upper City of the Second Temple era.

After the Romans destroyed the Second Temple, they set fire to the Upper City and massacred the inhabitants. An audiovisual show is shown in different languages, including English.

It's open Sunday to Thursday 9 am to 5 pm, Friday 9 am to 1 pm, and is closed Saturday; admission is US$2.20 (combined with the Israelite Tower and Wohl Archaeological Museum).

Nea Church

This was the New Church built by Justinian in 543. Its southern apse projects outside the city wall and it was once the city's second-grandest church, after the Holy Sepulchre.

Siebenberg House

This archaeological museum, at 35 Misgav Ladakh St (corner of HaGittit St), features various remains in the basement of a house. These include a Hasmonean cistern and parts of what may have been an aqueduct that carried water from Solomon's Pools to the Temple.

It's open Sunday to Thursday 9 am to 5 pm, with a 45-minute guided tour in English at noon only; admission is US$3.

Wohl Archaeological Museum – Herodian Quarter

Perhaps the Jewish Quarter's most impressive complex, this museum features more renovated examples of the wealthy Jewish neighbourhood in Herod's Upper City. The lavish lifestyle enjoyed by the Cohanim and public servants of the Second Temple period is represented by the frescoes, stucco reliefs, mosaic floors, ornaments, furniture and household objects on display.

It's open Sunday to Thursday 9 am to 5 pm, Friday 9 am to 1 pm, and admission is US$2.20 (combined with the Israelite Tower and the Burnt House).

St Mary's of the Germans

On the north side of the steps leading to the Western Wall, this is a 12th-century complex comprising a church, a hospital and a hospice. The entrance is to the church on

Misgav Ladakh St, just east of the Quarter Café.

Ophel Archaeological Garden
Just inside Dung Gate, these excavations at the southern wall of the Haram have uncovered 22 layers from 12 periods of Jerusalem's history. The garden is open Sunday to Thursday 9 am to 5 pm, Friday 9 am to 3 pm, and admission is US$1.40 (students US$0.70).

MUSLIM QUARTER
Largely overlooked by visitors, this quarter covers 30 hectares in the north-eastern sector of the Old City and is its most highly populated area.

The buildings tend to be dilapidated and many of the streets look uninviting, but there are a number of things well worth seeing, including some great Mameluke architecture, the first section of the Via Dolorosa and the Stations of the Cross, beautiful churches and examples of today's struggle between Israelis and Palestinians over the rights of possession.

St Anne's Church
Built in 1140 and generally agreed to be the best example of Crusader architecture in Jerusalem, this church is one of Israel's most popular. Byzantine tradition claims that its crypt enshrines the site of the home of Joachim and Anne, the parents of the Virgin Mary. Next to the church are the impressive ruins surrounding the Pool of Bethesda. These were the medicinal baths where clients of the God Serapis came hoping for a miracle cure. John 5:1-18 tells of Jesus healing a man who had been sick for 38 years.

The Crusaders took over the ruins of a 5th-century church destroyed by Caliph Hakim. They constructed a small chapel with a stairway leading down to the northern pool to allow pilgrims to venerate Jesus' miracle. Beside it they built the Romanesque church of St Anne to enshrine the Virgin's home and to serve as a chapel for a community of nuns.

Saladin turned the church into a Muslim

theological school in 1192; note his inscription above the door. Successive rulers allowed the church to fall into decay so that by the 18th century it was roof-deep in refuse. In 1856 the Ottoman Turks presented the church to France in gratitude for their support in the Crimean War and it was restored to its former glory.

Apart from its architectural beauty, the church is noted for its acoustics, and a prominent sign requests that only hymns are used for sound checks. A joint in the north wall indicates a medieval extension in the bare chapel. The crypt is older than the church; note how the pillars' foundations stand out from the original shape of the caves which once formed part of Serapis' sanctuary.

It's open Monday to Saturday from 8 am to noon and 2 to 6 pm (winter 2 to 5 pm), but is closed on Sunday; admission is free. The entrance is marked 'St Anne – Peres Blanc'; do not use the other door marked 'Religious Birthplace of Mary'.

Via Dolorosa
This road, holy to Christians, spans both the Muslim and the Christian quarters. Traditionally the route followed by Jesus as he carried his cross to Calvary, this road's sanctity is based on faith, not history. Its origins can be traced back to the days when Byzantine pilgrims, on the night of Holy Thursday, would go in procession from Gethsemane to Calvary along roughly the same route as today's Via Dolorosa, although there were no official devotional stops en route.

By the 8th century, some stops had become customary but the route had changed considerably and went from Gethsemane around the city on the south to Caiaphas' house on Mount Zion, then to the Praetorium of Pilate at St Sophia near the Temple and eventually to the Holy Sepulchre.

In the Middle Ages, with Latin Christianity divided into two camps, the situation became more complicated. One group located the Praetorium and the high priest's palace on Mount Zion, while the other placed them both north of the Temple, and so they followed totally different routes to the Holy

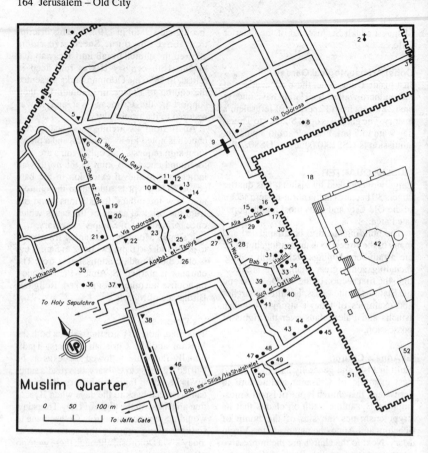

Muslim Quarter

0   50   100 m

To Jaffa Gate

To Holy Sepulchre

Sepulchre. The basic reason for their conflict was simply that one group had churches on the western hill, the other on the eastern!

In the 14th century, the Franciscans devised a walk of devotion following Jesus' steps in Jerusalem. This included some of today's stations but the starting point was the Holy Sepulchre. This became the standard route for nearly two centuries but eventually changed as a result of the enthusiasm of European pilgrims who had adapted the ceremonies according to the order of events in the gospels. Although the Christians resident in Jerusalem had also begun to follow the

gospels' order of events, they had only eight stations, whereas the Europeans had 14.

Pilgrims arriving in Jerusalem expected to find the same as they were accustomed to back home, and the European tradition eventually caught on. The Jerusalem Way of the Cross was extended in the 18th century to include stations within the Holy Sepulchre. However, the 1st, 4th, 5th and 8th stations were only given their present location in the 19th century.

Today's Via Dolorosa has little to do with historical reality, as it is more likely that Jesus was condemned to death by Pilate on

■ PLACES TO STAY

9   Notre Dame de Sion Ecce Homo Convent
10 Al-Ahram Hostel
11 Armenian Catholic Patriarchate Hospice
19 Al-Arab Hostel
20 New Hashimi Hotel

▼ PLACES TO EAT

5   Green Door Bakery
6   Felafel Stalls
14 Abu Shukri
22 Linda's Restaurant
37 Zalatimo Sweets
38 Pipe Cafe

OTHER

1   Solomon's Quarries
2   Church of St Anne
3   Lion's (St Stephen's) Gate
4   Damascus Gate
7   Station 2
8   Station 1
9   Ecce Homo Arch
12 Station 3
13 Station 4
15 Ribat Ala ed-Din el-Basir

16 Muslim Supreme Council
17 Bab en-Nazir
18 Haram esh-Sharif (Temple Mount)
21 Station 7
23 Station 6
24 Station 5
25 Turbatt es-Sitt Tunshuq
26 Serai es-Sitt Tunshuq
27 Ribat Bayram Jawish
28 Beit Sharon
29 Ribat Mansuri
30 Small Wall
31 Madrassa Jawhariyya
32 Ribut Kurd
33 Madrasa Muzhiriyya
34 Madrasa Arghuniyya
35 Station 8
36 Station 9
39 Suq el-Qattanin
40 Hammam esh-Shifa
41 Hammam el-Ayn
42 Dome of the Rock
43 Turba Turkan Khatun
44 Turba Sadiyya
45 Madrasa Tankiziyya
46 Khan es-Sultan
47 Turba Kilaniyya
48 Turba Madrasa Taziyya
49 Turba Barakat Kan (Khalidi Library)
50 Madrasa Turba Tashtimatiyya
51 Western Wall
52 El-Aqsa Mosque

the other side of the city at the Citadel, next to Jaffa Gate. This was Herod's palace and where Pilate normally resided in Jerusalem. Various Bible references to the trial taking place on a platform (Matthew 27:19) and in the open (Luke 23:4, John 18:28) support this theory as the palace is known to have had such a structure. A more probable route for Jesus to have taken would be east along David St, north through the Butchers' Market of today, and west to Golgotha.

Stations of the Cross
Every Friday at 3 pm the Franciscan Fathers lead a procession which attracts many pilgrims, tourists and souvenir salespersons. At other times the route is often crowded with tour groups and individuals, sometimes with replicas of the cross being carried.

The Stations are difficult to locate, despite their great importance to so many.

1st Station Inside the El-Omariyeh College, whose entrance is the door at the top of the ramp on the south side of the Via Dolorosa, east of the Ecce Homo Arch is the 1st Station. Entry is not always permitted so if you are asked to leave, however impolitely, don't be surprised. Jesus was tried here, but there is nothing of official Christian value to see. There is a great view of the Haram esh-Sharif through the barred windows on the upper level.

2nd Station In the Franciscan sanctuaries of the Flagellation and the Condemnation, the Church of the Condemnation to the left is the 2nd Station. Jesus was condemned here, and

the Chapel of Flagellation to the right is where he was flogged. The dome incorporates the crown of thorns and the windows of the chapel around the altar show the mob who witnessed the event. Built in 1929, it's open daily: April to September 8 am to noon and 2 to 6 pm; October to March 8 am to noon and 1 to 5 pm; admission is free.

3rd Station This is where the Via Dolorosa joins up with El-Wad Rd and marks the spot where Jesus fell for the first time while carrying his cross. Adjacent to the entrance of the Armenian Catholic Patriarchate Hospice, the station is marked by a small Polish chapel. The street is dominated by the excavated remains of the original Roman road.

4th Station Beyond the hospice, this station marks the spot where Jesus faced his mother in the crowd of onlookers.

5th Station As El-Wad Rd continues towards the Western Wall, the Via Dolorosa heads up to the west. Right on the corner, this is the spot where the Romans forced Simon the Cyrene to carry the cross. It is marked by signs around a door.

6th Station Further along the street, also on the left and easy to miss, is the place where Veronica wiped Jesus' face with a cloth. The Greek Orthodox Patriarchate in the Christian Quarter, displays what is claimed to be the cloth, which shows the imprint of Jesus' face.

7th Station This is where Jesus fell a second

time and is marked by signs on the wall on the west of Suq Khan ez-Zeit St, the main market street at the top of this section of the Via Dolorosa. In the 1st century, this was the edge of the city and a gate led out to the countryside. This is part of the argument supporting the claim that the Church of the Holy Sepulchre is the genuine location of Jesus' crucifixion, burial and resurrection.

8th Station Another station easy to miss. Cut straight across Suq Khan ez-Zeit St from the Via Dolorosa and ascend Aqabat el-Khanqa. Just past the Greek Orthodox Convent on the left is the stone and Latin cross marking where Jesus told some women to cry for themselves and their children, not for him.

9th Station Come back down to where the Via Dolorosa and Aqabat el-Khanqa meet and turn right (south, away from Damascus Gate) up Suq Khan ez-Zeit St. Head up the stairway on your right and follow the path round to the Coptic Church. The remains of a column in its door mark the spot where Jesus fell the third time.

Retrace your steps to the main street and head for the Church of the Holy Sepulchre. Inside the church you will find the remaining five stations.

10th Station As you enter the church, head up the steep stairway immediately to your right. The chapel at the top is divided into two naves. The right one belongs to the Franciscans, the left to the Greek Orthodox. At the entrance to the Franciscan Chapel is the 10th Station where Jesus was stripped of his clothes.

11th Station Still in the chapel, this is where Jesus was nailed to the cross.

12th Station In the Greek Orthodox Chapel, this is the site of Jesus' crucifixion.

13th Station Between the 11th and 12th stations, this is where the body of Jesus was taken down and handed to Mary.

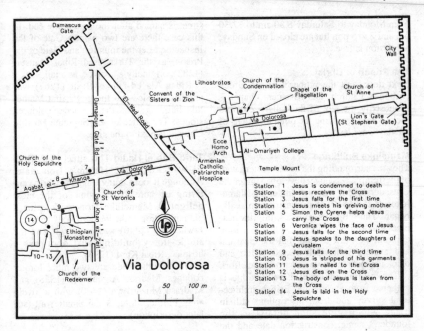

Damascus Gate

City Wall

Lithostrotos

Convent of the Sisters of Zion

Church of the Condemnation

Chapel of the Flagellation

Church of St Anne

El-Wad Road

Damascus Gate Rd

Via Dolorosa

Lion's Gate (St Stephens Gate)

Church of the Holy Sepulchre

Ecce Homo Arch

Al-Omariyeh College

7

Khanqa

Via Dolorosa

Aqabat el- 8

6

Church of St Veronica

4

5

Armenian Catholic Patriarchate Hospice

Temple Mount

9

Suq Khan ez-

14

Ethiopian Monastery

10-13

Church of the Redeemer

Via Dolorosa

0   50   100 m

Station 1	Jesus is condemned to death
Station 2	Jesus receives the Cross
Station 3	Jesus falls for the first time
Station 4	Jesus meets his grieving mother
Station 5	Simon the Cyrene helps Jesus carry the Cross
Station 6	Veronica wipes the face of Jesus
Station 7	Jesus falls for the second time
Station 8	Jesus speaks to the daughters of Jerusalem
Station 9	Jesus falls for the third time
Station 10	Jesus is stripped of his garments
Station 11	Jesus is nailed to the Cross
Station 12	Jesus dies on the Cross
Station 13	The body of Jesus is taken from the Cross
Station 14	Jesus is laid in the Holy Sepulchre

14th Station The Holy Sepulchre, the Tomb of Jesus. Walk down the narrow stairs beyond the Greek Orthodox Chapel to the ground floor and you will see that the Holy Sepulchre is to be found in the centre of the rotunda, which would be on your left if you were entering from outside. The actual tomb is inside the Sepulchre, beyond the initial Chapel of the Angel. Candles lit by pilgrims who make a donation dominate the small tomb, with the raised marble slab covering the rock on which Jesus' body was laid. Around the back of the Holy Sepulchre is the tiny Coptic Chapel where pilgrims kiss the wall of the tomb, encouraged by a priest who expects a donation. The Church of the Holy Sepulchre is described in the Christian Quarter section.

Ecce Homo Arch & the Convent of the Sisters of Zion

West of the crossroads on the crest of the slope as Via Dolorosa leads towards El-Wad Rd, an arch with a two-windowed room spans the street. Its northern end is preserved in the Convent of the Sisters of Zion. Beneath the convent, with its entrance to the right, facing the building and around the corner, are impressive excavations from the Roman period. The arch is traditionally, but improbably, the spot where Pilate looked down at Jesus to say, 'Behold your King!'

The arch was probably the eastern gate of the city when Herod Agrippa I (37-44) extended it northwards. After the Roman victory, the wall and gate were destroyed, but the debris protected the lower section. When Hadrian replanned the city in 135 he constructed a forum on this site, leaving the original gate in the middle of the pavement. For generations the complex had been connected with Herod the Great's Antonia fortress built around 37-35 BC and named after his Roman friend, Mark Anthony.

The excavations and access to the arch (not the one spanning the street) are open from Monday to Saturday 8.30 am to 12.30 pm and 2 to 5 pm, but are closed on Sunday; admission is free.

The Prison of Christ

Next door, and the property of the Greek Orthodox Church, this basement chapel is supposedly the site of the cellars, cut into rock, where Jesus and the other criminals of the day were held.

Mameluke Buildings

The area surrounding the north-western wall of the Temple was never developed under the Crusaders and it was only under the Mamelukes (1250-1517) that construction really began. The religious colleges, pilgrim hospices and tombs of this period require a little exploration work to find, but the clear-cut and austere stonework of red, white and black is most attractive and worth the effort.

The information about these buildings is gathered from an ongoing British architectural survey and from inscriptions still in place which give such details as the founder's name, construction date and the building's function. Most of them are now tenements and closed to the public.

However, the most interesting part of a Mameluke building is found in its ornate facade, normally dominated by a door with a larger recess to give extra shade and protection.

Jerome Murphy-O'Conner's good archaeological guide *The Holy Land* (Oxford University Press, 1986) covers this area in detail.

Aqabat et-Takiya

In this street is a palace, Serai es-Sitt Tunshuq (1382), which is now an orphanage. The domed tomb opposite, Turbatt es-Sitt Tunshuq, was built by the palace's original owner.

On the corner with El-Wad Rd is the last notable piece of Mameluke architecture built in Jerusalem, the Ribat Bayram Jawish (1540), which was a pilgrim's hospice.

Tariq Bab en-Nazir (Tariq Bab el-Habs)

Like the other main routes to the Haram, this street is named after the gate at the end. In this case there are two names: Gate of the Inspector, after the founder; and Gate of the Prison, as the Turks used Ribat Mansuri (1282), originally a hospice, as a jail.

Ribat Ala ed-Din el-Basir (1267) was another hospice and the city's first Mameluke building – note the absence of coloured stones. The office of the Supreme Muslim Council is next to the gate.

Tariq Bab el-Hadid

This street leads from El-Wad Rd to the Haram's Iron Gate. Although it looks uninviting, it is worth venturing up here to see some of the most delightful Mameluke stonework, plus a hidden section of the Western Wall. Madrasa Jawhariyya (1440) was a college, and the single-storey building next door was a hospice, Ribat Kurd (1293).

On the other side are two more former colleges: Madrasa Arghuniyya (1358), and Madrasa Muzhiriyya (1480) with a lovely arch. Further along is the Small Wall (see later description).

Suq el-Qattanin

Market of the Cotton Merchants, this vaulted passageway was built in the mid-13th century to provide an income for charities. Two 'Turkish' baths, Hammam el-Ayn and Hammam esh-Shifa, can be seen here.

Tariq Bab es-Silsila

The busy gate of the Chain St leads to one of the two access points to the Haram for non-Muslims, and becomes David St in the heart of the Old City markets. Look out for the restored Khan es-Sultan (1386) – a discreet entrance just up from the large 'Gali' sign leads into a courtyard surrounded by workshops.

Down towards the Haram, the Madrasa /Turba Tashtimutiyya (1382) is a mausoleum built by a top government official for himself. Further east is the Turba Kilaniyya (1352) and next door the Turba/ Madrasa Taziyya (1362). The Turba Barakat Khan, on the corner opposite, is now the Khalidi Library. Continue towards the Haram to see two more tombs, the Turba Turkan Khatun

(1352) and the Turba Sadiyya (1311). The open square outside the Chain Gate features the semi-domed entrance to the college Madrasa Tankiziyya (1328).

Small Wall

This site, also known as the Hidden Wall, is at the end of the last narrow passageway off Bab el-Hadid St, just outside the Haram's Iron Gate. It is marked by a small sign, visible from El-Wad Rd where Bab el-Hadid St begins. This section of wall, now part of a Muslim house, is the same Western Wall that thousands of Jews flock to a few hundred metres to the south. The Arabs living here don't seem to mind the traffic of visitors and have provided an outside light on their first floor to enable Jews to read their prayers.

When the Israelis took the Old City in 1967, they found that some of the stones from the wall here had been taken and used for construction work elsewhere. Note the toilet built next to the wall but now sealed off by the Israelis.

Beit Sharon

On El-Wad Rd across from the Jerusalem Star Restaurant (just north of the arch), this is the controversial home of the hawkish Israeli politician Ariel Sharon. Look for the IDF soldiers on guard outside. He purchased this property in the heart of the Muslim Quarter to highlight the right of Jews to live anywhere in Israel, specifically in this neighbourhood which is a symbolic centre for anti-Israeli sentiments. Nearby are other properties purchased recently by Jews, including yeshivas (religious schools) and family homes.

CHRISTIAN QUARTER

The Christian Quarter covers nearly 20 hectares in the north-western section of the Old City, and has a population estimated at 5000. In the same way that the Mamelukes clustered their buildings around the Haram esh-Sharif, the Christians centred around the Church of the Holy Sepulchre.

On higher ground than the rest of the Old City, this quarter is dominated by Christian institutions and many of its backstreets are full of grand buildings.

As you enter from Jaffa Gate, the first two streets to the north (left) – Latin Patriarchate Rd and Greek Catholic Patriarchate Rd – indicate the tone of the neighbourhood, named as they are after the offices there. The roads lead to St Francis St and in this area around New Gate the local Christian hierarchy resides in comfort.

The Franciscans' Holy Land headquarters is in St Francis St in the Monastery of St Salvador. Nearby, on Frères Rd, is the Frères College, run by the Catholic monks. In its cellar are ancient fortifications known as Goliath's Castle, dating from the 1st-century Jewish revolt against Rome. On Casa Nova St are the old and new Casa Nova buildings, both owned by the Franciscans. The old building is now administrative offices but was previously the main pilgrims' hostel. A wooden doorway inside is carved with the names of pilgrims who had stayed here and wanted to leave a permanent reminder of their visit to the Holy Land. The low pillar near the entrance was used by them to climb onto their donkeys. The new Casa Nova building is the replacement hotel (see Places to Stay in this chapter).

Christ Church

Located just across from the Citadel and the police station, this was the Holy Land's first Protestant church, consecrated in 1849. It was built by the London Society for Promoting Christianity Amongst the Jews (known today as CMJ: the Church's Ministry Among the Jews). The society's founders were inspired by the belief that the Jews would be restored to what was then Turkish Palestine, and that many would acknowledge Jesus Christ as the Messiah before He returned.

In order to present Christianity as something not totally alien to Judaism, Christ Church was built in the Protestant style with several similarities to a synagogue. Jewish symbols, such as Hebrew script and the Star of David, figure prominently at the altar and in the stained glass windows.

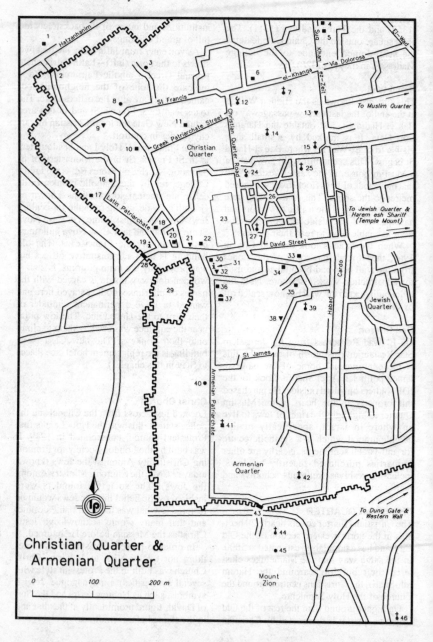

Christian Quarter & Armenian Quarter

0   100   200 m

Christ Church also features a hospice (see Places to Stay in this chapter).

Greek Orthodox Patriarchate Museum
On Greek Catholic Patriarchate Rd this museum (☎ 284006), presents some of the treasures of the patriarchate, and goes a little way towards presenting the history of this locally dominant church.

It's open Tuesday to Friday 9 am to 1 pm and 3 to 5 pm, and Saturday 9 am to 1 pm, but is closed Sunday and Monday; admission is US$0.70. Follow Greek Orthodox Patriarchate Rd north from Jaffa Gate all the way around to the east (right) and it is on the north side (left).

Church of the Holy Sepulchre
Despite the Holy Sepulchre being the central shrine of Christianity, this church is less

recognisable than many lesser sites. I have met several people wandering in and out without a clue of its status. Those who are aware of what it represents are often sorely disappointed. It does fail to stand out from its surroundings and is dark, cramped and noisy, but the un-Christian behaviour of some of the monks and priests who live and pray here is the most common cause for disappointment. Many a visitor is subjected to the rudeness of these supposedly holy men as they rush around praying and blessing, pushing and bumping startled bystanders as they go by.

The church is an ugly conglomerate of different architectural styles developed over the centuries, and generally agreed to be built on the site of Jesus' crucifixion, burial and resurrection. At the start of the 1st century this was a disused quarry outside the city

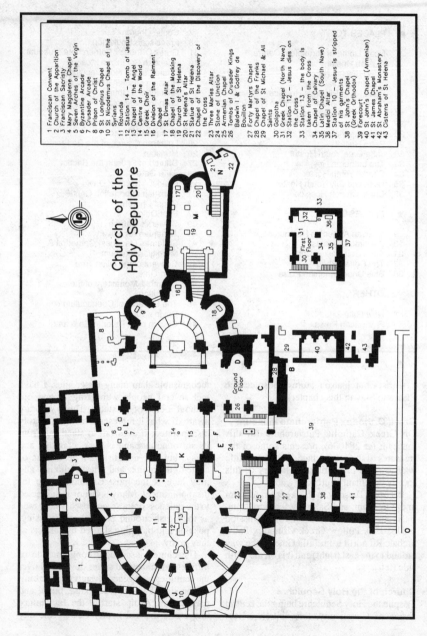

Church of the
Holy Sepulchre

1 Franciscan Convent
2 Church of the Apparition
3 Franciscan Sacristy
4 Mary Magdalene Chapel
5 Seven Arches of the Virgin
6 Byzantine Arcade
7 Crusader Arcade
8 Prison of Christ
9 St Longinus Chapel
10 St Nicodemus Chapel of the Syrians
11 Rotunda
12 Station 14 – Tomb of Jesus
13 Chapel of the Angel
14 Centre of the World
15 Greek Choir
16 Division of the Raiment Chapel
17 St Dimas Altar
18 Chapel of the Mocking
19 Church of St Helena
20 St Helena's Altar
21 Statue of St Helena
22 Chapel of the Discovery of the Cross
23 Three Maries Altar
24 Stone of Unction
25 Armenian Chapel
26 Tombs of Crusader Kings Baldwin I & Godfrey de Bouillon
27 Forty Martyrs Chapel
28 Chapel of the Franks
29 Chapel of St Michael & All Saints
30 Golgotha
31 Greek Chapel (North Nave)
32 Station 12 – Jesus dies on the Cross
33 Station 13 – the body is taken from the Cross
34 Chapel of Calvary
35 Latin Chapel (South Nave)
36 Medici Altar
37 Station 10 – Jesus is stripped of his garments
38 St John's Chapel (Greek Orthodox)
39 Forecourt
40 St John's Chapel (Armenian)
41 St James Chapel
42 St Abraham's Monastery
43 Cisterns of St Helena

A   12th century facade and entrance/exit.

B   These steps were the Crusader entrance to Calvary closed in 1187 to become the Chapel of the Franks.

C   Calvary: the 10th, 11th, 12th and 13th Stations of the Cross in the Latin and Greek chapels. Accessible via the steep stairs on the immediate right inside the entrance, their floor is level with the summit of the block of rock left in the old quarry - you can see/touch it beneath the Greek altar marking the 13th Station.

D   In the Chapel of Adam, downstairs, a window allows you to see the rock again. One legend has it that Adam was buried below Calvary and Jesus' blood dripped through this crack to anoint him. Crusader kings were buried in this chapel and the bodies of Godfrey de Bouillon and Baldwin I lay on the two benches near the door until 1810.

E   The Stone of Unction often causes pilgrims to miss the small stairway up to Calvary, and commemorates Jesus being anointed before burial. It is not the actual stone where his body was laid out. First appearing in the 12th century, the present stone dates from 1810.

F   This wall with the paintings has no structural or major religious function but would provide a fine view of the church and create more room if demolished. It was built after the 1808 fire to support the great arch which was cracked, and was immediately festooned with Greek icons. Despite recent restoration work making the wall unnecessary, a new one was built to allow the Greeks a place to hang their icons.

G   These two columns have been left in the same damaged condition as they were after the 1808 fire, while the rest of the 11th century piers and columns were restored. Looking closely you will see that one of the two has a rim around the top while the other has a rim around the base and its taper continues in the first one. This is because the massive 4th-century columns supporting the dome's drum were cut in half to be re-used to support the upper gallery added in the 11th century.

H   The tomb monument, understandably described as 'a hideous kiosk', dates only from the 19th-century. The 1808 fire had destroyed the previous 11th-century monument which replaced the rock tomb Hakim removed in 1009. You can queue up here to take a look inside.

I   Here you will find the Coptic Shrine at the back of the present tomb where you can see a very small section of the original (near the base).

J   This is the 4th-century wall and apse, now part of the Syrian Chapel.

K   The simplicity of the 12th-century Crusader church is here dominated by Greek Orthodox additions. Its upper gallery was included because of the corresponding gallery in the rotunda the previous century and is not normally found in churches of this period.

L   These two lines of different pillars were included by the 12th-century architect to preserve the remains of the original colonnade on the Byzantine courtyard's north side in front of the rotunda.

M   Follow the steps down to the crypt of St Helena. The stairway walls are marked by pilgrims' graffiti – several crosses scratched into the stone.

N   Only opened in the 12th century, the crypt's north and south walls are the foundations of the 4th-century basilica's nave. From this church it is believed that a narrow stairway led down to the cistern here, where the True Cross is reputed to have been found.

O   The attractive entrance to the Mosque of Omar; entrance is barred to non-Muslims.

walls. According to John 19:17 and 41-2, Jesus' crucifixion occurred at a place reminiscent of a skull, outside the city walls and with a grave nearby.

Archaeologists discovered tombs here similar to those found elsewhere and dated to this period, so the site is at least compatible with the gospel evidence.

Until at least 66 AD there had been a tradition for the Jerusalem community to hold celebrations of public worship at the tomb, in accordance with the Jewish practice then of praying at the tombs of holy persons.

Hadrian filled in the area in 135 to build a temple dedicated to Aphrodite, but the Christian tradition persisted and Constantine and his mother chose the site to construct a church honouring Jesus' resurrection. To make room for the new development, substantial buildings had to be demolished – a move of a mere 100 metres either way would have saved a lot of time and expense but the community insisted that this had to be the church's location. No other location ever won popular support until the Garden Tomb theory originated in 1883. Work on Constantine's church commenced in 326 and it was dedicated in 335. However, it was not fully completed until 348 due to the immense work involved in cutting away the cliff to isolate the tomb chamber.

Caliph Omar was invited to pray in the church when his forces took the city in 638 but he refused, generously noting that if he did his fellow Muslims would have turned it into a mosque. In 1009 the church was destroyed by the Fatamid Caliph Hakim, which no doubt, would not have happened if Omar had been less considerate before. Unable to afford the major repairs necessary, the Jerusalem community had to wait until 1042 when Constantine Monomachus' Byzantine Imperial Treasury provided a subsidy. It wasn't enough to pay for a complete reconstruction of the original church, however, and a large part of the edifice was abandoned, with an upper gallery introduced into the rotunda and an apse added to its eastern side to compensate. The open courtyard stayed basically the same and this was the church that the Crusaders entered on 15 July 1099 as the new rulers of the city. They made significant alterations, absorbing the courtyard into a Romanesque church attached to the unchanged rotunda. Therefore, the church is now a Crusader building, more or less.

A fire in 1808 and an earthquake in 1927 caused extensive damage, but due to the rivalry between the Christian churches it took until 1959 for the Latins, Greeks and Armenians to agree on a major repair programme. Progress was hampered considerably by disputes between the denominations, with accusations of certain parties trying to claim ownership of areas belonging to others.

The church is locked and unlocked every day by a Muslim – the church keys have been in the possession of a local Muslim family since the Ottoman Period when the Arabs claimed ownership of the building and charged the Christians a fee for keeping it secure. This fee is still payable to the family but is no longer a significant amount.

The Church of the Holy Sepulchre is open daily to anyone suitably dressed – the guards are very strict and refuse entry to those with bare legs, shoulders and backs, including men or women in shorts. The church is open daily 4.30 am to 8 pm (7 pm in winter). The main entrance is in the courtyard to the south and can be reached by two points: via Christian Quarter Rd or Dabbaga Rd, running from Suq Khan ez-Zeit St past Muristan. Another two possible entry points are via the roof (see Ethiopian Monastery later in this chapter).

Hidden Remains The 4th-century Church of the Holy Sepulchre was much larger than the present one and some interesting traces of it can be found in neighbouring buildings.

Russian Mission in Exile Just east of the Holy Sepulchre, on the Dabbaga Rd, between the Muristan and Khan ez-Zeit markets, is St Alexander's Church, which houses the Russian mission in exile. A much-altered triumphal arch dominates the visitors' area. It once stood in Hadrian's forum, built here in 135. Through the arch and to the left at the top of the steps you can see a section of the pavement which was once part of the platform of Hadrian's temple to Aphrodite.

A worn door sill is at the foot of the steps. It is often mistaken as the gate through which

Jesus left the city to reach Golgotha. St Alexander's Church is only open at 7 am on Thursday when prayers are said for Tsar Alexander III. The excavations are open from Monday to Thursday from 9 am to 3 pm; admission is US$0.60, and ring the bell.

Zalatimo's Sweets Set back from Suq Khan ez-Zeit St just north of the stairway leading up to the 9th Station is this small bakery. You should come here for its excellent products, but to help pass the time waiting to be served, ask to be shown the storeroom from where you can just about see the continuation of the Hadrianic and Constantinian wall.

Unfortunately, access to it has been blocked off by the recently built wall of the storeroom.

Ethiopian Monastery

Following the route to the 9th Station of the Cross, after the first left turn and as the street turns to the right, you'll see a small grey door below a green beam ahead of you. This opens onto a roof of the Church of the Holy Sepulchre. The cluster of huts here has been the Ethiopian Monastery since the Copts forced them out of their former building in one of the many disputes between the various Christian groups.

The quiet Ethiopian monks live amongst the ruins of a medieval cloister erected by the Crusaders where Constantine's basilica had been previously. The cupola in the middle of this roof section admits light to St Helena's crypt below. Access to the Church of the Holy Sepulchre is possible via two nearby points. One is through the Ethiopian Chapel (most of these monks do not speak much English but are very friendly, so ask for directions) and the other way is to go left out of the Ethiopian monastery and through the Copts' entrance.

Mosque of Omar & Khanqah Salahiyya

Adjacent to the Holy Sepulchre are these two mosques, and some speculation surrounds their matching minarets.

To the north, the Khanqah Salahiyya is on the site of the Crusader Patriarch of Jerusalem's palace. During its restoration in 1417 a minaret was added to the roof. The Mosque of Omar was built in 1193 to commemorate the caliph's prayers in the courtyard of the Holy Sepulchre in 638, but the minaret in its courtyard was only added between 1458 and 1465.

The tops of the minarets are identical in structure and materials. It is believed that they were meant to match – note that, despite the difference in ground level, a line joining their summits is absolutely horizontal. Also it has been shown that the mid-point of a line drawn between the minarets falls roughly at the entrance to Jesus' tomb in the Holy Sepulchre. This is thought to be intentional, although the purpose is unclear. It's suggested that perhaps the Mamelukes wanted to 'nullify' the Holy Sepulchre – it is the one site associated with Jesus that Muslims do not accept. Neither mosque is open to non-Muslims.

Lutheran Church of the Redeemer

Dominating the Old City skyline with its tall white tower, the present church was built in 1898 on the site of the 11th-century church of St Mary la Latine. The closed northern entrance porch is medieval and decorated with the signs of the zodiac and the symbols of the months. The tower is a popular attraction, and its narrow spiral staircase leads you up to excellent central views across the Old City and its surroundings.

It's open Tuesday to Saturday 9 am to 1 pm and 2 to 5 pm, Monday 9 am to 3 pm, but is closed Sunday; admission is US$0.65.

Church of St John the Baptist

Jerusalem's oldest church, it stands in a hidden section of the Muristan area and is usually overlooked, having been buried by the gradual raising of surrounding street levels. However, the entrance from Christian Quarter Rd is clearly signposted. This leads you into the courtyard of a more recent Greek Orthodox monastery where a monk will usually be present to open the church for you. Originally built in the mid-5th century, it was restored after the Persians destroyed it in

Christian Spires

614. In the 11th century the merchants of Amalfi built a new church which became the cradle of the Knights Hospitallers, using the walls of the earlier building.

The present facade with the two small bell towers is a more recent addition along with a few other alterations made to ensure the building's stability.

Pool of the Patriarch's Bath

This unsightly rubbish tip was a large reservoir believed to date from the Herodian period, but as no archaeological inspections have been made, little is known about it. A welcomed restoration project is long planned for this attractive location just to the north of the David St entrance near Jaffa Gate.

ARMENIAN QUARTER

The Armenian Quarter is often described as a miniature city within the Old City. With its own schools, library, seminary and residential quarters discreetly tucked away behind high walls, it is not unusual for visitors to walk straight through this area having seen nothing.

Armenia was the first nation to officially embrace Christianity, at the beginning of the 4th century. Its churches came under the jurisdiction of the Metropolitan of Caesarea and the country was represented in Jerusalem during the Byzantine period. An area permanently troubled by politics, the kingdom of Armenia disappeared at the end of the 4th century. This was the start of a continuing period of persecution and exile which culminated in the massacre of one and a half million Armenians by the Turks in 1915. The exiled community here enjoys a strong sense of unity based on their language and culture, both with strong roots in their church.

Two great saints of the early 5th century, Isaac and Mesrob, are credited with the creation of the sense of national identity which has survived these centuries of dispersal.

Armenian Compound

About 1200 Armenians now live in what used to be a large pilgrims' hospice. It became a residential area after 1915 when refugees from the Turkish massacres settled here. Its empty, wide courtyards are a rare sight in the Old City. It is basically closed to visitors, but you can telephone ☎ 282331 or ask at the entrance to St James' Cathedral to make an appointment for a visit.

St James' (Jacques') Cathedral

The carpets, the numerous lamps hanging in the air and the use of ceramic tiles are the dominant characteristics of this ornate church built and reconstructed in honour of St James the Great, the first martyred disciple who is believed to have been beheaded on this site.

The first church to honour St James was built here by the Georgians in the 11th century. This was built on the foundations of an oratory dedicated to St Menas, an Egyptian martyr, dating from the middle of the 5th century. The Armenians, in favour with the Crusaders, took possession of the church from the Crusaders in the 12th century. They restored the church between them. With a comparable devotion to St James, the Spanish identified with the Armenians and their donations kept the Jerusalem community alive in the 15th century. With the increasingly large numbers of pilgrims, the Armenians purchased adjoining property to house them.

The 17th-century porch was added when the entrance was moved. The pierced brass grills and strange pieces of wood and bronze were used to avoid a 9th-century ruling that forbade Christians to use bells.

Most of the interior's structural elements date back to the Middle Ages, but the central cupola's rib vaulting is typically Armenian. The four piers were squared off in the 17th

century to be decorated with tiles – this was a speciality of the Armenians.

The church is only open for services, held Monday to Friday, 3 to 3.30 pm, Saturday and Sunday 2.30 to 3 pm; admission is free.

Mardigian Museum

Housed in what was a theological seminary built in 1843, with an attractive courtyard enclosed by arched colonnades on two levels, this presents an uninspiring synopsis of Armenian history.

It's open Monday to Saturday 10 am to 5 pm, but is closed Sunday; admission is US$0.65. Enter from either the Armenian Patriarchate Rd or from St James' Cathedral.

Convent of the Olive Tree

Built around 1300 and a fine example of classical Armenian architecture, the site was claimed in the late 14th century to be that of the house of the high priest Annas, the father-in-law of Caiaphas (John 18:13). In the north wall a niche is claimed as the prison of Christ, an alternative to the Greek Orthodox choice on the Via Dolorosa, and in the 15th century the belief started that an olive tree outside the chapel to the north was where Jesus was tied and scourged.

Nearby and part of the chapel's north-east external corner, a stone with a trimmed margin and a central cavity is believed to be the same stone mentioned in Luke 19:40 which would have cried out had the disciples not praised God.

From St James' Cathedral, cut across the compound towards the library and the Mardigian Museum, down the steps into the narrow street and through the low gateway in the far wall. It is best to visit between 8 and 9 am, although until noon you should be able to find an Armenian nun from the adjacent convent to open the chapel for you; admission is free.

St Mark's Chapel

The centre of the Syrian Orthodox community, it also is the centre of certain traditions. The Syrian Orthodox believe it to be the site of the home of St Mark's mother, Mary, where Peter went after he was released from prison by an angel (Acts 12:12). The Virgin Mary is believed to have been baptised here, and according to some, the Last Supper was eaten here, not in the Cenacle on Mount Zion as is most popularly believed. One thing to look out for is the painting on leather of the Virgin and the Child attributed to St Luke. Its age is not known.

It's open 9 am to noon, Monday to Saturday, but is closed on Sundays; admission is free. From Armenian Patriarchate Rd head east along St James' Rd, turn north (left) onto Ararat St and the chapel is on your right, part of a convent. If the door is closed, ring the bell.

MOUNT ZION

Now meaning the part of the stern hill south of the Old City beyond Zion Gate, 'Mount Zion' in the Old Testament period referred to the eastern hill, now known as the City of David (II Samuel 5:7). The name change came in the 4th century, based on new interpretations of religious texts. Bordered on the west and south by the Hinnom Valley and on the east by the Tyropoeon Valley, Mount Zion has one of the city's most enchanting locations. Although now outside the city walls, the area was previously enclosed; first during the 2nd century BC. This compact area contains some of the most important sites in Jerusalem.

To reach Mount Zion, leave the Old City via Zion Gate or head for Zion Gate outside the city walls from either Jaffa or Dung gates. From the New City, Egged bus No 1 runs here via Mea She'arim and HaNevi'im Sts; Egged bus No 38 passes through the New City's centre.

The Cenacle of Coenaculum

Popularly thought to be the site of the Last Supper (*cenacle* is Greek for supper and *coenaculum* is Latin for dining hall), this is the only Christian site in Israel administered by the local government. Like so many traditions, that concerning the Cenacle is unreliable. It probably originated in the 5th century due to the other belief that it is the

room where the Holy Spirit first came down on the disciples at Pentecost.

Part of the complex where David's Tomb is located, the Cenacle was a site of Christian veneration during the Byzantine period. In the Middle Ages the Franciscans acquired it but were later expelled by the Turks. Although the Israeli Government now controls the site, the Franciscans still retain a deed of purchase dated 1335. Under the Turks the Cenacle became a mosque, and Christians were barred from entering, just as Jews were kept from David's Tomb.

To get there, head south from Zion Gate, bear right at the entrance to the Franciscan monastery (double doors marked 'Custodia Terra Sancta') then take the left path when the road splits. A discrete stairway behind a door to the left leads up to the Cenacle. Many visitors mistake the first large room for the real thing, but you need to walk across this big hall to enter the much smaller room where Jesus supposedly ate the Last Supper with his disciples (Matthew 26:26-35; Mark 14:15-25; Luke 22:14-38; John 13, 14, 15, 17; I Corinthians 11:23-25; Acts 1:12-26 and Acts 2:1-4).

It's open daily from 8.30 am to sundown, and admission is free. The Cenacle Chapel is open daily from 8 am to noon, and 3 to 6 pm. Special services are occasionally held; contact the Christian Information Centre for details.

David's Tomb

The entrance to David's Tomb is on the other side of the same building as the Cenacle. From Zion Gate head south and turn left at the Franciscan monastery door and it is on your right. There isn't a lot to see and the site's authenticity is highly disputable. However, it is one of the most revered of the Jewish holy places despite I Kings 2:10 telling of David's burial east of here within his own city.

It's open daily; in summer Saturday to Thursday 8 am to 6 pm, Friday 8 am to 2 pm; and in winter Saturday to Thursday 8 am to 5 pm, Friday 8 am to 1 pm.

Admission is free but beware of guides

forcing themselves upon you to explain away the empty spaces. As heads must be covered, cardboard yarmulkas are provided.

Museum of King David

This museum next to David's Tomb is associated with the Diaspora Yeshiva, the adjacent Jewish school for religious study. Some rather bizarre modern art is the main exhibit. A reason for its existence appears to be to raise money for the yeshiva – donations of at least US$1 are strongly encouraged.

It's hours are Sunday to Thursday 8 am to 6 pm, Friday 8 am to 2 pm and Saturday 8.30 am to 4.30 pm.

Chamber of the Holocaust

Opposite David's Tomb, this was the country's first holocaust museum. The presentation is not so lavish as that at Yad Vashem, but its chilling collection of artefacts is reinforced with a display of anti-Jewish propaganda produced since the holocaust.

It is open Sunday to Thursday 9 am to 5 pm, Friday 8 am to 2 pm, and is closed Saturday; admission is free, but donations are requested. A slide show (US$0.75) is given every two hours or so. Again, as heads must be covered, cardboard yarmulkas are provided.

Church & Monastery of the Dormition

This beautiful church is one of the area's most popular landmarks and is the traditional site where the Virgin Mary died, or fell into 'eternal sleep'. Its Latin name is Dormition Sanctae Mariae (Sleep of Mary). The current church and monastery, owned by the German Benedictine order, was consecrated in 1906. It was noticeably damaged during the battles for the city in 1948 and 1967.

The church's interior is a bright contrast to many of its older and duller peers nearby. A golden mosaic of Mary with the baby Jesus is set in the upper part of the apse; below are the Prophets of Israel. The chapels around the hall are dedicated to saints: St Willibald, an English Benedictine who visited the Holy Land in 724; the Three Wise Men; St Joseph,

whose chapel is covered with medallions featuring kings of Judah as Jesus' forefathers; and St John the Baptist. The floor is decorated with names of saints and prophets and zodiac symbols.

The crypt features a stone effigy of Mary asleep on her deathbed with Jesus calling his Mother to heaven. The chapels around this statue were donated by various countries. In the apse is the Chapel of the Holy Ghost, shown coming down to the Apostles.

The church is open daily from 8 am to noon and 2 to 6 pm; admission is free. The complex also has a pleasant café where cakes and drinks (including beer) are served.

Church of St Peter in Gallicantu

Almost hidden by the trees and the angle of the hill's eastern slope, the Church of St Peter at the Crowing of the Cock is the traditional site of the disciple Peter's denial of Jesus (Mark 14:66-72). It is also believed to be the site of the high priest Caiaphas' house, where Jesus was taken after his arrest (Mark 14:53). Archaeological findings show that a monastic church was built here in the 6th century.

The view from the church's balcony across to the City of David, the Arab village of Silwan and the three valleys that shape Jerusalem is reason enough to justify a visit. The church was built in 1931, but its cellars are Herodian and Roman steps lead down to the Gihon Spring from the garden.

The church is open Monday to Saturday 8 to 11.45 am and 2 to 5 pm (May to September 2 to 5.30 pm), but is closed Sunday; admission is free. The church is reached by turning east (left) as you descend the road leading from Mount Zion down and around to Sultan's Pool.

City of David

The oldest part of Jerusalem, dating back to beyond the 20th century BC, this is the confirmed site of the city captured and developed by King David. The excavations are the result of work, still continuing, that started in 1850.

Of interest to archaeologists, is a signposted path which leads around the excavations. These include the Canaanite citadel of the Jebusite town that David conquered, a fortress built by David, Jerusalem's Upper City where the wealthy resided and buildings destroyed in the Babylonian conquest of 586 BC once stood.

It's open daily from 9 am to 5 pm and admission is free.

From Dung Gate, head east (downhill), take the road to the right (just past the parking lot), then take a left along the path with the sign (just past the grocery store) and follow it down to the bottom of the hill where you turn right. If you don't see a sign, ask for directions as the slopes are too steep to want to get lost on. Continue downhill to reach Warren's Shaft.

Warren's Shaft

This was built by the Jebusites to ensure their water supply during a siege. It is just inside their city's defence wall and this is possibly where Joab entered the City of David (2 Samuel 5:8, I Chronicles 11:6). About 100 metres down from the entrance to the City of David excavations, a small museum features photos of the excavation work with explanations of the water supply situation as it used to be. A spiral staircase leads to a tunnel extending into the shaft, so bring a flashlight. The shaft is open Sunday to Thursday 9 am to 5 pm, Friday 9 am to 12.30 pm, but is closed Saturday; admission is US$1 (students US$0.65).

From Warren's Shaft, you can then proceed down to Hezekiah's Tunnel at the bottom of the hill.

Gihon Spring, Pool of Shiloah & Hezekiah's Tunnel

The Gihon Spring was the main reason why the Jebusites settled on the low Ophel ridge rather than choose the adjacent higher ground. *Gihon* means 'gushing', quite suitable as the spring acts like a siphon, pouring out a large quantity of water for some 30 minutes before almost drying up for between four and 10 hours. There is believed to be enough water to support a population of about 2500. The tunnel was built in about

700 BC by King Hezekiah to bring the water of the Gihon into the city and store it in the pool of Shiloah, or Siloam. Its purpose was to prevent invaders, in particular the Assyrians, from locating the city's water supply and cutting it off (II Chronicles 32). The tunnel's length is 533 metres (335 metres as the crow flies).

Although narrow and low in parts, you can wade through it; the water is normally about half a metre deep. Due to the siphon effect it does occasionally rise, but only by about 15 to 20 cm.

The entrance steps leading down to the water are medieval, built due to the ground level having risen over the years. After about 20 metres the tunnel turns sharply to the left, where a chest-high wall blocks another channel which leads to Warren's Shaft (this can be visited near the City of David excavations). Towards the tunnel's end the roof rises. This is because the tunnellers worked from either end and one team slightly misjudged the other's level. They had to lower the floor so that the water would flow. A Hebrew inscription was found in the tunnel, and a copy can be seen in the Israel Museum in the New City of Jerusalem. Carved by Hezekiah's engineers, it tells of the tunnel's construction.

You enter the tunnel at the Gihon Spring source on Shiloah Way, down in the Kidron Valley and just south of the rest house. Turn right as you get to the foot of the hill from Warren's Shaft.

It's open Sunday to Thursday 9 am to 5 pm, Friday 9 am to 3 pm, and is closed Saturday; admission is free. The wade takes about 30 minutes; wear shorts and suitable footwear. A torch (flashlight) is also required, although candles are normally available from the local shop or the caretaker.

KIDRON VALLEY

Apart from the wonderful views, the points of interest here are tombs. These can be reached by following the road north from the entrance to Hezekiah's Tunnel or by heading south from the Jericho Rd. The Arab village that clings to the eastern slope of the valley is Silwan. From north to south, the most prominent tombs are:

Tomb of Jehoshaphat
This 1st-century burial cave is notable for the impressive frieze above its entrance.

Absalom's Pillar
Also dated to the 1st century, the legendary tomb of David's son (II Samuel 15-18) is just in front of the Tomb of Jehoshaphat.

Grotto of St James or Bnei Hezir
Just beyond Absalom's Pillar, this is where St James is believed to have hidden when Jesus was arrested nearby. It is probably the burial place of the Bnei Hezir's, a family of Jewish priests (Nehemiah 10:21).

Tomb of Zechariah
Carved out of the rock next to the grotto with a pyramid-like top, this is where Jewish tradition believes the prophet Zechariah is buried (II Chronicles 24:20).

Valley of Jehoshaphat
Part of the Kidron Valley, this is the area between the Haram esh-Sharif and the Mount of Olives. Joel 3:1-2 relates to it as the prophesied site of God's judgement of humanity. Jehoshaphat in Hebrew means: 'God shall judge'. Based on this, a legend has arisen which tells of the Day of Judgement. All human beings will be assembled together on the Mount of Olives, with the Judgement Seat on the Haram opposite. Two bridges will appear across the valley between them, and everyone will have to cross either one depending on how they are judged by God. One bridge will be made of iron, the other of paper. The iron bridge will collapse and those who are sent across will die, whilst the paper bridge will hold those who were judged to be allowed to cross it and they will live eternally.

HINNOM VALLEY
Stretching east from below Mount Zion to the Kidron Valley, this was once the area for idols and child sacrifices (Jeremiah 7:31-32). Its name derives from the Hebrew Gei-Hinnom (Ravine of Hinnom), given to the site because of the sin and depravity practised here in ancient times.

Monastery of St Onuphrius (Aceldama)
Named after an Egyptian hermit famous for his very long beard – and for wearing nothing else! It is believed to be near to the Field of Blood which is either the land that the chief priests purchased with the 30 pieces of silver returned by Judas (Matthew 27:7-10) or the place where the repentant disciple hanged himself (Acts 1:18-19). To reach the Greek Orthodox monastery a long but scenic walk is required; either south from the Old City area or east from the New City, adjacent to the Cinemateque.

MOUNT OF OLIVES
Standing to the east of the Old City, the Mount of Olives is dominated by the world's largest Jewish cemetery and the many churches commemorating the events that led to Jesus' arrest and his ascension to heaven. The Arab village of Et Tur is on the summit – its name is Arabic for Mount of Olives.

One of the many 'musts' on a Jerusalem visit, a trip to the Mount of Olives is best started at the top. You can walk from East Jerusalem, or take the bus to avoid what most find a strenuous walk. Arab bus No 75 runs from the station on Suleiman St.

Most of the churches and gardens are open in the morning, before closing down for at least two hours and reopening again in the mid-afternoon. Visiting later in the day is special too; when the sun goes down you will see why Jerusalem is called 'City of Gold'.

Church of Ascension
Located next to Augusta Victoria Hospital and associated with the German Evangelical Church, this church features the 'Service for Tourists & Pilgrims', PO Box 14076, Jerusalem 91140 (☎ 287704; fax 894610).

Working closely with the German language congregation of the city, the church offers an opportunity to meet local Protestant communities of all languages. The church's 45-metre-high tower affords great views across to the Old City and the Judean Desert. The church itself features some noteworthy mosaics, paintings and masonry work. A cafeteria serves refreshments. It is open Monday to Saturday; admission to the church is free, to the tower US$2 (students US$1). Arab bus No 75 stops outside the hospital before heading south across the Mount of Olives to the village of El Tur.

From the New City, Egged bus Nos 23, 9, 28, 26 and 4A go to the Hebrew University on Mount Scopus; from the Goldsmith building stop it's about a 20-minute walk to the hospital.

Russian Chapel of the Ascension

The tallest structure on the Mount of Olives, it is closed to the public.

Mosque of the Ascension

The bus often stops just outside. If not, walk south for a few minutes to reach the mosque; it's on your left. Islam recognises Jesus as a prophet and this mosque is the Crusader reconstruction of the original church built before 392. Saladin authorised two of his followers to acquire the site in 1198 and it has remained in Muslim possession since.

The stone floor bears a mark believed to be Jesus' footprint. Perhaps the reason for its unconvincing appearance today is that pilgrims in the Byzantine period were permitted to take bits of it away.

Its opening hours vary, and the cost of admission is US$0.65.

Church of the Pater Noster

Continue south on the same road and on the bend is the site of the cave, also linked to his ascension, where Jesus spoke to his disciples. Queen Helena had the Church of the Eleona built – its name is a bastardisation of the Greek work *elaion*, meaning olives. After the commemoration site of the Ascension was moved northwards, the cave became exclusively associated with Jesus' teachings such as that recorded by Matthew 24:1-26. Destroyed by the Persians in 614, the site

later became known as the place where Jesus had taught the Lord's Prayer. This inspired the Crusaders to construct an oratory among the ruins in 1106. Based on an old tradition, attractive tiled panels display the Lord's Prayer in over 60 languages.

As you enter the gate, turn left and then

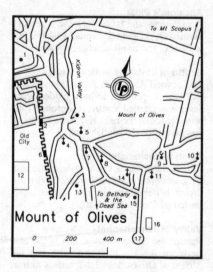

Mount of Olives

1 Rockefeller Museum
2 Lion's (St Stephen's) Gate
3 Mary's Tomb
4 St Stephen's Church
5 Church of the Assumption & Grotto
6 Golden Gate
7 Church of All Nations
8 Russian Church of Mary Magdalene
9 Mosque of the Ascension
10 Russian Orthodox Church
11 Church of the Pater Noster
12 Dome of the Rock
13 Tombs of Absalom & Jehoshaphat
14 Church of Dominus Flevit
15 Tombs of the Prophets
16 Seven Arches Hotel
17 Lookout

right. The tomb is of Princesse de la Tour d'Auvergne who purchased the property in 1886 and built the Carmelite convent. The actual cave can be reached by going around the cloister to the left, down some stairs and through the first door on the right.

It is open Monday to Saturday from 8.30 to 11.45 am and 3 to 4.45 pm, but is closed on Sunday; admission is free.

Seven Arches Hotel
Although a large gin and tonic can be most refreshing, the hotel is more renowned for its beautiful but controversial location than for its facilities and service. In front of the hotel, at the end of the road which runs along the top of the mount, is a viewing point from where many photographs of the Old City are taken.

A camel or two will often be available for rides and photo opportunities. The controversy surrounding the hotel is due to it being built over part of an ancient Jewish cemetery.

Tombs of the Prophets
Head back up the road a little and take the path down to these tombs, now in the backyard of the nearby house, whose owner is the caretaker. Buried here are the prophets Haggai, Zachariah and Malachi who lived in the 5th century BC.

It is open Sunday to Friday 8 am to 3 pm, and is closed Saturday; admission is free.

National Cemetery & Common Grave
This is the burial place of some of those who died in the Jewish Quarter battles of 1948.

Jewish Cemetery
This is the world's oldest and largest Jewish cemetery, dating back to biblical times. Its importance is based on the belief that this will be the site of the Resurrection of the Dead on the Day of Judgement when the Messiah comes (Zechariah 14:1-11).

Church of Dominus Flevit
Follow the path down to this church built by medieval pilgrims who claimed to have found the rock on the Mount of Olives where

Jesus had wept for Jerusalem (Luke 19:41). In 1881, the Franciscans built a chapel nearby as the Muslims would not allow them on the site.

When the existing church was built in 1954-55, excavations unearthed a 5th-century monastery and a large cemetery dating back to about 1500 BC. The cemetery has since been recovered but some tombs are still visible.

The view of the Dome of the Rock from the altar's window is particularly attractive. It is open daily from 8 to 11.45 am and 3 to 5 pm; admission is free.

Russian Church of Mary Magdalene
With its onion domes making it another attractive landmark, this beautiful church is open for very limited hours so check your schedule if you plan to pay a visit. Built by Alexander III and dedicated to his mother, the church is now a convent and has one of the city's best choirs. A section of the Garden of Gethsemane is claimed to be within the church's grounds.

It is only open on Tuesday and Thursday from 10 to 11.30 am; admission is free.

Church of All Nations & Garden of Gethsemane
From the Russian Church, continue down and turn left; the garden's entrance is on the left – not at the front by the main road. Built in 1924, this church, also known as the Basilica of the Agony, was financed by various countries, hence its popular name.

The successor to two earlier churches, the first was built in the 4th century but was destroyed by an earthquake in the 740s. The Crusaders built an oratory in its ruins but it was abandoned in 1345 for unknown reasons.

This is the popularly accepted site of the garden where Jesus was arrested (Mark 14:32-50). The garden has some of the world's oldest olive trees, but they probably do not date back to the time of Jesus. The mosaic on the church's attractive facade sparkles subtly in the evening sunlight.

The garden is open daily April to October

8 am to noon and 2.30 to 6 pm; and November to March 8 am to noon and 2.30 to 5 pm. Admission is free.

Mary's Tomb

On the main road turn right, and take the stairs to the right down to this tomb. A cupola supported by columns is a memorial to Mujir ed-Din, a 15th-century Muslim judge and historian. Mary was supposedly interned here by the disciples. A monument was first constructed in the 5th century but was repeatedly destroyed. The present monument is from the 12th century and is owned by the Greek Orthodox Church, whilst the Armenians, Syrians and Copts have shares in the altar.

It is open Monday to Saturday 6.30 am to noon and 2 to 5 pm, but is closed Sunday; admission is free.

St Stephen's Church

This Greek Orthodox Church is on the south side of the main road as it bends down and around from East Jerusalem and the Old City. Largely ignored by guides and visitors alike, it was completed in 1968. A 'modern Byzantine' church, it is near the site where Stephen, the first Christian martyr, was stoned to death. The two pleasant ladies who look after the church are happy to guide visitors around both the church and the chapel on the site where Stephen was slain.

There are also remains of the Roman road which led from the Golden Gate down to the Kidron Valley and an anonymous tomb cut into the rock. It is also a good place to ask questions about the Greek Orthodox Church. Ring the bell to see if anyone is in – there are no set hours. Admission is free.

MOUNT SCOPUS

With marvellous views of the city and the Judean Desert towards Jordan, a visit to this spot is well worthwhile. Mount Scopus' name is the Greek translation of the Hebrew word *hatsofim* (to look over).

Its strategic location has played a decisive role in the many battles for Jerusalem over the centuries. In 70 AD the Roman legions of Titus camped here, as did the Crusaders in 1099 and the British in 1917. In the 1948 War of Independence, Arab forces attacked from here.

One of the more intriguing aspects of the 1949 ceasefire was that Mount Scopus became an Israeli-held enclave in Jordanian territory. In addition to the Hebrew University campus and the military cemetery, other places of note here include Hadassah Hospital, renowned as one of the world's top medical centres, and the Mormon Brigham Young University, which opened against strong opposition from religious Jews. Take Arab bus No 75 to the Augusta Victoria Hospital, or Egged bus Nos 4, 4A, 9, 23 or 28 to the university.

Hebrew University

With its distinctive modern architecture dominating the hilltop, the Mount Scopus campus of the Hebrew University could interest you. The world's first secular Hebrew institute of higher learning, it was founded in 1925. After the War of Independence, the university was re-established at Giv'at Ram. After Israel's victory in the Six Day War of 1967, the Mount Scopus campus was renovated and expanded.

There are free guided tours in English at 11 am, lasting from 60 to 90 minutes, Sunday to Thursday. These leave from the Bronfman Visitors' Centre in the administration building. The modern Hecht Synagogue stands out as the major attraction for visitors.

WW I Cemetery

Soldiers from the British Commonwealth forces are buried here. Various remembrance services, including ANZAC Day (for New Zealanders and Australians) are held here, attended by the Mayor of Jerusalem, other local dignitaries and military personnel.

EAST JERUSALEM
Solomon's Quarries

Between Damascus and Herod's Gates, this vast cave beneath the Old City's north wall was part of a quarry that extended as far as what is now Suleiman St and the bus station.

It is possible that stone from here was used to construct the Temple (I Kings 5:15-17) and that Herod the Great (37-4 BC) used it.

In Jewish tradition the cave is known as Me'arat Zidkiyahu (Zedekiah's Cave), because the last king of Judah apparently used it as an escape route before being captured near Jericho by the Babylonians. The cave continues for over 200 metres beneath the Old City and offers cool refuge from a hot day, but there is little to see.

It's open daily from 9 am to 5 pm; admission is US$0.55 (students US$0.30).

Rockefeller Museum
Further east on the north side of Suleiman St, opposite the north-eastern corner of the Old City, this architectural delight is one of the leading archaeological museums in Israel. Established in 1927 as the Palestine Archaeological Museum, its exhibits range from the Stone Age to the 18th century.

The museum (☎ 282251, 285151) is open Sunday to Thursday 10 am to 5 pm, and Friday and Saturday 10 am to 2 pm. There are free guided tours at 11 am on Sunday and Friday. Admission is US$2.40. From the New City take Egged buses Nos 23, 27 or 99.

Friday's Arab Sheep Market
Seeing Beersheba's touristy Bedouin market on Thursdays may seem a waste of time, but this early morning get-together each Friday is a more authentic Middle Eastern spectacle. With the solid walls of the Old City as a backdrop, hundreds of kaffiyeh-clad Palestinian farmers bring their livestock to sell, and in the process provide a free show for those visitors who are not sleeping in after a wasted day in Beersheba. It's opposite the Rockefeller Museum on the north-eastern corner of the Old City wall, just walk through the impatient traffic jam caused by the market.

Garden Tomb
Many of you will end up either participating in or listening to earnest travellers' discussions regarding the most likely site of Jesus' crucifixion, burial and resurrection: either the Church of the Holy Sepulchre or the Garden Tomb. Certainly many find this to be the more pleasant site. As one Catholic priest was heard to say: 'If the Garden Tomb is not the true site of the Lord's death and resurrection, it should have been!' Also known as Gordon's Calvary, the site was first claimed as Golgotha by General Charles Gordon in 1883. The tomb found here, along with the hill's skull shape, convinced him of the site's authenticity.

Now owned by the Garden Tomb Association of London, the site has very friendly staff. During the summer months an interesting and often humorous free guided tour is given. Some argue that the Protestants in particular have supported the Garden Tomb theory due to the lack of their own holy site.

Go and see for yourself – it's open Monday to Saturday 8 am to 12.15 pm and 2.30 to 5.15 pm, but is closed Sunday; admission is free. On Sunday at 9 am an inter-denominational service with singing is held, which lasts about 50 minutes. From Suleiman St head north along Nablus Rd and turn right on Schick St.

St George's Cathedral
Named after St George, traditionally believed to have been martyred in Palestine early in the 4th century, this is the cathedral church of the Anglican Episcopal Diocese of Jerusalem and the Middle East. It was consecrated in 1910. During WW I, the Turks closed the church and used the bishop's house as their army headquarters. After the British took Jerusalem in 1917, the truce was signed here in the bishop's study.

The cathedral has two congregations, Arabic and English speaking, and the complex includes a popular guesthouse (see Places to Stay in this chapter) and school, St George's College (see Courses in the Facts for the Visitor chapter).

Stepping into the compound of this church, you leave the hustle of the city behind you and escape into a British oasis, a piece of the Mandate seemingly frozen in time. The church features many symbols of the British presence in Jerusalem: a font

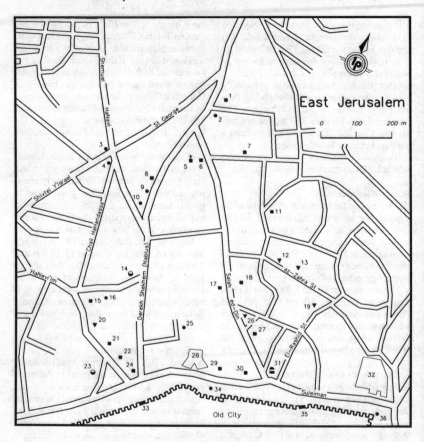

given by Queen Victoria, memorials to British servicemen, a royal coat of arms, an English oak screen and the tower built in memory of King Edward VII.

The guesthouse's beautiful garden is a great place to sit and reflect over a cup of tea. Continuing northwards along Nablus Rd, the complex is on the right. It has no set hours and admission is free.

Tombs of the Kings

Carry on northwards after St George's Cathedral to the end of Nablus Rd, turn right into Salah ed-Din St and the tombs are on the left by the corner. The first archaeologist to excavate the complex identified it as the Tombs of the Kings of Judah due to its majestic facade. The name has stuck, but it has since been proved that this is the 1st century tomb of Queen Helena of Adiabene, Mesopotamia. It was described by one scholar as one of the country's 'most interesting ancient burial places' but only archaeology buffs are likely to agree.

The area is open Monday to Saturday from 8 am to 12.30 pm and 2 to 5 pm, but is closed Sunday; admission is US$0.65 (students US$0.35).

<table>
<tr><th colspan="2">■ PLACES TO STAY</th><th colspan="2">OTHER</th></tr>
</table>

■ PLACES TO STAY

1	American Colony Hotel
6	St George's Cathedral Guesthouse
7	Christmas Hotel
8	YMCA East-Aelia Capitolina
11	Ritz Hotel
15	Ramsis Youth Hostel
17	Capitol Hotel
18	Lawrence Hotel
21	New Raghadan Hostel
22	Palm Hostel
24	Faisal Youth Hostel
27	New Metropole Hotel
29	Pilgrim's Palace Hotel
30	Rivoli Hotel

▼ PLACES TO EAT

12	Philadelphia Restaurant
13	Café Europe
19	Petra Restaurant
20	Arab Bakery
26	Abu Ali Restaurant

OTHER

2	Tombs of the Kings
3	Mandelbaum Gate
4	Tourjeman Post Museum
5	St George's Anglican Cathedral
9	British Consulate
10	US Consulate
14	Arab Bus Station (for Northern Destinations)
16	Armenian Mosaic
23	Sherut Station
33	Damascus Gate
25	Garden Tomb
28	Arab Bus Station (for Southern & Eastern Destinations)
31	Post Office
32	Rockefeller Museum
33	Damascus Gate
34	Solomon's Quarries & Zedekiah's Cave
35	Lion's Gate
36	Arab Sheep Market

Tourjeman Post Museum

Overlooking the former Mandelbaum Gate area, the only access point between the Jewish New City and the Jordanian Old City and East Jerusalem between 1948 and 1967, this museum is housed in an old Turkish house used by the Israelis as a frontier position. With the touchy theme 'a divided city reunited', it presents a distinctly Zionist picture of the period when the city was physically divided by walls and barbed wire between Israel and Jordan.

A little tricky to find, it is at 1 Chail HaHandassa St (☎ 281278). From the Damascus Gate area walk north up HaNevi'im St, turn right after the Ramsis Youth Hostel onto Chail HaHandassa St and it's on your left after a few minutes. Alternatively you can walk up Nablus Rd, take the road to the left of the US Consulate which takes you to the junction with Chail Handassa, Shivtei Y'Israel and St George Sts. From the New City take Egged bus Nos 1, 11 or 27.

The museum is open Sunday to Thursday, from 9 am to 4 pm, Friday and Saturday 9 am to 1 pm; admission is US$1.40.

Armenian Mosaic

Perhaps the country's loveliest mosaic floor, its design features various species of birds in the branches of a vine. Laid down in the 5th-6th centuries, the colours are still incredibly brilliant. The Armenian inscription where the apse should begin in what was a mortuary chapel, reads 'For the memory and salvation of the souls of all Armenians whose names are known to God alone'.

A sign referring to St Polyeuctus indicates this building just around the corner from, and behind Ramsis Youth Hostel in HaNevi'im St. It is open Monday to Saturday from 7 am to 5.30 pm, and is closed Sunday; admission is free.

NEW CITY
Ammunition Hill
This was Jordan's main fortified outpost on
the Jerusalem front and during the Six Day
War it was taken by the Israelis in the first
major battle for the Old City. The bunker
complex has been converted into a museum
of the war and a memorial to the many Israeli
lives lost in the fighting.

The museum is open Sunday to Thursday
9 am to 5 pm, Friday 9 am to 1 pm, closed
Saturday, and admission is US$0.85. Take
Egged bus Nos 9, 25 or 28 and ask for Giv'at
HaTahmoshet (Ammunition Hill). It is in a
small park east of Nablus Rd and the police
headquarters, and west of Levi Eshkol St
(☎ 284442).

UNRWA
South of Ammunition Hill, and on the same
side of the main road, this is the location of
UNRWA's public information office.

Inquire here (☎ 828451/5, Nablus Rd, PO
Box 19149) about arranging a visit to the
West Bank refugee camps (see the UNRWA
section in the Facts about the Country
chapter). Allow at least 48 hours; note that it
is closed Saturday afternoon and all day
Sunday.

Sanhedrin Tombs
Known to Christians as the Judges' Tombs,
the Sanhedrin was ancient Israel's supreme
court. Its 71 members sat in the Temple area
and are believed to be buried in this park.

The site is open Sunday to Friday from 9
am to sunset, and is closed Saturday; admission is free. Take Egged bus No 2, get off at
HaSanhedrin St and look for the attractive
park carpeted with pebbles, acanthus leaves
and fruit.

Biblical Zoo
Universally condemned as not worth a visit,
this ragged collection of creatures mentioned
in the Bible is located near the Sanhedrin
Tombs. Continue south on HaSanhedrin St
and turn west (right) on Bar-Ilan St.

From the New City centre take Egged bus
Nos 7, 15 or 27.

The zoo is open from Sunday to Thursday
9 am to 5 pm, Friday 9 am to 1 pm, Saturday
9 am to 3 pm, and admission is around
US$3.80 (students US$2.50).

For a Saturday visit, tickets must be purchased in advance due to the religious law
forbidding money transactions on Shabbat.

Mahane Yehuda Market
Generally cheaper than the competition in
the Old City, this Jewish food market is a
bustling hive of activity. About a km west of
Zion Square between Jaffa Rd and Agrippas
St, the market is an attraction in its own right
even if you don't want to do any shopping.

Stalls laden with fruit, vegetables, pickles,
cheese, fish and biscuits line the streets along
with cheap butcheries, bakeries and wholesale *mahkolets* (grocery shops). On Agrippas
St are several great places where you can
enjoy meat cooked 'on the fire', and these
are open from the early evening until early
morning.

The market is at its busiest on Thursday
and Friday with thousands scrambling to buy
the food needed for Shabbat. Mahane
Yehuda is Hebrew for Camp of Judah, and
its streets are named after fruits.

Mea She'arim
Possibly the world's most reluctant tourist
attraction, this ultra-orthodox Jewish district
is the only remaining example of *shtetl*
(ghetto) which existed before the Holocaust
in Eastern European Jewish communities. It
is just to the north of the downtown area and
was established in 1875.

Mea She'arim is Hebrew for One Hundred
Gates and is taken from Genesis 26:12, referring to Isaac farming the land and receiving
a hundredfold. At one time in its formative
years the district had its own defence walls
with, it is said, 100 gates in them.

Walking these streets is usually an eye-
opener: the residents mostly dress in
18th-century East European styles. They are
mainly devoted to religious study and are

often financed by fellow ultra-orthodox communities abroad. Because of the intensity of the religious aspect, this is the best place in the world for buying items of Judaica. There are also many bakeries producing traditional products.

Another result of the dominant interpretation of Jewish Law here are the attitudes towards strangers. Signs proclaim 'Daughters of Israel! The Torah requires you to dress modestly' and give details of what this all means. When you visit Mea She'arim you should conform to the residents' standards in your dress and behaviour. This means that women should not wear shorts or even long trousers, but a loose-fitting skirt and long sleeves. Men should wear long trousers. Do not walk arm in arm or even hand in hand with anyone, and kissing is definitely taboo. Most ultra-orthodox Jews dislike being photographed – in fact, their interpretation of Jewish Law forbids it.

The more extreme characters have been known to stone those, Jewish and non-Jewish, who break these codes of conduct, however unwittingly. Signalled or verbal objections are more common, though. These vary from the holding of a hand to the face to avoid being photographed, to the hissing of the word 'prostitute' at a young woman whose taste in fashion does not include a shaved head, wig and scarf. Needless to say, thousands of photographs are taken each week; just be discreet and aware of the possible response to your activities. Abiding by the request to dress discreetly is not too difficult though.

Mea She'arim is a few minutes' walk from both Damascus Gate and the Jaffa Rd/King George V St junction.

Ministry of Education Building

This 16th-century Italian renaissance-style beauty stands on Shivtei Y'Israel St, between HaNevi'im and Mea She'arim Sts. Built in the 1880s, it was once the Italian Hospital.

HaNevi'im (Prophet) St

An important street in the New City, right on the border with East Jerusalem, it honours the prophets of Israel, many of whom lived in the city, and is lined by some important and attractive buildings. It is also a useful street for travellers, being a convenient route between the Damascus Gate area, Mea She'arim, the Russian Compound and the New City's downtown area.

At the Damascus Gate end, by the lorry park, large numbers of Arabs gather in what is an unofficial outdoor employment agency. Every so often a car driven by a Jewish employer needing a worker for the day will cruise along, chased by job-seekers.

Ethiopian Church

Tucked away on the narrow Ethiopia St, this impressive domed construction would be a major feature in most cities, but in Jerusalem it is often overlooked. Built between 1896 and 1904, the church's entrance gate features the carved Lion of Judah. This emblem is believed to have been given to the Queen of Sheba, Ethiopia's queen, by Solomon when she visited Jerusalem.

This church opens daily, March to September from 7 am to 6 pm; and October to February from 8 am to 5 pm. Admission is free.

Opposite the church is the house where Eliezer Ben Yehuda lived and did much of his work on the revival of the Hebrew language. A plaque marking the house was stolen by ultra-orthodox Jews who strongly disapprove of the language's everyday use. Note the Ethiopian Consulate with its mosaic-decorated facade on your left as you descend HaNevi'im St towards the Old City.

Notre Dame of Jerusalem Centre

Opposite New Gate, this is one of the city's most attractive buildings. Built in 1887 by the Roman Catholic Assumpionist Fathers for French pilgrims, it suffered considerable damage during the 1948 War of Independence with some of the fiercest fighting taking place in this area. The south wing, facing the Old City, became uninhabitable due to bombing, and was used as an Israeli bunker and frontier post.

Unable to meet the costs of maintaining the property, the Assumptionists left in 1970, selling the property to a branch of the Jewish National Fund. They donated it to the Hebrew University as a students' residence. Amidst rumours of profiteering on the part of the fathers and others involved, the Vatican opposed the transaction and engaged in top-level discussions with the university, mayor, and even the prime minister.

Eventually, the property was sold to the Vatican at the price paid by the university, and Pope Paul VI instigated a major renovation programme, restoring Notre Dame as a pilgrim centre. Starting in 1973, it was completed in 1978, largely financed by American Catholics.

In its function as the Holy See's international pilgrim centre, Notre Dame today consists of a highly rated guesthouse (see Places to Stay in this chapter) and restaurant (see Places to Eat, also in this chapter), with an arts centre promoting traditional local Christian art. There is also a cultural centre under construction.

Daughters of Charity of St Vincent de Paul

On Mamilla Rd down from Jaffa Gate, this large convent is another of those wonderful Jerusalem buildings that gets lost in the crowd. The house at No 33 bears a plaque noting that Dr Theodor Herzl, the founder of political Zionism, stayed here during his visit to Palestine in 1898.

Russian Compound

Between Jaffa Rd and HaNevi'im St and dominated by the green domes of the Russian cathedral, this area was acquired by the Russian Church in 1860. In addition to the cathedral, facilities were constructed here for the many pilgrims who visited the Holy Land until WW I. The cathedral, closed to the public, occupies the site where the Assyrians camped in about 700 BC, and in 70 AD Roman legions assembled here during the Jewish revolt. In front of the cathedral, the 12-metre-high Herod's Pillar is believed to have been intended for Herod's

Temple. However, it broke and was abandoned here.

Nicknamed 'Bevingrad' by the Jews during the Mandate, after the unpopular (with them) British Foreign Secretary Ernest Bevin, the compound is home today to the central police station and law courts.

Hall of Heroism In the middle of the car park in the north-west of the compound, this museum commemorates the exploits of the Jewish underground paramilitary movement of the British Mandate period. A blindly patriotic tribute to the Haganah and its fringe organisations, it's housed in what was a British prison, complete with cells and gallows.

The hall is open Sunday to Thursday 9 am to 4 pm, Friday 10 am to 1 pm, but is closed Saturday; admission is US$2.

Ticho House

On Abraham Ticho St just off HaRav Kook St opposite Zion Square (☎ 245068), this is the former home of Dr Abraham Ticho and his artist wife, Anna. Now part of the Israel Museum, it's a popular combination of museum, art gallery, library and café; a particular favourite with local conservative ladies.

Dr Ticho, a Jew, was a leader in the field of ophthalmology and, during the British Mandate, was responsible for saving hundreds of Palestinian Arabs from blindness. Anna Ticho was an award-winning artist with Jerusalem the major inspiration for much of her work.

. Included in the exhibits is Dr Ticho's study and some documents and letters of interest, in particular dealing with his work for the Arabs, as well as his collection of Hanukkah lamps and Anna Ticho's art.

The house is open Sunday, Monday, Wednesday and Thursday 10 am to 5 pm, Tuesday 10 am to 10 pm, Friday 10 am to 2 pm, but is closed Saturday.

The library is open Sunday to Thursday 10 am to 4 pm, Friday 10 am to noon, and admission is free.

The café is open Sunday to Wednesday 10

am to 11.45 pm, closed Thursday and Friday, and open on Saturday from sundown to 11.45 pm.

Bezalel School of Art

Near the junction of King George V and Ben Yehuda Sts, at 10 Shemuel HaNagid St, this is Israel's premier art school, founded in 1906. It is named after the Old Testament artist Bezalel Ben-Ouri (Exodus 31:2-11).

Next door to the main school building, at 12 Shemuel HaNagid St, Artists' House (☎ 223653) features an art gallery, shop and a bar/restaurant.

The gallery is open Monday to Friday 9 am to 1 pm and 4 to 7 pm, Saturday and Sunday 10 am to 1 pm and 4 to 7 pm, and admission is free. The bar/restaurant is open daily, usually until after midnight.

Museum of the Potential Holocaust

Located at 31 Ussishkin St, between Keren Kayemet and Narkiss Sts, this museum features a display of racist propoganda featuring anti-Semitism.

The museum is open Sunday to Thursday 1 to 4 pm, closed Friday and Saturday, and admission is US$2. Egged bus Nos 17 or 19 will get you there.

Museum of Italian Jewish Art & Synagogue

A visit is recommended to enjoy the beauty of the architecture and artwork housed here. This includes an entire 18th-century synagogue brought from Italy. This is the only synagogue outside of Italy where the ancient Italian liturgy is performed.

The museum is at 27 Hillel St (☎ 24160), on the next street parallel to and south of Ben Yehuda St, down from King George V St.

It is open Sunday and Tuesday 10 am to 1 pm, Wednesday 4 to 7 pm, and admission is US$0.65. Shabbat services are held here.

Jewish Agency Building

On King George V St (named after the British monarch reigning when the Balfour Declaration was issued in 1917), this complex is topped by a menorah illustrating the age of the State of Israel. The Jewish Agency headquarters, it also houses the offices of the JNF and Keren Hayesod. During the British Mandate, this was the seat of the Jewish secondary government. On view are the Zionist Archives, the Golden Book (recording the names of donors to the cause), and occasional films.

The building is open Sunday to Thursday 8 am to 1 pm, closed Friday and Saturday, and admission is free.

Heichal Shlomo

Facing the Plaza Hotel and Independence Park at 58 King George V St, this complex is styled along the lines of Solomon's Temple. 'Heichal Shlomo' literally means 'Solomon's Mansion' and is the seat of the Chief Rabbinate of Israel and the Supreme Religious Centre. The emblem of the scales of justice is featured on both sides of the entrance.

The Wolffson Museum here features presentations of religious and traditional Jewish life; admission is US$0.65. The actual building is open Sunday to Thursday 9 am to 1 pm, Friday 9 am to noon, and is closed Saturday.

Great Synagogue

This is next door to the Heichal Shlomo and incorporated in the complex. Attendance at a Shabbat service is recommended here.

Rehavia & Komemiyut

These are amongst the city's more fashionable neighbourhoods, although the increase in the number of ultra-orthodox Jewish residents is said to be changing that. Most of the impressive properties display nameplates of the medical and legal professions. The official residence of the prime minister is here, on the corner of Balfour and Smolenskin Sts. Next door is the Rubin Academy of Music, and, at 6 Balfour St, the Schoken Library houses rare Hebrew prints and manuscripts.

The president's official residence is on HaNassi St, near the Jerusalem Sherover Theatre and the L A Mayer Museum of Islamic Art.

These neighbourhoods are basically between King George V St to the east and HaNassi Ben Zvi St to the west. Cutting through on foot to reach the Israel Museum, the Knesset building and the Monastery of the Cross, makes a pleasant stroll.

International Christian Embassy Jerusalem

At 10 Brenner St, Rehavia, this 'embassy' (☎ 669389/823) invites everyone to watch a free video explaining the reasons for its establishment, and in particular its participation in the Feast of the Tabernacles celebrations (see Religion in the Facts about the Country chapter).

The 'embassy' is open Monday to Thursday 9 am to 4 pm, Friday and Saturday 9 am to 2 pm, and is closed Sunday.

Jason's Tomb

In Rehavia's Alfasi St this is one of the city's most interesting tombs because its history is known in detail. Built in the early 1st century BC by Jason, the head of a wealthy family, it contains two or three generations of that family.

Archaeologists learned from this tomb of that era's expressions of belief in the afterlife. Cooking pots, complete with food, and lighting were provided in the individual graves and some dice were found – gambling in heaven? The porch's charcoal drawings of a warship in pursuit of two other vessels indicate that Jason or a son was a naval officer. Tomb robbers had struck before the great earthquake of 31 BC destroyed it. The pyramid over the porch is a reconstruction. Before it are three courts, the nearest of which is entered by a gate. Look through the iron grille to see the burial chamber. Eight shaft graves can be seen through the small opening on the left.

L A Mayer Museum of Islamic Art

This highly recommended museum is at 2 HaPalmach St in Rehavia (☎ 661291/2). The collection includes paintings, weaponry, miniatures and jewellery – no specifically Palestinian items are featured however.

The museum is open Sunday to Thursday 10 am to 5 pm, Saturday 10 am to 1 pm, and it's closed Friday; admission is US$2 (students US$1.35). Take Egged bus No 15 from the New City centre.

King David St

Also called David HaMelekh, this busy road runs south from the New City centre to the railway station and has several important landmarks, including Terra Sancta, the Hebrew Union College building, the King David Hotel and the YMCA. It leads to Herod's Family Tomb, the attractive Yemin Moshe and Mishkenot Sha'ananim neighbourhoods and Liberty Bell Park.

YMCA

The YMCA (☎ 227111, 223433/7) is on King David St opposite the King David Hotel. The distinctive tower is open Monday to Saturday 9 am to 1 pm, is closed Sunday, and admission is US$0.65.

The soccer stadium behind the main building is the home ground for the Jerusalem team, and enthusiastic crowds attend the matches. The complex also features swimming pool, tennis and other sports facilities, accommodation and a restaurant (see Places to Stay for Jerusalem in this chapter).

Herod's Family Tomb

The tomb is just south of the King David Hotel and overlooking the Old City. When archaeologists discovered it, little was found inside due to tomb robbers. Herod himself is not buried here but at Herodian, near Bethlehem.

Montefiore Windmill

The windmill is a pretty landmark adjacent to Bloomfield Park and opposite Mount Zion. A museum here is dedicated to Sir Moses Montefiore, the philanthropist who financed the adjacent neighbourhood project, and deals with 'his life and his work'.

It is open Sunday to Thursday 9 am to 4 pm, Friday 9 am to 1 pm, but is closed on Saturday.

Top: Ancient olive tree in the Garden of Gethsemane. Mount of Olives, Jerusalem (RE)
Left: Tombs at the Mount of Olives (RE)
Right: Mount of Olives (NT)

Top: Jewish women praying at the Western Wall, Jerusalem (NT)
Bottom: Palestinian mother and daughters climbing up to Dome of the Rock (NT)

Mishkenot Sha'ananim & Yemin Moshe

Montefiore's major contribution to modern Jewish development in the country – the first Jewish settlement outside the Old City walls. Now beautifully renovated and a real estate agent's dream. Artists' galleries attract many visitors to the area.

Liberty Bell Park

Just across from the Montefiore Windmill an exact replica of the Liberty Bell in Philadelphia is the central point of this three-hectare garden, which is used for picnics and public events.

St Andrew's Church

Also known as the Scottish Church, it was built in 1927 to commemorate the capture of the city and the Holy Land by the British in WW I. Owned by the Church of Scotland, the floor features an inscription to the memory of the Scottish King Robert the Bruce, who wanted to have his heart buried in Jerusalem when he died. He arranged that Sir James Douglas would bring the heart but en route the knight was killed in Spain, fighting the Moors. The heart was recovered and returned to Scotland where it is buried at Melrose, while the body is buried at Dunfermline.

House of Quality

Most noticeable here is the cable pulley stretching across to Mount Zion, put up in 1948 to secure a link with the Jewish forces struggling to survive against the Arabs. The House of Quality (12 Hebron St) is a showroom for goods made by local artists.

The house is open Sunday to Thursday 10 am to 6 pm, Friday 10 am to 1 pm, and is closed Saturday.

Cinemateque & the Jerusalem Film Centre

On Hebron Rd (☎ 715398), with great views across to Mount Zion, the Old City and the Hinnom Valley, this complex houses a small museum, library and archives relating to the film industry. It's open Sunday and Monday 10 am to 3 pm, Tuesday and Thursday 10 am to 7 pm, and Friday 10 am to 1 pm. It also houses the city's best cinema and a popular restaurant with a terrace to enjoy those views.

Sultan's Pool

Now a unique amphitheatre used for a variety of concerts, this was one of the city's three major water reservoirs and the site of a cattle market. On the roadside is a beautiful 16th-century water fountain, built during the Suleiman Period. Another example is on El-Wad Rd in the Old City's Muslim Quarter.

Haas Promenade & Hill of Evil Counsel

Providing another spectacular view of Jerusalem, this promenade is a popular place for Jerusalemites to visit at night. Nearby, on the east side of the Kidron Valley is the Hill of Evil Counsel. Now the site of the UN headquarters, it was the residency of the British High Commissioner for Palestine during the Mandate. Going further back, it is an alternate possibility for the site of the house of Caiaphas, the high priest who paid Judas to betray Jesus.

Kibbutz Ramat Rahel

Its location between Jerusalem and Bethlehem made this kibbutz a scene of bloody fighting during the 1948 War.

Today, that same location has helped the kibbutz develop itself as a full-scale tourist attraction. Its name means 'the Height of Rachel', referring to Jacob's wife whose tomb is in Bethlehem. It offers visitors a glimpse of life on the collective farm with tours, a guesthouse, restaurant and bar.

A museum has exhibits on the 1948 War; this is open 8 am to noon daily. Telephone ☎ 702555 for details about guided tour schedules and use Egged bus No 7 to get there.

Monastery of the Cross

Founded by King Bagrat of Georgia, it commemorates the tradition that the tree from which Jesus' cross was made grew here. Although the church is basically 11th century, various additions were made over time. The Greek Orthodox Church purchased the complex in 1685. In a valley that was once the vineyard of Jerusalem's Crusader kings, the monastery can be reached by walking through Rehavia along Ramban St, crossing Herzog St and following the path down the hillside.

From the New City centre take Egged bus Nos 9, 16 or 24; from Jaffa Gate, Egged bus No 19. Get off at the first stop on Herzog St and follow the path down.

The monastery is open Monday to Friday 9 am to 4 pm, closed Saturday and Sunday, and admission is US$0.65.

Israel Museum & Shrine of the Book

Israel's leading museum complex, it features various facets of Jewish history in several separate museums, a sculpture garden and the Shrine of the Book, which houses some of the Dead Sea Scrolls. With specific departments dealing with archaeology, Jewish ethnography, Jewish life, Jewish ceremonial art, primitive and Israeli art, old masters and Impressionists, modern art, ancient glass and period rooms, there is a lot to see. The Billy Rose Sculpture Garden includes work by Henry Moore and Picasso.

The Shrine of the Book is a distinctive building resembling a cover of the pots in which the 2000-year-old Dead Sea Scrolls were found in caves at Qumran, near the Dead Sea in 1947. The scrolls were written by Essenes, members of a mystical, ascetic Jewish cult. They are ancient editions of some books of the bible, and are of immense importance to Judaic scholarship.

Guided tours in English are included in the museum's admission price. They start from the main entrance and deal with a specific area rather than the whole complex – check the current schedule for the hours and the subjects covered.

The museum is open Sunday, Monday, Wednesday, Thursday 10 am to 5 pm (Shrine of the Book 10 am to 3 pm); Tuesday 4 to 10 pm, and Friday and Saturday 10 am to 2 pm.

Admission to the museum only is US$4, and to the museum and the Shrine of the Book US$5 (students US$2.50). Telephone ☎ 708873 for recorded information or check the tourist office and *Jerusalem Post* for details of special exhibits, lectures, concerts and events. You can get there on Egged bus Nos 9, 17 or 24.

Bible Museum

The latest addition to the New City's cultural scene, the museum is billed as 'a nondenominational centre for the appreciation of the history of the bible' and 'a guide to the cultures that make up the book'.

Dating from 6000 BC to 600 AD and presented chronologically, the exhibits include some two thousand artefacts. These range from mosaics and other art pieces, seals, ivories and bronzes to simple household items from all over Asia, Europe and Africa.

The museum is on Granot St, adjacent to the Israel Museum and near the Knesset.

It is open Sunday and Wednesday from 9.30 am to 9.30 pm; Monday, Tuesday and Thursday from 9.30 am to 5.30 pm; and Friday from 9.30 am to 2 pm. It is closed on Saturday, and admission is US$3.50.

Knesset

A few minutes' walk from the Israel Museum and overlooking the valley in which the Monastery of the Cross sits is HaKirya (The City), the government centre. Dominating the scene is the Knesset, Israel's Parliament, inaugurated in 1966. You can see the Knesset in session on Monday or Tuesday, 4 to 7 pm and Sunday and Thursday 11 am to 7 pm. The proceedings are mainly conducted in Hebrew, but occasionally in Arabic.

Free guided tours of the building are held on Sunday and Thursday 8.30 am to 3.30 pm. Take your passport. Egged bus Nos 19 or 24 will get you there.

Next to the bus stops opposite the Knesset is a bronze menorah, a gift from British supporters of the State of Israel. It is decorated with panels representing important figures and events in Jewish history.

Hebrew University

The Giv'at Ram campus of the university on

Brodetsky Rd, west of HaKirya and the Israel Museum, features a strikingly designed synagogue recognisable by its white egg-shaped cupola.

Other features of interest include the Academy of the Hebrew Language which displays the library and furniture of Eliezer Ben Yehuda, who was responsible for the revival of the Hebrew language. Also, the campus cafeterias provide very cheap food of good quality.

Free daily guided tours of the campus start at 9 and 11 am from the old Sherman Building. Take Egged bus Nos 24 or 28 to get there.

Model of Ancient Jerusalem

In the grounds of the Holy Land Hotel (☎ 630201) on Uziel St between Herzog St and Herzl Ave, is a huge 1:50 scale model of Jerusalem as it was in 66 AD, at the beginning of the Jewish revolt.

It's open daily (summer 8 am to 5 pm, winter 8 am to 4 pm) and admission is US$2.25 (students US$1.75). Use Egged bus No 21 to get to it.

Mount Herzl & Herzl Museum

Just to the north of Yad Vashem, this pleasant park is named in honour of the founder of political Zionism. He is buried here, along with his wife and parents and other prominent Zionist leaders. Nearby are the graves of the late prime ministers Levi Eshkol and Golda Meir, as well as the graves of Menachem Begin and of Ze'ev Jabotinsky (the latter founded and led the Revisionist movement and was the spiritual leader of the Irgun). Further on is a cemetery for Jewish soldiers killed in battle locally.

The Herzl Museum (☎ 531108) includes a replica of Herzl's Vienna study, library and furniture.

It's open Sunday to Thursday 9 am to 5 pm, Friday 9 am to 1 pm, and is closed Saturday; admission is free. Take Egged bus Nos 13, 18, 20, 23, 24 or 27 to get there.

Yad Vashem

On the Mount of Remembrance, by the edge of the beautiful Jerusalem Forest, is the Yad Vashem Memorial; from here there are pretty views towards the village of Ein Kerem. This is Israel's major memorial to the victims of the Holocaust. Yad Vashem (☎ 531202) means 'A Place and a Name', or 'A Monument and a Memorial', and is taken from Isaiah 56:5.

From the main road, follow HaZikkaron Rd to the entrance. Next to the car park is a café, administration offices and archives building featuring the most complete library dealing with the holocaust.

Avenue of the Righteous Gentiles

Leading off to the left, this and the surrounding gardens are a memorial to the non-Jews who risked their lives to save Jews. The trees bordering the avenue bear plaques in remembrance of certain individuals.

Remembrance Hall is a sombre construction with a mosaic floor inscribed with the names of the 21 largest concentration and death camps. Men's heads must be covered here and cardboard yarmulkas are provided.

On Holocaust Day (see Festivals & Holidays in the Facts about the Country chapter), the Martyrs and Heroes Remembrance Day Assembly is held here, attended by the President of Israel and other national leaders.

Pillar of Heroism This is a 21-metre-high memorial to honour the resistance fighters. Bordering the path leading here are inscriptions carved into stones which record their various acts of bravery.

Museum A comprehensive and harrowing presentation of the events of the Holocaust. You could easily spend many hours here, taking in the many photographs, documents, artefacts and other effects which bring home the realities once faced by the Jews.

Art Gallery Do not miss this often wonderful but always poignant collection of work produced under some of the most unbearable conditions imaginable.

Hall of Names Containing over three million pages of testimony by Holocaust victims who have registered here.

Garden of the Children of the Holocaust This is simply as suggested – a garden in remembrance of the child victims.

Valley of the Destroyed Communities Commemorating the European Jewish communities that were wiped out during WW II, this memorial is under construction nearby.

Yad Vashem is open Sunday to Thursday 9 am to 4.45 pm, Friday 9 am to 1.45 pm, and is closed Saturday; admission is free. Take Egged bus Nos 13, 17, 18, 20, 23, 24 or 27 to get there.

Hadassah Medical Centre
Often confused with its namesake on Mount Scopus, this is the Middle East's largest medical centre, famous for its synagogue featuring the Chagall Windows. These abstract stained-glass designs depict the 12 tribes of Israel based on Genesis 49 and Deuteronomy 33. Four of the current windows are replacements for those damaged during the Six Day War. Three other windows still contain bullet holes.

Beautifully situated to the south-west of Jerusalem, the centre overlooks the village of Ein Kerem and the surrounding green hills. The Bernice & Nathan Tanneabaum tourist reception centre is open Sunday to Thursday 8 am to 3.45 pm, Friday 8.30 am to 12.30 pm, and is closed on Saturday. Admission is US$2.50 (students US$1.50), which includes a guided tour (held every hour on the half hour). Take Egged bus Nos 19 or 27 to get there.

Ein Kerem
Now enveloped by the expanding New City whose ugly apartment blocks threaten to blot out the landscape, this picturesque village is dominated by attractive churches commemorating the traditional birthplace of John the Baptist and by the surrounding terraced slopes of the valley.

A visit to this village with its narrow streets and alleyways can be pleasantly combined with a walk in the adjacent Jerusalem Forest.

Church of St John This church is owned by the Franciscans and built over the grotto where St John was believed to have been born (Luke 1:5-25, 57-80). Steps lead down to the grotto with its remains of ancient structures and a Byzantine mosaic.

The church is open March to September, Monday to Saturday 8 am to noon and 2.30 to 6 pm; October to February, Monday to Saturday 8 am to noon and 2.30 to 4 pm, and is closed Sunday. Admission is free. It's on the street to the right of the main road.

Church of the Visitation Also Franciscan and built on the traditional site of the summer house of Zacharias and Elizabeth, the church was visited by St Mary (Luke 1:39-56). Note also the ancient cistern and, in an alcove, the stone behind which John supposedly hid from Roman soldiers. Upstairs is the apse of a Crusader church.

It is open daily 9 am to noon and 3 to 6 pm and admission is free. You'll find it on the street to the left of the main road, opposite that leading to the Church of St John. The spring which gives the village its name is nearby. The wall bears the words of the prophet Isaiah, 'Ho everyone who thirsts, come to the waters' (Isaiah 55:1).

Russian Church & Monastery Higher up the steep slope, this monastery (☎ 222565, 654128) can only be visited by appointment.

Getting There & Away To reach Ein Kerem you can go direct from the New City by Egged bus No 17 (every 20 to 30 minutes) or take Nos 5, 6, 18 or 21 to the Jerusalem Forest. Get off at the Sonol petrol station on Herzl Blvd, continue walking in the same direction and take the first right onto Ye'fe Nof and the second left, Pirhe Hen, to enter the forest. Head for the Youth Centre in the middle of the forest and from there the village is visible most of the way. You can

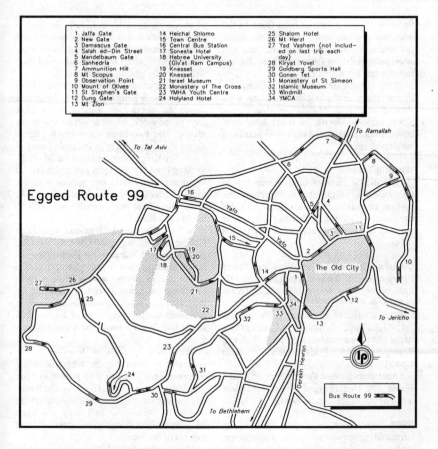

Egged Route 99

Map Legend:

1 Jaffa Gate
2 New Gate
3 Damascus Gate
4 Salah ed-Din Street
5 Mandelbaum Gate
6 Sanhedria
7 Ammunition Hill
8 Mt Scopus
9 Observation Point
10 Mount of Olives
11 St Stephen's Gate
12 Dung Gate
13 Mt Zion
14 Heichal Shlomo
15 Town Centre
16 Central Bus Station
17 Sonesta Hotel
18 Hebrew University (Giv'at Ram Campus)
19 Knesset
20 Knesset
21 Israel Museum
22 Monastery of The Cross
23 YMHA Youth Centre
24 Holyland Hotel
25 Shalom Hotel
26 Mt Herzl
27 Yad Vashem (not included on last trip each day)
28 Kiryat Yovel
29 Goldberg Sports Hall
30 Gonen Tet
31 Monastery of St Simeon
32 Islamic Museum
33 Windmill
34 YMCA

also reach Ein Kerem by walking down the slope from the Hadassah Medical Centre (from the stop for Egged bus No 19).

TOURS

The huge number of places of interest in Jerusalem and the wealth of history that surrounds them make an organised tour a good idea. This can be as an introduction to the city, or to give you a more detailed awareness of certain areas.

Coach Tours

A marvellous introduction to the city but flexible enough to be a great way to get around and visit the major sites is Egged Tours' Route 99, the Circular Line. This service takes you on a comfortable coach to 34 of the major sites, with basic commentary in English provided by the driver. A single ticket at US$1.30 allows you to enjoy the complete trip, and a one-day ticket at US$5 is valid for a day's unlimited travel on the Circular Line, enabling you to get off and back on at each stop. A similar two-day ticket costs US$6.50.

It operates Sunday to Thursday 9 am to 5 pm, Friday 9 am to 2 pm, with no service on

Saturday. The bus leaves Jaffa Gate on the hour, but you can board at any of the stops. It's a continuous circular route, and you eventually finish at the stop where the bus initially left from.

Other Jerusalem tours are offered by Egged Tours, including an aeroplane tour. Pick up their brochure from one of the Egged Tours offices. Details of other operators' coach tours can be found at the tourist offices and travel agents.

Walking Tours

An increasing number of travellers opt to take a walking tour to gain an insight into the various aspects of the city's history. Up-to-date details of the following and other walking tours are available at the tourist office.

David's 'City of David' Walking Tours

Enjoying one of the best reputations for Old and New City tours, David's Tours (☎ 522568, 818758, 4203580) leave from the Citadel courtyard (museum exit), outside Jaffa Gate. The 3½- hour Four Quarters tour of the Old City operates twice daily, 9 am and 2 pm, Sunday to Friday (US$7, students US$5).

Other tours include the Pre-Temple Period Route, The Underground City of Jerusalem and The Anthropological Route.

SPNI These tours are mainly hikes in the surrounding countryside but some cover unusual and interesting routes within the city (see the Information section in this chapter for more details about SPNI).

Archaeological Seminars Specialised Old City tours include the excavations at the City of David, below Temple Mount, the Western Wall and the Jewish Quarter. Each lasts two hours at US$7; three tours cost US$18. Tours depart from 34 Habad St, Jewish Quarter, Old City.

Free Walking Tours Every Saturday at 10 am the municipal tourist office organises a free walking tour to a specific site in the city.

Meet outside the office at 32 Jaffa Rd. Unfortunately such a free tour on a Saturday in Israel inevitably attracts a large crowd so, although the guides are well informed, you will often struggle to hear them.

The Sheraton Jerusalem Plaza Hotel (☎ 259111), on King George V St, corner of Agron St, offers free walking tours most days of the week, which are open to nonresidents. The two-hour tours often start a sherut-ride away. Meet in the hotel lobby at 9 am. The King Solomon Hotel (☎ 241433), on King David St across from the Montefiore Windmill, also offers free guided walking tours – check with reception for details. These three-hour tours usually start at 9.15 am in the lobby.

Jeffrey Seidel, an Orthodox Jew from Chicago now living in the Old City, runs the Jewish Student Information Centre (see the information section in this chapter) and is committed to giving young Jews a fresh awareness of being Jewish. Concerned by the increase in young Jewish assimilation, he organises free walking tours of Jewish sites in the Old City's Jewish and Muslim Quarters.

Non-Jews as well as Jews are most welcome to meet by the womens' water fountain in the Western Wall piazza, at 3 pm Sunday to Tuesday and Thursday. On Saturday the tour starts an hour before sunset, with no tour on Wednesday or Friday. The tours are informative, friendly and cover Jewish aspects of the area.

More controversial than your average sightseeing option, Ateret Cohenim, the extreme Zionist organisation whose aim is to take back the Muslim Quarter properties it feels rightfully belong to Jews, offers free tours of the neighbourhood. Call ☎ 895101 to inquire about joining the Underground Tunnel Tour and/or The Yeshiva Tour. Each lasts one to two hours, and are described by the organisation as 'fascinating and dramatic'.

PLACES TO STAY

Jerusalem has a wide range of accommodation in a variety of surroundings, and there are some real bargains available. You can choose between the unique and colourful Old City, which offers the country's cheapest hostels and some middle-range hospices and hotels; East Jerusalem, with cheap hostels and middle-range hospices and hotels right outside those Old City walls; and the New City, where most of the luxury and middle-range hotels are to be found, as well as a limited number of hostels and two of the best hospices.

The best location to stay in really depends on your requirements. The Old City and East Jerusalem tend to have the cheapest places, are more convenient for the major sites nearby, and the Arab bus stations and service taxi rank are there. However, some hostels and hospices have strict curfews, and being at least a good 20-minute walk from the New City's downtown nightlife, they are not suitable for those who want to stay out late. The intifada has made East Jerusalem a virtual ghost town after dark and on strike days, which can be a problem with nowhere to eat or shop. The Old City streets have always been slightly uncomfortable for women after dark, and now with the Arab uprising everyone should be a little wary there.

If an early curfew stops you from enjoying the New City's after-dark goings-on, then stay there. Likewise, if security concerns make you feel uncomfortable about the Old City or East Jerusalem, then the New City's for you, too. However, except for most Jewish and many American travellers, the less interesting surroundings and higher prices of the New City encourage most budget travellers to opt for the Old City and East Jerusalem. The two hospices within the New City boundaries, St Andrew's and Notre Dame, are also very popular.

If you plan to stay a week or more ask about reduced rates.

Places to Stay – bottom end
Old City Most of the Old City's budget accommodation is found near Jaffa and Damascus gates which is convenient as they are the main access points and well served by buses. Egged bus Nos 1, 3, 13, 19, 20 and

80 go to Jaffa Gate from the central bus station. No 27 takes you to the Arab station near Damascus Gate. Once you have learned the way to your accommodation, it is often quicker to catch a bus to Jaffa Gate and walk than to take the No 27 for the longer route to Damascus Gate.

In the vicinity of Damascus Gate, *Al-Arab* (☎ 283537) on Suq Khan ez-Zeit St is very popular. Bear right up Suq Khan ez-Zeit St and it's on your left just before the New Hashimi Hotel. Owner Abu Hassan is a friendly host, willing and able to give travel advice and directions to his guests. He also arranges visits to Palestinian refugee camps in the Occupied Territories. Dorm beds are US$4, singles/doubles US$11/22, and there is a kitchen. It has a 1 am curfew.

New Hashimi Hotel (☎ 284410), just a few doors along from Al-Arab, is quite pleasant and quiet in this busy market area. There's a comfortable lounge but no kitchen. Dorm beds are US$4, and singles/doubles are US$6/10. There is a flexible midnight curfew.

Al-Ahram Youth Hostel (☎ 280926) is on El-Wad Rd. From Damascus Gate bear left along El-Wad Rd and it's on your right, opposite the Via Dolorosa and the 3rd Station of the Cross. This popular hostel has generally on-the-ball Arab staff who do a good job. It's comfortable, cleaner than average and has a lounge, TV, music, roof terrace and kitchen. Free tea is often forthcoming. There are some great views but also the loud calls to prayer from the mosque next door. Dorm beds are US$4, less for a comfortable mattress up on the roof terrace. Winter prices are a little more to cover heating costs; singles/doubles here cost US$15/30. There is a midnight curfew.

The *Armenian Catholic Patriarchate Hospice* (☎ 284262), is on El-Wad Rd between the 3rd and 4th Stations of the Cross. From Damascus Gate bear left along El-Wad, and it's on your left just after the Via Dolorosa. It's quiet, clean, but sombre and uncomfortable, with no kitchen or lounge. The miserable staff make you feel as though you're at boarding school. Dorm beds are

US$5 and doubles start at US$20. It is closed from 1 to 3 pm, and has a 10 pm curfew.

Turn right off Suq Khan ez-Zeit St to find *JOC Inn & Teahouse* at 21 al-Khanqa St. Popular with a few who like the roof deck, kitchen, washing machine and cosy set up, but the would be pick-up joint of a café downstairs with its loud music is a turn-off for others.

Now to the Jaffa Gate area. *Petra Hotel* (☎ 282356), is at the start of David St, on the left as you enter Jaffa Gate. Despite its good location, a nice reception area with a TV lounge and attractive balconies overlooking Jaffa Gate and the Citadel, it's less popular than other places. During the winter months the cold really penetrates every corner, the staff are not particularly friendly or switched on, and the cooking facilities are limited. Dorm beds cost US$6 and there is a midnight curfew.

Beside the Christian Information Centre, *Jaffa Gate Youth Hostel* (☎ 898480), on al-Khattab St, is a popular, if crowded, alternative with a kitchen and TV lounge. Dorm beds are US$4, doubles US$14, and there's a midnight curfew.

For a couple of better hostels, head right from inside Jaffa Gate and go left on Maronite Convent Rd (look for the Coffee Shop on the corner). Follow the road around and turn right on St Mark's Rd. *Citadel Youth Hostel* (☎ 286273) is on your right. It has friendly management and is clean and comfortable. There's a small lounge, kitchen, and access to the roof, with one great room overlooking the Old City. Dorm beds are US$4, doubles US$16 and there's a midnight curfew.

The *Lutheran Hospice* (☎ 282120, 894734/5; fax 894610), St Mark's Rd, PO Box 14051, is just past the Citadel Youth Hostel and is on the opposite side. It is spotless, has excellent facilities, a kitchen, and a beautiful garden with views of the Holy Sepulchre. Dorm beds are US$6. It is closed from 9 am to noon, has a strict 10.45 pm curfew and a very quiet, Christian atmosphere.

Across from the Lutheran Hospice, head up Ararat St to the *Old City Youth Hostel –*

IYHA (☎ 288611). It has great facilities but, being more expensive than the competition, it's usually filled with school groups and not travellers. Dorm beds are US$8 (US$9 for nonmembers) and there's an 11 pm curfew.

The *New Imperial Hotel* (☎ 272400), on your left as you enter Jaffa Gate, was built in 1883. Now owned by the Greek Orthodox Church, its large rooms are clean but a bit jaded. It seems to exist solely for Greek pilgrims who fill the place at Easter. Singles/doubles are US$12/24.

East Jerusalem 'Hostel Row' is at the first stretch of HaNevi'im St across from Damascus Gate and opposite the service taxi rank. These hostels are among the best in Jerusalem – they need to be as the many travellers who stay here have to contend with the noise created by Arab men hanging around the adjacent wholesale stores at all hours, watching kung fu and wrestling videos played at full volume.

Faisal Youth Hostel (☎ 282189) is at 4 HaNevi'im St. This place is very popular and right outside Damascus Gate, which can be seen from the pleasant terrace. There's a lounge, dining area and a kitchen with free tea and coffee. The large dorms have painfully deformed beds at US$4; opt for a mattress on the floor or the terrace which cost less anyway. The few double rooms usually fill quickly and cost about US$12. There's a flexible midnight curfew.

Palm Hostel, next door to the Faisal at 6 HaNevi'im St (☎ 282189), has a pretty lounge with plants and a glass roof. There's a kitchen with free tea and coffee. It's closed from 10 am to 1 pm, has a flexible midnight curfew, dorm beds are US$4 and singles/doubles are US$7/11.

A few doors up, *New Raghadan Hostel* (☎ 282725), at 10 HaNevi'im St, is a comfortable, easygoing, basically clean place with a pleasant manager. There's a large lounge with soft chairs, a kitchen and a washing machine. The balcony and rooms on the upper floors have nice views of the

Old City. Dorm beds cost US$3, singles/doubles are US$6/12 and there's no curfew.

Ramsis Youth Hostel (☎ 284818), 20 HaNevi'im St, is often overlooked but is a decent place to stay if the others are full or you want some space. It has large rooms, high ceilings, kitchen, lounge and friendly staff. Dorms are US$4, and singles/doubles are US$12. There's a flexible midnight curfew.

New City These days the most popular choice (it's usually full during July/August) is the *Jerusalem Inn* (☎ 251294) at 6 HaHistradrut St, between King George V and Ben Yehuda Sts. Take Egged bus Nos 14, 17, 31 or 32. It's a clean and well-run converted apartment building in the heart of the downtown area. Under the same management, the larger *Jerusalem Inn Guest House* (☎ 252757) is at 7 Harkenos St. From Zion Square, head south on Jaffa Rd, go up Eliashar St (look for MacDavid's on the corner), up the steps at the end of the street and it's on the left. A converted hotel with masses of public space, it features a large lounge with plans for a bar/restaurant.

Neither hostel has a kitchen, but you can use the fridge, and breakfast, snacks, tea, coffee, beer and sodas are available. There's a midnight curfew, but a deposit will get you a front door key. Dorm beds are US$8, singles US$16, and doubles from US$22 to US$30.

A new place opened just as this edition was being researched. It is the *Ritz*, at 37 Jaffa Rd, between Steimatsky's Bookshop and Zion Square, above the Arizona Bar. It is very crowded and rather dingy, but currently the cheapest New City hostel. It has basic kitchen facilities and no curfew. Dorm beds are US$5, or it is US$3.50 on the roof.

King George Hostel (☎ 223498), 15 King George V St, between Jaffa Rd and Ben Yehuda St in the downtown area, is a 15-minute walk to Jaffa Gate. Take Egged bus Nos 7, 8, 9, 10, 14 or 31, and get off at first stop on King George V St. As Jerusalem's traditional hippy and psychedelic haven, it's cramped and dirty but a lot of people like it. Beer and snacks are available, and there's a kitchen and washing machines. Prices vary from time to time, with dorms around US$8. There is no curfew.

Jasmine (☎ 223032) is at 3 Even Sapir St, on the corner of Bezalel St. It is in a pleasant neighbourhood a few blocks way from the downtown area, so quite a walk from the Old City; take Egged bus No 17 from the central bus station. A bit shabby in a bohemian way, it has a kitchen, TV lounge and a ban on alcohol. There is no curfew, dorm beds are US$8, and singles/doubles cost US$22.

Sisters of the Rosary Convent (☎ 228529), 14 Agron St, PO Box 54 is run by friendly local nuns. It's a spacious, basic but adequate place to stay, in lovely quiet surroundings, 10 minutes' walk to Old City and downtown area. Dorm beds are US$10, and singles/doubles are US$20/30. There are some triples. Breakfast costs around US$4, and lunch or dinner is US$8. The curfew is at 10 or 10.30 pm. Take Egged bus Nos 7, 8 or 14 to the Plaza Hotel and walk down Agron St; it's on the right.

Bernstein Youth Hostel – IYHA (☎ 228286), 1 Keren Hayesod St, is at the junction of Agron/King George V/Ramban Sts. Take Egged bus Nos 7, 8 or 14. This place has good facilities and is clean, but not very friendly and is often busy with Israeli school groups. Its a 12-minute walk to Jaffa Gate and the New City downtown area. Dorm beds for members are US$10, and nonmembers pay US$11. It is closed from 9 am to 5 pm and there's an 11 pm curfew.

Hotel Nogah (☎ 254590, 661888) is at 4 Bezalel St. Its best to call ahead; ask for Mr or Mrs Kristal. Take Egged bus Nos 7, 8, 9, 10, 14 or 31 to King George V St, get off near Ben Yehuda St and then walk north one block. A popular choice, this is a clean and quiet apartment near the tourist office and alongside the Bezalel School and Artists' House (on the right). The comfortably furnished rooms share a well-equipped kitchen and bathroom. Singles/doubles are US$18/22. There's no curfew as guests get their own front door key.

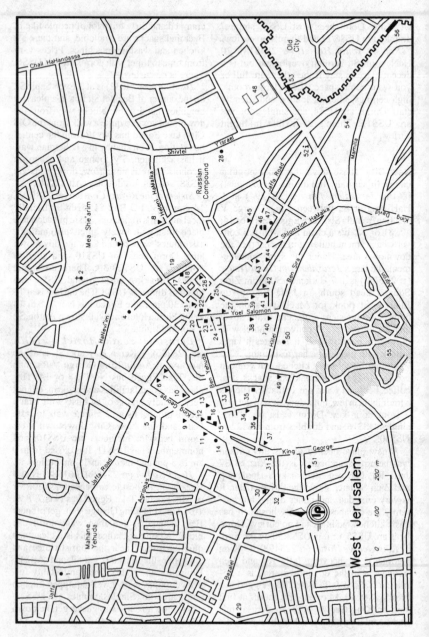

■ PLACES TO STAY

15 King George Hostel
16 Jerusalem Inn
18 Jerusalem Inn Guesthouse
22 Ritz Hostel
23 Kikar Zion Hotel
29 Jasmine Hostel
30 Hotel Nogah
35 Jerusalem Tower Hotel
48 Notre Dame of Jerusalem Centre

▼ PLACES TO EAT

1 Mahane Yehuda Market
3 Yemenite Felafel & Boureka Bakery
4 Ticho House Café
5 Abu Shabi & Micky
6 Uri's Ice Cream
7 Sefer VeSefel Bookstore Café
8 Heleni HaMalka St - Sergey, Glasnost & Gizmo Restaurants/Bars
9 Alla Gondola
10 Alumah Natural Food Restaurant
13 Sova Self-Service Restaurant
11 Marvad Haksamin
12 Fink's Bar-Restaurant
14 Carmel Ice Cream
19 Harkenos St - HaTorif (The Pie House), Mandy Tachi Chinese Restaurant, Shunra, Chess, Magritte & Nargila Yemenite Restaurant
21 Restaurant Europa
22 Arizona Bar
24 The Underground
25 The Mad Hatter
26 Queen's Hummus
27 Champs Bar

32 Artists' House
33 Ta'ami Hummus
34 Mamma Leone
37 Ta'amon Café
36 Ben & Jerry's Ice Cream
38 Tea House
39 La Belle
40 Gilly's
41 The Tavern
42 Ocean
43 Little Street of Pubs
44 Bistro Chez Pe'er
45 Hen
48 Notre Dame of Jerusalem Centre
49 Mamma Mia

OTHER

1 Mahane Yehuda Market
2 Ethiopian Church
4 Ticho House
14 Hamashbir Department Store
17 Student Travel ISSTA
20 Zion Square (Kikkar Zion)
28 Hall of Heroism
32 Bezalel School of Art
31 West Jerusalem Tourist Office
46 Post Office
47 Bezeq International Telephones
50 Museum of Italian Jewish Art & Synagogue
51 Tzavta Theatre
52 Municipal Tourist Office
53 New Gate
54 Daughters of Charity of St Vincent de Paul
55 Independence Park
56 Jaffa Gate

Hotel Eretz Israel (☎ 245071), is at 54 King George V St; take Egged bus Nos 7, 8, 9, 10, 14 or 31. It's just before the large white Plaza Hotel and the house with the facade covered in wheels; note the 'Hotel' signs. An elderly Orthodox Jewish couple (who are a little blunt) do a good job keeping a clean, quiet, comfortable guesthouse, popular with older Jewish visitors. No unmarried couples are allowed. There's a fridge but no kitchen. Singles/doubles are around US$22/28, but bargain hard. There's no set curfew but you are expected in by midnight at the latest.

Louise Waterman Wise Hostel – IYHA (☎ 423366), is at 8 Pisyah Rd, Bayit Gegan. Take Egged bus Nos 18 or 20 to Mount Herzl – about 30 minutes by bus from the New City centre. There's a midnight curfew so don't miss the last bus at about 11.15 pm. This hostel has a good reputation, and is in a lovely building near a forest on the outskirts of Jerusalem. There's a kitchen but no utensils. Rates are US$10 for members, and US$12 for nonmembers (both with breakfast). They also serve dinner, and it's good food for an IYHA hostel.

Ein Kerem Youth Hostel – IYHA (☎ 416282), is off Ma'ayan St. Take Egged bus No 17 to Ein Kerem and it is the last stop. Turn left on Ma'ayan St and follow the path. There's great scenery here in the Jerusalem hills. Rates are US$8 for members, US$10 for nonmembers and it is extra for breakfast, lunch or dinner. There's no curfew here but the last bus is at about 11.15 pm.

Mitzpe Rachel (☎ 702555; fax 733155), Kibbutz Ramat Rahel, MP North Judea, 90900. Egged bus No 7 brings you here, and it's about 10 minutes' south of the Old City. You might want to stay here while in Jerusalem to experience a kibbutz of today. Facilities include a swimming pool, tennis court, bar, lounge and they serve good food. Dorm beds in the kibbutz guesthouse are around US$15.

Places to Stay – middle
In this price range, Jerusalem's Christian hospices offer the best value. The best of these are as popular with nonbelievers as they are with pilgrims.

Old City Some hotels are also included here, with most of the accommodation found near Jaffa Gate.

Christ Church Hospice (☎ 282082; fax 289187), is at al-Khattab Square, PO Box 14037. From Jaffa Gate bear right (after the Citadel), up past the Christian Information Centre and before the post office on the corner on your left. The hospice entrance is next door on the site of Herod the Great's palace gardens, and is a part of a complex based around the oldest Anglican church in the Middle East. It has pleasant staff and is very clean, quiet and comfortable, with a pretty courtyard and nice public rooms. Singles cost from US$30 to US$35, and doubles from US$52 to US$64.

The very popular *Lutheran Hospice* (see Places to Stay – bottom end for directions and description) has singles/doubles at US$35/58 with breakfast provided.

The *Casa Nova Pilgrims' Hospice* is at 10 Casa Nova St, PO Box 1321 (☎ 282791). From Jaffa Gate take the second left, Greek Catholic Patriarchate Rd, and follow it until it becomes Casa Nova St. The hospice is on your left with St Francis St up on the right. Run by the Franciscans with the help of some officious Arab staff, it is clean and has vaulted ceilings and massive marble pillars in the dining room. The food is great and the rooms, mainly twins with bathrooms and central heating, are pleasant. The hospice is often full with European pilgrims. Singles/doubles are US$30/50, breakfast costs US$6 and there's an 11 pm curfew.

The *Greek Catholic Patriarchate Hospice* (☎ 282023), is on St Dimitri's Rd. From Jaffa Gate take the second left (Greek Catholic Patriarchate Rd which becomes St Dimitri's Rd) and the hospice is on the right on the bend. It's a bit unfriendly, but perhaps not if you're Greek. You get basic, comfortable singles/doubles for US$28/40, with breakfast included. Lunch costs US$6, dinner US$8 and there's an 11 pm curfew.

The *Gloria Hotel* (☎ 282431/2; fax 282401), is at Latin Patriarchate Rd. From Jaffa Gate take the first left and it's on the right. It has large, quiet, modern rooms, with nice views across the Citadel from the dining room. Singles/doubles cost from US$32/48, with breakfast and there's no curfew. On the same street is *Knights Palace* (☎ 282537), owned by the Latin Patriarchate. A grand looking place, albeit rather run down, singles/doubles are US$20/30 with breakfast included.

Notre Dame de Sion Ecce Homo Convent (☎ 282445), is at 41 Via Dolorosa. From Damascus Gate bear left along El-Wad Rd, turn left onto Via Dolorosa and it's on your left just after the first turning. It's very clean, with a study area and kitchen, but there are only double rooms at around US$35 with breakfast. It is closed from 10 am to noon, and it has a 10 pm curfew.

East Jerusalem This was where all the pilgrims to the Old City would stay before 1967, so there are several hotels, mostly on or around Salah ed-Din St.

One of the best accommodation deals in

the city, *St George's Cathedral Guesthouse* (☎ 283302; fax 282253), is at 20 Nablus Rd, PO Box 19018. Part of the St George's Cathedral compound, where Nablus Rd meets Salah ed-Din St, it's a 10-minute walk to Herod's or Damascus gates, and 20 minutes to the New City downtown area. Egged bus No 27 from the central bus station stops right outside. A delightful cloistered building with an attractive garden, it's an oasis of peace and quiet in a city that can often wear you out. The atmosphere is very relaxed and friendly, with no curfew. The comfortable rooms, most with private bathroom, cost US$25/40 for singles/doubles, with breakfast. Complimentary morning and afternoon tea are served in the garden. Ask about full and half-board rates.

YMCA East-Aelia Capitolina Hotel (☎ 894271), is at 29 Nablus Rd, just past the US Consulate (bear right) and on the left. The decor is dowdy but there are good facilities, including squash and tennis courts, and a swimming pool; singles/doubles are US$35/55. From here it's an eight-minute walk to Herod's or Damascus gates.

Pilgrims' Palace Hotel (☎ 284831; fax 894658) is adjacent to the bus station on Suleiman St, so rooms on that side are noisy. Overlooking the city walls between Herod's and Damascus gates, it's plain and dull but clean enough. Singles cost US$31, and doubles range from US$34 to US$46.

Rivoli Hotel (☎ 284871), on Salah ed-Din St, at the corner of Suleiman St, has adequate rooms, a nice lounge and a TV room. Singles/doubles here are US$20/32.

The *New Metropole Hotel* (☎ 283846), is at 8 Salah ed-Din St. This is a popular place for Muslim and Christian Arab pilgrims to stay. There are views of Mount Scopus, the Mount of Olives and the Rockefeller Museum from the pleasant roof garden. Comfortable air-con singles/doubles with good facilities cost US$25/35.

Capitol Hotel (☎ 282561), on Salah ed-Din St, opposite the Lawrence Hotel, has well-equipped air-con rooms with balconies which face the Mount of Olives. There's a bar and the hotel is popular with tours from

Europe. Singles/doubles are good value from US$35/45.

Lawrence Hotel (☎ 282585), at 18 Salah ed-Din St has basic singles from US$16 to US$20, and doubles from US$32 to US$38.

The *Christmas Hotel* (☎ 282588) on Salah ed-Din St is north of the cinema and on the corner on the right. It's clean and comfortable, with singles from US$31 to US$34, and doubles from US$52 to US$56.

New City The New City's middle-priced hotels are mostly found in three main areas: near the Old City, in or within easy walking distance of the downtown area, and in the vicinity of the Knesset and the Israel Museum.

Not far from the Old City, a personal favourite is *St Andrew's Hospice* (☎ 732401; fax 731711), PO Box 14216, which is in a lovely location near Bloomfield Park, overlooking Mount Zion, the Old City and the Hinnom Valley. You can take Egged bus Nos 5, 7, 8, 21 or 30 and it's near the train station. Belonging to the Church of Scotland, it has a friendly Scottish country house atmosphere – very comfortable and peaceful, with singles/doubles for US$35/55, with breakfast. It is popular, good value and is recommended. It is also about 12 minutes' steep walk to Zion or Jaffa gates, and 20 minutes' walk to the New City downtown area.

St Charles Hospice (☎ 637737), 12 Lloyd George St, PO Box 8020, is off Bethlehem Rd to the south of the Old City in the German Colony district. Egged bus Nos 4, 14, 18 or 24 will get you there. This German-run hospice offers clean, sparse but comfortable and peaceful surroundings and is usually full. Some rooms don't have private bathrooms. It costs US$28 per person in singles or doubles, with breakfast.

Another favourite of mine and terrific value is *Notre Dame of Jerusalem Centre* (☎ 894511; fax 271995), Paratroopers' Rd, PO Box 20531. Ideally located outside the Old City opposite New Gate and just a 10-minute walk from the New City's downtown area, Egged bus No 23 stops right outside.

This majestic and renovated Roman Catholic complex features a guesthouse with facilities more reminiscent of a good three-star hotel, which is how it is graded. Singles cost from US$24 to US$30, doubles from US$48 to US$60, and breakfast is provided.

The *YMCA* (☎ 227111), on King David St, opposite the King David Hotel, can be reached on Egged bus Nos 7, 8, 21 or 30. It's probably the best-looking YMCA in the world, with terrific architecture and nice grounds. Rooms are basic but comfortable, and free use of the pool, squash, tennis and gym facilities make it good value in comparison with the New City hotels. The restaurant is not great, though, and the staff can be officious. If you don't plan to use the sports facilities here, consider the recommended hospices. From here it's six minutes' steep walk down and then up to Jaffa Gate, or 12 minutes' walk to the downtown area. Singles cost from US$26 to US$31, doubles from US$44 to US$61, and breakfast is included.

Windmill Hotel (☎ 663111; fax 690964) is at 3 Mendele St, in the desirable Talkich district, or 15 minutes' walk to Old City and 25 minutes' walk to the downtown area. This is a popular, modern hotel catering for religious Jews with a strictly kosher restaurant and coffee shop. Singles cost from US$55 to US$91, and doubles from US$65 to US$92.

The modern *Kikar Zion Hotel* (☎ 244644; fax 244136) is right on Zion Square, the heart of the downtown area. With a swimming pool, gym, restaurant and bar, singles here cost from US$50 to US$56, and doubles from US$80 to US$83.

Jerusalem Tower Hotel (☎ 252161; fax 252167) is at 23 Hillel St – the street parallel with Ben Yehuda St, just down from the tourist office. It has good facilities with singles costing from US$55 to US$62, and doubles from US$70 to US$85.

The *Har-Aviv Hotel* (☎ 521515), 16 Bet Hakerem St, is south of the central bus station and west of the downtown area; take Egged bus Nos 6, 16 or 17. All rooms in this quiet, pension-style hotel have a terrace. It's family operated and great value with singles/doubles costing from US$25/40. To

get to the downtown area take Egged bus No 20 from Herzl Blvd.

Mitzpe Rachel, the guesthouse at Kibbutz Ramat Rahel has singles costing from US$46 to US$57, and doubles from US$66 to US$90 (see Places to Stay – bottom end for description and directions).

Places to Stay – top end

Jerusalem's luxury hotels are mainly in the New City with a couple in East Jerusalem – the Old City has no four or five-star accommodation. Most of Israel's new hotel rooms have been built in Jerusalem. The competition has resulted in many empty luxury rooms, so look out for bargain deals in the *Jerusalem Post* or shop around.

One of the country's few hotels with real atmosphere and class is the *American Colony Hotel* (☎ 285171; fax 283357), 1 Louis Vincent St, Nablus Rd, East Jerusalem. Once the home of a Turkish pasha, it is the city's only top-class Arab hotel and many prefer it to the more recognised King David Hotel. A sort of unofficial 'no-man's land', it has been adopted by journalists from all over the world as the place to stay when on assignment in this, the longest running and ultimate troublespot. It has beautiful Oriental architecture, a lovely swimming pool, a popular garden terrace and serves non-kosher food, including a renowned lunch-time buffet on Saturday.

The rooms vary in quality, and this is reflected by the range of prices – singles cost from US$50 to US$150, and doubles range from US$70 to US$170.

The *Hyatt Regency Jerusalem* (☎ 821333; fax 815947) is at 32 Lehi St. It is a bit out of the way but has great facilities, and is the latest addition to the luxury hotel lineup. Singles cost from US$89 to US$155, and doubles from US$98 to US$169.

Seven Arches (☎ 894455; fax 285384) is on top of the Mount of Olives, with the classic view over the whole city. Once you've savoured the view and explored the churches below, though, you've a long way to go to get anywhere. Formerly the Inter-Continental, it created a stir when it was built under the Jordanian regime as it stands over part of the Jewish cemetery. Business has not been great here and singles/doubles are a low US$70/80.

Opposite the YMCA is the *King David Hotel* (☎ 251111; fax 232303), at 23 King David St. Traditionally the country's top hotel, the facilities are here but the service and food are often disappointing considering its status. Despite this you may well meet royalty and heads of state in the elevator. Singles cost from US$126 to US$252, doubles from US$146 to US$272, and some rooms have Old City views.

Up the road, the *King Solomon Hotel* (☎ 241433), at 32 King David St, is the former Sheraton. A modern tower hotel overlooking the Old City, it boasts the city's only kosher Japanese restaurant. Singles/doubles cost US$95/110.

Overlooking Liberty Bell Park and the Old City, *Laromme Jerusalem Hotel* (☎ 697777; fax 6987268), is at 3 Jabotinsky St. This modern El Al-owned hotel enjoys a good reputation. Singles cost from US$78 to US$203, and doubles from US$92 to US$218.

Behind the YMCA, and within easy walking distance of the Old City and the downtown area, is the modern *Moriah Jerusalem Hotel* (☎ 232232; fax 232411), at 39 Keren Hayesod St. Singles cost from US$72 to US$120, and doubles from US$90 to US$160.

Overlooking Ha'Atzmaut Park, with its upper floors having views across the whole city, the *Sheraton Jerusalem Plaza Hotel* (☎ 259111; fax 231667) is at 47 King George V St. Very central and within walking distance of both the downtown area and the Old City, its kosher restaurants include the ultra-expensive Cow on the Roof. Singles cost from US$87 to US$202, and doubles from US$100 to US$215.

Opposite the Plaza Hotel, the *King's Hotel* (☎ 247133), at 60 King George V St, has singles costing from US$62 to US$85, and doubles from US$75 to US$98.

Between the central bus station and the Knesset is the *Jerusalem Hilton* (☎ 536151; fax 380575) at Giv'at Ram. It's the usual Hilton set-up, includes a health club, and has singles/doubles at US$135/170.

Long-Term Accommodation
B & B in a private home, or renting a room or an apartment are options taken by many travellers staying for several weeks. Contact the tourist office for the current list (see also Accommodation in the Facts for the Visitor chapter).

Staying in an Israeli home helps you to see the Israeli way of life close-up and, as with apartments, it can work out better value than a three-star hotel. Those with less money to spend should still consider finding an apartment if they intend spending two months or more in Jerusalem. If you look around you should be able to pay less rent than you would in a hostel, and you have privacy and independence.

To find a cheap room or studio, or someone who needs an extra person to share an apartment, scan the *Jerusalem Post* (especially the Friday edition). *Kol Ha'ir*, a Hebrew paper, is probably the best source for such places. It's in Hebrew so find someone to translate it. The stall holders in Mahane Yehuda Market often know somebody with a room to rent, so keep your eyes open for small signs in shop windows announcing a room to let. The notice-boards at the two campuses of the Hebrew University, the Israel Centre at the corner of Strauss and HaNevi'im Sts, and at Sefer VeSefel bookshop and café on Ya'Avetz St can also be good places to look.

Two services offer listings (in English) of properties for rent. She'al, at 21 King George V St (☎ 226991), is open Sunday to Thursday 8.30 am to 1 pm and 4 to 7 pm, Friday 8.30 am to noon, but is closed Saturday. Dehaf Ltd, at 43 Jaffa Rd by Zion Square (☎ 223941, 226335), is open Sunday to Thursday 9 am to 7 pm. Room Renting Ltd (☎ 633563) offers various standards of rooms and apartments by the night or for longer periods. Call in the afternoons and early evening except on Shabbat.

PLACES TO EAT
Old City

The Old City features various stalls, shops and vendors selling food items in the often crowded Arab markets. Pitta bread and bagels are sold everywhere, from carts and shops – check the going rate, as travellers are often overcharged.

In particular, you can buy bread/bagels at the bottom of the slope as you enter from Damascus Gate and at the end of David St, next to the Cardo. Good quality and well-priced fruits and vegetables can be bargained for, too.

Unfortunately, while the intifada continues, the Old City's Arab establishments and markets close after about 1 pm, and don't open at all on strike days.

Felafel The Old City's felafel is disappointing so stick with the cheapest place, a stall at the very bottom of the slope as you enter from Damascus Gate. It's straight ahead with the two main streets passing to the left and right of it, and charges about US$1.

Hummus Two of the world's best examples of hummus can be enjoyed here, both along the Via Dolorosa. By the 5th Station of the Cross, where the Via Dolorosa turns west (right), *Abu-Shukri* is opposite at 63 El-Wad Rd. Long-established, this simple, clean place is busy. Before the intifada, Israelis used to queue up to get in on Saturday. Continue up the Via Dolorosa towards Suq Khan ez-Zeit St and on the left near the top is *Linda's Restaurant*, which many feel produces hummus of equal quality.

In either place, you pay about US$2.50 for a plate of hummus with pitta and maybe olives or onions. For a little more, ask to have your plate of hummus served with pine nuts, meat and fancy garnish.

Pizza From Damascus Gate take the small street to the east (left) as you head for El-Wad Rd. A little further and on the left is the *Green Door* bakery. In a cavernous room dominated by the traditional oven, Mohammed Ali bakes for the local neighbourhood. For

travellers, his version of the pizza is a popular attraction, although those cats must put off more than a few potential customers. He will also use any ingredients that you care to bring along. The bakery is open daily from 4 am to 11 pm.

In the Armenian Quarter is the *Armenian Ararat Pizza Bakery*, also known as the *Blue Door*. From Jaffa Gate turn right across al-Khattab Square and up Armenian Patriarchate Rd, left down St James' St, left on Ararat St and it's on the left behind the unmarked blue door, next to the Ararat Grocery. Run by a friendly Armenian couple, Hagop and Nver Meveshian, the Blue Door is only open Wednesday from 11 am to 9 pm and Saturday 11 am to 5 pm and the sole product is 'lahmoajin' (Arabic for 'meat dough'), known as Armenian pizza. It consists of minced lamb mixed with peppers, tomatoes, herbs and spices spread over a pitta bread base and costs about US$1.

Restaurants & Cafés The *Coffee Shop*, next to the Christian Information Centre near Jaffa Gate, is a lovely place. Really clean, and decorated with Christian-theme Jerusalem tiles on the tables and walls, it features an all-you-can-eat salad bar for US$3, or US$4 with soup and bread. It's open Monday to Friday from 9 am to 6 pm, but is closed Sunday.

Abou Seif, on the left as you enter from Jaffa Gate, is a long-established good-value sit-down restaurant. They serve breakfast and have various Middle Eastern dishes for lunch, such as salads and stuffed vegetables, at around US$1.75 a piece, so you can eat quite reasonably. It is closed on Sunday.

In the Jewish Quarter, just up from the Western Wall on Tiferet Y'Israel St, the self-service *Quarter Café* (upstairs) has decent, reasonably priced kosher food in pleasant surroundings, with a great view across to the Dome of the Rock and the Mount of Olives from the upper level. You can get salads from US$4 and main meals, such as moussaka, from US$5. It's open Sunday to Thursday from 8 am to 6.30 pm, Friday 8 am to 3 pm, and is closed Saturday.

In the Christian Quarter, the nicely furnished *Yerevan Armenian Restaurant* on Frères Rd is more expensive, but provides a pleasant change from the usual. The use of herbs and spices make the chicken, kubbe and the Armenian pizza taste pretty good. It's in a quiet backwater near New Gate. From Jaffa Gate take the second left up Greek Catholic Patriarchate Rd and follow the road up to the left, passing Francis St on the right. It costs around US$15 for a set three-course meal.

At the *Lark Hotel Restaurant* just down the street on Latin Patriarchate Rd, similar Armenian fare is served for about the same price.

On Suq Khan ez-Zeit St, just north of the Holy Sepulchre turn-off, a juice bar serves carrot and orange juice all year round, and other juices in season.

Sweets On Suq Khan ez-Zeit St, you cannot avoid gazing at the honey-soaked delights of the many Arab pastry shops. However, due to the competition it can take some time for items to sell, and at US$1 a time you don't want to end up with anything but a fresh pastry.

For this reason, but also because it is highly rated by the Arabs for a special treat, try *Zalatimo's*, just back from the stairs leading up to the 9th Station of the Cross. This unremarkable looking little bakery produces some of the city's best pastry. Its speciality is the rich moutabak made to order by Abu Ali Hawash, the baker here for over 20 years. Super light pastry is kneaded and rolled over and over with a fresh cheese filling and served straight from the traditional oven with hot sugar syrup. Other sweets are available, but this is what people wait for – sometimes for over 30 minutes due to the made-to-order system. Quite filling, a single portion is often enough for two, at about US$1.35. It's open daily until the pastry is all used – usually by 11.30 am.

Bars Another side effect of the intifada on tourism has been the closure of the Old City's two bars. You can still get a bottle of beer at

many Old City restaurants and cafés but only one place currently serves draught beer. Head for the Jewish Quarter, and across from the Burnt House is *Tzaddik's Old City Deli*; it's open Sunday to Thursday until 9 pm, Friday until 2 or 3 pm, and is closed on Saturday. Kosher, they also serve roast beef sandwiches, hot dogs, chilli and pasta.

With the lack of after dark hang-outs and places for alcoholic refreshment in the Old City, I'm grateful to the reader who wrote in to mention *Mardik's Mini Market*. Located next door to the Armenian convent on Armenian Patriarchate St, the friendly staff sell bottled beer and wine at lower than average prices; they're open daily till 10 pm.

East Jerusalem

On HaNevi'im St, just north of the New Raghadan Hostel, a popular Arab bakery is open long hours producing delicious pitta bread and bagels. The cheaper cafés are uninviting; the cleanest and cheapest is next to the New Raghadan Hostel. *Nasser Eddin Bros* on Suleiman St, across from Damascus Gate, stock a wide range of dry goods for self caterers; they are closed Sunday.

Something of a cult amongst hummus freaks is the *Abu Ali Restaurant*. Although less than spotless, it is busy with local Arabs who eat lunch early, from 11 am, and IDF patrols continue to stop by for a bite to eat, too. Hidden away off Salah ed-Din St, head north from Herod's Gate and turn right along an alley at the sign for 'Ibrahim Dandis'; it's downstairs on your left. It's open daily from 6 am to about 2 pm. Tasty and inexpensive main meals are also served – simply wander into the kitchen and point out what you want from the various meat, rice and vegetable dishes kept hot on top of the stove. This is a typical Arab worker's eating place – no frills and cheap. Bank on US$4 for hummus and the works.

Café Europe, 11 az-Zahra St, east of Salah ed-Din St, serves tasty fast food, ice cream and shakes.

East Jerusalem traditionally provided Jerusalem's best Arab restaurants, and before the intifada Friday night would be busy with most Jewish competitors closed for Shabbat. With the drop-off in Jewish trade and tourists, though, the restaurants have really suffered and many have had to close. *Philadelphia Restaurant* (☎ 289770), at 9 az-Sahar St off Salah-ed Din St remains one of the best. Named after Amman as it was known in ancient times, it specialises in mazzas, the traditional appetisers, as well as grilled lamb dishes. A full meal costs about US$15, but individual dishes are less and the mazzas can be a meal on their own. To counter the effect of the intifada, another branch has opened in the New City (see New City later in this chapter).

Another top restaurant is the *Petra* (☎ 283655, 280510), 11 El-Rashid St, parallel to and east of Salah ed-Din St. The excellent set lunch or dinner costs about US$18.

The *National Palace Restaurant*, in the hotel of the same name, is a little more expensive, but is recommended. The food is wonderful, with mansaf being the speciality served on Friday. It costs about US$20 a head.

The up-market *American Colony Hotel* provides good food in exotic surroundings. The US$30 Saturday lunch-time buffet is popular.

New City

Jerusalem's New City has a vast number of eateries, many of which blend into an indistinguishable mass providing coffee and cakes, hummus and salad, felafel, pizza, shishlik, Ashkenazi fare or local interpretations of international styles. Amongst a high number of mediocre places, there are some cheaper options of high quality which are well worth the experience.

The Mahane Yehuda Market is where you can buy the cheapest food; even the Old City costs more. To save even more, learn to bargain and go along just as the market closes (about 7.30 to 8.30 pm Sunday to Thursday, and 3 to 4 pm Friday) when prices are at their lowest. It is closed on Saturday.

Elsewhere in the New City, the basement supermarket in the Hamashbir department store on King George V St on the corner of Ben Yehuda St has a good selection of bread and dairy products at regular prices, as well as other items not necessarily found in cheaper environments. Other convenient supermarkets are on Jaffa Rd between Strauss St and Zion Square and on the corner of Agron and King George V Sts, next to the Plaza Hotel.

Felafel Perhaps the best felafel in Israel can be had at the *Yemenite Felafel*, 48 HaNevi'im St. It's open Sunday to Thursday 10 am to 7 pm, Friday 10 am to 2 pm, but is closed Saturday. From King George V St head up Strauss St and bear right on HaNevi'im St. This mecca of felafel is on the left opposite the Russian Compound with a marvellous view of the green-domed Russian Cathedral at the end of the narrow street opposite.

Most New City felafel is sold on King George V St between Jaffa Rd and Ben Yehuda St. Just follow the trail of tehina, salad and squashed felafel balls on the pavement.

Shwarma Many of the places selling felafel also have shwarma. None of them really inspires a recommendation, but you will find the busiest of them on the corner of King George V and Agrippas Sts.

Hummus Available in most Oriental restaurants, the following enjoy particularly good reputations for hummus: *Ta'ami* (no English sign), 3 Shammai St parallel with and to the south of Ben Yehuda St; *Queen's*, second on the left from Jaffa Rd on Heleni HaMalka St – Elvis Presley is the apparent inspiration here; and *Rahmo*, beside the Mahane Yehuda Market, on the corner of Ha'Armonium St, off Agrippas St.

Pizza This fare is very popular here, with several outlets in the downtown triangle – but the quality doesn't seem to justify the enthusiasm of the Israelis and the Americans (who should know better with their superior product back home). For me, the best of a poor bunch are *Pizza Ami* on HaHistradrut

St, to the left as you walk up Ben Yehuda St, and *Apple Pizza*, at 13 HaRishonim St, off Ben Yehuda St.

Cafés These literally line the downtown streets, and attract their own clique of local regulars. They offer basic hot dishes and salads as well as a wide range of cakes, ice cream and beverages. When busy they are all as bad as each other, with inefficient service and even basic items such as coffee often of questionable quality.

However, some cafés enjoy a reputation of quality earned in the good old pioneering days of Zionism and still appeal to certain types. Often talked about is the *Atara* at 7 Ben Yehuda St, with its truly superb onion soup. The traditional hang-out for the literary set, it was the original haunt of *Palestine Post* (now *Jerusalem Post*) journalists before independence. It still attracts regulars from the press and intelligentsia during the day, but on a busy evening you'll not notice any difference between this and the other equally congested cafés. Another café of note is *Ta'amon*, at 27 King George V St, near the corner of Hillel St. Also a literary favourite, it's a lot more working class and less frequented by tourists and younger Israelis. More popular with the younger locals are the *Rimon* and *Akrai* and their neighbours on Luntz St, which leads off to the right from Ben Yehuda St coming up from Zion Square.

The *Ticho House* café, in the museum and library complex at 7 HaRav Kook St across from Zion Square, is very popular.

As well as the European-style street cafés, Jerusalem has some alternatives. In the Nahalat Shiva neighbourhood, built in 1891, the bohemian *Tea House*, at 12 Yoel Salomon St, is popular with local young hippy types who sit cross-legged on cushions and choose from the range of 30 herbal teas, blintzes and other desserts. It is open Sunday to Thursday Saturday 7 pm to 2 am but is closed Friday.

Sefer VeSefel (meaning Mug & Book), the bookstore on Ya'Avetz St, has a café noted for its ice cream, notice-board and magazine collection. The *Artists' House* at 12 Shemuel HaNagid has a pleasant café away from the mainstream. Also popular for its bar and for meals, it's a pleasant spot for coffee or tea and it stays open till late every night.

Away from the downtown area is the *Cinemateque* café (see Entertainment in this chapter) with its scenic location. It's also one of the few places open on a Friday evening.

Restaurants – cheap A great and inexpensive area to eat meat in the evening is along Agrippas St, south of Mahane Yehuda. Perhaps the best of the small grilled meat specialists are *Abu Shabi* and *Micky*. Simply look in the fridge and choose from various skewered meats and offal which are then grilled 'on the fire' and served with tehina, vegetable salad and pitta. Beer and wine are available. Each skewer costs US$2.50, and salad is US$2.50. They open Sunday to Thursday from 5 pm to 3 am, but are closed Friday and Saturday.

At 12 King George V St, the *Marvad Haksamin* (Magic Carpet) is always busy and provides a variety of inexpensive Oriental dishes such as hummus, tehina with eggplant, soups and grilled meats and stuffed vegetables from US$4. You can spend more on steak, liver and chicken. It's open all day Sunday to Thursday and lunch time Friday, but is closed Friday evening and Saturday.

A busy lunch-time favourite is *Hen*, 30 Jaffa Rd, across from the main post office (no English sign, next to two pastry shops). Israel's President Chaim Herzog is rumoured to have eaten here (as well as me) – and I don't blame him. Good, basic Oriental favourites again – salads, soups, stuffed vegetables and grilled meats. You can eat well on US$4 or spend more. It's open Sunday to Thursday 9 am to 6 pm, Friday 9 am to 3 pm, and is closed Saturday.

At 3 HaHistradrut St, to the right going up Ben Yehuda St, is *Sova*, a cheap self-service restaurant. The food won't win prizes but it will suit a low budget. Stews, casseroles and gefilte fish are usually on the Ashkenazi-type menu. It is open Sunday to Friday from 11 am to 8 pm, Friday 11 am to 3 pm, and is closed on Saturday.

One of Jerusalem's better known secrets is that one of the city's great kitchens is to be found at *Notre Dame*, opposite New Gate. The Vatican's complex features a coffee shop that's open all day and has a pleasant terrace, but the main restaurant is the place to go for some excellent food and pleasant, if basic, surroundings inside a truly grand building. It's open daily to non-residents for lunch and dinner, with a US$9 set menu.

Gilly's, on Yoel Salomon St at the corner of Hillel St, is a very popular Rumanian restaurant. Always packed, it's well worth getting in the line for a great dinner at about US$15 to US$30.

On Rivlin St next to the Tavern, *La Belle* is a pleasant French restaurant at about US$15 to US$20 per person. It is open Sunday to Thursday from 7 pm to late, Saturday 8 pm to late, and is closed on Friday.

For Hungarian food, try the *Europa*, upstairs at 48 Jaffa Rd, opposite Zion Square, which is around US$18 for a full three-course meal. Europa is open Sunday to Thursday from noon to 9.30 pm, but is closed Friday and Saturday.

Harkenos St is home to popular places where a decent meal can be had for about US$15: *HaTorif* (the Pie House) serves meat and vegetarian pies and salads, while next door is *Mandy Tachi*, a good Chinese restaurant. Next door is *Nargila*, part of a nationwide chain of inexpensive Yemenite restaurants. Very popular, a meal can cost as little as US$8. Many obviously like it, but the food is not so great and service can be erratic. Another Chinese restaurant worth a mention is *Tain-Lee-Chow*, next to the Kings Hotel and opposite the Plaza Hotel on King George V St. It's kosher and up-market, so expect to spend US$20 a head or more.

A sister to the original restaurant in Tel Aviv, *White Hall* (☎ 248408), at 8 Rabbi Akiva St, is a terrific steak house, and something of a rarity in Israel. The desserts here are 'extra special' according to one reader's letter. Expect to spend between US$20 and US$40 from a menu featuring steaks, burgers and a salad bar. There is a great value US$10 lunch menu.

For Italian food, try *Alla Gondola*, at 14 King George V St, opposite HaHistradrut St; *Mamma Mia*, 18 Rabbi Akiva St – head along the street opposite the Jerusalem Tower Hotel on Hillel St and turn right before the end; or *Mamma Leone*, 5 Hillel St. You can enjoy pasta, seafood and other dishes for between US$9 to US$15. All are open for dinner Saturday to Thursday, but are closed Friday.

Due to the drastic drop in business during the intifada, one of East Jerusalem's top Arab restaurants opened a branch in the New City. *Phildaelphia West* (☎ 731814), at 4 Kikkar Remez St, outside the railway station, is open daily, from noon to 11 pm. Lunch or dinner is US$15 to US$25 per person.

Restaurants – expensive

At the corner of HaHistradrut and King George V Sts, *Fink's Bar-Restaurant* (☎ 23 4523) is a largely hidden treasure, although it has its sizable band of enthusiastic regulars. Opened in 1933, it became the favourite watering-hole for British military and police officers during the Mandate, and Jewish underground fighters would frequent the bar to hear the gossip. Later, politicians took over, followed by the journalists. Now Fink's is the traditional hang-out for journalists, both local and from around the world who have been sent to Israel over the years to cover the various wars and political events. It was listed by *Newsweek* magazine as one of the world's top bars.

The place is notable not only for its well-stocked bar and consistently excellent Austro-Bavarian food, but for atmosphere, bonhomie and a quiet professionalism found nowhere else in Israel, and so rarely abroad. You can sit at the bar for a drink or try the speciality, goulash soup, described as a 'Jewish ploughman's lunch', or opt for a full dinner and choose from a wide range of meats, fish and desserts, along with an extensive wine list. With less than a dozen stools at the bar and only six tables, the place soon fills up and reservations are advisable. Expect to pay US$20 and up, plus wine. It is open from Saturday to Thursday from 6 pm till late, closed Friday, and offers a good-value set lunch served Sunday to Thursday from noon to 3 pm.

The *Mishkenot Sha'ananim* (☎ 251042, 254424), below the Montefiore Windmill, serves French cuisine combined with a few Moroccan appetisers. With plush surroundings and terrific views of the floodlit Old City walls, it's very nice but very expensive. An extensive wine list adds to the attractions offered on the menu. A set lunch is about US$30, eating à la carte starts from US$25, increasing to unprintable prices when you look at the vintage claret selection; it is closed Friday.

The proprietor, Moise Pe'er, has another restaurant, *Bistro Chez Pe'er* (☎ 231793, 252332), on Ben Shetach St, on the corner of Hasoreg St and across from Rivlin St. The set menu is US$15, eating à la carte starts from US$20, and the place is open daily for lunch and dinner.

For good fish, head for *Ocean* (☎ 247501) at 7 Rivlin St. Ocean opens daily for lunch and dinner and costs about US$25 to US$35 per person.

Vegetarian & Health Food Jerusalem has a couple of vegetarian eateries worth a mention that serve soups, salads, grains, casseroles, cakes, herbal teas, grain coffees and juices. Established for over 30 years, *Liber*, at 10 Ben Yehuda St, is a reliable site for good-value vegetarian food and refreshment. Also worth a visit is the *Alumah Natural Food Restaurant*, nearby at 8 Ya'Avetz St (the narrow alley linking Hillel St to 49 Jaffa Rd). It's open Sunday to Thursday from noon to 10 pm, but is closed Friday and Saturday.

Attention all peanut butter addicts, the country's finest can be found at the health-food shop at 76 Jaffa Rd (between Strauss St and Mahane Yehuda Market).

Bakeries All over Jerusalem, but in the district of Mea She'arim in particular, many bakeries produce the various types of bread, cakes and biscuits so popular with the locals. A favourite treat is to go along late in the evening and pick up a sticky bun or three, perhaps a chocolate-filled one as well for variety and another with currants – and don't forget the biscuits.

Convenient to the downtown area is the bakery on Peri Hadash St. Go up Strauss St from Jaffa Rd, take the first left along HaNevi'im St, right along Yeshayahu St and it's just down from the Edison Cinema on the left, by the musical instrument shop. On Thursday this and other bakeries are open all night to meet the demand for Shabbat.

For bourekas, try the bakery that makes nothing else, next to the Yemenite Felafel at 48 HaNevi'im St, opposite the Russian Compound. It is open Sunday to Thursday from 6 am to 7 pm, Friday 6 am to 2 pm, and is closed Saturday.

La Lavanaise, Baguette et Croissant on the right along Jaffa Rd heading towards Mahane Yehuda from Strauss St, is a bakery and café producing those light French delights.

Ice Cream *Ben & Jerry's* has a branch on Hillel St, down from King George V St. The softer *Carmel* is along King George V St, away from the street to the right of the Hamashbir department store and opposite Ben Yehuda St. At 51 Jaffa Rd, just below the King George V/Strauss Sts crossroads, is the small kiosk of *Uri's* with its popular soft variety. The café at *Kefer VeSefel*, the bookstore upstairs at 2 Ya'Avetz St, serves home-made ice cream along with chocolate brownies and other delights.

Bars Popular with tourists and an ever-growing Israeli market, Jerusalem's bars have played a considerable part in changing the face of the city's social life. Now it is possible to drink in a variety of establishments until the early hours seven nights a week (once unheard of). Most of the bars call themselves pubs, several play videos loudly, some are open from lunch time till the early hours while others only open in the evenings. On Friday and Saturday they all open a little later due to the Shabbat.

On Rivlin St, the *Tavern* was the original

Jerusalem pub. Still popular, it's looking a bit worse for wear. Further along Rivlin St, the *Mad Hatter* is a cosy place. Just across from the Tavern, and starting at the other end from 31 Jaffa Rd near the Shlomzion St junction, is the Little Street of Pubs – a narrow alleyway where *The Yard, Little Pub, La Lo's Pub* and *Pini's Pub* await you.

The pedestrianised Yoel Salomon St houses a few more watering holes. *The Rock* is candlelit and a little bohemian, the *Good Vintage Pub* plays videos, the more popular *Champs* plays videos, has a dartboard and is open daily from around 11 am, while the *Underground* caters to a younger crowd with videos and a disco downstairs.

Just around the corner at 37 Jaffa Rd, between Steimatsky's bookstore and Zion Square, *Arizona* opened in the summer of 1991 with loud music and lower than average beer prices.

A few late night bar/restaurants popular with the Israeli 'yuppie set' are to be found in the vicinity of the Russian Compound. *Sergey, Glasnost* and *Gizmo* on Heleni HaMalka St, and *Shunra, Chess* and *Magritte* on Harkenos St tend to fill up after 10 pm.

The *Artists' House*, in the Bezalel School of Art at 12 Shemuel HaNagid St, is a quieter drinking spot, open till late daily except Friday.

True bar-hopping aficionados will appreciate the unique ambience to be enjoyed at the legendary *Fink's* (see under Restaurants – expensive in this chapter).

To cater for those pangs of hunger which befall most drinkers when they leave a bar late at night, the *Kiosk* on Rivlin St, next to the Tavern, serves hot dogs and sandwiches till the bars close.

ENTERTAINMENT

Q *What is the best part of Jerusalem's nightlife?*

A *The road to Tel Aviv!*

Although most Tel Aviv residents will insist that this old joke still applies, Jerusalem has

changed considerably in the last few years. Be sure to read the *Jerusalem Post*, in particular the Friday edition, for an up-to-date and comprehensive list of events. Also check at the tourist offices for any special events or regular happenings, some of which will not be featured in the *Post*.

Throughout the year, Jerusalem is a major venue for special events, in particular national celebrations of Jewish festivals (see Festivals & Holidays in the Facts about the Country chapter) and the Israel Festival. Usually held sometime during May or June, this is a three-week programme of cultural events featuring music, theatre, and dance in outdoor historical sites such as the Citadel, Sultan's Pool and the Mount Scopus amphitheatre, as well as in more conventional surroundings.

In the Old City, the sound & light show at the Citadel is performed in the evening between April and November.

Evenings in the New City see most people head for the downtown area to promenade, sit outside cafés (however cold it may be) and people-watch. Ben Yehuda St is the main drag for this activity which reaches its peak on Saturday night, after Shabbat. The pedestrianised street is also busy with buskers, artists and jewellery sellers. A more scenic walk would be along King David St, past the floodlit YMCA, King David Hotel and the Montefiore Windmill, to enjoy the views of the Old City, Mount Zion and St Andrew's Church.

Cinema

Films from the US and Europe show up in Israel fairly soon after release, usually in the original language with Hebrew and French or English subtitles. The quality of the cinemas, in terms of comfort and sound and picture clarity, is often low, but they are not too expensive. The *Jerusalem Post* lists the current programmes and schedules but does not give you the cinemas' addresses. The Jerusalem Hilton, the Israel Museum and the Jerusalem Sherover and Tzavta theatres show films occasionally. See the *Jerusalem*

Post for details. These are the city's main cinemas:

Cinema 1 on Qiryat HaYovel, out past Mount Herzl en route to the Hadassah Medical Centre. Take Egged bus No 18 from King David St or Jaffa Rd – it's a circular route so you can catch it in either direction (☎ 415067).

Cinemateque on Hebron Rd, shows a variety of classics, avant garde, new wave, and off-beat films, with a festival each July. It's a membership cinema, but usually a sufficient number of tickets are available just before the performance. The complex of the cinema, café, archives and museum is tucked below Hebron Rd, down from St Andrew's Church and the railway station (☎ 724131).

Eden is at 5 Agrippas St, half a block on the left from King George V St (☎ 223829).

Edison is at 14 Yeshayahu St, from the crossroads with King George V St and Jaffa Rd, head up Strauss St, left onto HaNevi'im St, then right on Yeshayahu St and it's on your right, on the corner of Belilius St (☎ 224036).

Habira is at 19 Shamai St, one block south-east of and parallel to Ben Yehuda St (☎ 232366).

Kfir is at 97 Jaffa Rd, in the Klal Building (☎ 242523).

Merkaz Klal, is between King George V St and Mahane Yehuda St, on the left.

Orna is at 19 Hillel St near the Jerusalem Tower Hotel on the street south of and parallel with Ben Yehuda St and down from the tourist office (☎ 224733).

Or-Gil is at 18 Hillel St, near the Jerusalem Tower and the Orna cinema (☎ 234176).

Orion is at Shamai St, is one block south-east of, and parallel to Ben Yehuda St (% 222914).

Ron is at 1 Rabbi Akiva St, opposite the Jerusalem Tower on Hillel St (☎ 234704).

Semadar is at 4 Lloyd George St, in the German Colony, three blocks south of the railway station. Take Egged bus No 18 heading east along Jaffa Rd or King David St, and get off just after the station (☎ 633742).

Theatres

Most theatre is performed in Hebrew, with occasional foreign-language productions.

Jerusalem Sherover Theatre, is at 20 David Marcus St, in Rehavia. This modern complex features the classics and modern works. It is also the home of the Jerusalem Symphony Orchestra and the Israel Chamber Ensemble (☎ 667167).

Khan Theatre, is on David Remez Square across from the railway station entrance. In a converted and refurbished Ottoman Turkish caravanserai, this complex features mainly Hebrew plays in its theatre, along with a nightclub. Take Egged bus Nos 6, 7, 8 or 30 (☎ 721782).

Tzavta, is at 38 King George V St, behind the car park on the right from Ben Yehuda St, opposite the start of Independence Park. This small music-theatre club often features productions in English, and visiting entertainers are invited to audition for unscheduled performances. Tickets are often very affordable at US$2 to US$5 (☎ 227621).

Little Theatre, in the Jerusalem Hilton opposite the central bus station, presents plays in both English and Hebrew (☎ 536151).

Al-Masrah for Palestine Culture & Art PO Box 20462 and *Al-Kasaba Theatre* (☎ 8944052), PO Box 17218 are on Obaidah St, one block south of the American Colony Hotel off Salah ed-Din St, behind the Tombs of the Kings, East Jerusalem. This is the Palestinian cultural centre. Plays, musicals, operettas and folk dancing are performed here in Arabic, often with an English synopsis (☎ 280957).

Music & Folk Dancing

Classical music lovers are usually well catered to in Jerusalem. Binyanei Ha-Oomah (☎ 222481) opposite the central bus station and adjacent to the Jerusalem Hilton, is home to the Israel Philharmonic Orchestra and also stages other musical events.

Free classical performances and also folk dancing are held at the YMCA Auditorium, on King David St, opposite the King David Hotel. Free classical music can also be enjoyed at the Music Centre of Mishkenot Sha'ananim (alternate Fridays); the Church of the Dormition (Fridays); Beit Shmuel, part of Hebrew Union College, King George St, New City (Saturday morning). At the International Cultural Centre for Youth (ICCY) (☎ 664144/6, 630900, 669838) 12A Emek Refaim St in the German Colony, south of the city, the Pa'amez Teyman Folklore Ensemble presents Israeli folk dances, Yemenite, Hasidic and Arabic traditional dances, Israeli folk singing and Khalifa Arabic drummers. Sing along, dance along. Tickets are sold at the door and at many hotels.

The Hilton's Little Theatre occasionally

holds musical events. See the theatre list above for the Khan Theatre, which also features nightly shows of Israeli folk singing with the audience joining in with the singing and dancing, and Tzavta, which features a variety of musical styles.

For regular jazz music but with a variety of visiting artists performing rock, blues, country and folk, the Pargod Theatre (☎ 228819, 231765), at 94 Bezalel St, should not be missed.

In particular, Friday afternoons feature a free jazz jam session 1.30 to 5.30 pm. A US$3.50 cover charge applies most evenings.

Penny Lane (☎ 858202), 29 HaNevi'im St, entrance through the car park from the Russian Compound, is a pleasant bar/restaurant with live jazz or blues music most evenings. The food and service are so so, but the music can be worthwhile.

The Israel Centre, at 10 Strauss St on the corner of HaNevi'im St, features musical concerts, in particular Hasidic rock.

On Mount Zion, Asaf's Cave (☎ 716841) at the Mount Zion Cultural Centre, adjacent to David's Tomb, is the regular venue for the Diaspora Yeshiva Band who perform their widely appreciated brand of Hasidic rock in a mixture of Yiddish, Hebrew and English. Check for the current schedule and admission charge.

Discos

Of the New City bars listed earlier, the Underground and Glasnost feature dancing. Jerusalem's major dance spots, though, are located in the southern industrial neighbourhood of Talpiot. You'll need to take a taxi or hitch a ride with some young Israelis to get there. The current list of places to check out includes HaHunger, Exposé and Pythagoras.

What to do on Shabbat in Jerusalem

'Shabbat Shalom' in Jerusalem for the unobservant Jew and non-Jew is no longer a password to boredom. Jerusalem offers several options to enable you to make full use of the day and night. Most Israelis are

equally enthusiastic to escape the confines of the Shabbat laws. Before the intifada, they used to pour into the Old City to shop, see the sights and eat hummus and other Arab specialties, or visit Jericho and other places of interest in the West Bank. Nowadays, security fears have reduced their numbers drastically, and they mostly stay within the 'green line'.

Shabbat options for the traveller include:

Old City & Surroundings For most of the Old City, Mount Zion, the Mount of Olives and East Jerusalem, Shabbat is just another day, with markets, eating places and attractions open. The Western Wall is the destination of thousands of observant Jews, and the Jewish Quarter is completely shut down for the day. Be sure to be at the Western Wall to see the crowds, the singing and the dancing that welcomes the Shabbat on Friday at sunset, or visit a synagogue.

West Bank Courtesy of the Arab bus network and shared-taxi system, you can head for such West Bank attractions as Bethlehem, Jericho, Hebron, Ramallah or Nablus. The day is also as good a time as any to enjoy the stunning scenery on the Wadi Qelt hike (see Jericho and Bethlehem).

Dead Sea This is only a couple of hours drive away, and many people take an Egged bus down on Friday before the shutdown to enjoy the sea, the nature reserve at Ein Gedi or to climb Masada.

New City Most of the Jewish cafés and restaurants close early on Friday afternoon, along with most other businesses, offices and shops. The New City becomes a ghost town as buses fill up and traffic jams become the norm as Israelis head home or leave the city altogether. An increasing number of entertainment places have begun to open on Friday night, much to the annoyance of observant Jews. These include most of the bars on and around Yoel Salomon and Rivlin

Sts and the Russian Compound. Further out, the Cinemateque café is open as usual.

GETTING THERE & AWAY

Jerusalem is a busy crossroads for the Egged and Arab bus networks. The popular sherut/shared-taxi services make the city a convenient base from to take advantage of the small distances involved and visit many places of interest.

Coming from the north you can either take the Jordan Valley route, via Tiberias, Beit She'an and Jericho, to enter Jerusalem from the east (on the same road that you would use coming from the Dead Sea and Allenby/King Hussein Bridge), or you can take the less arid but perhaps more scenic route over the mountains, passing Jenin, Nablus and Ramallah.

From places in the west, such as Tel Aviv, Haifa and Ben-Gurion Airport, you enter the New City via a steady climb up into the Judean Hills, on the four-lane highway Weizmann Blvd.

It soon changes to become Jaffa Rd with the central bus station to the left. From the south you enter via Beersheba, Hebron and Bethlehem.

Air

Arkia flights depart from the airport at Atarot, north of the city. These connect directly with Eilat and Rosh Pinna, with further connections to Haifa and Tel Aviv. There are no flights on Saturday.

Bus

Egged The Egged central bus station on Jaffa Rd is where most people first arrive. Buses here connect to all the major areas in the country. Always busy, the inter-urban buses arrive in and depart from the main concourse, with the city buses operating from stops outside on Jaffa Rd and Zaiman St, reached by an underground walkway. Although the inter-urban buses usually fill up, you need only make reservations for the Eilat bus a day in advance.

Buses for the Dead Sea are always busy and seem to operate independently of official timetables. The simple rule is to make as early a start as possible.

The left-luggage office is on the opposite side of Jaffa Rd from the central bus station. It is open Sunday to Thursday 6.30 am to 7 pm, Friday 6.30 am to 3 pm, and is closed Saturday. The charge is US$0.80 per item per day.

Arab Buses The Arab buses run from two stations in East Jerusalem. Their schedules are not to be relied upon, but the last Arab buses usually leave the station by 6.30 pm.

Egged Buses

to	fare	time	frequency
Tel Aviv	US$2.90	50 minutes	at least every 10 minutes
Haifa	US$5.50	two hours	at least every hour
Eilat	US$10	4½ hours	a night service and three daytime runs
Dead Sea – Qumran	US$3	50 minutes	
Newe Zohar	US$4.30	2½ hours	
Ben-Gurion Airport	US$2.75	40 minutes	express at least every hour.

Arab Buses

to	fare	time	frequency
Hebron (No 23)	US$1.75	1 hour	every 40 minutes
Bethlehem (No 22)	US$0.45	20 minutes	every 15 minutes
Mount of Olives (No 75)	US$0.45	10 minutes	every 30 minutes
Bethany (No 36)	US$0.45	10 minutes	every 30 minutes

The main station is on Suleiman St, between Nablus Rd and Salah ed-Din St. The services and approximate prices are listed below.

The other station is on Nablus Rd, just up from Damascus Gate, on the left. Here, services operate to/from the West Bank north of Jerusalem, mainly Ramallah (No 18 – US$0.35) and Nablus (No 23 – US$1.35). Some Egged buses also run from this station.

Taxi

Sheruts/service taxis make an affordable alternative to the buses. In the New City regular services include the following main destinations:

Tel Aviv
   HaBirah, 1 HaRav Kook St, opposite Zion Square (☎ 534444)
   Kesher-Aviv (☎ 227366), 12 Shamai St, south east of and parallel to Ben Yehuda St; daily US$2.80 per person, Friday and Saturday US$4.25
Ben-Gurion Airport
   Nesher (☎ 231231), 21 King George V St, at the corner of Ben Yehuda St; US$10 to be picked up from your hostel/hotel; reserve one day ahead
Haifa & Eilat
   Yael Daroma (☎ 226985), Shamai St, next door to Kesher-Aviv; reservations a day in advance are normally necessary

In East Jerusalem, on the corner of HaNevi'im St and opposite Damascus Gate, the service taxi rank is where you arrive from/depart for Arab towns on the West Bank and in the Gaza Strip. Some approximate fares and journey times:

to	fare	time
Bethlehem	US$1.60	15 minutes
Jericho	US$2.70	30 minutes
Hebron	US$2.70	40 minutes
Ramallah	US$1.35	20 minutes
Nablus	US$5.60	1¼ hours
Gaza	US$6.60	1¾ hours

These service taxis operate daily and regularly from about 5 am until about 5 pm, after which time the service becomes less dependable with fewer passengers to fill the vehicles.

Train

Jerusalem's railway station (☎ 733764) is in David Remez Square, south of the Old City on the edge of the New City's German colony. This is the end of the line running from Haifa via Tel Aviv, and the service is daily except for Saturday.

The fare to/from Tel Aviv is about US$3, and to Haifa US$4. The ISIC discount is 20%. Several Egged buses run between the railway station and the New City. To reach the Old City it is perhaps just as easy to walk as it is to take a bus to the start of Jaffa Rd.

Hitchhiking

For Tel Aviv, stand on Weizmann Blvd down past Yirmiyahu St and queue up behind the usual IDF platoon with pointed fingers.

For Jericho and the Dead Sea, it's hardly worth the time and effort involved. You really need to take an Arab bus from East Jerusalem to get past the Mount of Olives and tooting taxi drivers. Get off along the Jericho Rd near Bethany or stay on the bus until you are on the fast stretch of road where the main bulk of Jewish traffic joins from the New City.

For Eilat, aim for Bethlehem, Hebron and Beersheba; stand on Hebron Rd by the railway station.

GETTING AROUND
To/From the Airport

Choose between buses, sheruts and 'special' taxis for the 45-minute run from Ben-Gurion Airport (see the Getting Around chapter).

Local Transport

Buses are the cheapest public transport, unless three or more people take a taxi.

At the central bus station, look above the main exit to see a display of all the destinations, routes and the location of the relevant bus stops.

AROUND JERUSALEM
Kennedy Memorial

South of the Hadassah Medical Centre and about 11 km from the city centre, this fine memorial to John F Kennedy sits atop Mount

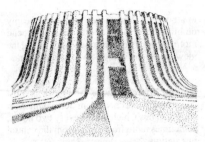

Kennedy Memorial

Orah. Egged bus Nos 20 and 50 stop a good 30-minute walk away.

Sorek/Avshalom Stalagmite & Stalactite Cave

The stunning Sorek, or Avshalom (or Absalom's), cave is some 20 km west of Jerusalem along the road from Ein Kerem. The predominance of limestone in the region has caused these geological formations, which are floodlit for effect and a popular attraction. The pleasant scenery en route from Jerusalem is almost worth an excursion itself.

No regular bus goes directly to the cave, but Egged Tours offer two half-day guided tours, each for around US$18.

Shoresh Junction

West of this junction on the Jerusalem-Tel Aviv highway, the road descends into a gorge. On both sides you can see the rusted remains of vehicles that were part of the Jewish supply convoys attacked by the Arabs during the 1948 siege of Jerusalem. Some have been daubed with red paint and inscriptions, and they form a memorial to the Jews who were killed here.

Abu Gosh

This peaceful and picturesque Arab village (13 km from Jerusalem and off the main highway to Tel Aviv) is significant because it is the site of Biblical Kiriath-Jearim (Town of Forests) where the Ark of the Covenant was located for 20 years until David moved it to Jerusalem (I Chronicles 13:5-8). The village is known from the time Joshua conquered it. Sheikh Abu Gosh once charged a toll on the caravans of pilgrims passing through on the way to Jerusalem. Before the new highway bypassed the village it was a popular beauty spot for Israelis, but now it sees less visitors.

Two interesting churches can be seen here. **Notre Dame de l'Arche** (Our Lady of the Ark of the Covenant) was built in 1924 and is a local landmark, with its statue of St Mary carrying the baby Jesus. It belongs to the French Sisters of St Joseph of the Apparition, and they believe that it stands on the site of Abinadab's house where the Ark was kept (I Samuel 7:1).

Ring the bell at the door of the adjacent building if no-one is about and the church is closed. The church is built on the same site as a larger Byzantine church, and you can see its mosaic floor inside and out. Reach the church from the top of the hill overlooking the village and facing Jerusalem. Turn right coming out of the Caravan Restaurant and up the hill. It's open daily from 8 to 11.30 am and 3.30 to 6 pm, and admission is free.

The **Crusader Church & Monastery** is one of the country's best preserved and most attractive Crusader remains. It was built about 1142 and destroyed in 1187. Used for many centuries as an animal shelter, it was acquired in 1859 by the French government, who placed it under the guardianship of the French Benedictine Fathers. Since 1956 it has belonged to the Lazarist Fathers. In the subterranean section of the building is a small spring. It is believed that the monastery stands on the remains of a Roman castle. A stone from it is displayed in the church and bears an inscription of the 10th Legion, a renowned Roman unit stationed in Jerusalem in the 1st century.

This is the monastery where you can apply to stay in the small hostel (separate accommodation for six men and two women) and experience life in a monastery first-hand. There are eight monks and nuns here. Telephone ☎ 42798 to be a monk, 343622 to be a nun, or come here to inquire. The complex is next door to the mosque, so look for the minaret in the valley. The sign outside reads: 'Eglise de Croisse – Crusaders' Church'. Ring the bell to enter. The monastery is open Monday to Wednesday, Friday and Saturday from 8.30 to 11am and 2.30 to 5.30 pm, but is closed Sunday and Thursday; admission is free, and donations are requested.

Places to Eat The *Caravan Restaurant* is halfway between the two churches and next

to a bus-stop. You can eat well and cheaply on hummus or stuffed vine leaves or spend more on meat and dessert whilst enjoying the view across the village towards Jerusalem.

Getting There & Away Abu Gosh is most conveniently reached from Jerusalem with an Egged bus which leaves every two hours, sometimes more frequently, from the central bus station.

Tel Aviv & the South Coast

TEL AVIV
(Population: 339,400)

Tel Aviv, which now includes the old Arab town of Jaffa within its municipal boundaries, is Israel's largest metropolis and its financial and business centre. Tel Aviv is often a disappointment at first glance, particularly if your point of entry is the central bus station with its crumbling buildings, filth, strange characters and general air of confusion. Initial impressions often convince people that the city is ugly, tasteless, noisy and chaotic. However, given a little time and a knowledge of where to go, Tel Aviv has much to offer the traveller.

Unfortunately, the inhabitants of Tel Aviv have a habit of comparing their city to New York; some even call it the Big Orange. Yes, Tel Aviv does boast a collection of cafés, bars and restaurants that attract large cliques of regulars; there are some distinctive neighbourhoods and a variety of options for having a good time: the vast beaches, the markets, parks, museums, concerts and galleries. However, the impact of the diverse backgrounds of its inhabitants, with so many countries represented in a population of just over a third of a million, is lessened by the fact that they are virtually all Jewish, as opposed to the Big Apple's melting pot. What does make Tel Aviv truly remarkable is the brief history that has led to its current size and capabilities.

Tel Aviv is the cultural and entertainment capital of Israel as well as its business centre. With the exception of the *Jerusalem Post*, all the newspapers are published here, as are most books. Tel Aviv is also the base for industry and the political parties.

Despite being a 45-minute drive from Jerusalem, many residents of Tel Aviv rarely visit the Holy City. Mostly nonreligious, they see Jerusalem as boring, inconveniently situated and basically not worth a visit. They prefer their city's hedonistic lifestyle without the shackles of centuries-old traditions that dominate the capital. Tel Aviv has a recognised black-market area, red-light districts, transvestites and a constant parade of would-be beautiful people posing furiously as they check out the competition on the beach, on the pavements and in the popular cafés and bars. It's hardly surprising, therefore, that the two cities are so separate.

History

The first modern Jewish city, Tel Aviv's history is brief but full of incident and rapid development. Compared to Jerusalem and its lengthy history of foreign dynasties and religions, Tel Aviv is a modern short story of Jewish drive and ambition coupled with town-planning blunders.

It first developed as a long narrow strip along the coast stretching north of Old Jaffa to the Yarkon River. Conditions in Jaffa in the late 19th century were cramped and unsanitary, and, with the city walls destroyed by the Turks, many inhabitants started to move north.

The minority Jewish community established two small districts: Newe Tzedek (1886) and Newe Shalom (1890). In 1906 with assistance from the Jewish National Fund, the Ahuzat Bayit group purchased 12 hectares to build a Jewish quarter north of Newe Tzedek. These 60 families (about 250 people) were led by Meir Dizengoff who foresaw a town of 25,000.

With the English garden city in mind, several town planners were invited to submit schemes and the one adopted in 1909 was from Professor Boris Schatz, founder of the Bezalel Art School in Jerusalem. His plan centred around what is now Herzl St. It was closed off at one end by the Gymnasia Herzlia (the first Hebrew secondary school), which was based on an ancient Jewish temple with Islamic influences.

The new town was given the symbolic name Tel Aviv, meaning Hill of Spring. It is the name of a town in Babylon mentioned in

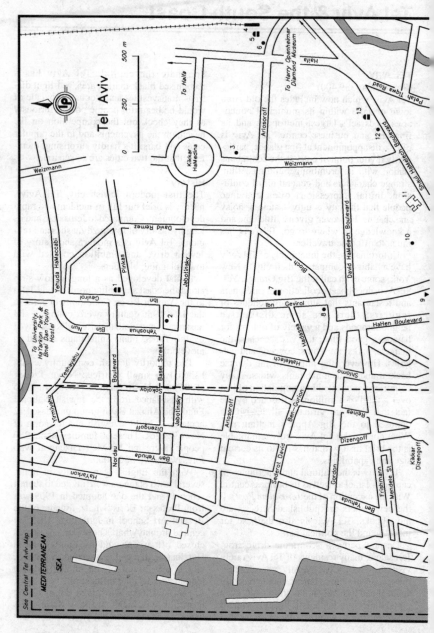

Tel Aviv

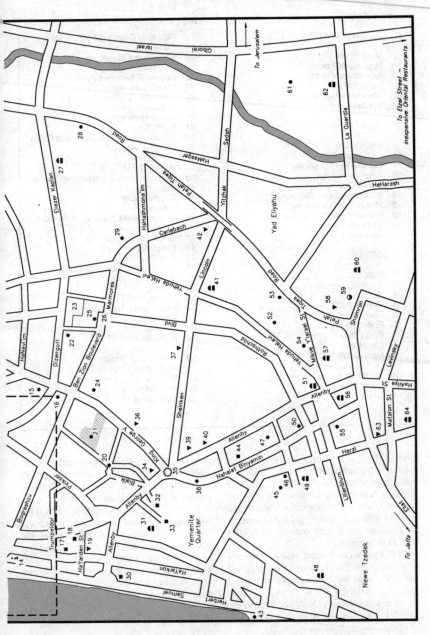

■ PLACES TO STAY

17	Moss Hotel
18	Hotel Ness Tziona
30	Ambassador Hotel
32	HaGalil Hotel
33	The Home Hostel
44	Nordau Hotel

▼ PLACES TO EAT

9	Shoftim Bar
19	Restaurant Alpin
34	Bezalel 'Felafel' Market
36	King George Bar
37	Tamar Café
39	2 Brenner Italian Restaurant
40	Midbar Bar/Restaurant
42	Family Yemenite Restaurant
58	Eli Melek Restaurant
63	Poondak Chem

OTHER

1	Post Office
2	Egyptian Embassy
3	Beit Lessin
4	Central Railway Station
5	Post Office
6	Parking
7	Post Office
8	City Hall
10	Moshav Office
11	Tel Aviv Museum
12	Australian Embassy
13	Post Office
14	Information
15	Dizengoff Centre (Shopping Mall)
16	Parking
20	Bialik Street Museums
21	Gan Me'ir
22	Helena Rubenstein Pavilion
23	Mann Auditorium
24	Jabotinsky Institute
25	Habima Theatre
26	Kikkar Habima
27	Post Office
28	National Parks Authority Head Office
29	Cinematheque
31	Post Office
35	Magen David Circle
38	Carmel Market & Yementine Quarter
41	Post Office
43	Dolphinarium
45	Parking
46	Shalom Tower (Ministry of the Interior - Visa Renewal)
47	Great Synagogue
48	Post Office
49	Post Office
50	Haganah Museum/IDF Museum
51	Main Post Office
52	Parking
53	Central Police Station
54	International Telephones & Poste Restante
55	Penguin Club
56	Post Office
57	Post Office
59	Central Bus Station
60	Post Office
61	Parking
62	Post Office
64	Post Office

Ezekiel 3:15. It was also the Hebrew title used by the translator of Theodor Herzl's book *Altneuland* (Old-New Land). In 1909 the area was simply a stretch of unspoilt coastline, and the photographs taken of the families gathered on the sand dunes to stake their claims are a stark contrast to today's urban environment.

WW I put an end to the new settlement's progress as the Turkish authorities expelled the Jews, who were then dispersed around Palestine. With the British victory the Jews returned and Tel Aviv rapidly became a town. In 1921 Jews fled the Arab riots in Jaffa to neighbouring Tel Aviv. Between 1909 and 1926 Tel Aviv grew from a settlement of 550 people in 65 houses to a town of 40,000 people in 3000 buildings.

Poor planning in these early stages is at the root of today's chaos, as each neighbourhood was designed in isolation. Allenby Rd, the new main street, was diverted to the seafront in order to reach a coffee house on the beach, instead of continuing north. The Newe Shanan district in the south was planned in the shape of a menorah merely because of the associated Jewish symbolism. Eclectic building styles flourished and Oriental and

Top: Station 4, Via Dolorosa – Jesus faces his mother (TW)
Left: Via Dolorosa (NT)
Right: The Citadel, Old City, Jerusalem (NT)

Top: Kidron from the Old City ramparts (Judean Desert behind) (NT)
Bottom: Church and Monastery of the Dormition, Mt Zion (NT)

Art Nouveau influences were encouraged by the friendship between Meir Dizengoff, who became the first mayor of Tel Aviv, and Bezalel's Professor Schatz. Contrary to the founders' dream of a quiet English garden city, Tel Aviv had become the country's main commercial centre and reflected the largely continental education of the immigrant architects.

In the 1930s, Tel Aviv absorbed mostly middle-class urban immigrants escaping Nazi Germany, and a new town plan was devised by a Scot, Patrick Geddes. He proposed housing for 70,000 on the garden-city model with little commercial activity. Streets were to run east-west towards the sea and Ben Yehuda and Dizengoff, the two main streets, were to run north. Lanes, leading to public areas, divided large apartment blocks. When put into practice, these plans were altered: spaces between the buildings and the public areas were decreased and commercial activity was allowed.

The 1936 Arab riots in Jaffa were a catalyst for the building of a port in Tel Aviv to reduce Jewish dependency on Jaffa's port. This was a major step in Tel Aviv's commercial development. Widespread use of the International-style of building made the city a centre of modern architecture in the 1930s. The designs of Bauhaus, Le Corbusier and Mendelsohn were dominant at this time and their influence is still evident today.

Tel Aviv was bombed by Italian and Vichy planes during WW II but largely escaped serious damage. It played host to about two million Allied troops though, and became a centre of the Zionist resistance against the British anti-immigration policies. In 1948, as the British pulled out, Jewish forces attacked Jaffa and after some bloody fighting most of the Arab population fled.

The early years of Israel's independence saw Tel Aviv struggling in an economic crisis: the population swelled from 195,000 in 1946 to 345,000 in 1951, and the city expanded east towards the Ayalon River and north across the Yarkon River. Large-scale public building housed the mass influx of new immigrants, but overcrowding was still common. Yad Eliyahu and HaTiqwa are examples of these building policies. Ramat Aviv, north of the Yarkon River, however, was planned with open space and large green areas.

Most of the city's public buildings were constructed in the 1960s during the economic boom and a US influence resulted in the profusion of tall buildings uncommon in this Mediterranean setting. With the drift towards the suburbs, the population of Tel Aviv dropped from 400,000 to 329,000 during the 1960s.

The economic crisis of the early 1970s halted public investment in building and the private sector took over, financing a spate of commercial and office buildings, shopping centres and apartment towers. The buildings of the 1980s are very different again, although the overall effect of dullness has continued. After its boundaries merged with the surrounding towns in the 1960s, Tel Aviv basically stopped expanding.

The city is now the centre of a metropolis and people commute to Tel Aviv from the suburbs and surrounding towns for work and entertainment.

Orientation

Tel Aviv-Jaffa is a large urban sprawl of connecting suburbs, such as Ramat Gan, Bnei Brak, Petah Tiqwa, Bat Yam and Holon, set on on a coastal plain. Most of your time will be spent in Tel Aviv's six km long and one-km wide central city area based on four main streets. These mostly run parallel to the sea.

From the seafront going to the east they are: HaYarkon, Ben Yehuda, Dizengoff and Ibn Gevirol Sts. These streets run virtually the entire length of the central city area, from the northern tip bordered by the Yarkon River, with HaYarkon and Ben Yehuda Sts extending down as far as Allenby Rd and the Yemenite Quarter; Dizengoff leading east from Dizengoff Square at a virtual right-angle to join Ibn Gevirol, which in turn continues south to intersect with Petah Tiqwa and Eilat Sts.

Allenby Rd is a fifth major street which

runs in from the seafront, intersecting with Ben Yehuda St and later King George St on its way towards the central bus station area, but stopping before it gets there.

Street numbers run from the seafront to the east, and from south to north. They are posted at most street corners, either on signs or on the sides of buildings.

Most of the major facilities and attractions, including hotels and hostels in all price ranges, can be found within the central city area. Not far away, the Tel Aviv University campus, the Diaspora and Ha'Aretz museums and HaYarkon Park are to the north, the central railway station is to the east, and to the south is the railway station for Jerusalem, Jaffa and the Newe Tzedek neighbourhood. The Dan bus system provides cheap connections between all of these areas, and it is possible to walk to many of the places of interest.

Information
Tourist Office The IGTO (☎ 660258/9) at 5 Shalom Aleichem St, between HaYarkon and Ben Yehuda Sts, is open Sunday to Thursday 8.30 am to 5 pm, Friday 8.30 am to 2 pm, but is closed Saturday.

Banks & Moneychangers Due to the current stability of the sheqel, Tel Aviv's black-market area is a lot quieter than it used to be. Go to the corner of Allenby and Yehuda HaLevi Sts, outside the main post office, to see the sleazy-looking characters whispering illegal transactions out of the sides of their mouths. Most of their business with tourists is done by buying goods, rather than by moneychanging. Selling to them is unlikely to get you a fair price, but changing money may save you the banks' charges.

However, unlike Jerusalem's legal Arab moneychangers, these guys do not accept travellers' cheques – they want cash only. The other hang-outs for touts are Lilienblum St and between the Ramada Hotel and Atarim Square on the seafront.

Banks are most easily found on Allenby, Ben Yehuda and Dizengoff Sts and normally open Sunday, Tuesday and Thursday from 8.30 am to 12.30 pm and 4 to 5.30 pm, Monday 8.30 am to 1.30 pm, Wednesday 8.30 am to 12.30 pm and Friday 8.30 am to noon; they're closed on Saturday.

The American Express office (☎ 294654) is at Meditrad Ltd, 16 Ben Yehuda St. It's open Sunday to Thursday from 9 am to 5 pm, and is closed Friday and Saturday.

Post & Telecommunications The main post office is at 132 Allenby Rd, on the corner of Yehuda HaLevi St, and is open Sunday to Thursday 7 am to 8 pm, Friday 7 am to 2 pm, and is closed Saturday. The poste restante is two blocks east at 7 Mikve

The Clocktower at Jaffa

Y'Israel St – bear right as you cross Allenby St to Yehuda HaLevi St. This is also the international telephone office, and is open Sunday to Thursday 8 am to 6 pm, Friday 8 am to 2 pm, and is closed Saturday. More central post office branches are on HaYarkon St, near the corner of Trumpeldor St, and at 3 Mendele St, between HaYarkon and Ben Yehuda Sts.

A more central location for international phone calls is the Bezek office at 13 Frishmann St, between HaYarkon and Ben Yehuda Sts. It is open Sunday to Thursday 9 am to 11 pm, Friday 8 am to 2 pm, and is closed Saturday.

Police The central police station (☎ 100) and the lost & found office is on the corner of Yehuda HaLevi St, three blocks east from Allenby on the right. From the central bus station, cross Petah Tiqwa Rd, head north, take the first left and it's on the left after two blocks.

Airlines For charter flight queries, contact a travel agency.

Aerolineas Argentinas
  5 Shalom Aleichem St (☎ 652253)
Air Canada
  26 Allenby St (☎ 5100579)
Air France
  1 Ben Yehuda St (☎ 6644333)
Air Sinai
  1 Ben Yehuda St (☎ 5104281)
Alitalia
  98 Dizengoff St (☎ 5449922)
American Airlines
  1 Ben Yehuda St (☎ 5104322)
Arkia
  Dov Airport (☎ 5412222)
  11 Frishmann St (☎ 6992222)
Austrian Airlines
  17 Ben Yehuda St (☎ 653535)
British Airways
  1 Ben Yehuda St (☎ 5101581)
Canadian Pacific
  1 Ben Yehuda St (☎ 652163)
Cathay Pacific
  43 Ben Yehuda St (☎ 5230414)
Delta Airlines
  32 Ben Yehuda St (☎ 290972)
Eastern Airlines
  92 Ben Yehuda St (☎ 234147)

El Al
  32 Ben Yehuda St (☎ 5141222)
Iberian Airlines
  14 Ben Yehuda St (☎ 290976)
KLM
  124 Ibn Gevirol St (☎ 5272722)
Lufthansa
  1 Ben Yehuda St (☎ 5101621)
Olympic
  13 Idelson St (☎ 294381)
Qantas
  1 Ben Yehuda St (☎ 652163)
SAA
  1 Ben Yehuda St (☎ 5102828)
Sabena
  72 HaYarkon St (☎ 654411)
SAS
  1 Ben Yehuda St (☎ 5101177)
Swissair
  1 Ben Yehuda St (☎ 5102626)
Tarom Rumanian Airlines
  1 Ben Yehuda St (☎ 662030)
Tower Air
  78 HaYarkon St (☎ 659421)
Turkish Air
  5 Shalom Aleichem St (☎ 652333)
TWA
  74-76 HaYarkon St (☎ 651212)
United Airlines
  117 Ben Yehuda St (☎ 5449555)
Varig
  5 Shalom Aleichem St (☎ 650567)

Foreign Embassies Unless otherwise stated, all of the following embassies and consulates in Tel Aviv are closed on Saturday and Sunday. Several of them maintain separate offices for passport and/or visa inquiries.

Argentina
  112 HaYarkon St (☎ 5271614)
Australia
  37 King Shaul Blvd (☎ 250451)
Austria
  11 Herman HaKohen St (off Frishmann St between Reines and Shlomo HaMelekh Sts) (☎ 246186)
Belgium
  266 HaYarkon St (☎ 454164)
Canada
  7 Habbakuk St (☎ 448162)
Denmark
  23 Bnei Moshe St (☎ 440405)
Egypt
  54 Basel St, just off Ibn Gevirol St (☎ 224152, visa information 464151); see the Getting There & Away chapter for visa information

Finland
  2 Ibn Gevirol St (☎ 250527)
France
  1 Ben Yehuda St (☎ 5101415)
Great Britain
  Consular Section, 1 Ben Yehuda St (☎ 5100166, 510660)
Greece
  35 King Shaul Blvd (☎ 259704)
Italy
  Asia House, 4 Weizmann St (☎ 264223)
Japan
  Asia House, 4 Weizmann St (☎ 257292)
Netherlands
  Asia House, 4 Weizmann St (☎ 257377)
South Africa
  2 Kaplan St (☎ 256147)
Spain
  3 Dubnov St (☎ 265217)
Sweden
  Asia House, 4 Weizmann St (☎ 258111)
Switzerland
  228 HaYarkon St (☎ 5464455)
USA
  61 HaYarkon St (☎ 654338)

Student Travel ISSTA (☎ 247164) is at 109 Ben Yehuda, corner of Ben-Gurion Blvd, and is open Sunday to Thursday 8.30 am to 1 pm, and 3 to 6 pm, Friday 8.30 am to 1 pm. It is closed on Saturday.

Bookshops Steimatzky's, at 103 Allenby Rd, is Israel's largest bookshop. There is another branch on Dizengoff between Frishmann and Gordon Sts. Quality Books, 45 Ben Yehuda St has second-hand paperbacks. Pollack's, 36 King George St, buys and sells second-hand books.

Libraries The British Council Library (☎ 214211) is at 140 HaYarkon St, opposite the Ramada Hotel. It has a reading room with English newspapers and magazines and is open to all, Monday to Thursday 10 am to 1 pm and 4 to 7 pm, Friday 10 am to 1 pm, closed Saturday and Sunday. The Shakespeare Coffee Shop here is a pleasant retreat from the traffic and humidity.

The Australian Embassy has a library which includes books on the subject of Israel, and newspapers and magazines from home. It is open Monday to Thursday 8 am to 4 pm, but is closed Friday to Sunday. The central public library is on King Shaul Blvd adjacent to the Tel Aviv Museum.

Camera Repairs Atarim-Video & Camera Repairs (☎ 280532), Atarim Square, shop No 352; Dorel (☎ 651254), 44 Nahalat Binyamin St; Bendak Zui (☎ 657495), 56 HaYarkon St; Camera (☎ 650376), 36 Allenby Rd; Hadar (☎ 615343), 112 Allenby Rd; Pe'er Laboratories (☎ 293689), 18 Ben Yehuda St.

Laundromats There are laundromats at 51 and 103 Ben Yehuda St, 45 Bograshov St, and 13 Allenby Rd. They are open Sunday, Monday, Wednesday, Thursday 8 am to 7 pm, Tuesday and Friday 8 am to 1 pm, and closed Saturday.

Camping Gear Lametayel (☎ 286894), in the Dizengoff Centre, is open Sunday to Thursday from 9.30 am to 7 pm, Friday 9.30 am to 1 pm, but is closed on Saturday.

Harry Openheimer Diamond Museum

Out of the downtown area, but worth a visit, is the Harry Openheimer Diamond Museum (☎ 576029) in the Diamond Exchange complex at 1 Jabotinsky St, north-east of the city in the suburb of Ramat Gan. The exhibits are thoughtfully presented and include working models, a film and a succession of lavish exhibits on loan. The museum is open Sunday, Monday, Wednesday and Thursday from 10 am to 4 pm, Tuesday 10 am to 7 pm, and is closed Friday and Saturday; admission is around US$2.25 (students US$1). Take Dan bus Nos 51, 68 or 69 from the Petah Tiqwa Rd stop across from the central bus station and HaNegev St.

Tel Aviv University

North of the Yarkon River, in Ramat Aviv, the university campus features some striking modern architecture and its departments cover the widest spectrum of all the country's universities, including fine arts, humanities, history, Jewish studies, law, medicine, the sciences, engineering, business and film-making.

Diaspora Museum

The museum, in Hebrew Beit Hatfusot (☎ 6462020), gives an interesting account of the diversity of Jewish life and culture in exile. Traditions, rituals and holidays among different Jewish communities are presented in an elaborate and innovative way, using techniques such as film, murals, slides, models, a computer and the chronosphere. The museum is unusual in that it is more concerned with reconstructing a way of life than with displaying treasures or artefacts from the past. There is a lot to see.

It's open Sunday to Tuesday and Thursday from 10 am to 5 pm, Wednesday 10 am to 7 pm, and is closed Friday and Saturday; admission is US$3 (students US$1.50). The chronosphere multi-screen audiovisual display costs a little more. Take Dan bus No 25 from Jaffa, the west side of Carmel Market, Allenby Rd between Magen David Circle and Moshavot Square, King George and Reines Sts on the corner of Frishmann St (near Dizengoff Circle), or near the IYHA hostel; or No 27 from the central bus station. Get off at the university, either Matatia Gate No 2 or Frenkel Gate No 7.

Land of Israel (Eretz Y'Israel) Museum

About one km south-west of the university campus (follow Ha'Universita St), this impressive complex consists of 11 small museums constructed around an archaeological site, Tel Qasile. The complex is open Sunday, Monday, and Wednesday to Friday 9 am to 1 pm, Tuesday 9 am to 1 pm and 4 to 7 pm, and Saturday 10 am to 1 pm. Admission is US$2 (students US$1.35). The museums include:

Tel Qasile Excavations & Pavilion This

mound was probably first settled by the Philistines in the 12th century BC. Three of their temples have been unearthed, as well as some of their town. There are also a few Crusader remains to be seen. In the pavilion is a collection of artefacts found at the site.

Glass Museum This museum houses one of the world's finest and most valuable glass collections, which traces the history of glass-making.

Kadman Numismatic Museum Housing a collection of ancient coins and also some displays of some pre-coinage currencies.

Ceramics Museum Deals with the history of pottery, its development over the centuries and its religious significance. The collection includes Gaza and Akko styles of Ilbriq pottery.

Nechustan Pavilion Features some of the finds from excavations of the ancient copper mines at Timna – the legendary King Solomon's Mines.

Man & His Work Pavilion A collection of ancient tools.

Folklore Pavilion Jewish religious arts, ethnic costumes, ceremonial objects and a Florentine synagogue's benches, pulpit and ark.

Alphabet Museum The most recent addition, showing the history of the development of alphabets and writing.

Lasky Planetarium This is housed in the the prominent domed building.

HaYarkon Park & River

The Yarkon River divides the coastal plain into the Sharon Plain to the north and the Shephela, the lowland plain to the south. In biblical times the river marked the border between the tribes of Ephraim and Dan. In the 1950s, water from here was siphoned off to irrigate the Negev Desert. The Reading Power Station's chimney on the western side of the river is a useful landmark.

The park's green expanse offers an alternative to the traffic noise and the beach parade, but the ugly electric pylons stop it from becoming too appealing. This is the site for outdoor concerts, either in the Wohl

Amphitheatre or, for bigger events, on the larger grass expanse.

It is possible to take a boat trip along the river or hire your own rowing boat, although the water is dirty and the surroundings unspectacular.

Beaches

One of Tel Aviv's main attractions is its lengthy stretch of white sand to which thousands of Israelis flock in good weather, with incredible scenes of overcrowding on Shabbat. The beaches are within easy walking distance of most accommodation, eating places and shops. Bear in mind, however, that drownings are a tragically regular occurrence due to a combination of the strong undertow and reckless swimmers overestimating their capabilities. Theft is a more widespread problem so try not to take any valuables with you when you go to the beach. The most crowded area is between the Hilton in the north and Opera Square to the south where Allenby Rd starts.

When the sun is out (and it usually is) the beaches are a sort of Israeli 'Copacabana', with all the local poseurs on parade. In the mornings, before the sun rises over the north of the city, a hardy group of old-timers congregate to swim and exercise; later in the day the beaches are dotted with people playing *matkot* (Israeli beach tennis). As the evening approaches, fishing enthusiasts take over, especially to the north of the marina and to the south of West Beach.

Religious Beach North of the Hilton Beach and before the old harbour is a stretch of beach reserved for religious bathers who want to be able to swim in a more modest style. On Sunday, Tuesday and Thursday only women are permitted to use the area and it is a good place for any women, Jewish or not, to enjoy a swim or to sunbathe without the constant attention of the amorous Israeli male.

West Beach & Charles Clore Park South of the failed dolphinarium complex, this beach is a popular site for Israeli families to camp and enjoy a barbecue. The café/restaurant on the beach is a popular late-night spot, and there are often groups of people enthusiastically dancing in the open air.

Squares

Atarim Square Also known as Namir Square, this ugly concrete jungle houses a complex of shops, offices, hotels, cafés, restaurants, bars, a cinema, a nightclub and a car park. Straddling HaYarkon St, it links Ben-Gurion Blvd with the beach. The landmarks are, from north to south, the Carlton, Moriah, Diplomat and Ramada hotels.

London Square This garden between HaYarkon St and Herbert Samuel Blvd opposite Bograshov St was built in 1940 and was dedicated to the citizens of London in recognition of their courage during the blitz attacks of the Battle of Britain.

HaYarkon St

Running the length of the downtown beaches and named after the river, this street houses Tel Aviv's luxury hotels and several embassies. As you head south the street becomes decidedly shabby, eventually entering the city's red-light district, which has definitely seen better days. Dominating the southern end of HaYarkon St, where Allenby Rd starts, is Opera Square and the Israel Opera building, the home of the Israeli parliament before it was moved to Jerusalem.

The bizarre-looking apartment building at 181 HaYarkon, across from the beach north of Atarim Square, is the subject of much critical comment, with its western facade festooned with sculptured designs. Check out the other side to see the tree mural incorporating the design of the building.

Independence Park (Gan Ha'Atzmaut), between the Hilton and Carlton hotels, is a gay hang-out at night.

Ben Yehuda St

Named after the man credited with the revival of the Hebrew language, this street was populated mainly by German Jews, who were among the most stubborn opponents of his ideas for a modern Hebrew language. Many of the children of these people now run the local shops while the older generation can be seen sitting and reminiscing outside the cafés here and on Dizengoff St. When they first arrived, HaYarkon St was just a path for the Arabs' camels, and Dizengoff St had not been built.

Ben-Gurion's House

At 17 Ben-Gurion Blvd (☎ 221010), on the seafront between Ben Yehuda St and Atarim Square, is the former house of Israel's first prime minister, David Ben-Gurion and his wife, Paula. Maintained more or less as it was when they lived here, the small rooms are simply furnished and contain part of Ben-Gurion's library of some 20,000 books as well as his correspondence with political leaders. The house is open Sunday to Thursday from 8 am to 2 pm, Monday and Thursday 5 to 7 pm, Friday 8 am to 1 pm, and Saturday 11 am to 2 pm; admission is free.

It is worth stopping on your way past one day, if only to practise your French and read Ben-Gurion's letter to Charles de Gaulle, written in 1964, predicting that in 10 to 15 years the USSR would be a democratic country.

Old Cemetery

On Trumpeldor St, east of Ben Yehuda St, is the cemetery where many victims of the 1921 and 1929 riots lie buried, as well as the Zionist leaders Max Nordau, Ahad Ha'am, Haim Arlosoroff, Shemaryahu Levin, the poets H N Bialik and S Tchernichovsky, and the first mayor of Tel Aviv, Meir Dizengoff.

Dizengoff St

Named after the city's first mayor (1910-37), this is Tel Aviv's prime street for people-watching and window shopping. In recent years, though, locals tend to agree that Dizengoff is not what it was, with more and more trashy stores and eating places opening up to replace of the up-market establishments that used to dominate, rather like London's Oxford St.

Little Tel Aviv The northern end of the street remains a more up-market area of shops, cafés and restaurants covering HaYarkon, Ben Yehuda and Yeshayahu Sts, known collectively as 'Little Tel Aviv'. On Shabbat and Jewish festivals, in particular Purim, the street is closed to traffic and is used as a children's playground and an extra seating area for the local cafés.

Along the length of Dizengoff St are some of the country's top cultural centres, such as the Mann Auditorium and the Habima and Cameri theatres.

Dizengoff Centre This multilevel shopping centre crosses the street, both above and below ground level, and has slowly developed into one of Israel's prime retailing areas. It houses cafés, two cinemas and several interesting shops.

Dizengoff Square & Fountain Officially named Tzina Square after the first mayor's wife, this is the raised circular plaza dominated by a modern water fountain. It was designed by Ya'acov Agam, a leading Israeli artist whose most prominent local work prior to this was the paint job on the Dan Hotel. Called 'Fire and Water', a flame periodically shoots up above the fountain while the coloured structure spins round with jets of water playing to the sound of recorded music. I think it looks awful, but it certainly attracts a lot of attention. The area immediately north of here is Dizengoff's most crowded, particularly on Saturday evenings after Shabbat.

Tel Aviv Museum

Part of an attractive modern development including the Law Courts and the municipal central library, the Tel Aviv Museum (☎ 261297) is at 27 King Shaul Blvd. It's a large museum and you'll need a few hours to see it all. Displays include paintings by Impressionists such as Renoir, Pissarro, Monet and Duffy, and Post-Impressionists such as Picasso, Kokoschka, Roualt and Matisse.

Films and special exhibits are often featured, so call by or check the *Jerusalem Post* and the tourist office for the current schedule. It is open Sunday to Thursday from 10 am to 9.30 pm, Saturday 10 am to 2 pm and 7 to 10 pm, and is closed Friday. Admission is US$4.50 (students US$1.75), and it includes access to the Helena Rubenstein Pavilion. To get there, take Dan bus No 18 from Trumpeldor St, Ben Yehuda St to Allenby St; Nos 28 or 70 from the central bus station; or No 32 from Allenby Rd, Ben Yehuda and Bograshov Sts.

Jabotinsky Institute

This is an historical research organisation, featuring a museum which presents the history and activities of the National Resistance Movement, founded and led by Ze'ev Jabotinsky. The several departments show his political, literary and journalistic activities, and also the creation of the Jewish Legion in WW I, the paramilitary force of the Revisionist Movement and their illegal immigration programme.

The museum is at 38 King George St on the 1st floor of the institute. As no signs are in English it can be difficult to find. It is open Sunday, Tuesday and Thursday from 10 am to 6 pm, Monday and Wednesday 10 am to 1 pm and 6 to 8 pm, Friday 10 am to 1 pm, but is closed on Saturday; admission is free.

Gan Me'ir

Sandwiched between King George and Tchernichovsky Sts, the lovely small shaded park of Gan Me'ir offers a pleasant respite from the heat and noise. Designed by Abraham Karavan in the mid-1930s and also named after the first mayor, it is now threatened by plans for an underground car park.

Allenby Rd

A Tel Avivian comparison is made here with New York's Wall St and Lower East Side. Forget it. Once Tel Aviv's main fashionable artery, it is now overshadowed by Dizengoff St although it still houses the city's main market places – the Boursa (stock market) and the Carmel Market.

Opened in 1917, the street was named in honour of the British general who, with the support of Arabs, liberated Palestine from the Turks. At that time the immediate area was basically an expanse of sand, but it soon became the heart of the commercial and social district. The bright lights and fancy shops are now found elsewhere but the major Israeli banks still have their main offices on or around Allenby Rd, with 'bargain basement' shops as neighbours. Beyond the southern end is the central bus station with its cheap shops and stalls.

Allenby Rd starts on the seafront in Opera Square and curves eastward through the decaying red-light district to intersect with Ben Yehuda and Pinsker Sts to form Mograbi Square.

Heading sharply south from here, Allenby Rd takes in the oldest bookstores; often you will see books sold from carts on the pavement.

Magen David Circle This busy junction is named after the six-pointed Magen David (Star of David) and is so-named because it is the point where six streets (King George, Allenby, Ben Yehuda, Sheinken, HaKarmel and Nahalat Binyamin) intersect. Freelance painters and decorators hang around the King George St side of the circle hoping for some work.

Great Synagogue On the corner of Allenby Rd and Ahad Ha'am St, the synagogue, built in 1926, is the domed building with stained-glass windows. It is one of the few obvious signs of the Jewish religion in the city.

Bialik St

With its attractive buildings, this small street running north off Allenby Rd near the corner of Ben Yehuda St, is one of Tel Aviv's much-overlooked backwaters. The street is named after Haim Nachman Bialik, Israel's national poet and the man behind the renaissance in Hebrew literature.

Reuven Rubin House This house is at No 14 (☎ 658961), on the right as you head from Allenby, and it is the former residence of the artist Reuven Rubin.

You can see an exhibition of his work and his private collection of photographs and furnishings here. It is open Sunday, Monday, Wednesday and Thursday from 10 am to 2 pm, Tuesday 10 am to 1 pm and 4 to 8 pm, Saturday 11 am to 2 pm, but is closed Friday; admission is US$0.70.

Bialik House At No 22 is Bialik's former home, which has now been converted into a small museum. It contains memorabilia connected with his life and work, along with occasional temporary exhibits. It's open Sunday to Thursday from 9 am to 7 pm, and Friday 9 am to 1 pm; admission is free.

Museum of the History of Tel Aviv-Jaffa At No 27, by the side of the circular fountain at the end of the street, this museum (☎ 653052) has photographs, models, a film (in English) and documents relating to the city's history. It's badly presented, which is unusual for an Israeli museum.

This museum is open Sunday, Monday, and Wednesday to Friday from 9 am to 1 pm, Tuesday 4 to 7 pm, but is closed Saturday; admission is around US$1.75 (students US$1).

Carmel Market
Tel Aviv's loud and crowded market is between Allenby Rd, on Magen David Circle, and HaYarkon St, cutting into the Yemenite Quarter. From Allenby Rd, the main market street is Carmel St, and you need to push your way past the first few metres of clothing and footwear stalls to be totally immersed in the atmosphere. This is probably best achieved by heading for the southern end where the fruit, vegetables and, in particular, poultry are bandied about to great effect. When in form, the stallholders have an amusing sales patter, singing songs to promote their goods and often joining in with one another.

For a change of pace, each of the narrow side streets specialises in a particular range of items, one favouring dry goods, another dried fruit, nuts and spices sold from sacks. As usual, good prices are to be had as the

market closes, and it's at its busiest in the pre-Shabbat rush.

On the other side of Allenby Rd is the Bezalel Market, between King George and Tchernichovsky Sts, specialising in eat-as-much-as-you-can felafel and cheap clothes.

Yemenite Quarter
Between Allenby Rd and the sea, Kerem Hatemanim (the Yememite Quarter), is one of the oldest areas of the city. Its crumbling buildings house some great eating places, mainly in the middle-price range but it's also possible to eat well here for less.

Rothschild Blvd
Named after the Jewish family of financiers in recognition of their support for the Zionist cause, the promenade of this pleasant boulevard is shaded along its entire length and is one of the city's more attractive places for a stroll. The boulevard goes from just south of Herzl St to Habima Square close to the theatre of the same name, the Mann Auditorium and the Helena Rubenstein Pavilion.

Founders' Monument Ornamented on one side with a bas-relief and inscribed on the other side with the founders' names, the monument illustrates the development of Tel Aviv in three phases:

1 1909-10 – Jewish workers starting to build on the sand

2 1910-18 – the Gymnasia Herzlia building, Tel Aviv's first major construction flanked by the first water tower and the residence of Meir Dizengoff

3 Tel Aviv today – the harbour, built in 1936 and an important factor in the Jewish struggle against Arab opposition, the Habima Theatre, Bialik House and modern apartment blocks in the background.

Independence Hall On 14 May 1948, Ben-Gurion declared the establishment of the State of Israel from this hall at 16 Rothschild Blvd, then part of the old Tel Aviv Museum

and previously Meir Dizengoff's home. It is
open Sunday to Friday from 9 am to 2 pm,
Tuesday also 4 to 7 pm, but is closed Saturday; admission is US$0.90 (students
US$0.75).

Haganah/IDF Museum At 23 Rothschild
Blvd this museum (☎ 623624) is the former
home of General Eliyahu Golomb, one of the
founders of the military organisation whose
history is recorded here. The Haganah
became an integral part of the IDF and exhibits mainly deal with its development over the
years.

The museum is open Sunday to Friday
from 9 am to 3 pm, but closed Saturday;
admission is US$1.30 (students US$0.75).

Habima Square
Linking Rothschild Blvd with Dizengoff and
Ibn Gevirol Sts, this is the centre of Israel's
cultural scene.

Helena Rubenstein Pavilion Around the
corner from the square at 6 Tarsat Blvd
(☎ 287196) and part of the Tel Aviv
Museum, this small museum features temporary exhibits by guest artists, both Israeli and
foreign. Admission is sometimes free
depending on the exhibit, but a Tel Aviv
Museum ticket is good for here, too.

Habima Theatre Now Israel's national
theatre (☎ 209888), the original company
was founded in Moscow in 1918 by
Stanislavsky and in 1928 it moved to Palestine and changed its name to Habima,
meaning 'the stage'. The group presented the
first Hebrew translations of works by
Shakespeare, Moliére, Shaw and O'Neill.
All performances are in Hebrew and simultaneous translation earphones are sometimes
available.

Mann Auditorium With a capacity of 3000,
the Mann Auditorium (☎ 299170) is the
country's major concert venue and home of
the Israel Philharmonic Orchestra. The
complex includes a pleasant garden, ponds
and an exterior mural.

White Gallery On the corner of Rothschild
Blvd and the square, this attractive complex
combines a café/restaurant and a New Age
bookshop.

Nahalat Binyamin St
'Never mind the price, feel the quality'. This
is the old textile and haberdashery centre,
which has been rejuvenated and is enjoying
a new lease of life with artists' street stalls
during the day and several popular cafés that
fill up into the night. On Friday, there is
music and dancing in the street to see in
Shabbat.

The name of the suburb, meaning Inheri-
tance of Benjamin, dates back to 1912 when
the poor artisans who settled here were
looking for financial backing to build their
houses. The Jewish National Fund was told
that the suburb would be named after
Benyamin Herzl, and the Rothschilds were
told it would be named after Baron Benjamin
de Rothschild.

Whoever ended up footing the bill, you
can still see that a great deal of money must
have been spent, as some of the architectural
delights of the city of Tel Aviv are to be found
here. Look upwards to see the fancy balconies and balustrades, in particular No 8,
Degel House; No 13, Levy House; No 16,
Rosenberg House; No 27, the Nordau Hotel;
and the Palatin Hotel on the corner of Ahad
Ha'am St.

Shalom Tower
Herzl St was the new city's first main road
and the centre of the social scene. Look out
for photographs of it 70 years ago to see how
it started. At the top of the street was Tel
Aviv's first building, the Gymnasia Herzlia,
built in 1909. As the first secular, Hebrew-
language secondary school, the Gymnasia
became a symbol of Jewish development,
acting as a cultural and economic stimulus
for the community and attracting many students from abroad, who were accommodated
in nearby hostels. The Gymnasia has now
been demolished and Israel's tallest building, the Shalom Tower, built in 1959, now
stands in its place.

The Shalom Tower includes a post office branch, supermarket/department store and the Ministry of the Interior's offices. For desperate tourists there is a terrible wax museum which tries to depict events and characters in Israeli history but fails dismally – the only convincing piece in the whole place is Moshe Dayan's eyepatch. More worthwhile is a visit to the top-floor observatory with its views of the city and, on a clear day, beyond.

Admission to the observatory is US$2.75, the wax museum US$3.20, or to both US$4. The tower is open Sunday to Friday from 9.30 am, but is closed Saturday.

Merkaz Mis-hari
At the southern end of Allenby Rd, dominated by Levinsky and Matalon Sts, is the wholesalers' market area, which dates back to 1925. Tel Aviv had previously relied entirely on its supplies from Jaffa but the problems between the Arab and Jewish communities put a stop to that. Most of the shops here are mini-warehouses crammed with an assortment of goods including toys and souvenirs and there are some good places to eat.

Newe Tzedek
One of the first quarters to be built in the new city in 1887, this area, south-west of Allenby Rd and the Shalom Tower is a delightful maze of narrow streets full of lovely old buildings of grand design. It fell into decay, became adopted by the textile industry which filled its northern streets with workshops and fashion showrooms, and is now 'in', with much renovation work being carried out. Well worth a casual wander, it has a theatre, cafés, restaurants and perhaps the city's best example of an old-style bagel factory.

Manshiye
An old Arab district largely destroyed during the 1948 War of Independence, it lies at the southern end of the Carmel Market.

Hassan Baq Mosque This mosque is now being renovated under the auspices of the

Ministry of Religious Affairs with criticism from some Jews – its minaret was used by Arab snipers during the war.

Industry House This building is part of a striking modern complex which is the first in a planned series of developments which will fill the now vacant stretch of coastline between Tel Aviv and Jaffa.

Etzel Museum
South of the West Beach along South Herbert Samuel Esplanade, in an attractive smoked-glass reconstruction within the stone shell of an older building, this museum (☎ 657180) presents a mainly photographic history of the Jewish victory against the Arabs in Jaffa in April 1948.

The museum is open Sunday to Thursday from 8 am to 4 pm, Friday 8 am to 1 pm, and is closed Saturday; admission is US$0.70.

Yad Eliyahu
This district east of the central bus station, across the busy dual carriageway, was established in 1946 by Jewish veterans of the British Army. It was named after Eliyahu Golomb, one of the Haganah's commanders.

HaTiqwa
To the south of Yad Eliyahu, this district's name means The Hope. It was established in 1852 by a group of American Seventh Day Adventists. Only five years later they were forced to disband the colony after either being stricken by disease or attacked by Bedouin (reports vary). The area is now a depressed Sephardic neighbourhood.

Its inexpensive meat restaurants and Iraqi bakeries are popular and well worth a visit (see the Places to Eat section under Tel Aviv in this chapter).

Art Galleries
Opening hours vary, but Tel Aviv's many galleries are often open for short periods of time, say 10 am to 1 pm and 5 to 8 pm.

Alef, 36 Gordon St; Israeli ceramics, silver, glass, · enamel, embroidery and weaving (☎ 239932)

Camera Obscura, 57 Allenby Rd; photography school gallery exhibiting work by students and top photographers (☎ 298291)

Christies', 2 Habima Square; regular exhibitions (☎ 204727)

Dervish, 7 Gordon St; folklore from various countries, wood, ceramics, carpets (☎ 227906)

Dvir, 26 Gordon St; Israeli art (☎ 232003)

Engel Gallery, 26 Gordon St; Israeli art (☎ 225637)

Gordon Gallery, 95 Ben Yehuda St; a leading Israeli gallery with a twice yearly auction held in the WZO Building on Kaplan St (☎ 240323)

Julie M Gallery, 7 Glickson St; Israeli art (☎ 295473)

Kibbutz Art Gallery 25 Dov Hoz St; all work produced by kibbutzniks (☎ 232533)

Sara Kishon, 31 Frug St; Israeli art (☎ 225069)

Sara Levy, 10 Pineles St; Israeli art (☎ 450202)

Proza, Dizengoff Central; 2nd floor bookshop with exhibits by art students

E Rosenfeld Gallery, 147 Dizengoff St; pleasant owner, top Israeli artists' work with regular exhibitions (☎ 229044)

Stern Gallery, 30 Gordon St; Israeli art (☎ 246303)

Tel Aviv University Mexico Building; exhibitions to inspire the art students here

Safari Park

This 100-hectare African animal reserve in Ramat Gan will only appeal to the desperate and easily pleased.

It is open October to May (Sunday to Thursday 9 am to 3 pm, Friday 9 am to 2 pm), June to September (Sunday to Thursday 9 am to 6 pm, Friday 9 am to 2 pm), but is closed Saturday. Dan bus Nos 30, 35 and 40 go there but you're only allowed to enter in closed vehicles.

Tours

Egged Tours offer a variety of guided tours of Tel Aviv-Jaffa and surrounding places of interest. They start with a half-day tour of Tel Aviv-Jaffa at around US$18 and a full-day tour at US$35. Coaches leave from here to other areas of the country as well.

Places to Stay

Virtually all of Tel Aviv's hostels and hotels are found in or around Ben Yehuda, HaYarkon and Dizengoff Sts and Allenby Rd. All these locations are within a few minutes' walk of the beaches, popular eating and shopping places and nightspots; a brisk walk or cheap bus ride should put you within easy reach of most other places of interest.

Two Dan buses leaving from the central bus station will get you to the general area. No 4 goes along Allenby Rd and Ben Yehuda St, and No 5 along Dizengoff St. When choosing a place to stay bear in mind that rooms facing the street can be noisy due to heavy traffic. For a change of scene, consider staying in Jaffa (see Places to Stay for Jaffa in this chapter).

Places to Stay – bottom end

Generally speaking, it seems that the majority of budget travellers fall into two categories regarding a visit to Tel Aviv. Most tend to stay for as short a time as possible, either to be close to the airport, or as a stopover en route to/from a kibbutz/moshav or simply to have a quick look at the city whilst devoting more time to other places. A significant number, though, become long-term 'residents', often finding a job to keep their heads above water. Some hostels are particularly popular with the latter community; these tend to be the more laid-back places, where the housekeeping is of less importance, the bar is busy, and the noise level is somewhat high.

For those who prefer quieter, cleaner accommodation, the following should appeal.

Greenhouse Hostel (☎ 235994), at 201 Dizengoff St, between Arlosoroff and Jabotinsky Sts, is a quiet, ultra-clean and nicely furnished place. This well-run treasure is often full so call ahead if possible. There's a TV lounge, kitchen and a pleasant rooftop bar open in the summer. Beds in the spacious dorms are US$8 (only four or five beds per room); lovely doubles cost from US$20 to US$30. It is closed from 10 am to 2.30 pm and there's no curfew.

Bnei Dan Youth Hostel – IYHA (☎ 5460719; fax 5441030), is at 32 Bnei Dan St. Take Dan bus No 5, get off on Yehuda HaMaccabi St, walk north two blocks, and it's across from the Yarkon River. The hostel is mainly used by Israelis, as travellers prefer the cheaper, more central private hostels. It

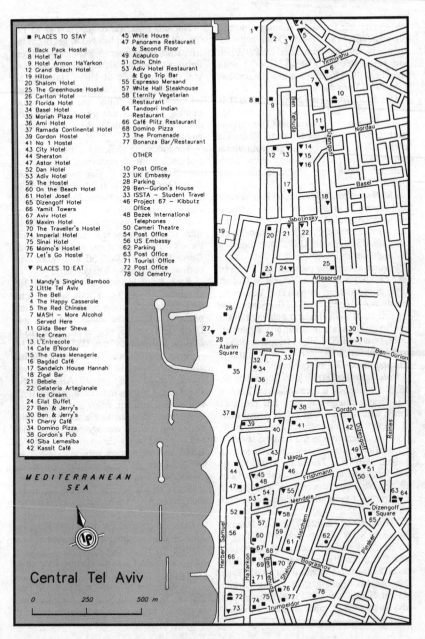

■ PLACES TO STAY

6 Back Pack Hostel
8 Hotel Tal
9 Hotel Armon HaYarkon
12 Grand Beach Hotel
19 Hilton
20 Shalom Hotel
25 The Greenhouse Hostel
26 Carlton Hotel
32 Florida Hotel
34 Basel Hotel
35 Moriah Plaza Hotel
36 Ami Hotel
37 Ramada Continental Hotel
39 Gordon Hostel
41 No 1 Hostel
43 City Hotel
44 Sheraton
47 Astor Hotel
52 Dan Hotel
53 Adiv Hotel
59 The Hostel
60 On the Beach Hotel
61 Hotel Josef
65 Dizengoff Hotel
66 Yamit Towers
67 Aviv Hotel
69 Maxim Hotel
70 The Traveller's Hostel
74 Imperial Hotel
75 Sinai Hotel
76 Momo's Hostel
77 Let's Go Hostel

▼ PLACES TO EAT

1 Mandy's Singing Bamboo
2 Little Tel Aviv
3 The Bell
4 The Happy Casserole
5 The Red Chinese
7 MASH – More Alcohol
  Served Here
11 Glida Beer Sheva
   Ice Cream
13 L'Entrecote
14 Cafe B'Nordau
15 The Glass Menagerie
16 Bagdad Café
17 Sandwich House Hannah
18 Zigal Bar
21 Bebele
22 Gelateria Artegianale
   Ice Cream
24 Eilat Buffet
27 Ben & Jerry's
30 Ben & Jerry's
31 Cherry Café
34 Domino Pizza
38 Gordon's Pub
40 Siba Lemesiba
42 Kassit Café

45 White House
47 Panorama Restaurant
   & Second Floor
49 Acapulco
51 Chin Chin
53 Adiv Hotel Restaurant
   & Ego Trip Bar
55 Espresso Mersand
57 White Hall Steakhouse
58 Eternity Vegetarian
   Restaurant
64 Tandoori Indian
   Restaurant
66 Café Piltz Restaurant
68 Domino Pizza
73 The Promenade
77 Bonanza Bar/Restaurant

OTHER

10 Post Office
23 UK Embassy
28 Parking
29 Ben-Gurion's House
33 ISSTA – Student Travel
46 Project 67 – Kibbutz
   Office
48 Bezek International
   Telephones
50 Cameri Theatre
54 Post Office
56 US Embassy
62 Parking
63 Post Office
71 Tourist Office
72 Post Office
78 Old Cemetry

MEDITERRANEAN SEA

Central Tel Aviv

0   250   500 m

has no cooking facilities, although you can get standard IYHA food. Dorm beds for members/nonmembers cost US$9/10.50, and singles/doubles are $21.50/33 with breakfast. It is closed 9 am to 5 pm and has a flexible 11 pm curfew.

Dizengoff Hotel (☎ 5242024, 220687), is at 11-13 Dizengoff Square, and the entrance is across from the cinema and Co-op supermarket, next to the felafel stand. There's a kitchen, bar, and a roof terrace with views across the square. There's no curfew, dorm beds are US$8, and singles/doubles are US$22.

The Hostel (☎ 287088), at 60 Ben Yehuda St, between Bograshov and Mendele Sts, is not so good and is on the 4th floor with no lift. It's clean enough, with a kitchen. Dorm beds are US$8, rooms US$17 and there's a midnight curfew.

Further along, the pleasant *No 1 Hostel* (☎ 5237807) is at 84 Ben Yehuda St. Get off at the third No 4 bus stop on Ben Yehuda St, and the hostel is just south of Gordon St. Use the side entrance and take the elevator to the top floor. There's a nice bar and a kitchen. Dorm beds are US$8.50, and doubles US$22 with breakfast. It is closed from 10 am to 1 pm, and there's a 1 am curfew.

Hotel Josef (☎ 280955), 15 Bograshov St, off Ben Yehuda St is nice and clean. There's a pleasant lounge-bar area but crowded dorms with beds for US$7. It is closed from 11 am to 1 pm, and there's a 1 am curfew.

As an alternative to the hostels, some of the smaller hotels can be within a traveller's budget. *Hotel Nes Tziona* (☎ 5103404), 10 Nes Tziona St, is a few minutes' walk from the first No 4 bus stop on Ben Yehuda St. It is quiet, and rooms with/without bathrooms are US$30/25.

Nordau Hotel (☎ 621612), at 27 Nahalat Binyamin St, is a lovely domed building in the heart of an architecturally interesting area. Unfortunately, the hotel is a bit grubby, has no kitchen and unenthusiastic staff. Take Dan bus No 4 and get off by the Carmel Market. Singles are US$13, doubles are just US$16 to US$22, and all have showers. There's no curfew.

HaGalil Hotel (☎ 655036), is at 23 Bet Yosef St. Take Dan bus No 4, get off at the fifth stop, cross over to 56 Allenby Rd, cut through the wide walkway and it's ahead of you on the corner of Hillel HaZaken St. Quaint, quiet, clean and comfortable, there's no kitchen but a fridge and tea & coffee-making facilities are available. Singles/doubles are US$16/25, there's no curfew, and ask for a key.

The following choices are the city's more laid-back options mentioned earlier, very popular with those staying awhile. *Gordon Hostel* (☎ 229870) is at 2 Gordon St, above the Terminal bar on the seafront and on the corner of HaYarkon St. It's a good place to learn about job opportunities. It has kitchens, some rooms face the sea with balconies and there's a roof terrace, bar and video room. Dorm beds are US$7.50 and there's no curfew. Take bus No 4 to get there.

Back Pack Hostel (☎ 458381), at 306 Dizengoff St, south of Yirmiyahu St is a bit tatty, but friendly enough. This can also be a place to ask around about finding a job. Dorm beds cost $5, singles are from $15 to US$20, and doubles from US$20 to US$24.

Away from the beach in the crumbling but attractive Yemenite Quarter is the *Home Hotel* (☎ 656736), at 20 Alsheich St. Rumoured for years to be closing soon, if it's still around you can enjoy a courtyard bar, video room, loud music, kitchen, free tea and coffee and friendly management. It provides some of the city's cheapest dorm beds at US$6, and offers some private rooms. Take bus No 4, and get off at the fifth stop before Bialik St. Cross Allenby and go down the walkway beside No 56. Take the first right, then left on Alsheich St and it's a few metres down on your left.

Let's Go Hostel (☎ 5289445) Hovevei Zion St, off Trumpeldor St, and east of Ben Yehuda St, is another cheapie with dorm beds for US$6. There's a kitchen, free tea & coffee and a small garden.

The Traveller's Hostel (☎ 25099), 38 Ben Yehuda St, between Shalom Aleichem and Bograshov Sts, is small and a bit crowded. It has no kitchen, but the secluded garden courtyard can be a bonus. Dorms are US$7, private rooms US$22, and there's no curfew.

Momo's Hostel (☎ 297421, 287471), at 28 Ben Yehuda St, between Trumpeldor and Shalom Aleichem Sts, has US$7 dorm beds, a kitchen and bar.

On the Beach Hostel, on the corner of HaYarkon and Bograshov Sts, is very crowded and grubby but is one of Tel Aviv's cheapest hostels; dorm beds are US$6.50.

There are a number of small hotels in the depressing red-light zone and, despite recent attempts to clean the place up, many travellers will find this area less than appealing. *Riviera Hostel* (☎ 656870, 653883), 52 HaYarkon St, on the corner of Allenby Rd, is a hotel now targeting the budget traveller. Dorm beds are US$6, private rooms are from US$23 to US$30, and there is no curfew.

Other options include, on Allenby Rd, *Sandi Hotel* (☎ 653889), the *Bell Hotel* (☎ 654291), the *Migdal David Hotel* (☎ 656392), the *Monopol Hotel* (☎ 655906), and, at 58 HaYarkon St, the *Hotel Eilat* (☎ 655368).

Places to Stay – middle

Unless otherwise stated, prices include breakfast and private bathrooms and can vary dramatically due to high-season rates. Most of these hotels are modern and uniformly anonymous with basic furnishings and small rooms.

A room with a sea view can make up for the lack of atmosphere; HaYarkon St, running parallel with the Mediterranean, is lined with hotels. The best value in this category is *Aviv Hotel* (☎ 5102784/5), 88 HaYarkon St, on the corner of Bograshov St. With only 20 rooms, it's often full so book in advance if you can. Singles cost from US$20 to US$25, and doubles are from US$35 to US$40. A little to the south, *Maxim Hotel* (☎ 653721), 86 HaYarkon St, has singles/doubles for US$30/49.

Ambassador Hotel (☎ 5103993; fax 657301), 2 Allenby Rd, actually faces the seafront. Some rooms here are larger than average; singles cost from US$35 to US$43, and doubles from US$50 to US$66.

The *Florida Hotel* (☎ 5242184), 164 HaYarkon St, is across from Atarim Square, and south of Ben-Gurion Blvd. Rooms are US$35/48 for a single/double. *Shalom Hotel* (☎ 243277, 249444; fax 235895), is at 216 HaYarkon St, north of the British Embassy and across from the Hilton. The Stagecoach Restaurant dominates its entrance. Singles cost from US$36 to US$40, and doubles from US$50 to US$65.

Hotel Armon HaYarkon (☎ 455271/3), at 268 HaYarkon St, is a small, smart looking place with singles costing from US$39 to US$43, and doubles from US$49 to US$56.

Away from the seafront, but in Tel Aviv that's rarely very far, are several other choices. Just half a block back from Atarim Square is the *Ami Hotel* (☎ 5249141/5, 231151) at 4 Am Y'Israel Hai St. Singles cost from US$45 to US$48, and doubles from US$56 to US$60.

Moss Hotel (☎ 651656), is at 6 Nes Tziona St, between Ben Yehuda and HaYarkon Sts. Take Dan bus No 4 to the first stop on Ben Yehuda St, continue walking in the same direction, turn left onto Idelson St and Nes Tziona St is immediately on the right. Moss Hotel is a pleasant hotel in a quiet location. There's a bar, coffee shop and dining room. Singles/doubles are US$45/55.

Adiv Hotel (☎ 229141; fax 229144), is at 5 Mendele St, between Ben Yehuda and HaYarkon Sts. This hotel has a popular self-service restaurant, which was closed for renovations at the time of writing. Singles/doubles are US$40/58.

A step up is the *City Hotel* (☎ 5246253; fax 5246250), 9 Mapu St, between Ben Yehuda and HaYarkon Sts. Singles cost from US$52 to US$62, and doubles from US$66 to US$85.

Places to Stay – top end

The seafront four-star hotels include the *Astor Hotel* (☎ 223141; fax 5237247) at 105 HaYarkon St, with singles costing from US$48 to US$66, and doubles from US$73 to US$90. Their award-winning restaurant features Israeli nouvelle cuisine.

Basel Hotel (☎ 5244161; fax 5440005), at

156 HaYarkon St, is across from Atarim Square, with singles costing from US$63 to US$73, and doubles from US$75 to US$94.

Grand Beach Hotel (☎ 241252; fax 5466589), 250 HaYarkon St, has its entrance on the corner of Nordau Blvd. It is a grand-looking place with singles costing from US$60 to US$100, and doubles from US$76 to US$139.

I met some visitors who recommended *Hotel Tal* (☎ 5442281; fax 5467687) at 287 HaYarkon St, where singles cost from US$58 to US$68, and doubles from US$69 to US$88.

A block back from the sea, but tall enough to offer some sea-view rooms is the *Sinai Hotel* (☎ 652621; fax 660297), at 11 Trumpeldor St, between HaYarkon and Ben Yehuda Sts. Singles cost from US$$66 to US$84, and doubles from US$77 to US$94.

Good value in this price range, *Regency Suites* (☎ 663266; fax 663276), at 80 HaYarkon St, is an all-suite property. Singles cost from US$105 to US$120, and the doubles (from US$120 to US$140) feature a lounge and kitchenette.

Tel Aviv's luxury hotels contribute to the ugliness of the city's seafront with their standard reinforced-concrete block profiles. Adjacent to the US Embassy is *Yamit Towers* (☎ 651111; fax 654719), 79 HaYarkon St. Singles/doubles cost from US$105 to US$120, and one/two bedroom suites cost from US$145 to US$265.

Dan Tel Aviv (☎ 5241111; fax 5249755), 99 HaYarkon St, was the city's first luxury hotel. It was recently renovated and is now adding an apartment wing. Singles cost from US$110 to US$210, and doubles from US$130 to US$230.

Tel Aviv Sheraton (☎ 5286222; fax 5280805), is at 115 HaYarkon St. It now enjoys a reputation as one of the best hotels in town, with singles costing from US$115 to US$205, and doubles from US$130 to US$220.

The northernmost of the luxury hotels, *Tel Aviv Hilton* (☎ 5202222; fax 5272711), is near Ha'Atzmaut Park. It also enjoys good word-of-mouth recommendations. Singles

cost from US$172 to US$196, and doubles from US$187 to US$226.

Three properties are adjacent to Atarim Square. The best is the *Carlton Hotel* (☎ 5201818; fax 5271043), at 10 Eliezer Peri St. Singles cost from US$85 to US$162, and doubles from US$96 to US$172.

The others are *Moriah Plaza Tel Aviv* (☎ 5271515; fax 5271065), 155 HaYarkon St (singles cost from US$94 to US$122, and doubles from US$114 to US$156) and the *Ramada Continental* (☎ 5272626; fax 5272576), 121 HaYarkon St (singles cost from US$85 to US$115, doubles from US$95 to US$135).

Dan Panorama (☎ 5190190; fax 658599), at 10 Y Kaufmann St, is a bit out of the way. South of the main beaches and the downtown area towards Jaffa, singles cost from US$80 to US$128, and doubles from US$94 to US$142.

Places to Eat

Carmel Market is the cheapest place for fresh fruit and vegetables. Two convenient supermarkets are: *Supersol*, on Ben Yehuda St, between Gordon and Mapu Sts (open Sunday to Thursday 7 am to midnight, Wednesday and Thursday for 24 hours, Friday 7 am to 3 pm, and closed Saturday); and the *Co-op* at Dizengoff Square.

The country's best cheese shop is *Shomorn* at 88 Nahalat Binyamin St, between Levinsky and Matalon Sts, in the Merkaz Mis-hari wholesalers' district. The best fishmonger is *The Four Fishermen*, 169 Ben Yehuda St, on the corner of Jabotinsky St; the cheapest is in Jaffa, on the corner of Yefet St, up past Said Abulafiah & Sons bakery.

Tel Aviv has an incredible number of fast-food outlets serving shwarma, felafel, pizza, hot dogs, burgers and ice cream. Much of it is mediocre at best and rarely good value for money. However, there are some places worth trying. Handy to the beach, Ben Yehuda St is home to several inexpensive cafés and kiosks where you can get a baguette sandwich for about US$3.

Felafel Tel Aviv's felafel is average at best, often consisting largely of breadcrumbs. Most popular (probably because you can eat as much of the extras as you like) are the self-service stalls around the Bezalel Market, off Allenby Rd across from the Carmel Market; and the two on Dizengoff Square.

Hummus & Shwarma The best places for hummus are in Jaffa, but if that's too far, try the Yemenite Quarter. Don't settle for the inferior shwarma available in Atarim Square, Allenby Rd, Ben Yehuda and Dizengoff Sts – Israel's best shwarma is sold at the *Poondak Chem* (see Restaurants – inexpensive under Tel Aviv in this chapter).

Cafés Tel Aviv's many cafés are not normally renowned for good and/or cheap food, but for pleasant surroundings, a pavement seat from which to people-watch, or as a trendy meeting place. Some are particularly worth checking out for different reasons.

One of the cheapest, which also serves some of the best coffee and cakes in town, is *Espresso Mersand* on Ben Yehuda St, at the corner of Frishmann St. It is close to the tourist office and most hostels and hotels, and attracts a unique collection of regulars. These include bohemian types, journalists, actors, models, and elderly German Jews or, more derisively, 'Yekkes'. The latter, who are known for their formality and highly developed sense of propriety, come in the morning and sit outside, passing comment on everything that happens.

Another Tel Aviv café with a clientele of character is *Kassit*, at 117 Dizengoff St, between Gordon and Frishmann Sts. This is the long-established bohemian hang-out whose past customers have included Frank Sinatra and Harry Belafonte. Today you'll rub shoulders with Israel's retired actors, comedians and musicians.

Among the more popular 'smart' cafés on Dizengoff St, *Acapulco*, on the busy corner of Frishmann St, and *Cherry*, on the corner of Ben-Gurion Blvd, stand out. Another nice one is *Café B'Nordau*, 230 Ben Yehuda St,

at the corner of Nordau Blvd. The florist next door provides a pleasant botanical setting.

The *White House* is handy for the beach on HaYarkon St, between Frishmann and Mapu Sts.

Tamar, on Sheinkin Street at the corner of Ahad Ha'am St, is a popular daytime café – which reaches a peak of overcrowding on Friday afternoon. This is a traditional Labour Party favourite and staff of Histradrut, the main union organisation, still patronise the place.

Vegetarian The unique tofu-cuisine at the Black Hebrews *Eternity*, 60 Ben Yehuda St, south of Mendele St, is well worth a try. Even avid meat lovers should at least sample the vegetable shwarma (US$3), cheaper and perhaps more enjoyable than the real thing.

Other dishes include vegetarian hot dogs, tamali, tofulafel, barbecue twist burgers, cheeses, yoghurts, ice cream and shakes. Prices here are good and the food is very tasty. It is open Sunday to Thursday, 9 am to 11 pm, Friday 9 am to 3 pm, and Saturday sunset to midnight.

Ice Cream The *Eternity* restaurant's popular all-vegetable ice cream should be tried. As well as tasting good, it isn't fattening!

Glida Beer Sheva, 249 Dizengoff St, just north-east of Nordau St and *Gelateria Artegianale*, 194 Ben Yehuda St, just below Jabotinsky St, are two of the city's best.

Ben & Jerry's have branches on Dizengoff St, on the corner of Ben-Gurion Blvd and on the beach below Atarim Square.

There are two *Manalitos* branches. Strangely, these Argentinian ice-cream makers are on the same stretch of Ibn Gevirol, albeit on opposite sides, between King Shaul Blvd, Kaplan and Marmorek Sts. Frozen yoghurt is currently popular and stores are found all over the city.

Bakeries Downtown Tel Aviv has a lot of places selling a variety of cakes and pastries. Opinions vary considerably about the best, many of which are also cafés. *Espresso Mersand* has a selection of home-made delights that are among the tastiest – it is on Ben Yehuda St, at the corner of Frishmann St. The *Kapulsky* bakeries at 166 Dizengoff St, next to the Cherry café, on the corner of Ben-Gurion Blvd and also at 37 Allenby Rd, on the corner of Tchernichovsky St, are also top contenders.

Tel Aviv's bagels are something of a tradition and you will see them being sold on the beach and on the streets later in the day and at night. Going along to the bakery to watch them being made is a great way to round off an evening. One of the most popular bakeries is at 11 Pines St in Newe Tzedek. From the Shalom Tower, follow Montefiore St to the south-west, turn left onto HaShahar St, veer right to the end of the block, right onto Yavniel St, turn left at the second stop sign, and the bakery is along the second street on the left.

The traditional Iraqi bakeries along Etsel St (see the Restaurants – inexpensive later in this chapter) in the HaTiqwa district are interesting to see. Here the large wafer-thin pitta are baked in the traditional ovens.

Restaurants – inexpensive In Merkaz Mis-hari at 41 Levinsky St, *Poondak Chem* (look for the 'Best Shwarma in Israel' sign), is a Turkish-owned workers' restaurant patronised by the local wholesale merchants. It offers a good range of excellent and inexpensive food. The shwarma (US$3) is the main event; also on the menu are hummus, 'ishkambe' (sheep's stomach soup), meat and offal grilled 'on the fire', steaks, salads, oriental sweets and draught beer. You can sit down or take away; it is open Sunday to Friday, lunch time only.

Another good lunch-time place is down the street. *Eli Melek*, 29 Levinsky St, west of Herzl St, is a Bulgarian workers' restaurant serving a variety of regional specialities. Appetisers go for US$3 to US$8; salads and pastas from US$8, with main dishes, mostly meats grilled or oven-cooked, US$8 to US$12.

More central, another two cheap lunch choices are the *Eilat Buffet*, on Ben Yehuda St at the corner of Arlosoroff St, or *Sandwich House Hannah*, 191 Ben Yehuda St, between Nordau and Jabotinsky Sts. Open all day, *Siba Lemesiba*, 77 Ben Yehuda St and opposite the No 1 Hostel, serves a variety of plain but inexpensive oriental dishes like hummus for US$2. Draught beer is also served here.

The *Adiv Hotel's* self-service restaurant, on Mendele St between Ben Yehuda and HaYarkon Sts, was closed for renovation at the time of writing. If it reopens as before, it will be busy with a popular US$4 buffet breakfast and a set lunch/dinner consisting of soup, salad, main course and dessert for around US$8.

A decent place, and handy to the beach, is the *Promenade* on Herbert Samuel Esplanade, just to the north of Trumpeldor St. It's open daily, and has a set menu for US$9.

The Yemenite Quarter features a number of inexpensive eating places – mainly the family-run, basic worker's type, serving simple oriental delights such as hummus, spicy meat soups and meat and offal grilled on the fire (US$5 plus). Popular are *Zion Gamliel*, at 12 Peduyim St, *Shimon's* on the corner of Peduyim St at 28 Yiche St, and *Oved's* on the corner of Peduyim and Nahali'el Sts. While the masses flood *Nargila's* a few doors along, *Family Kitchen* (no English sign), 11 Carkbach St, serves tastier Yemenite favourites. Nargila's has another branch on Mendele St, between Ben Yehuda and HaYarkon Sts, and is open 24 hours.

Inexpensive oriental food is also available in the run-down HaTiqwa neighbourhood, south-east of the central bus station. Etsel St is full of popular eateries and traditional Iraqi bakeries. Israelis flock here to eat. Meat and offal grilled on the fire are the speciality along with the usual hummus, tehina and vegetable salads and soups. The street has two of the best value restaurants around. *Aziz* (☎ 370911 – no English sign), 6 Etsel St, is open Sunday to Thursday from lunch time till 1 am, Friday lunch time only, and Saturday sunset to 1 am. They serve grilled cow's udder, lamb and chicken heart and shashlik, US$3 per skewer; turkey's testicles

US$3.50, and goat's liver US$6. Dessert and coffee are on the house.

More presentable (and therefore arguably less authentic) and also very popular, is *Yehuda Avazi* (☎ 973979), 54 Etsel St. They open at 11 am and serve until 6 am. The prices here are slightly higher than at Aziz, but you can still eat well from US$7. Wine and beer are served in both restaurants. Dan bus No 16 starts from Allenby Rd and stops at the beginning of Etsel St; otherwise it's a 15-minute walk from the central bus station. Head south along Har-Ziyyon St, left onto Levinsky St, cross the main highway to Haganah Rd and it's on the right.

On the northern stretch of Ben Yehuda are two welcome variations of the often predictable Ashkenazi restaurant. For a Polish theme in stylish surroundings try *Bebele*, on Ben Yehuda St near Jabotinsky St. Tasty dishes cost from US$6 to US$20. Nearby, *The Glass Menagerie* (no English sign), 226 Ben Yehuda, between Nordau and Jabotinsky Sts, is another attractive place with appetisers from US$2.50 to US$8, salads US$8, and main courses for US$10.

Of the proliferation of places specialising in blintzes, the most consistently rated are *Shoshana & Uri's Hungarian Blintzes* (☎ 450674), 35 Yirmiyahu St, east of Dizengoff St and *Hungarian Blintzes*, 114 Dizengoff St. Expect to pay about US$6 for the savoury, and US$5 for the sweet.

Tel Aviv has some pretty good pizza. *Big Mama*, 20 Rabbi Akiva St, in a side street by the Carmel Market, is open evenings only. Also worthwhile is *Domino Pizza*, on the corner of Ben Yehuda and Bograshov Sts.

A cheap Chinese restaurant is the *Long Sang*, at 13 Allenby Rd (near the seafront) with a US$7 set menu and individual dishes for about US$5. The Szechuan and Cantonese food isn't bad for the price. Another decent cheapie is *Chin Chin*, 42 Frishmann St, near the corner of Dizengoff St.

Restaurants – middle Many official tourist brochures for Tel Aviv glibly attach 'gourmet' and 'quality' tags to restaurants, but if you are tempted by their enthusiastic recommendations you will often be disappointed. Fortunately, there are some very good and even excellent exceptions. Some of these middle-range restaurants are not totally out of reach for those on a budget who want to treat themselves or just have a main course, a salad or dessert.

With such items as tomato soup with arak and St Peter's fish in papaya sauce, the *Panorama Restaurant* (☎ 5238913) in the Astor Hotel, 105 HaYarkon St near Frishmann St, serves Israeli nouvelle cuisine using unusual combinations of fresh local ingredients. It is good value at about US$20, and the restaurant is open daily. The *Second Floor* is their kosher section, serving dairy and vegetarian dishes.

For some of the country's best meat, perhaps *the* best, try *White Hall Steakhouse*, 6 Mendele St, between HaYarkon and Ben Yehuda Sts. Enjoy decent steaks, burgers and a salad bar from US$20 to US$40, with a great-value US$10 lunch menu. It is open daily.

Also good for meat are the city's better Rumanian restaurants. At 8 Malchei Y'Israel Square (by the City Hall), the *Romanesc Restaurant* (☎ 265581) serves a variety of delicious specialities of the country, such as grilled meats, liver and goulash. Run by an older couple, the small room is usually full by 8 pm, so arrive early; it's closed Friday evening. *Restaurant Alpin* (☎ 658412), 56 HaYarkon St, at the corner of HaYarden St, and *Mon Jardin* (☎ 5238694), 186 Ben Yehuda St, serve more of the same in an equally efficient fashion. These are open daily, noon to midnight. In either restaurant you can eat for US$15 to US$30.

L'Entrecote (☎ 230726, 834453), 195 Ben Yehuda St by Nordau Blvd, serves good French food. The three-course set menu is about US$16. It is closed after lunch Friday until Saturday dinner.

For French and Italian cuisine, try *Baobab* (☎ 203331), 43 Ahad Ha'am St, off Allenby Rd; it's closed for dinner Friday. A good Italian restaurant is *2 Brenner*, at 2 Brenner St, off Allenby Rd. Both charge about US$20.

The Yemenite Quarter houses several up-market versions of the workers' restaurants already mentioned. These serve the familiar meat, offal and salad specialities in more expensive surroundings. Three of the best are the *Zion* (☎ 657323), 28 Peduyim St, *Maganda* (☎ 659990), 26 Rabbi Meir St, and *Shaul's Inn* (☎ 653303), 11 Elyashiv St, which has a more expensive room upstairs. Count on spending about US$15 to US$30 in each place. They're closed Friday evening and Saturday lunch time, otherwise they stay open until midnight.

The *Café Piltz Restaurant* (☎ 652778, 657021), 81 HaYarkon St, adjacent to the Yamit Hotel, is a 1930s dinner-dance spot – a traditional Tel Aviv favourite. The French-style food and service do not usually live up to the nostalgic popularity of the place, but you can spend an enjoyable evening here, dancing in the old-fashioned Israeli way to the Piltz Orchestra on Monday, Thursday, Friday and Saturday evenings. It costs about US$30 per person.

Chinese food has long been popular in Tel Aviv. Most of the best choices are in the vicinity of Dizengoff St to the north. Try the *Red Chinese* (☎ 5448405), 326 Dizengoff St, where Ben Yehuda St ends. It is open daily for lunch and dinner; US$15 to US$20 for Szechuan cuisine and a few Thai dishes.

Tel Aviv's first Chinese restaurant was none other than *Mandy's Singing Bamboo* (☎ 451282, 458785), 317 HaYarkon St, north of HaSira St. It's still highly rated and priced similarly to The Red Chinese.

Opposite, at 300 HaYarkon St, on the corner of HaSira St, is *Little Tel Aviv* (☎ 450109). Decorated with cinema posters, this place has been in and out of fashion since it was opened by the same team responsible for Mandy's Singing Bamboo, namely Raafi Shauly and Mandy Rice-Davies.

Mandy achieved notoriety as one of the London call-girls (the other was Christine Keeler) who played a major role in the Profumo Scandal which brought down the British Conservative Government in the early 1960s. She later married Shauly, an Israeli entrepreneur, and they opened various Mandy's Chinese restaurants around the country and the two Cherry cafés in Tel Aviv. Shauly was also behind the failed dolphinarium. They have since divorced, but their flamboyant public image is still attached to their establishments today.

Little Tel Aviv serves a variety of dishes from salads, burgers, steaks, pasta and chilli, to crêpes, gateaux and ice cream. You can spend US$10 to US$30 depending on what and how much you eat. There's live music some evenings, and it's open daily till 12.30 am, later on Saturday.

For a change, enjoy an Indian meal at *Tandoori* (☎ 296185/605), 2 Zamenhof St, Dizengoff Square; a good value buffet lunch costs US$14.

Restaurants – expensive Serving French-style cuisine in a converted mansion in the attractive Newe Tzedek neighbourhood, *Karen*, (☎ 816565) at 12 Elat St, has a US$22 set lunch, with à la carte dinner about US$45.

Yin Yang (☎ 621833), 64 Rothschild Blvd, serves excellent Chinese cuisine. It is owned and run by Israel Aharoni, an Israeli who once taught juvenile delinquents on a kibbutz but, attracted by South-East Asia, ended up in Taiwan learning the language and the cuisine. He has published a Chinese cookery book in Hebrew and his restaurant has become widely recognised as the country's best in its category. A meal costs from US$20 to US$40; it is open for lunch Sunday to Friday, and for dinner every night.

The Twelve Tribes (☎ 5286222) is at the Sheraton Tel Aviv, 115 HaYarkon St. Inspired by ancient Israel's geography, history and biblical references, a rotating menu features some interesting gourmet dishes, all served in a plush setting. Expect to pay from US$25 to US$50.

Bars Tel Aviv's bars are extremely popular, especially late in the evening and towards the end of the week. Thursday night sees most Tel Avivians crowd their favourite watering holes, while on Friday and Saturday nights, hordes of suburbanites from such places as

Bat Yam and Holon arrive. Although most of the bars attract regulars from a particular social group or profession, it is often difficult to suggest specific places because the bar that is the 'in' place this month can be 'out' the next. Most of the places listed have established their popularity over some time and should still be in business when you get there.

At the time of writing, the most popular bar with travellers is *Ego Trip*, 7 Mendele St, between HaYarkon & Ben Yehuda Sts, next to the Adiv Hotel. With draught beer, loud music and late opening hours, it is crowded most nights.

Paris, Texas, 14 Frishmann St, between Ben Yehuda and HaYarkon Sts, is a dark, noisy bar & restaurant.

In 'Little Tel Aviv', where HaYarkon, Ben Yehuda and Dizengoff Sts join up with Yirmiyahu St, popular bars operate among the restaurants and designer boutiques. *MASH (More Alcohol Served Here)*, 275 Dizengoff St, is perennially popular with travellers. *The Bell* is in a mock-Tudor building at 281 Dizengoff St, at the junction with Ben Yehuda St.

Down from the police station on Dizengoff St, opposite Basel St, *Zigal* is named after a top police officer who uncovered corruption in the force.

Kassit (see Cafés for Tel Aviv earlier), at 117 Dizengoff St, between Gordon and Frishmann Sts, has a full bar that serves draught beer. It's a nice place to sit outside and watch your fellow patrons as well as the pedestrian traffic passing by.

Ben Yehuda St has some pleasant drinking places. Between Nordau and Jabotinsky Sts, look for *Bagdad Cafe*, *The Glass Menagerie* and *Bebele*, which serves draught Guinness (see Restaurants – inexpensive for Tel Aviv in this chapter).

Gordon's Pub, at 17 Gordon St near Ben Yehuda St, stands out from the crowd by showing cartoons on a 250-cm screen.

A backstreet behind Dizengoff Square, through the alley by the Nakniot Hakikar Restaurant, hides three late-night bars: *Long John Silver's*, *Revolution* and *The Backyard*.

Rock music is played in these dark places and they attract a young Israeli crowd.

Midbar (Desert), 6 Balfour St, off Allenby Rd, is packed with a younger Israeli crowd; it's open till very late. *The Boiling Box* at the Riviera Hotel, HaYarkon St by the corner of Allenby Rd, is also frequented by a younger late-night crowd. Rock videos are played loudly here.

A slightly older local crowd packs out *Terminal*, on the corner of Gordon and HaYarkon Sts.

Bonanza is the bar & restaurant on Trumpeldor St, to the east of Ben Yehuda St. This is the regular haunt of a more mature clientele, former Jewish underground and IDF officers and possibly arms dealers as well. During the week in the evenings, and on Shabbat during the day, these old warriors meet to drink, eat, reminisce and sing. On a good night, the place fills with the sounds of ad lib but heartfelt renditions of Edith Piaf classics and Zionist pioneer songs to piano accompaniment, as older couples dance in the old-fashioned way – not to be missed.

Another Tel Aviv classic is *The Happy Casserole*, 344 Dizengoff St. It has live Sephardic music every night, and this middle-aged crowd often ends up dancing on the tables.

If you feel like a busy, but quiet, no-frills working person's bar, head for *The King George* (no English sign, look for the Johnny Walker sign), 26 King George St, down from Allenby Rd; it's closed Friday.

Shoftim, on the corner of Ibn Gevirol and Shoftim Sts, is an old favourite with Israeli intellectuals, lawyers, and left-wing types.

Down on the West Beach (by Charles Clore Park, south of the dolphinarium), the popular *West Beach Restaurant* is open 24 hours – Israelis often pack the tables that overlook the sea and drink all night long.

Entertainment

Crowds of locals and visitors are out people-watching after dark, especially around Dizengoff Square and the seafront. The bars, cafés and restaurants fill up, and people also go down to visit Old Jaffa. For more organised activities, pick up a free copy of the leaflets *Events in the Tel Aviv Region* and *This Week in Tel Aviv* from the tourist office. *Jerusalem Post* also carries details of current entertainment in its Friday supplement.

Cinemas Many of the major cinemas show English-language films subtitled in Hebrew. Foreign-language films are also shown in some of the smaller cinemas. During the summer months, check to see if free films are being screened at night on the beach, near Allenby Rd.

Allenby, 58 Allenby Rd (☎ 657820)
Beit Lessin, 34 Weizmann St (☎ 216653)
Ben Yehuda, 77 Ben Yehuda St (☎ 222759)
Chen 1-5, Dizengoff Square (☎ 282288)
Cinema Club, Yirmiyahu St (☎ 5441708)
Cinemateque, 1 HaArka'a St, is part of the membership chain which shows a variety of classics, avant garde, new wave, and off-beat movies. A few tickets for nonmembers are sold just before the performance. Actress Goldie Hawn donated enough to have one of the screens named in her honour (☎ 210028, 210425)
Dekel, 2 Herzog St (☎ 443200)
Dizengoff 1-3, Dizengoff Centre (☎ 200485)
Esther, Dizengoff Square (☎ 225610)
French Cultural Institute, 111 HaYarkon St, occasionally shows French films.
Gat 2 Zetlin St (☎ 267888)
German Institute, 4 Weizmann St, occasionally shows German films (☎ 217266)
Gordon, 87 Ben Yehuda St (☎ 244373)
Hod, 101 Dizengoff St (☎ 226226)
Lev 1-4, Dizengoff Centre (☎ 288868)
Limor, 30 Ibn Gevirol St (☎ 260773)
Maxim, 48 King George St (☎ 287457)
Orly, 2 HaMaccabi St (☎ 284025)
Paris, 106 HaYarkon St, opposite the Dan Hotel, rotates classics by Fellini, Woody Allen and Monty Python, among others
Pe'er, 1 Yeshayahu St (☎ 443795)
Shahaf, Atarim Square (☎ 226645)
Tamuz, 17 Brodetsky St (☎ 412761)
Tayelet 1-3, 58 Herbert Samuel Blvd (☎ 657952)
Tel Aviv, Pinsker St (☎ 281181)
Tel Aviv Museum, 27 King Shaul Blvd, sometimes screens art films (☎ 261297)
Zafon, 18 Louis Marechal St (☎ 443966)
Zionist Organisation of America (ZOA) House,
   1 Daniel Frisch St (☎ 6959341/3)

Theatre & Dance Most of the theatre is

performed in Hebrew, with occasional foreign-language productions:

Bat Sheva Ballet 6 Yechieli St, Newe Tzedek
   (☎ 651471)
Cameri Theatre 101 Dizengoff St, entrance on
   Frishmann St (☎ 233335)
Suzanne Dellal Centre for Dance & Theatre 1
   Yechieli St, Newe Tzedek (☎ 659635/6)
Habima Theatre Habima Square, between Rothschild
   Blvd and Dizengoff St (☎ 209888)
Inbal Dance Theatre 6 Yechieli St, Newe Tzedek
   (☎ 653711)
Neve Tzedek Theatre 6 Yechieli St, Newe Tzedek
   (☎ 651241)
Ohel Shem Auditorium 30 Balfour St (☎ 296240)
Tzavta Theatre 30 Ibn Gevirol St (☎ 6950156)
Zionist Organisation of America (ZOA) House
   1 Daniel Frisch St (☎ 6959341/3)

Music & Dance A range of musical styles is performed in a variety of settings, clubs as well as discos, many of them with dancing. Like the bars, they go in and out of fashion very quickly, so ask around for the current places to check out.

Beit Lessin, 34 Weizmann St, for jazz, folk and
   popular music performances (☎ 256222).
Byblos Club, 128 Derekh St, Petah Tiqwa features a
   Wednesday jazz jam (☎ 5626270).
Dolphinarium Beach features free samba music with
   dancing from 11pm till early morning during the
   summer.
Mann Auditorium, Habima Square, between Rothschild Blvd and Dizengoff St. Home to the Israel
   Philharmonic, it stages a wide range of concerts
   (☎ 299170)
Penguin, 43 Yehuda HaLevi St, off Allenby Rd,
   attracts new wave/punk characters and features
   live acts on weekends and some week nights.
Sigal Club, 73 HaYarkon St. Wednesday is free samba
   night with dancing (☎ 5103040).
Soweto, 6 Frishmann St, plays reggae and African
   music with dancing (☎ 240825)
Wohl Amphitheatre, HaYarkon Park, is used for
   outdoor concerts.
Zavta Club, 30 Ibn Gevirol St, downstairs in the
   London Ministore Passage and on the corner of
   King Shaul Blvd for folk, jazz, blues, rock and
   classical
ZOA House, 1 Daniel Frisch St, corner of Ibn Gevirol
   St, has occasional performances of plays, folk
   singing and other concerts – and celebrates
   Israeli and US holidays (☎ 259341).

The cheapest place to dance is the *Samba*, a Latin American evening organised by Brazilian Jews who just love to dance. They play their collection of tapes from home over a not-too-brilliant sound-system in a variety of venues such as the West Beach. Ask around for the latest location.

The *Colosseum* disco is in the large circular building spanning Ha Yarkon St in Atarim Square. It was originally a supermarket and attracts a mainly young (14 to 18) crowd and plays commercial pop. Cover charges vary and sometimes include varying numbers of 'free' drinks. At least one night a week is free for women.

Some of the luxury hotels have nightclubs, such as *Herbie Sams* at the Yamit Tower and *Reflections* at the Sheraton, with dancing in the *Beach Bar* at the Grand Beach.

Visit the *Happy Casserole*, 344 Dizengoff St, where more 'bus station superstars' have the primarily Sephardic crowd dancing on the tables. The 'Little Tel Aviv' area often features great live music and dancing at some of the bars (see the earlier Bars section).

What to do on Shabbat in Tel Aviv-Jaffa
Many cafés, bars and restaurants in Tel Aviv-Jaffa are open on Friday nights and are very busy. As most shops and businesses rush to close early on Friday, many people hang out at their favourite café before the sun goes down.

On Friday afternoon, say between 1 and 3 pm, head for Nahalat Binyamin St. The pedestrianised streets are packed with artists' stalls and musicians, the cafés are full and there is usually dancing to see in the Shabbat.

Another great happening is the Friday afternoon/evening party on the Western Beach, towards Jaffa. South American residents play music from home and dance on the sand. There's no charge for turning up; food and drinks are available.

'Little Tel Aviv' (the northern end of Ha Yarkon, Ben Yehuda and Dizengoff Sts) Dizengoff Square and Old Jaffa are the busiest spots in the evening, along with the seafront. Charles Clore Park, by the West Beach, plays host to out-of-town visitors with their tents, barbecues and, occasionally, their guitars, bongos, ouds and tambourines. Cinemas are also open – the *Paris* puts on a special programme of film classics.

On Saturday, if the weather is fine, the beaches are packed solid. Despite the beautiful open countryside close by, large numbers of Israelis can be seen picnicking on the small grass area near the central railway station, surrounded by busy traffic.

All the city buses grind to a halt, but the minibus sherut service runs between Ben Yehuda St and Allenby Rd and Mercedes sheruts operate to Jerusalem and Haifa. The other available public transport is the United Services bus No 90, running from the Dan Panorama Hotel along Allenby Rd, Ben Yehuda, Bograshov, Dizengoff, Reines and Arlosoroff Sts to Herzlia up the coast.

The only place to buy provisions during Shabbat is the mini-market in Atarim Square, open till about 5 pm – prices are high, so stock up in advance from cheaper sources early on Friday.

Cheap eating places that stay open include the *Adiv Hotel's* self-service restaurant for breakfast, lunch and dinner; and the *Vienna* at 48A Ben Yehuda St and *Batia* at 197 Dizengoff St, corner of Arlosoroff St for traditional Jewish Shabbat dishes such as cholent and kreplach soup. The *Kassit* café & restaurant, 117 Dizengoff St, is also open throughout Shabbat.

Jaffa's eating and entertainment places are open and busier than ever.

On Saturday, the No 4 minibus operates along Ben Yehuda St and United bus No 90 allows you to visit Herzlia for the day.

Getting There & Away
With Ben-Gurion Airport close by, Tel Aviv-Jaffa is often the visitor's first stop. Just about in the centre of Israel's Mediterranean coast, the city is a popular choice as a base from which to visit other places in this small country.

The highway to the north leads to Haifa and Galilee, to the south, Ashdod, Ashkelon,

Gaza and the Negev. The busy highway to the east leads to Jerusalem.

Air Arkia flights depart from the Sde Dov. Airport, north of the Yarkon River and the Reading Power Station. These connect directly with Eilat and Rosh Pinna, with further connections to Haifa and Jerusalem. There are no flights on Saturday.

Bus The central bus station has long outgrown its original site. A new site is being developed nearby, and some routes now operate from the central railway station to spread the load. With the relocation of the station, and the pending merger of the Egged and Dan bus companies, routes are likely to change considerably.

Buses depart from the central bus station for Jerusalem at least every 10 minutes, and the 55-minute ride costs US$2.90. For Haifa, departures are every hour, more frequently at peak times, and the one-hour trip costs US$3. You can catch a bus to Beersheba at least every 10 minutes (US$4.25, 1½ hour), and there are four day buses and one night bus to Eilat (US$10, five hours).

The left-luggage office is on Finn St, beside the central bus station, and is open Sunday to Thursday, 6 am to 5.45 pm, Friday 6 am to 2.45 pm, and is closed Saturday. The charge is US$0.80 per item per day.

Buses for Jerusalem, Haifa and other destinations also leave from the central railway station.

Train Tel Aviv has two railway stations. The central railway station (☎ 254271) is for Haifa and the north and is at the junction of Haifa Rd, Arlosoroff St and Petah Tiqwa Rd. Trains run almost every hour between 6 am and 8 pm except on Saturday.

The service between Jerusalem and Haifa stops at the south railway station (☎ 922676) on Kibbutz Galuyot Blvd to the south of the city.

Taxi Sherut services operate from Salomon St, across from the central bus station, to the suburbs, Jerusalem (US$4) and Haifa

(US$4.50). On Saturday they leave from Moshavot Square on Allenby Rd and cost about an extra 20%. Service taxis to Gaza leave from Jaffa (one hour, US$7) from Yefet St, south of St Antonio's Church (take Dan bus No 10 from Allenby Rd).

Hitchhiking For Haifa and the north, stand on Haifa Rd north of the Yarkon River. For Jerusalem and the south, stand either by the junction in front of the south railway station or at the intersection of HaMesilla and Golomb Ludvipol Rds.

Getting Around
To/From the Airport See the Getting Around chapter. United Tours bus No 222 provides an excellent service between the city centre and the airport, and there are departures every hour.

Going out to the airport, the bus picks up passengers at the Dan Panorama Hotel, on HaYarkon St south of Allenby Rd (near the Riviera Hotel), north of Shalom Aleichem St (opposite the Yamit Towers Hotel), 104 HaYarkon St (opposite the Dan Hotel), 144 HaYarkon St (opposite the Diplomat Hotel), 196 HaYarkon St (opposite the Hilton), 248 HaYarkon St (near the Grand Beach Hotel), Weizmann St (corner of Pinkas St), central railway station, and Hatayasim Rd.

As already mentioned, the city bus company, Dan, is scheduled to merge with Egged. For Dan information call ☎ 561444. Currently, these are the major routes:

Dan bus No 4 goes from the central bus station via Allenby Rd, Nahalat Binyamin St, Carmel Market, Ben Yehuda St, and north Dizengoff St to the old port.
Mini bus sherut No 4 follows the same route as Dan bus No 4 for the same price. Its advantage is that it's more comfortable, taking only as many passengers as there are seats, and it's quicker – once it's full it only stops to let people off. It also operates on Shabbat (when the price doubles), between the northern end of Ben Yehuda St to the inter-urban sheruts at Moshavim Square.
Dan bus No 5 goes from the central bus station, along Allenby Rd, up Rothschild Blvd, along Dizengoff St, Nordau Blvd, Pinkas and Ben Yehuda, HaMaccabi Sts and back. Useful for the

IYHA hostel, the Egyptian Embassy, Habima Square and Dizengoff St hostels and other attractions.

Dan bus No 10 goes from City Hall via HaHen and Ben-Gurion Blvds, Ben Yehuda St, Allenby Rd and Herbert Samuel Blvd.

Dan bus No 20 goes from the central railway station along Arlosoroff, Dizengoff, Pinsker, Trumpeldor, HaYarkon, and Shalom Aleichem Sts. It returns from Shalom Aleichem St opposite the El Al building on Ben Yehuda St via Ben Yehuda, Bograshov, Tchernichovsky, Dizengoff and Arlosoroff Sts.

Dan bus No 25 goes from Tel Aviv University via the Diaspora Museum, Ibn Gevirol St, Allenby Rd, Carmel Market, Nahalat Binyamin St to Jaffa.

Dan bus No 41 goes from Levinsky St, near the central bus station, to the south railway station.

Dan bus No 46 goes from the central bus station via Yefet and Elat Rds to Jaffa.

Dan bus No 64 travels from the central railway station along Arlosoroff, Dizengoff, Pinsker and Trumpeldor Sts.

JAFFA

In Hebrew, it's *Yafo,* which is believed to be derived from either *yafé,* meaning beautiful, or the name of Noah's son, Japheth, who established the town after the flood. The Greeks called it *Joppa,* as does the Bible. This is the place where Hiram landed the Lebanese cedars for Solomon's Temple, and where the Old Testament Book of Jonah tells of Jonah's experiences with God and a whale. It was under Solomon that Jaffa became the nation's sea port and today it is believed to be the world's oldest working harbour.

Archaeologists have dug up remains here dating from the 18th century BC, making it one of the oldest cities in the world. The Egyptians conquered the place in 1468 BC by hiding in large, clay pots carried into the local market. Under Herod the Great, Caesarea became the main port, but Jaffa later returned to its pre-eminent position.

During the 12th century Jaffa underwent a particularly turbulent period: the Crusaders lost the city to Saladin, but then regained it under Richard the Lionheart, only to lose it to Saladin's brother, who slaughtered 20,000 Christians in the process.

After the Mamelukes conquered Jaffa in 1267 it remained in Arab hands, except for a brief period under Napoleon, until Allenby defeated the Turks in 1917.

By 1840 a wave of Jewish immigrants had settled in Jaffa and by the turn of the century, the town had become a gateway for the large-scale immigration of European Jews, many of whom founded colonies in the surrounding areas.

The first few decades of the 20th century were marked by mounting antagonism between the Jewish and the Arab communities of Jaffa and in 1929, 1936 and 1939 anti-Jewish rioting broke out. After the terror and hostility of the struggle for Jaffa in the 1948 War of Independence and in the wake of the Irgun's victory, most of the Arab population fled the town, leaving behind their homes and possessions.

Today Jaffa is dominated by Old Jaffa, an area of restored alleyways and gardens around the port, developed as an artists' quarter. Unfortunately the overall effect is a little sterile. Most of the galleries have not attracted the type of artists originally hoped for and there is a sense of emptiness here which only serves to highlight such unattractive aspects as the bright yellow lines painted on the steps of the alleyways, the ugly modern light fittings and the overall failure of the modern additions to complement their ancient surroundings.

Towards the end of the week, and reaching a peak on Friday, Old Jaffa's fish restaurants attract hundreds of Israelis who like to compare the atmosphere to Greece.

The rest of Jaffa is pretty much ignored, although the flea market enjoys a good reputation. However, it's worth spending an hour or so to continue south and east of Old Jaffa. Such an excursion can be rewarding as there are some excellent places to eat and some attractive buildings with a distinct European feel about them.

Yefet St

From Tel Aviv most people enter Jaffa via the Herbert Samuel Esplanade, ending up in the vicinity of the Ottoman clocktower on Yefet St, a continuation of the Esplanade. On the

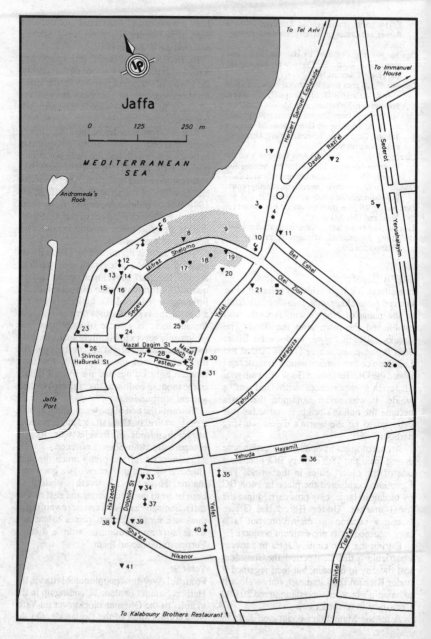

Jaffa

0   125   250 m

MEDITERRANEAN SEA

Andromeda's Rock

Jaffa Port

Shimon HaBurski St

Mazal Dagim St

Mazal Anch St

Pasteur

Mitraz Shelomo

Segev

Yefet

Merguza

Yehuda Hayarnil

Yehuda

Bet Eshel

Olei Zion

David Razi'el

Herbert Samuel Esplanade

Sederot

Yerushalayim

Shivtei Yisra'el

To Tel Aviv

To Immanuel House

HaTzedef

Dolphin St

Yefet

Sha'are

Nikanor

To Kalabouny Brothers Restaurant

Shelomo St leads pedestrians to Old Jaffa. Drivers continue along Yefet St, up the hill, and turn right as the road curves to the left. This will also take you down to the port area. The flea market is east of Yefet St and covers a few blocks – follow Olei Zion St, left from the clocktower as you enter Jaffa from Tel Aviv. After the clocktower and the turn-offs towards Old Jaffa and the flea market, Yefet St is dominated by the Arab bakeries and sweet shops.

At the top of the hill, the corner building on the right is the old French Hospital. Opposite, at No 23, is the Church of Scotland's Tabitha School; next door at No 25, is the College des Fréres with the former convent school and its round tower. The St Antonio's Church is at No 49. This church commemorates Anthonio of Padua, a 13th-century monk, one of the first Franciscans and their saint in the Holy Land.

Dolphin St

This pleasant street runs roughly parallel with Yefet St, down from the bridge towards the port entrance. There are a couple of galleries and restaurants and some attractive buildings, including the Maronite church and convent, the Greek Catholic church and the pillared building at No 19.

Beyond the street to the south stretches a much neglected area of Jaffa with some reminders of past glory. The grand old red-roofed houses were built by wealthy Turks in Italian and French styles.

Flea Market

Covering several streets south-east of the clocktower, this Jewish market (with its decent reputation for antiques and interesting oriental bits and pieces) requires several visits if you want to shop seriously, as new items regularly appear. Bargaining is the order of the day, and the stall-holders' traditional sales patter includes the one about making a quick first sale early on Sunday morning to bring good luck for the coming week. It's closed on Saturday.

right, and past the police station and the Mahmudiye Mosque (1812), Mifraz

Old Jaffa

Old Jaffa is at its best when seen from the water – the old buildings on the side of the hill provide a backdrop for the boats in the port and the tower of St Peter's Monastery caps the whole picture. The view from Old Jaffa up the coast towards Tel Aviv is spectacular. At least two visits are really necessary, during the daytime and at night, to see the main characteristics of the area. The galleries, restaurants and cafés are closed or very quiet during the day, but attract larger numbers once darkness falls.

Museum of Antiquities of Tel Aviv-Jaffa

This is at 10 Mifraz Shelomo St. This building was a Turkish administrative and detention centre but its vaulted ceilings and

Old porch, Jaffa

archways are now home to a display of local archaeological discoveries.

Facing the view up the coast to Tel Aviv, it's on the left across the paved courtyard coming up from the clocktower, or on the right as you walk down from Kedumim Square and St Peter's Monastery.

It's open Sunday to Friday from 9 am to 1 pm, Tuesday 4 to 7 pm, also Saturday 10 am to 1 pm; admission is US$0.90 (students US$0.75).

HaPisga Gardens Behind the museum, this grassy area has a small amphitheatre with a panorama of the Tel Aviv seafront as its backdrop. Excavations nearby have uncovered Egyptian, Israelite, Greek and Roman remains. The bizarre white sculpture on one of the hills, neo-Mayan in style, depicts the fall of Jericho, Isaac's sacrifice and Jacob's dream.

Kedumim Square A footbridge connects the gardens to Kikkar Kedumim, Old Jaffa's reconstructed centre dominated by restaurants, clubs and galleries. This was where the city's first Jewish hostel was established in 1840. It included two *mikvot* (ritual baths) and a synagogue. Libyan Jews have reopened the synagogue – it's on Mazal Dagim St, heading up to the left as you come down the steps from Kedumim Square and across from Simon the Tanner's House. Also in the square is another archaeological site showing remnants of catacombs of the 3rd century BC.

St Peter's Monastery This orange-painted Franciscan church was built above a medieval citadel on one side of Kedumim Square. It is open daily during October to February from 8 to 11.45 am and from 3 to 5 pm; March to September from 8 to 11.45 am and from 3 to 6 pm.

Simon the Tanner's House This is the traditional site of the house where the Apostle Peter was staying when he received divine instruction to preach to non-Jews (Acts 9:32-43) after he had brought Tabitha back to life.

It's at 8 Shimon HaBurski St at the bottom of the narrow alley leading down to the right at the foot of the southern steps of Kedumim Square.

In the courtyard you can see a well, supposedly used in Peter's day, and a stone sculptured coffin from the same period. Muslims later converted it into a wash-stand to use before praying at the mosque, which was built on the site in 1730. Now a private house, it is officially open daily from 8 am to 7 pm; just ring the bell and see if anyone answers. Admission is US$0.70.

You continue north along this narrow alley, called Nativ Hamazalot Lane, to the other side of St Peter's Monastery where there are various galleries, a Greek Orthodox church, and an Armenian church.

Galleries The central gallery area is south of the square and gardens along Mazal Dagim and Mazal Arieh Sts. They are mostly open in the evenings, and the Horace Richter Gallery attracts the most attention.

Israel Experience This tacky complex comprises a series of 'multi-media computerised techniques' to present Israel to the masses. The masses choose to stay away. Admission is US$6 (students US$4).

Port & Andromeda's Rock This is one of the oldest known harbours. It was mentioned by Hiram, King of Tyre, in conversation with Solomon (II Chronicles 2:15) and referred to in Jonah 1:3. For centuries this was where pilgrims to the Holy Land first arrived en route to Jerusalem and it was Palestine's main port.

Beyond its walls are the remains of the blackened rocks, the largest of which is named after Andromeda, the Greek mythological figure saved from being sacrificed to the Sea Monster by Perseus. Reconstruction of the port and the dredging of the approaches resulted in the rock being damaged.

At the weekend and on Jewish holidays, there is a US$0.50 entry fee to the port.

Walking Tour Every Wednesday, a free guided walking tour of Old Jaffa is organised by the Association for Tourism, Tel Aviv-Jaffa. Meet by the clocktower at 9.30 am; the tour ends at about noon.

Places to Stay
A pleasant Israeli couple have converted a beautiful old building, typical of the architecture found in Jaffa, into a lovely hostel. It's quite amazing how much work has gone into this place. The *Old Jaffa Hostel* (☎ 822370/16), 8 Olei Zion St, overlooks the flea market. Dorm beds are US$6, beds on the roof US$4.50 and private rooms US$12. There's a roof terrace and inexpensive meals are available. From Tel Aviv's central bus station, take Dan bus Nos 44 or 46, ask for the flea market, or Nos 10 or 25 to the Dan Panorama Hotel; from the airport, take United bus No 222 to the last stop, the Dan Panorama Hotel.

The other place to stay is the attractive Christian hospice *Immanuel House* (☎ 821459; fax 829817) PO Box 2773, Tel Aviv 61027. Built in 1884 by Baron Ustinov, Peter Ustinov's father, it was originally the Park Hotel. An integral part of Jaffa's prosperous German colony, Kaiser Wilhelm II was a guest here. Beautifully renovated and with a garden, it now comprises a pilgrims' hostel, study facilities and a worship centre for a Hebrew-speaking congregation. Dorm beds are US$9 with breakfast, and private rooms are US$22. Take Dan bus Nos 44 or 46 from the central bus station; get off at the Nechustan Lift factory (look for the sign), cross the street and go left on Auerbach St, the right on Bar Hofman St; the entrance is at the rear of the building.

Places to Eat
I wouldn't advise buying the Arab sweets displayed so prominently on the corner of Mifraz Shelomo St. Their turnover is far from prolific and so they are usually stale. The regular supply of car exhaust fumes no doubt plays a part in their condition.

On to much better things and something of a legend: *Said Abou Elafia & Sons* at 7

Yefet St is the furthest bakery past the traffic lights up from the foot of the hill. This was Jaffa's first bakery and from its establishment in 1880 it did good business catering for the nearby mosque, police station and the French Hospital. Now, with the family's fourth generation working here, the bakery is busier than ever with Jewish and Arab customers coming from miles around.

The main attraction is their version of the pizza, developed from a traditional Arab recipe of cracking a couple of eggs on top of pitta bread and baking it in the oven. The Abou Elafia bakers were the first to retail it and soon added the tomato, mushrooms, cheese and olives. The place really caught up with Israelis and many 'copy-cat' bakeries opened up. Right next door and further down the street, almost identical looking bakeries struggle to compete while the crowds choose to swarm around the original. The central bus station in Tel Aviv also has several pizza bakeries but none of them come close.

As well as the 'special pizza', regular items include 24 varieties of bread, such as pitta coated in either sesame seeds, or za'atar (spices) and olive oil, Iraqi, Arab and Persian breads, and 'zambuska' (a type of pastry filled with Bulgarian cheese or potatoes). Zambuska are often split open and an egg baked in its shell ('hamim' – making it brown when shelled) is stuffed inside and sliced up. The secret of Abou Elafia's success is apparently their policy of using only good-quality ingredients and the custom of still burning wood in the now gas-fired ovens to get a better flavour – whatever it is that they do, theirs is easily the best. This wonderful business is open Monday to Saturday from about 5 am right up to 2 am or even later. They are closed on Sunday, a good day for the competition down the street. Prices are good too, from about US$1.30.

For excellent ice cream, try Dr Leck, a dentist turned ice-cream maker, before the clocktower on the right-hand side entering Jaffa from Tel Aviv on Yefet St.

Two of the best eating places in Jaffa are of the inexpensive Arab sit-down variety, specialising in terrific hummus. Kalabouny

Brothers is at 132 Yefet St – continue past Old Jaffa and it's on the right just before the Hapoalim Bank on the corner, (no English sign). It's open from early in the morning till 4 pm, and serves hummus, foul, salad, chips, pitta and coffee; all for about US$6. At 1 Dolphin St, Abu Hassan (no English sign) does more of the same, less the chips.

On the same street, Le Relais is a pleasant French restaurant (expect to pay about US$30). In Old Jaffa, Le Toutouner, 1 Mazal Dagim St, is another decent French-style place (expect to pay about US$25).

Misu, 7 Raziel St (turn left before the clocktower), is a cheap Rumanian restaurant, open for lunch only, Monday to Friday, closed Saturday and Sunday. It has sparse surroundings but is excellent value and serves great food, including kebabs, sauerkraut, pitta and beer. The interesting menu also includes a cheap type of caviar as well as hummus, liver, steak and sheep's stomach.

Adjacent to the clocktower is Tripoli, specialising in couscous.

Michel's Aladdin, 5 Mifraz Shelomo St, on the right as you walk up towards Old Jaffa from the clocktower, is a popular oriental bar & restaurant in an 800-year-old building that was originally a Turkish bath. It has nice atmosphere and great Mediterranean views.

For Israelis, the main culinary attraction in Jaffa is fish and the approach to Old Jaffa off Mifraz Shelomo St has several outdoor restaurants, some of which also serve meat grilled on the fire. Although extremely popular with Israelis, I wasn't greatly impressed by the food, service or prices. Chez le Beau Shebti (the one with no English sign) was one of the most highly praised places that I came across; a meal of fish with salad, pitta and beer/wine comes to about US$20. You can eat much better for the same or less in Tel Aviv.

Il Patio is a pretty Italian restaurant at the southern end of Dolphin St serving homemade pasta and some delicious cakes. It costs about US$20 per person.

Younes on Kedem St (it's visible from the end of Dolphin St) serves a wide range of meats, fish, salads and desserts. Traditional, basic oriental food is served in pleasant surroundings.

One of Israel's best restaurants is Jaffa's *Al Hambra* (☎ 834453), 30 Jerusalem Blvd, a continuation of Hamered St coming from Tel Aviv. This serves mainly French cuisine, and costs from about US$40.

Entertainment
Jaffa offers quite a few choices for nightlife:

Caravan Club, Old Jaffa; oriental nightclub-restaurant with live bands and dancing (☎ 830200/828255).

The Cave, Kedumim Square, Old Jaffa; folk music (☎ 829018).

DJ, 15 Yefet St; disco (☎ 811545).

HaHamam Theatre, adjacent to the museum; another former Turkish bath, now a theatre for plays and musical events (☎ 813261).

HaKochav Ha'Adom, 15 Yefet St; Turkish and oriental music, open till very late (☎ 9613354).

HaTayavon, Jaffa Port; jazz (☎ 811176).

Metal Zone, Kedumim Square, Old Jaffa, below The Cave; open Thursday to Sunday only; Israel's first and only heavy metal bar.

Mivneh 5, Jaffa Port; Israeli music and dancing (☎ 814770).

Noga Theatre, Noga Square, 7 Jerusalem St, Jaffa; a restored beauty, staging various dramatic productions (☎ 813131).

Omar Khayyam, Kedumim Square, Old Jaffa; live oriental music (☎ 825865).

Getting There & Away
If you don't fancy a walk of some 45 minutes, the following buses go to Jaffa from Tel Aviv: Dan bus No 18 can be boarded on Dizengoff St, No 10 on Ben Yehuda St, and Nos 18 and 25 on Allenby Rd.

BAT YAM
(Population: 141,300)
Established in 1925, its name is Hebrew for Daughter of the Sea. The sandy beach is a popular attraction, and the town is also noted for its sizable Turkish community whose restaurants and nightclubs provide excellent food and entertainment, although apart from these there's really nothing of interest for the visitor.

Orientation & Information
Bat Yam is just to the south of Jaffa and can be reached by following Jerusalem Blvd through Jaffa until it becomes Rothschild Blvd. Leading down to the waterfront, this is Bat Yam's main thoroughfare. The street running parallel to the sea is Ben-Gurion Blvd where most of the hotels can be found. The municipal tourist office (☎ 589766) is on Ben-Gurion Blvd just to the north of the intersection with Rothschild Blvd in the same building as the Via Maris Hotel and the Kontiki Restaurant. It's open Sunday to Thursday from 8 am to 6.30 pm, Friday 8 am to 1 pm, and is closed Saturday. In winter they close between 1.30 and 4 pm on Monday and Wednesday.

Places to Stay
Bat Yam has no budget or luxury accommodation. The few hotels are along Ben-Gurion Blvd facing the sea, from Rothschild Blvd at the northern end to the last hotel at the southern end. All rooms have showers, some have bathtubs, and prices include breakfast.

Via Maria Hotel (☎ 860171), 43 Ben-Gurion Blvd, is a simple seaside hotel, near the tourist office. Here singles/doubles are US$20/35. A few doors down the street, is the *Bat Yam Hotel* (☎ 864373) at 53 Ben-Gurion Blvd where singles/doubles are US$33/40.

The highest-rated hotel in Bat Yam is the *Armon Yam* (☎ 5522424) at No 95; its rooms have balconies and are generally fitted out to a higher standard than the others; singles cost from US$39 to US$49, and doubles from US$45 to US$55.

Places to Eat
It's difficult to distinguish between Bat Yam's highly-rated Turkish restaurants and nightclubs. Among them is *Taverna Istanbul* at 61 Ben-Gurion Blvd, which features live music in the evenings and costs about US$30 per person for a good feed.

Getting There & Away
Dan bus Nos 10, 18, 25 and 26 provide a regular service to and from Tel Aviv, which

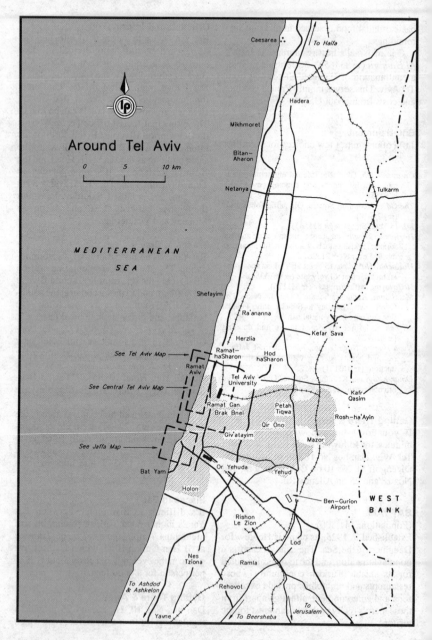

Top: Ethiopian monk & rooftop cell, Church of the Holy Sepulchre, Jerusalem (RE)
Left: The bell tolls for...? Church of the Holy Sepulchre (RE)
Right: The faithful gather at the Church of the Holy Sepulchre at Easter (RE)

Top: Shabbat on the beach in August, Tel Aviv (NT)
Bottom: A Haifa felafel stall (NT)

is five to 20 minutes away depending on which part you are going to.

HERZLIA
(Population: 90,000)
Named in memory of Theodor Herzl and established in 1924 as an agricultural centre, Herzlia was greatly affected by the rapid expansion of Tel Aviv to the south. As the city grew, the fine beaches here became more accessible and luxurious homes for diplomats and wealthy Israelis were built on the slopes overlooking the Mediterranean. Herzlia Pituah, the seafront area, becomes quite crowded on weekends.

Orientation & Information
Herzlia is 16 km north of Tel Aviv. Herzlia Pituah and the beaches are the only real attraction for the visitor. The town is dominated by luxury hotels and with many foreign diplomats residing in the neighbourhood, the beaches (which charge admission) are particularly popular with the trendy, more affluent set.

Basel St, Shalit Square and the seafront is the area to head for – the Sharon Hotel in among various cafés, bars and restaurants, is the major landmark and the beach stretches out from it in both directions. To the north and just a short walk away is Sydney Ali Beach, which is free and is often less crowded than surrounding beaches. Sharon Beach is next to the Sharon Hotel, Dabush Beach is near the Daniel Hotel and Accadia Beach is to the south by the Accadia Hotel. Coming in by bus, get off by the Green Door home and garden store or at the Sharon Hotel for the Sydney Ali or Sharon beaches. For the other beaches wait until the Accadia Hotel stop.

Sydney Ali Beach & the Caveman
The free beach boasts a unique attraction in addition to the sand, cliffs and nearby Roman ruins. Nissim Kahalon, known as the Caveman, has built an amazing house in the cliffside above the beach, where he has lived for about 10 years.

Formerly a plasterer, Nissim decided to opt for a healthy lifestyle in the open air and eventually decided on this spot to build his bizarre complex.

Relying as little as possible on regular building materials, he used bits and pieces found on the beach such as empty bottles, driftwood and tyres and mixed his 'cement' using sand, seawater and ash from his wood fire for strength. He has created his version of Noah's Ark, which serves as a bedroom and a pigeon house, topped off by a dinosaur sculpture. He has also tunnelled into the cliff to take advantage of the natural air conditioning. Nissim's future plans include a new 'flying saucer' bedroom design and an octopus sculpture above his café. He would also like to open a small school teaching sculpture using waste products.

Nissim can be persuaded to show you around his home, although he sometimes charges a small fee. The interior is a real eye-opener. He had to battle with the local authorities for some time to be allowed to stay, and he has only recently had electricity connected. He makes a living from his café, which does good business despite the steep prices. His lush garden is irrigated by the waste water from the bathroom. The wooden tables and benches on the café terrace are made from wood found nearby and are varnished using oil washed up on the beach. The palm leaves were donated by his affluent neighbours along the clifftop.

Sydney Ali Mosque, built by Saladin himself in the late 12th century and now being renovated, gives the beach its name. Apollonia, a Roman port, is a few hundred metres to the north but the few remains are not really worth a special trip. The Crusaders built battlements here, but they too are now rubble. Nearby you might find pieces of Roman glass from an ancient glass factory.

To reach Sydney Ali Beach, head north from the Sharon Hotel along Galei Thelet St, turn left along the dirt path just before the US Embassy residence, right along the clifftop, past the army installation, continue down the slope and turn left down the road to the beach – it's just over a 15-minute walk. Kahalon's cave is about 100 metres north of the entrance.

Places to Stay

Expensive hotels dominate and there is no budget accommodation. Prices include breakfast and vary between summer and winter.

The *Eshel Inn* (☎ 570208; fax 236926), across from the Sharon Hotel, provides one of the cheapest deals. Singles cost from US$25 to US$40, and doubles from US$30 to US$53. Another cheaper hotel with similar prices is the *Mittlemann* (☎ 72544), 13 Basel St, near Shalit Square.

At 29 Hamapilim St, the *Cymberg Hotel* (☎ 572179) is an attractive villa with a pleasant garden, lawn and verandah. It is nice and peaceful but only has 11 rooms. Hamapilim St is two blocks north of Shalit Square, running parallel with Basel St.

The *Tadmor Hotel* (☎ 57232; fax 574560), 38 Basel St, is staffed by hotel trainees. Singles cost from US$32 to US$52, and doubles from US$40 to US$74.

Of the luxury hotels, the *Daniel* (☎ 544444; fax 544675), dominates. It quotes from the Bible (Daniel 1:19) in its advertising and boasts an indoor pool, Dead Sea baths and a host of other facilities including a health and beauty spa. Lavish throughout, probably more so than any other Israeli hotel, singles cost from US$138 to US$158, and doubles from US$60 to US$200.

The *Dan Accadia* (☎ 556677; fax 571311) to the south has a pool, piano bar and synagogue. Singles cost from US$88 to US$236, and doubles are from US$102 to US$256.

The *Sharon* (☎ 575777; fax 572448) has singles costing from US$65 to US$145, and doubles from US$80 to US$158.

Places to Eat

You can try the *Caveman's* fish and/or salads which are surprisingly tasty, from US$6.

On Saturday the *Dabush Restaurant* is a popular hang-out for the 'in crowd'. It has good food, such as couscous and stuffed vegetables. It's the restaurant on the left of the Daniel Hotel's towers; the others nearby are also good.

Getting There & Away

United Tours bus No 90 leaves Tel Aviv from the Dan Panorama Hotel and passes along Allenby Rd, Ben Yehuda, Bograshov, Tchernichovsky, Dizengoff, Arlosoroff and Weizmann Sts. The ride costs about US$1 and takes under 40 minutes. The bus runs throughout Shabbat, making Herzlia a popular Saturday outing.

HOLON

(Population: 156,700)
This town was named for the barren sands on which it was established in 1935 (*hol* is Hebrew for sand). Dominated in its formative years by Polish textile workers immigrating from Lodz, Holon soon became an industrial city, turning out goods such as metals, leather and nylon as well as textiles.

Despite the industrialisation of the area, gardens, parks and tree-lined streets give the city a pleasant look. Holon is also notable for its tiny Samaritan colony.

BNEI BRAK

(Population: 110,400)
This Orthodox Jewish community was established in 1924 by Warsaw Hasidim. Joshua 19:45 mentions Bnei Brak as a city of the Dan tribe and during the Roman period it became a home to many famous sages of Israel and a centre of Hebrew study. Today the new city, with its numerous yeshivot, has once again become a centre for religious study. A sign of its status is the busy sherut service between here and Mea She'arim in Jerusalem.

PETAH TIQWA

(Population: 144,000)
Petah Tiqwa is Hebrew for Gate of Hope and it was the first Jewish agricultural settlement in Palestine – it's referred to as Em Hamoshavot (Mother of the Moshav). Jews from Jerusalem founded a moshav here in 1882 and were faced with considerable hardship

in the initial stages of development, relying heavily on financial support from Baron Benjamin Edmond de Rothschild. A stone archway honours his contribution to the town.

RISHON LE ZION
(Population: 139,500)
Meaning First in Zion, Rishon Le Zion was founded by Russian Zionists in 1882. After battling with agricultural problems and disease for five years, the settlers were given financial assistance by Baron Benjamin Rothschild – his first direct involvement with Zionism in Palestine. The vineyard and cellars that he helped establish are still among the town's major attractions.

Orientation
Coming south-east from Tel Aviv, the Carmel winery on Herzl St is just to the south of both the Egged and the Dan bus stops. Dan bus No 19 will drop you off on the corner of Herzl and Rothschild Sts and Egged will drop you off a little further down on Herzl St.

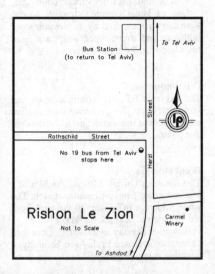

Bus Station
(to return to Tel Aviv)

To Tel Aviv

Street

Rothschild Street

No 19 bus from Tel Aviv
stops here

Herzl

Rishon Le Zion
Not to Scale

Carmel
Winery

To Ashdod

Carmel Winery
To arrange a guided tour of the winery telephone 942021/8. In the tour you get a brief explanation of Carmel's history and the vinification process as well as a tasting session to finish. Admission is US$0.90.

History Museum
Providing an insight into the pioneer spirit that drove the early Zionist settlers and the obstacles they faced, this museum is open Sunday to Thursday 9 am to 1 pm, Monday and Wednesday also 4 to 7 pm, and Saturday 6 to 9 pm; it is closed Friday. Admission is US$1.50.

It's located at 4 Ahad Ha'am St, the walk from the bus station is a history lesson in itself. Head for the pedestrian mall, turn left where you are flanked by buildings from the 1880s. On the right, notice the sign indicating the location of the old well. The museum's sound & light show is performed here. Cross the road open to traffic and continue to the top. Here is the old synagogue, built in 1885 and registered as a warehouse because the Turkish authorities would not allow a synagogue to be built.

It's open during the day so you should just step inside. The museum is to the right.

Getting There & Away
Get here on a Dan bus No 19 from Tel Aviv, which leaves from Shalom Aleichem St, between HaYarkon and Ben Yehuda Sts (across from the El Al building) and is the most convenient bus from the hostels and hotels. Egged bus Nos 200 and 201 leave from the central bus station. Many visitors follow a visit to the winery with a visit to the Weizmann Institute in nearby Rehovot.

REHOVOT
(Population: 90,000)
This quiet town is best known for the Weizmann Institute of Science. Established in 1890 by Polish Jews, *rehovot* means expanses and the name was taken from Genesis 26:22 to symbolise the community's aims to expand the Zionist settlements in Palestine.

Weizmann Institute of Science

This world-renowned centre was named after Israel's first president, Chaim Weizmann, on his 70th birthday in 1944. He was a leading research chemist, and the institute was established to provide facilities for research and study in the sciences. A free slide show explaining the institute's activities is shown in the Wix Auditorium at 11 am and 3.15 pm, Sunday to Thursday.

It's closed Friday and Saturday. There is a pleasant 80-hectare garden here.

Visitors' Section In Room 102 (☎ (08) 483597) of the Stone Administration Building (the first building on the left as you enter via the main gate), you can ask about the institute and pick up a variety of brochures. Phone in advance for a guided tour.

Weizmann House Follow the road away from the main gate and eventually bear right to reach the tombs of Weizmann and his wife, Vera, and the lovely house they lived in. Designed by the renowned architect Eric Mendelsohn, it was built in 1937 on this site because of the views across to the Judean hills in the direction of Jerusalem. Outside the house is the Lincoln limousine presented to Weizmann by Henry Ford II. One of only two ever made, the other was given to US President Truman.

It's open Sunday to Thursday, 10 am to 3.30 pm, and is closed Friday and Saturday; admission is US$1.

From the house you can leave the institute's grounds via the side gate, and follow HaNassi Harishon St back to Herzl St; the bus stop for Tel Aviv is on the right.

Places to Eat

The pleasant self-service *Estate Restaurant* just inside the gate near Weizmann House provides cheap food and drink – main meals, snacks, hot and cold drinks and beer.

Carvel, 176 Herzl St, serves up their popular American ice cream. Various felafel shops and cafés are here, too.

Getting There & Away

Egged bus Nos 200 and 201 leave frequently from Tel Aviv central bus station (US$1.25, 40 minutes), or you can pick up these buses at the Rishon Le Zion bus station (US$0.90, 10 minutes).

RAMLA

(Population: 53,200)

The only town in Israel that was founded and originally developed by Arabs, Ramla was an important crossroads between Damascus, Baghdad and Egypt, with the Jaffa to Jerusalem and the Haifa and Galilee to Beersheba roads converging here. It also has two railway lines running either side of it: Tel Aviv to Jerusalem and Haifa to Ashkelon.

Established in 716 by Caliph Suleiman, its name was derived from the Arabic word *aml* (sand). Until the arrival of the Crusaders in the 11th century, Ramla was the country's capital. In the Middle Ages it served as the first stop on the pilgrims' route from Jaffa to Jerusalem, and a small number of Christians have always lived there. After the 1948 War of Independence the Arab majority were forced to flee and were soon replaced by Jewish immigrants from various countries.

One of Israel's more attractive towns, Ramla is characterised by its pleasant stone buildings and streets lined with eucalyptus trees imported from Australia.

Orientation

The bus from Tel Aviv terminates at the bus station off Herzl Blvd, the main road; the five major sights of interest lie just to the north of this point.

Great Mosque

The Great, or Omari, Mosque (☎ 225081), was converted from a Crusader church. The white minaret can be seen to the west from the bus station, near the market.

It is open Sunday to Thursday from 8 to 11 am, but is closed Friday and Saturday; a donation is requested.

Church & Hospice of St Nicodemus & St Joseph Arimathea

Further north along Herzl Blvd, to the left, the clock-faced, square tower is a recognisable landmark. Turn left at Bialik St, and the entrance is through the first gate on your left. Ring the bell and one of the four monks living here will let you in.

According to Christian tradition, Ramla is the site of Arimathea, the home town of Joseph who arranged Jesus' burial with Nicodemus (John 19:38-39). Owned by the Franciscans, the church was originally built in the 16th century, although most of it was completed in 1902. Napoleon stayed in the church during his unsuccessful campaign against the Turks. If you ask, one of the monks will usually show you Napoleon's chambers.

The church is open Monday to Saturday from 8 to 11.30 am, and is closed Sunday; admission is free, and donations are accepted.

Tower of the 40 Martyrs

This was built in the 14th century as the minaret for the Jamal el Abias Mosque, which was built in the 8th century and has since been destroyed. It is sometimes referred to as the White Tower.

To reach it, continue north of the church along Herzl Blvd, turn left on Danny Mass St, and it's at the end on the left. Apparently in the morning a guard is on duty to let you in, but I never saw him. No doubt the view from the top would be worth the climb, although I imagine the steep stairway is not in good condition.

Pool of St Helena

On the other side of Herzl Blvd and further north, set in pleasant gardens, this 8th-century reservoir is on the right of Haganah St. To reach the water, enter the small building next to the blue and white murals. Named after the mother of the Roman Emperor Constantine, it is known as the Pool of El Anazia in Arabic and Breichat Hakeshatot, the Pool of Arches, in Hebrew. It was built for Harun

el-Rashid, of *A Thousand and One Nights* fame.

British War Cemetery

About two km outside Ramla to the east, is the cemetery where members of the British forces who defeated the Turks in 1917 are buried.

Market

Ramla's Thursday market has moved at least one reader to call it the best in the country.

Getting There & Away

Best visited from Tel Aviv, Egged bus Nos 411, 451, 452 and 455 all leave from the central bus station on Newe Sha'anan St. The fare is US$2 and it takes about 35 minutes. There are also regular express buses from Jerusalem. The Ramla bus station fronts onto Herzl Blvd.

LOD

Best known as the location of Ben-Gurion Airport, this is Ramla's sister city to the north. It dates to biblical times and shares a similar modern history. Much of its older section is derelict, but a visit to the traditional burial site of St George (the slayer of the dragon and patron saint of England) is the main attraction here.

The Church of St George is partially Crusader and was rebuilt by the Greek Orthodox Church in 1870. To get in, you usually need to persuade the caretaker to open it up; he lives in the Greek-style building across the cobbled lane. Next door to the church is another Crusader building, converted into a mosque in 1187. Again, some persuasion is required to get a caretaker to let you in.

A two-km walk north on Lod's main street leads you to the country's oldest bridge currently in use. Pass through the industrial site, look for the petrol station on your left and the signposted turn-off for Yagel and Zetan, and follow the road as it turns right and crosses the Ayalon River. This is the 14th-century Mameluke bridge. From here you can catch an Egged bus to Tel Aviv.

ASHDOD

(Population: 88,500)

Along with Gath, Gaza, Ekron and Ashkelon, Ashdod was one of the five great Philistine cities and an important cultural and religious centre.

The Greeks settled here, calling it Azotus, but they were conquered by the Maccabees in about 147 BC. An Arab village, Isdud, was later established here and the mound or tel which marks the site is about five km out of modern Ashdod. In the 1948 War of Independence, the Egyptian Army was forced back after a decisive battle nearby and some have drawn parallels between the Jewish victory and Isaiah 19:16-17. In the aftermath of the fighting the local Arab population was forced to leave the area.

The modern city of Ashdod was established in 1957 on what was desert sand by the seashore. It has developed quickly into a major port: its deep-water harbour has taken much work from Haifa and caused the closure of Tel Aviv's port. The navy's nautical school is here. Other industries based in Ashdod include cosmetics and textiles plants and a power plant which provides about half the country's supply of electricity.

Ashdod also serves as a major absorption centre for new Jewish immigrants.

Orientation & Information

A 'planned' city, Ashdod has little of interest for most people, dominated as it is by modern-style buildings, industrial sites and earnest attempts at gardening. The beaches are pleasant enough, and you can camp here – there are showers and no-one seems to mind.

Avi Haisman of the Bureau of Public Relations (☎ 52301), on the 7th floor of the municipality building next to the bus station, is very helpful but there's not a lot he can tell you. The post office is on the main street, Shavei Tzion, and a Steimatzsky bookshop is next to the bus station where there are a few uninspiring eating places.

Fatamid Fortress

Unfortunately, only a very small part of this pre-Crusader fortress remains and it is no longer very impressive. Known in Arabic as *Quleat El-Mine* (Fortress of the Port), the site was believed to be relatively recent until excavations unearthed bits of ceramic pottery. An early Arab document tells of Byzantine ships, which at the time were involved in trying to recapture Palestine, docking here to sell Muslim prisoners back to their families.

As the ships were sighted off the coast, smoke signals were sent up from the fortress here to let the families know. They would then collect their valuables to barter with the captors. You can still see portions of the four towers.

Take local Egged bus No 5 south and tell the driver where you want to go. The remains are now at the end of a row of houses on the city's outskirts.

Yaffa Ben-Ami Memorial Hill

From the top of the hill you have a good view of Ashdod and its surroundings. According to Muslim tradition, these ruins mark Jonah's tomb. He is believed to have settled in the area after his encounter with the whale.

Flea Market

If you happen to be in Ashdod on a Wednesday, you could take a look at the flea market on Lido Beach (the market lasts all day).

Places to Stay

Apparently included on Israel's master plan for tourist development, Ashdod currently has only two hotels, both somewhat expensive for what they provide, and both on Nordau St. The *Miami* (☎ 560573, 522085) and the *Orly* (☎ 521587) are both priced the same too – singles/doubles cost from US$30/50.

Places to Eat

Nowhere in particular stands out. *Felafel King* next to the post office, or buying provisions at the supermarket, usually win by default.

Getting There & Away

Tel Aviv is the nearest main centre; Egged buses run direct, and often continue to Ashkelon. You can also reach Ashdod from Beersheba and Jerusalem.

ASHKELON

(Population: 74,500)

Popular with many Israelis for its sandy beaches and national park, Ashkelon can be difficult for the budget traveller as it has no cheap accommodation.

Another major absorption centre, Ashkelon has a large community of Jews from North Africa, but there are also *olim* (new immigrants) from various countries around the world attending orientation classes during their first three months of residency in Israel.

Ashkelon's history involves a multitude of conquerors: the Philistines, the Israelites, the Greeks, the Romans, the Crusaders and the Muslims.

Under the Philistines, Ashkelon flourished, becoming one of the country's five major cities, its most important port, and an important caravan stop along the Via Maris, the famous trade route between Syria and

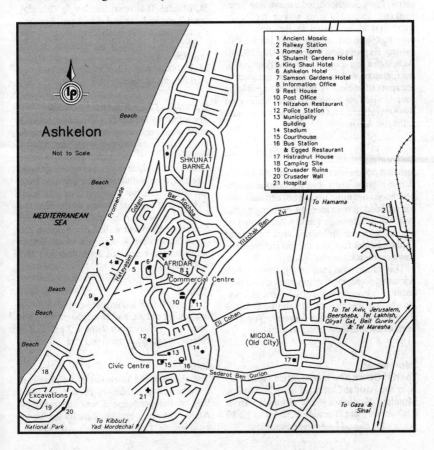

Ashkelon

Not to Scale

1 Ancient Mosaic
2 Railway Station
3 Roman Tomb
4 Shulamit Gardens Hotel
5 King Shaul Hotel
6 Ashkelon Hotel
7 Samson Gardens Hotel
8 Information Office
9 Rest House
10 Post Office
11 Nitzahon Restaurant
12 Police Station
13 Municipality
 Building
14 Stadium
15 Courthouse
16 Bus Station
 & Egged Restaurant
17 Histradrut House
18 Camping Site
19 Crusader Ruins
20 Crusader Wall
21 Hospital

MEDITERRANEAN SEA

Beach

SHKUNAT BARNEA

AFRIDAR
Commercial Centre

MIGDAL
(Old City)

Civic Centre

Excavations

National Park

To Hamama

To Tel Aviv, Jerusalem,
Beersheba, Tel Lakhish,
Qiryat Gat, Beit Guvrin
& Tel Maresha

To Gaza &
Sinai

To Kibbutz
Yad Mordechai

Egypt. It was also the centre of their culture and the stronghold of anti-Israelite feeling.

Under the Romans many grand buildings were constructed and Ashkelon is believed to be the birthplace of Herod the Great, who seems to have been particularly keen to embellish his home town. Ashkelon was also an important town to the Muslims, who called it the Bride of the East. Before the town was finally destroyed by Sultan Baybars in 1270, Ashkelon was the scene of several major battles between Muslims and Crusaders.

In the early 19th century an English aristocrat, Lady Stanhope, led excavations here, looking for gold and silver treasures rumoured to be buried in the area. Later diggings were carried out by the British Palestine Exploration Fund in the 1920s. Although a few foundations of various buildings, statues and columns were uncovered, the ruins of ancient Ashkelon have yet to be found. The few items that were uncovered were mainly used for building houses around Jaffa and Akko.

Orientation

Situated 56 km south of Tel Aviv, Ashkelon is not a large town, but its various neighbourhoods are quite spread out and each one has retained its own identity. Arriving by bus you will go through the old Arab town of Migdal and the industrial area of Ramat Eshkol, before reaching the bus station in the new commercial centre, Afridar.

This suburb was built in 1952 by a South African development company with the proceeds of donations from South African Jews. Nearby are the residential suburbs Shkunat Barnea, Zion Hills and Samson. You will need to use the local buses to get about.

Information

Tourist Office The tourist office (☎ 32412) is in the Afridar Centre. It is open Sunday, Monday, Wednesday and Thursday from 8.30 am to 1 pm, Tuesday 8.30 am to 12.30 pm, and is closed Friday and Saturday.

Post & Telecommunications The main post office and international telephones are at 18 Herzl St in Migdal. The offices are open Sunday to Thursday from 8.30 am to 12.30 pm and 4 to 6 pm, Friday 8.30 am to noon, but are closed Saturday. There are branches in the Afridar Centre, Samson, and near the bus station in the civic centre.

Other The Israel Discount Bank is on Ben-Gurion St, two blocks west of the bus station. Other banks are in Migdal, Afridar and Samson.

There is a laundromat (☎ 23431) at Herzl St, Migdal. It is open Sunday to Thursday from 7 am to 1 pm and 4 to 7 pm, Friday 7 am to 1 pm, and is closed Saturday.

The police station (emergency ☎ 100; information 34222, 24144) is on the corner of HaNassi and Eli Cohen Sts between Afridar and the bus station.

Byzantine Church & Mosaic Floor

These 5th to 6th-century Byzantine church ruins were uncovered in Ashkelon's newest neighbourhood, along with the nearby mosaic floor of the same period. Marble pillars and capitals lie around on the ground. The church is within walking distance from the city centre, but you can also take local bus No 5 to Shkunat Barnea from either the bus station or the Afridar Centre. Get off at Jerusalem Blvd and walk half a block to Zui Segal St. Bus No 4 stops one block further south on the corner of Jerusalem and Bar Kochba Sts.

Afridar

Here you'll find a courtyard containing two interesting old Roman sarcophagi. It's open Sunday to Friday from 9 am to 2 pm, and is closed Saturday; admission is free.

Migdal

The shabbier old town has more character than the rest of Ashkelon. Prior to the 1948 War of Independence it was inhabited by Arabs who were brought here by the Turks to work on Lady Stanhope's excavations.

Most of them were forced to flee to the Gaza Strip where many now live in refugee camps.

In today's Ashkelon, Migdal is the main shopping quarter, with a fruit and vegetable market on Monday and Wednesday and a produce, clothing and jewellery market on Thursday. You will also find some of Israel's cheapest felafel here. The market is off Herzl St, just past Tzahal St, down a narrow passageway to the left. Local bus Nos 4, 5 or 7 will take you to Migdal, or you could walk. A pleasant half-hour stroll along the road through an open field will bring you to the market.

National Park

This national park (☎ 36444) attracts large numbers of Israelis at weekends and holidays with its seaside location. It is dominated by excavations, as it is on the site of 4000-year-old Canaanite remains buried under the ruins of their successors' cities.

From the entrance at the north of the ancient city, the road passes through the 12th-century Crusader city wall which can be traced all the way round the site. In the south-western corner, the Tower of Virgins and the Tower of Blood have collapsed onto the beach. At the base of the cliffs are part of the sea wall with its granite columns protruding to the north of the towers. These were used for bonding purposes.

The site's oldest section is between the two car parks. Piled one on top of the other in the eroded cliff-face are strata from the Middle Bronze Age (beginning circa 2000 BC) to the Roman period. These can be clearly seen from the beach.

The ruins of two Crusader churches and one Byzantine church are found here, but all are unimpressive. The open-air auditorium was possibly a well, referred to in records dated 560.

A quadrangle, in the centre of the park, and marked by Roman columns, probably dates to the 2nd century, although it is often associated with Herod the Great. The columns are only partly visible because the excavators were obliged to replace the earth. The original floor level has been preserved

in a small section at the southern end and here you can see various parts of the building which have been collected. These include three major pillar reliefs: two of Nike, the winged goddess of victory on a globe supported by Atlas, and one of the goddess Isis with the child god Horus. Made of Italian marble, they date back to sometime between 200 BC and 100 AD.

Outside the park, to the north, take the first left after the main intersection. At the top of the cliff, after the road turns to the right there is a Roman tomb with places for four bodies, believed to have been built for a wealthy Hellenistic family in the 3rd century. Inside is a well-preserved fresco depicting Greek mythological scenes.

It's open Sunday to Friday from 9 am to 1 pm, Saturday 10 am to 2 pm, and admission is free.

Beaches

The national park's beach at the southern edge of the town has a grass lawn and the ruins. **Delilah Beach** is after the holiday village's beach, facing three islands within wading and swimming distance. **Barnea Beach** attracts the town's wealthier residents. For nude bathing, head for the **North Beach**. As with the whole Israeli Mediterranean coast, watch out for the strong undertow here.

A few km south of Ashkelon is **Kibbutz Zikim**. Nearby you can see the floating dock where tankers unload their oil. Unfortunately, they are responsible for the tar which often washes ashore – they illegally wash out their holds with sea water instead of using the more expensive chemicals.

Places to Stay

Camping is the only really cheap way to stay in Ashkelon. You can usually camp with no hassles in the national park or on the beaches if you are discreet. However, watch out for your valuables and do not camp on the kibbutz's beach. It is unsafe for women to camp alone. An official camping ground is adjacent to the national park. There are also bungalows. Despite above-average prices, the camping ground is usually full on weekends and holidays.

Renting a private room can be the cheapest deal outside of canvas-dwelling. Contact the tourist office, although sometimes prospective landlords will approach you at the bus station. Rooms vary in quality, and the prices are around US$15 to US$25 per person per night. Bargain hard, and see the room and facilities before agreeing to anything. Wandering around looking for a room can take forever, as most of these places are in Migdal and are unmarked.

Hotels in Ashkelon include the *Ashkelon Hotel* (☎ 34188), 7 South Africa Blvd – about 15 minutes' walk from the beach. Singles/doubles are US$20/27, with shower or bath. From the tourist office, walk through the National Gardens and turn left on South Africa Blvd.

The *Samson Gardens* (☎ 34666, 36641), 38 Hatamar St has singles from US$21 to US$24, and doubles from US$36 to US$41 (breakfast is included).

The *Shulamit Gardens* (☎ 36222; fax 36227), 11 Hatayasim St, has singles from US$55 to US$75, and doubles from US$70 to US$100.

Places to Eat

Migdal is the cheapest area to eat in. Some of the country's cheapest felafel is sold on Herzl St under the AGAG sign. At the intersection with Tzahal St, a small shop serves tasty Moroccan sandwiches. *Nitzahon*, across the street near the post office, has Ashkelon's best selection of grilled meat and the stuffed cabbage is great – you can eat well here from about US$4. A few inexpensive Moroccan places in this area are worth trying.

The Egged *self-service restaurant* at the bus station provides the usual excellent value for money, and the supermarket, two blocks west, provides various types of sandwiches – it's open Sunday and Monday 9 am to 7 pm, Tuesday to Thursday 9 am to 8 pm, Friday 8 am to 2 pm, and is closed Saturday.

Entertainment

If you decide to stay, the local nightlife involves a few bars, people-watching, a cinema, the beach and the national park. *Bayit Hakfari* (Village House), next to the clocktower in Afridar Square, is a pub popular with young Israelis.

The *Esther Cinema* (☎ 22659), in Giv'at Zion, usually shows English-language films. Check with the tourist office for the current schedule of events, which normally includes a few winter concerts.

Delilah Beach often sees tourists and residents alike gathering to drink beer and eat steak or pizza. The civic centre on HaNassi St holds a disco on Saturday night (small admission fee). Also on Saturday night in the national park, *Bustan Hazeytim* (Olive Grove), features dancing, folk-singing and sometimes magicians.

Getting There & Away

Ashkelon can be reached by Egged bus Nos 300, 301 or 311 from Tel Aviv (1¼ hours). It can also be reached by bus from Beersheba and Gaza.

Getting Around

You have to rely on the town's bus network to get around Ashkelon. For the beach, take No 13 – but only in July and August; Nos 3 and 9 will take you to within walking distance of the park behind the beach; Nos 4, 5 and 7 will take you to Zefania Square in the centre of Afridar – No 5 continues to Shkunat Barnea and all serve Migdal.

AROUND ASHKELON
Kibbutz Yad Mordechai

Established in 1943 and named after Mordechai Anilewicz, a commander of the Jewish Resistance in the Warsaw Ghetto uprising against the Nazis, this kibbutz features a statue of the defiant Anilewicz, grenade in hand.

Over the hill to the left of the kibbutz entrance is another monument to ferocious resistance – a rather bizarre reconstruction of the battle which took place on this site during the 1948 War of Independence. The scene shows how the kibbutzniks withstood the Egyptian Army's attack for five days, allowing precious time for Jewish forces to regroup in Tel Aviv. A few months later the kibbutz was recaptured by the Israelis.

There is also a museum which has exhibits illustrating the Jewish Resistance during the Warsaw Ghetto uprising, the Jewish community's life in Poland, and major local incidents of 1948.

It's open Sunday to Thursday from 8 am to 4 pm, Friday 8 am to 2 pm, and is closed Saturday; admission is US$1 (students US$0.80).

Egged bus No 19 runs between Ashkelon and Yad Mordechai – Sunday to Thursday at noon, 2.45 and 6 pm, and Friday at noon and 4.15 pm. The last return bus from the kibbutz is at 3.10 pm (12.40 Friday) so visitors need to take the noon bus from Ashkelon (US$0.75).

Qiryat Gat

A rapidly growing industrial town at the heart of the Lakhish region, Qiryat Gat lies about 22 km east of Ashkelon and can be reached by bus from there and also from Tel Aviv or Jerusalem. Established in 1954, it is named after the Biblical town of Gat which is believed to have stood nearby at Tel Gat, the hill to the north-east. This was a major Philistine city and the birthplace of Goliath.

The excavations here have been discontinued and there's little to see in the town. There are, however, some nearby sites of archaeological interest.

Beit Guvrin & Tel Maresha

Surrounding Kibbutz Beit Guvrin is a fascinating series of some 4000 caves, hidden by cacti and fig trees. There are also two archaeological sites nearby – Beit Guvrin and Tel Maresha.

Coming from Qiryat Gat, remnants of a Crusader castle can be seen by the roadside. The turn-off for the site is to the left from the kibbutz, beside a large tree. After a few metres the road forks. To the left is Beit Guvrin and to the right, about two km along, is the circular road leading to Tel Maresha.

The kibbutz is built on the site of a deserted Arab village, Beit Jibrin (House of Gabriel). Opposite is the remains of the ancient town of Beit Guvrin, which was an important town during Roman times. It is mentioned in Talmudic literature of the 3rd and 4th centuries and the Crusaders ruled here in the 12th century. Remains from a 3rd-century synagogue, Crusader artefacts and Greek objects of art from Beit Guvrin are on display at Jerusalem's Rockefeller Museum, and Byzantine mosaics found here are now in the Israel Museum, Jerusalem.

Among the ruins at Tel Maresha is the apse of the 12th-century Crusader church of St Anna. Sandhanna, the Arabic name for Maresha, is derived from this.

It is the caves, though, that attract the most interest. Some of them are natural, created as water carried away the soft limestone. Others, however, are thought to have been made by the Phoenicians as they dug for limestone to be used in the construction of Ashkelon's port between the 4th and 7th centuries. During the Byzantine period the caves were used by monks and hermits. St John the Baptist is said to have been one of those who carved crosses and altars out of the limestone here.

The easiest caves to explore are those west of Tel Maresha – you can see tracks leading from the road. Check each interesting hole in the ground that you see. Some of the caves have elaborate staircases with banisters leading down below ground level. The rows of hundreds of small niches suggest that they were used for raising small domesticated doves used in the worship of Aphrodite by the Sidonian colony between the 3rd and 1st centuries BC.

There are two burial tombs to the east of Tel Maresha, built by the Sidonians and dating from the 3rd to the 2nd century BC.

Public transport to the area is limited. Egged bus No 11 runs twice a day from Qiryat Gat, at 8 am and 5 pm (8 am only on Friday). Some of the Qiryat Gat to Hebron buses also pass by. Although there is no official stop, the driver will let you off in front of the kibbutz if you ask him.

Tel Lakhish

Between Beit Guvrin and Qiryat Gat, Tel Lakhish is archaeologically more important but visually less interesting than Tel Maresha. Lakhish was a fortified city before Joshua's conquest (Joshua 10:31). With its strategic location at the intersection of the road to Egypt and the approach to Jerusalem, many battles were fought nearby in ancient times. Nine levels of settlement have been revealed by excavations, but with the most interesting artefacts now displayed in museums in London and Jerusalem, there is little to see at the site itself. Lakhish is not on any major public transport routes – by bus you will need to get off on the Qiryat Gat to Beit Guvrin road and walk/hitch the two km.

NETANYA

(Population: 132,200)
Netanya is a popular seaside resort, famous for its good sandy beaches and quiet atmosphere. It's both the capital of the Sharon district, and a major industrial centre specialising in diamonds, citrus-packing and, with the country's only brewery, beermaking. Fortunately, the industrial sector of the city has been kept apart from the seafront, making Netanya an attractive city.

Named after Nathan Strauss, an American philanthropist, Netanya was established in 1929 as a citrus growing centre, soon developing as a holiday resort. In the early 1940s the British used it as a convalescent centre for the Allied armed forces. Now aimed at an older clientele, there are limited facilities for budget travellers, but those who choose to stay can enjoy a great climate, lovely surroundings and free entertainment almost every day during the summer.

Orientation

Quite a large place, Netanya is easy to get to know. The main coastal highway, Haifa Rd, links the city to Tel Aviv and Haifa. From Tel Aviv, you pass the railway station on your right just before the big intersection with Herzl St, Netanya's main east-west thoroughfare. The bus station is on Herzl St, six blocks to the west where Herzl meets Weizmann and Benyamin Blvds. A further six blocks bring you to Ha'Atzmaut (Independence) Square, the downtown area by the sea. The tourist office, eating places and shops are all in this area and the hotels are nearby.

Information

Tourist Office The Israel Government Tourist Office (☎ 27286), on the southwestern corner of Ha'Atzmaut Square, is open Sunday to Thursday from 8.30 am to 2 pm and 4 to 7 pm, Friday 8.30 am to 2 pm, but is closed Saturday. The municipal tourist office, on Lion Square, east of Ha'Atzmaut Square on Herzl St, is open Sunday to Thursday from 9 am to 1 pm and 5 to 7 pm, Friday 9 am to 1 pm, but is closed Saturday.

Its role is only to help with finding accommodation for tourists rather than to give general information.

Post The post office (☎ 41109), is at 59 Herzl St with branches in Ha'Atzmaut Square and at 15 Herzl St. The post office is open Sunday to Tuesday and Thursday from 7.45 am to 12.30 pm and 3.30 to 6 pm, Wednesday 7.45 am to 2 pm, Friday 7.45 am to 1 pm, and is closed Saturday.

Other Banks can be found along Herzl St. There is a laundromat at 28 Smilansky St, near the corner of Remez St (south of Herzl St). The police emergency telephone number is 100.

Beaches

Netanya's 11 km of free sandy beaches are the basis of the city's 'Riviera' label. The seven lifeguard stations dotted along the beach are an indication of how strong the currents are. The **Qiryat Sanz Beach** in the north is for religious Jews; there are separate bathing times for men and women.

Diamond Cutting Factory

An audiovisual programme is part of a free guided tour put on to attract potential buyers at the commercial National Diamond Centre showrooms at 90 Herzl St (☎ 624770). You can see diamonds being cut and polished here.

Citrus-Packing Houses
Inquire at the tourist office between January and March about visits to a citrus-packing house.

Places to Stay
Most hotel prices vary considerably between the low season (November to February), the regular (March to mid-July and September to October), and the high (mid-July to August and Jewish holidays). The further you are from the sea, the less you tend to pay, as well. Netanya has a large German-Jewish population and most of the hotels seem to be run by them. Empty rooms may mean that the low-season prices quoted here will apply in the high season too.

Places to Stay – bottom end
The *Landa Motel* (☎ 22634 – look for the sign 'Motel: Rooms to Rent'), 3 Jabotinsky Blvd, has doubles from US$25, including breakfast. It is close to the beach, and is south of Ha'Atzmaut Square.

Nearby, *Beit Orit* (☎ 616818), 21 Hen St, is a delightful hotel run by Swedish Christians. This place is nicely decorated and very comfortable, and is often filled by Scandinavian groups. Singles/doubles are US$15/23.

Places to Stay – middle
Netanya has over 30 listed hotels, most of which fall into the middle bracket.

In Ha'Atzmaut Square is the *Hotel Atzma'ut* (☎ 22562) to the south on the corner at 2 Ussishkin St; singles/doubles are from US$15/20. On the north side, the modern *Hof Hotel* (☎ 22825), has singles/ doubles for US$20/32.

To the south of the square, Gad Machnes St starts by the tourist office and is just across from the seafront. At No 9, the *Hotel Margoa* (☎ 624434; fax 623430) has singles costing from US$40 to US$53, and doubles from US$48 to US$63. At No 17, the *Grand Metropol Hotel* (☎ 624777; fax 611556) is

higher class, with singles costing from US$30 to US$55, and doubles from US$38 to US$65. It has a lower-grade sister hotel, the *Metropol* (☎ 624777) behind it, with cheaper rooms.

The *Palace Hotel* (☎ 620222), 33 Gad Machnes St, has singles/doubles from US$25/50. Behind the Palace, the small *Daphna Hotel* (☎ 23655), 29 Rishon-le-Zion St, has sparse, cramped double rooms for US$30. The nearby *Mitzpe-Yam Hotel* (☎ 623730; fax 616722), 4 Carlebach St, has singles/doubles for US$30/35.

At 25 Ussishkin St, the *Hotel Reuven* (☎ 23107), has a pool, pleasant gardens and typically gruff management; singles cost from US$25 to US$50, and doubles from US$34 to US$60.

North of Ha'Atzmaut Square, on King David St, the hotels include the *Ginot Yam* (☎ 341007; fax 615722), with singles costing from US$25 to US$50, and doubles from US$30 to US$65. Two blocks from the square, the *Topaz Hotel* (☎ 624555), has kitchen facilities available at extra cost; here singles/doubles are US$45/60.

Places to Stay – top end
The luxury *Dan Netanya* (☎ 30044), on Nice Blvd has singles/doubles which start at US$85/110. At *The Seasons* (☎ 618555; fax 623022), also on Nice Blvd, singles cost from US$70 to US$165, and doubles from US$90 to US$195.

Places to Eat
Budget visitors are not really catered for, and the cheapest options are the *Egged self-service restaurant* at the bus station, and the felafel stalls. There is a *street market* near the bus station on and around Zangwill St.

On Ha'Atzmaut Square and along Herzl St are several cafés and restaurants. *Pundak HaYam Grill Bar* at 1 HaRav Kook St, off Herzl St by the square, seems to be a bit better than most. Hummus, spaghetti and grilled meats are served here – the portions are good, and you can eat well from about US$7.

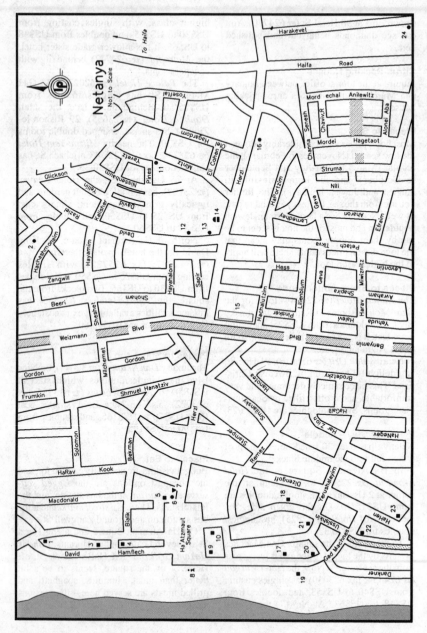

Netanya
Not to Scale

1	Topaz Hotel
2	Stadium
3	Galei Ruth Hotel
4	Ginot Yam Hotel
5	Hof
6	Hapoalim Bank
7	Pundak HaYam Grill Bar
8	Tourist Office
9	Hotel Margog
10	Atzmaut Hotel
11	First Aid
12	Police
13	Ohel Shem Auditorium
14	Post Office
15	Bus Station
16	Netanya Diamond Centre
17	Grand Metropol & Metropol
18	Hotel Reuven
19	Residence Hotel
20	Palace Hotel
21	Daphna Hotel
22	Landa Motel & Mitzpe-Yam Hotel
23	Beit Orit
24	Railway Station

Entertainment

Netanya is proud of its reputation for providing visitors with a wide programme of organised events. Most of it is geared towards older tourists – bingo, bridge, chess, and lawn bowls, for example.

During the summer months in particular, the range of activities available is wide and the crowds of visitors obviously appreciate it. The Netanya Orchestra plays free concerts

each Tuesday evening in Ha'Atzmaut Square and there is also free Israeli folk dancing in the square on Saturday evening. In the amphitheatre in King's Park, there are free films and concerts.

All year round, the Cinematheque, Ohel Shem Auditorium, 4 Raziel St, shows a film at least once a week.

Getting There & Away

Bus There are buses about every 10 minutes to and from Tel Aviv, a mere 20 minutes' drive away. Services to Haifa, Jerusalem and Ben-Gurion Airport run every 30 minutes and there are infrequent buses for Beersheba and Eilat.

To reach Caesarea, Meggido, Afulla, Nazareth or Tiberias, take a bus from Netanya to Hadera and change there for the required destination.

Train The commuter-filled Haifa to Tel Aviv and the less frequent Haifa to Jerusalem services stop at Netanya.

Taxi Sherut services operate from Herzl St by Zion Square to Tel Aviv and Haifa.

Getting Around

Most of the areas of interest can be reached on foot as they are centred around Ha'Atzmaut Square, the beach and the bus station. Arriving by train you will need to take a bus to the city centre.

Haifa & the North Coast

HAIFA

(Population: 245,900)

Haifa is Israel's third-largest city, the country's main port and industrial centre, and home to two major universities. It is also the world centre of the Baha'i faith. Set on the wooded slopes of Mount Carmel overlooking the sea, the upper section of the city includes some delightful residential areas. The panoramic views to the east across Carmel National Park and the city lights at night are enchanting.

It is often said that 'in Jerusalem they pray, in Tel Aviv they dance, in Haifa they work'. The lack of major attractions here means that few travellers spend much time in the city. However, Haifa's beaches are among the country's best and there are also excellent museums, art galleries and venues for music and theatre. In addition, there are quite a few places nearby that are worth a brief visit and the city makes a useful base for some day trips.

History

The city's name first appeared in 3rd-century Talmudic literature and although its origin remains obscure, it has been related to the Hebrew words *hof yafe* (beautiful coast). The Crusaders called the city 'Caife', 'Cayfe' and sometimes 'Caiphas', which suggests that the name Haifa may have evolved from Caiaphas, the high priest of Jerusalem at the time of Jesus, who waš was born in the city. In earlier biblical times, the prophet Elijah was here, as were the Phoenicians.

There is evidence that one of the earliest known Jewish communities came from this area. Their exposure to foreign influences eventually led them to speak a different style of Hebrew. As a result of their mispronunciation of many important words and their inability to differentiate between gutterals, rabbinical authorities decided that they should not officiate in synagogues or serve as readers of the Torah.

Haifa was an important Arab town during the Middle Ages, but early in the 12th century it was destroyed in battle when the Arabs teamed up with the small number of Jews to defeat the Crusaders. Nearby Akko superseded the town in importance, and when the Ottoman Turks took control of Palestine, Haifa was an insignificant village. Strangely, the Jews did not consider Akko part of the Holy Land, and the community used to come to Haifa to bury their dead.

By the early 19th century, Haifa's Jewish community had begun to increase. With the growth of political Zionism the town expanded quite dramatically, although early in the 20th century the population was still only 10,000. Its port area was marshland, sand dunes dominated the coastline and the slopes of Carmel were used to graze sheep.

In 1898, Theodor Herzl, the founder of political Zionism, visited Haifa and visualised what lay ahead for modern Haifa: 'huge liners rode at anchor ... serpentine road to Mount Carmel', and at the 'top of the mountain there were thousands of white homes and the mountain itself was crowned with imposing villas'. His predictions have proved amazingly accurate.

The construction of the Hejaz Railway between Damascus and Medina in 1905 and the later development of lines to Zemach, Akko and the south of the country, started Haifa's modern revival. During the British Mandate the modern port was constructed – a major task which involved reclaiming from the sea the land now occupied by the warehouses, port offices, railway lines and adjoining streets. Haifa then began its rapid transformation, becoming the country's shipping base, naval centre and oil terminal. For some reason, the British were the first to use Haifa's naturally sheltered position as a harbour; their ancient predecessors had chosen Caesarea, Atlit, Ahziv and Akko.

With its new port, Haifa became many new immigrants' first sight of the Promised

Land. Prior to the British withdrawal from Palestine, Haifa had become a Jewish stronghold and it was the first major area to be secured by the newly declared State of Israel in 1948. By that time new areas such as Bat Gallim, Hadar, Central Carmel and Newe Sha'anan had already sprung up, but the immediate post-independence rush of Jewish newcomers spurred the development of others like Ramot Remez, Qiryat Elizer, Newe Josef and Qiryat Shprinzak. Haifa became Israel's first industrial centre, and earned a reputation for liberalism. The mostly secular Jewish community is under considerably less pressure to follow religious laws than elsewhere. They also enjoy a better than average relationship with the local Arabs, who are mainly Christian. The intifada, though, has shown that there are definite tensions between the two groups.

Orientation

Haifa is basically divided into three main sections which become progressively more affluent as you ascend. Whether you arrive by bus, train or boat, the first place you will see is the port area. Next is the Hadar HaCarmel (Glory of the Carmel) area, which is known as Hadar for short. Most shops, businesses, eating places and hotels are here.

Finally, the Carmel district occupies the higher slopes of the city, and is characterised by pleasant residential streets. The Carmel district also has a small commercial centre called Central Carmel, with several hotels and restaurants.

With a few important exceptions, the major roads in Haifa run parallel to the coastline and are linked by a series of stairways, which saves a lot of unnecessary pavement-pounding. It is feasible to walk between some sections of the port area and Hadar, but the tiring slopes encourage you to use public transport to and from Central Carmel.

Information

Tourist Office Haifa has two IGTO offices – the one at the port (☎ 63980) is usually open to coincide with the arrival of ferries and cruise ships, while the main office

(☎ 666521/3) is at 18 Herzl St in Hadar. It is open Sunday to Thursday 8.30 am to 5 pm, Friday 8.30 am to 3 pm, and is closed on Saturday.

Municipal tourist offices are at four locations: the central bus station, open Sunday to Thursday 9 am to 4 pm, Friday 9 am to 1 pm, and closed Saturday; in Hadar (☎ 663056) at 23 HaNevi'im St, open Sunday to Thursday 8 am to 7 pm, Friday 9 am to 1 pm, and closed Saturday; in the City Hall (☎ 645359), 14 Hassan Shukri St, open Sunday to Friday 8 am to 1 pm, and closed Saturday; and in Central Carmel (☎ 83683), 119 HaNassi Ave, open Sunday to Thursday 9 am to 1 pm, Friday 8 am to 1 pm, and closed Saturday.

The Haifa Tourist Development Association (☎ 671645) is at 10 Ahad Ha'am St, just off HaNevi'im St in Hadar. There is also a Voluntary Tourist Service office here. It is open Sunday to Thursday 10 am to noon, and closed Saturday.

Banks & Moneychangers Haifa's port area is a popular haunt for black-marketeers, who offer a better rate than the banks – but they change cash only and there's a definite risk of being ripped off. Banks are easily found on Jaffa Rd, and in Hadar on and around HaNevi'im St.

The American Express office is in the port area at Meditrad Ltd (☎ 642267), 2 Khayat Square. The entrance is in the alleyway near Steimatzky's off Ha'Atzmaut St, just west of Khayat St. The office is open Sunday to Thursday 9 am to 5 pm, and is closed Friday and Saturday.

Post & Telecommunications The main post office, poste restante and international telephones are at 19 HaPalyam St in the port area. It is open Sunday to Thursday 8 am to 8 pm, Friday 8 am to 2 pm, and closed Saturday.

A more central branch is in Hadar at the corner of HaNevi'im and Shabtai Levi Sts; this branch is open Sunday to Thursday 8 am to 7 pm, Friday 8 am to noon, and closed Saturday. There is also a branch at the central bus station.

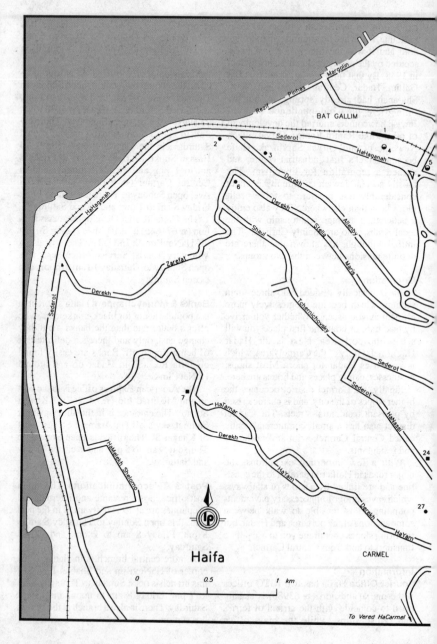

Haifa

0   0.5   1 km

To Vered HaCarmel

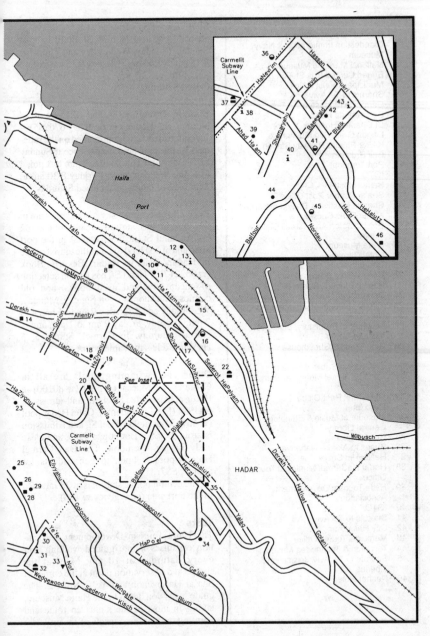

1   Central Railway Station
2   Clandestine Immigration & Navy Museum
3   National Maritime Museum
4   Egged Central Bus Station & Municipal Tourist Office
5   Sheruts to Tel Aviv
6   Carmelite Monastery
7   Ben Yehuda Hotel
8   St Charles' Hospice
9   Dagon Grain Silo Museum
10 Kikkar Plumer Railway Station
11 Beit Erdstein
12 Port Terminal
13 IGTO
14 Bethel Hostel
15 Sha'ar Palmer Post Office
16 Sheruts to Isfiya & Daliyat el Karmel
17 Kikkar Paris Subway
18 Beit HaGefen Arab-Israeli Cultural Centre
19 Haifa Museum
20 Hotel Carmelia
21 Chagall Artists' House
22 Central Post Office
23 Baha'i Shrine & Gardens
24 Dan Carmel Hotel
25 Tikotin Museum of Japanese Art
26 Nof Hotel
27 Museum of Prehistory, Biological Institute & Zoo
28 Beth Shalom Guesthouse
29 Mane Katz Museum
30 Gan Ha'em Subway Station
31 Central Carmel Municipal Tourist Office
32 Mt Carmel Post Office
33 Dvir Hotel
34 Museum of Music & Ethnology & Central Library
35 Hotel Talpiot
36 Buses to Akko & Nahariya
37 HaNevi'im Street Post Office
38 Hadar HaCarmel Municipal Tourist Office
39 Haifa Tourism Development Association
40 IGTO
41 Sheruts to Tel Aviv
42 City Hall
43 Municipal Tourist Office
44 Technion & Technodea Museum
45 Sheruts to Tel Aviv, Jerusalem & Tiberias
46 Nesher Hotel

SPNI The SPNI office is at 8 Menahem St (☎ 664135), near Nordau St. SNPI is open Sunday, Monday, Wednesday and Thursday 8.15 am to 3.45 pm, Tuesday 9.15 am to 4.45 pm, Friday 8.15 am to 12.30 pm, and is closed Saturday.

Student Travel ISSTA and ISIC are at 28 Nordau St, Hadar (☎ 669139, 670865) – several readers have commented on the rudeness of the staff here. Experience it Sunday to Tuesday and Thursday 8.30 am to 1 pm, 4 to 6 pm, Wednesday and Friday 8.30 am to 1 pm but, of course, it's closed Saturday.

Bookshops Steimatzsky's bookshops are in the central bus station arcade and at 82 Ha'Atzmaut St, near Khayat St in the port area, and at 16 Herzl St, near the tourist office in Hadar. Also in Hadar, Beverly Book (☎ 933217), 7 Herzl St, has a good selection of cheap new and used books, and old comics. The shop is open Sunday, Monday, Wednesday and Thursday 9 am to 1 pm, 4 to 7 pm, Tuesday, Friday 9 am to 1 pm, and is closed Saturday. In Carmel, Studio 5, 5 HaYam Rd has the same hours.

Other The swimming pools are all in Carmel. The Maccabee pool (☎ 80100) in Bikurim St is heated in winter, and admission is US$4 (less for students). Galei Hadar pool (☎ 667854) is at 9 HaPoel St, and admission is around US$3. Both open daily, and close early Friday afternoon. The Dan Carmel Hotel's pool is open to nonresidents for about US$7.

The central police station is at 28 Jaffa Rd in the port area (emergency ☎ 100).

Tours

The Haifa Tourism Development Association organises a free guided walking tour every Saturday at 10 am. Meet at the signposted observation point at the corner of Sha'ar HaLevenon and Ye'fe Nof Sts. The guide leads you down to the Haifa Museum, taking in most of the sights en route and pointing out various aspects of the city. Not mind-blowing, but it is a convenient way to get your initial bearings in Haifa.

Egged Tours offer a half-day tour of the city for US$15. They also offer tours to nearby Caesarea, Tel Aviv, Akko, Rosh Hanikra and the Druze villages.

Beaches

Haifa has some good beaches, most of which are to the north and the west – many are pay beaches, charging about US$2 per person per day. Closest is **Shaqet Beach**, reached on Egged bus No 41 from Hadar. **Bat Gallim Beach** is near the central bus station, and is rocky and not very attractive, although there is a free sandy stretch nearby. Egged bus No 41 also brings you here, or it is within easy walking distance from the central bus station. **Carmel Beach** is the best free beach in Haifa and worth the longer ride on Egged bus Nos 44 or 45 from Hadar. Zamir and Dado beaches are south of Carmel Beach.

Cablecar

This runs from near Bat Gallim Promenade up the Carmel's slopes to near the Carmelite Monastery. A recorded commentary in Hebrew or English gives a few facts about the surroundings en route, but the ride is short and leads from one unexciting place to another.

The cablecar is operational Sunday to Thursday 9 am to 11 pm, Friday 9 am to 3 pm, Saturday 4 to 11 pm, and the return trip is US$3.

To reach the lower station, you can walk the few blocks from the central bus station: take Ha'Aliya HaSheniya St. Egged bus No 45 speeds along Haganah Blvd; keep a lookout for the lower station to your right, as there is a bus stop just past it.

Clandestine Immigration & Navy Museum

This museum in a boat deals with the Zionists' illegal immigration during the British Mandate. The boat is the *Af-Al-Pi*, one of the many which attempted to run the British blockade. It's across the busy Haganah Blvd from the lower cablecar

station at 204 Allenby Rd (☎ 536249). The museum is open Sunday and Thursday 9 am to 4 pm, Monday to Wednesday 9 am to 3 pm, Friday 9 am to 1 pm, and is closed Saturday. Admission is US$0.70.

National Maritime Museum

Just up the street at 198 Allenby Rd, this museum (☎ 536622) deals with the history of shipping in the Mediterranean area. There are some interesting archaeological finds in the collection. It's open Sunday to Thursday 10 am to 4 pm, Saturday 10 am to 1 pm, and is closed Friday. Admission is US$2.50 (students US$1.80), and it is free on Saturday.

Elijah's Cave

Just across Allenby Rd from the National Maritime Museum, this is where Elijah is believed to have hidden from King Ahab and Queen Jezebel after he slew the 450 priests of Ba'al (I Kings:17-19). There is also a Christian tradition that the Holy Family once sheltered here. Also Elijah, in the guise of Khadar (The Green Prophet), is recognised by Muslims, so it's a holy place to them.

Pilgrims of each of these three faiths come here to pray, and Arabs in particular enjoy it as a picnic site. The cave is also believed to provide relief for nervous disorders.

The cave is open in summer, Sunday to Thursday 8 am to 6 pm, Friday 8 am to 1 pm, winter, Sunday to Thursday 8 am to 5 pm, Friday 9 am to 1 pm, but is closed Saturday. Admission is free.

It is possible from here to climb up the hill to reach the Carmelite Monastery.

Carmelite Monastery

This monastery on Stella Maris Rd belongs to the Carmelites, a Catholic order that originated in the area, taking its name from the mountain.

In the late 12th century, some Crusaders settled on the western slopes of Mount Carmel, wanting to live a hermit lifestyle in the caves here, just like the prophet Elijah.

Later, the Crusader hermits became part of the Jerusalem diocese and were called the Carmelites.

Over the centuries they have suffered from Muslim persecution, twice having to abandon their monasteries. The current site is built over what they believe to be a cave where Elijah lived. The ruins of a medieval Greek church, St Margaret's Abbey, and an ancient chapel, probably Byzantine, had to be cleared from the site first.

The monastery was used by Napoleon's forces as a temporary hospital during his unsuccessful campaign in 1799. When he retreated, the Turks massacred the wounded and the Carmelites were again driven out. When they were eventually allowed to return, they buried the dead in a garden tomb, and erected a memorial monument in the form of a pyramid.

The monastery was destroyed in 1821 by Abdallah, Pasha of Akko, and a new church and monastery were opened in 1836, and named Stella Maris (Star of the Sea).

Today the complex houses an extension of the International College of Theology of the Carmelites in Rome; the old building is now a hospice for pilgrim groups.

Paintings in the chapel's dome portray Elijah and the famous chariot of fire, King David with his harp, the saints of the order, the prophets Isaiah, Ezekiel and David, and the Holy Family with the four evangelists below. The cupola's base bears two texts from the Old Testament used in the mass service. The stained-glass windows portray Elijah in the desert, elevated in the chariot. The statue of Mary was made in two parts – the head in Genoa, Italy, in 1820, and the body about 100 years later, from Lebanese cedar.

A small adjoining museum contains ruins of former Mount Carmel cloisters dating from Byzantine and Crusader times. The museum is open daily from 8.30 am to 1.30 pm, and 3 to 6 pm. Admission is free.

Egged bus Nos 25 and 26 from Hadar and No 31 from Central Carmel stop nearby.

To walk down to Elijah's Cave, cross the car park to the left of the coastguard/military installation and follow the track. The convent of the Carmelites' female order is on Tchernichovsky St, around the corner from the monastery, and is closed to the public.

Sculpture Garden

This garden, by the junction of HaZiyonut Blvd, features bronze sculptures by Ursula Malbin.

Baha'i Shrine & Gardens

Haifa's most impressive attraction is the golden-domed Shrine of the Bab which is in the middle of the beautifully manicured Persian Gardens. It contains the tomb of the Bab, the man who is called the Martyr-Herald and the Forerunner of Baha'ism.

The shrine, completed in 1953, combines the style and proportions of European architecture with designs inspired by the Orient. It is constructed of Chiampo stone cut and carved in Italy, with monolithic columns of Rose Baveno granite.

The 12,000 eye-catching fish-scale tiles

Baha'i Shrine of the Bab

were made in the Netherlands by a process of fire glazing over gold leaf.

Take Egged bus No 22 from the central bus station, or Nos 23, 25, 26 and 32 from HaNevi'im or Herzl Sts (in Hadar) stop outside. The shrine is open daily 9 am to noon, with the gardens remaining open until 5 pm. Admission is free, but remove your shoes before entering.

Universal House of Justice

On the other side of HaZiyonut Blvd and higher up the hill, this impressive white marble building with a colonnade of 58 Corinthian columns, houses the nine Baha'is who form the co-ordinating body of all the faith's activities. They are elected by secret ballot every five years by members of the National Spiritual Assemblies of the Baha'is worldwide. Closed to the public, the building faces the Shrine of Baha'u'llah in Bahje, near Akko across the bay, and in its garden stand four Carrara marble monuments erected over the tombs of some of Baha'u'llah's relatives.

International Baha'i Archives

Another attractive construction in the Ionic style of classical Greek architecture, this is a private museum of Baha'i relics and historical material. Built of Chiampo stone from Italy with green roof tiles from the Netherlands, it, too, is closed to the public.

Mane Katz Museum

Mane Katz, an influential artist of the Paris Jewish Expressionist group, left his studio, works and collection to the city of Haifa where he spent the last years of his life. The museum (☎ 83482), at 89 Ye'fe Nof St, near the Dan Carmel Hotel, is open Sunday to Thursday 10 am to 1 pm and 4 to 6 pm, 10 am to 1 pm Saturday, and is closed Friday. Admission is free.

Tikotin Museum of Japanese Art

This museum (☎ 383554), at 89 HaNassi Ave, was established in 1959 after Felix Tikotin of the Netherlands donated his private collection of Japanese art to the city of Haifa. Exhibits include over 7000 items such as paintings, woodblock prints, drawings, lacquer work, metals and ceramics of both ancient and modern Japan.

The museum is open Sunday to Thursday 10 am to 5 pm, Saturday 10 am to 2 pm, and is closed Friday. Admission is US$2.50 (students US$1.80), and it is free on Saturday.

Gan Ha'em (Mother's Park), Zoo & Museum

With a small amphitheatre and an arcade of cafés, bars and shops, the park is particularly popular with the locals on Saturday. At its northern end is the zoo and museum complex (☎ 337833).

The zoo features animals indigenous to Israel, and the M Stekelis Museum of Prehistory, the Natural History Museum and the Biological Institute deal with aspects of the area's history and flora & fauna. The complex is open Sunday to Thursday 8 am to 4 pm, Friday 8 am to 1 pm, and Saturday 9 am to 4 pm (July to August – Sunday to Thursday 8 am to 6 pm). Admission is US$2, but it is less for students and children.

Haifa Museum

The Haifa Museum (☎ 523325), at 26 Shabtai Levi St, Hadar, is three museums in one. The **Museum of Ancient Art** includes sculpture, Egyptian textiles, Greek pottery, decorated oil lamps, terracotta figurines and coins from the time of the First Revolt against the Romans, items recovered from the sea off Haifa, and various exhibits from excavations. The **Museum of Modern Art** includes late 18th-century collections and contemporary Israeli paintings, sculptures, graphics and photographs; also graphic works by world- renowned artists from Europe, America and South-East Asia. The **Museum of Music & Ethnology** changes its exhibitions and displays musical instruments clothing, crafts and jewellery.

All three are open Saturday to Thursday from 10 am to 1 pm, also 6 to 9 pm Tuesday, Thursday and Saturday, and are closed Friday. Admission is US$2.50 (students US$1.80), free on Saturdays.

Chagall Artists' House

Works of contemporary Israeli artists are exhibited here, at 24 HaZiyonut Blvd on the corner of Herzlia St in Hadar (☎ 522355). The house is open Sunday to Thursday 10 am to 1 pm, and 4 to 7 pm, Saturday from 10 am to 1 pm, and is closed Friday. Admission is free.

Beit HaGefen Arab-Israeli Cultural Centre

This centre (☎ 525252) sponsors joint Arab-Jewish social activities, and could be worth a visit – check to see if there are any social events or lectures during your stay. It's in Hadar on the corner of HaGefen St and HaZiyonut Blvd.

Technodea Museum

Its full title is the National Museum of Science & Technology. On Balfour St in Hadar (☎ 671372), it specialises in interactive displays mainly aimed at the younger generation.

The museum is open Monday, Wednesday and Thursday 9 am to 5 pm, Tuesday 9 am to 7 pm, Friday 9 am to 1 pm, Saturday 10 am to 2 pm, and is closed Sunday. Admission is US$3.20 (students US$2.50). Walk uphill on Balfour St from Herzl St and it's on the right, opposite No 15.

Technion

The Technodea Museum is on the old campus of the Technion, Israel's leading technological institute. Built in 1912, this was the first building in Hadar, and was initially known as the Technion quarter. The Turkish-style building houses the school of architecture, while Technion City in Newe Sha'anan comprises other departments such as electrical and soil engineering, chemistry, building research, aeronautics and physics.

The Coler-California Visitors' Centre presents the history and achievements of the institute. There are films and exhibits of the institute's work, including the Lavi fighter plane, a laser disc video module, a laser hologram and a robot.

Just before WW I the Technion saw a bitter

controversy over the usage of modern Hebrew. Some of the school's German founders insisted that German was the only language suitable for teaching science. The students disagreed, refused to study, and eventually won.

It's open Sunday to Thursday 8.30 am to 2 pm, Friday 8.30 am to noon, and closed Saturday (☎ 293863, 210664).

To reach Technion City take Egged bus Nos 17 or 19 from the central bus station, No 19 from Herzl St, Hadar, or No 31 from Carmel.

Haifa University

On the summit of Mount Carmel with the best views of Haifa and far beyond, the modern university campus is dominated by the 25-storey Eshkol Tower. Designed by the renowned architect Niemeyer, it features a top-floor observatory and a museum in the basement. The Reuben & Edith Hecht Museum houses a collection of archaeological artefacts relating to Jewish history before the Diaspora.

The museum is open Saturday to Thursday 10 am to 1 pm, Tuesday also 4 to 6 pm, and is closed Friday.

Admission is free, and free guided tours of the museum are given Sunday to Thursday at noon, on Tuesday also at 5 pm, and on Saturday at 11.30 am. Free guided tours of the campus are available Sunday to Thursday between 8 am and 1 pm. On arrival, dial 2093 or 2097 on the internal telephone system to speak with the Public Affairs Department.

Take Egged bus No 92 from the central bus station, or Nos 24 or 37 from Herzl St, Hadar. Alternatively, walk the steep 20-minute climb from downtown.

Dagon Grain Silo

Not quite what most people come to Israel to see, but this grain silo might be worth a visit. The distinctive fortress-like construction at Pulmer Square on Ha'Atzmaut St near the port is the country's tallest industrial building. You can take a free guided tour of the plant to learn something about the other oldest profession: the cultivation, handling, storing and distribution of grain. There is also a small archaeological exhibit which is open to visitors only when the tours are given, which is Sunday to Friday at 10.30 am. It's closed Saturday.

Take Egged bus Nos 10, 12 or 22 to get to the silo.

Railway Museum
Housed in the old Haifa East railway station (☎ 531211 ext 2347), opposite 40 Hativat Golani Rd, in Ottoman buildings, the new museum features a collection of stamps, photographs, tickets, timetables and artefacts connected with the railways of this region. Rolling stock on display includes a 1922 saloon car and an 1893 coach brought from Egypt at the end of WW I and used as an ambulance by the British.

Old timetables remind you that you could at one time travel from here by train to Cairo via Qantara on the Sinai Peninsula, or head off to Beirut, Damascus or Amman.

The museum is open Sunday to Thursday 9 am to noon, and is closed Friday and Saturday. Admission is free.

Carmel National Park
Israel's largest national park covers the scenic southern slopes of Mount Carmel; it's known to locals as Shveytsaria HaK'tana (Little Switzerland). Renowned for its fertility, vineyards covered the area in ancient times and the name Carmel is derived from the Hebrew Kerem-El (Vineyard of God). For some pleasant walking or for a picnic, take Egged bus No 92 from the central bus station, Herzl St in Hadar or Central Carmel – when you see a nice spot, tell the driver that you want to get off.

Places to Stay – bottom end
There's not much to choose from, and most travellers end up at the pleasant and friendly *Bethel Hostel* (☎ 521110), 40 HaGefen St, west of Ben-Gurion Blvd. Take Egged bus No 22, get off at the first stop on HaGefen St, walk back past Ben-Gurion Blvd and it's on your right. It's quiet, comfortable and

very clean, with a strong Christian emphasis, and dorm beds cost US$8. There are no private rooms nor a kitchen, but there's a nice lounge with tea & coffee-making facilities, and a garden with basketball and table tennis. There's a reliable 7 am wake-up call, and everyone has to be out of the dorms by 9 am.

The hostel stays closed until 5 pm (4.30 pm Friday), although the lounge and garden remain open. Check-in is from 5 to 10 pm (Friday 4 to 9 pm) and there's a strict 11 pm curfew.

The *Carmel Youth Hostel – IYHA* (☎ 531944), at the south-western approach to the city, was closed and being used to house Soviet immigrants at the time of writing. If it is open by the time you reach Haifa, you might find it too isolated from the city anyway, but it is just across from the free beach.

Other factors not in its favour are the frequency of muggings in the area after dark, the absence of food shops or eating places nearby and its proximity to a cemetery. Egged bus No 43 goes right to the hostel from the central bus station about every hour and the equally frequent bus No 45 will drop you off on the main road nearby.

An often overlooked alternative is the peaceful *St Charles Hospice* (☎ 523705), 105 Jaffa Rd, which is owned by the Latin Patriarchate and run by the Rosary Sisters. It is housed in a beautiful building with rooms that are simple but comfortably furnished, has a lovely garden, and the place is kept spotlessly clean by the nuns. Dorm beds are US$13, singles/doubles US$15/28, and all include breakfast; curfew is at 10 pm.

Places to Stay – middle
Haifa's more expensive hotels are mostly spread between Hadar and Central Carmel. The latter provides the more pleasant surroundings, which compensates for it being further away from the central area.

Hadar At the basic but comfortable *Nesher Hotel* (☎ 640644), 53 Herzl St, singles cost from US$22 to US$25, and doubles from US$32 to US$37. Nearby, the *Hotel Talpiot*

(☎ 673753), 61 Herzl St, is more basic and the slightly less comfortable singles cost from US$18 to US$20, doubles from US$26 to US$29.

The *Hotel Carmelia* (☎ 521278/9), 35 Herzlia St, corner of HaZiyonut Blvd, is a nice-looking place, with a bar, dining room and patio. Singles/doubles cost from US$45/55.

Central Carmel The *Dvir Hotel* (☎ 389131; fax 381068), 124 Ye'fe Nof St, (Panorama Rd) is run by the Dan hotel group's training department and so the service is better than usual. The views are pleasant and the surroundings comfortable. Singles cost from US$44 to US$70. *Beth Shalom Guesthouse* (☎ 337481/2; fax 372443), at 110 HaNassi Ave, has singles/doubles for US$29/40. It's a comfortable German Protestant-run 'evangelical guesthouse', open to all, and provides good hotel-style facilities; book ahead as it's often full.

Vered HaCarmel (☎ 389236), 1 Heinrich Heine Square, is four blocks south of the Haifa Auditorium. Head along Moriah Blvd, turn down HaMayim St, the small street on the right. It's nice, in a quiet location and has a pretty garden terrace. Singles/doubles are US$32/40.

Going up a bit in style and price, the *Shulamit Hotel* (☎ 3242811; fax 255206), 15 Qiryat Sefer St, is further along Moriah Blvd. Singles cost from US$47 to US$55, and doubles from US$65 to US$78.

The *Marom Hotel* (☎ 254355), at 51 HaPalmach St, is further away from the centre of things; singles/doubles here cost US$32/45.

Places to Stay – top end
The *Dan Panorama Hotel* (☎ 352222; fax 352235) with its twin towers, dominates HaNassi Ave. Singles cost from US$78 to US$98, and doubles from US$92 to US$112. The top-price rooms have views over the city and the Mediterranean below.

The *Dan Carmel* (☎ 386211; fax 387504), at 87 HaNassi Blvd, is the city's top luxury hotel. Singles cost from US$102 to US$188,

and doubles from US$122 to US$208. At 101 HaNassi Ave, the *Nof Hotel* (☎ 354311; fax 388810) provides four-star comforts in the shadow of its five-star competition. Singles cost US$70 to US$100, and doubles from US$85 to US$120.

Places to Eat
Markets & Food Stores For the cheapest fruit and vegetables, shop at the market on Nahum Dobrin St, between Ha'Atzmaut and Nathenson Sts in the Wadi Nisnas Arab Quarter, west of Hadar. It operates Monday to Saturday and is closed Sunday. There's a small Jewish market near Paris Square, between Nahum Dobrin and Nathan Sts, open Sunday to Friday, and closed Saturday.

Khouri St in Wadi Nisnas has a couple of Arab groceries selling a wide range of foodstuffs. They're open Monday to Saturday, and closed on Sunday.

Felafel, Shwarma & Bakeries Apart from the Baha'i Shrine & Persian Gardens, one of Haifa's major attractions must be its street food, which is cheap, delicious and readily available. In particular, head for the corner of HaNevi'im and HeHalutz Sts where some of the country's best felafel is sold, alongside bakeries producing some delicious ring doughnuts, sticky buns and other delights. The bakery right on the corner seems to be the best of all.

Another felafel favourite is *Avraham, King of Felafel* (no English sign) at 36 Allenby St by Ziyonut St. For great shwarma, head for *Nimer, King of Shwarma*, 136 Jaffa St, some 200 metres north of the central bus station.

Cafés There are several pleasant *konditereis* (pastry shops and cafés combined) around Hadar. The *Ritz Conditoria*, 5 Haim St near Herzl St, is different to the rest. It serves draught beer and provides complimentary newspapers, and has an art gallery on the premises. It's open Sunday to Thursday 7.30 am to 11 pm, Friday 7.30 am to 3 pm, and closed Saturday.

Another nice spot for coffee, cake, and

salads which is open daily is the *Bank Café*, across from Gan Ha'em on HaNassi Ave, Central Carmel. On pedestrianised Nordau St, *Lehem*, at No 28, serves good coffee and cakes.

For juice, check out the popular *Beit HaPri* (House of Fruit) on Shemaryahu Levin St, corner of Herzl St (no English sign so look for the snowflake sign). This juice bar whisks up a variety of tasty shakes for about US$1.20, although you could sometimes die of thirst waiting to be served.

Restaurants – cheaper The Egged self-service restaurant at the central bus station provides the usual value for money, and there are several fast-food outlets at the station, too. In the market area by Paris Square are two fairly decent and inexpensive restaurants. At *Naim's*, 6 Eliyahu HaNavi St, you can eat well for about US$5 on soup and hummus, and spend a little more on grilled meat and offal. It's open Sunday to Thursday till 6 pm, Friday till 3 pm, and is closed Saturday. *Restaurant Shichmona*, 3 Nahum Dobrin St, has more of the same.

In Hadar, head for 30 Herzl St and *Haim Tzimhonia Vegetarian Restaurant – Dairy Farm Food*, only the latter part of which is written in English. Here you will find plain but tasty vegetarian dishes served in a fairly busy, though unexciting, atmosphere. You can eat for as little as US$3. The restaurant is open Sunday to Thursday 8 am to 9 pm, Friday 8 am to 2 pm, and is closed Saturday.

The *Balfour Cellar & Restaurant*, 3 Balfour St, up from Herzl St, is an old favourite, serving Ashkenazi dishes. A self-service snack bar keeps prices down, but you can eat in the restaurant for US$6 to US$15. It is open Sunday to Thursday, noon to 6 pm, Friday noon to 3 pm, and is closed Saturday.

Benny's, 23 HeHalutz St, is a sparse but clean oriental restaurant with hummus and other salads for US$5, and grilled meats from US$8.

In one of Hadar's nicest spots, *Beiteinu*, 29 Jerusalem St, inside the William Green Cultural Centre, is a self-service restaurant providing salads and Ashkenazi fare, but at lunch time only. It is open Sunday to Thursday, noon to 9 pm, Friday noon to 2 pm, and is closed Saturday. You can eat well for US$7.

Up in Central Carmel, *Ristorante Italiano* 121 HaNassi St, is a decent family-run place with pasta favourites and Middle Eastern dishes; US$5 to US$15. *Bagel Nash* at the intersection of HaNassi Ave and Wedgewood St, provides some decent options in the US$4 to US$8 range. This is open daily from 8 am to 10 pm.

Check out the two Technion campuses and Haifa University for the cheap food in their student cafeterias.

Restaurants – more expensive The port area has some decent food joints. One of the better places is the popular *Shmulik & Dany Restaurant* (☎ 514411), 7 HaBankim St, off Jaffa Rd about four blocks north-west of Paris Square. Interestingly decorated with Israeli art, it serves roasts and grills. Open for lunch only, Sunday to Friday, and closed Saturday, meals cost about US$18 per person.

Closer to Paris Square are a few Arab restaurants. Perhaps the best of these is *Abu Yusuf's* (☎ 663723) on the corner. The sign is only in Arabic and Hebrew, so look for the large windows and arches. Yusuf's is open daily, 7 am to midnight. You can eat a little or a lot from the wide selection of hummus, foul, kubbe, grilled meat, offal or fish. People tend to spend anything from US$8 to US$18 here for a full meal.

In Hadar, another decent Arab establishment, though more expensive, is the *Peer Amran Brothers Restaurant* (☎ 6657070) at 1 Atlit St, the third street to the left down HaNevi'im St from Masaryk Square. Luckily the food tastes a lot better than the attempt to create plush surroundings might suggest and you can expect to pay about US$18 per person. It is open daily from 7 am to midnight.

The best of Haifa's Rumanian restaurants is *Leon & Ioji Gratar Romanesc* (☎ 538073) at 31 HaNevi'im St, on the corner of Emek HaZetim St. It doesn't look much, but it deserves its reputation and you can eat well here for about US$15 per person. It is open daily for lunch and dinner until 11 pm.

The *Dvir Hotel* (☎ 389131), up in Central Carmel at 124 Ye'fe Nof St, serves a good set dinner for US$18 in its dining room (closed Friday). Being the Dan hotel group's training school, the food and service are of a high standard and you can enjoy the view of the city lights as you eat.

Bars A pleasant little bar is the pub-like establishment on Herzlia St, corner of HaNevi'im St – it has no English sign. This is one of the cheapest places to drink in Haifa, and you are given free pretzels to munch. Nearby is the *Studio 46* bar at 46 Pevsner St. Another pleasant drinking spot I found was up in Gan Ha'em at the *Garden* restaurant-bar-café (no English sign) in the arcade there.

Among bars in the port area are the suitably sleazy *London Pride*, at 85 Ha'Atzmaut Rd and *The Pub*, at 102 Ha'Atzmaut Rd. *Al-Pasha*, on Hammam al-Pasha St features energetic live music on some evenings.

Entertainment

Haifa is not renowned for its entertainment scene, but there are, however, usually a few things to do. Get a copy of the free leaflet, *Events in the Haifa & Northern Region*, from the tourist office. You can also dial 640840 after 4 pm for a recorded message listing that evening's events and the *Jerusalem Post* will include some of those details.

As anywhere else in Israel, people come out in the evening to stroll around. In Haifa, Panorama Rd (Ye'fe Nof St) enjoys a great view of the city and harbour lights. Also in Central Carmel, Gan Ha'em usually attracts a crowd, as do the shops further up HaNassi Ave. Bat Gallim Promenade, along the seafront, is also popular for an evening stroll. Hadar's felafel and ice-cream parlours along HaNevi'im and HeHalutz Sts, and the pedestrianised Nordau St, are usually busy too.

Cinemas Most cinemas feature current US and other imports, with a few Israeli films.

Amphitheatre 43 HeHalutz St, Hadar (☎ 664018)
Armon 18 HaNevi'im St, Hadar – just below the fountain (☎ 664848)
Atzmon 30 HaNevi'im St, Hadar (☎ 663003)
Chen 7 Shabtai Levi St, Hadar (☎ 666272)
Cinemateque 142 HaNassi Ave, Central Carmel in the Haifa Auditorium with a good selection of movie classics and oddities (☎ 347424)
Karen Or Hamehudesh 67 Herzl St, Hadar, entrance on Sokoloff St around the corner (☎ 663443)
Moriah Moriah St, Central Carmel (☎ 242477)
Orah 41 Herzl St, Hadar (☎ 664017)
Orly 4 Mahayanim St, Central Carmel (☎ 381868)
Peer Atlit St, Hadar – off HaNevi'im St (☎ 662232)
Rav Gat 1 & 2 Solel Boneh Square, Hadar – at the bottom of HaNevi'im St (☎ 646969)
Ron 67 HeHalutz St, Hadar (☎ 669069)

Theatres The Haifa Municipal Theatre, at the intersection of Pevsner, Trumpeldor and Yehoshua Sts in Hadar, presents regular performances in Hebrew. The nearby Zafit Café-Theatre (☎ 253641), at 23 Jerusalem St, corner of Ha'im St, is another drama venue. There is also usually a chamber music concert here at 5 pm on Saturdays.

Music & Dance The Haifa Auditorium, 142 HaNassi Ave, Central Carmel, is where the Israel Philharmonic perform in Haifa, and other classical concerts and opera are also staged here. The Al-Pasha (☎ 671309), Hammam al-Pasha St, just south of the main post office on Ha'Atzmaut St in the port area, regularly features Israeli folk singers and can be a lively spot – dancing on the tables and all that. In Central Carmel, the Rothschild Centre (☎ 382749), next door to the Haifa Auditorium, has folk dancing some evenings, as does the Newe Sha'anan campus of the Technion and the Haifa University. The students here also have regular film shows and discos.

Of the nightclubs, *Club 120* (☎ 382979), 120 Ye'fe Nof St, Central Carmel, seems to be the most popular. There is usually a cover charge (around US$3), and on Friday and Saturday it's packed. Women are admitted free Monday and Wednesday. Dado Beach is often a venue for free disco dancing from 8 pm until midnight on summer evenings.

What to do on Shabbat in Haifa

Timing a visit to Haifa to coincide with Shabbat is not a bad idea, as it is still possible to 'do' many of the sights. This is mainly due to the city's liberal approach to Jewish religious law, highlighted by the fact that some Egged buses actually operate throughout the day.

In the city itself, you have plenty of options, several of them free, to keep you busy on Saturday. The Baha'i Shrine & Gardens and the Haifa, Mane Katz, Japanese Art and National Maritime museums are all open in the morning – admission is free.

Then there is the free guided walking tour. Or take Egged bus No 23 from HaNevi'im St in Hadar up to Central Carmel where Gan Ha'em, the zoo, the museums and the café and restaurants are all open. In good weather the beaches are packed – Egged bus No 40 runs from Hadar.

The Arab market and grocers in Wadi Nisnas stay open, as do some of the felafel merchants, bakeries and cafés along HaNevi'im and HeHalutz Sts in Hadar.

There are also a couple of options for a Shabbat excursion from Haifa: to Akko, about 40 minutes away, and to the villages of Isfiya and Daliyat al-Karmel. Shabbat is the busiest day of the week for these two Druze villages with crowds of Israelis coming along to see the locals, their market and the nearby Mukhraqa Monastery. Sheruts operate from Eliyahu St, north of Paris Square in the port area.

Getting There & Away

For thousands of ferry and cruise-ship passengers, Haifa is the first port of call on a visit to Israel. Most of the city's other visitors arrive from Tel Aviv, Jerusalem or Tiberias, although there are bus services to several other areas. Haifa is also the original home of the country's railway network.

Air Arkia depart from the airport in the east of Haifa, which is in the industrial zone.

Flights connect directly with Eilat, with further connections to Tel Aviv and Jerusalem.

Bus The central bus station, on Jaffa Rd in the Bat Gallim neighbourhood of the port area, has inter-urban buses arriving and departing on the north side, and local buses operating from the south side. You can obtain bus information by phoning ☎ 515221.

The Jerusalem bus costs US$5.50, takes about two hours and departs every hour; there are extra services at peak times. The Tel Aviv bus costs US$3, takes about an hour and departs at least every hour; more frequently at peak times.

Buses for Akko and Nahariya depart from Daniel St, Hadar, as well as from the central bus station. Egged bus No 271 goes to Nahariya via Akko; No 251 goes to Akko only. The fare to Akko is US$1.25 and the bus takes 40 minutes; to Nahariya it is US$1.80 and a 55-minute ride.

Egged bus No 331 leaves from the central bus station while the more frequent Arab bus No 331 leaves from Paris Square.

The 'Department of Losses & Belongings Keepings' is opposite platform 10 in the central bus station – it's open Sunday to Thursday 8 am to 3 pm, Friday 8 am to 1 pm, and is closed Saturday.

Sherut Amal sheruts (☎ 66234, 522828) to Tel Aviv depart from 157 Jaffa Rd, next to the central bus station and from HeHalutz St, up from HaNevi'im St, from 6 am to late at night each day. Aryeh (☎ 673666) run a service to Tel Aviv from 9 Beerwald St in Hadar, and Aviv (☎ 666333) from 10 Nordau St in the same suburb; both cost around US$3.

Aviv and Amal both provide services to Jerusalem, but you need to book.

Kavei HaGalil (☎ 664442) to Akko and Nahariya depart from 16 HaNevi'im St in Hadar and from Kikkar Plumer St by the Dagon grain silo in the port area. The trip should cost about US$2.50.

The trip to Isfiya and Daliyat al-Karmel should cost around US$1.25 and sheruts

(☎ 664640) depart from the corner of Shemaryahu Levin and Herzl Sts and from Eliyahu St, down from Paris Square near the corner of Derekh Ha'Atzmaut in the port area. There are frequent services except on Friday when most shops and businesses in the Druze villages are closed.

The sherut to Nazareth also departs from Eliyahu St near the intersection with Derekh Ha'Atzmaut and costs around US$2.50. Departures are not as frequent as those to Tel Aviv, Akko and the Druze villages.

Train Haifa has three railway stations. Bat Gallim, the central railway station, is adjacent to the central bus station – take the underground passage next to bus platform 33. The old or Plumer Square railway station is between the ferry port entrance and the Dagon grain silo. The east railway station is further east along Derekh Hativat Golani. For train information, telephone ☎ 521211. The Jerusalem train leaves the central railway station at 7 am Sunday to Friday, and services to Tel Aviv leave almost every hour.

Hitchhiking For Tel Aviv, stand on Haganah Blvd at the intersection outside the central bus station. For Akko, stand on Histradrut Blvd at the intersection with Y'Israel Bar-Yehuda Rd, on the way out of the city centre towards the industrial zone. For Nazareth and the Galilee, stand by the same intersection but on Y'Israel Bar-Yehuda Rd.

Getting Around
Bus The main city bus routes (all Egged) are:

Baha'i Shrine & Gardens
    No 22 from the central bus station, and Nos 23, 25 and 26 from HaNevi'im and Herzl Sts, Hadar
Beaches
    No 44 from Allenby Rd, near the Bethel Hostel, to the free Carmel Beach
Bethel Hostel
    No 22 from the central bus station
Central Carmel
    No 24 from the central bus station and Herzl St, Hadar, and No 37, also from Herzl St
Hadar
    Nos 6, 19, 21, 24, 28 and 51 from the central bus station to Herzl St

University
    From the central bus station No 24 via Herzl and Arlosoroff Sts, Hadar, and No 37 via Arlosoroff St, Hadar, and Central Carmel

Carmelit Subway Closed several years ago for renovations, conflicting rumours suggest that Israel's only subway system will or will not reopen. The Carmelit provided an interesting, albeit limited, alternative to the bus service. Opened in 1959, the subway was built by a French company – Paris Square was named in their honour. Only 1800 metres long with six stations, its one line runs from Paris Square in the port area, straight up through Hadar to Central Carmel along the line drawn by HaNevi'im St (a rise of 275 metres). The six stations are:

1 Paris Square – lower station, port area.
2 Solel Boneh – near Khouri and Hasan Shukri Sts.
3 HaNevi'im – Shabtai Levi St, Hadar.
4 Massada – Massada St.
5 Eliezer Golomb – Eliezer Golomb St.
6 Gan Ha'em – upper station, Central Carmel.

DRUZE VILLAGES
The villages of Isfiya and Daliyat al-Karmel, on the slopes of Mount Carmel, are a popular attraction for Israelis as well as foreign visitors, providing an opportunity to observe and meet the Druze people and to wander around and shop in their village. The Druze have a reputation for being incredibly friendly and hospitable, and being invited into a house for tea or coffee and a bite to eat is not unusual.

The male elders are instantly recognisable by their thick moustaches, distinctive robes and Fez-style hat covered by a turban. Other religious Druze often sport a moustache, cropped hair and a flat, coloured hat. There are many Druze men, however, who choose to wear Western-style clothes, and look no different from Arabs or oriental Jews. Most of the women still wear the traditional long dark dress and white headscarf.

On Saturday, Israelis pour into the area and on Friday many places are closed. Visit during the week to have a chance of meeting the locals and to be able to get a seat in one of the restaurants.

Isfiya
(Population: 6600)

Built on the ancient Jewish village of Huseifa, Isfiya is the nearest of the two villages to Haifa (21 km). Although the town houses the now rather unimpressive remains of a 5th to 6th-century synagogue, the main interest in Isfiya is the Druze themselves. Rosh HaCarmel, the mount's highest peak, is nearby, and scenic views can be enjoyed in most directions.

Places to Stay The *Stella Carmel Hospice & Christian Conference Centre* (☎ 391692), is on the outskirts of the village. Originally built as an Arab hotel, it is in an idyllic setting and provides clean and comfortable accommodation in a quiet atmosphere. Dorm beds are US$10 (with breakfast), US$14 (half board), and US$20 (full board). Rooms cost from US$16 (with breakfast), US$20 (half board), and US$24 (full board). It is often full, so call ahead. The sherut from Haifa will drop you off on request.

Daliyat al-Karmel
(Population: 8800)

A few minutes' drive from Isfiya, Daliyat al-Karmel is the larger of the two towns and the last stop for buses and sheruts from Haifa. Although the market attracts a large number of visitors, I was disappointed by the high prices and the lack of locally produced goods on sale.

Beit Oliphant At the end of the main street, this was the home of the Christian Zionists Sir Lawrence Oliphant and his wife between 1882 and 1887. The Oliphants were among the few non-Druze to have a close relationship with the sect, and did much to help the community. In the garden is a cave where they hid insurgents from the authorities. The house was recently renovated and is now a memorial to the many Druze members of the IDF.

Mukhraqa About four km south of Daliyat al-Karmel is one of the country's most renowned viewpoints, the Carmelite Monastery of St Elijah, built to commemorate Elijah's showdown with the 421 prophets of Ba'al (I Kings 17-19). Climb to the roof of the monastery to enjoy the great views across the patchwork of fields of the Jezreel Valley.

The monastery is open from Monday to

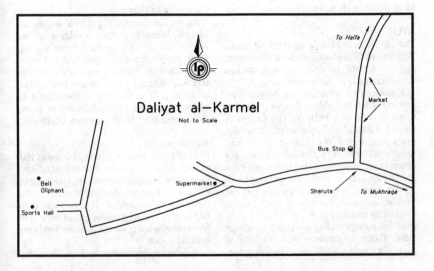

Daliyat al–Karmel
Not to Scale

Saturday 8 am to 1.30 pm and 2.30 to 5 pm, and Sunday 8 am to 1.30 pm only. Admission is US$0.45. There is no public transport so you have to walk/hitchhike from Daliyat al-Karmel. Bear left at the signposted junction or else you will end up miles away and be part of the view that you are meant to be admiring.

Getting There & Away

The Druze villages are a convenient day trip from Haifa. Egged bus Nos 92 and 93 run infrequently, Sunday to Thursday, from the central bus station and go via Herzl St, Hadar and Central Carmel. They take about 40 minutes to do the journey. However, the sheruts are far more frequent, run on Saturday, are more comfortable, take half the time and are actually a bit cheaper. They leave continually all day till about 5 pm from Eliyahu St, on the corner of Ha'Atzmaut St, in the port area.

Returning to Haifa, the sheruts become less frequent after about 5 pm and you run the risk of either a long wait for a stretch-Mercedes to fill up, or of being forced to pay more for a special taxi. The last bus back to Haifa leaves Daliyat al-Karmel at about 3.15 pm. Buses and sheruts pass through Isfiya en route between Haifa and Daliyat al-Karmel.

ATLIT

The old Haifa to Hadera coastal road passes Atlit and its Crusader ruins about 16 km from Haifa – in fact, in 1291, this was the last Crusader castle to fall to the Arabs.

Known in Latin as Castrum Pergrinorum and in French as Château Pelerin (Pilgrims' Castle), Atlit was built by the Crusaders around 1200. British-sponsored archaeologists excavated the site in 1930 and uncovered not only Crusader relics but others from the Persian, Hellenistic and Phoenician periods as well. An earthquake in 1837 seriously damaged the castle and the Turkish authorities removed much of the crumbling masonry to Akko and Jaffa to be used for reconstructing damaged buildings there. Today the castle is off-limits as it is part of a naval installation. The camp was originally built by the British to detain illegal Jewish immigrants.

EN HOD

Inland from Atlit, En Hod is an artists' village established in 1953 on the site of an abandoned Arab village. Founded by painter Marcel Janco (who was also one of the founders of the Dadaist movement), En Hod – meaning Well of Beauty – operates as a sort of cooperative.

The current site was designed and developed by painters, sculptors and potters who decided that this would be an ideal setting in which to live and work. They succeeded in turning it into an established artists' colony although many say that today's products are disappointing.

There are various working studios and Israelis come here to learn such skills as ceramics, weaving and drawing. The studios are mainly closed to casual visitors but there are some things to see.

En Hod Gallery

This exhibits works by the residents – it's open daily from 9.30 am to 5 pm; admission is US$0.45.

Janco-Dado Museum

This museum mainly exhibits works by Marcel Janco but other residents of the colony are also represented. From the top floor porch you can appreciate the view down towards Atlit – it was views such as this that inspired Janco to settle here. The museum is open Saturday to Thursday 9.30 am to 5 pm, and Friday 9.30 am to 4 pm. Admission is US$0.80 (students US$0.40).

Beit Gertrude

Next to the restaurant, a blue gate marks this small museum and memorial to past inhabitants of the village. This was the residence of Gertrude Krause, one of the founding members of the colony. The museum contains more locally produced artwork and hosts occasional concerts, lectures and other cultural events.

It is open September to June, Saturday

Top: Haifa panorama (NT)
Bottom: The port, Akko (NT)

Top: Mosque of el-Jazzar, Akko (TW)
Left: Baha'i Shrine of the Bab, Haifa (NT)
Right: Church of the Beatitudes, near Capernaum, Galilee (NT)

only from 11 am to 2 pm. At other times you can inquire at the En Hod Gallery and if they are not busy, they will let you in. Admission is free.

Roman Amphitheatre
Up the road from the restaurant, a small restored Roman amphitheatre is the venue for Israeli rock concerts on occasional Friday evenings.

Places to Eat
The *Artists' Inn Café* offers a variety of dairy dishes; they cost from US$5 to US$10.

Getting There & Away
Egged bus Nos 202, 222 and 922 go past the En Hod junction on the Haifa-Hadera coastal road. Buses are fairly frequent and the trip takes about 20 minutes from Haifa. From the junction, walk up the hill for about 10 minutes, and the village is on the right.

AROUND EN HOD
Yamin Orde
Just up the road past En Hod, the settlement of Yamin Orde commands pleasant views over the surrounding countryside and the sea.

Carmel Caves
These caves can be seen from the Haifa to Hadera road in a rocky gorge just to the north of Habonim (The Builders), a settlement founded by South African Jews.

In the 1930s British and US excavations uncovered relics indicating that the caves were inhabited during the Stone Age.

DOR
Still on the coast road, about 29 km south of Haifa, Dor is a modern settlement mainly populated by Greek Jews. It is next to the site of an ancient town and near the lovely sandy beach of Tantura.

Tel Dor
At the northern end of the beach, the ancient ruins of Dor are on a hill. The town probably dates as far back as the 15th century BC. It

was mentioned in an ancient Egyptian papyrus and was well known during King Solomon's reign. You can just about distinguish the ancient harbour and the fortress by the shore. There are Roman and Hellenistic remains and also the ruins of a 6th-century Byzantine church.

Tantura Beach
One of the country's loveliest and most peaceful beaches, it has four small, rocky islands which act as bird sanctuaries.

Places to Stay
The area is an ideal *campsite* and there are many appealing places to pitch a tent. Nearby is a *campsite* run by the Dor Moshav.

Getting There & Away
Take any of the several Egged buses going along the Haifa to Hadera road, and ask the driver to drop you off at Dor.

ZICHRON YA'ACOV
(Population: 7200)
About five km south-east of Dor, and renowned for its role in Israel's wine industry, Zichron Ya'acov (Jacob's Memorial), was established in 1882 by Rumanian Jews and is one of the first modern Zionist settlements.

Carmel Winery
From the bus station walk north (go out opposite the entry point) and turn left down Jabotinsky St, then turn right on HaNadiv St and the winery (☎ 90105) is signposted at the bottom of the slopes. Telephone to arrange a guided tour of the winery and a tasting session. Admission is US$0.80.

Aaronsohn House Museum
Aaron Aaronsohn was a noted agronomist and botanist who lived in Zichron Ya'acov, but he and his family were also leaders of the NILI network which spied on the Turks in WW I. Thus the museum not only houses his collection of Palestinian plants, but also tells the story of NILI.

It's open Sunday to Thursday 9.30 am to

1 pm, and is closed Friday and Saturday. Admission is US$1.25 (students US$0.80). Following Jabotinsky St down from the bus station, a paved pathway leads up to the left – the museum is up here on the right.

Rothschild Family Tomb

A beautifully designed garden surrounds the family tomb where the bodies of Baron and Baroness de Rothschild lie, having been brought over from France in 1954 aboard an Israeli warship and given a state funeral.

The setting is most appropriate: there are views across the Sharon Plain and the bordering mountains, the areas where their financial support helped establish several Jewish settlements, many of which are named after members of the Rothschild family. The tomb lies to the left just before the road approaches the town from the coast road.

Places to Eat

There is a small Egged *restaurant* at the bus station.

Getting There & Away

From Haifa take Egged bus Nos 202 or 222; from Netanya, Nos 707 or 708; and from Tel Aviv, Nos 872, 876 or 877.

CAESAREA

Now one of the country's most important archaeological sites, Caesarea was the Roman capital of Judea for almost 600 years. During this time it became one of the Roman Empire's great trading ports, and was later a Crusader city. It was renowned for the splendour of its buildings and today you can visit the remains, which include the Roman amphitheatre, aqueduct and hippodrome, and the Crusader city.

Archaeologists have learnt much about Caesarea's colourful history. For many years, the ancient accounts of the construction of Caesarea's Roman harbour had been treated with scepticism because of the high standard of engineering that would have been required to build it. Until recently no trace of the 20-hectare harbour could be found and historians refused to believe that it existed. Today we know that those ancient accounts were accurate, and that Caesarea is indeed one of the greatest engineering achievements of all time.

History

Herod the Great established the city of Caesarea in about 22 BC on the site of a 3rd or 4th-century BC Phoenician settlement called Strato's Tower. Naming it after the Roman Emperor Augustus Caesar, Herod apparently set out to create the most advanced city imaginable. Recent archaeological research suggests that in the pursuit of this desire he became increasingly tyrannical. It is highly likely that Herod's despotic behaviour was further reinforced by remorse at having executed his first wife and his suffering from a painful disease. Those who even questioned, let alone disobeyed, his orders were often executed.

For several years, hundreds of builders and divers worked round the clock to complete the project. To create the two lofty breakwaters which stretched for 540 metres on the south side and 270 metres on the north, stones of 230 cubic metres were lowered into the open sea, a technique not too dissimilar to that used to construct Mulberry Harbour in the Allied invasion of Normandy in WW II. Towers bearing colossal statues marked the entrance, and there was a massive oil-fuelled lighthouse. On land, the city enjoyed an advanced sewage system and a grid street pattern as well as a temple dedicated to Caesar, a palace, a theatre and the amphitheatre. The exact size of Herod's city is not certain because no outer wall has yet been discovered.

Archaeologists are still diving in the area and the coins and artefacts they recover amid Caesarea's sunken ruins continue to increase our knowledge of the Roman Empire. Pottery fragments indicate the volume of trade, and the coins with their emperor's face and dates show how long the city continued as a trading centre in competition with the better known Alexandria.

Caesarea became the local Roman capital

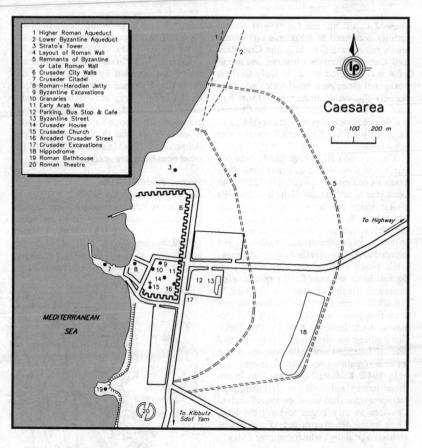

1 Higher Roman Aqueduct
2 Lower Byzantine Aqueduct
3 Strato's Tower
4 Layout of Roman Wall
5 Remnants of Byzantine
  or Late Roman Wall
6 Crusader City Walls
7 Crusader Citadel
8 Roman–Herodian Jetty
9 Byzantine Excavations
10 Granaries
11 Early Arab Wall
12 Parking, Bus Stop & Cafe
13 Byzantine Street
14 Crusader House
15 Crusader Church
16 Arcaded Crusader Street
17 Crusader Excavations
18 Hippodrome
19 Roman Bathhouse
20 Roman Theatre

Caesarea

0   100   200 m

To Highway

MEDITERRANEAN
SEA

To Kibbutz
Sdot Yam

after Herod's death, with Pontius Pilate residing here as prefect from 26 to 36 AD; an inscription bearing his name was found in the ruins of the theatre. Acts 10 in the Bible deals with Cornelius, a centurion of the Roman garrison here, who was the first Gentile converted to Christianity by Peter. Paul passed through the port several times on his missionary journeys and Acts 23-26 deal with these events.

A major cause of the First Revolt (66 to 70 AD) was the desecration of the synagogue here. Thousands of Jews were executed in Caesarea's amphitheatre when the Romans defeated the revolt. Later, after the defeat of the Bar Kochba Rebellion, the Romans used the amphitheatre to kill 10 Jewish sages.

At the beginning of the 3rd century a leading rabbinical school was founded which produced some of the top Talmudic intellectuals. In the 4th century a leading Christian theologian, the Greek Eusebius, was Bishop of Caesarea. He was the author of *Onomasticon*, the first biblical geography, invaluable in identifying many of the biblical sites.

After the city was taken by the Arabs in 640 it fell into disrepair. The harbour was allowed to silt up, but the coastal plain's fertility continued to make this one of the area's richest cities. In 1101 the Crusaders took Caesarea from the Muslims, and found what they believed to be the Holy Grail: a hexagonal green glass bowl which was supposedly the vessel from which Jesus had drunk at the Last Supper. Under the Crusaders, whose principal ports were at Akko and Jaffa, only a part of Herod's Caesarea was rehabilitated.

The city was to change hands between Arabs and Crusaders four times until King Louis IX of France captured it in 1251. That same year he added most of the fortifications visible today but he was defeated by the Mameluke Sultan Baybars in 1261. The inhabitants had hidden from their attackers in the citadel on the southern breakwater and escaped to Akko under the cover of darkness while peace negotiations were being conducted. In an apparent fit of pique at being deceived, Baybars destroyed the city. It remained deserted until 1878 when refugees from Bosnia (soon to become part of Yugoslavia) were installed here by the Turks. Their village was destroyed during the 1948 War of Independence with only the small mosque remaining beside the harbour.

In 1940, Kibbutz Sdot Yam was established nearby and during its first decade its members unearthed some remains of ancient Caesarea as they began to farm the land. Their initial discoveries led to a series of archaeological digs which continue today.

Orientation

Caesarea's remains spread along a three-km stretch of the Mediterranean coast about 3½ km from the old Haifa to Hadera road. Kibbutz Sdot Yam is at the southern end. North of here is the Roman amphitheatre, followed by the walled Crusader city with its citadel and harbour a half km further up the road. North of the Crusader city is Caesarea's oldest structure, Strato's Tower, and a km beyond that on the beach is the Roman aqueduct. Just inland from the Crusader city is the Byzantine street, behind the café and car park. Further inland, beside the road, is the

ruined Roman hippodrome. You will probably start from either the Roman amphitheatre or the Crusader city.

Caesarea's archaeological sites are maintained and operated by the National Parks Authority. Entrance to the Roman amphitheatre and the Crusader city is on the same ticket and there are ticket booths at both entrances. They open Saturday to Thursday 8 am to 6 pm, and Friday 8 am to 5 pm. Admission is US$3 (students US$2.30). The other sites have free access.

Roman Amphitheatre

Just beyond the ticket booth is a replica of the Pontius Pilate inscription. The original Herodian structure was modified and added to over the years: the semi-circular platform behind the stage was added in the 3rd century and the great wall with the two towers is part of a 6th-century Byzantine fortress built over

Roman statue at Caesarea

the amphitheatre's ruins. Unearthed in 1961, the amphitheatre is now used for concert performances.

Crusader City

Excavation continues here, as does the commercialisation of the complex, with a growing number of restaurants and souvenir shops.

To your right as you approach the ticket booth, you'll see that part of the guard tower has fallen into a moat, the work of Louis IX. Other visible defences include an L-shaped gate designed to slow down a charge, and the windows above where archers were stationed.

The cathedral was built over the site of Caesar's temple and was destroyed by the Arabs in 1291. Nearby are some Byzantine remains. Down by the harbour is the 19th-century mosque and the Crusader Citadel.

Jewish Quarter & Strato's Tower

Immediately to the north of the Crusader city wall is the Jewish Quarter with its 3rd to 5th-century synagogue remains. Also, foundations of houses from the Hellenistic period (4th to 2nd century BC) were found at the lowest level. The large wall in the sea below may have been part of the harbour.

Although it may seem logical to continue ·northwards up the beach to see the Roman aqueducts, it is easier to backtrack via the road past the Roman hippodrome and take the road to the left from there.

Byzantine St

In amongst the trees to the east of the Crusader city's entrance, behind the café and car park, is an excavated Byzantine street with two 2nd or 3rd-century statues. Some steps lead down to the street where an inscription in the mosaic floor attributes it to Flavius Strategius, a 6th-century mayor. The statues originally belonged to temples and were unearthed by the ploughs of local kibbutzniks. The white marble figure is unidentified but the red porphyry one is perhaps Emperor Hadrian holding an orb and sceptre.

Hippodrome

About one km east (inland) from the Crusader city is the rectangular ploughed field which is the neglected hippodrome. The best way to find it is to look for the modern arch by the roadside. Possibly built by Herod (Caesarea's horse races were apparently world-famous in the 4th century), the racetrack could accommodate 20,000 spectators.

It is best to reach the Roman aqueducts by continuing eastwards (inland) from here; take the next left turn (north) to the section of beach where the aqueducts are located, as it will save you a more difficult walk along the beach from the Crusader city.

Roman Aqueduct

Although most of it has been buried by sand, the aqueduct is about 17 km long. Built by the Romans in the 2nd century, it carried water from mountain springs to Caesarea.

Beaches

There's a free beach south of the amphitheatre near the Kayet U'shait holiday village. Watch out for the 'No Bathing' signs – here the water is dangerously polluted by the kibbutz's factory. Even in the safe area you should watch out for tar from the oil tankers. Swimming at the beach near the amphitheatre costs around US$3.

Places to Stay

Accommodation here is expensive and while free camping is possible on the beach, theft is common.

Kayit U'shait (☎ 61161, 62928) is a holiday village and guesthouse at Kibbutz Sdot Yam has comfortable singles/doubles for US$40/65. There is also a *campsite* – it's about US$6 per person, and no tents are provided.

The *Dan Caesarea* (☎ 362266/8; fax 362392) offers five-star luxury and service, with singles from US$80 to US$180, and doubles from US$94 to US$200. Facilities include a pool, tennis court, health club, sauna and golf course.

Places to Eat

There is an unexciting *café* across from the Crusader city.

Getting There & Away

From Haifa or Tel Aviv and Netanya take any Egged bus going along the coastal road to Hadera. Get off at the Caesarea intersection which is about 3½ km from the excavations. Unfortunately the local Egged bus No 76 is not that frequent and so you will often have to choose between a long wait or a long walk to reach the site.

AROUND CAESAREA
Moshav Beit Hananya

Near Moshav Beit Hananya on the coast north of Caesarea are Roman aqueducts. Continue north to **Tel Mevorah** where archaeologists are still uncovering Roman remains.

Kibbutz Ma'agan Michael

There are archaeological finds to be seen here, and it's a pleasant kibbutz to visit.

The kibbutz guesthouse has comfortable rooms with private bathroom for about US$25 per person, and breakfast is provided. Cheaper is the nearby *SPNI Field Study Centre* (☎ 99655) at the **Beit Safer Sadeh Nature Preserve**, but it's usually full. If there is room, you will usually be able to stay for about US$8 per person.

BEIT SHE'ARIM

About 19 km south-east of Haifa, the archaeological site of Beit She'arim features a network of burial caves and a few ruins from the 2nd century. It does not justify a major detour, but if you are in the area with time on your hands it's worth a visit.

History

An important town in ancient Israel, Beit She'arim was the meeting place of the Sanhedrin, the supreme court, during the 2nd century. It was also the home of Rabbi Yehuda HaNassi, compiler of the Mishnah, and he was one of the many famous and learned Jews buried here. Later, when Hadrian closed the area around Jerusalem to Jews, making it impossible for them to bury their dead on the Mount of Olives, Beit She'arim became the ideal alternative because of the reverence with which Rabbi Yehuda HaNassi was held. For over 100 years Jews from Palestine and the Diaspora brought their dead here for burial.

During the 4th century the town was destroyed by the Romans, presumably in the process of suppressing a Jewish uprising.

Over the centuries the many tombs here have been destroyed: the caves were looted and the catacombs gradually covered by layers of earth and rock, becoming hidden as the town and the burial grounds were forgotten. It was not until 1936 that archaeologists first discovered some of the town's remains, and more extensive exploration resumed after Israel's independence. Today's site is basically in two parts – the town's remains on the crest of the hill, and the tombs below.

Ancient Synagogue

Coming down the hill from the Haifa to Nazareth road, the ruins of this 2nd-century synagogue are on the left. Destroyed by the Romans around 350 as punishment for unrest, it was probably one of the largest synagogues in the country. A hoard of some 1200 4th-century coins was found in the two-storey building between the synagogue and the road.

Olive Press

About 100 metres further on are the ruins of a 4th-century olive press. Olives were stacked between two uprights on the circular stone and a heavy horizontal beam let into a notch in the wall acted as a lever to press out the oil which flowed from the circular groove into a plastered basin in the rock floor.

Basilica

Further up the slope from the road, the 2nd-century basilica's ruins show a basic rectangle divided by two rows of columns with a raised platform at the end opposite the doors, which opened onto a wide court.

Alexander Zaid Statue

Alexander Zaid was guardian of the surrounding area in the 1930s. He was killed during uprisings in 1936.

Museum & Catacombs

There are 31 catacombs here, and a small museum in an ancient rock-cut reservoir. The catacombs are slightly spooky caves – cool chambers filled with now-empty stone coffins.

They are open Saturday to Thursday, 8 am to 5 pm, and Friday 8 am to 4 pm. Admission is US$1.80 (students US$0.80).

Places to Eat

A *café* adjacent to the museum and car park is open for the same hours as the site.

Getting There & Away

Egged bus No 338 from Haifa to Qiryat Tivon is about a 30-minute ride. Get off by the King Garden Chinese restaurant and walk back up the hill to the sideroad on the left. Then take the first left (Hashomrin St), next Shikonella St, and proceed right following the signs downhill.

AKKO (ACRE)

Akko's picturesque Old City is an understandably popular tourist attraction, with Islamic minarets and domes and Crusader remains dominating the labyrinth of alleyways. There's also a small Arab market.

History

Akko's history is long and colourful. One of the world's oldest towns, it was first mentioned in Egyptian sacred texts of the 19th century BC when it was located on a mound, Tel el Fukhar, 1½ km north-east of the present Old City wall. Judges 1:31 mentions that in the 13th century BC the town remained in Phoenician control although the Israelites had conquered most of the country.

It stood on the border of the Jewish tribe of Asher, which managed to take it a few hundred years later. Always an important port, in the 4th century BC it assumed the stature that Tyre and Sidon had earlier enjoyed. This was probably due to Alexander the Great having established a mint here in 333 BC, which operated for 600 years. The name Akko is perhaps derived from the Greek word *aka* (cure), as the hero Hercules found herbs here to cure his wounds.

After Alexander's death, Akko was taken by the Egyptian Ptolemites, who called it Ptolemais. In 200 BC they lost it to the Syrian Seleucids who struggled to keep it until the Romans, led by Pompey, began two centuries of rule. As Ptolemais, the city is mentioned in the account of Paul's travels in Acts 21:7. At this time it was in decline as Caesarea developed.

In 636, the Arabs conquered Akko and, as Caesarea's port had silted up through neglect, Akko's regained its position as Palestine's leading port. When the Crusaders took the city they named it Jean D'Acre, because it housed the headquarters of the Knights of St Jean. It soon became the main link between the Latin kingdom and Europe, with the new rulers arriving in their ships from Genoa, Pisa, Venice and Amalfi.

In 1187, Akko surrendered to Saladin without a fight, but four years later Richard the Lionheart and Philip of France retook it, and it remained the capital of the Latin kingdom for another 100 years. During this time the city grew outside its original walls and the new walls enclosed an area three times the size of today's walled city. St Francis of Assisi and Marco Polo were among the VIPs who passed through, and Akko became more important as a trading port.

Due to this growth in trade, disputes arose over the succession of the king here and eventually open war erupted between factions living in the individually fortified quarters. Venice and Genoa fought sea battles within sight of the city, and in 1259 the Mongols, and in 1265 the Mamelukes attacked unsuccessfully. The Mamelukes attacked again in 1291, outnumbering the defenders 10 to 1. After a two-month siege, during which over 30,000 of its inhabitants escaped to Cyprus, Akko fell.

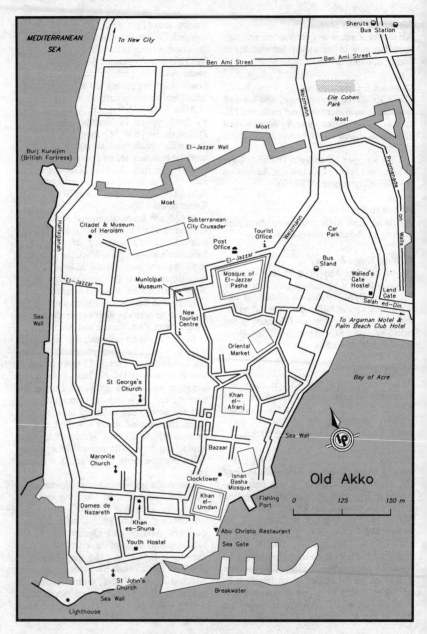

MEDITERRANEAN
SEA

To New City

Ben Ami Street

Ben Ami Street

Sheruts
Bus Station

Weizmann

Elie Cohen
Park

Moat

Moat

El-Jazzar Wall

Moat

Promenade
on Walls

Burj Kuraijim
(British Fortress)

HaHaganah

Citadel & Museum
of Heroism

Subterranean
City Crusader

Post
Office

Tourist
Office

Car
Park

El-Jazzar

Municipal
Museum

Mosque of
El-Jazzar
Pasha

Bus
Stand

Walied's
Gate
Hostel

Land
Gate

Salah ed-Din

El-Jazzar

Sea
Wall

New
Tourist
Centre

Oriental
Market

To Argaman Motel &
Palm Beach Club Hotel

Bay of Acre

St George's
Church

Khan
el-
Afranj

Sea Wall

Maronite
Church

Bazaar

Clocktower

Isnan
Basha
Mosque

Old Akko

Dames de
Nazareth

Khan
el-
Umdan

Fishing
Port

0   125   150 m

Khan
es-Shuna

Youth Hostel

Abu Christo Restaurant

Sea Gate

St John's
Church

Sea Wall

Breakwater

Lighthouse

The city lay in ruins and was neglected for the next 450 years until a local Arab sheik took advantage of the weak and corrupt Ottoman administration to establish a virtually independent fiefdom. Trade was encouraged and the port again developed. An Albanian mercenary, known as el-Jazzar (the Butcher) because of his cruelty, took over and continued the city's development. In 1799, Napoleon invaded Palestine and attempted to take Akko, but was repulsed by the English fleet under Sir Sidney Smith.

In 1832 Ibrahim Pasha, leading an Egyptian army, took Akko from the Turks and ruled Palestine and Syria from Akko until the British intervened on Turkey's behalf in 1840, and the Turks then ruled until Britain captured Palestine in 1917. The British set up their headquarters in Haifa and Akko's importance dwindled. They did establish Akko's citadel as their main prison in Palestine, and many Jewish resistance fighters were executed here. During the 1930s Akko became a hotbed of Arab hostility towards increased Jewish immigration and the notion of a Zionist state. Jewish forces captured Akko fairly easily in 1948.

Today the city has a large new town, but it is the Arab Old City which attracts visitors. Akko is often given as an example of how Jews and Arabs can live together in relative harmony. Foreign women, however, may still be subjected to sexual harassment.

Orientation

Because all the places of interest are in or near the Old City, you only need to get to know a small, albeit confusing, area. From the bus station it's a short walk to the Old City: turn left as you leave the station, walk one block to the traffic lights and turn right at Ben Ami St. After four blocks turn left at Weizmann St and you will see the walls of the Turkish fortress in the distance. You can choose where to enter the Old City. Either turn right after the moat and head for el-Jazzar St, with the el-Jazzar Mosque and the subterranean Crusader city, or walk straight ahead to explore the market or the port.

Information

Tourist Office The municipal information office is in the municipality building, 35 Weizmann St. Look for the grassy, palm-shaded piazza with the waterfall sculpture.

It's open Sunday and Wednesday 7 am to 12.30 pm and 4 to 6 pm, Monday, Tuesday and Thursday 7 am to 1.30 pm, Friday 7 am to 12.30 pm, and is closed Saturday.

The ticket office at the subterranean Crusader city sells a map of Akko and can give limited information. It's open Saturday to Thursday 9 am to 4.30 pm, and Friday 9 am to 12.30 pm.

Post & Telecommunications The main post office, poste restante and international phones are next door to the municipality building, at 11 Ha'Atzmaut St.

These facilities are open Sunday, Tuesday and Thursday 8 am to 12.30 pm and 3.30 to 6 pm, Monday and Wednesday 8 am to 2 pm, Friday 8 am to 1 pm, and are closed Saturday.

There is a handy branch in the Old City, next to the subterranean Crusader city, which is open in July and August from Sunday to Thursday 8 am to 2 pm, Friday 8 am to noon, and is closed Saturday; and from September to June, Sunday, Tuesday and Thursday 8 am to 12.30 pm and 3.30 to 6 pm, Monday and Wednesday 8 am to 1 pm, and is closed Saturday.

Other There are banks on Ben Ami St. The police station (☎ 91023 or 100) is at 2 Ben Ami St.

Walls & Gates

As you approach the Old City on Weizmann St, you first come to the wall and moat built in 1799 by Ahmed Pasha el-Jazzar after Napoleon's retreat. The sea wall was refaced at the same time, partly with stones from the Crusader castle at Atlit. It was originally built by the Crusaders in the 12th century. Other parts of the Crusader wall can be seen on both sides of Weizmann St, and were probably incorporated into the 18th-century defences. The 13th-century Crusader wall is now hidden by the new town – the Palm

Beach Club Hotel marks its easternmost point.

The Land Gate and the Sea Gate, now part of the Abu Christo Restaurant, are both from the 12th century.

Mosque of El-Jazzar Pasha

After passing the el-Jazzar wall and moat, turn right on el-Jazzar St and the mosque is on your left, its large green dome and minaret dominating the skyline. It was built in 1781 and the columns in the courtyard were looted from Caesarea.

Around the corner by the minaret, the small twin-domed building contains the sarcophagi of el-Jazzar and his adopted son, Suleiman, who ruled Akko from 1804 to 1819. To your left as you enter and across the courtyard, signs point to the underground reservoir. It's nothing too exciting, and here you can stroll along the walkways to see the pipelines and where rainfall was collected below.

The mosque is open Saturday to Thursday 8 am to 12.30 pm and 1.30 to 4 pm, and Friday 8 to 11 am and 2 to 4 pm. Admission is US$0.90. A guide will often try to force himself on you as you enter. If you don't want his brief tour tell him so immediately to avoid hassles when you leave. There are public toilets inside the complex.

Subterranean Crusader City

Across the street from the mosque is the entrance to the subterranean Crusader city. This area was the quarter of the Knights Hospitallers, and what was their street level is now eight metres below ground.

In the entrance halls, some of the huge columns are engraved with French fleur-de-lys, others with Turkish decorations.

From here you enter another hall, which once held a winepress, before entering the courtyard where the 30-metre-high citadel walls dominate.

Through the large Turkish gates to the left are the knights' halls. Turn right from here into the centre of the Crusader complex. In the ceiling is the cemented-over tunnel dug by Jewish prisoners in the British prison

above. Not knowing what lay beneath in the dark halls they returned to their cells to plot a more successful mass escape.

Today the halls are occasionally used for concerts and the annual Akko Underground Theatre Festival is aptly staged here.

Back through the courtyard you come to the Grand Meneir, the centre of the Crusader government. A narrow passage leads to the knights' dining hall – the Refectory (or Crypt) of St John. Next to the crypt's third column is a stairway leading to a long underground passage. It's not known what its original purpose was, but el-Jazzar planned to use it as an escape route if Napoleon captured the city. Following the passage you come to the rooms and courtyard of the Crusaders' Domus Infirmorum, or hospital. The Turks used the area as a post office so it's also known as Al-Bosta.

The subterranean Crusader city is open Saturday to Thursday 9 am to 4.30 pm, and Friday 9 am to 12.30 pm. Tickets are normally valid for both the subterranean Crusader city and the municipal museum. Admission is US$2 (students US$1.50).

Municipal Museum

Turn right out of the subterranean Crusader city, follow el-Jazzar St around to the left, and the museum is on the right. It occupies what was originally a Turkish bath, Hammam el Pasha, built by el-Jazzar in 1780 for the people of Akko. The exhibits include drawings, lithographs and engravings relating to Akko during the Napoleonic wars, and artefacts found locally, such as Crusader weapons. The museum generally has the same operating hours as the subterranean Crusader city, and the same ticket is valid for both.

Tourist Centre & Market

Continuing along the alley from the museum you come to the Tourist Centre, a renovated area now occupied by art studios and the inevitable souvenir stalls.

The actual market occupies a few narrow streets and is really tiny compared with its counterparts in other old cities. Its selection of shops, nonetheless, makes it a popular distraction.

Khan el-Umdan

This is the most attractive of Akko's caravanserais which once served the camel caravans bringing grain from the southern Golan to the port. Its name means Inn of the Pillars and it was built by el-Jazzar in 1785. You can easily find it by its tall clocktower which was erected in 1906 by the Ottoman sultan.

The ground floor housed the animals, and the people slept upstairs. The pillars are another example of the looting of Caesarea. The courtyard is now Akko's unofficial soccer stadium.

Fishing Port

South of Khan el-Umdan lies the fishing port. Especially in summer, it is possible to take a boat trip to enjoy the view of the city. Ignore the imaginative prices suggested by your would-be skipper – about US$2 to US$3 per person is the going rate.

Citadel & Museum of Heroism

On HaHaganah St, the citadel houses the Museum of Heroism, dedicated to the Jewish resistance fighters during the British Mandate.

Built by the Turks in the late 18th century on 13th-century Crusader foundations, the inmates of the prison included Baha'u'llah, founder of the Baha'i faith, and Ze'ev Jabotinsky, a leader of the Jewish underground in the 1920s.

Eight members of the Irgun were hanged here and other members staged a successful mass breakout in 1947. That scene in the movie *Exodus* was filmed here. The citadel also houses a mental hospital.

The museum is open Saturday to Thursday 9 am to 5.30 pm, and Friday 9 am to 12.30 pm. Admission is US$2 (students US$1.50).

Burj Kurajim

Although usually called the British Fortress, Burj Kurajim literally means Fortress of the Vineyards and it was built by the Turks on Crusader foundations. From here you can follow el-Jazzar's wall and moat across to the centre to make your way back to the bus station.

Beaches

Akko's nicest beach is Purple Beach (Hof Argaman), so named because of the dye that could be obtained from the snails that frequented the area in ancient times. With wonderful views of the Old City on the horizon, the beach is popular with Israelis, who happily pay the US$0.70 admission.

To reach **Purple Beach**, either get off the bus from Haifa when you see the Palm Beach Club Hotel and the Argaman Motel, or walk east from Land Gate along Yonatan HaHoshmonai St – about a 10-minute walk.

The free but unattractive **Walls Beach** is just down from Land Gate, and is popular with windsurfers. There is a changing room near the entrance to the beach.

Tours

Egged Tours have a day tour to Akko and Rosh Hanikra which departs from Haifa. The cost is US$37.

Places to Stay – bottom end

Most travellers make day tours to Akko from Haifa, or en route to/from Galilee, but it can be a convenient site to plan an overnight stop on your way around the country.

Walied's Gate Hostel (☎ 910410, 914700) currently provides the only budget accommodation in Akko. Located just outside the Old City, next to Land Gate on Salah ed-Din St, dorm beds are US$8, and singles/doubles are US$10/20.

Closed to the public at the time of writing as it was filled with Soviet immigrants, *Akko Youth Hostel – IYHA* (☎ 911982) is on the west side of the Old City, not far from the lighthouse. It is in a pleasant building which was the Turkish Governor's residence. It can be a bit difficult to find, despite signs here and there. When entering the Old City from the bus station head for HaHaganah St and walk down to the lighthouse. From here take the alley to the left, and the hostel is on the left. Beds are US$10 in dorms or double rooms, with breakfast included. The hostel is closed from 9 am to 5 pm, and there's an 11 pm curfew.

Places to Stay – middle

The two most noticeable places to stay in Akko are on Purple Beach. The *Argaman Motel* (☎ 916691/7; fax 916690) is a modern complex with free access to the beach and that great view; singles cost from US$36 to US$45, and doubles from US$56 to US$67. The adjacent *Palm Beach Club Hotel* (☎ 815815; fax 910434) has superior facilities, including a pool, sauna, tennis court and water sports; singles cost from US$50 to US$67, and doubles from US$70 to US$90.

On the north-eastern outskirts of Akko, *Nes Ammin* (☎ 822522; fax 826872) is a Christian-run guesthouse whose aim is to promote understanding between Christians and Jews. Singles cost from US$38 to US$48, and doubles from US$55 to US$73. It's off the Akko to Nahariya road about five km north of Akko.

Places to Eat

There are a few felafel and shwarma places along Ben Ami St and in the Old City, where there is also a bakery.

The fishing port is the most popular place for a sit-down meal. Fish is the obvious thing to order, and it is cooked simply, and served with salad. The best of an average bunch is probably *Abu Christo*, which costs around US$15 for one. It's open daily from 11 am to about midnight.

Getting There & Away

There are various Egged buses from Haifa, including No 271 which also runs to Nahariya. There is also a bus about every 30 minutes to and from Safed.

Don't forget that buses run between Haifa and Akko on Saturday.

AROUND AKKO

Bahje House & the Baha'i Gardens

The holiest site for followers of the Baha'i faith, this is where Baha'u'llah, the founder, lived after his release from prison in Akko and where he died in 1892. His tomb is in a lovely garden, similar in style to the one in Haifa. You can visit the garden daily, between 9 am and 5 pm. Bahje House, which contains a small museum, is open Friday to Sunday 9 am to noon, and admission is free.

Take Egged bus No 271 from Haifa, Akko or Nahariya. Unless you're a Baha'i, you'll have to use the entrance about half a km up the sideroad to the north of the main gate.

Turkish Aqueduct

On your right as you travel north on the Akko to Nahariya road is a long, arched, Roman-style aqueduct. Built by el-Jazzar in about 1780, it supplied Akko with water from Galilee's mountains.

Kibbutz Lochamei Hagetaot

Just north of the aqueduct, this kibbutz was established in 1949 by former resistance fighters from the ghettos of Germany, Poland and Lithuania. Their museum, **Ghetto Fighter's House** (☎ 920412), has artefacts related to Jewish communities in those countries prior to the Holocaust, and to the Jewish resistance movement.

The museum is open Sunday to Thursday 9 am to 4 pm, Friday 9 am to 1 pm, and Saturday 10 am to 5 pm. Admission is free, but donations are requested. Ask the bus driver to let you off – it's a short distance from the main road.

Nahal Shagur (Nahal Beit Hakerem)

Known by either name, this small river runs through an attractive valley. The SPNI have marked out a pleasant and only slightly arduous 12-km hike which follows the river bed, and it makes a good day trip from Akko. Note that the walk is not possible when the river is flowing.

The hardest part is negotiating a couple of steep drops which become waterfalls in season. With these in mind, it is inadvisable to go alone in case you twist an ankle or worse. Also, be sure to take plenty of water.

Take Egged bus No 361 (which leaves Akko for Gilon about every 30 minutes), and get off at the intersection for Gilon. It's marked by the Spanish-Jewish sign for Nahal Beit Hakerem. Take the steps by the sign down to the river bed and head right (west). For a short hike, take the path to the left to head back to Gilon when you reach the first steep drop. Otherwise, follow the river bed to the path which leads up to the road between Yasur and Alihud. Turn left to hitch back to Akko.

NAHARIYA
(Population: 28,600)
One of Israel's quietest seaside resorts, Nahariya is particularly popular with Jewish honeymooners on the Lag B'Omer holiday in spring, as this is the only day a Jew can marry during the six weeks between the Passover and Shavuot holidays.

Established in 1934 by German Jews escaping Nazism, Nahariya was western Galilee's first Jewish settlement. The town itself has nothing much of interest except the pleasant beach, but it is close to the grottoes of Rosh Hanikra, the beach and national park at Ahziv, the Crusader castle at Montfort, and Peqi'in.

Orientation
A small place, Nahariya is centred around its main street, the two-lane HaGa'aton Blvd, which has an unimpressive stream running down the middle of it. Here are the bus and railway stations, tourist office, shops, banks, cafés and restaurants, cinema, and, at the western end, the beach. Most of the hotels are towards this end of town.

Information
Tourist Office The IGTO (☎ 929800) is on the ground floor of the municipality building just west of the bus station on HaGa'aton Blvd.

It's open Sunday to Thursday 8 am to 1 pm and 4 to 7 pm, Friday 8 am to 1 pm, and is closed Saturday.

Post & Telecommunications These are at 40 HaGa'aton Blvd (☎ 920180), west of the bus station on the opposite side.

These facilities are open Sunday, Monday, Wednesday and Thursday 7.45 am to 12.30 pm and 3.30 to 6 pm, Tuesday 7.45 am to 2 pm, Friday 7.45 am to 1 pm, and are closed Saturday.

Police The police station (☎ 920344, emergency ☎ 100) is on Ben Zvi St, just off HaGa'aton Blvd, east of the railway station on the opposite side.

Beaches
Follow HaGa'aton Blvd westwards and it leads to Nahariya's sandy beaches. **Galei Gallil** is the main beach, sectioned off with a swimming pool and a few amusements. Admission is US$2.50. Head south or further north for a pleasant and free stretch of sand and sea.

Canaanite Temple
Not really worth the 20-minute walk, the 4000-year-old remains of a Canaanite temple can be seen to the north of Galei Gallil.

Museum
Also uninspiring, this small collection of local archaeological finds, seashells and modern art is on the 5th floor of the municipality building, near the bus station.

This small museum is open Sunday to Friday 10 am to noon, Sunday and Wednesday 4 to 6 pm, and is closed Saturday. Admission is free.

Places to Stay – bottom end
There are no true travellers' hostels as such here. Among the cheaper hotels, *Sirtash House* (☎ 922586), at 22 Jabotinsky St, is recommended by readers, with nice, clean singles/doubles for US$11/18. *Motel Arieli* (☎ 921076), at 1 Jabotinsky St, near the corner of HaGa'aton Blvd, has two-person bungalows for US$18, and double rooms in the main building for US$26. *Kalman Hotel* (☎ 920355; fax 923556), at 27 Jabotinsky St, has singles from US$35 to US$40, and doubles from US$45 to US$58. Affiliated

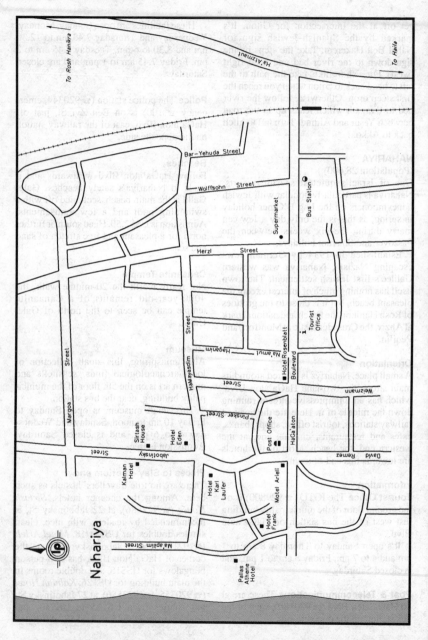

Nahariya

To Rosh Haniqra

To Haifa

Ha'Atzmaut

Bar-Yehuda Street

Wolffsohn Street

Bus Station

Supermarket

Herzl Street

Tourist Office

Hotel Rosenblatt

Na'amut

HaGefen

Weizmann

Pinsker Street

Post Office

HaGa'aton

David Remez

Margoa Street

Sirtash House

Hotel Eden

Jabotinsky Street

Kalman Hotel

Hotel Karl Laufer

Motel Arieli

Ma'apilim Street

Hotel Frank

Pallas Athene Hotel

with the IYHA, it has some doubles for around US$28.

Nahariya has several private homes where people let rooms. Look for the signs on Jabotinsky St in particular, or ask at the tourist office. Prices hover around US$20 per person, but can be higher during July and August, or much lower depending on your bargaining skills.

Places to Stay – middle

Hotel Eden (☎ 923246; fax 823741), on Mayasdim St at the corner of Jabotinsky St, is modern and slick-looking, which makes it stand out from the rest. Pleasant enough, singles cost from US$44 to US$49, and doubles from US$55 to US$71.

At the *Hotel Rosenblatt* (☎ 820069; fax 928121), 59 Weizmann St, singles cost from US$40 to US$50, and doubles from US$50 to US$70. With similar prices, *Panorama Hotel* (☎ 920555), at 6 Ma'apilim St, is one block north of HaGa'aton Blvd. It is a nice, modern hotel with sea views and a rooftop terrace.

Hotel Frank (☎ 920278; fax 925535), 4 HaAliyah St, off Ma'apilim St, has balconies, sea views and friendly staff. Singles cost from US$45 to US$57, and doubles from US$60 to US$79.

Places to Stay – top end

Nahariya has two four-star hotels. *Pallas Athene Hotel* (☎ 828222; fax 828111), 28 Ma'apilim St, has a rooftop sundeck, a sauna, and a billiard table. The *Carlton Hotel* (☎ 922211; fax 823771), HaGa'aton Blvd, is west of the bus station. It's modern and attractive with some tasteful interior design and a pool, solarium and jacuzzi. In both places, singles cost from US$58 to US$72, and doubles from US$80 to US$100.

Places to Eat

There is the Supersol supermarket on HaGa'aton Blvd, at the corner of Herzl St, and the bus station has an Egged self-service restaurant.

Elsewhere, standard quality felafel or hummus is available. Nahariya lives up to its 'typical Israeli seaside resort' tag by having a shortage of decent eating places. Although HaGa'aton Blvd has cafés and restaurants which attract the crowds, the food and service are usually mediocre. An exception is the *Donan Restaurant* (☎ 923956), 32 HaGa'aton Blvd, which is a pleasant little Rumanian grill with tables indoors or seating out on the pavement. It serves dishes such as grilled meats and fish from about US$15 to US$25.

The only other places I could recommend here are both Chinese. The *Singapore Chinese Garden* is one block north of HaGa'aton Blvd on Mayasdim St, corner of Jabotinsky St and across from the Yarden and Eden hotels. It has nice decor and good service and costs about US$15 for a full meal, although you could eat for less. The *Chinese Inn Restaurant*, 28 HaGa'aton Blvd is on the 2nd floor and you enter by the stairway at the rear. It's cheaper at about US$10 per person. Both places are open for lunch and dinner.

For draught beer, there are a few places along HaGa'aton Blvd and its offshoots. *My Pub*, across from the bus station on HaGa'aton Blvd, and *Tropigan*, further along and upstairs, are the popular choices.

Entertainment

Other than the *Hod Cinema*, on the corner of Herzl St and HaGa'aton Blvd, the main nocturnal activity is to promenade along HaGa'aton Blvd and sit at one of the cafés there to people watch. Alternatively, take a stroll along the beach.

Tropigan features live music on Friday and Saturday evenings, and the *Carlton Hotel* has a popular disco.

Getting There & Away

There are buses to and from Akko and Haifa every 30 minutes and the irregular train service to Haifa.

Getting Around

Although the beach and all accommodation is within walking distance of the bus and railway stations, it makes sense to hire a bicycle on HaGa'aton Blvd. This costs about US$4 per day, which is about what you would pay in bus fares to reach Ahziv and Rosh Hanikra, and you are not dependent on the irregular local buses. On Shabbat it is the only way to travel!

An expensive alternative to the bus and bicycle are the horse carts which presumably provide a living for their owners, although the unhealthy-looking horses don't seem to benefit from the deal. It costs US$10 for a 15-minute ride.

AROUND NAHARIYA
Ahziv
The short stretch of coastline between Nahariya and Rosh Hanikra is known as Ahziv. Once one of the towns of the Asher tribe in ancient Israel, it was also a Phoenician port, and Bronze Age remains have been found here.

Ahziv Beach About four km north of Nahariya on the road to Rosh Hanikra, this pleasant beach with its changing rooms, sunshades, showers and snack bar is free, although there is a fee for car parking.

Ahziv National Park Just a little further north, this area of parkland is on the site of an 'abandoned' Arab village. You can see traces of a Phoenician port and use the beach. There are changing rooms and a snack bar at the beach but admission of US$5 (students US$2.50) is charged.

It's open April to September, Saturday to Thursday 8 am to 5 pm and Friday 8 am to 4 pm; October to March, Saturday to Thursday 8 am to 4 pm and Friday 8 am to 3 pm.

Ahzivland In 1952, Eli Avivi settled in an old Arab house by the beach just north of the national park and declared his land to be an independent state, which he called 'Ahzivland'. Since then he has established a museum housing his varied collection of artefacts found nearby, some of which date from the Phoenician, Roman and Byzantine periods. The museum is opened daily, April

to September 8 am to 5 pm, and October to March 8 am to 4 pm. Admission is US$1.70.

Eli also has a very simple hostel that is expensive for the little he provides. A simple slab of foam rubber on the floor costs US$13, and ground space outside US$8.50. However, judging by the visitors' book there are people who are happy to stay here, most of them Israeli. Passport stamp collectors may want to get an Ahzivland stamp.

Campsite Across the road from Ahzivland is a *campsite* (☎ 921792, off-season 92 3366), with small, basic two-person cabins for US$18 and four-person cabins for US$30. If you have your own tent you pay US$5 per person. There is a supermarket, showers and toilets.

Yad Le Yad In 1946, 14 Haganah soldiers were killed trying to blow up the railway bridges on this stretch of the line when attempting to cut British communication links. A monument to them stands by the road.

Kibbutz Gesher HaZiv Named after the bridge incident, this settlement (☎ 927711) was established in 1949 by a group of Americans and Israelis. It was one of the first kibbutz to raise its children at home with their parents rather than in separate accommodation. There is a *guesthouse* with comfortable singles/doubles for US$60/90, with breakfast provided. There is also a restaurant open to nonresidents. Look for the signpost at the intersection on the coastal road.

Rosh Hanikra
On the sensitive Israel-Lebanon border (photography could be risky), the caves at Rosh Hanikra (Cave of the Grotto) are a popular tourist attraction. Carved by the sea at the base of the tall white cliff, this series of caves was enlarged by the British for a railway and by the Israelis to improve access for visitors. They are at their most interesting in bad weather when the sea is wild.

Think twice about swimming here – it is

illegal and dangerous. There are strong currents and the strictly out-of-bounds Lebanese territorial waters (along with shoot-first Lebanese border guards) are close by.

The only practical way to reach the caves is by cablecar, which operates Saturday to Thursday 8.30 am to 6 pm, and Friday 8.30 am to 4 pm. The US$6 fare is as steep as the cliff.

Places to Eat There are two cafeterias, one by the car park, down from the border and the other at the top of the hill, by the cablecar.

Getting There & Away Only a couple of the buses from Nahariya go direct to the site (stopping at the foot of the hill), and normally you have to walk the three km from the junction. This is another good reason for renting a bicycle in Nahariya, although that last stretch is an uphill struggle.

Peqi'in

A predominantly Druze village, Peqi'in has had a Jewish community for many centuries which, according to tradition, has never been exiled from the Holy Land. In 1936, though, the political situation forced them to leave the area and only a small number returned after Israel's independence. There is also an Arab community here.

The village is believed to be where Rabbi Shimon Bar Yochai and his son, Eliezer, hid from the Romans in the 2nd century to escape a decree which made it illegal to study the Torah. The tradition is that they stayed in a cave here for 13 years, during which the rabbi compiled the Zohar, the most important book in Jewish mysticism. Outside the cave a freshwater spring and a carob tree miraculously appeared. The two are said to have fed on the fruit from the tree, drunk from the spring and embedded themselves in the sand up to their necks while they spent all their time studying the Torah.

The traditional cave of Rabbi Shimon Bar Yochai is now holy to religious Jews. Also to be seen are the spring (trickling unattractively through a modern-day pipe into a

Seal of the Crusader Kings

pool), an ancient synagogue now housing a museum, the Jewish community's old cemetery, and an old flour mill and oil presses. The village is a maze of twisting streets and it is hard to find these visually disappointing sites. To save time, stop off at the Druze café next to the bus stop by the entrance to the village for a free map, directions and a friendly chat.

Places to Eat Peqi'in's food speciality is *pitta-eem-leben*. This is wafer-thin pitta bread served with a soft, sour, white cheese which is mixed with olive oil and dill. Two cafés opposite each other compete to serve you.

The *Jewish Community Restaurant* on your left as you arrive from Nahariya was here first. Despite its name, it is owned by Arabs, and the old lady has been baking the pitta for over 30 years. Across the street by the bus stop, the friendly Druze man set up his operation about eight years ago, with his sister doing the baking. The Arabs charge a bit less, about US$2. You can also order hummus and very good coffee at both cafés.

Getting There & Away Egged bus No 44 runs about every hour from Nahariya (45 minutes). You should get off at the old village Peqi'in Atika, not the modern settlement of Peqi'in Hadasha, the stop before.

Beit Jan

Another friendly Druze community, this

small village enjoys lovely views of the surrounding countryside and receives a lot fewer visitors than those near Haifa. Take Egged bus No 44 from Nahariya, stay on after Peqi'in, then get off three km later at the Beit Jan junction. From here the village is a 2½-km walk or hitchhike.

Montfort

Montfort is not the most impressive of Israel's Crusader castles, but it is interesting and a visit here involves a pleasant hike. Originally built in 1226 by the French Courtenays, its name was changed from Montfort (Strong Mountain) to Starkenburg (Strong Castle) when they sold it to the Teutonic knights, the Templars and the Hospitallers. They modified the castle, which became their central treasury, archives and Holy Land headquarters, although it had no real strategic value. In 1271 the Muslims, led by Baybars, took the castle after a previous attempt (five years earlier) had failed. The Crusaders retreated to Akko and the castle was razed.

There is little to see today. To the right of the entrance is the governor's residence, with the tower straight ahead. The two vaulted

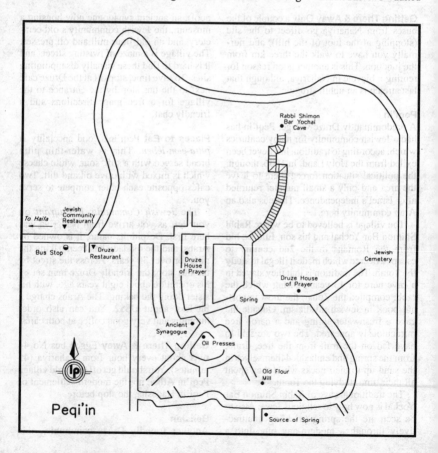

Peqi'in

To Haifa

Jewish Community Restaurant

Bus Stop

Druze Restaurant

Druze House of Prayer

Rabbi Shimon Bar Yochai Cave

Jewish Cemetery

Druze House of Prayer

Spring

Ancient Synagogue

Oil Presses

Old Flour Mill

Source of Spring

chambers to the right are the basement of the knights' hall; next to them is the chapel. It's open Saturday to Thursday 8 am to 5 pm, and Friday 8 am to 4 pm. Admission is US$1 (students US$0.70).

Getting There & Away From Nahariya take a bus to Goren and ask for the park. From here you will see the castle in the distance, about a 1½-hour walk. Another, perhaps more interesting (albeit strenuous), way to get there is by the Ma'alot bus from Nahariya. Get off at Mi'ilyah, and walk through this large Arab Christian village. After the turn off for Hilah, a small Jewish village, the road deteriorates into a dirt path. Follow the signs and scale the cliff to reach the fort.

Galilee & the Golan

Taken from the Hebrew word *galil* (district), Galilee is probably the most popular area of the country with visitors, as well as locals, due to its rich combination of beautiful scenery and religious heritage. This is Israel's lushest region, with green valleys, forests, farmland and, of course, the Sea of Galilee itself.

To the north of Galilee is another area of outstanding natural beauty – the Upper Galilee and the Golan. This region is covered later in this chapter.

Galilee

Galilee is often labelled 'the Land of the Bible' as it was here that Jesus did most of his preaching and where Jewish scholars produced the rabbinical texts, the Talmud, the Mishnah and the Kabbalah.

The Zionist pioneers first settled here because of the fertile land, in particular around the Sea of Galilee and in the Jordan and Jezreel valleys. Galilee's northernmost Jewish communities have had to exist under the continual physical threat of terrorist raids from Lebanon and Syria and artillery bombardments. It is often easy to forget that a large percentage of Israel's Arab residents still live here, although many were forced to leave before and during the 1948 War of Independence.

JORDAN RIVER

Despite its biblical background and status as Israel's longest river and major water source, the Jordan is often a disappointment. First-time visitors usually expect to find something more expansive than the small and muddy desert stream that it is for much of its length.

Throughout the scenic Jordan Valley drive between Tiberias and Jerusalem, the nearest

you get to actually seeing the river is the trail of trees that cluster around its meandering course. The most attractive parts of the river are north of the lake, at Banyas in the Golan and Tel Dan in Upper Galilee.

There are three main sources of the Jordan: the Senir River (Hasbani in Arabic) which rises in Lebanon; the Banyas and the Dan River. The origin and meaning of the name 'Jordan' are not so clear. A 1300 map of Palestine shows the river with two sources: Jor and Dan. Another theory is that the name comes from the Hebrew *yored Dan* (descends from Dan).

NAZARETH
(Population: 46,300)
Generally believed to be the home of Mary and Joseph before the birth of Jesus, and where they returned to raise him after fleeing to Egypt, Nazareth usually fails to match the high expectations of pilgrims and tourists. The several important churches are unfortunately overshadowed by the unattractive and rapidly expanding town and its busy streets.

Today Nazareth is notable for its important Christian shrines and as a main centre of the Christian mission movement in the Holy Land with its many smaller churches, convents, monasteries, schools, orphanages and hospitals. Nazareth also stands out as a place where Sunday is the Sabbath and not Saturday, so be sure to check individual shops and businesses for opening hours.

One of the country's largest Arab towns, it is known in Arabic as *en-Nasra*, in Hebrew *Natsrat*. It now includes Nazareth Illit, or Upper Nazareth, the newer Jewish town. This started to develop in 1957 with the establishment of factories, including textile and engineering plants.

Because of its large Arab population, Nazareth has been strongly affected by the intifada, with many businesses responding to the call for strikes. More prosaically, the old problem of Arab men versus foreign women

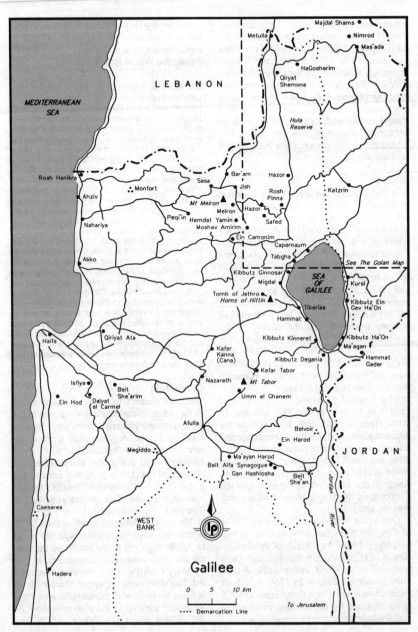

MEDITERRANEAN
SEA

LEBANON

Majdal Shams
Metulla
Nimrod
Mas'ada
HaGosherim
Qiryat
Shemona
Hula
Reserve

Rosh Hanikra
Bar'am
Hazor
Ahziv
Monfort
Sasa
Jish
Katzrin
Rosh
Pinna
Mt Meiron
Meiron
Hazor
Nahariya
Peqi'in
Hemdat Yamin
Safed
Moshav Amirim
Akko
Ein Camonim
Capernaum
See The Golan Map
Tabgha
Kibbutz Ginnosar
Migdal
SEA
OF
GALILEE
Kursi
Tomb of Jethro
Horns of Hittin
Kibbutz Ein
Gev Ha'On
Tiberias
Hammat
Haifa
Qiryat Ata
Kafer
Kanna
(Cana)
Kibbutz Kinneret
Kibbutz Ha'On
Ma'agan
Hammat
Gader
Kefar Tabor
Kibbutz Degania
Isfiya
Ein Hod
Beit
She'arim
Nazareth
Mt Tabor
Dalyat
el Carmel
Umm el Ghanem
Afula
Belvoir
Ein Harod
Megiddo
JORDAN
Ma'ayan Harod
Beit Alfa Synagogue
Gan Hashlosha
Beit
She'an
Caesarea
WEST
BANK
Jordan
River

Galilee

0   5   10 km

Hadera
To Jerusalem

···· Demarcation Line

is particularly apparent here. All women visiting Nazareth should make a point of not dressing or behaving in a way likely to either excite or cause offence (read the Women Travellers section in the Facts for the Visitor chapter). This is not easy when even nuns have been harassed. I would not want to deter women from visiting Nazareth, but they should be prepared for some pretty unpleasant verbal harassment at the very least if they do not follow my advice. John 1:46 can still be accurately applied.

History

It is thought that Nazareth had a Christian community until the 3rd century. However, after that it seems to have been largely ignored by pilgrims until the late 6th century when it was written by a pilgrim from Piacimya that many miracles took place here and that a synagogue had kept the book in which Jesus learnt to write, and the bench he had sat on. It was apparently too heavy for Jews to lift, but the Christians were quite able to carry it about. The site of Mary's home had become a church and the beauty of the Jewish women of Nazareth, supposedly the prettiest in the country, was credited to her, being a relation of theirs. More churches were built over the next century. Nazareth was a Jewish city at this time.

The Crusaders made Nazareth their capital of Galilee in the 11th century. In 1099, Tancred dedicated a church to the Annunciation, and another church around this time was dedicated to the angel Gabriel. After the Crusaders' defeat at the Horns of Hittin in 1187 pilgrims were still able to visit Nazareth due to a series of truces, but by the 13th century the danger from Muslim attack was too great.

Due to the benevolent Druze emir Fakhr ed-Din, the Franciscans were able to buy back the ruins of the Church of the Annunciation in 1620 and a Christian presence was re-established, albeit under difficult and often hostile conditions. In 1730, they built a new church which was demolished in 1955 to be replaced by the modern version that you see today.

During the British Mandate, Nazareth was the administration's headquarters in Galilee. Israeli forces took the town on 16 July 1948 during the War of Independence.

Did Mary & Joseph Hail From Nazareth?

Christian tradition states, and therefore most people believe, that Jesus' parents were from Nazareth. However, there are strong arguments against this, despite Luke 2:4-5 saying that Nazareth was their home town. Matthew 2 has been interpreted as saying that they lived in Bethlehem and only went to Nazareth on their return from Egypt. There are other arguments against tradition. Joseph was from a Judean family, and Mary was a relative of Zechariah, a priest who would have lived near the Temple in Jerusalem. If they were from Nazareth, it would have perhaps made more sense for them to return there to escape Herod then to go to Egypt. For Judeans, however, Egypt was a common place of refuge (I Kings 11:40, II Kings 25:26, Jeremiah 26:21). If she lived in Nazareth, it would be unlikely that a Jewish girl such as Mary would have travelled alone for three days to visit Zechariah and Elizabeth (Luke 1:39-40), but it would have been a normal event if she lived nearby.

It is suggested that the family and other relatives moved to Nazareth after Herod's death because the King's son, Archelaus, was proving to be as much of a threat as his father had been. Luke was aware that Jesus had been brought up in Nazareth (Luke 4:16) and that the other relatives also lived there (Matthew 13:55-6), so maybe he was simply assuming that Mary and Joseph had been born here.

Orientation

The town's main attractions are concentrated in the centre of the old Arab town, not in the industrialised Nazareth Illit. The modern Basilica of the Annunciation (commonly referred to as 'the basilica') is an obvious landmark, and due to the almost complete absence of street signs, you will need to use it and the other prominent churches to find your way around. You are almost certain to lose your way in the market.

The main street in Nazareth is Paul VI St which runs from the junction with the Haifa to Afulla highway to the south, up through the old Arab town with its churches, to end by Mary's Well where it becomes Namsawi Rd. The other most important street to know is Casa Nova St which intersects with Paul VI St and runs up to the market in front of the basilica. The tourist office and the best accommodation and eating places are here and the bus station is nearby.

Actually, Nazareth's bus station is merely a couple of shop-fronts containing information and left-luggage offices and a bus stop on either side of the street, just north of where Casa Nova St intersects, so don't waste time looking for a 'proper' bus station. The Hamishbir department store, Bank Hapoalim and the Paz petrol station are the landmarks here.

The market and eastern section of the Arab town are built on a very steep slope which you will have to get used to climbing if you want to visit any churches, monasteries or schools up here – there are no convenient roads with buses.

Information
Tourist Office The IGTO (☎ 73003) is on Casa Nova St, across and down from the basilica. It is open Monday to Friday 8.30 am to 5 pm, Saturday 8.30 am to 2 pm, and is closed Sunday.

Post & Telecommunications The main post office is north of the basilica, a couple of blocks west of Mary's Well.

It is open Monday and Wednesday 8.30 am to 2 pm, Tuesday, Thursday and Friday 8 am to 12.30 pm and 3.30 to 6 pm, Saturday 8 am to 1 pm, and is closed Sunday.

There is a branch office on Paul VI St south of the town centre by the Nazarene Church.

Other The Bank Hapoalim branch on Paul VI St by the bus station and next door to the Hamishbir department store is perhaps the most convenient.

The bank is open Monday and Tuesday 8.30 am to 12.30 pm and 4 to 6.30 pm; Wednesday and Saturday 8.30 am to 12.30 pm; Thursday 8.30 am to 12.30 pm and 4 to 6 pm; Friday 8.30 am to noon; and is closed Sunday.

There is a Barclays Discount branch just north of the basilica up past St Joseph's Church. The police station (☎ 74444 or 100) is near Mary's Well.

Tours
Egged Tours include visits to Nazareth with various tour options starting from Haifa, Tel Aviv and Jerusalem.

Basilica of the Annunciation

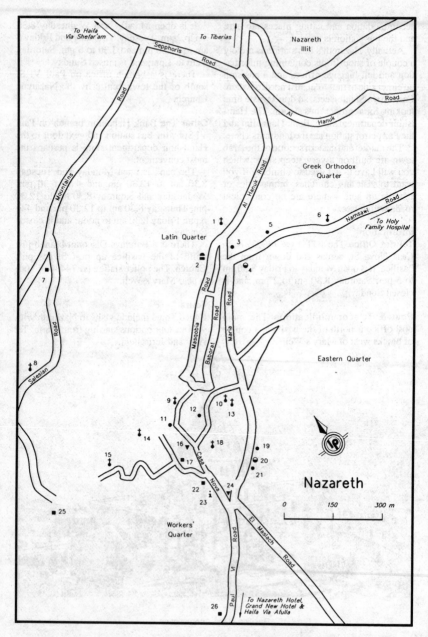

1	St Gabriel's Church
2	Post Office
3	Mary's Well
4	Buses to Cana
5	Frank Sinatra Brotherhood Centre
6	Church of Christ
7	Franciscan Sisters of Mary
8	Salesian Church & School of Jesus the Adolescent
9	Greek Catholic Synagogue Church
10	St Joseph'a Church
11	Old Market
12	Bank
13	Franciscan Monastery
14	Mensa Christi Church
15	Sisters of St Charles Borramaeus Convent
16	Mahroum's Sweets
17	Sisters of Nazareth Convent
18	Basilica of the Annunciation
19	Bank
20	Bus Station
21	Petrol Station
22	Casa Nova Hospice
23	Tourist Office
24	Astoria Restaurant
25	Fréres de Betharram Monastery
26	Hotel Galilee

Basilica of the Annunciation

Although it looks to me a bit like a misplaced lighthouse, the basilica's modern architectural style is a bold and striking contrast to its older environment. It's one of the world's most holy Christian shrines, as it's built on the traditional site of the Annunciation (Luke 1: 26-38), a cave, or perhaps house, where Mary lived.

Built in 1969 on the site of an 18th-century church demolished in 1955, there are basically two churches in the modern complex, incorporating the remains of even earlier buildings. Using the main entrance from Casa Nova St, you are on the lower level which contains these archaeological excavations. The bronze doors are decorated with scenes from the life of Jesus. In the centre of the underground church is the apse of a 5th-century Byzantine church. Behind it is the triple apse of a 12th-century Crusader church. Also to be seen here are the square

pre-Constantinian baptistry and, down a flight of steps, the mosaic floor which was the cave floor in the Byzantine period.

To reach the upper, modern level, use the stairs near the main entrance. The colours of the stained-glass windows here are highlighted against the bare stone. It is the basilica's collection of murals depicting Mary and the Baby Jesus, donated by Christian groups from all around the world, which is its most popular feature. Leave the upper level via the northern door to come out into a courtyard facing Terra Sancta Monastery which houses the Franciscan monks who maintain the basilica. Under the courtyard lie more excavations of ancient Nazareth.

Legend has it that when the Muslims captured Nazareth in 1263, they intended to convert the Crusaders' Church into a mosque. However, angels appeared and carried the building across the sea to Italy. Today the Italian town of Loretto is known as the Nazareth of Italy and contains the church mentioned in the legend, which was first heard of in the 15th century.

No visitors are allowed inside the basilica during services, otherwise it is open April to September, Monday to Saturday from 8.30 to 11.45 am and 2 to 5.45 pm, Sundays and holy days 2 to 5.45 pm; October to March, Monday to Saturday 9 to 11.45 am and 2 to 4.45 pm, Sundays and holy days 2 to 4.45 pm. Admission is free. Most of Nazareth's other churches have the same visiting hours.

St Joseph's Church

Just up Casa Nova St from the basilica and monastery is St Joseph's Church, built in 1914 and occupying the traditional site of Joseph's carpentry shop. This belief probably originated in the 17th century and today's church was built over the remains of a medieval church. Down in the crypt you can see an underground cave used for grain storage in pre-Byzantine times.

Sisters of Nazareth Convent

Up the side street, across from the basilica with the Casa Nova Hospice on the corner, this convent is on the right. It operates a school for deaf and blind Arab children as well as providing accommodation for travellers in its hospice and hostel, and the convent boasts one of the best examples of an ancient tomb sealed by a rolling stone. It lies under the present courtyard and can only be viewed by appointment.

Market

At the top of Casa Nova St is the Arab market occupying a maze of steep and narrow, winding streets. Unfortunately, it is dominated not by shops crammed with exotic bargains, but by an open drain running in the middle of the street. This is seemingly provided for the benefit of the donkeys which carry goods up and down the hill.

Greek Catholic Synagogue Church

In a prominent position in the market, this church is beside the synagogue traditionally believed to be where Jesus regularly prayed and later taught (Luke 4:15-30).

Mensa Christi Church

Built in 1861, this small Franciscan church contains a large rock known in Latin as *Mensa Christi* (Table of Christ). Tradition has it that Jesus dined here with his disciples after the Resurrection. It is north-west of St Charles Borramaeus Convent; the Maronite Church and Ecumenical Christian Child Care Centre are nearby.

St Gabriel's Church & Mary's Well

The story surrounding this Greek Orthodox church and the nearby well conflicts with that of the basilica. According to this tradition, the angel Gabriel appeared before Mary while she was fetching water – not when she was in what is now the grotto in the basilica. The church was built in the late 17th century on the site of earlier churches and the crypt at the far end contains the source of the spring supplying the nearby well. The church is about a 10-minute walk north of the basilica, two blocks west of where Paul VI St ends.

Mary's Well, also known as the Virgin's Fountain, is now an unimpressive faucet

down from St Gabriel's Church by Paul VI St. Some believe that the angel Gabriel appeared here and the water is said to have powers of healing.

Basilica & School of Jesus the Adolescent

Built in 1918 in 13th-century style, this is probably the most beautiful of Nazareth's many churches. It belongs to the French Salesian Order and its attractive architecture, both inside and out, and the impressive views of the town below and surrounding countryside could justify your hiking up the steep slope to reach it. It's next door to the Salesian school.

Chapel of Fright

Luke 4:29-30 tells of when the people of Nazareth tried to throw Jesus off the top of a hill. In the southern part of the town, the Franciscan Chapel of Fright, or Notre Dame de l'Effroi, is built on the supposed site from where Mary watched this event. The nearby hill is known as the 'precipice' or the Leap of the Lord. Look for the signposted gate in the wall on Paul VI St, opposite the Galilee Hotel. The church is behind the wall, beyond St Claire's Convent.

Places to Stay

The *Sisters of Nazareth Convent* (☎ 554304) provides by far the best cheap accommodation in town. Up Casa Nova St, turn left after the Casa Nova Hospice across from the basilica and it's up the street on the right. It's the door marked by the sign 'Religieuses de Nazareth – Sisters of Nazareth'. With beautiful architecture and a delightful cloistered courtyard, this is a peaceful haven and one of the cleanest places that you will find anywhere. There's a tastefully furnished lounge-dining room and kitchen; dorm beds cost US$6. There are also singles/doubles for US$14/24 with meals available for those staying in private rooms.

The dorms are open all year round, but the wing with the private rooms is closed during late January and throughout February. For the rest of the year, peaking at Easter and in the summer, it is busy with pilgrim groups from Europe so you would be well advised to make a reservation if possible. The dorm is rarely full – check in after about 4 pm. You are expected to be out by 9 am and there is a strict 9 pm curfew. Although Nazareth may not be all that popular with visitors, the convent is such a nice place to stay that many choose to make it a base from which to visit other parts of Galilee. You are officially limited to a maximum stay of three nights in the dorm but this rule is sometimes waived.

The alternatives to the Sisters of Nazareth's hospitality are generally more expensive, and usually less friendly and comfortable. Coming a fairly close second, though, is the *Casa Nova Hospice* (☎ 571367), across from the basilica on Casa Nova St. Belonging to the Franciscans, it is very popular with, and usually filled by, pilgrim groups. The hospice is excellent value, providing pleasant rooms and serving good food. It costs about US$20 per person with breakfast; inquire about half and full board. The curfew is at 10.30 pm.

There are other Christian institutions that provide accommodation, but they have limited facilities which are specifically for pilgrims. These include the *Frères de Betharram Monastery* (☎ 570046) with singles/doubles for US$18 per person, including breakfast and lunch, and the *Sisters of St Charles Borramaeus Convent* (☎ 554435), above the Carmelite Convent up on the western slopes. You may be able to get cheaper dorm beds at both of these.

Nazareth also has three hotels to provide a secular but not great alternative to the religious establishments. The modern *Hotel Galilee* (☎ 571311) on Paul VI St about five minutes' walk south of the basilica, has singles/doubles for US$22/35, and is the most central and probably the nicest of the three. The *Nazareth Hotel* (☎ 572045) is out of the way, on the edge of town at the inter-section of the Haifa to Afulla highway; singles/doubles are US$31/40. Further out towards Haifa is the *Grand New Hotel* (☎ 73020/1, 73325) on St Joseph St, where singles/doubles are US$32/42.

Places to Eat

The best places to eat in Nazareth are undoubtedly in the Christian hospices. Failing that, the next best thing is to cook for yourself.

The market is the place to buy fresh veg-etables and fruit, and there are grocery shops and bakeries along Paul VI St in both direc-tions from Casa Nova St. Between the basilica and the bus station are several good felafel stalls, whilst a place for some hummus and/or a bottle of beer is the *Astoria Restaurant* on the corner of Casa Nova and Paul VI Sts.

Just up the street, across from the basilica, *Mahroum's Sweets* enjoys a reputation as the best place in town for baclava and other honey-soaked pastries. Several places have the same name, but the original is the one nearest to the basilica.

Getting There & Away

Bus Nazareth is a stop en route for several buses that cross Galilee. Remember that because the bus station here consists of an insignificant couple of bus stops, you could easily miss it and end up going through the town without realising it. Keep a lookout for the basilica, the Hamishbir department store, the Hapoalim Bank and the Paz petrol station.

There are buses about every hour to Tiberias (34 km), Afulla (six km), Akko (14 km) and Haifa (35 km), and less frequently to Tel Aviv and just twice a day to Jerusalem. Stand outside the Hamishbir department store for the Tiberias bus; for all other desti-nations stand on the other side of the street.

The Egged information office is open Sunday to Thursday 4 am to 7 pm, Friday 4 am to 3 pm, and is closed Saturday. The left-luggage office next door is open Sunday to Thursday, 7.30 am to 5 pm, Friday 7.30 am to 1 pm, and is also closed Saturday.

Sheruts Sheruts to Tiberias leave from in front of the Hamishbir department store. For Haifa and Tel Aviv sheruts, go to the street by the side of the Paz petrol station. You will also get sheruts coming through Nazareth from Haifa, Tiberias and other places which are looking for extra passengers, so keep a lookout for them at the bus station.

Getting Around
All of the sights are within walking distance of the bus station, as are most of the places to stay.

AROUND NAZARETH & TIBERIAS
Cana
Known today as Kafer Kanna, this Arab town, seven km north-east of Nazareth on the road to Tiberias, is the purported site of Jesus' first miracle (John 2:1-11) when he changed water into wine at a wedding reception. It was also where he told the official that his son was cured (John 4:46-54) and it was the home town of the disciple Nathanael (John 21:2).

Franciscan Church This was built in 1881 on the traditional site of Jesus' first miracle. It contains an old jar of the type that contained the water he turned into wine. Under the church floor you can see a fragment of a mosaic pavement that bears an ancient Jewish Aramaic inscription.

St Nathanael Chapel Also belonging to the Franciscans and near their church, it is built on the traditional site of the disciple Nathanael's house.

Greek Church This contains ancient stone vats that some believe were involved in Jesus' first miracle. The painting on the wall, believed to date from 1849, portrays the miracle.

Getting There & Away Arab buses leave about every 45 minutes from near Mary's Well in Nazareth to go to Cana. Alternatively, Egged bus No 431 between Tiberias and Nazareth regularly passes the village – ask the driver to let you off. The Greek Church is nearest the main road, the Franciscan church and chapel are in the town centre.

Horns of Hittin
About 14 km east of Cana, heading towards Tiberias, the Horns of Hittin can be seen to the north. This long and low horn-shaped hill was where the Muslims, led by Saladin, defeated the Crusaders on 4 July 1187 and took control of most of the Holy Land in one of history's most important battles. There is nothing much to see here, but those with a keen interest might want to visit the summit; reached via a sideroad and a track two km from both Kibbutz Lavi and Zomet Poriyya.

At the foot of the Horns of Hittin is the traditional site of the Tomb of Jethro, holy to the Druze who make a pilgrimage here on 25 April.

Mount Tabor
With glorious views across the multi-coloured patchwork of fields of the Jezreel Valley, Mount Tabor is the traditional site of the Transfiguration of Jesus (Matthew 17:1-9, Mark 9:2-8 and Luke 9:28-36). This was when Jesus was seen by some of the disciples to be talking with the prophets Moses and Elijah. Two large churches on the summit, Franciscan and Greek, commemorate the event.

Neanderthal people came here from 80,000 to 15,000 BC to make flint tools, but because of the lack of water they were unable to settle; they worked here and lived elsewhere. The first Biblical mention of Mount Tabor is Judges 4:5-16, in relation to Deborah and Barak's victory over Hazor in 1125 BC. Judges 46:18 makes Mount Tabor a symbol of Nebuchadnezer's might. Hosea 5:1 relates to the altars built here to the heathen gods. In 218 BC the Egyptian soldiers stationed on the mount's summit were enticed down into the valley to be slaughtered by the Syrian forces of Antiochus III who were feigning retreat. In 67 AD the Romans under General Placidus did much the same to defeat the Jews who, led by Josephus, had fortified their position.

It is suggested that the Transfiguration

was first linked to the site at the beginning of the Byzantine period. Mount Hermon in the Golan Heights was another contender, along with the Mount of Olives.

A Byzantine church was probably still standing when Benedictine monks were installed on the mount in 1099 by the Crusaders. They were massacred in a Turkish attack in 1113 that also saw their buildings destroyed. They later returned to build a new church and monastery which survived an attack by Saladin in 1183, but the nearby Greek church of St Elijah was destroyed. However, the Benedictines were forced to leave after the Crusaders' defeat at the Horns of Hittin in 1187.

The Muslims then built their own fortress on the mount and, as it was on the site of the Transfiguration, it inspired the 5th Crusade. Although a Crusader siege in 1217 failed, the Muslims dismantled the fortress because they realised that it would continue to be a serious provocation. Later in the 13th century a series of truces made it possible for Christians to return to the mount but in 1263 they were expelled by King Baybars.

Church of St Elijah Built in 1911, this church stands next to the Franciscan basilica although the access roads are some distance apart. The Cave of Melchizedek, its entrance marked by an iron door in the wall just after the turn-off for the Greek church, is where he received Abraham (Genesis 14:17-20), according to a medieval tradition.

Basilica of the Transfiguration The entrance to the Franciscan complex is through the main gate of the Muslim's 13th-century fortress, restored in 1897. Its defence wall, including 12 towers, goes all the way round the summit. About 150 metres inside the gate to the right is a small chapel. Built on Byzantine foundations it commemorates the conversation between Jesus and his disciples after the Transfiguration (Mark 9:9-13). The cemetery to the north is medieval, the one to the south 1st century.

At the end of the drive is the basilica (built in 1924), definitely one of the Holy Land's most beautiful churches, both inside and out. Its highlight for me is the lovely mosaic of the Nativity. On the right of the piazza, in front of the basilica, stands the Franciscan monastery and hospice; on the left are remains of the Byzantine monastery.

No visitors are allowed inside the basilica during services, otherwise it is open April to September, Monday to Saturday 8.30 to 11.45 am and 2 to 5.45 pm; and Sunday and holy days 2 to 5.45 pm. From October to March, it is open Monday to Saturday 9 to 11.45 am and 2 to 4.45 pm; and Sundays and holy days 2 to 4.45 pm. Admission is free.

Panorama With its height of 580 metres, Mount Tabor commands stunning views in all directions. To the north are the mountains of Upper Galilee with Mount Hermon slightly to the east, and in front of it the Horns of Hittin just above the Sea of Galilee further to the east. Nazareth can be seen to the west, with Mount Carmel beyond, and the Samarian mountains blend in from the south round to the east.

Getting There & Away Mount Tabor can be reached most easily by bus from Tiberias, with all Tel Aviv buses stopping at the turn off for the mount. Coming from Nazareth (50 minutes), you need to change buses at Afulla, where you can also connect with buses to most of the major destinations in Israel. However, the Mount Tabor bus from Afulla is infrequent, so check the schedule to avoid a long delay, especially for the return bus.

All buses drop you off at the bottom of the steep and winding road that leads up to the summit; the climb takes about 30 minutes on foot. At the top the turning to the left leads to the Greek church; go straight ahead to reach the Franciscan basilica.

MEGIDDO

Megiddo is best known as Armageddon, the Biblical symbol for the last great battle on earth (Revelation 16:16). The name Armageddon is derived from the Hebrew Har Megiddo (Mount of Megiddo) and it is an important city in ancient history. Today

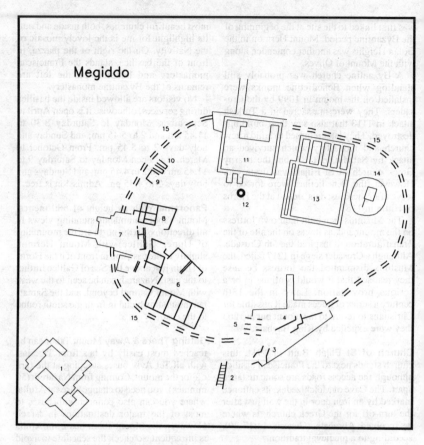

Megiddo

you can visit the archaeological site of Megiddo, maintained by the National Parks Authority, and see the remains of 20 distinct historical periods, from 4000 to 400 BC.

Due to its strategic location at the head of the ancient trade route from Egypt to Syria and Mesopotamia, Megiddo was the scene of important and bloody battles throughout the ages, right up to the 20th century.

Megiddo is first mentioned in the written records of an Egyptian king. Hieroglyphics on the wall of Karnak Temple in Luxor detail the battle that Thutmose III fought at Megiddo in 1468 BC. The account of his

victory includes the capture of 924 enemy chariots. Megiddo remained a prosperous Egyptian stronghold for at least 100 years. Judges 1:27 tells of it being too strong for the invading Israelites to take and it probably fell to David. Under Solomon, in the 10th century BC, it became one of the kingdom's major cities (I Kings 9:15). Megiddo was known then as the Chariot City and excavations have shown relics of stables where Solomon kept thousands of chariots and horses.

Also known as the Way of the Sea, it later became the Roman Empire's Via Maris, a

1	Museum
2	Staircase & Outer Gate
3	Gate - 15th Century BC
4	Gate - 18th Century BC
5	Gate - King Solomon's era
6	Holy Precinct
7	Chalcolithic Temple
8	Residence of Commander of King Solomon's Chariots
9	Observation Point
10	Building - King David's era
11	Palace - King Solomon's era
12	Grain Silo
13	'City of Chariots' - King Solomon's era
14	Water system
15	City Wall - Israelite Kingdom era

vital military zone. By the 4th century BC it had become uninhabited, inexplicably losing its importance as a city. Its strategic importance remained though, and among those armies who fought here were the British in WW I. On being awarded his peerage, General Allenby took the title Lord Allenby of Megiddo. More recently, Jewish and Arab forces fought here during the 1948 War of Independence.

The archaeological site, despite being signposted, is a bit confusing – a plan is available (about US$0.35) and the museum by the entrance contains a few exhibits that explain some of the site's history and how it used to look. One of the excavations is the preserved 9th-century BC water system. This consists of a shaft sunk 30 metres through solid rock to a tunnel of 70 metres. This hid the city's water source from invading forces, rather like Hezekiah's version in Jerusalem. There is no water to slosh through here, though. Save the tunnel till last as it leads you out of the site into the car park.

The site is open Saturday to Thursday, 8 am to 5 pm, and Friday 8 am to 4 pm. Admission is US$2 (students US$1). There is a snack bar and café in the museum.

Getting There & Away
The site is a 10-minute walk from the signposted intersection on the main road between Haifa and the junction of the Afulla to Hadera highway. There are several buses from Haifa that pass by. Buses from Tiberias to Tel Aviv also pass by. Megiddo can also be reached from Nazareth via Afulla. If you want to combine visits to Megiddo and Mount Tabor from Nazareth, it makes sense to make an early morning start and head for Mount Tabor, then return to Afulla for a connecting bus to the Megiddo intersection.

Ein Harod
About 30 km east of Afulla on the road to Beit She'an, a sideroad on the left leads one km up to a kibbutz, a campsite and an IYHA youth hostel. This is the site of Gideon's victory over the Midianites (Judges 7) around 1050 BC.

The kibbutz, established in 1921, features an archaeological and natural history museum and an art gallery which often stages some impressive exhibitions.

Places to Stay The *Ma'ayon Harod Youth Hostel – IYHA* (☎ 531630), has dorm beds for US$9 (members) or US$10.50 (non-members). The campsite (☎ 531604) charges about US$7 per person – no tents are provided.

Getting There & Away Buses going between Afulla and Beit She'an pass the signposted turn-off.

Beit Alpha Synagogue
East of Ein Harod (five km), a sideroad leads to two adjacent kibbutzim, Beit Alpha and Heftziba. In 1928, kibbutzniks uncovered the remains of a 6th-century BC synagogue while digging an irrigation channel. Its mosaic floor is in good condition and is one of the country's best Jewish relics.

The floor consists of three panels. The upper panel shows religious emblems including menorahs, shofars, and the *lulav* (bundle of branches) and *etrog* (citrus fruit). A zodiac circle with the seasons symbolised in each corner makes up the central panel. Abraham's sacrifice is illustrated in the lower panel.

It's open Saturday to Thursday 8 am to 5 pm, and Friday 8 am to 4 pm. Admission is US$1.05 (students US$0.75).

Members of the Makoya, a Japanese Christian sect, study Hebrew on the kibbutz, and their lovely little Japanese garden can be seen up the hill from the synagogue, beyond the swimming pool.

Sachne (Gan HaShlosha)

This is a pleasantly landscaped park with spacious lawns, trees and natural pools connected by gentle waterfalls. The water, with a year-round temperature of 28°C, comes from a spring (*sachne* is Arabic for warm), and the park is known in Hebrew as Gan HaShlosha (Garden of the Three) in memory of three Jews killed here by Arabs in 1938. It's a popular place for a swim or a picnic. There is a snack bar and café, too.

It's open April to September, Saturday to Thursday 8 am to 5 pm, Friday 8 am to 4 pm; October to March, Saturday to Thursday 8 am to 4 pm, Friday 8 am to 3 pm, and admission is US$5 (students US$2.50). One km south-east of Beit Alpha, get off the bus by the signposted side road and it's a short walk to the park's entrance.

Museum of Regional & Mediterranean Archaeology This museum (☎ 586094) houses a good collection of artefacts relating to the country's ancient history and that of neighbouring countries.

It is open Sunday to Thursday 8 am to 2 pm, Friday 8 am to 1 pm, and Saturday 10 am to 1 pm. Admission is US$0.70. The museum is a 10-minute walk up the road behind the park in Kibbutz Nir David.

Getting There & Away Take Egged bus Nos 412 or 415 from Afulla or Beit She'an. Getting off at the right place can be difficult. Look for the orange signs by Kibbutz Heftziba, not Kibbutz Beit Alpha, which is one km closer to Beit She'an.

BEIT SHE'AN

The attractions here are the country's best-preserved Roman amphitheatre and an archaeological museum featuring a Byzantine mosaic floor. On a busy trade route, Beit She'an was an important ancient city and has been continuously occupied for over 5000 years. Excavations have revealed 18 superimposed cities on an 80-metre-high section of ground.

Stone Age people settled here and the first real town was established circa 3000 BC; its name is mentioned in 19th-century BC Egyptian texts. Proof of the Egyptian influence is provided by the excavations; this was one of the strongholds from which the country was controlled by the Pharaohs. In the 13th century BC, the Israelite tribe of Manasseh inherited the area (Judges I:27), losing it to the Philistines in the 11th century BC after the Israelites' defeat on nearby Mount Gilboa, when King Saul's body was hung on the city walls (I Samuel 31).

Jewish sages wrote 'If the Garden of Eden is in Israel, then its gate is at Beit She'an' (Eirubin 19a). Despite being subjected to the heat of the Jordan Valley, the nearby Harod River and the usually sufficient rainfall make this a highly fertile area with thousands of

Bust - Tel Beit She'an

Top: Rock hyrax, Ein Gedi (TW)
Bottom: Fruit shop in Jericho (NT)

Top: The Wilderness of Zin, Negev (NT)
Bottom: Maktesh Ramon, Negev (NT)

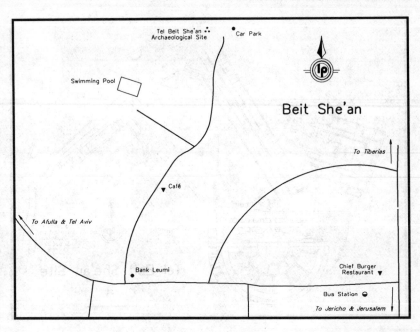

acres of crops. However, the modern day town of Beit She'an is not at all attractive.

Roman Amphitheatre & Byzantine Street
Not to be confused with the main site, these ruins are just a short walk from the bus station. The amphitheatre was used for gladiatorial contests and had 12 rows of seats for 6000 spectators in all. Only three rows can be seen today. The Byzantine street dates from the 5th century AD and connected this area with the main town. A Greek inscription notes that the drainage system dates from 522 AD.

Tel Beit She'an
The extensive site is about 800 metres from the bus station. Head west, left, and follow the road as far as the Bank Leumi, then turn right to go downhill through the park to the site.

There is a swimming pool over to the left,

which is open daily, 9 am to 7 pm; admission is US$2.75.

A hill on the northside of the site offers fine views of the ruins. With restoration work still continuing, it's open April to September, Saturday to Thursday 8 am to 5 pm, Friday 8 am to 4 pm; October to March, Saturday to Thursday 8 am to 4 pm, Friday 8 am to 3 pm and admission is US$3 (students US$1.50).

Theatre The large theatre dates from the Byzantine era and is the best preserved in Israel. It held 6000 spectators and the lower rows have been restored.

Baths The extensive Byzantine bath buildings covered over half a hectare with a paved courtyard and surrounding porticos, paved with mosaics and marble. At the end of the baths building a Byzantine structure sheltered a beautiful 6th-century mosaic of Tyche, the goddess of prosperity and good fortune. It was stolen in 1989.

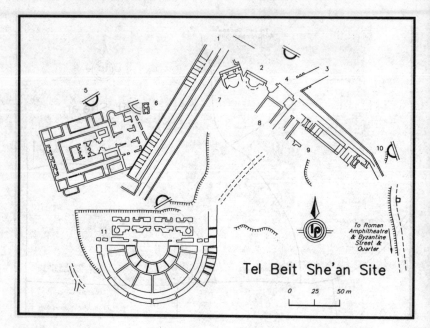

Tel Beit She'an Site

0   25   50 m

To Roman
Amphitheatre
& Byzantine
Street &
Quarter

1   Colonnaded Street
2   Nymphaeum
3   Colonnaded Roman Street
4   Monument & Junction of Two Streets
5   Bath Building
6   Tyche Mosaic
7   Roman Temple
8   Basilica
9   Portico from Roman Period
10 Byzantine Street & Shops
11 Theatre

Street & Temple A colonnaded street paved with slabs in a herringbone pattern runs north-east from the theatre. The columns on the western side once supported a portico in front of a row of shops. On the east side of the street is a ruined temple which collapsed in an 8th-century earthquake.

Other Structures Another colonnaded street is flanked by the foundations of a nymphaeum, a basilica, a Roman portico and the remains of a Byzantine street of shops.

Places to Eat

There is a snack bar in the bus station, and across the street are some cafés and felafel stands. On the road leading down to the site is another café.

Getting There & Away

Beit She'an is a stop-off point for the Tiberias-Jerusalem bus and there are also regular services between here and Afulla, making it accessible from Nazareth.

BELVOIR

This is an attractive destination for a brief visit, with its 12th-century Crusader castle ruins and great views over the Jezreel Valley, the Jordanian Gilead Mountains and, on a clear day, even the Sea of Galilee and Mount Hermon.

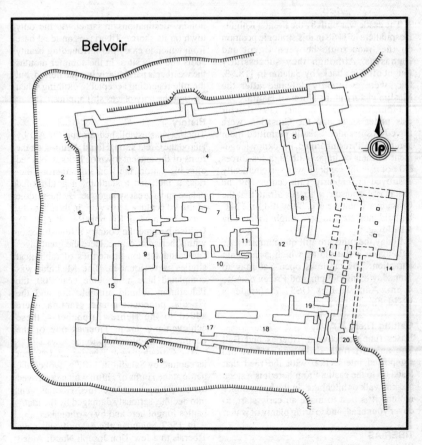

Belvoir

1 Moat (Western)
2 Moat (Northern)
3 Inner Corner Tower
4 Northern Court
5 Workshop
6 Postern Gate
7 Central Court
8 Outer Water Cistern
9 Inner Western Gate
10 Inner Southern Vault (Refectory)
11 Kitchen
12 Eastern Court
13 Eastern Vault (Stores & Stables)
14 Outer Eastern Tower
15 Outer Western Gate
16 Moat (Southern)
17 Postern Gate
18 Southern Vault
19 Inner Eastern Gate (Stores & Stables)
20 Outer Eastern Gate

The castle was built by the French Knights Hospitallers in 1168 in this strategic position on the trade route between Egypt and Damascus. Although they successfully fought off two attacks by Saladin in 1182-3, they were eventually defeated after the Muslim victory at the Horns of Hattin.

From July 1187 to January 1191 Belvoir was under siege and the Crusaders were forced to surrender. Saladin permitted them to retreat to Tyre unharmed, in acknowledgement of their courage. Although his forces did not raze the castle, it was systematically destroyed in the early 13th century by the Sultan of Damascus who was afraid that the Crusaders would return. They did, in 1241, but did not stay long enough to do any rebuilding.

Today the ruins are still quite impressive, although it is the setting which is the main attraction. The castle is open Saturday to Thursday 8 am to 5 pm, and Friday 8 am to 4 pm. Admission is US$1.75 (students US$0.90).

Getting There & Away

Buses running between Tiberias and Beit She'an will only drop you off at the signposted intersection with the road that leads up to the castle. From here it is a steep six-km walk or hitchhike. In the hot summer months it is best to make an early start, to cover your head, and to bring plenty of water.

TIBERIAS

(Population: 29,500)

The Sea of Galilee is one of the most popular holiday destinations in Israel. As the only town on its shores, Tiberias is an ideal base from which to enjoy the surrounding beauty spots and holy sites. In the summer months the weather is particularly hot and humid, but the rule regarding acceptable clothing when visiting the holy places still applies.

History

Tiberias was established around 20 AD by Herod the Great's son, Herod Antipas, on the ruins of the ancient town of Rakkat. Named after his patron, the Roman Emperor Tiberius, it included a stadium, a gold-roofed palace and a great synagogue. By the middle of the 1st century, Jews were in the majority, and after the Bar Kochba Revolt (132-5), Galilee became the country's Jewish sector with Tiberias its centre. Here the great sages came and the top academies of rabbinical studies were founded. The Mishnah was completed here around the year 200, the Palestinian Talmud around 400, and the vowels, punctuation and grammar were added to the Hebrew alphabet – these achievements made Tiberias one of the country's four cities holy to the Jews.

The Crusaders took Tiberias in 1099, but its capture by Saladin in 1187 provoked the battle at the Horns of Hittin which destroyed the Latin kingdom. After this, Tiberias went into decline, seriously damaged by the many battles fought here and by earthquakes.

In 1562 Suleiman the Magnificent gave Tiberias to a Jew, Don Joseph Nussi. Aided by his mother-in-law, Donna Grazia, he attempted to revive the town as a Jewish

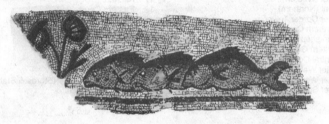

Fish & Lotus Mosaic

enclave. Historians disagree about his success: some say he made Tiberias flourish for 100 years, others that he failed completely. In the 18th century Daher el-Omar, an Arab sheikh, established an independent fiefdom in Galilee, and Tiberias was an integral part of it. He was assassinated in 1775 and an earthquake in 1837 demolished the town.

The Jews of the First Aliyah (at the end of the 19th century) mostly settled in Tiberias, and with the expansion of the Zionist movement many more immigrants have arrived, particularly since Israel's independence.

Following their 1948 defeat, Syrian troops positioned on the Golan Heights intermittently shelled Israeli targets to the north and east of Tiberias and Israel subsequently took the Heights in the 1967 Six Day War. In the 1973 Yom Kippur War, Syria attacked the Israeli installations on the Heights but were eventually defeated again. As a result of these and other border incidents, it is only over the last 15 years that the area around the Sea of Galilee has been fully developed as a tourist attraction. Tiberias in particular has become more and more commercialised. Unfortunately, this has meant a proliferation of gaudy buildings, as hotels and eating places compete to win business. Tiberias is not a good-looking town, but the surrounding natural beauty still manages to reign supreme.

Orientation

On the south-western shore of the Sea of Galilee, Tiberias is a small and easy place to get to know. There are three basic sections: the Old City, which is the all-important downtown and hostel area by the lakeside; the residential Qiryat Shemuel up the hill to the north; and Beit Ma'on, atop the hill.

Old City Do not expect to find a lovely walled section and quaint stone buildings à la Jerusalem or Akko. Invaders and earthquakes ensured that Israeli architects would have the opportunity to slap up an incongruous mix of styles with only a few reminders

of the ancient past interspersed between them.

Most visitors arrive at the bus station on HaYarden St. Two blocks down towards the lake is HaGalil St which, with HaBanim St, runs parallel to the water and is the main street. Along here are the shops, banks, post office and tourist office. The hostels and some hotels are nearby.

Qiryat Shemuel HaBanim St continues up the hill to the north, changing to become first Alhadif St, then Yehuda HaNassi St and finally Nazareth Rd. Dotted amongst the maze of curving streets are most of the middle-range hotels. This district is named after Sir Herbert Samuel, a prominent Jew and the first British High Commissioner of Palestine.

Beit Ma'on Up here you have the best views of Tiberias. Apart from one hotel and a cinema, there is little else for the visitor.

Hammat South of the Old City, HaGalil St changes to become Eliezer Kaplan Blvd and follows the shoreline two km to Hammat. Here there are natural hot springs and important ancient Jewish tombs and a synagogue. The road continues to circle the lake where various campsites occupy the shore.

Information

Tourist Office At the time of writing, the IGTO (☎ 720992) was scheduled to move to a new location in the vicinity of the Plaza Hotel. Its hours should remain the same: Sunday to Thursday 8 am to 6 pm, Friday 8 am to 2 pm, closed Saturday.

Post & Telecommunications The main post office is on HaYarden St (☎ 21515), across from HaGalil and HaBanim Sts. It is open Sunday, Monday, Tuesday and Thursday 8 am to 12.30 pm and 3.30 to 6 pm, Wednesday 8 am to 1.30 pm, Friday 8 am to noon, and is closed Saturday.

For international telephones, go to the Bezek office, which is off the Midrahov, and adjacent to Big Ben pub. It is open Sunday

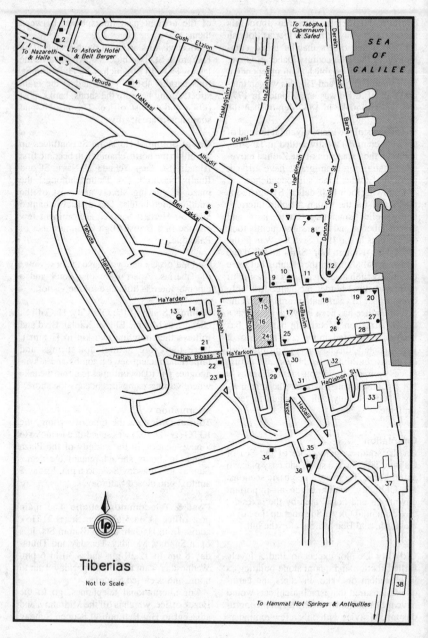

Tiberias

Not to Scale

1	Eden Hotel
2	Pe'er Hotel
3	HaGalil Hotel
4	Continental Hotel
5	Ministry of the Interior
6	Rambam's Tomb
7	Crusader Castle
8	Lamb & Goose Restaurant
9	Cinema
10	Post Office
11	Meyouhas Youth Hostel (IYHA)
12	Church of Scotland Hospice
13	Bus Station
14	Bicycle Hire
15	Felafel Shops
16	Shim'on Park
17	Felafel Shops
18	Supermarket & Shopping Area Ha'Atzmaut Square
19	Terra Sancta Hotel
20	Karamba Restaurant
21	Hotel Toledo
22	Sweitzer Hostel
23	Adina's Guesthouse
24	El Farsi Restaurant (Shishlik)
25	Shipoday Himelreh Restaurant (Shishlik)
26	Great Mosque
27	Ferries
28	Caesar Hotel
29	Maman Restaurant
30	Aviv Hotel/Hostel
31	Pub Row
32	Jordan River Hotel
33	Plaza Hotel
34	Maman Hostel
35	Guy Restaurant
36	Nahum Hostel
37	Galei Kinneret Hotel & Au Bord du Lac Restaurant
38	Gai Beach Hotel

to Thursday 8.45 am to 10.45 pm, and Friday 8 am to 2.30 pm; it's closed Saturday.

SPNI During the summer an information stand operates at the Beit She'an junction south of the lake. Inquire here about camp-sites, hikes, and almost anything – the staff are very helpful.

Other Camping equipment can be hired from Gal-Cal (☎ 20123), on HaShiloah St in

front of the bus station. It's open Sunday to Thursday 7 am to 7 pm, Friday 7 am to 4.30 pm, and is closed Saturday.

HaGalil St houses various bank branches, a Steimatzsky's bookshop and Blumfield's laundromat. For police, phone ☎ 92444, emergency 100.

Tours
Tiberias Although there is little to see of the town's historical past, there are a couple of free guided tours that go a little way to pointing out the evidence.

On Wednesday and Saturday meet in reception at the Plaza Hotel for a 10 am start (English and German are spoken). On Sunday, also at 10 am, meet in reception at the Galei Kinneret Hotel for a guided tour of 'Biblical & Roman Tiberias'. Check whether these tours are in operation during your stay in town – they normally take place only during summer.

Sea of Galilee, Upper Galilee & Golan With the distinct lack of public transport in the region, taking an organised tour often makes a lot of sense and can even be cheaper than doing it yourself.

Popular with travellers are the taxi tours offered by two local guides that each take in the Sea of Galilee, Upper Galilee and Golan. Opinions vary on who offers the best tour for your dollar. Max Bullhorn (☎ 793588) and Moshe Cohen (☎ 721608) each charge US$25. Starting out from Tiberias at about 8.30 am and returning by about 4 pm, they manage to fit in most of the essential sites. For those on a tight budget, this might seem out of reach but you will see in one day, and in relative comfort, what would take at least three days and a lot of hitchhiking or waiting around for the infrequent buses to do by yourself. Both tours can be booked at the Tiberias hostels and hotels.

Egged Tours cover some of the same area for US$22, leaving from Tiberias bus station on Tuesday, Thursday and Saturday. They have similar tours leaving from Haifa for US$37, and Tel Aviv for US$40 to US$43.

SPNI offers some guided camping hikes

in the area. Although a bit more expensive, they do take you to some great out-of-the-way places that you probably would not find on your own and that are usually inaccessible by bus or car.

Tomb of Rabbi Akiva
Above the Old City, beyond Qiryat Shemuel and the police station, a white dome covers the cave-tomb of Rabbi Akiva. Born in 50 AD, he was one of the great Jewish scholars, and was killed by the Romans for his role in the Bar Kochba Revolt in 135 AD.

Tombs of Rabbi Moshe Ben-Maimon & Rabbi Yohanan Ben-Zakkai
About two blocks on the right up Yohanan Ben-Zakkai St, a continuation of HaGalil north of HaYarden St, these two tombs testify to the holy status of Tiberias.

Better known by his acronym Rambam, Ben-Maimon was born in Spain in 1135 and was one of the 12th century's highly regarded sages. An Aristotelian philosopher, physician, astronomer and scientist, he died in 1204.

Ben-Zakkai founded the Yavne Academy and was Palestine's most eminent sage when the Romans destroyed Jerusalem in the 1st century. Near to his tomb are the tombs of Rabbi Eliezer the Great, a prominent 2nd-century scholar; Rav Ammi and Rav Assii who lived in the 3rd century; and Rabbi Isaiah Horowitz, who died around 1630.

Old City Walls & Castle
Remnants of the black basalt wall, built by Daher el-Omar in 1738, can be seen in the Old City. The section now housing an art studio, gallery and restaurant, north of the tourist office on Alhadif St, is sometimes called the Crusader Castle. It was possibly built later on in the 18th century by Daher el-Omar's son, Chulabi.

Great Mosque
In the middle of shopping arcades, this mosque was also built by Daher el-Omar in the mid-18th century. It is generally believed that its construction was partly paid for by

the town's Jewish community, presumably grateful to the sheikh for being permitted to return.

St Peter's Church
This Franciscan church, commonly called Terra Sancta, was built in the 12th century by the Crusaders. The Muslims converted it into a mosque and the Turks used it as a caravanserai before it became a church again. In 1870 it was rebuilt, in 1903 enlarged and in 1944 restored. Its two main points of interest are the boat-shaped nave (relating to Peter's fishing origins), and the courtyard built by the Polish soldiers stationed here during WW II. It's open daily 8 to 11.45 am, and 2 to 5 pm. Admission is free. There is also a hostel here. The church entrance is on the promenade.

The Galilee Experience
Located on the waterfront (☎ 723620; fax 723195), this 37-minute 'multi-image attraction' presents the history, geography and spiritual significance of the region in a state-of-the-art slide show. Operated by a group of Christian believers, admission is US$6 (students US$5).

With hourly screenings in English, and daily screenings in German and French, it's open Sunday to Thursday from 8 am to 10 pm, Friday 8 am to 4 pm, and for limited hours Saturday evening. The complex also features an art gallery, a café, a souvenir shop and bookshop.

Church & Monastery of the Apostles
South of the Plaza Hotel by the waterside, this Greek Orthodox complex is on the site of a Byzantine monastery that was destroyed by the Persians in the 7th century. It was replaced and then destroyed again several times over the years; today's building was restored in 1975.

Three monks live here and are sometimes available to let you in when you ring the bell. There are four chapels beyond the pleasant walled courtyard. One chapel is dedicated to St Peter, one to the disciples, one to Mary

Magdalene and the one in the ancient round tower to St Nicholas.

Hot Springs

The hot springs, containing high amounts of sulphuric, muriatic and calcium salts, are believed to have excellent curative powers for such ailments as rheumatism, arthritis, gout, and nervous and gynaecological disorders. The springs have been known for thousands of years – in biblical times a town called Hammath was built around the springs (Joshua 19:35). Its name was taken from the Hebrew *ham* (hot), and it was part of the territory of the Naphtali tribe.

Different legends surround origins of the springs. Some believe that they were formed during the great flood of the Bible when the hot middle of the earth rose up; others say that it was here that Jesus cured many sick people. Perhaps the most imaginative story credits King Solomon with the springs' creation. This legend has it that the king was approached by a group of sick men who begged him to find a cure for them. Solomon sent a group of demons to heat the water at the springs, making them deaf so that they would not hear the news of his death and stop working. It seems more likely, however, that the hot springs were first enjoyed by Stone Age people some 10,000 years ago.

In 110 AD, Roman emperor Trajan had a coin struck dedicated to Tiberias, with the image of Hygea, the goddess of health, shown sitting on a rock enjoying the water. The springs were also mentioned by Idris, an Arab writer who lived during the Crusades, and recommended by the Ramban to his patients. Bathing and therapy facilities in Tiberias date back to these times and were much appreciated by those well-known bath-lovers, the Romans and the Turks.

Today there are two complexes. The older one across the road from the lake, Tiberias Hot Springs, is for people with serious skin problems. The more modern Young Tiberias Hot Springs nearby is open to the general public. You don't need to suffer from any particular ailment to enjoy a good soak or massage.

They open Sunday to Thursday 8 am to 8 pm, Friday 8 am to 2.30 pm, and Saturday 8.30 am to 8 pm. There are various options at various prices. For example, a dip in the thermal pools costs US$10, a massage US$15, and a combined pool and massage is US$20. Prices are a little higher on Saturday. Egged bus Nos 2 and 5 stop outside, or you can walk the two km from the city centre.

Ancient Synagogue of Hammat

Behind the hot springs, away from the lake, the Ernest Lehman Museum displays the reconstructed ruins of the ancient town of Hammat. The highlight is the synagogue with its mosaic floor, dating to the 2nd or 3rd centuries. It's open daily 8 am to 5 pm, and admission is US$0.90.

Tomb of Rabbi Meir Ba'al Hanes

Up the hill from the museum and the hot springs is one of Israel's holiest places for Jews, the tomb of the 2nd-century rabbi who helped to compile the Mishnah. A pupil of Rabbi Akiva, he became renowned as 'the Miracle-Maker' due to the legends telling of his miraculous rescue of his sister-in-law, held captive by the Romans.

The tomb is marked by two synagogues, the one on the left Sephardic, and the other Ashkenazi. In the courtyard of the Sephardic synagogue is a pillar topped by a large bowl. Four days before the Lag B'Omer holiday a bonfire is lit here on the Pesach Sheni (second Passover). Crowds of religious Jews visit throughout the year to pray. It is a tradition that God will answer the prayers of pilgrims who have personal problems.

Places to Stay

Tiberias offers some of Israel's better hostels, a lovely Christian hospice in the middle-price range, and one of the country's best top-end hotels. Note that you can choose between staying in Tiberias itself or in more peaceful and scenic surroundings on the shores of the adjacent lake (see Places to Stay in the Sea of Galilee section).

Places to Stay – bottom end

The hostels are all within walking distance of the bus station. Due to the fierce competition between them, you will often have touts greeting you as you get off the bus. Be aware that prices are subject to dramatic changes – up during Jewish holidays when Israelis flock here and down immediately afterwards when nervous proprietors outbid each other to attract the travellers.

It is best to ask around to see what the going rates are before agreeing to a price. All these places charge about the same, unless stated otherwise: dorm beds from US$7 to US$8, doubles from US$18 to US$26; add about 25% for the holidays.

One of the most popular hostels in town seems to be *Nahum Hostel* (☎ 721505) on Tavor St, which doesn't raise its prices during the holidays. From the bus station bear right along HaShiloah St and follow it round to the left where it intersects with Tavor St. Nahum Hostel is across Tavor St to the right. It has a rooftop terrace and bar where videos are played in the evening, a kitchen, and there are bicycles for hire. Some larger rooms are great value for families and small groups. There's a flexible midnight curfew.

En route to Nahum Hostel, as you take HaShiloah St round to the left and down the hill on the right, you come to a favourite alternative, *Maman Hostel* (☎ 792986). A nice-looking place with its garden and terrace, it has a kitchen, bar, clean showers and a tiny swimming pool. They also have some great value larger rooms. There is a flexible midnight curfew.

Not as popular with travellers as it is with Israelis, *Shweitzer Hostel* (☎ 721991) is on the right as you head up HaShiloah St from the bus station. There's a kitchen and no curfew. A little further along is the more pleasant *Adina's Guesthouse* (☎ 722507). Run by an Orthodox Yemenite family, this is a family house with separate kitchen and bathroom facilities for guests, and a terrace. You have a key so there's no set curfew. It has private rooms only, and there are no dorm facilities available.

From the bus station, walk down HaYarden St to the centre of town for the other hostels. Turn right on HaGalil St to find the *Aviv Hotel/Hostel* (☎ 722031, 723510) on the corner of HaYarkon St. This may be Israel's longest building. There's a lounge and two kitchens, bike hire and no curfew.

A couple of hostels overlook the lake. *Terra Sancta* (☎ 722955) is in the building adjacent to St Peter's Church. The entrance is on the other side, up the stairs on HaYarden St just up from the water. It has a kitchen and a terrace with nice views, but it's a bit spartan.

Further south along HaBanim St, near the Plaza Hotel, is the *Lake Castle Hostel* (☎ 721175). It has a kitchen, bar, views of the lake and bike hire.

Back to HaYarden St and across from the supermarket is the *Meyouhas Youth Hostel* (☎ 721775, 790350; fax 720372). One of the country's nicest IYHA hostels, it has a TV room, but no kitchen facilities for guests. Dorm beds cost US$5.50 for members, and US$7 for nonmembers. Breakfast at US$3.50 is mandatory, and other meals are available. Reception is open 6.30 to 9 am and 4 pm to midnight. Between October and March there's a midnight curfew, and from April to September it's 1 am.

The *Church of Scotland Hospice* has what was a pleasant hostel with dorm beds and a kitchen. Closed at the time of writing, inquire about rates and availability (see Places to Stay – middle).

Places to Stay – middle

Just past the Meyouhas Youth Hostel towards the lake is the *Church of Scotland Hospice* (☎ 723769, 721165; fax 790145). A lovely place; it has friendly staff, is comfortably furnished, and has good facilities including a garden and private beach. B&B is US$25 per person in larger than average singles/doubles. The main gate is locked at 10.30 pm but guests can get their own key. With the lack of comparable alternatives, this place can be full, especially at weekends and holidays, so book ahead if you can.

Elsewhere, hotel rooms seem overpriced when compared to some of the private rooms available in the better hostels. Close to the bus station is the *Hotel Toledo* (☎ 721649). Turn right up HaShiloah St and right again up HaRab Bibass St. Singles/doubles are US$40/50.

HaEmek Hotel (☎ 720308), at 17 HaGalil St, three blocks south of Ha'Atzmaut Square, is basically furnished and is clean enough, with singles/doubles from US$18/36. Next door is the *Panorama Hotel* (☎ 720963), a little more basic with singles/doubles from US$22/30 – breakfast and other meals are extra and can be taken in the restaurant downstairs. Continuing south along HaGalil St you come to the *HaGilal Hotel* (☎ 720007) at No 4 above the Haroe Pub & Restaurant. It's nice enough, with singles/doubles at US$24/36.

Most middle-range hotels are up in Qiryat Shemuel, a bit out of the way unless you have a car. Some of them do have great views across the lake, though.

Among the best of these is the *Pe'er Hotel* (☎ 791641), 2 Ohel Ya'acov St. Some of its rooms have balconies which face the lake, and there's a restaurant and nightclub; singles cost from US$45 to US$60, and doubles from US$60 to US$75.

Next door is the *Eden Hotel* (☎ 790070; fax 722461), and further up the street on the corner with Naiberg St is the *Astoria Hotel* (☎ 722351; fax 722352) with similar facilities and prices. *Beit Berger* (☎ 720850) is recommended by readers. Located across from the Astoria, this private pension has air-con rooms with bath and a fridge for US$20.

Another of the better places here is the small *Hotel Ron* (☎ 720259), at 12 Ahad Ha'am St. It's modern and simple with good service, food and views; singles/doubles are US$30/50. The *Hotel Daphna* (☎ 792261/4; fax 724484) is just off Yehuda HaNassi St on Ussishkin St; singles/doubles are US$40/58.

Moving down the hill towards the Old City you come to the *Continental Hotel* (☎ 20018) on Alhadif St, at the corner of Tabur HaAretz St. It's a small, older place,

with a homey atmosphere; singles cost from US$33 to US$38, and doubles from US$52 to US$58.

South of Tiberias, by the hot springs, are two nicer hotels. The first you come to is the swish-looking *Ganei Hammat Hotel* (☎ 792890, 724443). Owned by the proprietors of the hot springs, it has four-star status; singles cost from US$64 to US$90, and doubles are as much as US$122. In addition to the nearby spa and sauna facilities, there is a piano bar, nightclub and tennis courts. Further south is the pleasant *Ganei Menorah Hotel* (☎ 792770; fax 790101), set in nicely kept grounds with lovely lake views. A peaceful place, singles cost from US$33 to US$38, doubles from US$52 to US$58.

Places to Stay – top end
The long-established top hotel in Tiberias is the *Galei Kinneret* (☎ 792331; fax 790260) at the southern end of the Old City overlooking the lake. Mentioned in books by Leon Uris, James D McDonald, Taylor Caldwell and Edwin Samuel, it has a touch of class not found elsewhere in town. The facilities include an outdoor pool, gardens, water sports and a fine restaurant. Singles cost from US$95 to US$155, and doubles from US$112 to US$170.

The other downtown top-end hotels contribute to the ugliness of the city. The *Moriah Tiberias Plaza* (☎ 792233; fax 792320) is in the centre of the Old City, singles cost from US$95 to US$155, and doubles from US$110 to US$170. Just to the south is the *Jordan River* (☎ 721111; fax 722111); singles cost from US$104 to US$112, and doubles from US$127 to US$140.

Places to Eat
There is a small food market on HaGalil St by the Aviv Hotel/Hostel with more stalls up the hill off HaRab Bibass St. The market is open Sunday to Friday, and is closed on Saturday.

The most convenient supermarket is by the Great Mosque and is open on Saturday. Its hours are Sunday to Thursday from 7 am to 6.45 pm, Friday 7 am to 3.30 pm, and Saturday 8 to 10 pm.

The place for felafel is HaYarden St between the bus station and HaBanim St. Several little shops compete here, and allow you to help yourself to salad. Take a look to see which has the best selection.

These shops close by 7 pm during the week, 2 pm on Friday, and most stay closed on Saturday, although one or two sometimes open in the evening.

In the bus station the *Egged self-service restaurant* has the usual cheap choice.

For great shishlik sandwiches (in pitta bread with salad) go to *El Farsi*, the grubby kiosk (no English sign) on the corner of HaGalil and HaRab Bibass Sts. It is closed Saturday, open Sunday to Friday for lunch (until that day's meat supply runs out), and is very popular. Sandwiches cost about US$2.25, and soft drinks and beer are sold – you can eat here or take away.

Across the street, opposite the Aviv, is another place serving shishlik sandwiches. Beside the market stalls with low tables and chairs out front, *Shipoday Himelreh* (no sign) charges US$2.50 for a sandwich and also serves soft drinks and beer. Open Sunday to Thursday 8 am to 11 pm, Friday 8 am to 3 pm, it's closed Saturday.

Restaurants – more expensive A St Peter fish dinner in Tiberias is not likely to be a gastronomic highlight. The Old City waterfront houses attractive fish restaurants where you pay about US$7 to US$9 for the fish, and US$12 to US$15 for a full meal.

At the northern end of the waterfront promenade is *Karamba*, a popular fish and vegetarian place with pleasant canework tables and chairs set outside amongst eucalyptus trees. Here you can enjoy soups or crepes (US$3.50), baked potatoes (US$4), vegetables au gratin (US$5), salads (US$5) and desserts (US$4.50). Karamba is open daily from about noon till very late.

On Donna Gracia St, up past the IYHA hostel with the Crusader castle wall as a backdrop, the *Lamb & the Goose* is a nice looking place which is open Sunday to

Thursday, noon to 1 am, Friday noon to 3 pm, and Saturday sunset to 1 am. It serves oriental dishes such as salads at US$1.50, and meat grilled on the fire from US$7 to US$12.

For more oriental food, visit the *Guy Restaurant* on the right along HaGalil St as you head out of Tiberias to the south. Here you have salads (US$2.50), soups, stuffed vegetables and vine leaves, spiced meatballs (US$4), and grilled meats (US$7 to US$12). Sit inside or outside on the terrace. The restaurant is open Sunday to Thursday noon to midnight, Friday noon to sunset, and Saturday sunset to midnight.

Also on HaGalil St, across from the Aviv Hotel/Hostel, is *Maman*, also with oriental food at similar prices and hours.

For decent Chinese and Thai cuisine, try *The House* (☎ 20226). It's on Gdud Barak Rd across from the beachfront hotels as you head north from Ha'Atzmaut Square. A full meal can cost between US$20 to US$30 and it's open daily for dinner only, 5 pm to midnight.

The best restaurant in town is at the Galei Kinneret Hotel. *Au Bord du Lac* serves French cuisine in a pleasant room, decorated with some great artwork, and with a lovely lake view. It is kosher, and closed Friday.

Bars 'Pub Row' is HaQishon St between HaGalil and HaBanim Sts, with three popular watering holes, *Little Tiberias* and *Avi's Restaurant* open from 1 pm to 2 am and the *Studio Pub* open from 5 pm to 2 am. On Saturday they open later.

To the north, by the Great Mosque arcade, are a few cafés with outside tables. Open daily, *Big Ben* is a pleasant pub-style bar where you are given free olives/popcorn with your beer.

The rooftop bar at *Nahum Hostel* still has the cheapest beer and shows videos.

If you are up late, *Karamba* down on the waterfront is often still open at 3 am and is where the staff from other restaurants go for a nightcap. With its shaded garden of eucalyptus trees overlooking the lake, it's nice here at any time.

At the southern end of HaGalil St you will

find the *Haroe Pub-Restaurant*, underneath the Panorama Hotel.

Entertainment
The cafés and bars in and around the Great Mosque arcade and the waterfront promenade in the Old City are where the crowds form in the evening. Check the tourist office for special events. The Ein Gev Music Festival, at Passover, and the Sea of Galilee Festival, held in the summer, attract a lot of attention.

With varying degrees of success there are a few discos/nightclubs, call them what you will. These include the *Castle Inn* on the waterfront, the *Blue Beach* (summer only), *Jordan River Hotel*, and the *Pe'er Hotel*. Admission varies between US$3 and US$7.

You'll find the *Gil Cinema* on HaYarden St across from the felafel shops, the *Aviv* in Qiryat Shemuel on Bialik St, and the *Hen* up above the Old City in Beit Ma'on, near Jabotinsky St.

What to do on Shabbat in Tiberias
With no buses running, your mobility is limited but you do have a few decent options if you are not inclined to abide by the Jewish law.

Starting with the transport problem, it is possible to hire a bicycle on Friday to use during Shabbat. The roads around the lake are mostly flat, but do bear in mind the heat – go easy on yourself and drink plenty of water.

If the weather is fine then it may be too hot to do anything too energetic, so you will probably be happy just to lie in the sun or go swimming in the lake. Otherwise you can cycle up to Tabgha where the churches are all open and free. Capernaum is open too, for a small fee. In the other direction you can visit Kibbutz Degania and Beit Gordon, the museum. If you are really energetic you could cycle all the way around the lake.

If you don't mind hitchhiking and risking a long wait, you can go to Hammat Gader for the day. If you do, make as early a start as possible to stand a better chance of getting a ride. Remember that Saturday sees the place packed with Israelis.

Finally, you can go on an organised tour – Max Bullhorn, Moshe Cohen and Egged Tours all operate on Shabbat.

On the food front, the popular eating and drinking places open as usual on Friday evening for their busiest night of the week. However, stock up on food at the market and supermarket on Friday morning because on Saturday virtually everything is closed until the evening.

Those of you with a car should consider a visit to Hemdat Yamin for Issak's classical music recital, followed by lunch at Dalia Cohen's or Ein Camonim (see Around Safed in this chapter).

Getting There & Away
Tiberias and the Sea of Galilee are usually reached via Nazareth, Safed or the Jordan Valley, with some visitors arriving from Haifa, Jerusalem and Tel Aviv by bus.

Bus From the Tiberias bus station there are regular services to Safed, Nazareth, Beit She'an, Afulla, Haifa, Tel Aviv and Jerusalem. When leaving town, check the current timetable to avoid missing the last bus, as services stop comparatively early, eg Jerusalem 5 pm, Haifa and Tel Aviv 8 pm, and Safed 6.30 pm. The left-luggage office is outside the bus station at the end of the row of offices as you turn right. It's open Sunday to Thursday 7.30 am to 3 pm, and is closed Friday and Saturday.

Although you can easily see it, getting to Upper Galilee and Golan is not so easy. From the bus station you have to take a bus to the Rosh Pinna junction and change there, which can involve a lot of waiting around.

Sheruts Outside the bus station and across the grass is where a few sheruts leave in the morning for Nazareth and occasionally Haifa. At other times you might find one looking for passengers to subsidise the journey back, but don't count on it.

Getting Around

In town you should be able to walk to most places, although if you stay up the hill in Qiryat Shemuel your legs would no doubt prefer you to use the bus. Bicycle hire is popular here and with good reason. As long as you can deal with the heat, go for it. It's 55 km all the way round the Sea of Galilee – a nice day out, but start early to beat the heat. You can rent bicycles from some of the hostels any day, or from the store just outside the bus station – they are closed Saturday. Expect to pay about US$7 for the day.

Another way to get about is by ferry. Lido Kinneret Sailing Co (☎ 721538, 720226) and Kinneret Sailing Co (☎ 721831) both operate cruises, evening disco cruises and special departures. By special arrangement they also operate between Capernaum and Tiberias (☎ 20248, 218131 in Tiberias or 58007/9 in Ein Gev), or check at the ticket office at each quay for current details.

SEA OF GALILEE

A freshwater lake fed by the Jordan River, the Sea of Galilee lies 212 metres below sea level and, in a good summer, the lake can be as warm as 33°C. Its length is 21 km and its width opposite Tiberias nine km; its greatest breadth is 13 km, its circumference 52 km and its depth about 49 metres – this can change depending on the sometimes unreliable rainfall in the region. Not just a natural beauty spot, it is Israel's major water supply.

It has been known by several different names. The Old Testament calls it the Sea of Kinnereth (Numbers 34:11, Joshua 12:3, 13:27) which is linked to the Hebrew word *kinnor* (harp). Some say that the lake is shaped like a harp, others that its waves make the sound of a harp. Arab poets called it the Bride, the Handmaiden of the Hills and the Silver Woman. The New Testament calls it the Sea of Galilee (Matthew 4:18, 15:29, Mark 1:16, 7:31), the Sea of Tiberias (John 6:1, 21:1), the Sea (Mark 2:13) and the Lake (Luke 8:22). Josephus, the 1st-century Jewish historian, called it the Lake of Gennesar. In Israel today, it is popularly known as the Kinneret.

There are over 20 species of fish found in the lake and fishing is still an important industry. The unique St Peter fish is enthusiastically recommended in Israeli restaurants although most now comes from fish farms rather than the lake.

Prehistoric tribes are known to have lived by the lake, in the Amud Caves south-west of Tabgha. The oldest human skull found in the country was discovered here in 1925. It was that of a man who lived in the Palaeolithic period, circa 100,000 BC. Bet Yerah, north of Kibbutz Degania, was an important Canaanite city 5000 years ago. Capernaum became the lake's most important site when Jesus made what was then a fishing village the centre of his ministry in Galilee. With the destruction of Jerusalem and Galilee's emergence as the new centre of Jewish life, the lakeside saw the establishment of schools of religious study and synagogues went up at Capernaum, Hammat Tiberias and Hammat Gader. The Byzantine period saw Christians flock here, and new churches were built in Heptapegon (Tabgha), Capernaum, Bet Yerah, and, on the eastern shore, Kursi and Susita.

Since the Syrian defeat in the Yom Kippur War, the lake has seen many new developments, particularly in tourism. There's been a proliferation of campsites, and amusement parks with giant water-slides.

Orientation

Nine km south of the Old City of Tiberias is the point where the Jordan River flows from the lake, in the grounds of Kibbutz Degania, the first-ever kibbutz. On the eastern shore, virtually opposite Tiberias, is another well-known kibbutz, Ein Gev, with its ferry boats, restaurant and campsite. Continuing north you come to the Luna-Gal amusement park on the way to where the Jordan River enters the lake. On the north-western shore is Capernaum and the ruins of its ancient synagogue where Jesus taught. Coming south is Tabgha with its two churches commemorating the Primacy of St Peter and the multiplication of the loaves and fishes. Overlooking them is the Mount of Beatitudes where Jesus gave the Sermon on the Mount.

Between here and Tiberias are the ancient ruins of Migdal, where Mary Magdalene, one of Jesus' followers, was born.

Beaches

Although the best things in life may be free, the best beaches on the lake are not. However, if you don't like the idea of paying as much as US$6 for a well-maintained stretch of shore with pleasant facilities, then you should either head for the harbour wall to the south of the Plaza Hotel, or leave Tiberias altogether and either walk, hitch-hike or take a bus further south, beyond the hot springs, and stop when you see an appealing site.

Man in the Galilee Museum – Yigal Alon Centre

In 1986, with the water level of the lake at its lowest for years, an ancient boat was found buried under an exposed section of the lake bed by the Kibbutz Ginnosar. It has been dated to somewhere between the 1st century BC and the 1st century AD. The wooden boat had become porous after the centuries spent in its muddy grave and it is now undergoing a nine-year restoration programme. In addition to the boat, the museum features an exhibit on the people of the region, and a tribute to the Israeli statesman Yigal Alon.

To get here, take Egged bus Nos 459, 841 or 963 from Tiberias bus station and get off at the orange signpost reading 'N of Ginnosar Guesthouse'. Walk one km along the side-road towards the lake and follow the signs to the museum. It is open Sunday to Thursday 9 am to 5 pm, Friday 9 am to 1 pm, and Saturday 9am to 4 pm; admission US$1.75.

Migdal

The lakeside road, six km north of Tiberias, passes ancient Migdal, or Magdala, birth-place of Mary Magdalene. Its name is Hebrew for 'tower', and it was named after the defence tower which dominated the important fishing village. A tiny, white-domed shrine marks the site.

Minya

Following the lakeside road, one km north from Migdal, a side road leads eastwards to Minya. Here you will find the ruins of a 7th-century palace. There are remnants of a western room with a mosaic floor, and on the south-eastern side a mosque with its *mihrab* (niche) facing Mecca. This is the most ancient Muslim prayer place in Israel.

Tabgha & the Mount of the Beatitudes

Generally considered to be the most appropriately beautiful and serene of the Christian holy places in the country, this site has managed to escape much of the commercialisation of modern Israel. Tradition locates three of the New Testament's most significant episodes here: the Sermon on the Mount, the Multiplication of the Loaves & Fishes, and Jesus' post-Resurrection appearance where he conferred the leadership of the church on Peter.

Tabgha is an Arab version of the Greek name Heptapegon (Seven Springs), and it is given to the small valley that lies south of the main road 12 km north of Tiberias. A side-road branches off to the right towards the lake and runs through the valley and past Capernaum to continue the circuit of the water, while the main road continues north towards Rosh Pinna.

Church of the Multiplication of the Loaves & Fishes This pleasant complex belongs to the German Benedictine Order and includes an adjacent monastery and pilgrims' hospice as well as the church. Today's church building dates back only to 1936 and the monastery to 1956. These modern additions were constructed on the site of a 5th-century Byzantine church whose well-preserved mosaic floor is probably the most beautiful in the country. Underneath the present floor are the remnants of a 4th-century church. The larger mosaic depicts a variety of flora & fauna, nearly all of which was found locally at the time it was made. The exception is the lotus flower which appears in several scenes. Along with the round tower, representing a Nilometer used to measure the water level of the lake, these touches show the influence of the Nilotic (Nile-like) landscapes that were popular in Hellenistic and Roman art.

The mosaic immediately in front of the altar depicts two fish flanking a basket of loaves. As the name implies, the churches were built on the traditional site where it is believed Jesus fed 5000 people with five loaves of bread and two fish (Mark 6:30-44).

The church is open Monday to Saturday 8.30 am to 5 pm, Sunday 9.15 am to 5 pm, and admission is free.

Church of the Primacy of St Peter This is where it is believed that Jesus appeared for the third time after his Resurrection (John 21). The modest black basalt church was built in 1933 by the Franciscans on the site of a late 4th-century church that was destroyed in the 13th century. At the base of the newer walls, at the end furthest away from the altar, you can clearly see the ancient wall on three sides. The flat rock in front of the altar is believed to be the table at which Jesus and his disciples ate, and it was known to Byzantine pilgrims as Mensa Christi (Christ's Table).

Outside the church, by the water, are steps cut out of the rock. Some say that this was where Jesus stood when the disciples saw him, but they were possibly cut in the 2nd to 3rd century when this area was quarried for limestone. Six double, or heart-shaped, column bases lie below the steps, although they are sometimes underwater if the lake level is high. These were probably taken from nearby buildings and intended to commemorate the 12 disciples. First mentioned in a text of 808 AD, they are known as the 12 Thrones. The church is open daily from 8 am to 5 pm and admission is free.

Church of the Mount of Beatitudes On the hill across the road from the entrance to the Heptapegon are the remains of a 4th-century church. Abandoned in the 7th century, it was eventually replaced in 1937 by the present structure on top of the hill that is now known as the Mount of Beatitudes. It is believed that this is where Jesus gave the Sermon on the Mount (Matthew 5-7) and also where he chose his disciples (Luke 6:12).

Owned by the Franciscans, whose nuns live in the adjacent hospice, its octagonal shape symbolises the eight beatitudes (Matthew 5:3-10), and the seven virtues (justice, charity, prudence, faith, fortitude, hope and temperance) are represented by symbols in the pavement around the altar. From the gallery you have some of the best views of the lake, particularly towards Tiberias to the south, and Capernaum, with the red domes of the Greek Orthodox monastery beyond, to the east. It's open daily from 8 am to noon and 2.30 to 5 pm; admission is free.

Springs These powerful springs lie to the east of the Church of the Primacy and with a bit of searching you can locate a pleasant little waterfall for a refreshing shower on a hot sticky day.

Getting There & Away Egged bus Nos 459, 941 and 963 leave from Tiberias bus station and speed northwards, past Migdal and Minya. Just before the bus stop at the Tabgha turn-off on the right, the road passes an electric power plant on the right as you climb a steep slope. Watch out for this so that you have time to remind the driver that you want to get off at Tabgha. The Egged school of grand prix driving seems to teach its drivers to build up speed here to negotiate the approaching steep climb.

From this bus stop follow the sideroad as it bends round to the left, with the Church of the Multiplication a few minutes' walk on the right. Continuing along the road above the lay-by is a rough path that leads up the slope to the Church of the Beatitudes. Alternatively, you can stay on the bus till the next stop, which is by the turn-off for the Beatitudes church. After the Tabgha turn-off the road turns away from the lake and zig-zags up the steep hill before reaching the turn-off marked by the orange sign reading 'Hospice of the Beatitudes'. Follow this sideroad to the church. From here you can walk down the slope to reach the Church of the Primacy. Read on to learn how to reach Capernaum from here.

CAPERNAUM

Capernaum is a Greek rendering of the Hebrew Kefar Nahum (Village of Nahum). Who Nahum was is not known. Medieval Jewish tradition suggests that the name refers to the prophet whose burial place was said to be here. Capernaum is best known, though, as the home of Jesus when he started his ministry (Matthew 4:12-17, 9:1, Mark 2:1). There are several other references to the town in the New Testament, including Jesus teaching in the synagogue (Mark 1:21), getting rid of a man's evil spirit (Mark 1:23-26), curing Peter's step-mother (Mark 1:29-31), the leper (Luke 5:12-16), the centurion's servant (Luke 7:1-10) and the paralytic (Mark 2:11-12, Luke 5:17-25), and walking on the water and discussing the bread of life (John 6:16-59).

The town's known history goes back to the 2nd century BC, although evidence of its existence in the 13th century BC has been found. Jesus is believed to have decided to move from Nazareth because his first converts (Peter and Andrew) lived here. There seems to have been a strong Christian presence here in the 2nd century, according to both rabbinical texts and archaeological discoveries. By the 4th century the town had expanded towards the hills with the buildings becoming more substantial. After the Arab conquest around 700 the town was destroyed and never again inhabited.

In 1894, the Franciscans purchased the site and set about restoring the ancient synagogue and other remnants found here. Unfortunately, they appear to have been influenced by the Israeli 'school of Holy Land tackiness' and built an ugly chapel that resembles a flying saucer hovering above the ruins.

Museum

The Franciscans' open-air archaeological museum features some impressive ruins. The

site is now clearly signposted, with detailed accounts of the major ruins.

Synagogue Not the synagogue frequented by Jesus, the specific date of this house of worship is still a mystery and a source of some debate amongst archaeologists. The discovery of coins and pottery on the site suggest that it was built in the late 4th century on top of early 4th-century buildings.

However, this evidence is not conclusive, with some archaeologists believing that it was erected in the late 2nd or early 3rd centuries.

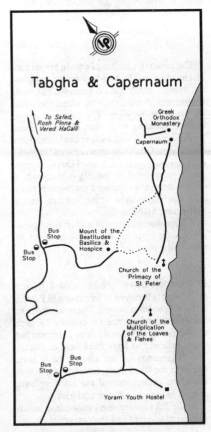

Tabgha & Capernaum

Coin from Capernaum

The building consists of a main prayer hall and an annexe. The hall features an impressive Roman facade and a column with a Greek inscription. Worshippers sat along the walls on the stone benches. The entrance to the annexe, standing to the east of the hall, had a nicely carved lintel, with an eagle and palm tree design. Other carvings are seen throughout the synagogue: the Star of David, a palm (once the symbol of Israel), a menorah, a wagon that may represent the ancient Holy Ark that carried the Torah, an urn, and a half-horse, half-fish figure.

A large stone flour mill and an olive press are among various ancient remnants to be seen in the courtyard.

St Peter's House The ruins of a church mark what is believed to have been St Peter's home where Jesus stayed. The house dates to sometime between the 1st century BC and the 4th century. A mosaic floor decorates the room believed to have been host to Christ. The beginnings of the church have been traced to the 4th century, when the room was made the centrepiece of the building with special entrances, an arch and roof.

In the 5th century, the surrounding buildings were levelled and the octagonal church was built, with a mosaic floor marking the room where Jesus had stayed.

It's open daily from 8.30 am to 4.15 pm. Admission is US$0.65. Modest dress is required – no shorts, bare shoulders, etc. There are toilets and a snack bar outside.

Greek Orthodox Monastery
From the museum walk back to the road, turn right and walk about two km to the next turn-off. With its peeling paint it looks better from a distance and there is little to see here. The two monks may be around but they don't seem too keen on visitors.

Getting There & Away
From the Church of the Beatitudes you have a pleasant walk across the fields to Capernaum. Just follow the various tracks down the hill and aim for the red domes of the Greek Orthodox monastery. To reach the museum, walk down the signposted side road; it's at the end. From Tabgha just follow the road three km to the east to reach the turn-off for the museum, and keep going for the Greek Orthodox monastery.

Vered HaGalil
As the road to Rosh Pinna continues northwards from the Mount of Beatitudes, it steadily climbs to reach sea level just before the intersection with the road to Almagor. Here an orange signpost directs you to Vered HaGalil (Rose of the Galilee), a stud farm and riding stable which offers horse-riding and guesthouse facilities (see Places to Stay). The American-style complex enjoys a good reputation and is beautifully situated in great riding country. You can go on trail rides for US$15 per hour, or for US$28 a half day and US$40 for a full day.

Korazim
Continue east along the road from Vered HaGalil and after four km you come to the ruins of ancient Korazim. There was a Jewish town here in the 1st century and along with Capernaum and Bethsaida its people were condemned by Jesus for their lack of faith (Matthew 11:20-24).

Although it probably benefited from Galilee's influx of Jews after the destruction of Jerusalem (132-5 AD), with rabbis commenting on its excellent wheat, records show that the town was in ruins by the 4th century and occupation ceased in the 8th century.

Among the remains is a black basalt synagogue of the 3rd to 4th century, similar in style to the limestone one at Capernaum.

Beyond Korazim to the east, the ground is covered with large basalt rocks. Many of these are 'dolmens', large blocks of broad and flat stone placed on other stones and used as burial chambers between 6000 and 4000 BC.

The road continues to meet the road encircling the lake with the Jordan River meandering down through a marshy area nearby.

Beit Yerah & Kinneret Cemetery

Following the lakeside road some nine km south of Tiberias, just south of the Afulla junction you come to a hill where, up on the left by the water, excavations have revealed the remains of a 3rd-century Roman fort and the ruins of a 5th-century Byzantine church and synagogue. There was a settlement here as early as 4000 BC but after about 2000 BC the site was unoccupied until the late 6th century BC. It developed greatly in the Hellenistic period (332-63 BC) and continued through the Roman and Byzantine periods.

The nearby cemetery belongs to Kibbutz Kinneret and among those buried there are Berl Katsenelson, a leader of the Jewish labour movement, and the Hebrew poets Rahel and Elisheva.

Baptism Site

Kibbutz Kinneret, just east of Beit Yerah, has built a baptism site (along with vending machines, a snack bar and a souvenir shop) south of the bridge crossing the Jordan River where it leaves the Sea of Galilee. This is not the site where Jesus was baptised – that is at al-Maghtes near Jericho, but its location in the sensitive militarised zone near the West Bank-Jordan border puts it out of bounds to pilgrims.

Kibbutz Degania

The world's first kibbutz, Kibbutz Degania is known as Em Hakevutsot (Mother of the Cooperative Villages). Located between the Jordan River and the Beit She'an junction, there are in fact two kibbutzim here.

The original, Degania A, is marked by a Syrian tank parked outside the main entrance just off the main road – a souvenir from the 1948 War of Independence when the kibbutzniks, armed only with molotov cocktails and rifles, defeated an enemy tank column.

Beit Gordon Dedicated to the memory of the father of the kibbutz movement, A D Gordon, this archaeological and natural history museum complex is in the grounds

Friezes

of Degania A, and is open Sunday to Thursday 9 am to 4 pm, Friday 9 am to 1 pm, and Saturday 9.30 am to noon. Admission is US$1.20.

The entrance to the museum is on the lakeside road where there is a car park. On Saturday the entrance here is closed to cars (pedestrians and cyclists can still get through) and you should drive through the main entrance (marked by that tank).

Cemetery The Degania Cemetery is on the bank of the Jordan River and includes a section for the soldiers killed in action locally. Leading Zionists are also buried here, including A D Gordon, Otto Warburg, Arthur Roppin and Leopold Greenburg.

Hammat Gader

One of the highlights for many visitors to Galilee, and a regular attraction for locals, the Hammat Gader complex is eight km south-east of the Sea of Galilee (21 km from Tiberias). In a pleasant parkland setting along with Roman ruins, a crocodile park and amusements, the hot sulphur springs here provide a cheaper alternative to the indoor baths at Tiberias. Although the sulphur smell can be a bit pungent at times, this is a great opportunity to experience the sensation of a natural hot spring.

The facilities include a modern pool with massage jets, a waterfall, and an area with black mud which is reputed to be good for the skin. The springs are first mentioned by the geographer Strabo (63 BC - 21 AD).

Hammat Gader is in the valley of the Yarmulk River on the sensitive border with Jordan and you will see lots of barbed-wire fences and sentry posts competing with the natural scenery. The Hebrew name Hammat Gader is derived from *ham* and the name of the nearby ancient city of Gadara, now a part of Jordan under the modern name of Umm Qeis. In Arabic it is called El Hamme.

The site was probably occupied as early as 3000 BC and again in the Roman and subsequent periods. The partially reconstructed Roman ruins are quite impressive and include various bathing areas, such as a smaller pool reserved for lepers and the hottest spring – 51°C – which is called in Hebrew Ma'ayan HaGehinom (Hell's Pool) and in Arabic Ain Makleh (Frying Pool). There is also a ruined 5th or 6th-century synagogue just west of the Roman baths and past the picnic area. From the top of the excavation site you have a fine view of the valley crossed by the bridge that used to carry the Haifa to Damascus railway.

The alligator park was started off with denizens imported from Florida but they are now born and raised in the hot-house by the entrance to the pools.

Hammat Gader (☎ 751039) is open Saturday to Thursday 8 am to 4 pm, and Friday 8 am to 3 pm. Admission is US$8 which gives access to all the amenities, with some extra health and beauty facilities (provided in the pool area at various prices).

Egged buses from Tiberias station are not that frequent so you need to make an early start to get the most out of your admission fee. Buses from Tiberias depart Sunday to Thursday 8.30, 9 and 10 am, and Friday 8.30 and 9.30 am.

Departures from Hammat Gader are Sunday to Thursday 11 am, noon, 1 and 2.15 pm, and Friday 11.30 am and noon. No buses run on Saturday. It's best not to miss the last bus back to Tiberias although you will usually find a refreshed Israeli family to give you a lift.

Kibbutz Ha'On

Its name meaning strength, this kibbutz was established in 1948. Next to the holiday village here is an **ostrich farm**. It is open to visitors Sunday to Thursday 9 am to 6 pm in the high season, 9 am to 5 pm in the low season, and Friday 9 am to 1 pm all year round. Entrance is US$5 (students US$3) in the high season, and US$3.75 (students US$2) in the low season.

Kibbutz Ein Gev

Established in 1937 by German and Czech pioneers, this kibbutz is renowned for its 5000-seat amphitheatre which is the setting for major music festivals. As well as its vineyards, banana plantations, date groves and fishing, the kibbutz makes a good living from tourism. They run the ferry service on the lake, and the 45-minute Tiberias to Ein Gev crossing is very popular with Israeli holidaymakers. At the kibbutz is an over-rated restaurant, a swimming pool and a campsite.

Kursi
Seven km north of Ein Gev, the Kursi archae-ological site features the remains of the largest Byzantine monastery in the Holy Land. This is the traditional site of the miracle of the swine (Luke 8:26-39; Matthew 8:23-34), when Jesus exorcised the body of a man and the spirits possessed a herd of swine grazing nearby. They then stampeded into the Sea of Galilee and were drowned. The site has also been identified as ancient Kurshi, a centre of idol worship which is mentioned in the Talmud.

Probably built in the 5th century, the walled monastery measured 145 by 123 metres, and has been partially reconstructed. At a nearby rock, assumed to be close to the spot where the miracle took place, additional excavations include a chapel paved with three separate layers of mosaics, columns, a damaged inscription and a bench which overlooks the Sea of Galilee.

A basilica was a major feature of the complex, with a nave and two side aisles divided by two rows of columns. Outside the monastery, you can see the remains of roads and buildings that served visiting pilgrims. It was damaged during the Persian invasion of 614, and many of the settlement's build-ings were destroyed. The monastery was reconstructed, only to be destroyed by fire in the 8th century. This was the end of the site's role as a place of Christian pilrimage. During the 9th century, the church ruins were used by Arab settlers as dwellings and storage rooms.

The kursi site (☎ 731983) is open from April to September, Saturday to Thursday 8 am to 5 pm, and Friday 8 am to 4 pm; from October to March, Saturday to Thursday 8 am to 4 pm, Friday 8 am to 3 pm; and admission is US$2 (students US$1). The Ein Gev bus from Tiberias usually continues on and can drop you nearby.

Luna Gal
On the north-eastern shore of the Sea of Galilee this is the largest of the water-slide complexes. It is open daily, but the admis-sion prices are steep. The hours are 9 am to 5.30 pm (US$12); 2.30 to 5.30 pm (US$8.25), or 7 pm to midnight (US$12). Take Egged bus Nos 18, 21 or 22 from the Tiberias bus station.

Places to Stay
An attractive alternative to Tiberias for many visitors is to stay outside the town for at least some of their time in the region. This allows you to be closer to places of greater interest, ie Tabgha or the beaches, or to experience a kibbutz guesthouse, Kibbutz Ginnosar, or Vered HaGalil stud farm, or to camp on the lakeshore.

North Beaches Following Gdud Barak Rd north from the Old City are some beach-front hotels. With its own stretch of private beach and a garden with a swimming pool, the *Quiet Beach Hotel* (☎ 721441, 720602), is perhaps the best of these; singles cost from US$34 to US$77, and doubles from US$52 to US$130.

Kibbuttz Ginnosar The four-star graded *Nof Ginnosar Guesthouse* (☎ 792161; fax 792170), run by the kibbutz, provides com-fortable accommodation in its lakeside location. It offers gardens, a private beach and water-sports facilities –it is very quiet and unhurried. Singles cost from US$53 to US$64, and doubles from US$70 to US$88. Just south of Tabgha, the kibbutz is off the main road from Tiberias, and clearly signposted.

Tabgha Twelve km from Tiberias and in the peaceful vicinity of the important Christian holy places is the pleasant *Karei Deshe-Yoram Youth Hostel – IYHA* (☎ 720601). This place is well worth considering if you want to spend some time in the immediate area. Set in attractive grounds with eucalyptus trees, a rocky beach and a few peacocks, the rooms are clean and air-conditioned, the management pleasant and the food good. Dorm beds are US$6 for members, and nonmembers pay US$7.50. There's also a family-sized room, meals are available, or there's a kitchen for self-catering; no curfew is imposed.

Egged bus Nos 459, 841 and 963 stop on the main road nearby. Get off at the orange 'Tabgha' signpost and walk straight down the sideroad, past the turning to the left, and the hostel is at the end.

A delightful place to stay for its peace and quiet, spotless rooms and lovely surroundings is the *Mount of the Beatitudes Hospice* (☎ 20878) 12365 Doar Na, Hevel Korazim. Due to reopen in 1992 after extensive renovations, the hospice overlooks the church and has fine views across the Sea of Galilee. Run by friendly Franciscan nuns who provide tasty food, rates should be around US$20 per person.

Egged bus Nos 459, 841 and 963 pass by. Get off at the orange 'Hospice of the Beatitudes' sign and walk up the one-km long drive. Down the hill are the churches of Tabgha and the ruins of Capernaum.

Vered HaGalil The 'guest farm' (☎ 935785; fax 934964) has lovely accommodation in Swiss-style chalets along with the horse-riding facilities. Singles/doubles cost US$22/38 in the bunkhouse, cabins are US$35/65, and a suite is US$45/85. The restaurant is very good and dinner costs about US$15. It is usually possible to camp out on the lawn for free and use the shower and toilet facilities if you go riding. Get off the bus from Tiberias at the signposted Korazim junction.

Camping If you thought camping was an alternative to paying high prices, think again. Campsites on the shores of the Sea of Galilee, mostly run by kibbutzim, are quite expensive. However, although there are still

a few areas around the lake where you can pitch your tent for free, the campsites are very popular with Israelis.

The *Ein Gev Holiday Village* (☎ 51177, 58027) is about 1½ km south of the kibbutz entrance. It is set amidst pleasant parkland and there is a rocky beach, boats and canoes for hire, crazy golf, cafeteria and restaurant. Prices go up considerably for the summer months and Jewish holidays. There are sites (US$14 per two people, US$6 per extra person), little bungalows and caravans/trailers fitted out with showers, toilets and kitchens; the latter work out at around US$28 per person.

The *Kibbutz Ha'On Holiday Village* (☎ 57555) is five km further south on the lakeside. With your own tent you pay from US$17. A caravan/trailer with shower, toilet and kitchen costs from US$60 for four, rising steeply during weekends, the summer months and Jewish holidays.

By the junction for Hammat Gader, and two km further south, is the *Ma'agon Vacation Centre* (☎ 51360, 51172). There are no camping facilities here, just caravans and trailers. These cost from US$15. This is the top windsurfing centre in Israel.

TIBERIAS TO SAFED
Moshav Amirim

Located off the east side of main road No 866, between Safed and the junction with main road No 85, this unique vegetarian co-operative is renowned for its popular restaurant and collection of guesthouses with breathtaking views of the Sea of Galilee below.

Dalia Cohen (☎ 989349) is the restaurant, run by Dalia herself. Her place is open daily (weekends only in the winter) from 8 am to 8 pm. Breakfast is US$11, and lunch and dinner (set menu) are US$18. It's a good idea to call ahead to be sure that she is open and has a table.

Among the individually operated guesthouses, *Zahi Guesthouse* (☎ 989170/270, 980434) stands out with its tastefully decorated rooms, although none have views of the lake. Yoram Zahi also operates jeep tours of the region, with prices around US$20 to US$30 per person (when the jeep is full). The moshav has a central reservations system, so call 989571 for any of the guest houses here. Singles/doubles are US$48 with breakfast, US$105 half board, and US$135 full board.

Due to the lack of public transport, you need a car to get here, but it's only a 20-minute drive from Safed, and 40 minutes from Tiberias.

Hemdat Yamin

Just across the road from Amirim is Moshav Shefer. One of the residents here is Issak Tavior, a classical pianist who gives recitals in his home/studio, Hemdat Yamin (☎ 989085). He charges US$10 per person, with refreshments included.

His regular weekly performance is at 11.30 am on Saturday, but you should call ahead to check and to inquire about other performance dates. Issak regularly performs for visiting groups and VIPs.

The experience of listening to his playing in such wonderful surroundings, with a beautiful hill-top location overlooking the mountains and the Sea of Galilee, perhaps followed by a meal at Dalia Cohen's or Ein Camonim, is highly recommended.

Ein Camonim

Located on the northern side of main road No 85 between Tzomet Hananya and the turn-off for Kadarim, this small family-run goat farm operates a popular restaurant that's well worth a visit.

It's open daily from 11 am to 9 pm, and the terrific set meal consists of a variety of superb goat cheeses, homemade bread, salad, wine, dessert and tea & coffee. Good value if you're hungry, you can eat and drink as much as you like for US$14 (☎ 989894 /680). Again, you need a car to get here, but it's only a 30-minute drive from either Safed or Tiberias.

SAFED

(Population: 21,000)

Set high amongst the beautiful scenery of the Galilee mountains, is the holy city of Safed. It's picturesque and peaceful with its maze of quaint cobbled streets, artists' quarter and a rich heritage of Jewish mysticism, and is on most travellers' itineraries. Alternatively spelt Safad, Tzfat, Tsfat, it may be a day trip from Tiberias, a stop-off en route between Galilee and the coast, or somewhere to stay a little longer.

History

Safed was in the territory assigned to the Napthali tribe after Joshua's conquest of the land of Israel. During the First Temple period it was one of the hill-top towns and villages where *masu'ot* (beacons) were lit. Starting in Jerusalem, these fires acted as signals to let the country know about the beginning of a new month or holy day. During the First Revolt (66-73 AD), Safed was fortified by Josephus, leader of the Jewish forces in Galilee.

In the 2nd century Jewish mysticism, or Kabbalism, was expanded in this area. Kabbalah is a very complex subject. The name comes from the Hebrew root *kbl* meaning 'to receive' and it originated near Safed with Rabbi Shimon Bar Yochai who wrote the Zohar (Book of Splendour), a major book of Jewish mystical teachings. Religious Jews believe that they should bring *kedusha* (holiness) into everything that they do. In order to apply this theory to their daily lives, the Kabbalists sought to discover exactly what God wanted them to do so that they could serve him perfectly.

During the Crusader occupation Fulke, King of Anjou, built a citadel here in 1140 to control the highway to Damascus, calling the town Saphet. It was destroyed by Saladin, rebuilt by the Knights Templar and destroyed again by Baybars in 1266. He made the town the capital of Palestine's northern district and it became known as Safat or Safad.

A Jewish community gradually formed, reaching the height of its fame in the mid-16th century with the arrival of leading Kabbalists from Spain. During the 'Golden Age' of Spain, Kabbalah had flourished

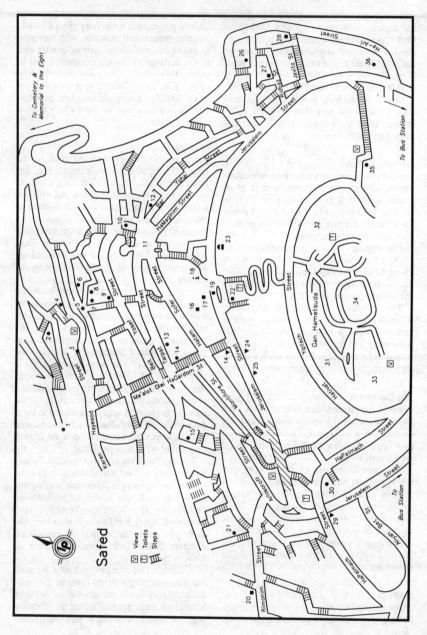

Safed

☑ Views
Ⓣ Toilets
▥ Steps

To Cemetery &
Memorial to the Eight

■ PLACES TO STAY

16 Central Hotel
17 Beit Nathan
20 Rimon Inn
26 Ascent Institute of Tsfat
27 Hadar Hotel

▼ PLACES TO EAT

13 Big Mo's Dairy Experience
24 Felafel Baruch
25 Palermo
28 Carmel Hotel

OTHER

1 Ha'Ari Mikveh (Ritual Bath)
2 Ha'Ari Sephardi Synagogue
3 Hameiri House
4 Banna Synagogue
5 Simtat Alsheikh (Blue-Painted Street)
6 Kikkar Abbo
7 Alsheikh Synagogue
8 Abuhav Synagogue
9 Yosef Caro Synagogue
10 Ha'Ari Ashkenazi Synagogue & Mikveh
11 Kikkar HaMaginim
12 Chernobyl Synagogue
14 Rehov Ma'alot Olei HaGardom
15 General Exhibition Hall
18 Tourist Office
19 Davidka Memorial
21 Zvi Assaf Printing Museum
22 Former British Police Station
23 Post Office
29 Café California
30 Shem Va'Ever Cave & Synagogue
31 Remains of Citadel Wall
32 Remains of Citadel Wall
33 Remains of Crusader Citadel
34 Citadel
35 Israel Bible Museum
36 War Memorial

air, became spiritual virtues. Some of the most famous and learned figures in Jewish history lived and studied here during this period.

The first printing press in the Holy Land, and in Asia, was set up in Safed and the first Hebrew book was printed in 1578.

The town went into decline in the 18th century after a plague in 1742 and an earthquake in 1759 compelled many Jews to leave. However, the arrival of Russian Hasidim, beginning in 1776, opened the second golden age of Safed. At its peak, the town's population reached 15,000, supporting as many as 69 synagogues. In 1837 another earthquake destroyed most of the town, killing up to 5000 people. Most of the survivors left. The town was restored, and when WWI broke out, Safed's Jews numbered 10,000. Due to a combination of typhoid, starvation and poor administration by the Turkish authorities, there were only 3000 left by the war's end.

Up until this time, violence between the Arab and Jewish communities here had been sporadic. With the growth of nationalistic aspirations on both sides, however, Arab attacks on the Jews became increasingly frequent. In 1929, inspired by the Mufti of Jerusalem, a wave of anti-Jewish riots swept Palestine. Between 29 August and 1 September that year, 21 Jews were killed in Safed, with 80 wounded. This totally changed the Arab-Jewish relationship in the city.

At the start of the 1948 War of Independence Safed's Jewish population was less than 2000, mainly elderly religious people. From February 1948 the town's Jewish quarter was under Arab siege and even with Palmach reinforcements those able to defend it numbered only a fraction of the Arab force of some 6000. In early May 1948 the outnumbered Jews defied the odds to defeat the Arabs who then abandoned the town. The Jews referred to their victory as the 'Miracle of Safed'.

After the creation of the State of Israel, Safed's population increased. The religious Jews were joined by Jewish artists, attracted not only by the town's beauty and its Jewish

throughout the Iberian Peninsula but the anti-Jewish riots in 1391, the Inquisition and the expulsion of 1492 all brought it to an end. Safed succeeded Spain as a world centre of Jewish learning and culture.

Rabbi Shimon's tomb being nearby was Safed's attraction to the Kabbalists, and the town's natural attributes, chiefly the fresh mystical heritage, but also by the availabilty of cheap accommodation and studio space that was available.

Over the years, with its combination of beautiful surroundings and temperate climate, the town has become a popular summer resort, although its tourist trade has suffered since the the Sea of Galilee was made more accessible after the Six Day War. Meanwhile, religious Jews continue to visit the graves and synagogues of the great Kabbalists. Today, 25% of Safed's population are recent immigrants from the former Soviet Union and Ethiopia.

Orientation

The highest town in the country, Safed is situated at over 800 metres above sea level on a series of hilltops. Basically consisting of three main areas, there is the town centre on one hill, south Safed on another, and Mount Cana'an to the east.

Mount Cana'an is Safed's highest point at 950 metres above sea level. With its views and forest it is an attractive part of town, with picnic sites and observation points. South Safed has little to offer the traveller except the IYHA youth hostel and a swimming pool.

Most of your time in Safed will be spent in the town centre, which is small enough to cover on foot. The town's main thoroughfare is Jerusalem St which completes a circle right around the area. The central bus station is just below Jerusalem St, to the east. From here you can go either to the left or to the right to reach the sights. The centre can be split into three sections: Gan HaMetsuda, the park area with the remains of the Crusader fortress standing atop the hill and encircled by Jerusalem St; the old city, or synagogue quarter, to the north-west – a compact cluster of narrow streets winding their way around the slopes and connected by a series of steep stairways; and the artists' quarter, immediately to the south of the Old City on the other side of Ma'alot Olei HaGardom St, which is the main stairway down the slope from Jerusalem St.

Information

Tourist Office The IGTO is in the lobby of the municipality at 50 Jerusalem St (☎ 920961). Climb the stairs from the central bus station and turn right – it's at the top of the hill and on the right. It is open Sunday to Thursday 8 am to 6 pm, Friday 8 am to 1 pm, and is closed Saturday.

School children in Safed

Post & Telecommunications A convenient branch office is at 37 Jerusalem St, and the main office and poste restante is on HaPalmach St. Look for the radar dish next door, visible from the corner of Aliyah Bet St.

The office is open Sunday to Tuesday and Thursday 8 am to 12.30 pm and 3.30 to 6 pm, Wednesday 8 am to 1.30 pm, and Friday 8 am to noon.

Other Bank branches are on Jerusalem Street west of the Citadel. They open Sunday, Tuesday and Thursday 8.30 am to 12.30 pm and 4 to 6 pm, Monday and Wednesday 8.30 am to 12.30 pm, Friday 8.30 am to noon, and are closed Saturday.

The Emek Hatchelet swimming pool is east of the town centre, off Ha'Atzmaut Rd just across from the central bus station. Open in the summer only, Sunday to Friday 7.30 am to 4 pm, Saturday 8.30 am to 4 pm, the admission is US$1.80 (students US$1). In South Safed an indoor pool is open all year round. Take Egged bus Nos 6 or 7.

For police, ☎ 930444 or 100.

Tours

Highly recommended to gain a deeper insight into Safed's status as a holy city and the centre of Jewish mysticism is the 'Magical Mystical Tour', a walking tour offered by Shlomo Bar-Ayal (☎ 974597). Charging a reasonable US$7 per person, US$5 to students, Shlomo gives a good two hours of interesting commentary on various aspects of Safed's history.

The tour starts at the tourist office Sunday to Thursday at 9.30 am and 2 pm and on Friday at 9.30 am. Call Shlomo ahead during the quieter winter months to check the current schedule. Tours on Shabbat and in the evening are by prior arrangement only.

Shlomo also offers a 'Bubbe Maise tour'. Popular mainly with Jewish visitors, this emphasises the many folk stories that have originated in Safed.

Contact the information office at the central bus station for details of Egged Tours' local itineraries. They run tours to local Jewish religious sites and to the Golan Heights, the Sea of Galilee and Hammat Gader.

Israel Bible Museum

From the central bus station, climb the stairs to Jerusalem St, bear right up the hill and after the municipal offices on the left you come to the Israel Bible Museum (☎ 973472) which is on the slopes of Gan HaMetsuda, across from the smaller park to the north.

Once the home of a Turkish pasha, the 120-year-old building is now home to the work of American Jewish sculptor and artist, Phillip Ratner. He has established a museum of his sculpture, painting, lithography and tapestry, which depict scenes from the Bible. There is also a collection of the sculpture of Henryck Glicenstein.

It's open Sunday to Thursday 8 am to 6 pm, Friday 8 am to 2 pm, and Saturday 10 am to 2 pm. Admission is free, but donations are accepted.

Gan HaMetsuda – Citadel

This is the pleasant park and viewpoint at the summit of Mount Safed – the Citadel. It was here that the signal beacons were lit and where Josephus built his fortifications, but today it is the remains of the 12th-century Crusader fortress that are evident (Jerusalem St follows the line of the Crusaders' city wall). In 1986 pottery fragments were accidentally unearthed, which have been dated to the time of Abraham – a major excavation is planned once funds have been raised.

From the Citadel you can enjoy marvellous views, with the Sea of Galilee visible on a clear day. Around Safed is the largest forest planted by the Jewish National Fund – before 1948 there were hardly any trees in the area.

Synagogue Quarter

Along with the surrounding views, the old city is Safed's major attraction. Resign yourself to losing your way amongst the network of meandering narrow streets, courtyards and steep stairways.

The synagogue quarter is centred on

Defenders' Square (Kikkar HaMaginim). In the good old days charcoal was sold here for heating; now it is Safed's main meeting place, known simply as 'the Kikkar'. What is now the Tiferet Gallery was the headquarters of the Haganah during the 1948 War of Independence. The kikkar is just off Jerusalem St, down the slope along HaMeginim St.

Safed's Kabbalist synagogues have their holy arks set in their southern rather than eastern walls so as to face Jerusalem. They are usually open throughout the day to visitors, and admission is free although donations are requested. Suitable clothing must be worn and cardboard yarmulkas are provided.

Ha'Ari Ashkenazi Synagogue Just down from the kikkar, this is one of two synagogues dedicated to 'the Ari', one of the major figures of Jewish mysticism. Ari (Lion) is an acronym of his name, Adoni (or Ashkenazi) Rabbi Itzhak Luria.

Born in Jerusalem in 1534, Rabbi Itzhak moved to Cairo where he quickly mastered conventional Jewish teachings and began to study Kabbalah. In 1569, after some 12 years of study, he brought his family to Safed so that he could study with the Ramak – Rabbi Moshe Cordeviero, the leading teacher of mysticism at the time. When he died, the Ari took over and taught the secrets of the Torah to a select group of students until his death in a sudden plague in 1572.

The Ha'Ari Ashkenazi Synagogue was built after his death on the site of the field (in those days it was outside the Old City) where the Kabbalists would gather to welcome Shabbat. There is no mezuzah on the synagogue entrance because the Ari had consecrated the area. The original building was destroyed in the 1852 earthquake.

The olive-wood ark was carved in the 19th century and represents over 10 years' work. It was painted about 30 years ago. The *bimah* (pulpit) bears a shrapnel hole from an Arab attack during the 1948 siege. The synagogue was packed at the time but nobody was hurt – the hole is now stuffed with messages to God à la Jerusalem's Western Wall.

At the rear of the synagogue, in a small room, is a chair carved at about the same time as the ark – it is Kise Eliyahu (Elijah's Chair). Legend has it that any Jewish couple who sit here will have a son within a year. Unfortunately, the synagogue is frequented by an old man who often forces himself upon unsuspecting visitors as a tour guide. Although he can be loud and rude, he is harmless enough so just ignore him.

Caro Synagogue Rabbi Yosef Caro was another leading Kabbalist. He was born in Spain in 1488 and after the expulsion of the Jews in 1492 he moved to the Balkans, arriving in Safed in 1535. He later became the chief rabbi here, but he attained fame for his important written works which included the Shulchan Aruch, basically an extensive blueprint for living a Jewish life.

So influential are his teachings and their interpretations of the Jewish Law that today's rabbis consider his opinions when dealing with contemporary questions.

Destroyed in the 1837 earthquake and rebuilt around 1847, the synagogue stands above Rabbi Caro's yeshiva. The ark contains three ancient Torah scrolls: the one on the right is from Persia and is about 200 years old; the centre one, from Iraq, is about 300 years old; and the scroll on the left, from Spain, is over 500 years old.

Alsheikh Synagogue Not always open, this synagogue is named after Rabbi Moses Alsheikh, another leading Kabbalist. Dating from the 17th century, it's the only synagogue that survived the 1827 earthquake intact. The walls along this street are traditionally painted an attractive blue – a colour which represents royalty and heaven.

Abuhav Synagogue This synagogue is believed to have been built by followers of Rabbi Yitzhak Abuhav in the 1490s, using a plan based on the Kabbalah. The four central pillars represent the four elements which, according to Kabbalists, make up all of the creation. The dome has 10 windows to represent the Commandments, pictures of the 12 tribes of Israel which represent Jewish unity, illustrations of the musical instruments used in the Temple, pomegranate trees (which traditionally have 613 seeds – the same number as the commandments in the Torah), and the Dome of the Rock, a reminder of the Temple's destruction. The silver candelabrum hanging opposite the central ark is a memorial to the Holocaust victims.

Legend has it that when the 1837 earthquake struck, the entire synagogue was destroyed except for the wall next to, and the arch over, the ark which still houses the Torah scroll written by Rabbi Abuhav. The large wooden ark is on your right as you enter, and the scroll is only used on Rosh HaShanah, Yom Kippur and Shavuot.

Banna Synagogue Named after Rabbi Yossi Banna (the Builder) who is buried here, this synagogue is also known as the Shrine of the White Saint – in Hebrew Hatsadik Halavan. This is based on a legend that tells of the time when an Arab governor of Safed ruled that the Jews had to use only white chickens for the Yom Kippur ceremony. The distressed Jews prayed at Rabbi Banna's tomb for a way out of the problem and the result was that all the black chickens turned pure white. Another version of the legend has it that the Jews were told to bring to the governor a certain number of white chickens, or face expulsion.

The synagogue contains the Torah scroll that is carried in the traditional procession to Meiron every Lag B'Omer.

Kikkar Abbo This small square, marked by a Star of David made out of pine needles, is where the Hasidim start their procession to Meiron on Lag B'Omer.

Ha'Ari Sephardic Synagogue On the lower slopes of the Old City, just up from the cemeteries, this synagogue is built on the site where Ari prayed. The small room on the left in the back is said to be where he learned the mystical texts with the prophet Elijah. In the 1948 siege, the synagogue was one of the key positions held by the Jewish defenders.

Cemeteries
Below the Old City on the western slopes, down from the Ha'Ari Sephardic Synagogue and facing Meiron, lie three adjoining cemeteries. The small building to the left of the path that leads down from the synagogue is its gents' mikveh (ritual bath).

The oldest of the cemeteries contains the graves of many of the famous Kabbalists who believed that Safed's pure air would benefit the souls of those buried here and fly them immediately to the Garden of Eden. Among those buried here are: the Ari; his teacher Cordoviero (Ramak), author of *Pardess Rimmonim* (Grove of Pomegranates); Shlomo Alkavets, composer of the hymn *Lecha Dodi*; Yosef Caro; Ya'acov Beirav, who attempted to re-establish the Sanhedrin (the Supreme Court) in Safed in 1538; and Moshe Alsheikh.

The domed tomb was built by the Karaites of Damascus and is believed by them to contain the body of the biblical prophet, Hosea. Legend has it that also buried on this hill are Hannah and her seven sons, martyred by the Greeks on the eve of the Maccabaean revolt. The sudden feeling of fatigue experienced when you climb the hill is said to be due to walking over their graves.

The more recent cemeteries contain victims of the 1948 siege, and at the bottom of the slope, seven of the eight members of the Irgun and Lehi who were hanged by the British in Akko Prison. The eighth is buried at Rosh Pinna, where he lived.

Hameiri House
Just up the slope from the cemeteries and the Ha'Ari Sephardic Synagogue, this complex comprises a museum, a research institute and a 'centre for educational tourism'.

The building dates back to 1517 when the Spanish Jews had begun arriving in Safed. They built it as a centre of Kabbalistic study. Partially destroyed in the earthquakes of 1759 and 1837, the house was restored between 1850 and 1860 by immigrants from Persia and North Africa. In the early 1900s the Sephardic Chief Rabbis and Sephardic Law Court were based here.

During WW I it served as accommodation for Jews made homeless or injured by the war and Safed's first Hebrew school was established here. During the Arab riots of 1929 and the late 1930s, parts of the building were destroyed, and the occupants killed, and it was eventually abandoned. The Jewish underground used it to store weapons and as a place to train between 1940 and 1948, and its ruins were a strategic Jewish position in the Arab siege.

Between 1959 and 1984 it was restored by Yehzkel Hameiri, a fifth-generation Safedian, who has gradually transformed it into today's museum and institute which documents the town's history. Having collected material for some 30 years, Mr Hameiri has put together a variety of documents, papers, ancient books, utensils from homes and workplaces, clothes, furniture and holy objects from over the years – all of which show how Safed's Jewish community has lived. There are also photographs, recordings and video tapes of both sites and older residents – a wide variety of material for display and research.

The aim of the **museum** is to give an understanding of Safed's Jewish community of the last century – the lifestyles of earlier generations and their struggle to survive. The museum is open Sunday to Friday 9 am to 2 pm, and is closed Saturday. The **institute** provides a wide variety of material on the history of Safed's Jewish community and also publishes studies relating to the town's heritage.

Run in cooperation with the Ministry of Education, university research institutes and the IDF, the **Centre for Educational Tourism** includes classrooms and a lecture hall with audiovisual facilities, all available for seminars and tour groups. Guest lecturers and accommodation can be arranged. For more details, contact Hameiri House (☎ 971307), PO Box 1028, Safed.

Davidka Memorial

Found by a bus stop on Jerusalem St, across from the former British police station and overlooking the Old City, this war memorial incorporates an example of the Davidka, a primitive and unreliable mortar made by the Jews and used to great effect in 1948. Somewhat dangerous to use, it did little physical damage but the story goes that it made such a loud noise that it scared the living daylights out of the Arabs.

Ma'alot Olei HaGardom St

This is the wide stairway that separates the synagogue quarter to the north from the artists' quarter to the south. Its name is Hebrew for 'Those Who Went Up On the Gallows', after seven Irgun terrorists hanged by the British whose bodies were carried down here en route to the cemetery. The stairway was built by the British after the 1929 Arab riots, to divide the town and keep the Arab and Jewish communities apart. Tarpat St, running from south to north along the slope, is the main street where the Arabs rioted in 1929. Note the ruins of 16th-century Jewish houses which were built using stones removed from the Crusader wall up the hill.

Look across Jerusalem St from the steps towards Gan HaMetsuda – on the roof of the opposite building is a British gun position with a searchlight. Further north is the former British police station, riddled with bullet holes. For many years it was an income tax office, and obvious jokes are made about the real reason for the bullets.

Artists' Quarter

South of Ma'alot Olei HaGardom St, this is the old Arab Quarter, now largely inhabited by artists. You may be disappointed with the work produced, but I am told that the local art scene is going through a transitional period and is on the way up with new blood coming through.

The steepness of the slopes may soon wear out any enthusiasm for gallery-hopping. The Ora Gallery, at 1 Beit Joseph St in the synagogue quarter, features work produced by religious artists, including some geometric acrylic paintings by Jacques Kaszemacher. This French Hasidic Jew, a fascinating character, is often here in the morning. Back in the artists' quarter, an abandoned mosque houses the general exhibition which features a representative selection of Safed's art. Often run by the artists themselves, the galleries' opening hours vary.

Zvi Assaf Printing Museum This houses exhibits of Jewish printing. The museum is open Sunday to Thursday 10 am to noon and 4 to 6 pm, Friday and Saturday 10 am to noon, and admission is free.

Shem Va'Ever Cave

Back on Jerusalem St, climb the stairs up to the bridge that carries HaPalmach St to reach this holy cave where Noah's son and great grandson supposedly studied the Torah.

According to Muslim tradition, it was here that a messenger told Jacob of the death of his son, Joseph. The Arabs therefore call the cave the 'Place of Mourning', and they believe that the messenger lies buried here.

Places to Stay

Safed's accommodation scene is not great. This has been made worse with many hotels closing, now filled with recent arrivals from the former Soviet Union and Ethiopia. Hoteliers put up their rates by some 15% to 20% during summer when the city offers a pleasant cool alternative to the heat of the lowlands. In the winter, it's too cold for most people and Safed does a good impersonation of a ghost town.

Places to Stay – bottom end

South Safed is where you will find the *Beit Binyamin IYHA Youth Hostel* (☎ 921086, 973514). Take Egged bus Nos 6 or 7 from the central bus station or walk for 25 or so minutes – it's near the Amal Trade School. B&B (mandatory) is US$8.50 (nonmembers US$9.50). Other meals are normally provided only if a group is staying here.

In the town centre there are a few private homes with rooms to rent – usually around US$20 per person. The tourist office has a list. Standards vary from those places that look as if they have remained untouched since the last earthquake to those that could be considered comfortable.

Shoshanna Briefer is a Rumanian lady with distinct grey-black hair who rents out beds (from US$8) in a couple of dingy apartments with kitchen facilities south of the artists' quarter. Very friendly and helpful, Shoshanna has lived in Safed for some 20 years and is a great source of information for the traveller. Look for her at the central bus station where she often waits to greet potential guests. If you don't see her or, even less likely, she doesn't see you, climb the stairs up to Jerusalem St, turn left and follow the road up to the bridge, climb the stairs and cross over the bridge heading south, away from Gan HaMetsuda. Take the first alley to your right, then take the alley that runs diagonally in the same general direction as the road. The apartments are towards the end – one is on the left, behind a large green metal door, the other is across the street on the right, with a grey door, about two-thirds of the way along.

For Jewish travellers, another option is *Ascent Institute of Tsfat* (☎ 971407; fax 921942), 2 Ha'Ari St. From the central bus station, turn right and take the first street on your right. Turn right again on Ha'Ari St and Ascent is on your left after a few minutes. In a renovated former hotel, this complex has a lovely hostel (there's a fridge but no kitchen) with visitors strongly encouraged to attend regular classes in Jewish mysticism. Arrangements are made for Shabbat meals with local families, hikes and city tours. Dorm beds are US$9, private rooms US$26, with a US$2 rebate for those attending daily classes. Non-Jews are accommodated if with a group of Jews, but if alone they will be set up elsewhere.

Places to Stay – middle & top end

Down below the Davidka Memorial on Jerusalem St, *Beit Nathan* (☎ 920121) is sometimes open with singles/doubles for about US$20 per person.

Up Jerusalem St, to the right from the central bus station and past the public garden on the right, you come to Javitz St, a series of steps leading down the slope. At No 8, the *Carmel Hotel* (☎ 920053) is in a modernised old building. The rooms are plain but clean and comfortable, some with great views. Singles/doubles are US$30/45. *Hotel Hadar* (☎ 930068) on Ridbaz St, offers a higher standard; singles cost from US$33 to US$36, and doubles from US$44 to US$50.

The top hotel in town is the *Rimon Inn* (☎ 920665; fax 920456), located in the artists' quarter. Singles cost from US$58 to US$88, and doubles from US$68 to US$98.

Places to Eat

Safed is no culinary centre, but there are a few places that are better than the rest.

There is a fruit and vegetable market on Monday and Tuesday morning in front of the main post office (cross the bridge and head south, away from the Citadel) and a supermarket on HaPalmach St (turn left from the central bus station).

On the pedestrianised part of Jerusalem St, after the tourist office, various eating places can be found. For decent felafel, head for *Felafel Baruch*, and for 'the Galilee's best pizza', try *Palermo*.

In the synagogue quarter, *Big Mo's Dairy Experience* offers kosher fast food including pizza, bagels, blintzes and sandwiches. Run by Orthodox Jews from the USA, current sports news from home is provided for patrons. *HaKikkar Restaurant*, upstairs in the kikkar, is a nice room decorated with local art. It was closed on my last visit; see if it has reopened. It used to be a pleasant place for a bottle of beer, a hot drink or a bite to eat, with hummus and other salads and hot vegetarian dishes from US$5.

Back on Jerusalem St, the *Café California* sounds interesting. They serve hummus, etc (US$2.50) or more substantial meals from about US$6.

Entertainment

The *Wolffson Community Centre*, on HaPalmach St near the market, is the venue for occasional chamber music concerts throughout the year, and a musical workshop in the summer. Check the tourist office for the schedules of any current local events.

Some of the art galleries are open during the evening and a stroll around the Old City can be pleasant.

Each July/August, Safed hosts the Klezmer Festival. For three to five days, thousands of Israelis flock to the city to enjoy a busy lineup of Jewish soul music. Depending on your outlook, it's either a great time to be here, or a great time to be somewhere else. Accommodation is hard to find at this time; you could be better off visiting Safed from Tiberias or some other nearby location, but note that the heavy traffic makes getting in and out of Safed a lengthy ordeal during the festival.

Getting There & Away

Safed is about one hour from Tiberias by bus with buses every hour until 7 pm (4 pm Friday). There are other services to Haifa and Akko every half hour (two hours) until 9 pm (5.45 pm Friday), only three a day to Tel Aviv (otherwise change at Haifa) and only one a day to Jerusalem (otherwise change at Rosh Pinna).

Getting Around

Safed's centre is close enough to the central bus station and compact enough to make walking the best way to get around. To reach Mount Cana'an take local Egged bus Nos 1, 1-3, 1-4 or 3; take Nos 2, 2A or 6 to South Safed.

AROUND SAFED
Meiron

This small Orthodox Jewish settlement lies nine km north-west of Safed and is the site of the tomb of Rabbi Shimon Bar Yochai, 2nd-century author of the Zohar. His son, Ele'azar, is also buried here.

On the eve of Lag B'Omer, crowds of Orthodox Jewish pilgrims take part in a traditional procession that starts in Safed's synagogue quarter and ends here at the tomb in Meiron.

In the north of the village is the almost intact facade of a 2nd-century **synagogue**.

Nearby is the **tomb of Rabbi Yohanan Hassandlar**. Another great 2nd-century sage, he was also known as the Shoemaker.

Top: Star window, Hisham's Palace (Khirbet al-Mafjar), Jericho (NT)
Bottom: Hisham's Palace, Jericho (NT)

Top: Nablus from Mount Gerizim (NT)
Left: St George's Monastery, Wadi Qelt (NT)
Right: Arab girls, Hebron (NT)

Not far from the grave is a cave where he supposedly worked as a cobbler.

The path leads down to a **cave** where it is believed that Hillel the Elder, a famous Jewish scholar who lived in Jerusalem in the 1st century BC, is buried with his disciples. The cave is often mentioned by medieval pilgrims.

Beside the tombs of Rabbi Shimon and his son and Hillel's Cave lies a deep gorge. Beyond it, on top of the hill, is the **tomb of Rabbi Shammai** and the rock known as the **Throne of the Messiah**. According to tradition, when the Messiah comes he will sit on this rock and Elijah will blow a trumpet to announce the event.

Jish

This Arab village four km north of Meiron is notable because most of its inhabitants are of the Maronite faith and originally came from Lebanon. This was an important town in ancient times, known as Gush Halaav (Abundance of Milk). Yohanan, a leader of the Jewish Revolt against the Romans in 66 AD, came from here, and the town was renowned for its olive oil.

On the outskirts of the village are the **tombs of Shamai'a & Avtalion,** two famous Jewish sages who taught in Jerusalem at the beginning of the 1st century. The remains of a 3rd or 4th-century **synagogue** can be seen in a small valley two km east of the village.

Bar'am

In this 'abandoned' Arab village are the oldest and perhaps most impressive remains of an ancient synagogue in the country. Dated to the 2nd century, legend has it that Queen Esther is buried in the grounds here.

Bat Ya'ar

Beautifully located in the Birya Forest, this activity centre (☎ 921788) offers visitors a steak restaurant, trail riding, jeep tours, country walks, children's activities and rapelling. You need a car to get here; from Safed take the road north-east to Amuka (see The Golan map).

Upper Galilee & the Golan

A relative lack of frequent public transport makes this area north and east of the Sea of Galilee much less accessible than other parts of Israel. However, its outstanding natural beauty and historical sites should be more than enough to encourage you to make the effort to explore.

The best way to visit the area depends on how much time and money you have, and whether or not you have your own car. This is one of the parts of Israel where it can be most advantageous to have your own vehicle. You can see a lot of the area in one day by car, but you would be rushed and would miss out on some great hikes with waterfalls and pools to swim in. Two days at least would be better to do it some justice.

Those who have limited time and money might decide to paticipate in one of the tours mentioned in the Tiberias section, and visit the area for a day with a guide to point out the major places of interest. Those with time but no money may want to rely on buses and hitchhiking to get around.

Beyond Tiberias and Safed, the only budget accommodations are in Tel Hai, near Qiryat Shemona, and in Katzrin, which does

Hoopoe

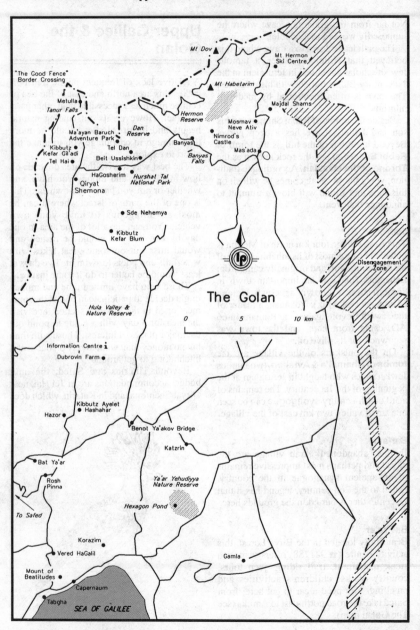

mean having to spend a fair bit of your time moving from place to place. For those with sufficient funds, there are some pleasant kibbutz guesthouses in other areas.

Recent years have seen giant strides made in developing the region as a leisure and tourist destination. With the intifada resulting in fewer foreign visitors, this has meant attracting Israelis from the south with guesthouses and speciality restaurants in scenic locations, and soft-adventure activities like inner-tube floating, kayaking, horse and donkey riding, even ice skating, as well as the more obvious natural and historic attractions with hikes, birdwatching and archaeological sites.

ADVENTURE ACTIVITIES IN GALILEE

Here is a quick reference for the main adventure activities to be enjoyed in the region (see the appropriate section in this chapter for more details):

Inner Tube Floating, Rafting & Kayaking

Floating down rivers in inflated car inner tubes is a lot of fun, very popular with Israelis and well worth a try (see the Hula Valley section). Try the following:

Ma'ayan Baruch Adventure Park (☎ 951390)
Huliot Jordan Rafting Park (☎ 946010)
Kibbutz Kefar Blum (☎ 948755; fax 948555)

Ice Skating

Ma'ayan Baruch Adventure Park – see the Hula Valley section in this chapter
Canada Centre – Metulla Sports Centre (☎ 950370) – see Metulla in this chapter

Horse & Donkey Riding

Bat Ya'ar (☎ 921788) – see Around Safed in this chapter
Kibbutz Ayelet HaShahar (☎ 932302; fax 934777) – see the Hula Valley section in this chapter
Baba Yona (☎ 937555, 935747; fax 935069), Yesud Hama'ala – see the Hula Valley section in this chapter
Vered HaGalil (☎ 935785; fax 934964) – see the Sea of Galilee in this chapter

Skiing

Hermon Ski Resort (☎ 981337) – see Mount Hermon in this chapter

ROSH PINNA

The busy junction at Rosh Pinna is the main point of entry to the region, with roads converging from Haifa, Akko and Safed from the west and Tiberias from the south. If you choose to travel by bus in the region you will often have to change here. Proceeding north from Rosh Pinna the road heads up to Metulla on the Israel-Lebanon border via Qiryat Shemona. Galilee's major airport is nearby.

Rosh Pinna Pioneer Settlement Site

This site (☎ 936603/913) is up the hill, just to the west of the Rosh Pinna junction. Rosh Pinna was the first settlement in Galilee, established in 1882. Although there are no major sights here, the original old houses have been renovated and it is an attractive spot for a meal or drink at the local pub. The discovery of wild wheat in the area by the leading Jewish botanist Aaron Aaronsohn in 1906 was an important development in the research of the origins of cultivated cereals.

Griffon

Places to Stay

Rosh Pinna Youth Hostel (☎ 937086) is currently closed with Ethiopian immigrants being housed there. There are a few B&B places, at about US$25 per person; just look for the signs.

BENOT YA'ACOV – JORDAN BRIDGE

Just north of the Rosh Pinna junction, a sideroad leads to the east and Kibbutz Kefar HaNassi. A little further north, another sideroad leads to the east. Passing the small settlement of Mahanayim it comes to Mishmar HaYarden (Guard of the Jordan) after 11 km. This is Galilee's oldest moshav, established in 1890. It was captured and destroyed by the Syrians in 1948 and rebuilt after the area was returned to the Jews under an armistice agreement.

After another two km the road leads to a bridge over the Jordan River, called Benot Ya'acov, 'Daughters of Jacob', as this used to be the place where they crossed the river on their way to Canaan from Mesopotamia. This has also been the site of much conflict over the years. It marked the border between the Latin Kingdom of the Crusaders to the west, and the Muslims to the east and many battles were fought here during the 12th century. In 1799 Napoleon's forces were entrenched here to prevent Turkish reinforcements from reaching Akko which was under siege from the French. WW I saw the Turks in action here again, and in 1918 they were defeated in their campaign to liberate Syria. During the 1948 War of Independence there was severe fighting here between Syrian troops and Zionist groups. The Six Day War saw Israeli troops cross the bridge on their way to capturing the Golan Heights and the surrounding area was regularly shelled.

From the bridge, the road leads up to the Golan Heights. A turn-off to the north leads through the scenic Hula Valley and after five km a turn-off to the south leads to Katzrin, the new 'capital' of the Golan.

HAZOR

Back on the Rosh Pinna to Metulla road, after nine km you come to the excavations of ancient Hazor. It is mentioned in ancient Assyrian and Egyptian records from as early as the 19th century BC, and it was the most important town in northern Canaan when the Israelites conquered the area (Joshua 11:10-13, 19:36) in the 13th century BC. In the late 10th century BC, Solomon made it one of his chariot towns (I Kings 9:15). It was captured by the Assyrians around 732 BC (II Kings 15:29) and they razed it to the ground.

Hazor Museum

Across the road from the tel (ancient mound) by the entrance to Kibbutz Ayelet HaShahar, is the Hazor Museum. This houses an exhibit of two pre-Israelite temples, a scale model of ancient Hazor and a selection of artefacts.

It's open Sunday to Thursday 8 am to 4 pm, Friday 8 am to 1 pm, and is closed Saturday. Admission is US$1.20.

Places to Stay

The four-star guesthouse at *Kibbutz Ayelet HaShahar* (☎ 932611; fax 934777) is one of the nicest in the country. Set in pleasant gardens with good facilities, including a swimming pool, there is a good restaurant, art gallery and free lectures on kibbutz life. Singles cost from US$57 to US$64, and doubles from US$67 to US$84.

Getting There

Egged buses running between Tiberias or Safed and Qiryat Shemona will drop you off; be sure to ask for Tel Hazor to avoid being guided to the town of Hatzor HaGlilit, near Rosh Pinna.

HULA VALLEY & NATURE RESERVE

This beautiful valley between the Galilee and Golan mountains was once a huge malarial swamp dominated by Lake Hula, the northernmost and smallest of the three lakes fed by the Jordan. In order to provide rich, well-watered land for intensive agricultural development, the Israelis implemented a massive engineering project here in the 1950s to drain the lake and the surrounding swamps. In addition, there was a plentiful supply of peat to be dug out of the former lake bed.

However, another result of the Hula project was to endanger a unique plant and wildlife habitat. The Hula is the northern-most point in the world where papyrus reed grows wild, and the region's characteristic flowers are the white water lily and the yellow pond lily. These were threatened, along with great numbers of birds and animals, from small waders to pelicans, sea eagles, otters, jungle cats, boar and many other creatures. The valley is a migratory station for birds, with many coming from as far as Scandinavia, Russia and India.

This threat spurred a small group to form the Society for the Protection of Nature in Israel (SPNI) in 1953 which launched a successful campaign to retain an area of the swamp as a nature reserve. The result of their initial campaign is the Hula Nature Reserve (☎ 937069), a unique wetlands reserve and wildlife sanctuary.

The Visitors' Centre features a flora & fauna museum. It's open daily 8 am to 4 pm in the summer, 8 am to 3 pm in the winter, and closes an hour earlier on Friday and on holidays. The reserve itself is open Saturday to Thursday 8 am to 5 pm, Friday 8 am to 4 pm and admission is US$3 (students US$1.50). There are free guided tours on Saturday, Sunday, Tuesday and Thursday between 9.30 am and 1.30 pm.

Buses running between Rosh Pinna and Qiryat Shemona will drop you off at a signposted junction about 2½ km from the entrance to the reserve – you have to walk or hitchhike from there.

Dubrovin Farm
North of Tel Hazor, this is a reconstructed Jewish settlers' farm (☎ 93445/937371) from the turn of the century.

In addition to the buildings and tools on display, there is a pottery workshop, an audio-visual presentation and a restaurant.

It is open in summer, Sunday to Thursday from 8 am to 6 pm, Friday from 8 am to 3 pm; in the winter Sunday to Thursday from 8 am to 5 pm, Friday from 8 am to 2 pm; and

is closed Saturday all year. Admission is US$3, which is deducted if you eat at least a main course in the restaurant.

Buses running between Rosh Pinna and Qiryat Shemona will drop you off at a signposted junction on main road No 90, about four km from the farm – you have to walk or hitchhike from there.

Adventure Activities
Hula Valley is the main location for some soft-adventure activities that have become extremely popular with Israelis in recent years.

The Ma'ayan Baruch Adventure Park (☎ 951390), at Kibbutz Ma'ayan, features inner-tube floating, rafting, kayaking and ice skating. Located in the north of the valley, look for the signposted exit off main road No 99, north of Qiryat Shemona. Other venues for these pursuits are Huliot Jordan Rafting Park (☎ 946010), at Kibbutz Sde Nechemia, and Kibbutz Kefar Blum (☎ 948755; fax 948555). For both of these places, look for the signposted turn-off heading south-east from Qiryat Shemona from main road No 90.

The following places both offer horseriding: Baba Yona (☎ 937555; 935747, fax 935069) at Yesud Hama'ala, located south-east of the Dubrovin Farm, east of main road No 90; and Kibbutz Ayelet HaShahar (☎ 932302; fax 934777), located north-east of Hazor. For both sites, look for the signposted exits off main road No 90.

All of these locations involve several km walking from the closest bus stop, but hitching can be possible.

Places to Stay
Kibbutz Ayelet HaShahar (☎ 932302; fax 934777) has a four-star guesthouse with horseriding and jeep trips available. Singles cost from US$57 to US$64, and doubles from US$67 to US$84. Its located south of the Dubrovin Farm, east of main road No 90.

North of the Hula Nature Reserve and three km along a sideroad to the east of main road No 90, *Kibbutz Kefar Blum* has a three-star guesthouse (☎ 943666; fax 948555). There is a swimming pool, and opportunities for fishing, birdwatching and jogging. Singles cost from US$47 to US$59, and doubles from US$58 to US$82.

Places to Eat

The restaurant at the Dubrovin Farm (☎ 937371) is popular with Israelis, and serves decent food in an authentic, rustic atmosphere. Expect to spend from US$20 to US$30 a head.

QIRYAT SHEMONA
(Population: 21,000)
This town's name is Hebrew for Town of the Eight, after the eight Jewish settlers killed at nearby Tel Hai in 1920. The town was a more recent target for Palestinian terrorist attacks in the 1970s. This is Upper Galilee's 'big town' and its administrative and transport centre.

A standard Israeli new town, it has the familiar wide main boulevard, carefully laid-out residential districts, and bus station. Its most prominent feature is a children's playground made from three old army tanks that have been painted in bright colours.

Information

The post office is just south of the bus station on Tel Hai Rd and has international telephone facilities. Bank Hapoalim is nearby.

Places to Stay

There's only the *Hotel North*, also called *HaTzafon* (☎ 944703). Across the street from the bus station, it is a three-star establishment with a bar, lounge and pool; singles/doubles are US$50/65.

Places to Eat

The choice is limited. There is an open-air market on Tel Hai Rd, north of the bus station and a supermarket to the south, behind Bank Hapoalim. Felafel and shwarma are sold nearby, there is a pastry and snack shop near the Hotel North and a basic oriental-type restaurant near the petrol station to the south. Another option is the *Sin-Galil* (China-Galilee) Chinese restaurant.

Getting There & Away

Qiryat Shemona is a major junction. Tel Hai, Metulla and the Israel-Lebanon border are to the north; the Hula Valley and Rosh Pinna to the south; and Hurshat Tal, Tel Dan, and such Golan attractions as Banyas, Nimrod Castle, Mount Hermon and Katzrin to the east. Check bus routes and timetables carefully before setting off and stock up on food, especially for Shabbat.

TEL HAI

Just north of Qiryat Shemona, off the Metulla road, is Tel Hai. It was an incident here in 1920 that led to the naming of the nearby town and the status of Josef Trumpeldor as a Zionist hero.

Born in Russia in 1880, Trumpeldor served in the Czar's army where he lost an arm, and was decorated for gallantry. He later founded the HeHalutz Jewish pioneer movement. In 1912 he immigrated to Palestine and with his self-styled Zion Mule Corps fought with the British Commonwealth forces in the disastrous Gallipoli campaign. Returning to Palestine after the war, he established Tel Hai (Hill of Life) in 1917 as a shepherds' camp. Three years later it was attacked by Arabs, and eight of the settlers were killed, including Trumpeldor, whose reported last words were: 'It is good to die for our country.'

Cemetery

The death of those eight settlers has since been made a symbol of political Zionism and Trumpeldor in particular is a model of courage and heroism – a sort of Jewish Lord Nelson. A statue of the Lion of Judah, with Trumpeldor's famous last words inscribed on it, marks the military cemetery where the eight are buried. The 11th day of the month of Adar is 'Tel Hai Day' and Israeli youngsters make an official pilgrimage to the graves to honour the eight.

Museum

The original settlement's watchtower and stockade have been converted into a museum showing its history and purpose. An audiovisual show in English will usually be screened for a small group on request.

The museum is open in summer Sunday to Thursday 8 am to 1 pm and 2 to 5 pm, but is closed Friday and Saturday. In winter, it is open Sunday to Thursday 8 am to 4 pm, Friday 8 am to 1 pm, and Saturday 9 am to 2.30 pm. Admission is US$1.65 (students US$1.20).

Places to Stay
The *Tel Hai Youth Hostel – IYHA* (☎ 940043) is a cheaper alternative to staying in Qiryat Shemona. It offers dorm beds for US$6.75, and rooms from US$20. Meals are available and reception is open from 5 to 7 pm.

Getting There & Away
Take Egged bus Nos 20 or 23 from Qiryat Shemona, or walk the three km.

KIBBUTZ KEFAR GIL'ADI
One km to the north on the road to Metulla from the Tel Hai turn-off, Kibbutz Kefar Gil'adi has a museum and a guesthouse. It can also be reached via a track from the Tel Hai cemetery.

Museum
Just inside the gates to the kibbutz is Beit HaShomer (House of the Guardian), an IDF museum documenting the history of the early Zionist settlers' regiments in the British Army during WW I.

It's open Sunday to Thursday 8 am to noon and 2 to 4 pm, Friday and Saturday 8.30 am to noon, and admission is US$0.20.

Places to Stay
At the three-star *kibbutz guesthouse* (☎ 941414/5; fax 951248), singles cost from US$47 to US$59, and doubles from US$58 to US$82.

METULLA
Established in 1896 with a grant from the Rothschild family, this frontier town's name is Arabic for 'overlooking'. While the Jewish residents continue to farm, grow fruit and keep bees, it is their town's location that

makes it important. Right on the border with Lebanon, it lives up to its name, overlooking the barbed-wire and concrete fortifications and Iyon Valley on the other side.

Good Fence
On the Israel-Lebanon border near Metulla, the 'Good Fence' refers to an Israeli medical clinic providing treatment (and referrals of serious cases to Israeli hospitals) for residents of southern Lebanon. Since 1976, over 230,000 Lebanese have crossed the border for medical attention courtesy of the Good Fence. Lebanese Christians and Druze are also permitted to visit relatives and hold jobs in Israel, commuting each day from Lebanon through the checkpoint.

Although Metulla has developed as a small-scale mountain resort with its slow pace and cooler climate, it is the Good Fence that is the major attraction here. Situated to the west of town you can see the checkpoint and, across the border, several Lebanese Christian villages. To the north-west is Beaufort Castle, once the Crusaders' but more recently a PLO artillery position.

Nahal Iyon Nature Reserve
Straight ahead on the main road, with the Good Fence to the left, this is a small wood and picnic area. Some pretty waterfalls are special attractions here.

The deep gorge of the Iyon River is east of the Qiryat Shemona to Metulla road. Two km before you enter the town is the largest and most attractive of the **Tanur Falls**. Some 18 metres high and surrounded by rocky walls, Tanur or Oven is so-called because the density of mist that it creates when in full flow supposedly resembles billowing smoke. The fall is reduced to a trickle during the summer months, although the deep pools below it are still good for a cool swim. The Iyon River continues to flow southwards where it later joins the Jordan. Further on, past the gate and down some stone steps, is a path leading to the Iyon Waterfall. During the summer, it runs completely dry, bar a few stagnant pools.

Egged bus No 20 will drop you at the turn-off if you ask; from there it's a few minutes' walk to the park. Follow the trail past Tanur and you will see two smaller falls before ending up in Metulla after about 45 minutes.

In Metulla you can find the **Canada Centre**, otherwise known as the Metulla Sports Centre (☎ 950370). In addition to the country's largest ice skating rink, it houses a heated swimming pool, water slides, squash, gymnasium, firing range, table tennis, sauna and health centre.

Places to Stay
There is no budget accommodation in Metulla. At the *Hamavri* (☎ 940150), singles cost from US$30 to US$42, and doubles from US$40 to US$52. Ask here about concerts at Kibbutz Daphna. The *Sheleg HaLevanon Hotel* (☎ 944015/7; fax 944018) has tennis courts, two swimming pools, a bar & restaurant and garden patio. Singles cost from US$45 to US$50, and doubles from US$62 to US$70. The older-style *Hotel-Pension Arazim* (☎ 944143/5; fax 944666) is perhaps more comfortable. Well-run and very clean, it has a swimming pool and tennis courts, bar and restaurant. Singles/doubles cost US$54/75.

Places to Eat
In addition to the hotels mentioned above, there are snack bars serving felafel near the Good Fence and a restaurant across from the HaMavri Hotel, where you pay about US$8 for a meal.

Getting There & Away
Egged buses run from Tiberias, Rosh Pinna and Qiryat Shemona.

HURSHAT TAL NATIONAL PARK
Main road No 99 heads east from Qiryat Shemona, across the Iyon River and then the Senir River, one of the principal sources of the Jordan River, to reach Hurshat Tal National Park after some five km.

A popular and, therefore, often crowded picnic spot, this forested area is famous for its ancient oaks. According to Muslim legend, 10 of Mohammed's messengers once rested here. With no trees around at that time to provide shade or a hitching post for their camels, they pounded sticks into the ground to fasten their mounts. Overnight the sticks grew into trees and in the morning the holy men awoke to find themselves in a beautiful forest. With some of them believed to be about 2000 years old, the oaks tower over the park with its lawns, pools and waterfalls. The Dan River has been diverted to create a series of pleasant but cold swimming pools.

The park is open daily, April to September from 8 am to 5 pm; October to March from 8 am to 4 pm; it closes an hour earlier on Friday and the eve of holidays. Admission is US$2.

Egged bus Nos 25, 26 and 36 from Qiryat Shemona will drop you off here.

Places to Stay
The *Hurshat Tal Camping Ground* (☎ 940400) is 100 metres up the road, on the banks of the Dan River. Tent space costs US$8 per person, and bungalows are available: three-bed US$35, four-bed US$42 or five-bed for US$48. The three-star guesthouse at nearby *Kibbutz HaGosherim* (☎ 945231; fax 945234), established by Turkish Jews in 1948, is graded three-star and has a swimming pool; singles cost from US$47 to US$59, and doubles from US$58 to US$82.

Places to Eat
Dag al Hadan (☎ 950225/6), enjoys a good reputation with Israelis, serving trout caught from the nearby Dan River. It is open Sunday to Thursday from noon to 6 pm, and Friday and Saturday from noon to midnight. Expect to spend about US$20 to US$30 per person.

TEL DAN
When the land of Israel was divided after Joshua's conquest, the Dan tribe received territory in the coastal plain near Jaffa (Joshua 19:40-6). Unable to hold it against the chariots of the Philistines, they headed north to occupy a Canaan city-state called

both Leshem (Joshua 19:47) and Laish (Judges 18:27). Its name was then changed to Dan. Laish is mentioned in Egyptian Execration Texts of the 19th century BC, in the mid-15th century BC list of cities conquered by Thutmose III, and in documents from Mari across the desert on the Euphrates. In the Old Testament, 'from Dan to Beersheba' is the standard expression defining the northern and southern limits of the Promised Land (Judges 20:1, I Samuel 3:20, II Samuel 3:10, 17:11, 24:2).

The Arabs call the site Tal el-Kadi (Hill of the Judge), based on a legend that tells of the creation of the Jordan River. Before the Jordan existed, there were three streams, each flowing in a different direction. A quarrel broke out between them as to which was the largest and the most important. Unable to reach an agreement, the streams asked God to decide. God sat on a small hill between them and told them that he loved each of them and that they should join together to form the biggest river. This they did and the Jordan was the result.

There are excavations in a pleasant nature reserve – with some 40 hectares it is comparatively small. Many small springs nourish the dense forest, and it is an enchanting place for a walk and a picnic. It's open daily, in summer 8 am to 5 pm, in winter 8 am to 4 pm, and admission is US$2.

Egged buses from Qiryat Shemona will take you to the nearby Kibbutz Dan; continue up the main road and turn left at the orange sign to the reserve which is a three-km walk or hitchhike.

Beit Ussishkin Museum

Close to the Dan Nature Reserve, Kibbutz Dan houses this museum (☎ 941704), named after the director of the Jewish National Fund and featuring audiovisuals, dioramas and other exhibits covering the flora & fauna, geology, topography and history of the region. There is also a birdwatching centre here.

The museum is open Sunday to Thursday 9 am to 4 pm, Friday 9 am to 3 pm, and Saturday 10 am to 4 pm. Admission is US$2 (students US$1).

BANYAS

Just two km or so inside the Golan area, Banyas is an ancient cave sanctuary to Pan, the god of the countryside, flocks and herds. Banyas is an Arabic corruption of the Greek word Paneas. A spring bursts from a crack below the cave and is one of the principal sources of the Jordan River. The water actually originates from the slopes of Mount Hermon.

In 200 BC the Seleucids of Syria defeated the Ptolemites of Egypt to take control of Palestine. In 20 BC the Roman Emperor Augustus gave the area to Herod the Great and on his death it passed to his son Phillip, who built his capital here, Caesarea Phillipi. Matthew 16:13-20 tells of Jesus visiting the area when he told the disciples that the church would be built on Peter, the rock. In 1129 the Crusaders held Banyas, an important site as it controlled the road between Damascus and Tyre. The nearby Nimrod Castle was part of their fortifications. With the eventual defeat of the Crusaders the site reverted to its original significance. When the Israelis took it in 1967 there was only a village of some 200 inhabitants.

There is not really that much to see, although the Canaanites and later the Greeks built shrines and temples here. The niches in the cliff face next to the cave were cut during the Graeco-Roman period to receive statues and although there have not been any organised excavations here there are columns, capitals and blocks scattered around the site showing that this was an important 1st-century city. To the north of the spring a room of an Herodian building can be seen, and above the cave to the north (left) is the Weli el-Khader (Tomb of St George), a Muslim saint, which is sacred to Muslims and Druze. Across the main road are some Crusader ruins.

Run by the National Parks Authority, the site is open daily from 8 am to 6 pm; admission is US$0.75. Along with the nearby Banyas Waterfall, this is the region's most popular site but the public transport situation is not good.

Banyas Waterfall

About a km from the park is this lovely waterfall. Follow the path which starts near the stream in the park. Take the right fork just past the bakery, and you come to a pool built by the Syrian Army. Past the pool you come to three paths – take the middle or right paths to the waterfall. Although in winter the water crashes down with more ferocity it is too cold for most people to dive in, whereas in the summer it is most refreshing. Needless to say, it is a very popular site so try to come here early and avoid visiting on Shabbat and Jewish holidays.

Getting There & Away

Egged bus No 55 travels from Qiryat Shemona via Banyas to the Golan only twice a day with the last bus back to Qiryat Shemona leaving Banyas around noon. An alternative, apart from hitchhiking, is to walk the five km west to Kibbutz Dan where bus Nos 25, 26 and 36 run a bit more often and until a bit later; check the schedules.

NIMROD CASTLE

Less than two km north-east of Banyas, this is the biggest and best preserved of Israel's Crusader castles. Nimrod also enjoys some of the country's finest views from its prominent position, with the Hula Valley below and Mount Hermon to the north.

The castle was named after the biblical Nimrod (Genesis 10:8-10) to whom legend attributes its construction. In fact, Baldwin II had it built in 1129 by Reiner Brus to protect Banyas from an attack from Damascus. It took him three years, which was not bad going judging by the size of the stones that had to be hauled up the steep slopes. However, in 1132 the castle was lost to the Damascenes, who had it taken from them in 1137 by an Arab rival, Zengi, who wanted control of Damascus.

In 1140, the Crusaders and Arabs teamed up to win back the castle after a month-long siege, but their alliance ended in 1154 when

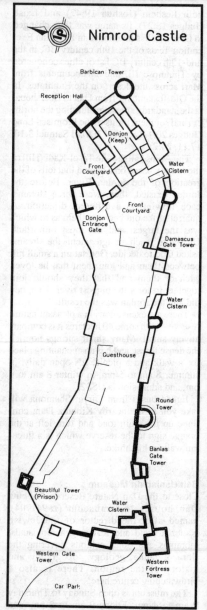

Nimrod Castle

- Barbican Tower
- Reception Hall
- Donjon (Keep)
- Front Courtyard
- Water Cistern
- Front Courtyard
- Donjon Entrance Gate
- Damascus Gate Tower
- Water Cistern
- Guesthouse
- Round Tower
- Banias Gate Tower
- Beautiful Tower (Prison)
- Water Cistern
- Western Gate Tower
- Western Fortress Tower
- Car Park

Zengi's son, Nur ed-Din, won control of Damascus. He twice attempted to take Nimrod in 1157, but had to retreat both times when a Crusader relief force impersonated the US Cavalry and appeared on the horizon just in the nick of time. He succeeded at his next attempt in 1164, with the garrison surrendering before the Crusader army could return from Egypt.

During the 5th Crusade (1217-21) it was dismantled but was later renovated by sultans of the Ayyub Dynasty during the early 13th century. There are 10 Arabic inscriptions which tell of this work, and in fact most of the remains seen today are from this period.

By 1260 the castle was under the Mameluke Sultan Baybars who constructed a citadel built from massive stones and decorated with inscriptions. From the 14th to the 16th centuries the castle served as a jail for political prisoners. After that it was abandoned and used as a cow shed and sheepfold by local farmers.

In the Six Day War it was first used by the Syrians as an observation post and a mortar position, and then by the Israelis. Both parties seemed keen to avoid damaging the impressive remains.

The site (☎ 942360) is open April to September, Saturday to Thursday 8 am to 5 pm, Friday 8 am to 4 pm; October to March, Saturday to Thursday 8 am to 4 pm, Friday 8 am to 3 pm; admission is US$3 (students US$1.50).

Getting There & Away

The most convenient way is to take a sherut from Qiryat Shemona, costing about US$3. Alternatively, the Egged bus running between Qiryat Shemona and Katzrin will drop you off nearby. You can also hike up the hill from Banyas – give yourself about 1½ hours each way, cover your head and take plenty of water. A footpath starts from just above the spring.

MOUNT HERMON SKI CENTRE

There are suprisingly decent, albeit limited, skiing facilities here on the country's highest mountain (2766 metres). The snow season is usually late December to early April and the slopes are pretty crowded on the weekend. There are four runs from the upper station, the longest being about 2½ km and all designed for the average to fairly good skier. Separate chairlifts take skiers and onlookers up from the base station. A shorter chairlift takes you up to a gentler run, with nursery slopes at the bottom of the hill.

Prices are as bad as you probably expect them to be. A round trip on the non-skiers' lift is about US$12. If you want to ski, the average daily cost of equipment hire, lift tickets and admission to the slopes is over US$70 per person. With most Israelis hiring their equipment, you need to get here early to ensure that your boots fit.

It is open between 8.30 am and 3.30 pm, depending on the conditions – telephone ☎ 981337 to check.

Place to Stay

At the *Moshav Neve Ativ Holiday Village* (☎ 941744), guests stay in members' homes and meals are served in the guesthouse dining room, a pleasant, country-style place complete with large fireplace and a great view down to Nimrod Castle and the Hula Valley. There is a disco/bar, billiard and pool room, and horseriding is available. Singles/doubles are US$50/90, rising on weekends and with mandatory half or full board at busy times. Holiday village guests get free admission to the slopes, use of the chairlift, and free skiing lessons.

Getting There & Away

The infrequent Egged bus No 55 runs up here from Qiryat Shemona and Katzrin.

DRUZE VILLAGES

Majdal Shams and Mas'ada are the two largest Druze villages in the area. Unlike those on Mount Carmel, these Druze are fiercely anti-Israel and they have protested against the occupation and subsequent annexation of the area ever since Israel took the Golan Heights from Syria in 1967.

Not only have they refused to accept

Israeli citizenship, they actively support Syria and there have been several violent anti-Israeli demonstrations here over the years. As well as their definite political differences, these Druze are also more traditional, having had less contact with the Western world. However, they are just as super-friendly to visitors and although the ramshackle villages are not exactly attractive, the surrounding countryside is and the people themselves can make a visit a wonderful experience.

Majdal Shams
(Population: 5900)
Majdal Shams (in Arabic, Tower of the Rising Sun), the Golan's largest town, stands near the Syrian border. There is a UN building on the next hill across the valley, and an adjacent white stone with a red mark denotes the border. Captured by the IDF in 1967, Majdal Shams' residents have relatives just across the border. On Friday they go down and shout across to one another, as separated families do in Rafah in the Gaza Strip.

Majdal Shams has a couple of inexpensive restaurants serving such things as felafel, hummus and grilled meats and salad. The Ram Pool is a crater lake that I find rather unattractive but with a restaurant and boats available for hire, it's considered a beauty spot by others. You'll find the village two km below the ski facilities.

QUNEITRA VIEWPOINT
About 15 km south from Mas'ada, the road heads towards Quneitra, the abandoned Syrian town, but skirts around it and reaches a high mound with an observation point. From here you can look across to Syria and the UN-patrolled border.

Quneitra was the Syrians' 'capital' of the Golan. It was mostly inhabited by Circassians, Muslim immigrants from the Caucasus. Captured by the Israelis in 1967,

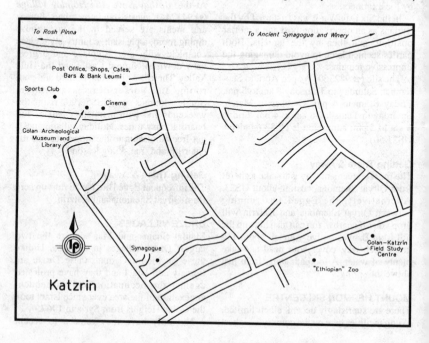

it was subsequently returned under the cease-fire agreement but has since remained a ghost town. Damascus is a mere 30 km north-east of here.

KATZRIN
(Population: 2500)
Established in 1977 and also known as Qazrin, Kazrin, etc, the name is Hebrew for Forts, originally from the Latin *castra* (fortress). It's about four km down a road that heads south off the Rosh Pinna-Quneitra road. The new 'capital' of the Golan, Katzrin is as near to an ideal base from which to explore the area as you can get, especially for those on a tight budget.

Planned in the shape of a butterfly, with the wings as neighbourhoods and the body as the commercial district, it is far from fully grown, having a projected population of 10,000. Set amongst a bleak landscape it is not an attractive town, but its decent facilities do provide good living conditions by Israeli standards – further enhanced by government grants and allowances for those who live and work here.

Orientation
The town lies to the south of the main road. The main street leads straight ahead past the shopping centre (which has a post office, bank, supermarket, eating places, cinema, museum and sports facilities) to the southern edge of the town. To the left is the SPNI field school, the only accommodation in Katzrin.

Information
The post office is open Sunday, Tuesday and Thursday, 7.45 am to 12.30 pm and 3.30 to 6 pm, Monday, Wednesday and Friday 7.45 am to 2 pm, and is closed Saturday.

The nearby Bank Leumi branch is open Sunday, Tuesday and Thursday 8.30 am to 12.30 pm and 4 to 6 pm, Monday, Wednesday and Friday 8.30 am to 12.30 pm, and is closed Saturday.

The swimming pool is open daily 10 to 5 pm, and admission is US$2.70.

Things to See
The **Golan Archaeological Museum** has some interesting exhibits. Many of the artefacts on display come from the site of ancient Katzrin which was one of the original Jewish settlements in the Golan.

It's open Sunday to Thursday 9 am to 2 pm, Friday 9 am to 1 pm, and Saturday 10 am to 2 pm. Admission is US$1.20 (students US$0.90).

You can visit the site of ancient Katzrin, with its 3rd-century **synagogue**. From the new town, return to the main road and head south (turn right). After about a 15-minute walk, it is on the opposite side of the road.

The turn-off to the north (left) passes the only petrol station in the Golan and leads to the new industrial area and the renowned **Golan winery**. At the time of writing, plans were being made to provide tours of the new outdoor winery where the prize-winning and much talked about Yarden wines are made. Telephone ☎ 961841/8 for more current information.

Back in town, a small **zoo** has been set up west of the field school by an Ethiopian resident.

Places to Stay
The SPNI's *Golan-Katzrin Field Study Centre* (☎ 961352) has a modern, clean and comfortable guesthouse for US$16 per person. It's often full, so phone ahead to make a reservation. To the south it has a campsite with basic bungalows for around US$8 per person or tent sites for US$4.

It is best to go straight to the main building of the field school regardless of where you want to stay. If no-one is around (not unusual), leave a note and your stuff. The staff are friendly and helpful to travellers who are keen to explore the area. They will happily tell you about natural beauty spots to visit, such as waterfalls, springs and rivers. Most of these places require a few hours hiking, but nothing too strenuous.

Places to Eat
In the shopping centre there are a few cafés serving felafel, salads and grilled meats;

some serve draught beer. Their main trade is provided by the IDF, with soldiers from nearby positions pouring in. Most of the staff are Druze from nearby villages.

The town's supermarket is open Sunday to Thursday 8 am to 6 pm, Friday 7 to 3.30 pm, and is closed Saturday.

Getting There & Away

There are infrequent buses from Tiberias and Qiryat Shemona.

DVORAH WATERFALL

The road from Katzrin heading north-east (left) joins the Benot Ya'acov Bridge to Quneitra road. Turn right to head towards Quneitra and a sideroad after one km leads down to this attractive waterfall. Turn off after about two km. The **Gilabon Nature Reserve** between here and Hulata is another pleasant area of forest.

YA'AR YEHUDIYYA NATURE RESERVE

Stretching down to the Sea of Galilee from Katzrin, this lovely area boasts some of the country's most attractive hikes. The source of Nahal Zavitan, the Zavitan River, the trails follow the water and you see some pretty waterfalls and amazing rock pools. These feature interesting hexagonal formations, caused by the rapid cooling of molten rock and known as Brekhat HaMeshushim, the Hexagon Pond.

To get here, either walk, hitch or drive two km south from Katzrin till you see the sign for the reserve and head for the car park.

Nahal Zavitan

One of the reserve's highlights is this four to five-hour hike. Possible all year round, it involves some generally light walking with an opportunity for a refreshing swim.

Entering the car park, turn right to continue north on foot or by car along the blue-marked semi-paved road for 1½ km. Look for the lava flow and electricity pole to your left and park here. Bear to your left along the blue-marked dirt road heading west.

The road splits after about one km; take

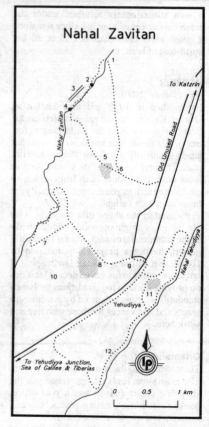

Nahal Zavitan

To Katzrin

Old Unused Road

Nahal Yehudiyya

Yehudiyya

To Yehudiyya Junction, Sea of Galilee & Tiberias

0   0.5   1 km

1 Zavitan River Bed
2 Hexagonal Basalt Formations
3 Aqueduct
4 Zavitan Falls & Swimming Hole
5 Hirbet Sheikh Hussein (Abandoned Arab Village)
6 Fork in Trail
7 Alternative Walk to Nahal Zavitan
8 Eucalyptus Grove
9 Parking & Entrance
10 Yehudiyya Forest
11 Yehudiyya
12 Nahal Yehudiyya Walk

the black-marked trail to the right and head
north for 1½ km. You should see a slope and
the end point of a lava flow to your right. The
trail heads down onto the western bank of
Nahal Zavitan, then follows the stream. Here
you can see the aqueduct built by local Arab
villagers who left the area as a result of the
fighting in 1967. About half a km down-
stream, you reach two of the large pools
featuring unique hexagon formations in the
basalt. These were caused three million years
ago when the lava cooled quickly and the
basalt cracked into these interesting shapes.

Nahal Zavitan continues and runs into
Nahal Meshushim where Berakhat Hameshushim features the country's best
examples of these amazing hexagons. You
follow the trail across Nahal Zavitan to walk
beside the aqueduct and after half a km come
to another pool with hexagonal formations.
From here, follow the red-marked trail to
look out over a 25-metre waterfall. Head
down to the right to reach Nahal Zavitan via
the blue-marked trail. This can be extremely
slippery in winter. You can reach another
pool under the waterfall by crossing the
stream. Head back up the blue-marked trail
to reach the top and continue along the wadi
to arrive at the Black Canyon.

Beautiful but dangerous, enough careless
hikers have fallen to their deaths here to
make unauthorised access illegal for safety
reasons. Continue along the red-marked trail
that bypasses the Black Canyon by taking
you along the western bank to Nahal Zavitan.

Follow the blue-marked trail past a memorial site to reach a dirt road. Follow this to
reach the abandoned Arab village of Hirbet
Sheikh Hussein and eventually to return to
the starting point.

GAMLA

Believed to be the ruins of ancient Gamla,
this spectacular site has great views overlooking the Sea of Galilee and is well worth
a visit.

On 12 October 67 AD the Romans began
to besiege Gamla, a Jewish city on the slopes
of the Golan. With the Jewish Revolt against
Rome, thousands of the rebels fled north to
Gamla seeking refuge. Three legions of the
Roman Army followed them and massacred
4000 Jews, while the remaining 5000 committed suicide by leaping over the cliff. As
in the similar events at Masada, two women
survived.

Our knowledge of Gamla is based on the
account of its siege by the 1st-century historian, Josephus. This includes descriptions of
the location and layout of the city, and it was
with this information that the site 15 km
south-east of Katzrin was chosen. However,
it is not certain that this is the right place –
some archaeologists believe that a site near
Jamle on the Syrian side of the current Golan
border is more likely.

The name Gamla is derived from the word
'camel' and the chosen site here does bear a
likeness to the ship of the desert. In accordance with Josephus' account, the ruins lie
on a rock plateau (the camel's body) joined
to the hillside by a narrow ridge (the camel's
tail). One aspect of this site that clashes with
Josephus' account is the citadel. Here it is
west of the hump, but he wrote that it was
south. Authentic or not, it is an impressive-
looking place, particularly from the Golan
looking south-west with the Sea of Galilee
down below in the distance.

Getting There & Away

Egged buses running between Tiberias and
Katzrin pass by the turn-off to the site (at
least twice a day). Otherwise you can try to
hitch the 15 km from Katzrin.

Dead Sea

A unique natural phenomenon, the Dead Sea is a major attraction for visitors. It is well-known for its high salt density that makes it impossible for bathers to sink. In addition, the water contains many minerals that, along with the climate, provide various health-giving properties.

Over recent years the region has been developed as a health resort with a slowly increasing number of spas, clinics and hotels.

There are plenty of other things to see and do as well as floating and feeling good. There are the archaeological sites at Qumran where the Dead Sea Scrolls were found, and Masada, Herod's mountaintop fortress and the Jewish Zealots' last stronghold in their revolt against Rome. Going back to nature, there is the outstanding scenery in the barren mountains of the Judean Desert to the west, and the mountains of Moab in Jordan to the east. A direct contrast to their desert surroundings are the lush green oases of the Ein Feshka and Ein Gedi nature reserves.

History

Awareness of the Dead Sea's unique qualities goes back to at least the 4th century BC when the Nabateans collected bitumen with special boats which swept bitumen from the surface. This was sold to the Egyptians, who used it for embalming, and written records show that this industry continued well into the Roman period.

Such luminaries as Aristotle, Strabo, Pliny, Tacitus, Pausanius and Galen all mentioned the sea's physical properties.

During the Byzantine and Crusader periods there was a lot of marine traffic here, but subsequent legends (eg that no birds could fly over it) inspired by a Sea of the Devil label, meant that it was left alone until the US Navy explored it in 1848. Ancient times also saw various religious ascetics and political fugitives choosing to hide out among the caves and the isolated mountain-tops that surround the Dead Sea. The future King David, King Herod, Jesus and John the Baptist were among them.

However, the Dead Sea remained desolate and unexploited until the 1920s, when mineral exploitation began. Soon two plants were producing half of Britain's and most of the Commonwealth's potash needs. During the 1948 War of Independence, the Qalya plant was destroyed as that area fell to the Jordanians. The Sodom plant remained in Jewish hands despite a siege that lasted some months until the IDF eventually arrived.

Despite the mass immigration and the programme of consolidating the areas gained by the new Jewish state, the first few years after independence were not good for Israel's development of the region. About 75% of the Dead Sea was in Jordanian hands, as were the freshwater supply, the roads and a considerable part of the evaporation pans at Sodom. It took time for a new road and a new supply of fresh water to be provided to the plant and it was not until 1952 that work there was resumed.

The Israelis have not yet fully exploited the enormous potential here for moneyspinning tourist and health facilities. The luxuries of modern roads and air-conditioned vehicles make it easy to overlook the fact that the region is a barren desert with an inhospitable climate and physically cut off from the rest of Israel by mountains. The heat and aridity and the political factors – half the area is in the occupied West Bank – have all played their part in making Israel's planners leave the area alone, with more attention focused on the coastal plain, the north, Eilat, and even on the Negev.

Geography

In Hebrew, Yam HaMelah (Sea of Salt), the Dead Sea is the world's lowest point at over 400 metres below sea level. Its actual water level fluctuates, losing about one metre each year, but its approximate total size at present is 65 km in length and 18 km across at its widest point. After the 1948 War of Independence only about a quarter of the Dead Sea fell to the new State of Israel, but as a result of the Six Day War, almost half of it is now under Jewish control, with the border between the Israeli-occupied West Bank and Jordan running virtually straight down the middle.

The Dead Sea is fed mainly by the Jordan River, supplemented by smaller rivers, underground springs and floods. With no outlet, the inflow of water is balanced by a high rate of evaporation due to the constant hot temperature. The water arrives with normal mineral concentrations (mainly magnesium, sodium, calcium and potassium chlorides) but the evaporation causes them to rise dramatically. The water's salt concentration is about 30% (compared to 4% for ordinary sea water) making it easy to sit up in and comfortably read this book. There are 11 species of bacteria that manage to survive in the Dead Sea, but no fish.

The original lake was four or five times the size of today's Dead Sea and in the early 19th century it was about as low as it is now. Fluctuations in the water level were once due only to natural conditions, mainly the variation in the rainfall. With the construction of Israel's National Water Carrier system, the natural balancing act of the Dead Sea was disturbed. Inspired by the Israelis, the Jordanians built a similar project on the Yarmuk River, and together the two neighbours have deprived the Dead Sea of over 600 million cubic metres of water per year. This has resulted in the Dead Sea's southern basin drying up completely and the length of the sea has been shortened by over 25 km.

Today, all the water to the south of Masada is being pumped there by the Dead Sea Works Ltd on the Israeli side, and by the Arabic Potash Corporation on the Jordanian side – you will see the canals dug into the dried out sea-bed.

There are two very different sections of the Dead Sea. The northern basin is over three times the size of the southern one, and a lot deeper – about 400 metres. The southern

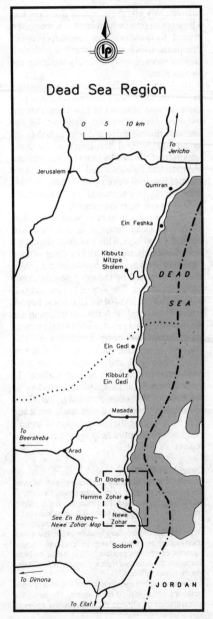

Dead Sea Region

0   5   10 km

To Jericho

Jerusalem

Qumran

Ein Feshka

Kibbutz Mitzpe Shalem

DEAD

SEA

Ein Gedi

Kibbutz Ein Gedi

Masada

To Beersheba

Arad

En Boqeq

Hamme Zohar

See En Boqeq–Newe Zohar Map

Newe Zohar

Sodom

To Dimona

JORDAN

To Eilat

basin is only about six metres deep and has a higher salt level which creates iceberg-like crystal formations. The Lashon (Tongue) Peninsula, which juts out from the Jordanian eastern shore, now completely separates the two sections.

Both the Israelis and the Jordanians exploit the Dead Sea's mineral wealth, which supplies vast amounts of raw chemicals for industry, agriculture and medicine. Of the various minerals extracted here, potash (used as an agricultural fertiliser) is the most important, followed by bromine, magnesium chloride and industrial and table salts. More recent industrial developments here include solar energy power stations using salt ponds to absorb and store the sun's heat.

An ambitious project to build a Mediterranean to Dead Sea Canal was proposed several years ago. This involved digging a water conduit over 100 km long with a pumping station and a hydroelectric power station, powered by the steep descent down to the Dead Sea. The aim of the project was to maintain the level of the Dead Sea, furnish water to be used in further developing the Arava Valley and provide additional electricity. There have been variations on this concept of a canal, including a Red Sea to Dead Sea Canal and another between the Mediterranean and the Sea of Galilee. To most observers, all such ideas seem too far fetched to be taken seriously, but those involved believe such a plan could work and that, by requiring the co-operation of Israel's neighbours, it would help bring peace to the region.

Dead Healthy?

Compared to regular sea water, the water of the Dead Sea contains 20 times as much bromine, 15 times as much magnesium and 10 times as much iodine. Bromine, a component of many sedatives, relaxes the nerves, magnesium counteracts skin allergies and clears the bronchial passages while iodine has a beneficial effect on certain glandular functions. Various cosmetic companies produce ranges based on Dead Sea products because of their reputation for health and beauty rejuvenation.

The hot sulphur springs and mud deposits provide treatment for a variety of ailments. The heat, the concentration of salts on the skin and the enforced relaxation are all helpful, particularly for muscular and joint conditions such as rheumatism and arthritis, fractures, several skin diseases and for those who simply want to unwind and be indulged.

The Dead Sea air is extremely dry, the temperatures are high all year round, and rainfall averages only five cm a year. Due to the low altitude, there is 10% more oxygen in the air than at sea level, and the lack of urban development has kept it free of pollution. All of this increases the body's metabolic rate and has a bracing effect. The misty evaporation haze over the Dead Sea contains large amounts of the water's bromine and this supposedly has a soothing effect.

Despite the high temperatures and around 300 cloudless days a year, the high atmospheric pressure filters the sun's burning ultra-violet rays which makes it harder to get sunburn. The intense, naturally filtered sunlight is used to help cure psoriasis, a severe skin disease.

Despite all the talk there are some who have found that the Dead Sea makes them feel ill rather than healthy. Certainly the water does have a few qualities that are not too appealing.

Firstly, don't shave just before bathing here, or expose any cuts or grazes to the water – it really stings. The high salt content will probably let you know about tiny scratches you never knew you had. Remember to wear shoes as most of the beaches have sharp stones. The magnesium chloride gives the water a revolting bitter taste – it's not surprising that no fish live in it. Whatever you do, don't swallow it or get any in your eyes.

The calcium chloride makes the water feel smooth and oily to the touch. You may want to avoid getting your hair wet as it becomes both smelly and sticky. When you get out after your float, a residue sticks to your body that many find unpleasant. The bathing beaches have freshwater showers, although some locals prefer not to wash it off immediately, believing that their skin benefits from the minerals.

The hot sulphur springs can be dangerous to those with blood pressure problems and for certain treatments a medical examination is compulsory.

Although it is harder to get sunburnt in the Dead Sea region, it is not impossible. I met a few pink people who had wrongly presumed that their fair skins were safe and didn't use a sunscreen – so be warned.

Things to See & Do

Before setting off to visit the Dead Sea, there are several factors to be considered that will greatly affect your enjoyment of the area.

Many travellers make the big mistake of regarding the Dead Sea as simply one place to visit. Instead, it covers a fairly large area with different things to see and do at various widespread points. Unless you have your own car or take an organised tour, you are dependent on the buses which do not run as frequently as you might like. Also, it is important to realise that with the area still in the early stages of development, there is a shortage of inexpensive places to stay and places to eat. Finally, the hot desert climate makes it even more essential that you arrange things so that you are not waiting endlessly for a bus, rushing around trying to cram in all the places that you want to visit, or having to pay more than you can really afford for accommodation and food.

Enjoying the sensation of floating in its water is the major attraction of the Dead Sea. The nicest place for this is the well-kept sandy beach at En Boqeq by the main hotel area, or at Hamme Zohar, a little further south. However, if you are short of time you may be better off using the beach at Ein Gedi. After the obligatory float, the next popular thing to do is to visit Masada. Coming a close third is the Ein Gedi Nature Reserve. For those of you short on time, the quickest way to enjoy the three popular attractions is to spend a night here. Coming from Jerusalem, take the early bus down and visit Ein Gedi's nature reserve and beach, then head for Masada to spend the night. You can then beat the heat and reach the top early the next morning and still have most of the day to move on elsewhere. Coming from Eilat or Beersheba, you reach Masada first. Spend the night here, reach the top first thing in the morning, then head north to Ein Gedi's nature reserve before it closes in the early afternoon, and end the day with a float before heading up to Jerusalem. If you have an extra night to spare, stay over at Ein Gedi so that you can reach the nature reserve early in the morning when it's cooler and less crowded, and to give yourself more time to enjoy the beautiful surroundings of the region.

Visits to Qumran and Ein Feshka come lower on the scale of 'musts' for most people, although they are worth a visit if you have the time.

If you look around, you can help yourself to free Dead Sea mud and salt crystals along the shoreline, otherwise you need more time and more sheqels to use the hot springs and clinics.

Deciding where to stay in the Dead Sea region or even whether to stay here at all is another dilemma, particularly for shoestring travellers. The IYHA hostels at Ein Gedi and Masada are by far the cheapest places, but they are over double the price of private hostels in nearby Jerusalem, so many choose to sleep rough, either on the beach at Ein Gedi or atop Masada à la zealot. Remember that by paying in US dollars, you save on the 15% VAT at IYHA hostels. Others choose to make day trips from Jerusalem and 'do the Dead' in stages, but the cost of the return bus fares and the extra travelling time should be taken into account. There is also a campsite at Ein Gedi, but sites are hardly cheaper than the hostels, nor is the Ein Gedi field school which is usually filled by SPNI members anyway. For those with hotel budgets, there are several choices at En Boqeq and Hamme Zohar, or the kibbutz guesthouses at Ein Gedi and Metzoke Dragot.

As with accommodation, there is a distinct shortage of inexpensive food in the Dead Sea region – to save a small fortune bring plenty of food. There are no supermarkets or grocery stores and the cheapest place to eat is the café at Hamme Zohar, hardly worth a special trip. Elsewhere, the self-service restaurants at the various sites provide snacks and meals from about US$5. By comparison, the basic but filling meals dished up by the IYHA hostels are excellent value.

Lastly, try to avoid the Dead Sea at weekends and holidays when it can be unpleasantly crowded.

Orientation

The entire west coast of the Dead Sea, about 90 km in length, is accessible from Israel. This is served by a single main road that starts in the north from the main Jerusalem-bound highway, and follows the shoreline southwards to Sodom, continuing to Eilat, with intersections heading west to Beersheba via Arad and Dimona. Some of the distances you will travel are:

Jerusalem-Qumran	40 km
Qumran-Ein Feshka	3 km
Ein Feshka-Ein Gedi Nature Reserve	34 km
Ein Gedi Nature Reserve-Ein Gedi Kibbutz	2 km
Ein Gedi Kibbutz-Ein Gedi Spa	2½ km
Ein Gedi Spa-Masada	15 km
Masada-En Boqeq	15 km
En Boqeq-Hamme Zohar	3 km
Hamme Zohar-Newe Zohar	1½ km
Newe Zohar-Sodom	12 km
Sodom-Beersheba	78 km
Sodom-Eilat	185 km

The road from the Jerusalem-bound highway intersects with the shore-side road that runs down from the outskirts of Jericho from the east via Qalya, with its crumbling remains of the old potash industrial plant, a Jordanian military camp and holiday centre. It now all belongs to the nearby Kibbutz Qalya which has developed the site as a leisure resort. The road continues southwards towards Qumran and passes through a not particularly appealing section of shoreline. In the distance are black and red-hued mountains. Up here is the Qumran archaeological site with the excavations of the Essene settlement and caves. Continuing southwards, you come to the Ein Feshka Nature Reserve with its fresh-water pools and bathing beach.

Ein Gedi is the next major place of interest. The attractions are spread out over four km and they all answer to the name of Ein Gedi, so it is important to get off the bus at the right place to avoid a long, hot walk or wait. The nature reserves, field school and youth hostel are to the north, on the west side of the road. Next stop, one km further south, are the bathing beach, restaurant, campsite and petrol station. Another 2½ km to the south is the turn-off for Kibbutz Ein Gedi, with the Ein Gedi Spa complex 2½ km beyond.

The archaeological site of Masada is at the end of a side road, overlooking the area where the Dead Sea is divided in two by the receding water level. There are restaurants, souvenir shops and a youth hostel here.

Back on the shore road and continuing south, you come to the pleasant En Boqeq

area. With the nicest beach on the Dead Sea, it is the region's most developed site with hotels, restaurants and medical clinics. Another three km further south is the Hamme Zohar section. This features the top of the range Moriah Dead Sea Spa Hotel with its own beach and comprehensive medical and health facilities. Just south of the hotel are the Hamme Zohar Thermal Baths, the Kupat Holim Hot Springs and another nice beach.

Another 1½ km leads to Newe Zohar, a sparse, messy area with new and old buildings including a failed hotel and museum. Beyond here is the Arad junction, with the main road continuing to Sodom, past the Dead Sea Works Ltd plant.

'Attraction' Operated by three local kibbutzim, this is the Dead Sea's first 'aqua' amusement park, along the lines of those that are so popular with the Israeli public at the Sea of Galilee (☎ 942393). The attractions include various water slides, inner-tube floating, swimming pools, a bathing beach with mud deposits, and a cafeteria. Admission for the day is US$11; it's open daily from 9 am to 5 pm, March to October only. In the winter, only the beach is open.

Getting There & Away

Although you can reach the Dead Sea by direct bus from Haifa, Tel Aviv, Beersheba, Arad, Dimona and Eilat, the most comprehensive service is from Jerusalem's central bus station. Note that the buses stop on request at all the major sites. It is important, however, that you keep a sharp eye out for the place that you want. The Egged drivers speed along so fast that you can fly past Qumran or Ein Feshka, for example, without realising it.

In Jerusalem, the Old City tourist office is a better place to go for the current Dead Sea bus schedules than the hectic central bus station.

On Saturday, no buses operate until the late afternoon. The exception is a bus that leaves from Beersheba for Ein Gedi at 7 am, stopping on the way at Arad at 7.45 am and Masada at 8.30 am.

QUMRAN

The Dead Sea Scrolls have been described as 'the most important discovery in the history of the Jewish people'. In early 1947, a Bedouin shepherd accidentally found them stored inside some earthenware jars in the caves here. They are now on display at the Shrine of the Book, part of the Israel Museum in Jerusalem.

Subsequent excavations revealed the community centre of the Essenes, a Jewish sect. They lived in the nearby caves (and in tents and underground chambers) from about 150 BC until 68 AD, when the Romans dispersed them. The area was inhabited as early as the 8th century BC by the Israelites, but was abandoned because of an earthquake. The Essenes lived communally, with a farm on the plain above the cliffs. Some of them worked the land and tended sheep, others made pottery or wrote. Most of their time was taken up by studying the Old Testament and other religious literature. They chose to settle here to get away from the

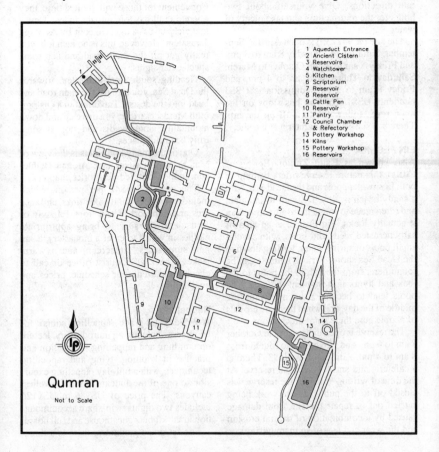

1 Aqueduct Entrance
2 Ancient Cistern
3 Reservoirs
4 Watchtower
5 Kitchen
6 Scriptorium
7 Reservoir
8 Reservoir
9 Cattle Pen
10 Reservoir
11 Pantry
12 Council Chamber & Refectory
13 Pottery Workshop
14 Kilns
15 Pottery Workshop
16 Reservoirs

Qumran

Not to Scale

Jewish establishment which was too liberal for them.

For a good view of the settlement, head for the watchtower. From here you can see the aqueduct, channels and cistern systems that ensured the water supply. Elsewhere is a refectory, a council chamber, the scriptorium where the Dead Sea Scrolls were probably written, ritual baths, a pottery workshop with kilns, and a cemetery.

The caves themselves are higher up and none of those in which the Dead Sea Scrolls were found are marked. If you interrogate the ticket office staff you might be given accurate directions. Give yourself about two hours for the return climb and take plenty of water.

The site (☎ 942235) is open April to September, Saturday to Thursday 8 am to 5 pm, and Friday 8 am to 4 pm; October to March, Saturday to Thursday 8 am to 4 pm, and Friday 8 am to 3 pm; admission is US$3 (students US$1.50). The bus stops on the main road; follow the turn-off up the hill. There is a self-service cafeteria at the site.

EIN FESHKA

Also known as Einot Zuqim (Spring of Cliffs), this nature reserve offers bathing in both freshwater pools and the Dead Sea, with a sandy beach nearby. Difficult to imagine, and often made to sound more attractive than it actually looks, Ein Feshka is an area of salt-encrusted reeds and grass, with several small pools of spring water, leading down to the Dead Sea shore. Various animals can be found here, from the fish in the pools to the ibex and hyrax that frequent the area. The pools tend to become a bit murky by the middle of the day, and when there are crowds of people here there's not much room.

The reserve is open daily, April to October 8 am to 5 pm, and November to March from 8 am to 4 pm. Admission is US$3. There is a cafeteria and snack bar in the reserve. At the time of writing, much of the reserve was closed off to the public due to work being carried out to repair the site from damage caused by a combination of natural erosion and the wear and tear of so many visitors.

METZOKE DRAGOT

Grandly calling itself the 'International Centre for Desert Tourism', Metzoke Dragot (☎ 964501/4; fax 964505) is operated by Kibbutz Mitzpe Shalem and offers various exciting tours and activities in the Judean Desert, either with or without accommodation. They are highly recommended by those who have experienced it. Note that the prices quoted here were valid for the 1991 season, and that tours and courses are offered for specific days, and not on a daily basis.

Desert Safaris

Convenient for those with limited time, they operate a full-day tour into the Judean Desert that picks up passengers in both Tel Aviv and Jerusalem. However, this is no rush job; you really get off the main road and see some spectacular sights.

Heading south from Jerusalem towards the Dead Sea, you turn off the main road and head into the desert. Travelling in a custom-built Mercedes truck, you drive up and down mountains, along wadis and stop at some truly beautiful places.

One of the many highlights is the view of Mar Saba Monastery (see Around Bethlehem in the Occupied Territories chapter).

The cost is US$42 per person, which includes lunch, hot and cold drinks, entrance fees and transport to and from Tel Aviv or Jerusalem. Be sure to bring appropriate clothes in which to enter a monastery, a sun hat, sunglasses, sunscreen, and a warm jacket. Check at a tourist office or call to check the current tour schedule, prices and availability.

Rappelling

A 2½-day 1st-grade rappelling course for beginners includes an introductory lecture on climbing and rappelling, instruction and practise in knotting, tying and rappelling techniques, with a full-day rappelling excursion to one of the Judean Desert's loveliest canyons. The price of US$86 to US$126 includes two nights twin-share accommodation in the kibbutz guesthouse and full board.

For 1st-grade graduates, there is a three-day 2nd-grade advanced course, costing from US$96 to US$140, including food and board. Combining both courses you pay from US$165 to US$260.

Rappelling day trips to various canyons in the Judean Desert are available to graduates at US$30 per person. There is also a five-day rappelling tour to the East Sinai for US$275.

Rock Climbing

You can take a basic rock climbing course here with the Israeli Alpine Club. The three-day course teaches the principals of free and aid climbing. Graduates can join Metzoke Dragot's climbing trips, and enjoy a year's membership of the Israeli Alpine Club. The price is US$165, including food and board.

Places to Stay

The kibbutz has a simple guesthouse, with singles/doubles for US$35/48.

Getting There & Away

Egged buses will drop you off on the main road by the signposted turn-off, but be aware that it's a good hour's steep climb to the kibbutz, which is beautifully located on a cliff overlooking the Dead Sea.

EIN GEDI

One of the country's most attractive desert oases, Ein Gedi (Spring of the Kid) has been developed by the Israelis into a major tourist site. There are two adjoining nature reserves that preserve the lush area of freshwater springs, waterfalls, pools and tropical vegetation to provide beauty spots and a haven for desert wildlife. Rich in biblical history as well, there are ancient remains of the early settlements here. The beach is one of the most popular in the Dead Sea, although this is due more to its proximity to the oasis than to its own qualities – it's rocky rather than sandy. Owned by the nearby kibbutz, the Ein Gedi Spa is probably the most popular venue to experience the Dead Sea's various health qualities.

With all of the above combined with the youth hostel, field school, restaurant, campsite, kibbutz guesthouse and a petrol station,

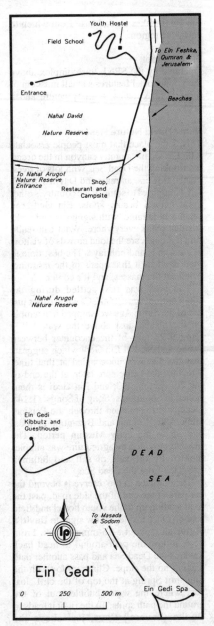

Ein Gedi

0   250   500 m

Ein Gedi makes a good base from which to enjoy the region.

Field School

Operated by the SPNI, this complex above the youth hostel features a small museum of local flora & fauna, a study centre and a hostel.

Nahal David Nature Reserve

This is the place that most people associate with Ein Gedi – a pretty canyon in the desert overlooking the Dead Sea, with lots of trees, plants, flowers, animals and David's Waterfall. Compared to some of the country's other great natural beauty spots, Ein Gedi can seem a little tame, with signposts and well-trodden paths everywhere. What can really ruin it though, are the loud crowds of visitors at weekends and holidays. The best time to visit is when it first opens in the morning. You beat the masses, and it's cooler.

The area was first settled during the Chalcolithic Age (3000 BC) when tribes just out of the Stone Age worshipped in a temple on the plateau just above the waterfall. I Samuel 24 tells of the encounter between David and Saul at Ein Gedi which suggests that the site was unoccupied at that time. Israelites did settle here later, at the end of the 7th century BC, and Ein Gedi is mentioned in Solomon's 'Song of Songs' (1:14). Occupation continued through the Persian, Hellenistic, Roman and Byzantine periods, and up to the early Muslim period. The income provided by agriculture was supplemented by the sale of salt and bitumen extracted from the Dead Sea.

The entrance to the reserve is beyond the car park at the end of the side road, past the road leading up to the youth hostel and field school. Once inside, follow signs to **David's Waterfall** – about a 15-minute walk. From here, follow the path around to head back towards the Dead Sea and pass another path leading up the slope. Climb up to reach the Shulamit Spring at the top of the cliff. Just past where the water bubbles out of the ground the path splits. To the right it leads to **Dodim (Lovers') Cave**, just above the

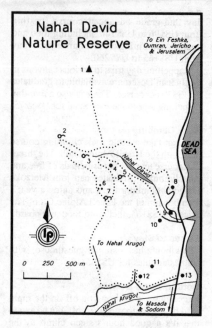

1	Mt Yishai
2	Springs & Dry Canyon
3	David Spring
4	David's Waterfall & Dodim Cave
5	Shulamit Spring
6	Chalcolithic Temple
7	Ein Gedi Spring
8	SPNI Field School & Start of Walk
9	Youth Hostel
10	Entrance to the Reserve & Car Park
11	Ancient Synagogue
12	Tel Goren
13	Entrance to Nahal Arugot Nature Reserve

waterfall in a lovely setting. Give yourself about 40 minutes to walk there and back. To the left, the steep path leads up to the fenced-in **Chalcolithic Temple ruins** – about a 10-minute climb.

Continuing down the slope, signs point to the **Ein Gedi Spring**. After about 25 minutes you come to a spring, surrounded by trees and reeds. Find your way through these to join another path. Go left to return to the main entrance, or go right to **Tel Goren**, the remains of the first Israelite settlement here. After another 20 minutes, you pass traces of ancient agricultural systems, including a watermill. Beyond Tel Goren are the ruins of an **ancient synagogue** (2nd or 3rd century BC). Continue down to the road and either turn right to reach the Nahal Arugot Nature Reserve by the car park or turn left to reach the main road, a 15-minute walk. From here it's a 10-minute walk northwards along the main road to return to the bus stop and the turn-off to the main entrance.

The Nahal David Nature Reserve is open daily, in the winter from 8 am to 3 pm (you have to vacate the reserve by 4 pm), and in the summer from 8 am to 4 pm (you have to vacate the reserve by 5 pm). Admission is US$3. You can leave heavy bags at the entrance. Eating is not allowed in the reserve and you must keep to the paths. Note that you are not allowed to visit Ein Gedi Spring and Dodim Cave after 2.30 pm.

Nahal Arugot Nature Reserve
For those with more time and more energy, this adjacent reserve provides another lovely waterfall. The **Hidden Waterfall** involves a round-trip hike of about 1½ hours. Another 30-minute hike beyond the Hidden Waterfall leads you to the Upper Pools.

The Nahal Arugot Nature Reserve closes one hour earlier than Nahal David reserve. There is a separate entrance, open at the weekend and on holidays; admission is also US$3. Follow the signposted turn-off from the main road, about three km south of the youth hostel, up to the car park for the start to the trail.

Dry Canyon Hike
This is a beautiful six-hour hike that takes you beyond the area of the Nahal David Nature Reserve that most visitors see. It involves some straightforward walking over

Ibex

slightly rough ground, with a few steep slopes to tackle and some scrambling over rocks here and there.

Regular sports shoes are suitable footwear – sandals are not. It can be muddy underfoot in places, especially in winter, and you can also end up getting your feet wet wading through shallow water.

Flash floods are a danger in winter, with a rush of water seeming to come from nowhere. It may not be raining here, but if it rains in the hills further west, say in Jerusalem, then a flash flood can be the result. Keep an ear out for the sound of rushing water and be ready to climb to higher ground. Take plenty of drinking water with you.

The hike starts at the end of the road leading up past the field school. Follow the black on white painted trail markers showing the way past reconstructed agricultural terraces. After half a km the trail reaches an intersection to the right; go straight ahead, now following red painted markers. As you climb up the small cliff, you can look down to the lush greenery between the David and Window waterfalls. The trail leads down to the dry canyon through a small gully. Take the left path down Nahal David, with the springs a little further along. The canyon gets deeper and narrower and stakes have been provided to help you get past the waterfall.

The canyon ends at the picturesque **Window Waterfall**, which overlooks Nahal David. Come back to the stakes to climb the small ravine to the south. After a hundred metres you come to a trail running parallel to the dry canyon. Turn left on this green marked trail, taking a right up the small hill. The view here looks down on Ein Gedi and the Chalcolithic Temple below.

Follow the trail on your right down to the temple. About 250 metres to the right is the **Ein Gedi Spring**. You may well see the hyrax here, along with such birds as the Tristram's grackle. The spring produces from 36 to 72 cubic metres of water per hour.

From the spring, you can choose to either return to Nahal David via the upper part of the reserve and/or the Shulamit Cave, or continue down through Tel Goren and past the ancient synagogue, with/without a stop at the upper part of the reserve and the cave.

To reach the upper part of Nahal David, take the wide path north from the spring, passing underneath the ledge with the **Chalcolithic Temple**. After 350 metres you intersect with the trail; continue straight down the southern bank and come to Nahal David spring, with the Window Fall's overhang nearby. Take the path to the right across the stream until you reach a large boulder at the top of David's Fall. You can climb down the ladder to reach **Shulamit Cave**.

To return to Nahal David, follow the path to your left and head down through Ein Shulamit. The path eventually reaches **David's Fall**, the reserve's biggest attraction for most visitors. Follow the path from here to reach the main entrance and parking lot.

To continue south, return to the Ein Gedi Spring and pass through a tunnel created by overhanging reeds. Note the ruins of a **Crusader flour mill** here. Follow the yellow marked trail, heading south-east, and crossing a dirt road. Take a right on the next dirt road you come to, and exit through the gate.

To your left is a war memorial. The adjacent ruins are **Tel Goren**, dating from the late 7th century BC and the 5th century. Follow the dirt road till it intersects with a paved road. Turn left and pass by Tel Goren and the former field school and kibbutz buildings. This road connects the entrance to Nahal Arugot with the main road. At the next intersection, turn left, and go through the gate. After about 100 metres, the road curves to the left. Head down to the right for another 100 metres and cross the fence to reach the ancient synagogue. Return to the paved road to make your way down to the main road, where you finish the hike about three km south from where you started.

Ein Gedi Beach

The public beach is beyond the petrol station and shops. The adjacent camping resort has a more pleasant private beach – nonresidents can use it for US$3.

Ein Gedi Spa

Further south, these therapeutic bathing facilities use hot sulphuric water from nearby mineral springs. There is a beach here, and a decent vegetarian restaurant. The complex belongs to the adjacent kibbutz whose guesthouse residents have the use of the facilities included in their room and board – nonresidents pay US$12, which includes mud, use of the private beach, and the sulphur pools.

Places to Stay

You can sleep for free by the beach, but watch your gear as several incidents of theft have been reported.

The *Beit Sara IYHA* hostel (☎ 584165) charges members/nonmembers US$9/10. Reception is open from 7 to 9 am and 5 to 7 pm. Dinner costs about US$5 and is served from 7 to 8 pm.

The *hostel* at the field school (☎ 84288, 84350) is usually full; reservations can be made here, or at SPNI offices. Beds cost US$12.

Back by the beach, the popular *Ein Gedi Camping Village* (☎ 584342) has tent space for US$6 per person and cabins for doubles for US$43, plus $9 for each extra person. There is a self-service restaurant, a mini-market for supplies and a clubhouse with a snack bar, TV and video lounge.

The guesthouse at Kibbutz Ein Gedi (☎ 584757/8) is one of the most popular in the country, with its combination of location and facilities. Surrounded by the patches of green trees and crops, with gardens, a swimming pool and the hot spa all included in the price, it gives value for money. Terms are half board only; singles cost from US$66 to US$94, and doubles from US$89 to US$101. Note that guests clean out their own rooms.

Places to Eat
The best value, apart from self-catering, is the youth hostel. The self-service restaurant by the camping ground serves basic food at prices which are reasonable, but still too high for many budget travellers. A wide range of snacks and meals, hot and cold, are available here. Ein Gedi Hot Spa has a pleasant self-service vegetarian restaurant. You can eat here from US$5 to US$15; it closes at 4.30 pm.

MASADA
Combining a spectacular setting with a dramatic history, the mountaintop fortress of Masada is well up on the list of 'musts' for visitors to Israel. However, the comparatively high prices for admission and the cablecar have inspired several visitors to label the site 'a blatant tourist rip-off'.

History
In Hebrew, Metzuda (Stronghold), the summit was first fortified by Alexander Jannaeus (103-76 BC) to defend his southeastern border. Herod the Great took it in 43 BC and, inspired by fears of either a Jewish revolt or Cleopatra of Egypt having him killed by Mark Anthony, he had this formidable and luxurious palace refuge built around 35 BC. It included a casement wall around the summit, defence towers, storehouses, an advanced water-storage system,

barracks, arsenals, public baths, and villas with swimming pools. With its desert location, steep ascent, elaborate fortifications and luxurious facilities, the construction of Masada was an amazing feat of design, engineering and construction. They don't build 'em like this anymore! After all that work, in 4 AD Herod died of natural causes without needing to use his desert hideaway.

In 66 AD the First Revolt started when a group of Jewish Zealots captured the fortress from the Romans, who had occupied it since Herod's death. Masada played no major role in the revolt itself, but when the Romans raided their villages, it became a Jewish refuge with the original Zealots joined by their families and other refugees from the fighting.

The revolt ended in 70 AD when the Romans captured Jerusalem. Masada, however, remained under the control of the Zealots for another three years. The Roman authorities did not see them as an immediate threat, but eventually the Roman army advanced on the fortress, determined to capture what was now the last Jewish stronghold in Palestine. With eight camps around the base of the mountain and up to 15,000 men, Flavius Silva laid siege. There were 967 men, women and children atop Masada.

After the Romans had built a ramp on the western side and managed to reach the defence wall, the Zealots chose to commit mass suicide rather than surrender. Taking lots, 10 were chosen to kill all the others, then nine of them killed themselves, leaving the survivor to set fire to the palace before killing himself. Food had been stacked up in the courtyard to show that the Zealots had not died because of starvation. When the Romans stormed the complex, they found two women and five children who had survived by hiding and who told them what had happened. With all the other Jews expelled by Titus when he captured Jerusalem, this was the end of that era of the Jewish presence in Palestine. Byzantine monks occupied the site during the 4th and 5th centuries.

Although there was a written record of the defeat of the Zealots, courtesy of Josephus,

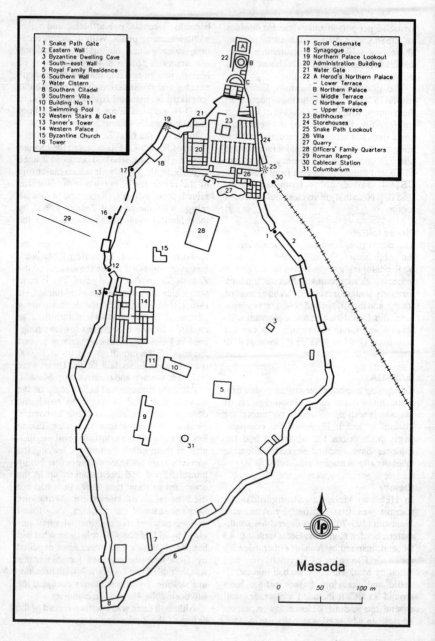

1 Snake Path Gate
2 Eastern Wall
3 Byzantine Dwelling Cave
4 South–east Wall
5 Royal Family Residence
6 Southern Wall
7 Water Cistern
8 Southern Citadel
9 Southern Villa
10 Building No 11
11 Swimming Pool
12 Western Stairs & Gate
13 Tanner's Tower
14 Western Palace
15 Byzantine Church
16 Tower

17 Scroll Casemate
18 Synagogue
19 Northern Palace Lookout
20 Administration Building
21 Water Gate
22 A Herod's Northern Palace
    – Lower Terrace
   B Northern Palace
    – Middle Terrace
   C Northern Palace
    – Upper Terrace
23 Bathhouse
24 Storehouses
25 Snake Path Lookout
26 Villa
27 Quarry
28 Officers' Family Quarters
29 Roman Ramp
30 Cablecar Station
31 Columbarium

Masada

0   50   100 m

a Jewish historian, Masada's location had been forgotten and it was not until the early 19th century that it was rediscovered. In 1807 it was seen from a boat on the Dead Sea, but not identified. In 1838 it was seen from Ein Gedi and identified correctly, and in 1842 it was climbed for the first time. Various small excavations took place during the late 1950s, and in 1963 a major programme commenced. The site was not only excavated and preserved, but partially rebuilt.

The story of the siege at Masada has been adopted as a symbol for the modern State of Israel with the oath that 'Masada shall not fall again'. Israeli schoolchildren visit the site as a part of their curriculum and some IDF units hold their swearing-in ceremonies here. On my last visit, some Israelis told me about an interesting, and because of the political value accorded to the Masada episode, extremely controversial theory that the events as described never actually happened. This is partly based on the possible unreliability of the historian Josephus, a Jewish traitor who collaborated with the Romans, and whose account is the sole written record of the siege. In addition, the remains of fewer than 30 Zealots' bodies have been found. Also, as strictly religious Jews, suicide would have involved them breaking Jewish law. Why would Josephus make up such a story, though, I wonder?

Things to See

Depending on your level of interest in archaeology, you could be up here for hours. A line of black paint indicates the original remains and the reconstructed parts.

(1) Snake Path Gate The stone slab floor, wall benches, guardroom and white plaster walls made to resemble marble, are typical of Masada's gates.

(2) Eastern Wall This section of the Herodian wall allows you to see how it was designed, with an outer and inner wall connected by partitions and the occasional tower. Herod's layout was, as befitting a

king, rather spacious, and the Zealots built partitions to create more living quarters for themselves.

(3) Byzantine Dwelling Cave Monks built this living space in an existing crater, believed to have been a quarry for plastering material.

(4) South-East Wall In this section of the wall, there's a tower with a little room built on to it. Inside, a small niche bears what might be a Roman inscription.

(5) Residence of the Royal Family One of a few examples of the luxurious residential villas built for Herod. Designed around a courtyard, it had a wide roofed hall at the southern end, separated by two pillars. Frescos cover the walls of the three rooms here. Again, the Zealots divided up the large rooms to accommodate their large numbers.

(6) Southern Wall There's a lookout tower here, with what was probably a bakery added by the Zealots. Strictly religious, the Zealots built ritual baths for themselves. The bath here has a dressing room next to it (note the narrow niches for clothes). The southern gate led to cisterns and caves outside the wall.

(7) Water Cistern This is an example of Herod's clever water supply system that was necessary to allow such a community to live in comfort in this barren location. There are another 12 cisterns up here, on the western slope.

(8) Southern Citadel This defended Masada at its weakest spot.

(9) Southern Villa An unfinished Herodian structure, the Zealots built more living quarters around it. One of the rooms has been restored to the state it was in when excavated, with pots left beside the kitchen hearth. A long hall with benches was built on to the north by the Zealots and may have been used as a study hall.

(10) Building No 11 The Zealots dug water reservoirs out of this Herodian villa's floor.

(11) Swimming Pool This pool illustrates the level of luxury enjoyed by Herod.

(12) Western Stairs & Gate This is where you enter if coming from the Arad road. From this side of the mountain you look west to Wadi Masada. Turn left to pass through the Western Gate and the wall that surrounds the whole site. The gate you see today is Byzantine. The Herodian gate and the gate the Romans breached are to the north.

(13) Tanner's Tower This is believed to have been where the Zealots treated hides, with basins built into the walls to store the liquids needed for the job.

(14) Western Palace This was both a royal residence and a ceremonial site. The western wing had storerooms and a kitchen, with an underground system of cisterns. The northern wing, built around a courtyard, had servants quarters, storerooms and workshops. The southern wing was for royalty, with waiting rooms, a throne room, bed chambers, and a bathhouse.

(15) Byzantine Church Dating from the 5th century, this consisted of a hall and three rooms. It had a tiled roof, glass windows, and a mosaic floor.

Mosaic

(16) Tower Byzantine monks constructed the wall around this tower, which was built out of sandstone.

(17) Scroll Casemate Archaeologists found several items of value left by the Zealots here, including scrolls, silver coins, a prayer shawl, weapons and sandals.

(18) Synagogue This is the oldest synagogue found anywhere in the world, and the only one dating from the time of the Temple. Pillars supported the roof, and you can see the base of the wall that divided the large hall.

(19) Northern Palace Lookout Enjoy the spectacular views north to Ein Gedi and the various wadis making their way to the Dead Sea. Herod's Northern Palace is below on the lower slopes of the mountain.

(20) Administration Building The Zealots built a ritual bath in this Herodian courtyard. As per strict Judaic law, rainwater was collected in the southern pool until it reached a certain level. It then trickled through a slit into another pool, and could then be used for the ritual immersion. The Zealots washed in the smaller pool to the west before taking the ritual bath.

(21) Water Gate With another great view to the north, this gate also featured a stone floor, benches around the walls for people to sit on while waiting, and the walls were covered with white plaster to imitate marble.

(22) Herod's Northern Palace Spectacularly built on three separate terraces on the northern slopes of the mountain, this was the king's private villa.

The lower terrace featured a courtyard, bordered by a double row of columns. Frescos covered the walls to imitate marble, and the small bathroom's floor was heated. Evidence of the Zealots' fate was found here: archaeologists dug up the skeletons of a man, a woman and a child, and the plaited scalp of another woman, along with a prayer shawl, arrows, and armour. The middle and upper terraces were Herod's private quarters. The upper terrace had black and white geometrically designed mosaic floors. Fragments of the wall and ceiling frescos can still be seen.

(23) Bathhouse Herod's luxurious bathroom boasted pillars, a black and red mosaic floor, a dressing room with frescos on the walls and ceiling and a black & white tiled floor, a lukewarm room with a pink and black tiled floor and more frescos, a cold room with just a pool, and a hot room, with another fancy mosaic floor.

(24) Storehouses This is where a years' worth of supplies were kept. Archaeologists found hundreds of storage jars here.

(25) Snake Path Lookout Look down to see the Snake Path, and across to the Dead Sea to the point where it is now split in two.

(26) Villa A residential villa at the time of Herod, it boasted a courtyard, pillars, and spacious rooms. The Zealots later divided up the rooms to house themselves.

(27) Quarry Some of the stone used in Masada's construction came from here.

(28) Officers' Family Quarters Here, three separate living quarters lead off a central courtyard. Again, the Zealots built more rooms within the existing setup. Valuable remains were found here, including silver coins, indicating that probably the wealthier Zealots lived here.

Sound & Light Show Staged each Tuesday and Thursday between April and October at 9 pm on the Arad side of the mountain, the 50-minute performance costs US$9. Call ☎ (057) 955052, 958993, 959333 for the current schedule. It's performed in Hebrew; you can rent earphones for simultaneous translation into English, French, German and Spanish. Access is from Arad only, and you need a car to get there.

Places to Stay
The *Isaac H Taylor – IYHA* hostel (☎ 584349), by the Masada bus stop, provides standard, simple accommodation for around US$10.50, with breakfast included. There is no kitchen; dinner costs US$5 but must be ordered before 6 pm, otherwise bring plenty to eat and drink or be prepared to rely on the nearby restaurants and snack bar. The hostel is closed from 8.30 am to 5 pm; check-in time is from 5 to 7 pm.

Sleeping out on top of Masada is a popular idea. Sadly, a young kibbutz volunteer fell to his death in 1986, so the authorities discourage you from staying up there for the night.

These days, a large group of travellers can normally be found spending the night by the snack bar, ready to head up the mountain before sunrise.

Places to Eat
Up the hill from the hostel are two restaurants and a snack bar. You can get a basic but filling set meal for about US$7; sandwiches cost about US$3.

Getting There & Away
To reach the top you can take the cablecar or climb up either of the two footpaths. The cablecar operates daily from 8 am with the last one returning from the top at 4 pm (Friday 2 pm).

The easier of the two paths is the Roman Ramp, but it is inconveniently built on the western side and can only be reached from Arad. Starting across from the cablecar station on the south-eastern side, the steeper and longer Snake Path is more widely used. It can be hard-going and, depending on your capabilities, you can run, walk or stagger up in anything from 15 minutes to over an hour.

Coming down can be as hard, if not harder, than going up, so remember the one-way ticket option on the cablecar. Top up with water before you start out, even though there is drinking water available on the summit. The heat really does get going by about 10 am, so the earlier you set off, the better, or plan your visit for later in the afternoon. The sunrise over Jordan and the Dead Sea can be lovely and well worth seeing from the summit.

The site is open daily from sunrise to 4 pm. Admission is US$4.50 (students US$3.50); the cablecar is an additional US$6.50 for the round trip (students US$3.70); and is US$4 one-way (students US$2.50).

EN BOQEQ

The pleasant beach here makes this tourist complex, with its hotels, restaurant and clinics, the nicest place for a 'dip in the Dead'.

Places to Stay

There's no budget accommodation here. The hotels boast facilities such as easy access to the beach (or their own private beach), freshwater swimming pools, sports and health facilities, a clinic and nightclubs.

At the three-star *Tsell Harim* (☎ 58 4121/2; fax 584666), singles cost from US$65 to US$78, and doubles from US$84 to US$100. At the *Lot Hotel* (☎ 584321/8; fax 584625), singles cost from US$73 to US$87, and doubles from US$90 to US$102.

Among the four-star properties, the *Moriah Gardens* (☎ 584351; fax 584383) has singles from US$88 to US$101, and doubles from US$120 to US$130. At the *Hod* (☎ 584644; fax 584606), singles cost from US$112 to US$120, and doubles from US$126 to US$135. The *Galei Zohar* (☎ 584311/4; fax 584503) has singles from US$70 to US$129, and doubles from US$80 to US$150. It also has self-contained apartments aimed at those needing to visit the Dead Sea each year for medical treatment, and are available on a sort of time-share deal.

An in-house dermatological clinic and a spa centre for rheumatic treatment make this establishment extremely popular.

The *Ein Bokek* (☎ 584331/4; fax 584162) has singles from US$75 to US$90, and doubles from US$90 to US$120.

Places to Eat

If you are staying here, eat in your hotel, otherwise there are a number of pleasant self-service restaurants which serve various meals, snacks and draught beer.

HAMME ZOHAR

This health and tourist complex fronts another pleasant beach. The Moriah Dead Sea Spa Hotel dominates, but a little to the south are two baths with more modest facilities.

Hamme Zohar Thermal Baths has a private beach and an open-air sulphur pool – admission is US$6 and various treatments are available. Away from the beach, the Kupat Holim Hot Springs is more clinical

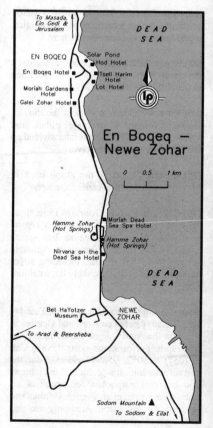

with a hot pool (US$8) and sulphur or air bubble bath (US$9); it also offers massages.

Places to Stay
The two luxury properties here are where many of the promotional photos for the Dead Sea are taken. Their private beaches with freshwater pools, indoor sea-water pools and other spa facilities, along with the tennis courts, cinema and nightclub, all make these the top places to stay on the Dead Sea.

At the *Moriah Dead Sea Spa Hotel* (☎ 584221/2, fax 584238) singles cost from US$101 to US$124, and doubles from US$128 to US$162. Further south, at the *Nirvana on the Dead Sea* (☎ 58426; fax 584345), singles cost from US$101 to US$170, and doubles from US$123 to US$189.

Places to Eat
In direct contrast to the trappings of its five-star neighbour, the unassuming *café* next door to the Moriah is the cheapest on the Dead Sea. Nothing exciting, just snacks including sandwiches and bottled beer.

NEWE ZOHAR
This messy development of buildings is the 'regional centre' for the Dead Sea with administration offices, emergency services, and a museum. A hotel opened here in 1985 but has since closed. There is a 24-hour petrol station at the junction with the road to Arad.

Bet HaYotzer Museum
Also known as the Dead Sea Museum, this was established under the auspices of the Dead Sea Works Ltd and shows the geographic make-up of the Dead Sea, its history and industrial development. At the time of writing, the museum was only open for groups by appointment with the Dead Sea Works Ltd (☎ 665111).

SODOM
Dominated by the unsightly Dead Sea Works Ltd plant, this area is traditionally thought to be the site of Sodom and Gomorrah, the wicked biblical cities that God destroyed with fire and brimstone (Genesis 18, 19). However, they were probably located further east in what is now Jordan. The reasons for today's industrial activity are highlighted by the salty surroundings.

The interesting sights are off the beaten track. With only the infrequent Eilat buses passing by, it's best to either have your own car or to take an organised tour – the SPNI offer some of the best. With your own car, you can follow the signs for a scenic drive with an eerie landscape and great views of the Dead Sea.

Sodom Mountain & Caves
This 11 km by three km mountain range is 98% salt. In most climates, salt dissolves and disappears, but in the dry Dead Sea region these salt rocks remain. The run-off water that collects on the surface cuts through to form a unique series of potholes that drain into a maze of caves.

The largest of these is next to a noticeable salt rock formation that has been dubbed 'Mrs Lot' in reference to Lot's wife who was turned into a pillar of salt for looking back at God's destruction (Genesis 19:26). Access to these caves is only possible with a guide, due to the danger of avalanches.

Nahal Prazim & Flour Cave is an interesting canyon which has been carved out of soft limestone into a variety of shapes by water currents. The **Flour Cave** is so called because of its powdery chalk lining.

The Negev

The Negev Desert accounts for almost half of Israel's land area. Although *negev* means 'dry land', it's far from being a simple expanse of sand. Starting by the Dead Sea where the Judean Desert ends, the northern Negev is a region of low sandstone hills, steppes and fertile plains with canyons and wadis. Moving south, the central Negev is drier and more mountainous – an area of bare rocky peaks, lofty plateaus and more canyons and wadis. The most outstanding features are the world's three largest craters, caused by millions of years of erosion. The Arava Valley is an extremely parched stretch of land to the east on the Israel-Jordan border.

At the Negev's southern tip are the grey-red Eilat Mountains and beyond is Egypt's Sinai Desert. The Negev is, in geographic terms, a natural extension of the Sinai.

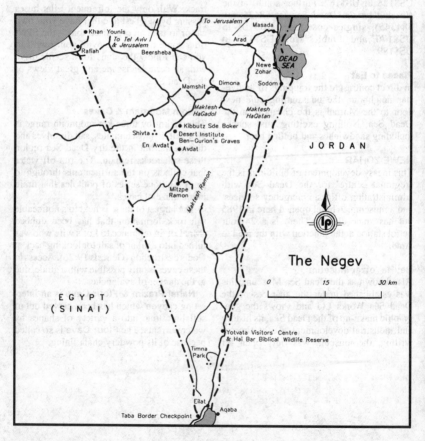

The Negev

Most of the Negev remains largely uninhabited and there are only a handful of towns. However, the harsh environment is dotted with an increasing number of Jewish settlements, mainly kibbutzim and moshavim but also 'Nahal' military projects (military service combined with agricultural work in marginal areas).

Established somewhat longer are the estimated 70,000 Bedouin who still live in tents and breed camels and livestock. The Israeli government seems to be trying to lure them away from their nomadic traditions by providing permanent housing and welfare facilities. You will hear more, though, about the progress made by the Jewish settlers in their bid to make the desert 'bloom'.

David Ben-Gurion, Israel's first prime minister and dubbed 'father of the Negev', was one of the first to publicly recognise the strategic importance and economic potential of the region. Under his leadership a development programme of sorts was launched with the basic aim of transforming a wilderness where nothing grows into much needed farmland. One of Ben-Gurion's popular quotes was 'If the State does not put an end to the desert, the desert may put an end to the State.'

Settlements were established in the middle of nowhere and, after much painstaking trial and error, results have been achieved. As you travel around the desert you will suddenly come across agricultural oases where the water piped down from the Sea of Galilee has been put to good use.

The Negev is often overlooked by visitors or simply seen through a bus window en route to or from Eilat. However, just a short distance away from the main roads there are several spectacular natural beauty spots and archaeological sites that are well worth a visit.

Major roads in the Negev are limited to two highways heading south to Eilat – the one from the Dead Sea is the most direct and the fastest, the other from Beersheba goes via Sde Boker, En Avdat and Mitzpe Ramon. Linking the Dead Sea and Beersheba is a road via Arad and another via Dimona.

With the Sinai Desert back under Egyptian control, the Negev became the 'playground' of the IDF. Military manoeuvres, both on the ground and in the air, regularly contribute to the scenery and soldiers are everywhere.

The Negev is a harsh desert, but due to its rapid development visitors can easily be lulled into a false sense of security and forget to follow the safety guidelines for a desert environment. It really is best to make an early start, to avoid physical exertion in the middle of the day (say noon to 3 pm), to cover your head and to drink plenty of water. Presumably due to the demands of IDF personnel, bus services pass by most of the places of interest – check the timetables to avoid too much waiting around.

Negev Tourism Development Authority

As part of a plan to exploit the tourist potential of the Negev, in March 1988 the Israeli government decided to give 38% grants to investors in tourism projects, and that US$30 million would be invested in tourism development over the next five years. The Negev Tourism Development Authority was founded to oversee this policy, with its head office in Beersheba at 1 Sold St (☎ (057) 671539; fax 671538), and a branch office in Tel Aviv at 7 Mendele St (☎ (03) 5272444/5; fax 223266). Visitors with special interests in the region might find the organisation a better source for information than the local tourist offices.

ARAD

(Population: 15,500)
On the road between Beersheba (48 km) and the Dead Sea (28 km), Arad is a new town even by Israeli standards. Established in 1961 after the discovery here of natural gas, Arad is one of the more attractive of Israel's preplanned towns, with pedestrian and motor traffic separated as much as possible in residential quarters. Situated on a high plateau (620 metres above sea level), it has commanding views of the desert and, in the distance, the Dead Sea.

Renowned for its cool, dry and pollen-free air, Arad is promoted as an ideal health resort for those suffering from asthmatic and respiratory difficulties. Arad, however, offers nothing much to either see or do and so most travellers limit any time spent here to changing buses en route to or from the Dead Sea.

Orientation

Arad's bus station on Yehuda St is easy to miss as there is no actual building, just a hut. Look instead for the police station next door. Across the street is the pedestrianised commercial centre with shops, eating places, the tourist office, banks, post office and a cinema.

If you choose to stay overnight the youth hostel is just a five-minute walk to the east, as is one of the hotels.

Information

Tourist Office The IGTO (☎ 958144) is in the commercial centre. It is open Sunday to Thursday 9 am to noon and 5 to 8 pm, Friday 9 am to noon, and is closed Saturday.

Post & Telecommunications These are in the commercial centre and are open Sunday to Thursday 7.45 am to 2 pm, and Friday 7.45 am to noon.

Other There are banks in the commercial centre. East of the commercial centre, off Yehuda St on HaSport St is an outdoor and an indoor pool. The police station (☎ 957044 or 100) is next door to the bus station on Yehuda St.

Things to See & Do

In Arad itself there are no real sights. In the industrial quarter to the south, the Abir Riding School (☎ 954147) offers horse-riding facilities and there is a pleasant lookout at the far eastern end of Ben Yair and Moav St, by the Masada Hotel.

Opposite the tourist office, the Matnas Cultural Centre hosts various activities including folk dancing, chess, bridge and a youth club. The Orion Cinema, in the commercial centre, is another possible source of entertainment.

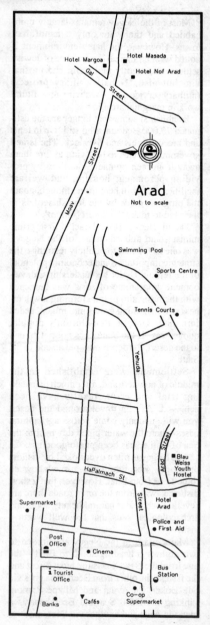

Arad
Not to scale

Hotel Margoa
Hotel Masada
Hotel Nof Arad
Swimming Pool
Sports Centre
Tennis Courts
Blau Weiss Youth Hostel
HaPalmach St
Hotel Arad
Supermarket
Police and First Aid
Post Office
Cinema
Bus Station
Tourist Office
Banks
Cafés
Co-op Supermarket

Visitors' Centre

Located by the commercial centre, the Visitors' Centre (☎ 954409) includes a museum which focuses on the archaeology of nearby Tel Arad. The exhibits include a sound & light show. It is open Saturday to Thursday from 9 am to 5 pm, Friday from 9 am to 4 pm, and admission is US$3.

Places to Stay

The IYHA's *Blau Weiss Youth Hostel* (☎ 957150) is on the corner of HaPalmach and Arad Sts. From the bus station walk east (past the police station) up Yehuda St, and follow the signs to turn right on HaPalmach. It's clean and quiet with kitchen facilities, and meals are available. Dorm beds cost US$9.50. It's closed from 9 am to 5 pm and there's no curfew.

The nearby *Hotel Arad* (☎ 957040; fax 954525) is basic but clean and comfortable – singles/doubles are US$27/44. There are a couple of more expensive hotels two km further east and each has a swimming pool. At the three-star *Nof Arad* (☎ 957056/8), singles cost from US$36 to US$47, and doubles from US$48 to US$64. The four-star *Margoa* (☎ 957014; fax 957778) has a clinic for the climatic treatment of asthma. Singles cost from US$54 to US$61, and doubles from US$68 to US$80.

Places to Eat

The commercial centre is where you will find what Arad has to offer. There are two supermarkets; the Co-op across from the bus station and Supersol across from the tourist office. Various places sell felafel, pizza, etc, or you can spend more and eat at one of the sit-down cafés.

Getting There & Away

With only a few buses connecting Beersheba to the Dead Sea, you will often have to change at Arad. From here there are fairly frequent buses to Masada (45 minutes), Ein Gedi (one hour) and Beersheba (45 minutes).

Remember that on Saturday morning a special bus runs from Beersheba to Ein Gedi via Arad and Masada. Egged provides this service primarily for the locals who would otherwise be unable to benefit from the Dead Sea's health facilities.

TEL ARAD

As it is the country's best example of an Early Bronze Age city, keen archaeologists will find Tel Arad worth a visit. It's located some 10 km west of modern Arad.

First mentioned in the Old Testament accounts of the Israelites' attempts to penetrate into the Promised Land from the south (Numbers 21:1-3, 33:40, Joshua 12:14), ancient Arad was an important fortress guarding the southern approaches to the country.

Covering several hectares, the excavations are clearly marked and an information leaflet is available (US$0.30). They are open April to September, Saturday to Thursday 8 am to 5 pm, Friday 8 am to 4 pm; October to March, Saturday to Thursday 8 am to 4 pm, Friday 8 am to 3 pm; and admission is US$1 (students US$0.65).

Buses going between Arad and Beersheba pass the orange signposted turn-off for Tel Arad – from here it's a two-km walk.

BEERSHEBA

(Population 122,300)
Not a particularly attractive town for visitors, with little in the way of impressive sights, Beersheba is the 'capital' of the Negev and the region's transportation hub. It is, however, a good example of the progress made by Israel in developing the desert. In 1948 this village with some 2000 inhabitants was in the middle of nowhere. Today's urban sprawl of drab apartment blocks surrounded by dusty gardens belies the fact that this is a 'frontier town' in a truly harsh environment.

History

Beersheba is mentioned several times in the Old Testament in its definition of the limits of ancient Israel: 'from Dan to Beersheba' (Judges 20:1, I Samuel 3:20, II Samuel 3:10, 17:11, 24:2). It is an important town because of its association with the Patriarchs: the name is explained by Genesis 21:25-33 as

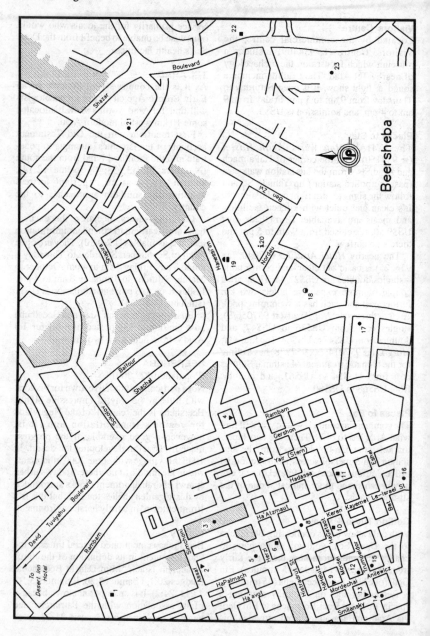

Beersheba

Boulevard

Shazar

•22

•23

•21

Ben Zvi

HaHistadrut

Nordau

i20

•19

•18

•17

Sprinzak

Balfour

Shachar

SOKOLOV

Rambam

Gershon

Yair (Stern)

Ramban

•7

Hadassa

Eshel

•11

HaAtzmaul

•16
Bialik St.

Keren Kayemet Le–Israel St.

Mordei

Simchoni

•3

HaSne'erot

•8

•10

Trumpeldor

HaTe'ulvul St.

Herzl

•6

•5

•9

•12

•15

Anilewicz

Assaf

•2

Mordechai

•13

•14

HaPalmach

Smilansky

•1

Ha'avot

To
Desert Inn
Hotel

David Tuvyahu Boulevard

1	Beit Yatziv Youth Hostel (IYHA)
2	Konditoria
3	Negev Museum
4	Papa Michel Restaurant
5	Police
6	Arava Hotel
7	Jade Palace Chinese Restaurant
8	Keren Kayemet Le-Israel (Main Street - Shops, Cafés & Sheruts)
9	Bluebird Restaurant
10	Aviv Hotel
11	Hotel HaNegev
12	The Wall Nightclub
13	Tahanah
14	Smilansky St (Art Galleries & Cafés)
15	HaSimta (The Alley) Nightclub & Gibatti's Pub-Pizza
16	Abraham's Well
17	Bedouin Market
18	Bus Station
19	Post Office
20	Tourist Office
21	Town Hall
22	Hotel Zohar
23	Negev Research Institute

meaning 'the well of the seven' or 'the well of the oath' in its account of Abraham's treaty with Abimelek the Philistine.

The Patriarchs lived and worked in the surrounding area which was later assigned to the tribe of Simeon. However, its history goes further back, as far as 4000 BC and the Chalcolithic Age. Excavations reveal that these people, who had introduced domesticated sheep to the Negev and moved away in about 3000 BC, were skilled at crafts.

David built a fortified town here, on the site of a small fort erected by his predecessor Saul, during his campaign against the Amalekites (I Samuel 14:48, 15:29). The ancient site is almost five km north-east of the modern town which was first settled during the late Roman period.

Until the late 19th century, Beersheba was just a collection of wells used by the Bedouin. The Turks then established a small town here which served as an administrative centre for the Negev's Bedouin tribes.

In 1917 towards the end of WW I it fell to Allenby's British forces as they advanced north to win control of Palestine. It was recaptured after a spectacular and celebrated charge by units of the Australian Lighthorse. Part of Palestine's Arab section in the UN Partition Plan, Beersheba was captured by the Egyptian Army at the very start of the 1948 War of Independence but the Israelis took it on 21 October in 'Operation 10 Plagues'.

During the early years after Israel's independence, Beersheba was compared to a 'Wild West frontier town' due to its stark location and the tough, adventurous types it apparently attracted. Today, however, you need a good imagination to picture it as such a place.

Orientation
The downtown area, where you will find most of the shops, eating places and accommodation, is in the Turkish Old Town about 15 minutes' walk south-west of the central bus station. One of its main streets is Keren Kayemet Le-Israel St. The rest of Beersheba is post-1948 and mainly residential, with the civic centre and Ben-Gurion University to the north and the market just south of the central bus station. Tel Beersheba, the ancient town, is five km outside to the east.

Information
Tourist Office The IGTO (☎ 36001/2) is on Nordau St, across from the entrance to the central bus station. It is open Sunday to Thursday 8 am to 3 pm, Friday 8 am to 1 pm, and is closed Saturday.

Post & Telecommunications The main post office is just north of the central bus station at the corner of HaNessi'im and Nordau Sts. It is open Sunday, Monday, Wednesday and Thursday 7.45 am to 12.30 pm and 3.30 to 6 pm, Tuesday 7.45 am to 2 pm, Friday 7.45 am to 1 pm, and is closed Saturday. There are also branches in the central bus station and in the Old Town, on the corner of Histradrut and Hadassa Sts.

Other Various bank branches are on and around Keren Kayemet Le-Israel St. The swimming pool at the IYHA hostel is open daily 9 am to 4 pm and costs US$3 for guests, US$4 for visitors. The pool at the Desert Inn Hotel is open to nonresidents (except on Saturday), and admission is US$4.

The police station (☎ 37444 or 100) is on Herzl St in the Old Town.

Market
Thursday is the day for Beersheba's much talked-about Bedouin Market. Traditionally this is when hundreds of the Negev's Bedouin Arabs come into town to buy and sell their livestock, food, carpets, clothes and jewellery to anyone who is willing to barter and buy, be they Israelis, tourists or each other.

It used to be truly authentic but now features such things as T-shirts and electronic goods, and an Israeli market sets up alongside. Only very early in the day can you really hope to capture something that resembles a Bedouin scene – the show starts about 6 am. It is just south of the central bus station where you can see the arched rooftops across the main road.

Negev Museum
In one of the more attractive areas of Beersheba, this museum (☎ 39105) at 18 Ha'Atzmaut St, Old Town, occupies an old Turkish mosque in a park – look for the minaret.

The exhibits include a history of the town itself as well as a series of archaeological artefacts from the whole Negev region. There is also a section on Bedouin culture, a collection of medieval maps of the Holy Land, and a 6th-century mosaic floor depicting animals in its geometric design. You can climb the minaret for a view which shows where the town abruptly ends and the desert begins. You are not allowed to take photographs up here because of the adjacent military installation.

It's open Sunday and Monday 8 am to 2 pm, Tuesday 8 am to 1 pm, Wednesday and Thursday 8 am to 5 pm, Friday 8 am to 1 pm, and Saturday 10 am to 1 pm. Admission is US$2 (students US$1).

WW I Cemetery
Located adjacent to the IYHA hostel, this is the largest British WWI cemetery in Israel. Most of those buried here were members of Australian and other Commonwealth regiments who were killed in action against the Turks.

Abraham's Well
At the southern end of Keren Kayemet Le-Israel St, near the riverbed, is a very unimpressive reconstruction of Abraham's Well. It is said to be the site where Abraham and Abimelech made their transaction. It is open daily 8 am to 7 pm, and admission is free.

Town Hall
The modern town hall, north of the central bus station along HaNessi'im St, dominates the skyline with its distinctive tower. Is it meant to resemble a clenched fist or a spanner? Due to the potential for suicide attempts the tower is only open to visitors by appointment.

Ben-Gurion University of the Negev
The university's Research & Development Authority deals with the desert environment, so the subjects studied here include artificial rainmaking, desalinisation of water, solar energy, and the chemical and biological conditions necessary for desert life. The university campus is architecturally interesting, and guided tours of the main campus (☎ 61111) and the desert studies facilities (☎ 78382) can be arranged.

Negev Palmach Brigade Memorial
North-east of the town on a hill, this is a bizarre and confusing modern tribute to the Jewish soldiers killed whilst taking Beersheba from the Egyptians in 1948. Hebrew inscriptions explain the significance of the images, which include a tent, a well, battle maps, a narrow passage, a bunker, a bird, a watchtower, an aqueduct, and a snake that represents the evil enemy.

Also known as the Andarta Memorial, it is difficult to reach by public transport. Near the Arad road, you can get off Egged bus No 388 and walk the ¾ km, or take local bus No 4 to the railway station and cut across the tracks to reach the hill. Admission is free and there is a café at the site.

Tel Beersheba

The site of the ancient town, this is some five km north-east of modern Beersheba on the Jerusalem road. Here you can see remains of city walls and houses – it's a good idea to visit the Negev Museum first to have a better idea of what it's all about. Next to the ruins is a Visitors' Centre with a cafeteria, a restaurant and a small museum dealing with the Bedouin. The site is open daily 9 am to 5 pm; admission is free.

To reach Tel Beersheba, take the twice-daily Egged bus to nearby Tel es-Sab, a new Bedouin village that is part of the Israeli programme to encourage the nomads to change to a more permanent address.

Places to Stay

Beersheba has a limited selection of accommodation. The *IYHA Beit Yatziv Youth Hostel* (☎ 77444) is the cheapest and is a clean, modern complex with a swimming pool, pleasant gardens and no curfew. The hostel is in the Old Town, a 20-minute walk from the central bus station. From the main entrance turn left and left again on HaNessi'im St, go straight over the crossroads onto Herzl St (either of the two streets leads to the Old Town), and turn right on Ha'Atzmaut St – the park on the corner contains the Negev Museum and its minaret. The hostel is on the left-hand side of the street after HaTivat HaNegev St. Local bus No 13 stops nearby but only runs about every 45 minutes.

The hostel is rarely full, and you have a choice of dorm beds for US$8.50 (members US$7.50) or US$9.60 (members US$8.60) in rooms with private bathroom. An adjoining guesthouse has singles/doubles for US$26/33. All prices include breakfast. Lunch and dinner are available – if you want them, make a point of telling the staff when

you check in and don't be late. The US$6 meals are good value.

The hotels tend to offer a lot less of a deal than the youth hostel. Also in the Old Town, the *Hotel HaNegev* (☎ 77026), at 26 Ha'Atzmaut St, is a scruffy old building, with basic singles for US$20, and doubles from US$30 to US$38. Over on Histradrut St, near Keren Kayemet Le-Israel St and one block down from the police station, the *Arava Hotel* (☎ 78792) has singles from US$17 to US$20, and doubles from US$28 to US$30. At 48 Mordei HaGetaot St, at the corner of Kerem Kayemet Le-Israel St, *Hotel Aviv* (☎ 78059) has singles/doubles for US$20/30.

Up past the Civic Centre, on Shazar Blvd, is the more respectable *Zohar Hotel* (☎ 77335/6). Modern and with decent facilities, it's a good deal at US$25/42 for singles/doubles.

Beersheba's top hotel is the four-star *Desert Inn* (☎ 424922; fax 412772) to the north of the Old Town in what is now a residential area, but was once the town's outskirts. It has a pool and a tennis court. Singles cost from US$44 to US$69, and doubles from US$60 to US$92.

Places to Eat

Apart from the Egged self-service restaurant at the central bus station, the nearby Qanyon shopping mall and the felafel stalls at the Bedouin market, the Old Town is where you will find most eating places. On and around Keren Kayemet Le-Israel St are cafés that serve the standard versions of grilled meats and salads, along with ice-cream parlours and fast-food outlets. Nowhere here really stands out as being better than anywhere else, although the *Province Art Gallery & Coffee Shop*, 99 HeHalutz St, makes for a pleasant change of scene.

For fruit and vegetables visit the market or the grocery stores in the Old Town. Just behind the police station, the *Konditoria* bakery serves lovely pastries.

Sh'va Tea House-Restaurant (☎ 71454), at 25 Smilansky St, is open daily from about 7.30 pm to 2 am or so. Set in a lovely old building decorated with *objet d'art*, this is a nice spot for a drink or a meal. There is a bar with draught beer, and live music is on some evenings.

The *Jade Palace Chinese Restaurant* (☎ 75375), Histradrut St, corner of Yair (Stern) St, is another of the nicer places in town – about US$15 for a full meal, but you could get away with less. *Papa Michel Restaurant*, further north on Histradrut St, near Ramban St, serves French-style food from about US$15 per person.

Entertainment
While Beersheba lacks things for the visitor to see and do during the day, it deserves credit for being a pleasant place to spend an evening. Strolling around the Old Town, with its tree-lined side streets and collection of cafés, restaurants, bars, galleries and clubs is suprisingly pleasant. Most of the locals seem to congregate on and around Keren Kayemet Le-Israel and Smilansky Sts.

The renowned local orchestra regularly performs at the S Rubin Music Conservatory and the Bet Ha'am (☎ 73478) often stages productions at the Beersheba Theatre. For these, and any other happenings, check the free *This Week in the South* leaflet available at tourist offices.

There is a collection of clubs/pubs on and around Trumpeldor St, mainly catering to a younger Israeli crowd. Although they open as early as 8 pm, they don't fill up till 11 pm. On Trumpeldor St, check out *Little Beersheba*, at No 6, *HaSimta (The Alley)* and *Gibatti's Pub-Pizza* next door at No 16, and *Ha Biktah* at No 21. *The Wall*, at No 15, is decorated with a Gerald Scarfe mural from Pink Floyd's album. At 4 Smilansky St, *Tahanah* has a windmill on the roof.

Catering to an older crowd, *Bluebird*, at 18 Mordechai Anilewicz, is a folklore bar & restaurant with live entertainment.

Getting There & Away
Bus Buses run almost continuously to and from Tel Aviv, about every 30 minutes to Jerusalem, and almost hourly to Eilat. There are also frequent services to Dimona and

Arad, with only the occasional through bus to the Dead Sea and also to Gaza.

On Saturday morning, an Egged bus leaves Beersheba for Ein Gedi, via Arad and Masada.

Sherut Ya'ed Daroma (☎ 39144), 195 Keren Kayemet Le-Israel St, operate sherut services to Tel Aviv (US$5, every hour), Jerusalem (US$5, every 45 minutes) Sunday to Thursday 6.30 am to 7 pm, Friday 6.30 am to 2 pm, but no Saturday service, and Eilat (US$10; 10 am and 2 pm) Sunday to Thursday only. There may be Arab service taxis going to Gaza from near the central bus station (about US$7).

Getting Around
You can easily walk from the central bus station to the Old Town and the market, otherwise the local buses leave from outside the central bus station's main entrance.

AROUND BEERSHEBA
Museum of Bedouin Culture
With Israel's push to develop the Negev, the nomadic existence of the Bedouin and all its traditional trappings is fading fast. This museum's aim is to preserve and present samples of this dying culture to the public.

Bedouin from the Negev and the Sinai have donated a variety of traditional items such as clothes, household utensils, tools and jewellery to make this a beautiful collection well worth a visit.

Other attractions include a 12-minute audiovisual programme detailing the Bedouin existence in the Negev and Sinai, a demonstration of traditional home-making activities like bread-making and weaving, and a traditional Bedouin tent of hospitality where visitors can sit with a Bedouin man, sip coffee and discuss his peoples' nomadic lifestyle.

There is also an archaeological section with a display of the cave culture dating from the Mishnaic and Talmudic eras. It features caves from the Chalcolithic, Israelite, Hellenistic, Roman and Byzantine periods.

The museum (☎ 918597, 913322; fax

919889) is part of the Joe Alon Regional &
Folklore Centre, named in memory of a
founder of Israel's airforce who was murdered in Washington, DC. The centre is a
combined museum, research institute and
field school. It is open Saturday to Thursday
from 9 am to 4 pm, Friday 9 am to 2 pm, and
admission is US$3.

The complex stands on the property of
Kibbutz Lahav. Established in 1952 as a
border settlement on the edge of the West
Bank, occupied at that time by Jordan, the
kibbutz now has one of the country's largest
pig farms.

Getting There & Away The kibbutz is near
Kibbutz Dvir, both off a sideroad that intersects with the Beersheba to Qiryat Gat road.
From Beersheba, Egged bus No 369 to Tel
Aviv passes the intersection quite often –
from here it's an eight-km hitchhike to the
kibbutz. Bus No 42 runs directly to the
kibbutz, but only once a day. Check with
Egged for the current schedule.

Bye Bye Bedouin

Critics of Israel's development of the Negev region
tend to be cynical about the latest wave of attractions
featuring the fascinating culture of these nomadic
people. The adoption by the Israeli tourist industry of
such Bedouin symbols as 'traditional Bedouin
hospitality', 'Bedouin tents', 'Bedouin meals',
'Bedouin handicrafts' etc, at a time when Israel's
domestic policies are resulting in their speedy demise,
is a sore point for many observers.

Shivta (Subeita)

Unfortunately not on the regular bus
network, this is one of the Negev's most
impressive archaeological sites. Some 58 km
south-west of Beersheba and in the middle
of nowhere, the area was first settled in the
1st century by the Nabateans. The people are
noted for their irrigation skills in an area
where the average annual rainfall is less than
90 mm.

In the 4th century, Shivta had expanded to
become an important Byzantine town on the
caravan route between Egypt and Anatolia.
Today's ruins include churches, houses, tiled
streets, and water and drainage systems. In

the 7th century the Arabs took the town and
did not destroy any of the earlier Christian
constructions.

After a further two centuries, Shivta was
abandoned due to problems with the water
supply. Being so isolated, its ruins escaped
being pillaged over the years by people on
the lookout for ready-cut stone, which is why
the buildings are in such good condition.

The site is open Saturday to Thursday 8
am to 5 pm, and Friday 8 am to 4 pm. From
October to March, the site closes one hour
earlier. Admission is US$2 (students US$1).

Getting There & Away You can take the
infrequent Egged bus No 44 from Beersheba
to Nizzana, get off at the 'Horvot Shivta' stop
and walk the remaining 8½ km. With little
traffic about, hitchhiking can be a lengthy
exercise. From the Nizzana road, the turn-off
to Shivta has two lanes and is paved only for
the first 2½ km. It then narrows considerably, passing a track to an army installation
on the left after a km.

DIMONA
(Population: 26,600)
Established in 1955 and named after the
biblical town of the tribe of Judah (Joshua
15:22), Dimona is one of the better-known
development towns. Its harsh desert location
was the cause of considerable controversy as
many thought that the climate would prove
to be too fierce for people to live and work
here. However, the initial brave collection of
tents has developed into today's bleak collection of apartment blocks. Dimona's
original settlers worked at the nearby chemical plants of the Dead Sea Works, but now
the town also has glass-making, ceramics
and textiles as local industry, along with
Israel's nuclear reactor.

Unless you're involved in espionage, the
sole attraction in Dimona is the controversial
Black Hebrew settlement. A visit is highly
recommended – you can telephone ☎ 55400
or simply ask any of the staff in the Eternity
Restaurant in Tel Aviv or the Hebrews you
meet selling jewellery. It's best not to simply
turn up, as they are suspicious of strangers

and prefer to have advance notice to prepare a place for you to stay, if required. The Black Hebrews occupy what was originally an absorption centre where they live a virtually self-contained lifestyle. However, they welcome visitors to discuss how they live, their aims and beliefs. There is no set price to spend a night here, but you should be prepared to give about US$20 per person for room and board.

Getting There & Away
With frequent buses from Beersheba (40 minutes) Dimona is not difficult to reach. There are also occasional buses from Arad and Mitzpe Ramon. From Dimona's central bus station, the Hebrew settlement is only about 10 minutes' walk along Herzl St.

AROUND DIMONA
Mamshit
Another Nabatean, Roman and Byzantine city, Mamshit is visually less impressive than Shivta, but it is particularly renowned for the engineering skills used in its construction.

The Nabateans built their city here in the 1st century and it was later used by the Romans. Six km south-east of Dimona, an abandoned British police station marks the site where the Romans built a series of dams to store rainwater to supply the town's inhabitants all year round. Razed by the Muslims in the 7th century, the site is dotted with explanatory signs and an information leaflet is available. The excavations include Nabatean remains, reservoirs, the dams, watchtowers, Roman military and Byzantine cemeteries, jewellery and coins, churches and mosaics.

The site is open April to September, Saturday to Thursday 8 am to 5 pm, and Friday 8 am to 4 pm; October to March, Saturday to Thursday 8 am to 4 pm, and Friday 8 am to 3 pm; and admission is US$2 (students US$1).

Getting There & Away
Any of the Egged buses heading to Eilat via Dimona will drop you at the signposted turn-off for the site.

Mamshit Camel Ranch
With a reputation as one of the better desert tourist centres in the Negev, this is located near the Yamit Plain and the Mamshit archaeological site.

Camel safaris, 4WD tours, rappelling and hiking are offered here, primarily for groups but also for individuals. Guests are accommodated in a large Bedouin-style tent, made of goat hair and wool. Traditional Bedouin hospitality is provided, with Bedouin hosts serving their terrific cuisine, coffee and tea, and entertaining guests with music, playing the *rababah* (fiddle), and *sumsimaya* (guitar). Modern bathroom facilities are provided. Guests tend to stay three nights on average, paying about US$50 a night per person. This includes full board and guided activities.

There are no buses going near the ranch, so you need a car to get here. Contact their Tel Aviv office (☎ 476920, fax 476920) for reservations: PO Box 53113, Tel Aviv 61530.

KIBBUTZ SDE BOKER
One of the best known of the kibbutzim, Sde Boker was established in 1952 by pioneers who planned to breed cattle in the desert; its name is Hebrew for 'Ranchers' Field'. Although the initial aims have not been totally fulfilled, the kibbutz is often seen to be a success, judged by its appearance as a lush oasis in the middle of the desert with its fruit orchards and zoo. Its main claim to fame though, is that it was here that David Ben-Gurion chose to live when he retired as prime minister in 1953. Only 14 months later he returned to the political scene and went on to serve a second term as prime minister, returning to kibbutz life in 1963. He died here in 1973.

South of the kibbutz and overlooking the Wilderness of Zin is the Sde Boker campus of the Ben-Gurion University, with the graves of Ben-Gurion and his wife and the En Avdat Springs nearby.

You will see three separate turn-offs for Sde Boker: heading south from Beersheba you first come to the turn-off to the main entrance of the kibbutz, then the turn-off for the Ben-Gurion Home (where he and his wife lived, now a museum) and, finally, the turn-off for the university campus, the Ben-Gurion graves and En Avdat.

Ben-Gurions' Home
Only slightly more regal than their fellow kibbutzniks' quarters, the small hut where David and Paula Ben-Gurion lived has been maintained as a museum. Kept basically as it was when they were here, there is a collection of letters, photographs and books on display in the simply furnished rooms.

It's open Sunday to Thursday 8.30 am to 3.30 pm, Friday 8 am to noon, and Saturday 9 am to 1 pm. Admission is free. A café nearby serves meals and snacks, including fruit grown on the kibbutz.

Zoo
This small collection of animals is found near the Ben-Gurion Home. From the museum and café, instead of turning right along the sideroad back to the main road, turn left past the tennis courts, turn right and the zoo is on your right. Feeding time is around 2 pm.

Ben-Gurions' Graves
From the bus-stop outside the entrance to the university campus, the graves of Ben-Gurion and his wife are reached by turning right then following the arrows to the left on the Hebrew signs. From here you have great views eastwards across the Wilderness of Zin, and southwards over to En Avdat.

Ben-Gurion University
The Sde Boker campus of the Ben-Gurion University, still in its initial stages of development, contains the Jacob Blaustein Institute for Desert Research, the Blaustein International Centre for Desert Studies, and the Ben-Gurion Research Institute. The latter boasts the most comprehensive archives dealing with Israel's first prime minister and, therefore, much of the country's history. It is the advanced level of knowledge of the desert achieved by the other institutes that is of most importance here.

For a guided tour of the campus, whose departments include desert hydrology, salinity & water engineering and desert meteorology, telephone ☎ 35333. Much of the work carried out is unique and has international significance with its aims to solve the problems of desert development.

Sde Boker SPNI Field Study Centre
Also on the university campus, this field school is primarily responsible for nature conservation in the area. This includes Maktesh Ramon (a crater), En Avdat and other desert springs.

The field school staff are extremely knowledgeable and enthusiastic and, once you have shown your interest, they will tell you all about the local wildlife and where and when to see it. This will include griffin vultures having their breakfast of raw meat provided by the field school, ibex and other animals coming to drink at a spring, and sooty falcons nesting in the cliff side.

You should also inquire here about the various hikes in the desert where you can see a lot of this natural activity as well as some beautiful scenery. Although often filled by groups, the guesthouse here is sometimes available for travellers – it's worth asking about if you want to spend some time in the area.

EN AVDAT
This is one of the highlights of the Negev and missed by most visitors as it is hidden from the main road. En Avdat is one of those freaks of nature – a pool of icy water in the hot expanse of desert, fed by waters that flow through an intricate network of channels. Dominated by a steep, winding canyon, reaching it involves an easy hike through the incredible scenery. At the very least, you should stop off for a few minutes to admire the view from the observation point.

The area on top of the cliffs is where prehistoric tribes camped for over 100,000 years. They lived in huts made from branches and the concentration of flint tools stands out from the soil here – especially on the northern rim of the canyon. Here and nearby, archaeologists have found evidence of dwellings from the Upper Palaeolithic and Mesolithic periods (35,000 to 15,000 BC).

Wilderness of Zin Nature Trail

Outside the main entrance to the Sde Boker campus of the Ben-Gurion University, an orange 'En Avdat' sign points the way. Follow the zig-zagging road down into the Wilderness of Zin until it ends at the car park. Follow the path that leads off beyond, and about 40 minutes after leaving the campus you will see the large cave up on your right. Ibex and gazelles can often be seen along here, too. Simply follow the water and after another five minutes you will come to a spring. Despite the warning sign, many enjoy a refreshing dip. If tempted, be aware of the danger caused by the extreme difference in temperature between the hot sun and the cold water.

This is a dead-end, so come back the way you came and on your left look out for steps cut into the rock leading up the cliff (hidden behind a tree). Climb the steps to the paved ledge where there's a great view.

Carry on walking and after another few minutes you will reach the top of a waterfall. In the winter, this waterfall can be quite spectacular.

Some more steps have been cut into the rock to lead up the cliff to the right (not always easy to find – look for the caves up above). There is a steep climb up steps cut into the cliff to reach the top of the canyon, or you can head back to the car park. I think the best views of all are from the steps, rather than at the very top, so be sure to take a good look around before the end of the climb. A short distance away an observation point has been provided.

The whole hike usually takes two to three hours, allowing plenty of time for relaxing by the springs.

The main road is a 10 to 15-minute walk along a side road from the observation point. You come out south of the university campus

– unfortunately there is no bus stop here but you can usually hitchhike to either Mitzpe Ramon or Beersheba quite easily, or at least get a lift to Sde Boker or Avdat where you can catch a bus.

For those who just want to visit the observation point, look out for the signpost, north of the Avdat archaeological site, south of Sde Boker (no bus stop, remember).

Entrance to En Avdat is free if you are on foot. Drivers are charged US$3 to park here. The site is open April to September, Saturday to Thursday 8 am to 5 pm, Friday 8 am to 4 pm; and October to March, Saturday to Thursday 8 am to 4 pm, and Friday 8 am to 3 pm.

AVDAT

Not to be confused with En Avdat, this is the well-preserved Nabatean, Roman and Byzantine city perched atop a nearby hill that dominates the desert skyline. The rich combination of impressive ruins and incredible vistas makes the steep climb well worth the effort.

Built by the Nabateans in the 2nd century BC as a caravan stop on the road from Petra and Eilat to the Mediterranean coast, Avdat was taken by the Romans in 106 AD. Prosperous throughout the Byzantine period, the city was abandoned in 634 when it fell to the Muslims. The ruins include Nabatean burial caves, a pottery workshop and a road, a Roman camp, and a Byzantine bath-house, wine press, house, church, monastery and castle. The site (☎ 550954) is open April to September, Saturday to Thursday 8 am to 5 pm, Friday 8 am to 4 pm; October to March, Saturday to Thursday 8 am to 4 pm, Friday 8 am to 3 pm; and admission is US$3 (students US$1.50). The bus stops outside on the main road; follow the turn-off past the petrol station.

Desert Run-Off Farms Unit

Some would say that the achievements of the Israelis in developing the desert pale by comparison with those of the Nabateans who, about 2000 years ago, managed to create great cities in the same harsh environment, but with a lot less in the way of technical knowledge and equipment. Their systems of desert agriculture inspired the establishment in 1959 of an experimental farm which can be seen below the archaeological site. It's closed to the general public, but you can telephone ☎ 88484 if you are interested in the work being done here.

Part of the Ben-Gurion University's Desert Farms Unit, the work carried out here includes the study of Nabatean farming techniques. Basically these involved the 'run-off' rain water that has not been absorbed by the soil. The chosen catchment area was divided into sections by low walls built at an angle across the sloping sides of the wadi. As well as dividing the run-off into manageable quantities, this enabled the farmers to direct it into specific fields. They also collected the stones on the slopes into heaps, which increased the run-off from light rains by as much as 40%.

The overall effect was that a specific field could receive the water equivalent to an annual rainfall of 300 to 500 mm (which is

Calcolithic Wand

comparable to the Jerusalem region) despite the average annual rainfall in the Negev being less than 90 mm.

Places to Eat
The large and dirty roadside *restaurant* down from the entrance to the archaeological site serves a set three-course meal for US$7; sandwiches and snacks are also available. Most importantly, the beer is cold.

Getting There & Away
On the Beersheba to Mitzpe Ramon road, Avdat lies 10 km south of the Ben-Gurion home, and 23 km north of Mitzpe Ramon. Buses pass by in each direction about every hour or so, and some continue to Eilat.

MITZPE RAMON
(Population: 7000)
The word *mitzpe* is Hebrew for lookout and this small town, which began in 1956 as a camp for a 17-member road-building co-operative, is named after the nearby cliff that looks over the massive Ramon Crater – the Maktesh Ramon.

Intended to be part of the desert development programme, the town failed to take off as planned due to the lack of employment opportunities, and scores of apartments lie empty despite various attempts at incentive schemes.

In 1986, the government announced that Mitzpe Ramon would be an income tax-free zone in a vain bid to attract new businesses and residents. Other plans involve the promotion of the area's unique geological, ecological and archaeological sites and its clear, dry air as tourist attractions. A top-end hotel is due to be built on the edge of the Maktesh Ramon.

In recent years the population has swelled from 3,000 to around 7,000 with the mass immigration of Soviet Jews. This has created problems with massive unemployment – which is now about 20%.

The Maktesh Ramon is the centre of attention for most visitors to Mitzpe Ramon. A few would also be interested in Tel Aviv University's astronomical observatory which lies to the north-west of the main street (☎ 88133 to inquire about access).

Mitzpe Ramon is the best place to base yourself for visits to the adjacent Maktesh Ramon, Avdat, En Avdat and Sde Boker.

Orientation
Standing on the northern edge of the Maktesh Ramon, the town is very small with little in the way of sights and amenities for the visitor. Leading from the Beersheba to Eilat road, the main street is a wide dual carriageway which passes the small collection of shops, a bank, swimming pool and cultural centre, with sideroads connecting with the residential quarters. The new youth hostel and the visitors' centre are to the south, overlooking the Maktesh Ramon. The town's only hotel is a little further west. All these places are within easy walking distance of each other.

Information
There is no tourist information office here, but the staff at the visitors' centre and the manager at the youth hostel are usually able to help out with general queries.

The post office is behind the swimming pool and supermarket in the arcade. It opens Sunday to Tuesday and Thursday 8 am to 12.30 pm and 3.30 to 6 pm, Wednesday 8 am to 1.30 pm, Friday 8 am to noon, and is closed on Saturday.

Bank Hapoalim, in the arcade beside the swimming pool, is open Sunday and Tuesday 8.30 am to noon and 4 to 6 pm, Monday, Wednesday and Friday 8.30 am to noon, Thursday 8.30 am to noon and 4 to 6 pm, and is closed Saturday.

The library is on the main street, west of the shops, the indoor swimming pool and cultural centre.

For police, telephone ☎ 100. The petrol station closes at 6 pm, and is closed Saturday.

Visitors' Centre
Perched right on the edge of the Maktesh Ramon, this attractive modern structure houses a museum whose aim is to explain everything you want to know about the massive and intriguing crater. It does the job quite well with a slide show and an exhibition of charts, illustrations, photographs, models and samples.

Admission is US$3, which is worthwhile

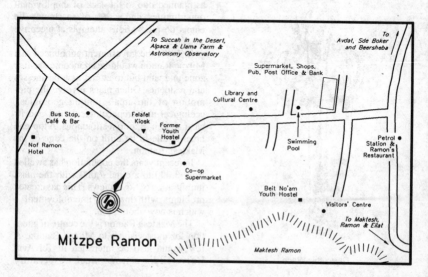

Mitzpe Ramon

spending to learn about this natural phenomenon. While difficult to describe without going overboard, it is said to remind visitors a little of the Grand Canyon and the moon. The centre is open Saturday to Thursday 9 am to 4.30 pm, Friday 9 am to 2 pm.

Camel Lookout

West of the youth hostel, along the edge of the Makhtesh Ramon, there is a lookout, constructed to resemble a camel. Offering more crater vistas, it will especially appeal to children.

Maktesh Ramon

The crater's vital statistics are: 300 metres deep, eight km wide, 40 km long. Known in Arabic as Wadi Ruman, it offers you a unique opportunity to walk through the successive stages of the earth's evolution in reverse, a unique and strange experience with a mass of different colours and shapes. Although the ceramics and cement industries are represented by a mine or two and there are plans to further exploit the area's mineral wealth, the crater remains largely unspoilt.

A few nature trails have been marked out which lead through some of the most attractive and interesting sections. At the time of writing, the only maps of the crater were in Hebrew, but plans are afoot to publish versions in English and other languages. For current details ask at the visitors' centre.

En Sharonim – Nahal Gewanim This trail in the Maktesh Ramon is recommended as one of the best by the staff at the visitors' centre. The various rock formations seen along the way and the variety of colours are simply awe-inspiring. Taking about 4½ to 5½ hours, the walk covers occasionally steep rocky terrain and is usually walked in very hot conditions. Do not overestimate your stamina – take along plenty of water, wear a head covering and start as early in the day as possible.

To reach the trail, take the south-bound Egged bus from Mitzpe Ramon (to Eilat). Get off when you see the second orange signpost on the left-hand side of the road in the crater – about 10 minutes' drive from town. You will pass mines on both sides of the road just before you get to the two signs. There is no bus stop, so tell the driver when you want to get off.

Follow the jeep track away from the road for about 30 minutes, then take the right fork after the electricity pylon on the left.

At the top of the steepish slope follow the green-on-white trail markers to your left. This narrow path takes you along the ridge, giving you excellent views across the crater to your left. There is a pleasant shaded spot for that necessary drink and rest after about 10 minutes – climb up to your right here. It should have taken you about an hour to reach this spot from the road.

After a further five minutes, the path splits in two, but both the high and the low paths go the same way. Scramble up the rock face briefly to the top of the ridge for a commanding view in all directions. Here you can see all at once the variety of contrasting rock formations and colours with the maze of wadis and canyons winding through them. If you took the high path, climb down after about 20 minutes to join the low path to save an even steeper descent later. It's possible to take either of the three paths here as they all join up eventually to lead down to a wadi.

Follow the wadi to the right and around to the left. After 25 minutes it narrows considerably with large and small caves on both sides of the canyon. Another 15 minutes and you come to a Hebrew signpost. Follow the track just past it to the left, leading away from the wadi. The track forks after five minutes; take the left track leading to the sign with the coloured trail markers. Go straight ahead following the blue-on-white trail markers.

After 20 minutes you should reach another signpost. Again, go straight ahead and then follow the path to the left. Follow the wadi for 20 minutes and you will come to a couple of water holes. Follow the track to the left 10 minutes from here – there is a blue-on-white sign. After five minutes you will come to a jeep track going left to right with a signpost. Go to the left and after 25 minutes you will reach the electricity pylon that you passed at the start of the walk. Go to the right here and the road is 30 minutes away.

Hitchhike back to Mitzpe Ramon – it shouldn't take too long. .

Scenic Pass This is part of the Trail of Israel, a series of hikes designed to run the length of the country. It is a leisurely and very scenic two-hour hike that takes you down into the Maktesh Ramon to the Carpenter's Workshop (see later description) and onto the main road. From the youth hostel, follow the path along the edge of the crater until you see the sign pointing down. Follow the green trail markings and you eventually come to the Carpenter's Workshop. Continue to reach the main road, where you can either hitch back to town, or flag down one of the infrequent buses.

Carpenter's Workshop Shortly after the road from Mitzpe Ramon zigzags down into the crater, an orange signpost points to this site of geological interest, half a km to the right.

To be honest, I wasn't bowled over by what I saw (for me the surrounding scenery is more impressive) but a couple I met were – perhaps they were keen geologists. This unique rock formation has been shaped by pressure and is said to resemble wood. The rock eventually breaks up into pieces, but amongst the rubble you can see unbroken parts.

Follow the jeep track from the road that ends with a car park. From here take the path up the hill to the left (past the refuse bins). This leads you around the hill to a wooden observation platform which gives you a close-up look at the rocks in question. You can either take the Eilat bus or hitchhike from Mitzpe Ramon, or stop here on your way down on the Scenic Pass hike.

Other Craters The Negev's other two craters are just south of Dimona and not accessible by public transport. **Maktesh HaQatan** is the smallest. Roughly circular in shape, it looks more like it was caused by a massive meteor than the slow process of erosion. **Maktesh HaGadol** is the easier of the two to reach. Both are worth a visit if you can get to them.

Alpaca & Llama Farm
These cameloids were flown here from Chile by a young Israeli couple, Ilan and Na'ama Dvir. Inspired by their love for South American wildlife and culture and for Israel, they went to a lot of trouble to set up their farm. Starting with 188 creatures, they now have about 300. They are being raised for their wool, which is for sale. If your timing is right, you can see such activities as shearing, washing, spinning, weaving, and children can ride on a llama cart. Llama safaris in the desert are planned!

Other animals are also to be found here for various reasons. Geese provide a security system, Scottish border collies act as 'sheepdogs', guinea fowl and chickens serve as exterminators of harmful pests and worms, and Pyrenees mountain dogs live with the herd to protect them from wolves, hyaenas and leopards – a genuine threat in this area.

Visitors are welcome, the farm is open Saturday to Thursday, in the summer from 9 am to 5 pm, in the winter from 9 am to 4 pm, and on Friday from 9 am to 2 pm. Admission is US$3 (telephone ☎ 588047 for information or to schedule a visit at another time). To get here, look for the signs on the road that heads west out of town.

Zell Midbar
Desert Shade (Zell Midbar) is one of the new wave of desert tour centres that are springing up in the Negev. It offers desert tours via camel and/or 4WD, rappelling, accommodation in large Bedouin-style tents with terrific views across the Maktesh, and 'traditional Bedouin hospitality'. It mainly caters for groups of Israeli schoolkids (rather them than me), but individuals are welcome to call (☎ or fax 586229) or stop by and inquire about their tours.

Here are some examples of the services provided, with prices per person: camel safaris, US$5 per hour; 4WD safari in the Maktesh Ramon, two hours US$9, four hours US$12. See Places to Stay for accommodation details. Desert Shade is located a few hundred metres north of the petrol station, east of the main road at the end of a dirt road.

Places to Stay

The modern *IYHA Beit No'am Youth Hostel* (☎ 88443) is a great place to stay and the manager is pleasant. Beautifully located near the edge of the Maktesh Ramon, just a short walk from the Visitors' Centre, dorm beds cost US$7.50/9 for members/nonmembers. Singles/doubles are US$23 for members, US$26 for nonmembers, and triples US$31.50 for members and US$36 for nonmembers, with breakfast. There are no kitchen facilities for guests.

For something completely different, consider a stay at the unique and wonderful *Succah in the Desert* (☎ 586280), PO Box 272, Mitzpe Ramon. Located some seven km west of the town, this is a collection of seven *succot* (small dwellings) that have been built on the rocky slopes of a wadi amidst some typically beautiful desert scenery. With 'recreation of the soul' the inspiration, there is one larger succah that houses a kitchen, lounge and dining area. This is where guests can relax during the day. There are materials for painting and drawing, pottery, musical instruments, reading and the like, and it is not unusual for guests to spend the evening enjoying good conversation and singing.

The other six succot provide the accommodation. They are spaced about 150 metres apart, with capacity for six to 12 guests at a time (a maximum of two guests per succah). All the succot are tastefully furnished with rugs and other fabrics and are very comfortable, cosy and romantic; if only the average hotel room was up to this standard! Bathroom facilites are limited to using the desert that surrounds you; each succah is supplied with a trowel, an earthenware water jar, bedding, candles and solar-powered lighting. There is one shower, heated by solar energy.

How much for this experience? Aimed primarily at locals, 'membership' of the succayah family costs about US$205 per person as a one-time joining fee. This covers a five-day stay in one succah with full board. After that, the daily rate is US$20 without meals. 'Passers by' are charged US$47 per night per person with breakfast. The second person in a succah pays 10% less. Prices are 10% higher on Shabbat and Jewish holidays, less for groups and longer stays. Delicious vegetarian food is served, to nonresidents as well: breakfast or lunch costs US$3 to US$6, dinner US$8, and a Shabbat dinner US$11. You can also cook for yourself; each succah has a place to build a fire and utensils are available.

To get here, you can always walk from Mitzpe Ramon, but if you call ahead, you will be met off the bus and picked up by 4WD. It's a good idea to call ahead to be sure of a succah, especially at weekends and on holidays. Note that the phone is in town; you leave your message on the machine and the staff drive into town each day to shop, do the laundry, top up with water, meet those guests arriving by bus and to check for messages.

Places to Eat

There are two supermarkets in town. The Co-op across from the old youth hostel building is open Sunday, Monday, Wednesday and Thursday 8.30 am to 1 pm and 4 to 6 pm, Tuesday and Friday 8.30 am to 2 pm, and is closed Saturday. Its larger competitor, in the arcade beyond the bank, is open Sunday to Thursday 9 am to 1 pm and 4 to 7 pm, Friday 8.30 am to 1 pm, and is closed Saturday.

For decent felafel, head for the kiosk across from the main bus stop, which closes at about 6 to 7 pm. The café by the main bus stop serves basic Oriental dishes, and the snooker bar here serves draught beer and snacks.

Pub Haveet (Harvest), in the arcade between the bank and the supermarket, is a pleasant bar for a drink or a meal. It is open daily for most of the day, and has a good tape/CD collection; a friendly crowd gathers

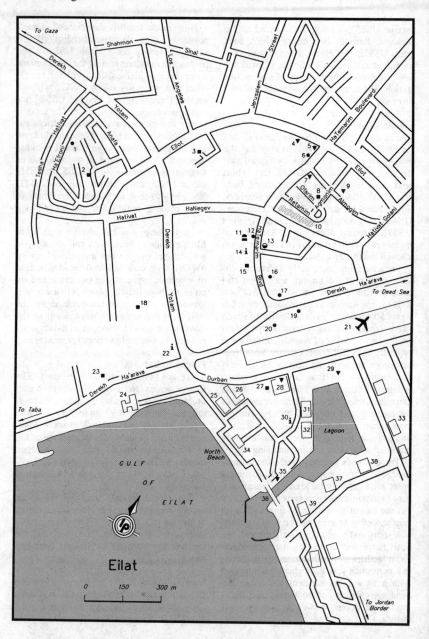

Eilat

0   150   300 m

■ PLACES TO STAY

2 Esther's Apartments
3 Shelter Hostel
8 Max & Merran's Fawlty Towers Hostel
10 Sinai/Red Mountain/Shalem & Taba Hostels
15 Etzion Hotel
18 Adi Hotel
23 IYHA Youth Hostel
24 Red Rock Hotel
25 Neptune Hotel
26 Galei Eilat Hotel
27 Dalia Hotel
31 Shulamit Gardens
32 Caesar Hotel
33 Americana Eilat Hotel
34 Moriah Eilat
37 Lagoona Hotel
38 King Solomon's Palace
39 Queen of Sheba Hotel

▼ PLACES TO EAT

4 Hard Rock Café
5 Coop Supermarket
7 Felafel Boutique
9 Pat Bar & Country Road
28 La Coquille
29 Teddy's
35 Oasis Restaurant
37 Tandoori Restaurant

OTHER

1 Egyptian Consulate
6 Laundromat
11 Post Office
12 Ministry of the Interior (Visa Renewal)
13 Central Bus Station
14 Municipal Tourist Office
16 Red Canyon Centre
17 Shalom Centre
19 Petrol Station
20 Airport Terminal
21 Runway
22 New Tourist Centre
30 IGTO
36 Marina Bridge

on some nights. There are two adjacent cafés serving fast food, kebabs and ice cream.

There is another café near the Visitors' Centre, called *Tsukit* (Cliffy, in English, inspired by the Cheers character and its location overlooking the Maktesh Ramon).

Next to the petrol station, *Ramon's Restaurant* serves decent food. It's open Sunday to Thursday from 5 am to 8 pm, Friday from 5 am to 4.30 pm, and is closed Saturday.

Getting There & Away

Mitzpe Ramon lies 23 km south of Avdat and 136 km north of Eilat, via the Gerofit crossroad. Egged bus No 392 stops here en route between Beersheba and Eilat. Other buses run between the town and Beersheba, with stops at Avdat, Sde Boker and occasionally Dimona. Arkia flights link the town with Tel Aviv and Eilat.

EILAT

(Population: 26,300)

Less than 45 years ago this was a tiny desert outpost. Inspired by the hot climate and its Red Sea location, the Israelis have developed Eilat into their southernmost town and a major resort.

For many visitors to Israel, Eilat is a must on the itinerary. Promoted as a centre of hedonism, it is one of the few places in the country where religion does not occupy centre stage. Instead of synagogues, mosques and churches, it is sun-worshipping, water sports and nightlife that dominate.

Unfortunately, Eilat is not all that it is cracked up to be. As a result of its speedy development the town is a mass of hastily built and ugly architecture that fails to blend in with the beautiful natural surroundings. Even when you look out to sea, the horizon is usually dotted with cargo ships waiting to dock at the port here, and across the strait at nearby Aqaba. Another Eilat turn-off is the large number of entrepreneurs attracted by the 'boomtown' image. Too often in Eilat you will find yourself paying out and feeling hard done by.

Eilat is a free trade zone, with no VAT. As a result, many items are cheaper than elsewhere in the country. However, the average visitor will not feel too much benefit as accommodation and food prices are not all that different; only luxury goods offer any real savings.

History

Mentioned in the Old Testament as Elath or Eloth, the Israelites stopped here on their way from Egypt back to the Promised Land (Deuteronomy 2:8). It was the port used by King Solomon as his gateway to the Far East trade routes (I Kings 9:26); the Queen of Sheba landed here when she journeyed to Jerusalem to see Solomon; King Jehoshophat of Judah built his unsuccessful navy here; and King Uzziah rebuilt the town (II Chronicles 26:2) which later fell to the Syrians (II Kings 16:6). After this the town was to change hands several times over the centuries.

In 1116, the Crusaders conquered the town, losing it to Saladin some 50 years later. With the development of the port of Aqaba by the Turks, Eilat's importance declined and it became a backwater. Right up until the end of the British Mandate it was simply a small police outpost in the desert. Captured by the Israelis on 10 March 1949 in the last military operation of the War of Independence, it was deemed by the new state as a vital port, with its strategic location on the Red Sea and its access to the eastern routes.

There are a few things that travellers visiting Eilat should be aware of. Firstly, the high rate of thefts here. You will probably meet or hear of people who have had valuables or even whole backpacks stolen. This happens mostly to those who sleep on the beach, but also in hostels. Therefore, be very security conscious at all times.

Eilat's police have something of a reputation for unfriendly behaviour. Be sure not to be caught jaywalking – easily done with the absence of traffic lights at key junctions between the beach and the town. Fines are often slapped on ignorant tourists, especially in the vicinity of the bus station. It would seem prudent to avoid behaving in any way that could be interpreted as unlawful. Despite their tough image, the police still tolerate the crowds who sleep on the beach and who congregate in the bars of the new tourist centre at night. A few brawls have occurred here so perhaps in the eyes of the police, all travellers are the same as the rowdy minority.

Finally, beware of offers to change money. A few travellers have been robbed of their cash by sharp operators, so only change money with a bank or a hostel manager.

Orientation

There are five basic areas in Eilat: the town itself on the slopes leading down to the sea, the hotel area with the lagoon, marina and main beaches, and to the south the port, Coral Beach and the border with Egypt at Taba.

Town The main street is HaTemarim Blvd – here you will find the bus station with the Commercial Centre and municipal tourist centre opposite. Up the hill to the north is the sherut rank, and down the hill is the airport.

There are a couple of malls on the west side of the street towards the airport (both recognisable by their distinct design) which are home to a variety of shops and eating places. The Shalom Centre is topped by what look likes a spacecraft landing on its roof, while the Red Canyon Centre is shaped like a Bedouin tent.

Across the street is the Commercial Centre, an older complex of shops and eating places that also houses the post office, international telephones and the municipal tourist office. South of the airport, before you reach the hotel area, the New Tourist Centre is a plaza of cafés, restaurants and bars. Further north, beyond the central bus station, you will find most of the hostels.

Hotel Area East of the airport, the hotel area is spread around a purpose-built lagoon and marina with the most accessible beaches nearby, known collectively as the North Beach. There are also various eating, drinking and dancing places to be found here amongst the middle and top-end hotels.

Coral Beach Dominated by the Coral Beach Marine Reserve, a stretch of protected beach five km south of the town, you find the underwater observatory and aquarium, dolphinarium, glass-bottomed boat trips, a mock Wild West town, campsites, and more hotels and restaurants.

Taba Another two km further south, this

stretch of the coast was the subject of a diplomatic tug-of-war which the Egyptians won and so the border with Egypt is now that little bit closer.

Information

Tourist Office The IGTO (☎ 34353) is in the Khan Amiel Centre, across from the Caesar Hotel near the marina.

The municipal tourist office (☎ 72268, 76737) is in the Commercial Centre across from the bus station and is open Sunday to Thursday 8 am to 6 pm, Friday 8 am to 1 pm, and is closed Saturday.

Post & Telecommunications These facilities are in the Commercial Centre, and are available Sunday to Tuesday and Thursday from 8 am to 12.30 pm and 4 to 6.30 pm, Wednesday 8 am to 1.30 pm, Friday 8.30 am to noon, and are closed Saturday.

The Bezek office is next door for international telephone and fax services. It is open Sunday to Thursday 7 am to 1 pm and 4 to 10 pm, Friday 7 am to 1 pm, and is closed Saturday.

Banks Bank Leumi is on HaTemarim Blvd across from the bus station by the municipality building, and is open Monday to Friday from 8.30 am to noon, Sunday, Tuesday and Thursday 5 to 6.30 pm, and is closed Saturday. There is an Israel Discount Bank at the Shalom Centre by the airport, and it's open Sunday to Thursday 8.30 am to noon, Sunday, Tuesday and Thursday 4 to 5.30 pm, and is closed Saturday.

Egyptian Consulate This consulate (☎ 76882) is in a residential area at 68 Ha'Efroni St. See the Getting There & Away chapter for visa information.

Other Steimatzsky's bookshop is in the bus station, and is open Sunday to Thursday 9 am to 7 pm, Friday 9 am to 2 pm, and is closed Saturday. Bronfman sells used books in the Commercial Centre, across from the bus station near the tourist office. They're open Sunday to Thursday 8 am to 1 pm and 5 to

7.30 pm, Friday 8 am to 1 pm, and are closed Saturday.

The library is found in the Philip Murray Cultural Centre, across from the corner of HaTemarim Blvd and Hativat HaNegev St. It's open Sunday, Monday, Wednesday and Thursday from 10 am to 6.45 pm, Tuesday 1 to 6.45 pm, Friday 9 to 11.45 am, and is closed Saturday.

The Gill laundromat, corner of Eilot St and HaTemarim Blvd, is open Sunday to Thursday 8 am to 1 pm and 4 to 7 pm, Friday 8 am to 1 pm, and is closed Saturday.

The police station (☎ 72444/5, 100) is on Avdat St, at the eastern end of Hativat HaNegev St. This is where many travellers end up going to report a theft.

Beaches

Eilat's hot climate and seaside location are its main attraction, and most visitors spend their time lying out in the sun and cooling off in the water. If you are not en route to/from the adjacent Sinai, try not to miss a glimpse of the underwater scenery of colourful coral and fish — perhaps best experienced by snorkelling or scuba diving, but also possible by visiting the observatory, or taking a trip on a glass-bottomed boat or a submarine.

The most convenient beach is North Beach by the hotel area, but it's also the most crowded and has little in the way of coral and fish. You need to head south to Coral Beach for this. There are some private beaches. Popular with Israelis, they don't charge admission, earning their income from their café, bar, deck chairs and sun lounges. *Raffi Pipson* is just north of Coral Beach, next to Aqua Sport. *Eddie's Beach* is down towards Taba.

Dolphin Reef

The management of this complex prefer not to have it labelled as a dolphinarium. An apparently sincere exercise in ecotourism, they purchased dolphins from Russian and Japanese fishing interests and brought them to the Red Sea with the aim of eventually releasing the mammals into the open water.

There are training demonstrations when

visitors can see the dolphins. Admission costs US$6, which includes the use of the private beach facilities, documentary films, and the dolphin training sessions. It's also possible for you to 'meet' the dolphins. For US$11 you can join the trainers to help feed the dolphins, for US$23 you can swim with the dolphins, or certified divers can dive with them, and for US$55 nondivers can get an introductory dive with the dolphins. Snorkelling and scuba gear is available for hire.

Located to the south of the port, Dolphin Reef (☎ 71846) is open daily from 9 am to 5 pm. The pub-bar stays open till the early morning.

Coral Beach Nature Reserve
Beyond the well-kept stretch of sand and under the clear blue water lie coral and fish whose beauty has to be seen to be fully appreciated. The reserve is open daily 8 am to 5 pm and admission is US$3.50. Snorkelling and scuba gear is available for hire.

Aquarium & Yellow Submarine
South of the Coral Beach Nature Reserve, the Coral World Underwater Observatory & Aquarium offers another opportunity to see the sea. A pier leads 100 metres out and 4½ metres below the water to a glass-walled chamber. The complex also includes aquaria, and a museum which tell you all about the fish that are to be seen. It's open Saturday to Thursday 8.30 am to 5 pm, Friday 8.30 am to 3 pm, and admission is US$8.

A new addition is the Yellow Submarine, a real submarine that dives to 30 metres to give you a closer look at the underwater world. The 50-minute dive costs US$38.

William's House
A private residence (☎ 72727), this now houses a small exhibition of Israeli art. Call for opening hours, and admission is free. Said to be Eilat's oldest property, this was originally the home of a British geologist who lived here during WW II.

Ostrich Farm
Located up the sideroad, towards Wadi Shlomo, this farm has some 30 ostriches and other animals such as goats, ponies and peacocks. There is a café and in the evening a sound & light show is put on. Admission is US$2.

Texas Ranch
Across the street from the nature reserve, Texas Ranch is an unimpressive mock Wild West town inspired by the resemblance of the local terrain to that of American cowboy country. It was originally built as a movie set, and features a saloon bar and coffee house. The complex offers horse-riding at US$15 for 40 minutes, and US$30 for a half-day ride. Half-day camel rides are also available for US$30, with a Bedouin meal included. Admission to the ranch is US$3, which includes a beer or soft drink at the saloon.

Israel Palace Museum
Only those suffering from sunstroke or parents with easily satisfied children will find this place worth a visit. It uses dioramas with little dolls to present a history of the Jews. Located next to the Caesar Hotel by the lagoon, it's open in the summer on Saturday to Thursday 9.30 am to noon and 5.30 to 9.30 pm, and Friday 9 am to 1 pm. In the winter it opens from Saturday to Thursday 9 am to noon and 4 to 8 pm, and Friday 9 am to 1 pm. Admission is US$3.50 (students US$2).

Eilat Express
Popular with children, this miniature train runs along the North Beach, from the Galei Eilat Hotel to the Luna Park. The 35-minute ride costs US$2.

International Birdwatching Centre
Eilat is the best place in the world to watch the migration of birds. The peak migration periods are in spring and autumn. In particular, migrating birds of prey are an impressive attraction and over a million raptors of about 30 different species can be seen in season. In addition, some 400 species

of songbirds, seabirds and waterfowl have been recorded migrating through here.

The International Birdwatching Centre (☎ 74276), PO Box 774, City Centre, located across from the central bus station and up from the Commercial Centre, co-ordinates all activities of research, surveys, tours and educational work in the area with the ultimate aim of promoting interest in the conservation of birds. The centre offers visitors a variety of activities, regardless of their depth of knowledge. Observation points and hiking trails have been established and guided hiking tours include the observation of the various birds and a visit to a ringing station. Lasting for two hours, the tours are good value for US$5.

Other facilities include rental of field glasses, literature and background material, participation in migration surveys, lectures and nature films.

The observation points, ringing stations and hiking trails are in the vicinity of the salt ponds to the east of the town and in the northern fields of Kibbutz Eilot. Each spring, the centre organises the Migration Festival which attracts birdwatchers from all over the world. Contact the centre for details.

Scuba Diving

Despite the enthusiastic PR, Eilat's waters do not offer world-class diving. 'Serious' divers should head to the nearby Sinai Desert for that, and Sinai dives are easily arranged with Eilat's dive shops. However, most visitors find Eilat a great place to snorkel and to be introduced to the joys of scuba diving. Many choose to take an introductory dive or to enrol in a certification course during their stay here.

With an office located by the marina in the King Solomon's Palace Hotel and their dive shop opposite Coral Beach, Red Sea Sports Club (☎ 79685; fax 73702), King's Wharf, North Beach, is one of Eilat's major dive operators. Located next to Coral Beach, Aqua Sport (☎ 34404; fax 33771), PO Box 300, is a good alternative and a little less expensive. Both charge about US$40 for an introductory dive. Designed for nondivers,

this includes a training session and dive with an instructor and all equipment. A diving course leading to PADI open-water certification lasts six days and costs US$250 in a group class, US$500 in a private class (minimum of three) or US$750 (minimum of two). These rates include all equipment except mask, snorkel and fins, which can be hired for about US$6 per day.

Certified divers can consider Red Sea Sports Club's six-day Manta Ray live aboard from US$700 to US$770, including full board and unlimited diving. Aqua Sport offers a one-day Sinai Diving Cruise for US$40 with lunch and two dives, and Diving Camping Safaris along the Sinai coast at US$260 for three days, or US$410 for five days. Prices include a guide, sleeping bag and mattress (you sleep under the stars), transportation, full board, tanks, weights and air refills.

Both operators have accommodation for divers who use their services. The Red Sea Sports Club Hotel (☎ 73145; fax 74083) is located across the road from Coral Beach. Singles cost from US$54 to US$66, and doubles from US$66 to US$88. A little further north, Aqua Club Hostel costs US$10 a night for a bed in a four-bed room.

Windsurfing

Both Aqua Sport and Red Sea Sports Club rent out windsurfers, on Coral and North Beach respectively. Expect to pay about US$11 per hour, US$40 for five hours and US$200 for a week. Sailing dinghies, underwater scooters and other equipment can also be rented.

Glass-Bottomed Boats

The modern *Jules Verne Explorer* (☎ 34668, 77702; fax 34924) operates from the marina. A two-hour cruise costs US$15. From a pier just to the north of Coral Beach, Tour Yam (☎ 721113) has older boats.

Cruises

Cruises along the coastline are a popular option, either by yacht or motorboats. Expect to pay from US$20 for a half-day cruise, the best of which head south to the Sinai coast.

Contact Yehoshua Tours (☎ 73024), Poolster Charter Sailing (☎ 76485), or Yacht L'Amie & Jadran (☎ 74815) in the marina, Ya'alat Tours (☎ 72167) in the New Tourist Centre or Johnny Desert Tours (☎ 72608, 76777; fax 72608) in the Shalom Centre.

Desert Hikes

Overshadowed by the activities on the beach and underwater, there are some marvellous hiking possibilities in the Eilat region. The colourful mountains and valleys just outside the town have been enthusiastically explored by SPNI personnel, and marked nature trails enable visitors to see the most interesting of the beauty spots. Contact the staff at the Coral Beach Nature Reserve or the field school for details about recommended hikes. Most of these cannot be reached by bus, so you need a car.

When you go hiking in the desert be sure to abide by the safety guidelines: follow a marked path, take sufficient water, cover your head, beware of flash floods and avoid the Israel-Egypt border area and army installations – do not take photographs or hike at night near here.

Mount Tsfachot Circular Trail This almost circular hike is within reach of nondrivers and is best enjoyed towards the end of the day. It involves about three hours of easy walking to give you a superb view of the Gulf of Aqaba and the four countries whose borders meet here: Israel, Egypt, Jordan and Saudia Arabia.

Take bus No 15 and get off by the Texas Ranch. Follow the sign pointing to Wadi Shlomo and pass by William's House on your right. Walk upstream along the dirt road for about two km, ignoring the numerous side paths, until you see the concrete buildings on your left. Now vacant, they were used to quarantine animals. Go left along Wadi Tsfachot and follow the green trail markers. You pass by a dry waterfall on your right, and after 300 metres the path forks with a black marked trail veering off to the

right. Keep going straight ahead on the green marked trail for another 200 metres. It then turns to the left and starts to climb quite steeply. Head up this path and keep climbing for about 15 minutes to reach the summit at about 278 metres.

From here you can enjoy that view. The Sinai is to the south – look for the Crusader castle on Coral Island. Across the gulf are the Jordanian port city of Aqaba and the Saudi border. To the north-east, the greenery of Kibbutz Eilot and the reefs off Coral Beach can also be seen. Although the sunset can be beautiful from here, hikers are advised not to return after dark as the trail can be difficult to follow. The path continues down to bring you to the field school on the main road.

Places to Stay

Although Eilat is often referred to as a winter resort, its season actually lasts all year round. From November to March, the coolest months with an average daytime temperature of 24°C, the town is at its busiest and reaches an unbelievable peak of overcrowding at Passover. At this time it seems that most Israelis head south. You would do well to stay away from Eilat for that week, and the week before and after as well.

From April to October, with the average temperature zooming up to 36°C, the town is filled mainly with Israelis, and reaches another peak of popularity at Sukkot. Not only is it hard to find a place to stay, but when you do, you will usually find that the price has been doubled or trebled. Other Jewish holidays can present the same problems.

Places to Stay – bottom end

Unlike most resorts, Eilat also encourages budget travellers to visit with several hostels and by allowing them to doss on the beach – this liberal approach to the use of its beaches has given Eilat a permanent community of 'beach people'. For those tempted to join them, remember that there is a high theft rate on Eilat's beaches and if you sleep near the beach-front hotels you will also share your bed with the rats who are attracted by the refuse areas.

Avoid the rodents but not necessarily the thieves by heading east of Sun Bay Camping or south of the Red Rock Hotel. There are toilets and tent pitching is allowed here.

Those who wish to pay for a campsite can choose between heading east towards the Israel-Jordan border, or south towards the Israel-Egypt border. Local bus No 1A's last stop is outside *Sun Bay Camping* (☎ 73105), beyond the hotel area and overlooking the beach. Some 750 metres from Jordanian soil, you pay US$15/20 for singles/doubles (with breakfast) in basic bungalows or US$3 to pitch your own tent.

Most of Eilat's hostels charge ridiculously high rates. Young Israelis, who flock here more than ever before (and not just on the Jewish holidays), seem prepared to pay whatever they are asked. Prices, therefore, can vary considerably from time to time and beds can be scarce at peak times. Travellers are often greeted on arrival at the bus station by hostel touts who have been known to fight over prospective guests. Private room renters may also approach you. Be sure to see any accommodation before deciding to stay there.

Another negative aspect of the town is the sizable community of travellers who find themselves stuck here with no money and having to work illegally to get by or to be able to afford to leave. Many of them frequent the bars and tend to make a nuisance of themselves, making some hostels uncomfortably noisy and unkempt for others. I met several travellers complaining about being unable to find a cheap place to stay that was clean and quiet.

Max & Merran's Fawlty Towers Hostel (☎ 72371), at 116/1 Ofarim St, stands out from a dismal selection of cheapies. It's probably the only private hostel that neither charges through the roof nor tolerates drunkenness and excessive noise. There is a ban on alcohol on the premises, but the atmosphere is far from puritanical. In fact, it's a very easy-going and friendly place. There's a lounge with a TV and VCR, and the owner keeps a good selection of videos. There's also a kitchen with free tea & coffee. It could

do with another bathroom to reduce the long queues, but otherwise it's fine.

A dorm bed costs US$7, and it's closed from 9 pm to 1 am for cleaning. From the bus station, turn right up HaTemarim Blvd, cross Hativat HaNegev St and Retamim St, turn right across the 'grass' area to the end of the dead-end street, and that is Ofarim St. The hostel is down on the left.

Eilat's *IYHA Youth Hostel* (☎ 72358), south of the New Tourist Centre, costs a little more but is pleasant enough, clean and quiet. Dorm beds for members/nonmembers are US$9/10, with breakfast.

Most of the private hostels are clustered around the bus station. Dorm beds can vary from US$8 to US$15, and are sometimes even more. Expect to pay anything from US$25 to US$50 for a private room. These places are all invariably clean.

On Hativat HaNegev St are the *Sinai Hostel* (☎ 72826), *Red Mountain* (☎ 74936, 72021), *Shalem Hostel* (☎ 76544), and *Taba Youth Hostel* (☎ 74072, 75815).

One block north, on Retamim St, are *Nathan's White House Hostel* (☎ 76572) and *The Village*. Also, there's the *Aviv/Spring Hostel* (☎ 74660) is on the corner of Ofarim and Agmonim Sts. *The Home* (☎ 71001), at 108/2 Agmonim St, has beds for US$7 but I heard many travellers complaining about noisy, overcrowded dorms and the dirty bathrooms and kitchen facilities here.

The Shelter (☎ 32868), 149 Eshol St, is a very clean, quiet and pleasantly furnished hostel operated by a Christian organisation. If you are a believer and happy to attend bible readings and listen to sermons on a daily basis, then this is a marvellous place. At US$6 for a dorm bed, it's also the best deal in Eilat. There is a kitchen and a midnight curfew. As it is located in a residential area, it can be tricky to find. From the bus station, turn right up HaTemarim Blvd, left at the lights on Hativat HaNegev St and cut through to Eshol St.

Opposite Coral Beach by the Hotel Caravan, *Carolina's Camping* (☎ 75063) has bungalows for US$9 per person, doubles for US$17, the cleanest bathrooms and showers around, and a basic cafeteria. It may appeal to those who plan to spend time on Coral Beach, costing US$3 per person with your own tent. Local bus No 15 stops nearby.

Remember that Coral Beach is some distance away from the town if you plan to enjoy Eilat's nightlife.

You can also go to the municipal tourist office in the Commercial Centre and ask them for the current list of residents with rooms to rent.

Divers should consider the Aqua Club Hostel (see Scuba Diving in this chapter).

Places to Stay – middle

Eilat's hotels, unlike the hostels, are answerable to the Ministry of Tourism and so prices are more regulated. However, they still go up by over 30% for the winter and on Jewish holidays.

Next to the municipal tourist office in the Commercial Centre and across from the bus station, is the *Etzion Hotel* (☎ 74131; fax 76138). It has a sauna, pool and nightclub, with singles from US$60 to US$70, and doubles from US$74 to US$87.

Up the hill and behind the New Tourist Centre off Yotam Blvd, the *Adi Hotel* (☎ 76151/3; fax 76154) is fairly well hidden; look for the red and white 'ADI' sign on its wall. Singles cost from US$35 to US$42, and doubles cost from US$46 to US$55.

In the expensive hotel area by the lagoon, there are some more moderately priced beds available. Near to the Galei Eilat Hotel, the *Dalia Hotel* (☎ 34004; fax 34072) has singles from US$38 to US$44, and doubles from US$55 to US$65. The *Americana Eilat* (☎ 33777; fax 34174) has a pool, nightclub and tennis with singles from US$40 to US$53, and doubles from US$50 to US$72.

Further east, the *Blue Sky Holiday Village* (☎ 73953/4) has caravans equipped with a bathroom and kitchenette for US$38/48 for singles/doubles.

Out by Coral Beach, the *Caravan Sun Club Hotel* (☎ 71345/6; fax 74083) is moderately priced considering its facilities, including a pool, diving, windsurfing, boating, cycling, tennis and horseriding.

Singles cost from US$42 to US$53, and doubles from US$50 to US$72.

Esther's Apartments (☎ 74575, 75206), at 41 Nesher St, is an agency with various properties on their books. Expect to pay about US$60 for a two-bedroom villa for up to four people. Divers should consider the *Red Sea Sports Club Hotel* (see Scuba Diving in this chapter).

Places to Stay – top end

Eilat's top-end hotels are generally of large and brash design, with swimming pools, nightclubs and various sports and social activities. You can usually save money by booking a package through a travel agent or an airline.

Red Rock Hotel (☎ 73171; fax 71530), south of the main beach, has singles from US$60 to US$80, and doubles from US$100 to US$130.

In the hotel area by the lagoon, the *Caesar* (☎ 33111; fax 32624) has singles from US$68 to US$102, and doubles from US$90 to US$124. At the *Shulamit Gardens* (☎ 33999; fax 34140) singles cost from US$85 to US$100, and doubles from US$110 to US$130. On the opposite side, the more up-market *Lagoona* (☎ 33666; fax 33744) has singles from US$99 to US$131, and doubles from US$131 to US$179.

Next door is Eilat's top-priced hotel, the *King Solomon's Palace* (☎ 34111; fax 34189) where singles cost from US$145 to US$184, and doubles from US$165 to US$225.

By North Beach, the *Queen of Sheba Hotel* (☎ 34121; fax 34126) overlooks the Red Sea and singles here cost from US$60 to US$70, and doubles from US$85 to US$110. The *Moriah Eilat* (☎ 32111; fax 34158) has singles from US$112 to US$155, and doubles from US$140 to US$180. The *Neptune* (☎ 34333; fax 34389) has singles from US$76 to US$168, doubles from US$110 to US$195. The *Galei Eilat* (☎ 34222; fax 34184) has singles from US$61 to US$183, and doubles from US$82 to US$139.

Out by Coral Beach, the *Club Inn*

(☎ 75122/3) is a complex of villa apartments set around a pool with tennis and other sports facilities. Two-bedroom villas, with lounge and kitchenette, cost from US$84 to US$180, and breakfast is not included.

Places to Eat

Eilat's food scene is simply diabolical – good eating places are as hard to find as a rainy day. With the heat, appetites tend to be smaller anyway and many travellers are happy to buy food from a supermarket and prepare their own snacks or sandwiches. A convenient Co-op supermarket is on Eilot St, at the corner of HaTemarim Blvd. In the Commercial Centre, near the tourist office, the Mini-Supermarket is more expensive, but is open for longer hours, including Shabbat.

Eilat's bakers win the prize for baking Israel's smallest pitta bread. When you order felafel here, the pitta is so tiny that there is hardly any room for the salad. The best and some of the cheapest felafel I tasted in town was from a little stall called *Felafel Boutique* on HaTemarim Blvd, up the hill from the bus station and just below Almogim St. It is open Sunday to Thursday 10 am to 10 pm, Friday 10 am to 2 or 3 pm, and is closed Saturday.

The bus station's *Egged self-service restaurant* provides the usual inexpensive meals, which is even more appreciated in Eilat. It is open from 4 am till 4 pm (3 pm on Friday), and is closed Saturday.

Near Max & Merran's Fawlty Towers Hostel, the *Country Road* provides basic snacks and meals (see Bars) and is probably the cheapest place in Eilat. At the corner of Eilot and Jerusalem Sts, *Pat Bar* is a bakery and dairy restaurant with low prices.

The *Oasis Restaurant* (☎ 72414), to the left of the western end of the marina bridge, provides decent salads for US$6, and meat or fish dishes from US$9.

Neither the Shalom Centre nor the New Tourist Centre have a truly recommendable eating place. Ice cream, waffles, pizzas and blintzes dominate here, as well as cafés which serve shishlik and kebab.

The local branch of the *Nargila* chain

provides value for money and passable Yemenite food; it's across from the Shulamit Gardens Hotel.

The *Fisherman House* (☎ 71330), across from the glass-bottomed boats' pier at Coral Beach, offers a self-service meal of fish, chips, salad and bread. It is average quality at best, but you can eat as much as you like for US$7.

More up-market are the *Lotus Chinese Restaurant* (☎ 76161) by the Caesar Hotel near the lagoon, and *Mandy's Chinese Restaurant* (☎ 72238) at Coral Beach. A meal costs from US$15 to US$20 here.

Al Hayam Lebanese Grill (☎ 74147/8), in the Phinat Eilat Centre on the promenade, has received great reviews from readers. Other decent places include *La Coquille* (☎ 73461) behind the lagoon for French cooking, and *Tandoori*, King's Wharf below the Lagoona Hotel, for Indian cuisine.

Bars Not surprisingly, the bars are popular both after dark and during the day when the hot sun can be too much to handle.

In the Shalom Centre, *Tropicana* serves draught beer and shows free videos.

The crowds tend to congregate in the New Tourist Centre and by the marina, especially at night. Two British-style pubs in the New Tourist Centre are the *Red Lion* and *The Tavern*, but can be too crowded and rowdy for some. Next to The Tavern, *Lido Pub* has a popular dancefloor and, unlike the discos, there is no cover charge. The mock Tudor-style *Teddy's*, behind the lagoon, is more sedate, as is *The Yacht Pub*, part of the King Solomon's Palace Hotel complex, which features live music that varies in quality.

West of the footbridge, across the lagoon and by the marina bridge, is *Yatush-Ba-Rosh*, a popular bar whose name translates literally to Mosquito in the Head.

There are some seedy looking bars up near the hostels. On the corner of Almogim and Agmonim Sts, the *Peace Bar* is a hang-out for locals, unemployed builders and some travellers. Come here early in the morning to try for a job on a building site, or later for inexpensive food and draught beer. Next door, the *Country Road* offers more of the same. The *Hard Rock Café* is another British-style pub, at 179 Eilot St.

For most eating and drinking places, Shabbat is just another day and they are open as usual.

Entertainment

Eilat's evenings are based around the bars and eating places of the Shalom Centre, the New Tourist Centre and the hotel area. Pick up the free *What's On in Eilat* leaflet from the tourist office to find out what else is happening. Some of the big hotels regularly put on such happenings as Hebrew lessons, belly dancers, films and videos, dancing lessons and lectures.

The Cinemateque at the Philip Murray Cultural Centre shows a usually good choice of films, and concerts and shows are staged here, too. Alternatively, the Cinema Eilat is next to the post office.

There are several nightclubs, or discos, and opinions differ as to which is the best. These include *Spiral*, by the marina bridge and above the Yatush-Ba-Rosh bar, *Sheba's* at the King Solomon's Palace Hotel and *Aquarium* at the Caesar Hotel.

Cover charges hover around the US$11 mark and dress codes normally rule out shorts, sandals and general beach-type attire. Nightclubs don't really start filling up until 10 pm or later and remain open till 2 am or when people leave. With no cover charge, the dance floor at *Lido Pub* in the new tourist centre was packed on my last visit (see Bars earlier).

Getting There & Away

Air Arkia flights depart from the central airport, connecting to Jerusalem and Tel Aviv (US$80).

Bus Eilat has express bus links with Jerusalem via the Dead Sea (4½ hours), Tel Aviv via Beersheba (five hours) and Haifa (6½ hours). It is often necessary to make reservations at least three days in advance – if you are unable to get on a Jerusalem or Tel Aviv bus, go to Beersheba and change there.

If you want to stop off in the Negev en route, Beersheba buses pass through Mitzpe Ramon and will also drop you at Avdat and Sde Boker. All buses pass by the Timna Valley National Park, Hai-Bar Biblical Wildlife Reserve and the Yotvata Visitors' Centre.

If you are heading to or from the Sinai, local bus No 15 runs between Eilat's central bus station and Taba. The Israeli border checkpoint is open 24 hours, but this is subject to change and you will want to time your crossing to be able to find transport on the other side. There are irregular Egyptian buses running from the border to Sharm el Sheikh and St Catherine's Monastery – only one or two a day. Ask around for the current rough schedule and aim to get there in plenty of time as they are reliably unreliable. Don't forget the US$10 departure tax, to be paid in Israeli currency. If you are only visiting the Sinai, no Egyptian visa is necessary, just a valid passport; you will have to buy some Egyptian currency.

You must get a visa from the Eilat consulate or the Tel Aviv embassy if you want to visit any other part of Egypt (see the Getting There & Away chapter).

Sherut Yael Daroma, (☎ 72279) run a good value sherut service from Almogim St, up the hill from the bus station. It's faster and the fares are only slightly higher than Egged. Cars regularly speed up to Jerusalem and Tel Aviv via Beersheba. You will usually have to make reservations at least three days in advance.

Getting Around

Bus Local bus No 15 is the most used service, running every day between the bus station and Taba via the hotel area and Coral Beach. Distances within the town are not so great and many people walk everywhere. If you don't want to, bus Nos 1, 2 and 3 run between the town and the hotel area, with No 1A running between the town and Sun Bay Camping, towards the Israel-Jordan border.

Taxi Especially when there are two or more

of you, Eilat's taxis can be an inexpensive and comfortable way to get around.

Although distances are short, much of the town is on a hill and, worn out by the heat, you could well decide to take a smart Mercedes ride rather than walk. Fares tend to be about US$3 to US$5.

Bicycle The heat may prove to be too much of a deterrent, but you can hire a bicycle for about US$8 a day in front of the Queen of Sheba Hotel by the lagoon.

AROUND EILAT

Unfortunately most of the many wonderful places of natural beauty near Eilat can only be reached by private transport, and with the high temperatures and infrequent traffic, hitchhiking is impractical. However, you can reach some marvellous places by bus.

The area's incredible landscape is due to the Great Syrian-African Rift which terminates here with the Arava Valley. The result is a desert environment with glorious colours and a surprising variety of flora & fauna.

Of the Negev's 1200 recorded plant species, only 300 exist in this southern, more arid, area. These include palms, acacia, tamarisk, pistachio and the very rare horseradish tree. The animals found here include gazelles, wolves, foxes, ibex and Israel's largest bird, the almost extinct lappet-faced vulture.

There are also many archaeological sites in the area which show that ancient people managed not only to live here, but also dug copper mines in these harsh surroundings.

Places that should be seen if you have a car or decide to take a tour include **En Netafim**, a small spring at the foot of a 30-metre waterfall which attracts many animals who come to drink; the **Red Canyon**, one of the area's most beautiful sights, 600 metres long, one to three metres wide at its narrowest and some 10 metres at it deepest; and **Moon Valley** which is Egyptian territory but can be seen from the Red Canyon.

Here are some places that can be reached by public transport:

Around Eilat

Timna Park

A popular excursion 30 km north of Eilat, this area of the desert is some 60 sq km. Timna Valley is the site of biblical copper mines (mining began here around 4000 BC). There are some really stunning desert landscapes with multicoloured rock formations here.

Among the things to see are the ancient copper mines, which now consist of sandstone arches and caves, underground shafts and galleries. About three km away are some Egyptian and Midianite rock drawings. Other signs of ancient life include copper smelting camps and the ruins of the 14th-century BC Temple of Hathor.

More striking, though, are the natural phenomena here. King Solomon's Pillars are a series of sandstone ridges caused by gradual erosion on a 50-metre-high cliff face. The aptly named rock formation, the Mushroom, is, again, caused by erosion.

Information about walks is available at the park's entrance. A lot of km are involved in walking around the park, so allow three to eight hours. It is open daily from 7.30 am till dark. Admission is US$3.50 per person for those travelling by car; those arriving on foot or by bicycle are admitted free.

Getting There & Away Any bus heading to or from Eilat passes the turn-off for Timna Valley. From the main road it is a 2½-km walk to the park's entrance. Make as early a start as possible to beat the heat and, as usual, take plenty of water and cover your head.

Hai-Bar Arava Biblical Wildlife Reserve

Hai-Bar is Hebrew for Wild Game and this wildlife reserve on 8000 acres of salt flats was created to establish breeding groups of wild animals threatened by extinction.

Although the reserve was inspired by the desire to reintroduce animals mentioned in the Bible, other creatures are also found here.

Guided tours of the reserve are available by minivan, and you cannot go on foot or in your own vehicle. Lasting about 1½ hours, these tours operate at 9 am, 10.30 am, noon and 1.30 pm and cost US$6.50 per person, which includes admission to the Visitors' Centre. In order to see more animals at feeding time, you are advised to take one of the earlier departures.

The main source of information (☎ 76018) on the entire Eilat area, the **Yotvata Visitors' Centre** features an audiovisual presentation that describes the region's natural attractions and an exhibition of maps, diagrams and photographs on the zoology, botany, geology, archaeology and history of the settlement here. It's open daily from 8 am to 3 pm. Admission to the Visitors' Centre is only US$2.

A cafeteria, run by the adjacent kibbutz, serves some of the local dairy produce. All buses to and from Eilat pass by the reserve.

Taba

This is a controversial pocket of land that Israel and Egypt continued to argue about long after the Camp David accord. Taba was eventually given back to the Egyptians in 1989. The pleasant public beach has freshwater showers, there is a private beach, *Rafi Nelson Village*, and the luxury *Taba Hilton Hotel* (☎ 79222). The hotel's telephone is considered a local call from Eilat, and there is a hotel minibus shuttle from the border crossing. You don't need an Egyptian visa to visit, just a passport. Israeli currency is accepted.

To get to Taba take local bus No 15 to the last stop. Private cars are permitted to enter Taba and the Sinai from Israel, but taxis and rental cars are not.

The Occupied Territories

As used here, the term Occupied Territories refers to the areas commonly known as the West Bank and the Gaza Strip. The West Bank is officially called Judaea and Samaria by Israel. These areas were occupied by Israel during the Six Day War and have remained in political limbo ever since, neither annexed outright by Israel (as were East Jerusalem and the Golan Heights), nor granted autonomy.

The military administration set up by the Israelis in 1967 is based on regulations first introduced by the British during the Mandate, against which the Zionists had themselves rebelled. IDF patrols are a constant aggravation to the Arab population and you will sense the tension just below the surface, even more so than in East Jerusalem and Nazareth.

In effect, though, the West Bank is a part of Israel. The pre-1967 border, known as the 'green line', is not marked by any signs, let alone a border post, and most Israelis would be hard pressed to point out where Israel ends and the West Bank begins. The Gaza Strip,

being smaller and more isolated from the Israeli population, is different. Gaza and Israel are like night and day and heavily armed border posts make it easy to tell where you are.

The Occupied Territories are seen by the majority of Palestinians as land that rightfully belongs to them. Israeli opinion is basically split between those who see this land as rightfully a part of Israel, those who feel that it should be returned to Palestinians in exchange for a peace treaty, and those who would agree with the land for peace concept but fear that it would recreate a situation that would lead to a major war. There can be no doubt that the occupation of the West Bank and the Gaza Strip has resulted in greater security for the Jewish State, creating a buffer zone between them and hostile neighbours. Since 1967, the number of terrorist raids here has fallen considerably.

Since the Arab intifada began in late 1987, and especially with the most recent round of peace talks initiated by the USA, Israeli attitudes to the Occupied Territories have polarised. Some of those thankful that an Israeli delegation is at last talking to its neighbours are more willing than ever to consider trading land for peace. Others are more determined than ever that the land should stay under Israeli control. Palestinian support for Iraq during the Desert Storm debacle swayed many liberal Israelis to take a more hardline approach to the concept of giving land and autonomy to the Palestinians.

The intifada also means that many Arab businesses, including hotels and restaurants, have responded to the call for strikes and operate for restricted hours.

The Occupied Territories are more rural and less developed than the rest of Israel and the scenery is often superb. There are more of the clichéd everyday scenes of the Middle East to see here, with Arab women balancing shopping on their heads, donkeys managing to convey even heavier loads (note that the donkey handlers are nearly always young boys or old men), and the ever-present stretch Mercedes and Peugeots sounding their horns.

West Bank

An integral part of any visit to the Holy Land, this region includes such familiar place names as Bethlehem, Jericho and Hebron. Amidst dramatic landscapes you will find the Mount of Temptation, the birthplace of Jesus, and the Tombs of the Patriarchs.

Covering an area of less than 6000 sq km, the West Bank consists of a diverse range of geographic regions. Starting from the edge of the Jezreel Valley in the north, the Samarian Mountains are a range of green and brown peaks with a distinct red soil, with olive and fruit trees, tobacco, livestock and the occasional Arab village on the terraced slopes. Nablus is the major town here. The Judean Hills are dominated by Jerusalem.

Descending eastward towards the Dead Sea, the Judean Hills become the savage scenic splendour of the Judean Desert. Moving down into the Jordan Valley you come to Jericho, a lush oasis with a distinctly hotter climate. Often overlooked is the fact that the shore of the Dead Sea, almost as far south as Ein Gedi, is part of the West Bank. This includes Qumran, where the Dead Sea Scrolls were found, and Ein Feshka, the freshwater spring. These areas are covered in detail in the Dead Sea Chapter.

To the west, the Judean Hills end where the Negev Desert begins, and you will find Bethlehem and Hebron, surrounded by hillsides of lush vineyards, orchards and olive trees set amongst the rocky brown terrain.

The Israelis officially designate the West Bank by the biblical names Judea and Samaria in the linguistic war. As you travel around you will see fortified Jewish settlements, military installations, periodic roadblocks and refugee camps that only begin to indicate the reality of the situation

here. These aspects cannot be ignored, but do not allow them to deter you from visiting the region.

Most travellers base themselves in Jerusalem and make day trips to destinations in the West Bank. Because of the intifada, the hotels in Ramallah and Nablus have been closed to foreigners from time to time.

Unless otherwise stated, the telephone area code for the West Bank is 2, the same as Jerusalem.

JERUSALEM TO JERICHO

The main attraction on the road between Jerusalem and Jericho is the dramatic change in scenery and temperature as you experience the rapid descent from 820 metres above sea level to 395 metres below sea level in less than an hour. You also pass by Bethany and the Inn of the Good Samaritan with their New Testament connotations; the Wadi Qelt, a nature reserve with a natural spring where you can bathe in a pool under a waterfall, hike along an aqueduct to a monastery built into the cliff face of a canyon and continue walking to Jericho; and see Nebi Musa, the tomb of Moses according to Muslim tradition.

Arab buses to Jericho leave East Jerusalem via the western slopes of the Mount of Olives and pass through Bethany. Egged buses leave the central bus station and head around the Mount of Olives to the north to join the Jericho road beyond Bethany.

Bethany

On the western slopes of the Mount of Olives, Bethany is renowned as the site of the resurrection of Lazarus (John 11:1-44). A Franciscan church commemorates the traditional site of the miracle performed by Jesus. Bethany is also named as the place where Jesus was anointed, much to the disapproval of his disciples (Matthew 26:6-13, Mark 14:3-9, John 12:1-8). The church features some impressive mosaics, one of which illustrates the resurrection. Built in 1954, this is the fourth church to occupy the area. The first was constructed in the mid-1st century,

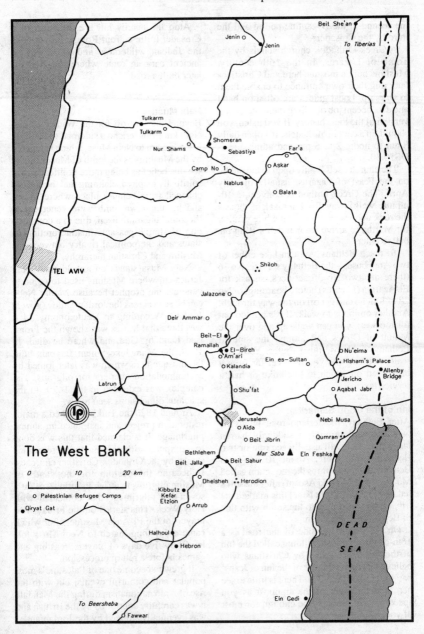

The West Bank

0   10   20 km

o Palestinian Refugee Camps

the second in the Byzantine period and the third by the Crusaders.

A Greek Orthodox church stands by the Tomb of Lazarus. In the 16th century, Muslims built a mosque here and Christians later dug their own entrance to enable them to worship. Local guides are often on hand and do a decent job of telling their interesting version of the local history. If you listen, you should tip a couple of sheqels. It's open daily 8 am to noon, 2 to 6 pm and admission is US$0.30.

The church itself is only open to the public on the Feast of Lazarus, usually in early April. The Greek Orthodox convent, a 10-minute walk away from Jerusalem, boasts the rock upon which Jesus sat while waiting for Martha to arrive from Jericho. Ring the bell to enter.

To reach Bethany you can take either of two Arab buses – the Bethany service, No 36 (there are two No 36 services, so ask for El-Azariya (Lazarus) before boarding) or No ·28 to Jericho and get off on the way through. Another option is to walk. If it's not too hot (or too wet), you can walk up and over the Mount of Olives and around the side to Bethany, or choose other routes. You can't really get lost, and you're never far from a busy road on which to hitchhike or hail a service taxi.

Inn of the Good Samaritan

After Bethany, the Jericho road winds its way eastward through a suddenly barren landscape. You will usually see one or two Bedouin camps here. About 10 km from Bethany the road climbs the mountain called Ma'ale Adumim (Red Ascent) after the soil's reddish tint. In ancient Israel this marked the tribal border of Judah to the south with that of Benjamin to the north.

On the right-hand side of the road is a 16th-century Turkish building called the Inn of the Good Samaritan by Christians who believe that this is the site of the inn of Jesus' parable (Luke 10:25-37). There is little to see here and the sight of the signpost as you speed by will probably be enough for most of you.

Atop the nearby hill are the ruins of a Crusader fortress, Tour Rouge. It overlooks the Judean wilderness and what was an ancient caravan route where the Romans later built a road.

Nebi Musa

Beyond the turn-off for the Wadi Qelt and eight km from Jericho a sideroad to the right leads 1½ km to Nebi Musa, which is revered by the Muslims as the tomb of Moses. Some see this belief as being more politically than spiritually inspired, claiming that the site has changed from being a place where Moses and his unknown tomb were venerated to 'become' the tomb itself, due to a combination of simple peasants misinterpreting its status and the political rivalry between the Muslim and Christian hierarchy.

Nebi Musa stands on an old road from Jerusalem where Muslims used to come to venerate the prophet because Mount Nebo can be seen across the Jordan Valley (now in Jordan). According to Deuteronomy 34 it was there that Moses was shown the Promised Land by God and where he died. In 1269, the Mameluke Sultan Baybars built the mosque here which was later joined by accommodation quarters for pilgrims. The complex was extended in the 1470s to the spacious dimensions seen today.

Around 1820 the Turks launched a major restoration project and instigated an annual pilgrimage. It is claimed that this was done to compete with the Easter ceremonies staged by the Orthodox Christian churches. It became the custom for thousands of Muslim pilgrims to arrive in Jerusalem for a seven-day pilgrimage that coincided with Holy Week. This started on the Friday with prayers at the El-Aqsa Mosque, after which came a day-long march to Nebi Musa followed by five days of prayers, feasting and games before a return procession.

It grew to become one of Palestine's most popular and colourful events, but with the rise of Arab nationalism during the Mandate it was carefully controlled by the British and was eventually stopped by the Jordanians.

In the belief that this is the tomb of Moses, many Muslims choose to be buried here.

Tradition also identifies two of the tombs in the large cemetery as those of Moses' shepherd, Hassan er-Rai, and of Aisha, who was Mohammed's favourite wife.

With the landscape of the Judean Desert an impressive backdrop, Nebi Musa is worth seeing. There is a resident watchman who expects a donation; US$1 per person should satisfy. There are no set hours.

To get there, look for the signpost on the main road to Jericho. It's a two-km walk from the bus stop.

WADI QELT & ST GEORGE'S MONASTERY

The hike through the Wadi Qelt to Jericho, with a stopoff at St George's Monastery along the way, is understandably popular. If you don't fancy the long trail through the canyon there is a more direct road leading past the monastery on its way to Jericho.

A wadi is a rocky watercourse that is dry except in the rainy season, and the Wadi Qelt runs through a steep canyon surrounded by limestone and chalk cliffs, the barren terrain dotted with clumps of trees and foliage.

Wadi Qelt Hike

Taking about four hours, this hike involves some straightforward walking over slightly rough ground with a bit of scrambling over rocks here and there. Regular sports shoes are suitable footwear – sandals are not. In winter it is often muddy underfoot in places and you can end up getting your feet wet wading through shallow water throughout the year. Flash floods are a danger in winter, with a sudden downpour being followed by a rush of water. Keep an eye on the weather and be ready to climb to higher ground.

Take plenty of water and cover your head. Also remember to take suitable clothes for the visit to the monastery. Although the monks will usually provide some unflattering rags for you to cover your legs and arms, you will show more respect by providing

your own. The Wadi Qelt is much warmer than Jerusalem though, so you might prefer to carry them to slip on when you get there.

At the turn-off on the Jerusalem to Jericho road, follow the sign to the monastery. After five minutes the road forks at another sign for the monastery pointing to the right. This is the direct route that avoids the wadi, so go to the left and after 100 metres turn right onto the dirt track that winds down to the valley, with a marvellous view before you. After 25 minutes you arrive at the spring, Ein Qelt, and the nature reserve. The aqueduct here carries spring water from Ein Fuwwar, a few km west of here, to Jericho. It was restored by the British, but note the ruins of the Herodian aqueduct.

Further along the wadi to the left you will find some picturesque bathing possibilities; climb up the opposite bank and turn right though for the monastery and Jericho. Following the path beside the aqueduct you will see occasional red on white painted trail markers showing the way. The paint must have been in short supply as they often appear at intervals lengthy enough to make you wonder whether you are still heading in the right direction.

After following the aqueduct for about 40 minutes the trail leads down to the wadi; this can be tricky if there is a lot of water. After another 45 minutes you'll pass under the ruined arches where the Herodian aqueduct crossed the canyon. Follow the wadi a little further and around the next bend you will see the monastery.

After visiting the monastery stay on the same side of the wadi, with the trail climbing high above the bed. Look out for the first sight of the Jordan Valley after about 25 minutes as you pass caves once used by hermits and the ruins of other monasteries. The trail later splits; you can either follow the wadi or climb up the other side.

If you choose the latter route, you find yourself by a largely abandoned refugee camp where young children insist that they be paid for saying 'shalom – baksheesh'. Head for the road that passes the mosque (look for the minaret) and follow it through the melon and banana fields to the main road by the restaurant and military camp.

Follow the wadi to the main road and you will pass the Tulul Abu el-Alaiq excavations. On both sides of the wadi and very easy to miss (well, they were for me), these are the remains of Hasmonean, Herodian and Roman winter palaces and villas.

At the main road, which is Jerusalem Rd, turn left to enter Jericho.

St George's Monastery

The more direct route to the monastery is the right fork on the turn-off from the Jerusalem to Jericho road, as directed by the orange signposts. Look out for the metal cross that marks the monastery's location. Steps lead down into the canyon and the road continues and eventually passes the previously mentioned refugee camp and mosque, intersecting with Jerusalem Rd by the restaurant and military camp.

The monastery, named after St George of Koziba, was first built in the late 5th century, based on a small oratory built by hermits in the early 4th century. The Wadi Qelt's numerous cave-dwelling hermits would attend the divine liturgy on Saturday and Sunday. It was virtually abandoned after the Persians swept through the valley and massacred the 14 monks, but it was restored by the Crusaders in 1179. A pilgrim in 1483 wrote that he only saw ruins here, and reconstruction began in 1878 and was completed in 1901 by the Greek Orthodox Church.

The traditions surrounding the monastery include St Elijah stopping here en route to the Sinai, and St Joachim weeping here because his wife Anne was sterile and then having an angel announce to him the news of the Virgin Mary's conception.

The oldest part of the building is the 6th-century mosaic floor of the Church of St George and John. The skulls of the martyred monks are kept here and a niche contains the tomb of St George. The larger church was added by the Crusaders during their 12th-century renovations. Dedicated to the Blessed Virgin, it features a black, white and red double-headed Byzantine eagle. Most of

the paintings and icons seen today date from the latest reconstruction but the doors at the centre of the iconostasis also date back to the Crusaders.

It's open Monday to Saturday 8 am to 5 pm, but the hours can be flexible. Admission is US$1.

Places to Eat

Top up with water at the monastery, after which *Wadi el-Kalt Cafeteria & Restaurant* at the Jerusalem Rd intersection serves draught beer and soft drinks to thirsty hikers. Prices are higher than average.

Getting There & Away

Take Arab bus No 28 from East Jerusalem or any Egged bus that is heading for the Dead Sea or Jericho from Jerusalem's central bus station. Tell the driver that you want to go to the Wadi Qelt and/or the monastery and keep an eye out for the orange signpost after about 25 minutes.

JERICHO

(Population: 7000)

Reputedly the world's oldest town, Jericho is best known for the biblical account of Joshua and the tumbling walls. A popular destination for visitors, especially in the winter when its warm climate is a pleasant alternative to the cold and rain in Jerusalem, its ancient ruins are surpassed by the shabby beauty of their surroundings. Often compared to Egypt, Jericho is a lush oasis of colour, with fruit and flowers abundant amongst the greenery; quite a contrast to the desert valley setting which, at 250 metres below sea level, makes it the world's lowest town.

History

The Old Testament Book of Joshua tells how Jericho was the first town captured by the Israelites when, after years in the wilderness, they sent in spies, crossed the River Jordan nearby, laid siege and caused the walls to collapse by the sound of their priests' trumpets.

Prior to the arrival of the Israelites around

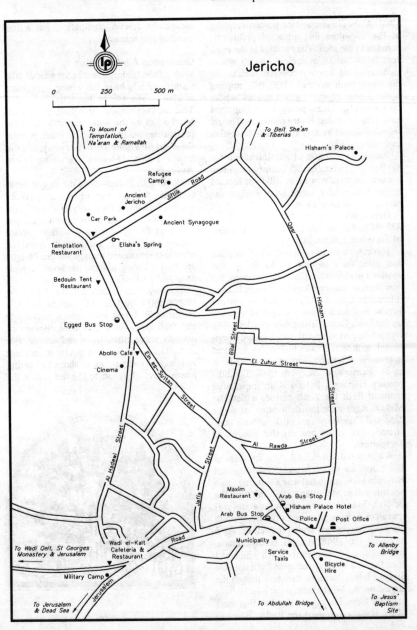

Jericho

0   250   500 m

To Mount of
Temptation,
Na'aran & Ramallah

To Beit She'an
& Tiberias

Hisham's Palace

Refugee
Camp

Jiftlik   Road

Ancient
Jericho

Car Park

Ancient Synagogue

Temptation
Restaurant

Elisha's Spring

Bedouin Tent
Restaurant

Oasis

Hisham

Egged Bus Stop

Abollo Cafe

Cinema

En es-Sultan   Street

Bilal   Street

El Zuhur Street

Street

Al   Rawda   Street

Al Hadewi Street

Jaffa

Street

Maxim
Restaurant

Arab Bus Stop

Hisham Palace Hotel

Arab Bus Stop

Police

Post Office

To Wadi Qelt, St Georges
Monastery & Jerusalem

Wadi el-Kalt
Cafeteria &
Restaurant

Road

Municipality

Service
Taxis

To Allenby
Bridge

Military Camp

Jerusalem

Bicycle
Hire

To Jerusalem
& Dead Sea

To Abdullah Bridge

To Jesus'
Baptism
Site

1200 BC the climate and the perennial spring of Ein es-Sultan had attracted prehistoric nomads to the area. They settled at the adjacent Tel es-Sultan, or ancient Jericho, where archaeologists have uncovered remains of the town built around 7000 BC, making Jericho one of the known places where people changed from being wandering food gatherers to settled food producers. The tel was abandoned as a result of the Babylonian exile around 586 BC.

Becoming a centre of administration for the Persians in the late 6th century BC, there is a settlement of some sort still to be located in the area where those who worked the plantations were housed.

During Alexander the Great's rule (336 to 323 BC), Jericho became the private estate of the ruling sovereign.

Mark Anthony gave the oasis to Cleopatra and after their suicide in 30 BC it was awarded to Herod the Great by Octavian, the new Roman leader. Herod had been leasing it from the Queen of Egypt, and he now put in new aqueducts to supply his winter palace by the Wadi Qelt at Tulul Abu el-Alaiq. The Byzantine period saw the area heavily populated, with synagogues built at Na'aran and near ancient Jericho, and monasteries such as St George's in the Wadi Qelt. The 8th-century Hisham's Palace is an impressive remnant from the Arab period, whilst the Middle Ages saw the cultivation of sugar cane and Crusader sugar mills, and the construction of churches on the Mount of Temptation.

When Saladin defeated the Crusaders in 1187, Jericho was left undefended against Bedouin raids and what was a thriving town became a desolate village. It wasn't until the British Mandate that Jericho's natural resources were again used effectively with the development of fruit production. As a result of the 1948 War of Independence, Jordan gained control of the town which had been flooded by Arab refugees from the new State of Israel. Refugee camps, amongst the largest on the West Bank, were hastily built to house them. During the Six Day War most of the refugees crossed the Jordan River to escape the Jewish occupation, but a few hundred still remain.

Orientation & Information

With all the 'oldest town in the world' talk, visitors usually have the wrong impression of what to expect when they arrive in Jericho. The archaeological site that is ancient Jericho lies on the northern outskirts of the present-day Arab town. The other popular sights are also quite a distance away, and this makes it difficult to see everything in one visit.

Coming from Jerusalem the Egged buses continue through the town and pass by ancient Jericho on their way to Tiberias; the Arab buses' last stop is downtown. Here you will find the main square with its police station (☎ 92251), municipality building, service-taxi rank and moneychanger. Nearby are shops, eating places, the hotel, bicycle shop and post office.

The way to reach the sights is to follow the loop formed by Qasr Hisham St and Ein es-Sultan St. Lined with garden restaurants and fruit shops with colourful displays of oranges, other citrus fruits and melons, Ein es-Sultan St forks just south of ancient Jericho and there are more shops and eating places here. The road to the left passes the

Tree of Life

turn-off to the Mount of Temptation with its monastery; the road to the right passes the ancient synagogue and intersects with Qasr Hisham St which leads past Hisham's Palace.

Deciding the order in which to 'do' Jericho is important as you want to avoid any unnecessary backtracking with the high temperatures and humidity making you feel sluggish.

Moving in an anticlockwise direction is the popular choice: head north up Qasr Hisham St to Hisham's Palace, then west to the ancient synagogue and ancient Jericho. Here you can refresh yourself at one of the eating places before heading down Ein es-Sultan St to return to town. The basic loop covers a distance of about six km, with the Mount of Temptation about two km further north.

You need to be both an early starter and a fast mover to conquer the heights of the Mount of Temptation in addition to that lot unless you have a car or take a taxi.

Alternatively, if you reach Jericho via the Wadi Qelt, you can make your way to the less exhausting sights and return later to scale the Mount of Temptation and see whatever else you missed.

Hisham's Palace

Known in Arabic as Khirbet al-Mafjar, these impressive ruins of a hunting lodge are better known as Hisham's Palace due to Umayyad Caliph Hisham ibn Abd al-Malik being credited with their construction. However, it is now thought more likely that his nephew and successor, al Walid ibn Yazid, was responsible. He was assassinated after only a year in power and the palace was never completed. It came to be used as a quarry of cut stones by the locals, although in the 12th century a programme of restoration was started, possibly by Saladin.

The architectural style and motifs show a strong Persian influence. Jerusalem's Rockefeller Museum displays much of the ornate plaster work, but the remaining highlights include the lovely mosaic floors, stucco floral patterns and the elaborate

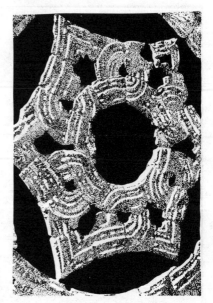

Stone window, Hisham's Palace

system of channels and vents used to provide steam to the hot-rooms, pools and baths. The large monument in the middle of the central court was built by the archaeologists. Intended as a window, it shows how the Umayyads adapted the motifs they found in the places they conquered. This star is Roman.

The site (☎ 922522) is open April to September, Saturday to Thursday 8 am to 5 pm, and Friday 8 am to 4 pm; October to March, Saturday to Thursday 8 am to 4 pm, and Friday 8 am to 3 pm; and admission is US$3 (students US$1.50).

Ancient Synagogue

An orange signpost points to the modern building at the end of the gravel road. Inside is the mosaic floor of a 5th or 6th-century synagogue. This pictures a menorah with the Hebrew inscription Shalom al Israel (Peace Upon Israel).

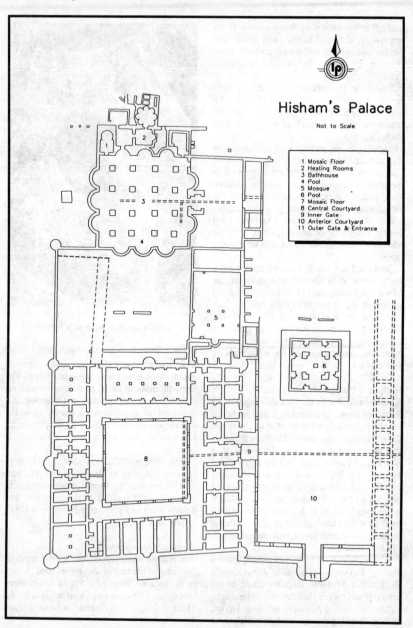

Hisham's Palace

Not to Scale

1 Mosaic Floor
2 Heating Rooms
3 Bathhouse
4 Pool
5 Mosque
6 Pool
7 Mosaic Floor
8 Central Courtyard
9 Inner Gate
10 Anterior Courtyard
11 Outer Gate & Entrance

It's open daily, although the attendant's hours are erratic. Seemingly absent, he will often arrive as if from nowhere to unlock the door and think of a suitable fee. Pay no more than US$2.

Ancient Jericho (Tel Jericho)

Only archaeology buffs are likely to be impressed by the sight of the Tel Jericho or Tel es-Sultan excavations.

The fact that they reveal the remains of a stone tower constructed around 7000 BC is interesting, as it is the only known structure from the Stone Age.

A good imagination is required to put together a picture of the ancient town whilst taking in the signposted trenches and mounds of dirt. The tel grew to its present height due to successive towns being built on top of the previous one. The mud-brick wall at the tel's summit is not one of those brought down by Joshua's trumpets as initially believed. It has now been dated as being 10 centuries before the arrival of the Israelites.

The site (☎ 922909) is open April to September, Saturday to Thursday 8 am to 5 pm, and Friday 8 am to 4 pm; October to March, Saturday to Thursday 8 am to 4 pm, and Friday 8 am to 3 pm; and admission is US$3 (students US$1.50).

Ein es-Sultan

Across the street from ancient Jericho is Ein es-Sultan, or Sultan's Spring, also known as Elisha's Spring. This will only quench your thirst, not your appetite for impressive sights; there is little to see except a shabby building and a UN sign barring admission. This is the spring traditionally associated with II Kings 2:19-22 which tells of Elisha purifying the water with salt.

Producing 76 litres per second, the

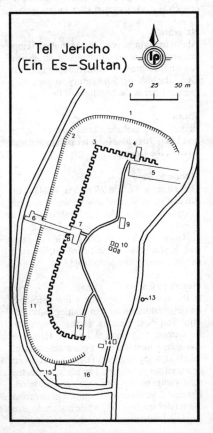

Tel Jericho
(Ein Es–Sultan)

0   25   50 m

1	Retaining Wall
2	Glacis Middle Bronze Period
3	City Wall Early Bronze Period
4	Stratigraphic Section 1952-1957 Excavations
5	Stratigraphic Section 1930-1936 Excavations
6	Stratigraphic Section 1952-1957 Excavations
7	Stratigraphic Section 1952-1957 Excavations
8	Tower & Wall 8th Millennium BC
9	Observation Point
10	Iron Age Structures
11	Glacis Middle Bronze Period
12	Stratigraphic Section 1952-1957 Excavations
13	Spring of Elisha (Ein es-Sultan)
14	Toilets
15	Entry
16	Parking

spring's water is distributed around Jericho's fields by a complex gravity-flow irrigation system.

Mount & Monastery of Temptation

Traditionally associated with the first and third temptations of Jesus by the Devil (Matthew 4: 1-11), the Crusaders called the mountain Mont Quarantana (Mount of Forty) which the Arabs modified to Qarantal.

Similar in style to St George's in the Wadi Qelt, the Greek Orthodox monastery clings to the cliff. Rebuilt around the same time (1874-1904), it dates back to the 12th century when two churches were constructed, one here and the other on the summit. Both are known to have been in ruins by the 14th century. The monastery is built around the original church which is believed to be the cave where Jesus fasted and refused to turn stones into bread. The stone on which he supposedly sat during the confrontation with the Devil is here.

Construction of a replacement church was started on the summit in 1874 with only the surrounding wall being completed. On this site in the 2nd century BC the Syrian General Baccides built the Castle of Dok and it was here that Simon Maccabaeus was assassinated by his son-in-law Ptolemy, the governor of Jericho, in 134 BC.

The mount is deceptively further north of

Neolithic skull

ancient Jericho than it looks, so give yourself plenty of time if walking or cycling. The summit is officially out of bounds but if you ask nicely (a sheqel or three sometimes does the trick) the attendant may let you through the back door of the monastery. It's well worth the extra 20-minute hike to the top for the knockout view of Jericho and the Jordan Valley, with the Dead Sea to the south and the Mount of Olives to the west. The combination of the view and the quiet stillness is superb.

In summer it's open Monday to Saturday, from 8 am to 5 pm (winter 7 am to 2 pm and 3 to 4 pm), and is closed Sunday. The cave-church is usually closed after 11 am.

Na'aran

About two km beyond the Mount of Temptation are the scanty remains of an ancient Jewish settlement. Close to the springs of Ein Duq, the 4th or 5th-century synagogue's mosaic floor is the highlight of the site.

Tours

Egged Tours include a brief visit to Jericho on a US$33 day tour from Jerusalem that also takes in the Dead Sea.

Places to Stay

The *Hisham Palace Hotel* (☎ 922414) on Ein es-Sultan St is the sole choice of accommodation in town. A large, shabby place, it offers small singles/doubles for US$18.

Bargaining should get you lower rates and, if you make the initial effort, the staff can be friendly and hospitable.

Places to Eat

In the town itself there are a few cafés and felafel/shishlik joints, but nothing outstanding. The best deal is at the *Temptation Restaurant* near ancient Jericho. Here you can help yourself from a good selection of salads (US$5) or meats (US$8) in pleasant and cool surroundings. The place across the road (with no English sign) is also good. Draught beer is served in chilled glasses and the felafel sandwiches, while not cheap, are large and delicious.

The garden restaurants on Ein es-Sultan St rarely seem to have enough trade to survive but they can be worth a splurge to enjoy Palestinian meat specialities and salads. Look out for the *Bedouin Tent Restaurant* with its bizarre water wheel based on a Drott mechanical digger.

The prices of the fruits attractively displayed outside the stores here are much higher than those in Jerusalem.

Getting There & Away
Arab bus No 28 runs daily from the Suleiman St station in East Jerusalem about every 20 minutes. The last bus leaves Jericho at about 4.30 pm. The faster Egged buses operate from Jerusalem's central bus station to pass through Jericho en route to Beit She'an and Tiberias. They can drop you off near the ancient archaeological site as they head north on Ein es-Sultan St. The returning buses can be flagged down here until late in the evening.

Service taxis operate from the rank opposite Jerusalem's Damascus Gate – US$3 for the pleasant 30-minute drive. In Jericho they operate from the town square, usually until about 5.30 pm. You can find taxis after this time but with a shortage of passengers you may have to fork out for a higher fare.

Getting Around
With the distance involved between the town and the sights, cycling is a popular mode of transport. The roads are relatively flat and traffic free, so decide for yourself whether the heat is easier to bear on foot or on the saddle of a rented boneshaker. The bicycle shop is on al-Madaras St, just off the town square. If you bargain hard, you should pay about US$5 for the day. A passport or a similar suitable document may be asked for as security.

AROUND JERICHO
Jesus' Baptism Site
You'll see old-style milestones pointing the way to the traditional site of Jesus' baptism on the Jordan River. With a picturesque 19th-century Greek Orthodox monastery nearby, it is unfortunately in a military zone normally out of bounds to visitors. Two exceptions are in January, when the Greek Orthodox celebrate Epiphany, and the third Thursday in October when the Roman Catholic Church is permitted to celebrate Jesus' baptism. Contact the Christian Information Centre in Jerusalem for details.

Dead Sea
Apart from special taxis, there is no direct public transport between Qumran, Ein Feshka and Jericho. You can change at the Almog junction, where the turn-off to Jericho intersects with the main road from Jerusalem. The Dead Sea is dealt with in a chapter of its own.

BETHLEHEM
(Population: 35,000)
For most travellers with a Christian background (however distant or remote), a trip to the Holy Land without visiting Bethlehem is unthinkable, even if only to please a pious relative back home. Rachel's Tomb, the romance between Ruth and Boaz, and Samuel's call to the shepherd-boy David to be King of Israel, all make Bethlehem sacred to the Jews.

Unfortunately, many visitors are disappointed by what they find here. Modern-day Bethlehem is a cynic's delight, with Manger Square, Manger St, Star St, Milk Grotto St, Shepherds' St, two Shepherds' Fields and three Christmases. The uninspiring Church of the Nativity marking the birthplace of Jesus is occupied by Christian factions who regularly fight over its possession. On top of all that is the argument that Mary and Joseph did not journey down from Nazareth to find that all the rooms in town were full, but were in fact locals. For thousands of pilgrims, however, these are mere technicalities which are secondary to the significance of simply being in this holy place.

After the almost mandatory visits to holy sites, there are excellent excursions just outside the town. Although disappointing

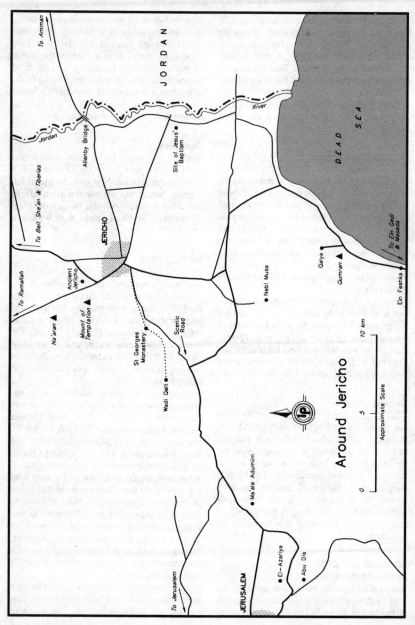

Around Jericho

Approximate Scale

0   5   10 km

itself, Bethlehem is beautifully located on the edge of the fertile Judean Hills and the barren Judean Desert.

More than making up for any disappointment with the town are sights such as Mar Saba Monastery in its stunning desert location; Herodion, the intriguing palace complex of Herod the Great which sits atop a volcano-like peak with outstanding views of the surrounding landscape; the pretty, neat terraces of Cremisan's vineyards and olive trees; and the attractive village of Beit Jalla. With Jerusalem's Jaffa Gate only 10 km to the north, it is all within easy reach.

History

First mentioned in the 14th century BC, Bethlehem is a well-known biblical town – Rachel the Matriarch died here (Genesis 35:19) and Ruth and Boaz romanced here (Ruth 1-4). It was through David that Bethlehem gained its initial importance. He was born here, a grandson of Ruth and Boaz, and worked as a shepherd until the prophet Samuel called him to be King of Israel (I Samuel 16).

Micah 5:1-2 prophesied the birth of the Messiah in Bethlehem and the birth of Jesus is held by Christians to have been its fulfilment. However, for almost two centuries after Jesus' death, Bethlehem was a centre of paganism. On 31 May 339, the town's first church was dedicated by Queen Helena on the site of today's Church of the Nativity and Bethlehem became a great monastic centre. It was here that St Jerome translated the Old and New Testaments into the Vulgate, the Catholics' authoritative version of the Bible (which remained so until the 20th century).

In keeping with the history of the land, Bethlehem has changed hands many times. The Romans, Byzantines, Arabs, Crusaders, Mamelukes, Turks, British and Jordanians have all preceded the current Israeli administration. Throughout these centuries of often hostile non-Christian rule, the town has remained a largely Christian community and a centre of pilgrimage. The skyline is today dominated by churches and an increasing number of mosques and, like Nazareth, Bethlehem is a centre of the Christian mission movement with convents, schools, monasteries, orphanages and hospitals.

Bethlehem & Bedlam

After defeating the Crusaders, Saladin allowed two Catholic priests and two deacons to return to Bethlehem. In 1247 the Bishop of Bethlehem travelled to England to beg for money and the Sheriff of London set up a hostel in Bishopsgate for the visiting clergy to stay in while they were there. It was later converted into a lunatic asylum and the name 'Bethlehem' was corrupted into 'Bedlam'.

Orientation

Bethlehem lies just to the east of the Jerusalem to Hebron road. Manger St intersects here, with Rachel's Tomb opposite, to wind south to Manger Square. This is the town centre, dominated by parked cars, tour buses and taxis, and here you will find the Church of the Nativity, tourist office, police station, post office, shops, hotels and eating places. Milk Grotto St heads off to the south-east, past the Milk Grotto Chapel. Paul VI St heads uphill to the north-west, with the museum, outdoor market and more shops and hotels along the network of winding streets.

The two Shepherds' Fields are almost two km east of the town, beyond the village of Beit Sahur. The monasteries of Theodosius and Mar Saba lie seven km east (and then another seven km further east), with Herodion eight km to the south. The village of Beit Jalla lies west of Hebron Rd, with Cremisan beyond it, up the steep hill.

Information

Tourist Office The IGTO (☎ 742591) is on the west side of Manger Square next to the post office. It's open Monday to Friday, from 8 am to 5 pm (summer), 8 am to 4 pm (winter), Saturday 8 am to 1 pm, and is closed Sunday. During Ramadan the hours are Saturday to Thursday 9 am to 2.30 pm, closed Friday.

Bethlehem

0   150   300 m

To Jerusalem

Hebron Road

To Hebron

Children Street

S O S Road

Manger Street

Star Street

Orient Star

al-Baten Street

Paul VI Street

Star Street

Manger Street

Beit Sahur Street

Shepherds Street

Atan Street

Farahiya Street

Milk Grotto Street

To Shepherd's Fields & Herodian

1	Rachel's Tomb
2	Petrol Station
3	Zsu Zsu Restaurant
4	Paradise Hotel
5	SOS Children's Village
6	The Holy Land Christian Mission
7	St Joseph's Pension
8	King David Cinema
9	King David's Well
10	Handal Hotel
11	Bethlehem Star Hotel
12	Petrol Station
13	Bus Station
14	Lawrence Restaurant & Hamburger House
15	Museum
16	Police
17	Palace Hotel
18	Casa Nova Hospice
19	Greek Orthodox Convent
20	Market
21	Manger Square
22	Minibuses to Solomon's Pools
23	Church of the Nativity
24	Tourist Office
25	Post Office
26	Al-Andalus Hotel
27	Coptic Orthodox Church
28	Armenian Convent
29	Franciscan Convent Pension
30	Milk Grotto Chapel

account of their long journey to Bethlehem, and their failure to find suitable accommodation. Luke 2:7, which reads 'she laid him in a manger because there was no place for them in the inn', in the Greek translation can be taken as 'she laid him in a manger because they had no space in the room'.

Many homes in Bethlehem were, and still are, built in front of caves. Although the gospels don't mention a cave, 2nd-century historians do speak of the cave in which Jesus was born. Therefore, it is suggested that Joseph and Mary, probably living with Joseph's parents, used the rear area of the house where the birth took place. Such a cave would have been used as an animal shelter in bad weather.

Church of the Nativity

Probably even more of a disappointment to visitors than the Church of the Holy Sepulchre, this is, nonetheless, generally agreed to be the likeliest site of the nativity. One of the world's oldest churches, it is built like a citadel over the cave where it is believed that Jesus was born.

Emperor Constantine's 4th-century church was altered considerably by Emperor Justinian around 530. His aim was to create a major shrine that would overshadow all others, including those in Jerusalem. Apart from the roof and the floor, which have been replaced several times, the basic structure of his church has remained in use to the present day.

On 6 June 1099, the Crusaders captured the church, a major prize. They crowned their kings here and between 1165 and 1169 and embarked on a major restoration programme, renewing the interior decoration and replacing the roof. Under Saladin the church was respectfully preserved, but with his defeat by the Mamelukes in the 13th century came the start of a long period of abuse which lasted right through to the end of the Ottoman period at the beginning of the 20th century. Infrequent repairs and systematic looting, along with an earthquake in 1834 and a fire in 1869 that destroyed the cave's furnishings, all took their toll.

In winter, the church is open daily from 8 am to 5 pm (7 am to 6 pm in summer), and admission is free. The adjoining Church of St Catherine and the underground caves are closed daily from noon to 2 pm.

Post & Telecommunications These facilities can be found on the west side of Manger Square, next to the tourist office, and are open Monday to Saturday 8 am to 5 pm, and are closed on Sunday. During Ramadan the hours are Monday to Thursday and Saturday 9 am to 3 pm, and it is closed Friday and Sunday.

Other There are banks on Manger Square and on Paul VI and Manger Sts. The police station (☎ 741581, 100) is on Manger Square as well.

Away in a Manger & All That

Contrary to the popular version of the nativity, it is strongly argued that Mary and Joseph were natives of Bethlehem, not Nazareth, and that they only moved to Galilee to escape the clutches of Herod's son on their return from Egypt. This interpretation of Matthew 2 claims that Luke was mistaken in his

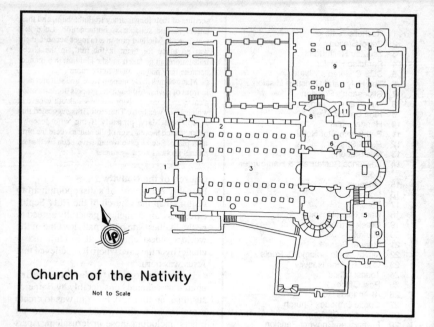

Church of the Nativity

Not to Scale

1 The main entrance to the church is through a small door. This is one of three 6th-century entrances, the others have been blocked up. The Crusaders first reduced its size to prevent attackers from riding in. Later, either during the Mameluke or the Ottoman period, it was made even smaller to prevent looters from driving their carts inside.

2 If there is a long queue of visitors slowly working its way through the tiny main entrance, you can save time by taking the entrance to the left and turning right as you come out onto the cloistered courtyard. The door here leads into the church.

3 The red limestone pillars here may date back to the original 4th-century church. They were decorated by individual Crusaders with paintings of saints. Wooden trapdoors are usually left open to reveal the original 4th-century mosaic floor.

4 Exit to the Greek Orthodox Monastery.

5 Greek Orthodox Monastery.

6 Entrances to the Grotto of the Nativity.

7 Armenian Chapel.

8 Entrance to the Church of St Catherine.

9 The Franciscan Church of St Catherine was built in 1881. It is here that the Midnight Mass is held on 24 December and broadcast around the world.

10 Entrance to the caves.

11 Statue of St Mary.

Battle of Bethlehem

More than any other shrine in the Holy Land, the Church of the Nativity is the centre of a bitter struggle between the various Christian factions over the rights of possession as expressed in the 'status quo'.

The Greek Orthodox, the Armenians, and the Roman Catholics grudgingly share the church. The fact that they each celebrate Christmas at different times indicates how well they get along.

Over the centuries, blood has been spilled on more than one occasion in the dispute over the church. The Greek Orthodox-controlled Grotto of the Nativity is still blocked off by a thick steel door which was designed to keep out the Roman Catholics.

In recent years, the most talked about dispute has been between the Greeks and the Armenians. This involves the system of cleaning, or sweeping, the church. By common consent, sweeping is the symbol of ownership in the holy places – therefore, if a member of one faction touches an area that is claimed by another, all hell breaks loose, if you'll pardon the expression. In this case, the sweeping of an area of wall above the entrance to the grotto is the problem. The Armenians object to the Greeks climbing up a ladder, perching on a beam and sweeping this particular strip of once-white masonry. On 29 December, the 'Annual General Cleaning Day', tempers tend to get rather frayed. In 1984 there were violent clashes as Greek and Armenian clergy fought running battles with staves and chains that had been hidden beneath their robes. Amidst accusations and counter accusations of 'bully boys' being hired for the day to take part in the violence, the Jewish authorities frantically tried to find a diplomatic solution.

The result was that the Greeks were able to sweep, but without actually walking along the beam. The Greek Patriarch was not happy and wrote a stiff letter of protest to the Israeli Governor of Judea and Samaria – the 'status quo' continues to be a cause of controversy.

Milk Grotto Chapel

A few minutes' walk along Milk Grotto St on the south side, this Franciscan chapel is where tradition has it that the Holy Family sheltered on their way to Egypt. It is said that while Mary was breast-feeding the baby Jesus, some of the milk fell to the floor. According to some versions of the tradition, this caused the rock out of which the cavern is built to turn chalky white. Women come here to pray in the belief that the white stone helps their lactation, and packets of the powdered stone are sold to pilgrims. The chapel is open daily 8 to 11.45 am and 2 to 5 pm. Admission is free; for attention, ring the bell in the courtyard.

Bethlehem Museum

On Paul VI St, just up from Manger Square and on the north side, this small museum has exhibits of traditional Palestinian crafts and costumes. It's open Monday to Saturday 10 am to noon and 2.30 to 5.30 pm, and is closed Sunday. Admission is US$1.

Market

Across from the Syrian Orthodox Church on Paul VI St, a short way up from Manger Square, the market is a small affair with stalls catering to the everyday needs of locals rather than tourists.

King David Cinema & King David's Well

On Star St, about half a km north of Manger

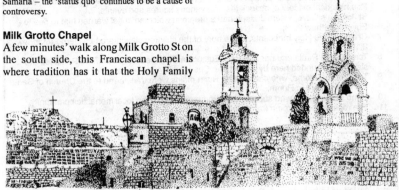

Basilica of Nativity

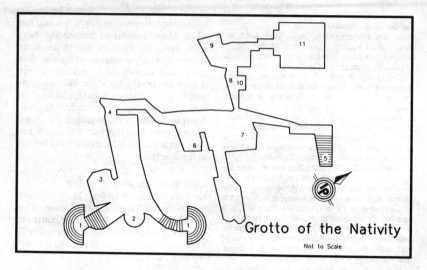

Grotto of the Nativity

Not to Scale

1 Entrances from the church above.
2 The site of the nativity, marked by a star. The Latin inscription reads Hic De Virgine Maria Jesus Christus Natus Est (Here Jesus Christ was born of the Virgin Mary). Kissed by many pilgrims, the star and its inscription were installed by the Catholics in 1717. The Greeks removed them in 1847, but were ordered to put them back by the Turkish authorities in 1853. The quarrel over the star was one of the causes of the Crimean War (1853-56) when Russia fought against Turkey, Britain and France.
3 Here is where Jesus supposedly 'laid in a manger'. The actual manger believed to have been used is now kept in the Church of Santa Maria Maggiore in Rome.
4 Normally the gate here is locked. To reach the nearby caves, head back up the stairs to the church and use the other entrance in the Church of St Catherine.
5 These steps inside the Church of St Catherine lead down to caves which tradition, with little historical evidence, associates with various figures and events.
6 St Joseph's Cave, where Joseph had a dream in which an angel warned him to flee to Egypt (Matthew 2:13).
7 Chapel of the Holy Innocents, in memory of the children slaughtered by Herod (Matthew 2:16).
8 Tombs of St Paula and her daughter Eustochia. A noble Roman woman, Paula led the sisterhood founded here by St Jerome. She died in 404, her daughter in 419.
9 Tomb of St Jerome, who died in 420. His remains were transferred to the Church of Santa Maria Maggiore in Rome.
10 Tomb of Eusebius, who succeeded Jerome as head of the local monastic community.
11 The room where Jerome translated the Bible.

Square, the King David Cinema presents a film, *Jesus*, which is a virtual word-for-word dramatisation of Luke's gospel. Poorly acted and directed, the film isn't as wonderful an experience as the Christian organisation responsible for it would have you believe.

Even more of a nonevent are the three restored water cisterns in the car park outside the cinema. They are associated with II Samuel 23:13-17 which relates the tale of the thirsty David offering the water to God as a sacrifice.

Rachel's Tomb

One of Judaism's most sacred shrines, also revered by Muslims and Christians, this is the tomb of the matriarch Rachel, wife of Jacob and mother of Benjamin (Genesis 35:19-20). Inside a plain, whitewashed building built by Sir Moses Montefiore in 1860, the tomb attracts people who pray for fertility and a safe birth. You will often find Sephardic Jewish women here weeping and praying.

It's at the intersection of Hebron Rd and Manger St and all buses between Jerusalem, Bethlehem and Hebron pass by. It is open Sunday to Thursday 8 am to 5 pm, Friday 8 am to 1 pm, and is closed Saturday. Admission is free; men must cover their heads, and cardboard yarmulkas are provided.

Places to Stay

Bethlehem's accommodation choice is somewhat limited (some things never change) and at Christmas and Easter you will need to plan ahead to be sure of a place to stay. Most people prefer to stay in Jerusalem with its wider choice and often lower prices.

Along Milk Grotto St, beyond the chapel, you'll find the *Franciscan Convent Pension* (☎ 742441). The pleasant nuns provide basic but clean and comfortable accommodation. Dorm beds are US$6, and when they're full floor space is US$3.50. Singles or doubles are US$15 per person, with breakfast included. Curfew is 9 pm for men, and 8 pm for women.

Near the King David Cinema, *St Joseph's Pension* (☎ 742483), on Manger St, is run by friendly Syrian Catholics. Singles or doubles are about US$10 per person, floor space when full can be negotiated for about US$3.50. Curfew is 11 pm.

Part of the Church of the Nativity complex is the recently renovated Franciscan *Casa Nova Hospice*. This lovely place is the nicest

looking in town but you will often have to deal with the holy bureaucracy of the staff to get in. Great facilities and good food make it worth the effort. It costs US$23 for half board, US$26 for full board plus a 15% surcharge in busy periods. Curfew is at 11 pm.

The *Al-Andalus Hotel* (☎ 741348) is upstairs on Manger Square. It has clean rooms and facilities but it's a bit depressing. Singles/doubles are US$18/32, with breakfast included. Curfew is at 11 pm. Expect to pay about 25% more at Christmas.

On Manger St, just down from the Church of the Nativity, the *Palace Hotel* (☎ 742798) was built by the Greek Orthodox. It's a bit rundown but is clean, and has singles/doubles for US$22/32. In the quiet summer months you can bargain for less.

There are some more hotels among the narrow streets to the north-west of Manger Square off Paul VI St. The *Bethlehem Star* (☎ 743249) on al-Baten St, has singles/doubles for US$18/32, with breakfast included. The *Handal* (☎ 742494) has singles/doubles for US$18/30, with breakfast included. Add 20% extra to these prices for Christmas and Easter.

Places to Eat

Bethlehem in Hebrew is Beit Lechem (House of Bread), and in Arabic Beit Lahem (House of Meat).

A few felafel merchants compete on the steps leading up from Manger St to Manger Square. Try the market or the various grocery stores nearby for provisions. The *Reem Restaurant*, down the side street past the bakery on Paul VI St, is inexpensive with hummus and other salads for about US$1.50.

For cheap draught beer head north along Manger St to the *Hamburger House*; the proprietor is a Palestinian who recently returned from Chile. Between the bus station and Manger Square, the *Lawrence Restaurant* serves good home-made burgers with salad and chips for US$2.50. The beer glasses are chilled, which is never a bad sign. Lawrence is an artist who specialises in mother-of-pearl and has had exhibitions of his work.

One of the best meat restaurants anywhere is *Zsu Zsu*, next to the Nissan Store on Manger St, down from Rachel's Tomb. Named after the extrovert proprietor, you can enjoy some of the tastiest shishlik and kebabs you're likely to find around here. Look at spending US$6 to US$12 per person.

Getting There & Away
Arab bus No 22 runs frequently from East Jerusalem and stops outside Jaffa Gate en route. Its about a 40-minute ride. Service taxis from outside Damascus Gate take half that time. The last bus leaves Bethlehem at about 6 pm; taxis can be found after this time but you will often have to pay a special price due to a lack of fellow passengers.

Arab bus No 23, running between Jerusalem and Hebron, passes by Rachel's Tomb, as do Egged buses that go to Hebron and Qiryat Arba.

As it is so close, walking from Jerusalem to Bethlehem is a popular option. At Christmas there is an official procession, but the two to 2½-hour, downhill-all-the-way hike is pleasant all year round. Follow Hebron Rd out past the Jerusalem railway station and eventually you will emerge into the country-side. Pass the Greek Orthodox Elias Monastery and you will see Bethlehem ahead of you.

Getting Around
With the exception of Rachel's Tomb, the sights are within easy walking distance of the bus station and taxi rank. If you want to visit the tomb, it is perhaps best, if coming from Jerusalem, to stop here, rather than stay with the bus or taxi to the town centre. With the frequent bus service, you can then easily continue to the centre to see the other places of interest.

Christmas is Cancelled
To protest against Israeli policy in combatting the intifada, the local Christian hierarchy have cancelled Bethlehem's traditional Christmas festivities in recent years. Even before the intifada, Christmas Eve in Bethlehem meant enduring a very tight security setup with checkpoints, body frisks, IDF patrols, marksmen on rooftops, etc.

Check with Jerusalem's Christian Information Centre for current details of the Christmas celebrations in Bethlehem.

AROUND BETHLEHEM
Beit Jalla, Gillo & Cremisan
Past Rachel's Tomb in the direction of Hebron, a road heads west up the hill to the pleasant Christian Arab village of Beit Jalla. The road continues to the summit of Har Gillo, believed to be biblical Gillo, the home of King David's counsellor, Anhithophel. With great views of Jerusalem it is a popular picnic site. Back down the slope, a sideroad leads to the attractive Salesian monastery of Cremisan (☎ 742605), renowned for its wine and olive oil.

Getting There & Away Arab bus No 21 runs from Jerusalem to Beit Jalla. From here it is a steep walk to either the summit or the monastery.

Ruth's Field & Shepherds' Fields
The village of Beit Sahur stands one km east of Bethlehem. Nearby, the Field of Ruth is traditionally associated with the events of the Old Testament Book of Ruth. In Hebrew, Beit Sahur means 'Village of the Watching' and the Roman Catholics and the Greek Orthodox each have their own Shepherds' Field associated with the shepherds mentioned in Luke 2:8-18.

The Roman Catholic site features a Franciscan chapel built in 1954, designed to resemble a shepherd's tent. There are ruins of a Byzantine monastery nearby, destroyed by the Persians in 614.

The Greek Orthodox site features a 5th-century church built over a cave with a mosaic floor. Often closed, there is an admission fee of US$2 when the caretaker is there to let you in.

Getting There & Away Arab bus No 47 leaves from Manger St by the police station for Beit Sahur. The respective fields are about a 20-minute walk further east from the village, beyond the fork in the road. Take the right fork for the Greek Orthodox field, left for the Roman Catholic.

Alternatively, you can walk the three or four km from Bethlehem.

Mar Saba Monastery

One of the most impressive buildings in the Holy Land because of its combination of architecture and location, this Greek Orthodox monastery is strictly closed to women, but the outside alone is worth a visit.

The monastery is on the steep bank of the Kidron River in the proverbial middle of nowhere, which in this case is the Judean Desert. Unless you have your own car, you will have to walk the eight km from where the bus stops in the village of Abusiye.

Just before the last stop there is another monastery. Overlooking Abusiye, the large Monastery of Theodosius or Deir Dosi is built over a cave where the three wise men supposedly rested on their way home from Bethlehem. It was founded by St Theodosius and accommodated 400 monks by the time he died in 529. Restored in 1893, only one monk and a nun live here now (they are genuinely brother and sister, I am told), and they will often refuse access. There is little to see anyway; some 7th-century mosaics and skulls of monks massacred by Persians are stored underground.

Mar Saba Monastery was founded in 482 by St Sabas (439-532). He had been living in a cave (look for the cross and letters A and C on the opposite side of the wadi), but with an increasing number of disciples he needed more room. The Persians massacred the occupants in 614 but the monastery managed to continue, with its 'golden age' occurring in the 8th and 9th centuries. However, until as recently as the 19th century the monks were still subjected to hostility, occasionally resulting in murderous attacks. After an earthquake in 1834 caused considerable damage the buildings were almost completely reconstructed, hence their impressive appearance today.

The body of St Sabas is displayed in the main church. It had been removed by the Crusaders but was returned by Pope Paul VI in 1965. More skulls of monks massacred by the Persians can also be seen. The adjacent Tower of St Simeon, built in 1612, is sometimes open to women and a path runs past here down into the wadi, which is rather smelly (courtesy of the Jerusalemites who use the river as a sewer). You should make a point of crossing over to the other side for the superb view of the monastery. It is mainly this that makes the hot hike worthwhile. There were some 5000 men living over here in the caves before the monastery was built.

To enter the monastery, pull the bell chain by the blue door. To enter, you must be suitably dressed (and of acceptable sex) – with the heat it's best to bring long pants to slip over shorts when on arrival. There are no set opening hours and the monks will normally let you in. However, on Sunday and at mealtimes your rings may be ignored. Saturday is relatively busy with an influx of other visitors, so a morning visit during the week is best.

Getting There & Away Take Arab bus No 60 from Bethlehem bus station to Ubudiyeh, the last stop, or get off by the Monastery of Theodosius. The last bus back to Bethlehem leaves Ubudiyeh at about 4 pm. From here follow the road east. After one km it forks; take the left branch. You will be hassled by children demanding baksheesh until you leave the outskirts of the village.

The six-km walk takes 1½ to two hours each way. Bring plenty of water – you can get a refill from the monastery for the return. Hitchhiking is possible, although there is little traffic, and you will be especially grateful of a ride for the steep climb back from the monastery.

Warning

Due to the strong anti-Israeli sentiments of the local villagers, many incidents of stone throwing have been reported by tourists visiting both the Shepherds' Fields and Mar Saba. It is, therefore, strongly recommended that you check with the tourist offices in Jerusalem before setting out to see if the situation has improved. For Mar Saba, consider joining an organised tour such as those operated by the SPNI or Metzoke Dragot (see the Dead Sea chapter).

Herodion

Built by Herod the Great between 24 and 15 BC, the Herodion palace complex occupies the top of a hill reshaped as part of the construction programme. About 100 metres above the surrounding area and looking rather like a volcano, it offers more great views and the remains of the citadel.

A lavish and luxurious place in its day, a stairway of white marble led up to the ring of round towers enclosing apartments, baths and a garden. It is not certain whether Herod was buried here as he had instructed. During the First Revolt (66 to 70 AD) the Jewish rebels attacked the Herodion and sheltered here. During the Second Revolt (132 to 135) they used it as an administrative centre. In the 5th century, Byzantine monks established a monastery among the ruins.

The site is open April to September, Saturday to Thursday 8 am to 5 pm, and Friday 8 am to 4 pm; October to March, Saturday to Thursday 8 am to 4 pm, and Friday 8 am to 3 pm; and admission is US$3 (students US$1.50).

Getting There & Away The Bethlehem tourist office often seems to indicate that you can only reach the Herodion by taxi. Although infrequent, there are buses that can drop you near the site. Ask a few locals and use the most popular answer to determine which bus and when. Bus No 52 was the one I caught, but on a previous visit I took No 47 from Manger St to Beit Sahur and changed there. Egged bus No 66 also stops nearby.

Another alternative is simply to walk and hitchhike. The Herodion stands about eight km south of Beit Sahur – take the right fork past the Greek Orthodox Shepherds' Field.

Wadi Khareitun

Two km south-west of the Herodion the road crosses a wadi where you can see some prehistoric caves – follow the path on the right-hand side to get a good view as the wadi deepens. Continue for three km to the end of

the path and you will come across the ruins of a Byzantine monastery established in the 4th century by St Chariton and remaining in use up to the 12th or 13th century.

Still occupied by Bedouin, the first cave was home to prehistoric families from around 80,000 BC. The second cave has not

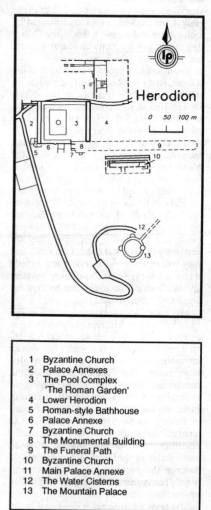

1   Byzantine Church
2   Palace Annexes
3   The Pool Complex
    'The Roman Garden'
4   Lower Herodion
5   Roman-style Bathhouse
6   Palace Annexe
7   Byzantine Church
8   The Monumental Building
9   The Funeral Path
10 Byzantine Church
11 Main Palace Annexe
12 The Water Cisterns
13 The Mountain Palace

been excavated, but the third cave is the most important. This cave provides archaeologists with the earliest evidence of the use of fire in Palestine and was first occupied in the Lower Palaeolithic period (500,000 to 120,000 BC).

BETHLEHEM TO HEBRON
Solomon's Pools
Eight km south of Beit Jalla, a turn-off to the east leads to these large reservoirs and a Turkish fort. The trees and shrubs helped to make this a popular picnic site before the intifada, and there is a café here.

Legend associates the pools with Solomon (Ecclesiastes 2:6); others date them to Herod. The aqueducts supplied Jerusalem with water right up to the early years of the State of Israel. The fort was built around 1540 to defend the water supply.

Getting There & Away From Manger St, Bethlehem, take Arab minibus No 1 to Dashit, the nearby Arab village. You could also take Arab bus No 23 or the Egged buses which run between Jerusalem and Hebron.

Kefar Etzion
Continuing south to Hebron, after seven km a sideroad to the right leads to Kefar Etzion, a religious kibbutz. First established by religious Zionists in 1943, it was destroyed by the Arabs in 1948 and most of the settlers were killed. In 1967 the settlement was re-established, with some of the new settlers being the children of those killed almost 20 years before.

There is a museum here highlighting the history of Jewish settlement in the Etzion region, which is the Judean hills between Jerusalem and Hebron.

Frequent Egged buses from Jerusalem go to the kibbutz.

Halhoul
Just outside Hebron, the main road passes through the small Arab village of Halhoul. The Tombs of Nathan and Gad (I Chronicles 29:29) are located here.

HEBRON
(Population: 70,000)
As the burial place of Abraham, Isaac and Jacob, the city of Hebron is holy to Jews, Muslim and Christians. The Cave of Machpelah/Tomb of the Patriarchs, the main focal point for locals and visitors alike, plays no small part in making the predominantly Arab city a centre of fierce opposition to the Jewish occupation in general and to Jewish settlement in Hebron in particular.

As well as this important shrine, Hebron is worth a visit for its interesting old quarter with one of the country's most colourful and authentic markets. Due to the controversial re-establishment of a Jewish community in Hebron, along with the problems of Jews and Muslims having to share such a major shrine, tensions in the city are worse than in, say, Bethlehem or Jericho.

Note that there are no suitable places to stay in Hebron.

History
Evidence has been found of a settlement in Hebron around 2000 BC making it one of the oldest cities in the world. It was at Hebron that God made a covenant with Abraham that he would be the father of the Chosen People (Genesis 17). When his wife Sarah died, Abraham purchased the Cave of Machpelah and the field in which it stood from Ephron the Hittite as a burial place, paying 400 silver sheqels (Genesis 23). When Abraham died, his sons Ishmael and Isaac buried him here as well. Isaac and his wife, Rebecca, were also buried here, as were Jacob and his wife Leah (Genesis 49:29-32; 50:7-9, 12-14).

Numbers 13:17-33 tells of the spies sent by Moses who came to Hebron and returned carrying grapes and other fruits from the region, and II Samuel tells of David's consecration and reign as king in Hebron and of Absalom's rebellion.

The Cave of Machpelah dominates Hebron's history and the succession of conquerors have left their mark. Throughout the centuries a small Jewish community had existed in relative peace amongst the Arabs. However, the late 19th century saw the start

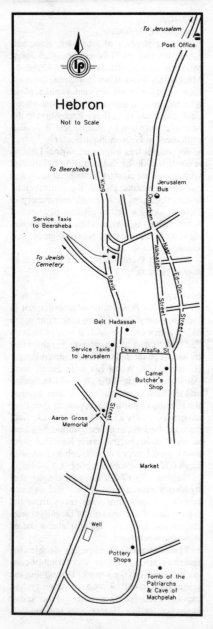

Hebron

Not to Scale

To Jerusalem
Post Office

To Beersheba

King Omaher St

Jerusalem Bus

Service Taxis to Beersheba

Naser Alkhetib

Ed-Din Street

To Jewish Cemetery

David Street

Beit Hadassah

Service Taxis to Jerusalem

Ekwan Alsafia St

Camel Butcher's Shop

Street

Aaron Gross Memorial

Market

Well

Pottery Shops

Tomb of the Patriarchs & Cave of Machpelah

of political Zionism and Hebron's Jewish population increased with the arrival of immigrants from Eastern Europe. In the wave of Arab riots that swept Palestine in August 1929 the violence in Hebron was especially fierce.

The majority of the Jews were killed and the few survivors were forced to abandon the city and were evacuated to Jerusalem.

After the Israeli victory in the Six Day War, some religious Jews were keen to re-establish a Jewish presence in Hebron, regardless of the fierce opposition from fellow Jews as well as Arabs. However, the Israeli Government banned Jews from settling in Hebron, not wanting to cause further upheaval. This served merely to make these religious Jews even more determined. Unable to live in the city, they eventually reached a compromise with the government and in 1972 established Qiryat Arba, a large settlement right on the edge of Hebron, just one km from the Cave of Machpelah. Not surprisingly, this development did not go down at all well with the Arabs. The Jewish settlers were also far from satisfied with this situation – they still wanted to live in Hebron proper, regardless of the obvious danger of violent resistance from the Arabs.

In 1979 Miriam Levinger, mother of 11 and one of the original Jewish settlers, led a group of women and children from Qiryat Arba into the city and illegally occupied the dilapidated Beit Hadassah, Hebron's old Hadassah Hospital in the ruined Jewish Quarter.

They refused to leave, and their eight-month 'sit-in' in protest at the government's policy succeeded in securing official permission for Jews to live in Beit Hadassah, a decision that eventually led to Jewish settlement in Hebron proper being allowed. These events were surrounded by much controversy and tragic violence, highlighted by the murder of six yeshiva students by Arabs in 1980 and revenge attacks by Jewish terrorists, whose subsequent capture and imprisonment caused further controversy.

There are about 40 Jewish families living in Hebron, surrounded by hostile Arab neighbours and you will see the odd Israeli flag draped outside a building in defiance of their opposition. Despite the hardships of living under such conditions there is a waiting list of Jews wanting to join them. Meanwhile the local Arabs seem to be more and more resentful of what they see as an invasion of their home and the ever-present patrols, watchtowers and checkpoints of the IDF.

Orientation & Information

The main areas of interest – the Cave of Machpelah, the Jewish Quarter and the market – are within easy walking distance of each other and of the bus stops and taxi ranks. The post office, bank, and police station (☎ 97144, 100) are on King David St, further north.

Bearing in mind the political climate and the religious traditions of Hebron, visitors should act and dress sensibly.

Cave of Machpelah & Tomb of the Patriarchs (Haram el-Khalil)

Sacred to all three monotheistic faiths, to Jews it is second only to Jerusalem's Western Wall and to Muslims it comes second in the Holy Land only to Jerusalem's Haram esh-Sharif.

Meaning 'double-cave', the name Cave of Machpelah leads visitors into expecting something quite different from the large, imposing structure that resembles a fortress. It stands over the cave purchased by Abraham because according to tradition he learned through divine inspiration that Adam and Eve were buried here. His wife, himself, his sons and their wives (except Ruth) were also buried here.

Around 20 BC, Herod the Great sealed off the cave and built the haram. Legend has it that King Solomon, assisted by *jinns* (Muslim genie-like spirits) did the work. You can see the chiselled borders of the massive Herodion stones. The original building had no roof, and by the southern wall of the Hall of Isaac you can see the Herodion rain-gutter carved into the stone floor.

The exact location of the cave underneath

the shrine is not known. The stone cenotaphs were only designed to represent the tombs and do not necessarily reflect their true location. A popular theory is that they lie underneath the cenotaph of Abraham.

In the late 6th century a Byzantine church was created here by enclosing the Hall of Isaac. Jews were permitted to build a synagogue in what is now the courtyard between the Hall of Isaac and the cenotaphs of Jacob and Leah. The church was converted into a mosque after the Arab conquest of 638, but the synagogue remained.

When the Crusaders conquered Hebron in 1100 they destroyed the synagogue, converted the mosque back into a church and massacred the Jews and Muslims.

When the Mamelukes conquered the city in 1260 they converted the church back into a mosque and permitted Jews to return to Hebron, but still denied them access to the haram. Instead, Jews could go no further than the seventh step on the eastern outer wall. This stairway was destroyed after 1967 when Jews were able to enter for the first time in centuries but you can still just about see where it was – the wall is blackened by candle smoke. The Mamelukes built the mosque and tomb of Joseph, and closed for good the entrance to the cave which had been explored by the Crusaders.

The shrine's status remained relatively unchanged until 1967. Since the 1929 massacre there had been no Jews in Hebron, and the Jewish settlers are keen to tell of how the first Jew re-entered the shrine. On Wednesday 7 June 1967, the IDF had conquered Jerusalem's Old City during the day, and Bethlehem that evening. They camped at Kefar Etzion in readiness to advance onto Hebron. At dawn, the army's chief chaplain, Rabbi Goren tried to find the officer who would lead the troops into the city, wanting to be the very first Jew to return to Hebron. Unable to find him, the rabbi ordered his driver to proceed ahead of the army. They arrived in Hebron to find the streets deserted with white flags of surrender hanging from most of the windows. The Arab population, presumably in view of the Jewish victories elsewhere and the likelihood of a fierce and bloody battle due to previous confrontations in Hebron, had decided not to fight. In what has been described as the most unusual victory of the Six Day War, the chaplain 'conquered' Hebron.

Under the surrender agreement supervised by Moshe Dayan, Israeli Defence Minister in 1967, the administration of the shrine has remained under Muslim control, with equal Jewish access permitted. The area still remains under military supervision with IDF soldiers on permanent guard.

The Djaouliyeh Mosque was built in 1320

and leads into the courtyard. Its present layout is due to the Mamelukes who constructed the cenotaphs of Jacob and Leah in the 14th century. In 1967 the Israelis installed the synagogue separating the 9th-century cenotaphs of Abraham and Sarah. In the Hall of Isaac, the mosque that had previously been a Byzantine and a Crusader church, a well-like hole is the sole entrance to the underground passage that is above the cave. Each morning the Muslims lower a lamp down here. The Crusaders' entrance was sealed in 1394.

Next to the mihrab is a lovely minbar

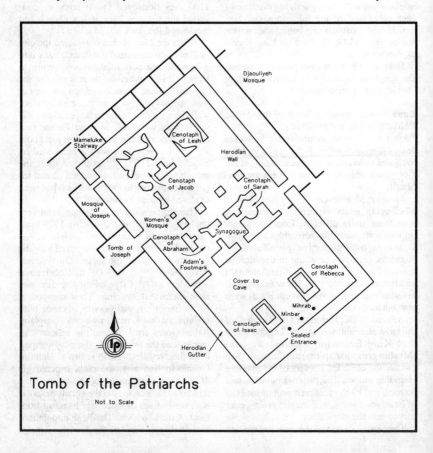

Tomb of the Patriarchs

Not to Scale

carved out of wood. Made in 1091 for a mosque in Ashkelon, it was donated by Saladin in 1191. The cenotaphs of Isaac and Rebecca were installed by the Mamelukes in 1332, along with the marble frieze. The 14th-century women's mosque includes a small shrine where Arab legend has it that Adam prayed so much that his foot left a mark in the stone. Nearby, another mosque contains the cenotaph of Joseph.

The site is open Saturday to Thursday 11 am to 7 pm, and is closed Friday (except for Muslims). Admission is free; cardboard yarmulkas are provided and suitable clothing must be worn. During the daily Muslim prayers, access to the mosques is limited to Muslims only, though free access to the rest of the building remains.

Jewish Community of Hebron

The religious Jews so keen to re-establish the Jewish presence in Hebron are labelled extremists, warmongers and worse by their critics, many of whom are fellow Jews. They are certainly well organised, as shown by their success in establishing Qiryat Arba and reversing the government's policy regarding the Jewish presence in Hebron.

The Jewish Community of Hebron (JCH) is their representative body whose basic aim is to promote and develop their cause. An active public relations department publishes a newsletter, *Hebron Today*, and offers tours of the city to show what they are trying to achieve. They also lobby politicians and prospective supporters in the Diaspora for financial, political and spiritual support.

Whether you are Jewish or not and whether you agree, disagree or have no opinion at all on the subject, it is well worth trying to join one of Gary Cooperberg's guided tours of Hebron to hear the settlers' argument and see for yourself the places involved.

In his capacity as PR Director of Hesder Yeshiva, a part of the Nir College of Judaic Studies in Qiryat Arba, Gary offers these tours primarily to the school's benefactors. Subject to availability, travellers are welcome to join his groups so write or call

for his current schedule: PO Box 107, Qiryat Arba, 90100 (☎ 961775/6; fax 961778 office; ☎ 961813 home). These tours last two to three hours, starting no later than 10 am. Give him as much notice as possible.

For large groups, he charges US$10 per person, which includes lunch. With enough advance notice, Gary will do a private tour, charging about US$100. Payable to the yeshiva and split between a few curious travellers, this is good value.

The re-established Jewish community is centred on four main areas within the city centre:

Beit Hadassah Complex On King David St, this was the Hadassah Hospital, forced to close in 1929. It has been restored and converted into JCH offices, a museum and residential apartments.

Next door to the left, Beit Chason was, until 1929, the home of Ben-Zion Gershon, the pharmacist-doctor of the hospital who had the downstairs apartment, and Rabbi Chason, former Chief Rabbi of Hebron, who lived upstairs. This, too, has been renovated and converted into new apartments.

To the right, Beit Hashisha is a new building erected in memory of the six yeshiva students killed by terrorists in 1980. Next door is the Beit Shneerson building.

Jewish Quarter Centred around the 16th-century Avraham Avinu Synagogue, the Jewish Quarter, abandoned after the 1929 massacre and destroyed by the Jordanians in 1948, is now being restored.

Beit Romano Constructed in 1867 as a rest-home for elderly Jews, this later became a yeshiva. The Jordanians used it as a girls' school. Today it is the home of the Shavei Hebron Yeshiva, also established in memory of Jewish victims of Arab terrorists. Families as well as students now live here.

Admot Yishai Close to the ancient Jewish cemetery, this is the latest settlement in Hebron. Believed to be the site of the original

Jewish settlement in the city, its name is derived from the belief that Yishai, David's father, was buried nearby.

Market

Hebron's market is made special by the authentic Middle East scenes that can be observed here. With the marvellous backdrop of Crusader and Mameluke facades, vaulted ceilings, tiny shops and narrow alleyways, crowds of Arabs go about their everyday business, many in traditional clothes.

Among the most unusual/revolting things to see/avoid is the butcher's shop selling camel meat. The ship of the desert can be seen moored to a meat hook, with that expression of nonchalance still on his face, hanging upside down while his intestines and feet are arranged on the shop floor to be sold separately.

Birket el-Sultan

An unattractive well or reservoir just west of the Cave of Machpelah, the Pool of the Sultan, is believed by some to be where David hanged the assassins of Saul's son (II Samuel 4:12). It is now empty of water and has become an unofficial rubbish dump.

Places to Eat

Take your pick from the various establishments around the market and the felafel and foul carts.

Those who are interested can eat camel meat. Ask the butcher which restaurant he has recently sold meat to – don't ask at the restaurants themselves, they'll say anything to make you buy something.

Getting There & Away

Arab bus No 23 operates regularly between Jerusalem and Hebron via Rachel's Tomb at Bethlehem. Egged also have less regular buses which go via Qiryat Arba. For only a little more, service taxis operate between Hebron and Jerusalem (opposite Damascus Gate) and are quicker and more comfortable.

They also operate less frequently to and from Beersheba.

AROUND HEBRON

Qiryat Arba

(Population: 5000)

The name of this controversial Jewish settlement just north of the city centre means Town of the Four, referring to the four couples who are believed to be buried in Hebron: Adam and Eve, Abraham and Sarah, Isaac and Rebecca, and Jacob and Leah. There is little to see here except the contrast between the crowded city and the settlement's modern apartment blocks, wide streets and gardens behind a barbed-wire perimeter. Egged buses stop here between Jerusalem and Hebron.

Nearby, an unfinished mosque symbolises the tensions in and around Hebron. Beautifully designed, its construction was halted by the Israelis who believed that the main reason for a new mosque in an area with few Muslims would be to draw Arabs to move closer to Qiryat Arba and thus create a new round of potentially violent confrontations with the Jewish settlers.

Oak of Abraham

An oak tree, two km west of Hebron, marks the legendary site where Abraham pitched his tent (Genesis 18:1). In the Middle Ages, pilgrims used to remove pieces from the tree for good luck charms, so there is not a lot to see now and the trunk is protected by steel braces, wire and nails. A nail in the coffin of the tree's authenticity is its probable age of only 600 years. The Russian Orthodox Church owns the site and its monastery is nearby.

Susiya

Set amidst attractive scenery are these extensive remains of a Jewish village from the Talmudic period. Still being developed as a tourist site, with nothing labelled in English at the time of writing, the highlight of the ruins is the ancient synagogue's mosaic floor.

It's open Sunday to Thursday from 9 am to 4 pm, Friday 9 am to 1 pm, and is closed Saturday; admission is US$2. There are terrific views looking east towards the Dead Sea.

Egged buses from Qiryat Arba and Beersheba go past the site, while the Arad bus can drop you at the Yatir junction (ask the driver) and you can walk or hitch from there. You can also try to hitch from Qiryat Arba by standing at the Hebron exit.

JERUSALEM TO RAMALLAH
Heading north from Jerusalem, the road passes over Mount Scopus in the direction of Ramallah, first coming to the village of **Shu'fat**. Today this is dominated by a refugee camp with a population of over 5000 displaced Palestinians. Across to the west, with the mountains in the distance, you can see Samuel's Tomb just above the modern suburban developments. In the Middle Ages, Jews came here for solemn religious celebrations and it is where the Crusaders had their first glimpse of Jerusalem – they called it Mount Joy.

Shu'fat is the site of biblical Gilbeah, Saul's capital. King Hussein of Jordan started to build a villa here but its construction was interrupted by the Six Day War – it's now used by the IDF. Several other pleasant homes can be seen in what was a cool summer retreat for wealthy Arabs.

El-Bireh
After passing Jerusalem Airport and Tel Nashe (biblical Mizpeh), you drive under the 'Welcome to El-Bireh' archway just south of Ramallah, and 14 km north of Jerusalem. Perhaps the first caravan stop on the ancient Jerusalem to Galilee route, there is little to see in this relatively affluent Arab suburb. An exception is the headquarters of the Inash El-Usra Society.

Inash El-Usra Society Established in 1965, this Palestinian women's organisation aims to improve women's general standing in the local community, to help the needy, and to preserve and develop Palestinian culture such as folklore and handicrafts. These aims have been put into practice by setting up vocational training centres. The society also has production centres which provide employment in these trades for Palestinians, with profits going to charity.

There is a wide range of other activities including an orphanage, child care, sponsorship of students otherwise unable to afford university education and other financial support schemes.

Perhaps of most interest to travellers is the Inash el-Usra society's Palestinian Folklore & Research Centre. Initiated in 1972 with the aim of preserving, studying and developing Palestinian folklore, this facility produces publications including the *Society & Heritage* journal, studies of villages, and books on such subjects as traditional costumes, architecture and food. It stages folkloric festivals in El-Bireh and is compiling an archive of materials. Worth a visit is its museum in the society's El-Bireh headquarters.

The society has no official political role or policy and its general aim is to improve the lot of Palestinian women. However, the inevitable view of its membership is that Israel's occupation of the West Bank and the Gaza Strip is unjust and that there should be an independent Palestine free of Jewish rule.

For more information and to arrange a visit to the society's headquarters and museum, contact the Inash El-Usra Society, El-Bireh, PO Box 3549, West Bank (☎ 952876/544). To get there it is most convenient to take a special taxi from Ramallah (about US$4).

RAMALLAH
(Population: 25,000)
Arabic for Heights of the Lord, Ramallah and its environs are among the more affluent areas of the West Bank region, as can be seen by the houses and gardens. Before the Israeli occupation it was a summer resort popular with wealthy Jordanians. Calling it the 'Switzerland of Jordan', they came here to escape the heat of Amman.

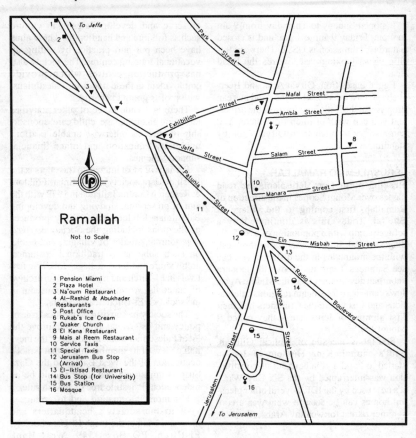

Ramallah
Not to Scale

1 Pension Miami
2 Plaza Hotel
3 Na'oum Restaurant
4 Al–Rashid & Abukhader
  Restaurants
5 Post Office
6 Rukab's Ice Cream
7 Quaker Church
8 El Kana Restaurant
9 Mais al Reem Restaurant
10 Service Taxis
11 Special Taxis
12 Jerusalem Bus Stop
   (Arrival)
13 El–Iktisad Restaurant
14 Bus Stop (for University)
15 Bus Station
16 Mosque

To Jaffa
Park Street
Mafal Street
Exhibition Street
Ambia Street
Jaffa Street
Salam Street
Patunia Street
Manara Street
Ein Misbah Street
Radio Boulevard
Al Nahoa Street
Jerusalem Street
To Jerusalem

Things to See & Do

There are no real sights in Ramallah. It is a
jumping-off point, however, for other places
of interest.

While here, a brief walkabout is worthwhile to get a glimpse of another Arab town
in the Occupied Territories. As you check out
the various shops, buildings and eating
places, you will often be approached by
locals curious to know where you are from
and keen to talk about life in the West Bank.
Next to the bus station is the small market,
with the Abu Nasser Mosque nearby. Non-

Muslims are not allowed to enter; be wary
of the attendant if you get too close.

Places to Stay

Note that Ramallah's hotels may be closed
to foreigners. Anyway, with Jerusalem and
its superior choice of accommodation
nearby, it is unlikely that you would choose
to stay in either of Ramallah's hotels. It's not
that they are so undesirable, they just fail to
compete in terms of cost, cleanliness and
facilities. Both on Jaffa Rd, the *Pension
Miami* (☎ 952808) has singles/doubles for

US$20/30, and the *Plaza Hotel* (☎ 952020) has singles/doubles for US$12/20.

Places to Eat
Ramallah has some good eating places, mostly inexpensive. On Jaffa St, the *Al-Rashid* and the *Mais al Reem* restaurants both serve excellent felafel (served stuffed with spiced onion), shwarma and kubbé. Their colourful and fancy salad displays show up their sloppy competitors elsewhere. For some reason, Ramallah's felafel is finger-shaped.

Two establishments compete for the 'best hummus in town' award. They provide other choices, too. The *El-Iktisad Restaurant* (no English sign) on Radio Blvd is a grubby place dishing up hummus, pitta and pickles for about US$2.50, with meat US$5. Also available are soup and hot main dishes such as kebabs in tehina, and okra (a beef stew served with rice and vegetables). The cleaner *El Kana Restaurant* on Salam St does a great plate of hummus and also specialises in shishlik and kebab.

Getting There & Away
Arab bus No 18 runs from the Nablus Rd bus station in East Jerusalem and takes about 40 minutes. The service taxis from opposite Damascus Gate take only 10 minutes. The last bus leaves from Ramallah for Jerusalem at about 6 pm with service taxis running till about 9 pm.

RAMALLAH TO NABLUS
Beit-El (Bethel)
On the road to Nablus, this is biblical Bethel (House of God), the site of Jacob's dream about a ladder (Genesis 28:10-17), and the home of Deborah (Judges 4:4-6). In reality, there is little for the visitor to see here. There is a hill called Jacob's Ladder but you will need to have it pointed out for you to find it.

The nearby Jewish settlement of Beit-El might be of interest if you want to know more about the religious and political ideals of the West Bank settlers. Egged bus No 70 runs here from Jerusalem.

Shiloh (Seilun)
Continuing north, you come to the Arab village of Sinjil. The name comes from the original Crusader settlement here, called St Giles. After five km you come to the sparse ruins of ancient Shiloh. It was here that the Tabernacle and the Holy Ark rested before the conquest of Jerusalem (Joshua 18:1-9; I Samuel 1:3; I Samuel 4; Jeremiah 7:12; Psalm 78:60).

NABLUS
(Population: 75,000)
Another centre of violent Palestinian opposition to Israel, Nablus is the largest West Bank town. Beautifully situated between the scenic mountains of Gerizim and Ebal, it has the typical appearance of a modern-day Arab town with a mix of old and new lifestyles, highlighted by the contrast between the tall office blocks and the narrow streets of the casbah.

As in Hebron, travellers should always bear in mind strong anti-Israeli sentiments of the local population. For most Jews, these have made Nablus a 'no-go' area.

History
First settled around 4500 to 3100 BC by Chalcolithic people, Nablus stands adjacent to another of the world's oldest towns. Mentioned in early biblical times when it was called Shechem, it was here that Abraham came in about 1850 BC and received the promise of the Land of Israel (Genesis 12:6-7), Jacob purchased a field (Genesis 33:18-19), Joshua gathered his people to renew their covenant (Joshua 8:30-35, 24:1-29), and Joseph was buried (Joshua 24:32). Ancient Shechem lies to the east, just outside the Arab town of Nablus. Israel, however, officially calls Nablus by the biblical name of Shechem.

In the 9th century BC, the town's importance lessened when the northern kingdom's capital moved from Shechem to Samaria, near the Arab village of Sebastiya. The name Nablus is derived from Flavia Neapolis, the Roman colony built here in 72 AD.

The New Testament tells of Phillip, Peter

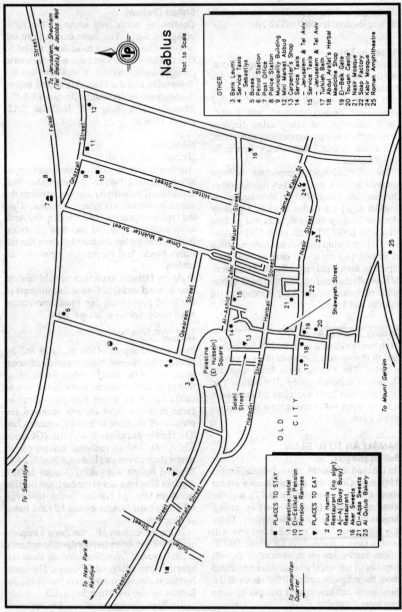

Nablus

Not to Scale

To Jerusalem, Shechem
To Jerusalem (Tel Belata) & Jacobs Well

Faisal Street

Ghazzali Street

Hitten Street

Omar el Mukhtar Street

Qawareen Street

Jamei el Kabir Street

Zafer el-Musri Street

Nasir Street

Al-Ashid Street

Hanbali Street

Shawayen Street

Palestine (El Hussein) Square

Salahi Street

Hadadin Street

OLD CITY

To Mount Gerizim

To Sebastiya

To Nasr Park & Rafidiya

To Samaritan Quarter

To Samaritan Quarter

Ghirnata Street

Sultan Street

Palestine Street

OTHER

3 Bank Leumi
4 Service Taxis
5 Buses — Sebastiya
6 Petrol Station
7 Post Office
8 Police Station
9 Municipality Building
12 Mini Market Abbud
13 Carpenter's Shop
14 Service Taxis — Jerusalem & Tel Aviv
15 Service Taxis — Jerusalem & Tel Aviv
17 Turkish Bath
18 Abdul Arafat's Herbal Medicine Shop
19 El-Beik Gate
20 Nouqala Coastie
21 Nasr Mosque
22 Soap Factory
24 Kabir Mosque
25 Roman Amphitheatre

■ **PLACES TO STAY**

1 Palestine Hotel
10 El-Estikial Pension
11 Pension Ramses

▼ **PLACES TO EAT**

2 Foul Hamis Restaurant (no sign)
13 Aj-Aj (Busy Busy) Restaurant
16 Aker Sweets
21 El-Aqsa Sweets
23 Al Qutub Bakery

and John spreading Christianity in the region (Acts 8:4-25). The Byzantine period saw churches built on the site of ancient Shechem and on Mount Gerizim.

Evidence of the Crusader presence was obscured by an earthquake in 1927 which virtually wiped out the town, and by the removal of the cut stones by the locals for building purposes.

Nablus became a main centre of industry and commerce in Palestine, with several soap factories, goldsmiths and other businesses, and with the surrounding farmers coming into town to sell their products.

Orientation & Information

The main road runs east-west through Nablus, and the town centre is to the south, based around Palestine/El Hussein Square. Buses and service taxis arrive and depart from near here. The police station (☎ 100) and post office (open Saturday to Wednesday 8 am to 1 pm and 3 to 5 pm, Thursday 8 am to 1 pm, and closed Friday) are across from the municipality building to the north, with the hotels nearby.

Just south of Palestine/El Hussein Square is the Old City. Nasir St, running east-west, is the main thoroughfare here. Behind it are the slopes of Mount Gerizim, holy to the Samaritans. Mount Ebal stands to the north. On the eastern outskirts of Nablus, about three km from the town centre, is the site of ancient Shechem (Tel Balata) with Jacob's Well and Joseph's Tomb.

The spectre of the occupation hangs over the town, with IDF patrols, anti-Israel graffiti and a general air of discontent. The visitor can still experience something of the authentic Arab Palestine in Nablus, however, especially in and around the Old City.

Being predominantly Muslim, the market, shops and businesses are closed on Friday afternoon. Saturday is a particularly busy day with crowds of Arabs who live in Israel coming to shop.

Old City

Besides the colourful market, there are other interesting sights to look out for as you wander through the labyrinth of narrow streets and alleyways of the Old City. Another sign of the troubled times are the barricades put up here by the IDF to help suppress disturbances.

Markets & Shops Markaz el-Tujari is the goldsmiths' market, just north of the Nasir Mosque. At 82 Nasir St, between Salahi St and el-Beik Gate, Abdul Arafat's little shop sells herbal medicine. Down on Salahi St you can see the carpenter's workshop where the green-painted handcarts are made.

Soap Factories Nablus is the centre of the Arab soap-making industry with over 40 factories. It is usually possible to visit one and see how the soap is made. Although some modern technology is now used, the production process is still traditional. One of the more interesting factories is also the most convenient.

Al-Bader (Full Moon) Soap at 20 Nasir St has been here for over 250 years and exports to other Arab countries via Amman. The soap's basic ingredients are caustic soda and olive oil. They once used local olive oil but the quality is very good and therefore too expensive; it is more economical to buy Italian. By the way, the soap is particularly good for dandruff.

Turkish Bath At 70 Nasir St is Hamam Lesjid, the oldest working Turkish bath in the country. Built around 1480 at the start of the Ottoman period, it is one of six in Nablus. It isn't in very good condition but is worth a look. The old man who works here speaks only Arabic but there may be someone else around who can explain to you how it all works.

The bath is open daily from about 7 am to 2 pm, and still has a few regular customers. At one time most of the town would have used public baths such as this.

Touqan Castle One of the grandest buildings in the Old City is this Turkish mansion. It's now privately owned, but usually visitors are welcome to look at the architecture and garden. Whilst not brilliantly maintained, you can still appreciate something of its former glory. From Nasir St walk south through el-Beik Gate and the entrance is up the slope on your left.

Mosques

There are something like 30 minarets that dominate the Nablus skyline. Nasir Mosque is in the centre of the market; Kabir Mosque is the largest with its beautiful arch at the corner of Nasir St and Jame' el Kabir St. One tradition has it that this is the site where Joseph's brothers showed their father, Jacob, the blood-stained coat of many colours to convince him that his favourite son was dead. Non-Muslims aren't permitted inside the city's mosques.

Amphitheatre

On the slopes, tucked away behind the markets and houses, is an excavated Roman amphitheatre. At the time of writing there were no explanatory signs.

Samaritan Quarter

Nablus is home to the Samaritans (for more information see Population & People and Religion in the Facts about the Country chapter). They live in a small western section of the town and their synagogue houses what they claim to be the world's oldest Torah scroll, dated to the 13th year of the Israelites' settlement in Canaan.

Shechem

To reach Shechem, take the main road three km east from the town centre and follow the signposts. It's possible to walk or take a taxi. The bus will drop you nearby.

Tel Balata The remains of biblical Shechem, dated to between 1650 and 1550 BC, are not that impressive to non-archaeologists.

Jacob's Well A little further east is the Greek Orthodox convent of Jacob's Well. A Byzantine church was first built here in 380, but it was destroyed in 529. The Crusaders erected a replacement and in 1914 the Russian

Orthodox Church began to rebuild it. WW I stopped them and the Greeks took control of the building, which remains uncompleted. In its crypt is the deep well believed to be the one where Jesus met the Samaritan woman (John 4) on the land purchased by Jacob (Genesis 33:18-20). It's open Monday to Saturday 8 am to noon and 2 to 5 pm, and is closed Sunday; admission is free.

Joseph's Tomb Just north of Jacob's Well is the traditional site of Joseph's Tomb. The simple white-domed building, similar in style to Rachel's Tomb in Bethlehem, is believed to be where Joseph's remains were carried to from Egypt (Joshua 24:32). Holy to Jews and Muslims, it used to be controlled by the Muslims but the Israeli authorities took it over and now IDF soldiers are on guard. The tomb is open daily from 6 am to 6 pm. Admission is free.

Mount Gerizim

Sacred to the Samaritans, Mount Gerizim (881 metres above sea level) offers a superb panoramic view of the town and the surrounding countryside.

The Samaritans spend the 40 days of their Passover up here, living in the houses just below the summit. The highlight of their celebrations is the bloody sacrifice of sheep. You can see where the ceremony takes place, just to the south of the road.

Following the instructions given in Exodus 12, they kill the sheep, pour water over them, strip off the fleece, extract the fat, and burn both. Each sheep's forefoot is then cut off and given to the priests. After being cleaned and salted, the sheep are put on a spit and roasted. After prayers, the sheep are eaten by the Samaritans who must be fully clothed and wearing shoes. The meat bones must not be broken, and everything that is edible has to be eaten quickly. When they have finished eating they gather up the bones, hooves, horns and spits, in fact everything that came in contact with the sacrificial altar, and solemnly burn it all. This deeply religious event now attracts a crowd of bemused tourists.

Further north is where the Samaritans believe Abraham sacrificed Isaac, disputing the tradition that it took place on Mount Moriah in Jerusalem.

No buses go up the mountain, so you either have to walk (say two hours) or take a taxi (about US$10).

Places to Stay

Because of the intifada, the hotels in Nablus are usually closed to foreigners. They were never very popular with travellers anyway, providing inferior accommodation to their Jerusalem counterparts. The cheapest is the *El-Estiklal Pension* near the municipality building. Beds in the large rooms cost US$6. Nearby is the slightly less inviting *Pension Ramses* with beds for US$7.

Although intended as a step up, the *Palestine Hotel* (☎ (053) 70040) on Shwetereh St offers little more in the way of cleanliness or comfort. Despite a distinguished past with a guest-book signed by the President of Tunisia and the King of Jordan, its price of US$18 per person is over the top due to the musty state of the large, bare rooms.

Places to Eat

Along with soap, the Nablus speciality is sweets. These include all the various pastries, halvah and Turkish Delight, but in particular kanafe (cheese topped with orange wheat flakes and soaked in honey). The best bakery at which to try this rich delicacy is *El-Aqsa*, next to Nasir Mosque and across from the soap factory on Nasir St in the Old City. *Aker Sweets*, on Hitten St, has a number of followers, too. A decent-sized slice costs about US$1.

In the heart of the Old City market, on Salahi St across from the carpenter's workshop, is an unobtrusive plain-looking restaurant. Called *Aj-Aj* which means 'Busy-Busy' (no English sign), it serves great hummus, and also laban, a delicious cheese salad dip and omelettes. *Juma Saih* (no English sign) on Ghirnata St, near Atimad Taxis, also serves great hummus. For the best foul in Nablus, head for *Foul Hamis* (no English sign), on 39 Palestine St. It's on the right towards the end as you walk from the square.

Self-caterers can choose from the produce available in the market. For bread, the best bakery is *Al Qutub* (no English sign) at 20 Nasir St.

Although inconveniently situated away from the town centre, the Christian area of Rafidya to the west boasts some of the better places to eat. *Quick Meal* on Rafidya St serves various versions of fast food and is popular with the locals. *Abu-Bedou* is said to have the best shwarma in town, while *Arz 14* wins the prize for its ice cream.

Due to Islamic law, beer and other alcohol is not sold in the cafés and eating places, although a few stores do stock it. If you buy some, be sure not to upset the locals by drinking in public. A good place to head for is *Mini-Market Abbud* on Faisal St, a few hundred metres east of the municipality building. Specialising in US and British 'luxury imports' ranging from confectionery and cigarettes to cosmetics and toiletries, it also stocks cold beer and the manager is a friendly host to thirsty travellers who are welcome to sit, sip, chat and listen to music.

Getting There & Away

Arab buses run to Nablus from East Jerusalem (Nablus Rd station) via Ramallah. The journey takes two to 2½ hours which makes the service-taxi option (1¼ hours) very appealing. Buses also run to and from Jenin and Afulla in the north, and service taxis also run to and from Jaffa.

AROUND NABLUS
Sebastiya

This quiet little Arab village stands about 15 km north-west of Nablus up on the scenic slopes of the Samarian hills. Just above it on the summit of the peak lie the impressive ruins of Samaria, the capital of the ancient Israelite kingdom.

Omri, King of Israel, established the city here in 876 BC (I Kings 16:24). It was greatly improved by his son Ahab, who built various great buildings and fortifications. In 724 to 722 BC the Assyrians invaded and destroyed the Israelite kingdom. Samaria's citizens were deported and it became a provincial capital under the Persians. Razed in 108 BC and restored in 57 BC, it came to Herod in 30 BC who renamed it Sebaste (Greek for Augustus) and initiated a new construction programme. It eventually declined with the development of Nablus. The Israelite, Hellenistic and Roman ruins include an amphitheatre, temple, palace, towers, columns and a hippodrome.

The site (☎ 942235) is open April to September, Saturday to Thursday 8 am to 5 pm, and Friday 8 am to 4 pm; October to March, Saturday to Thursday 8 am to 4 pm, and Friday 8 am to 3 pm; and admission is US$3 (students US$1.50).

Inside the village is a Crusader church (dating from the 12th-century) that was converted into a mosque by Saladin. Built on the site of a ruined 5th-century church, it contains two tomb chambers. The prophets Elisha and Obadiah are believed to be buried here, along with the head of John the Baptist – the prophet Yahya to the Muslims. The Nabi Yahya Mosque is on the east side of the square.

Places to Eat There is a café outside the archaeological site, and another in the village square.

Getting There & Away No buses run direct to Sebastiya. Instead, take a service taxi from near Palestine/el-Hussein Square (US$0.70). You can also take the Arab bus from Nablus to Jenin or Egged buses from Netanya to Shavei-Shomron and get off at the turn-off for the village. From here it's a steep two-km climb.

JERUSALEM TO TEL AVIV
Latrun
About halfway between Jerusalem and Tel Aviv lies Latrun. Its popular wine-producing monastery enjoys views of many biblical sites: Emmaus, Ayalon, Bethoron, Gezer,

Modin, Lydda and Sorec. Also nearby is Canada Park, a result of the tree-planting programme initiated by the Jewish National Fund. Latrun means Home of the Good Thief; it is believed to have been the home of one of the thieves crucified with Jesus.

A modern highway cuts through the area, and to the west (the left-hand side heading towards Tel Aviv) is the attractive Latrun Monastery, and to the east (the right-hand side) is Canada Park and the ruins of the Emmaus church.

In the 1948 War of Independence, the Arabs closed the road here, thus cutting off supplies to Jerusalem. It was not until the Six Day War that the Israelis took Latrun.

Going further back in time, the area has seen its fair share of conflict. Greeks and Romans, Arabs and Crusaders and the British and the Ottoman Turks have all passed through en route to Jerusalem.

Latrun Monastery It was founded in 1890 by the French Trappist Order of monks as a contemplative monastery. It is now widely renowned for its wine, as well as its lovely location, architecture and gardens.

The winemaking started in 1899. The monks reclaimed and cultivated the land and planted olive groves, grain fields and vegetable gardens as well as the vineyards. In the rocky areas pine trees and cypresses were chosen. In WW I the monks were expelled by the Turks, but they were able to return, and in 1926 the present monastery was constructed.

Visitors are welcome to enjoy the gardens, the architecture and to buy the wine, spirits, vermouths and the olive oil produced here. The shop by the gate is open Monday to Saturday 8.30 to 11.30 am and 2.30 to 4.30 pm; it is closed Sunday.

Emmaus Church Above the ruins rises the monastery formerly belonging to the Beit-Haram Brothers, but now functioning as the French Prehistorical Research Centre. The church commemorates Christian tradition that this is where Jesus appeared to two of his disciples after his resurrection (Mark 16:12-13, Luke 24:13-31).

Canada Park This park is one of the country's many beautifully forested areas, and you can wander around and picnic here. You can find a well-preserved Roman bath near the church, dating from around 640. Various water holes, conduits and the remains of an amphitheatre are also to be found in the park.

Getting There & Away Latrun can be reached most easily by bus from Jerusalem, with service every 30 minutes. From Tel Aviv only one bus (in the morning) passes through, although you can change at Ramla where there are frequent connections. Remind the driver that you want to go to Latrun before he flies past.

The Gaza Strip

The Gaza Strip is just that, a narrow stretch of land on the Mediterranean coast south of Ashdod, with the Negev Desert to the east and the Sinai Desert to the south. Only about 50 km long and as little as six km wide, it can't boast the holy places or natural beauty spots found elsewhere, standing out instead as a largely ignored, tragic consequence of the Palestine Problem.

Rather than fascinating ruins and lovely views, you are confronted with an area of squalid and overcrowded living conditions with crumbling towns and refugee camps having to cope with one of the world's highest birth-rates. The Strip's population doubles each generation and by the year 2000 it is expected to reach 900,000.

The Gaza Strip has three main towns, of which Gaza is the largest (often called Gaza City or Gaza Town to avoid confusion). The others are Khan Younis and Rafah. There are also eight refugee camps and about 20 Jewish settlements. These settlements are rarely discussed overseas; events in the West Bank tend to dominate the headlines. Over 2500 Jewish settlers have made the strip their home, mainly in the Gush-Katif area to the south.

There is a very different quality to the Gaza Strip than to the West Bank, and it is not just the desert terrain and climate. It is a quality of neglect and helplessness and the atmosphere of hatred towards Israel for its role in the events that have caused this situation. Over 60% of the residents here are refugees, representing about 20% of the entire Palestinian refugee population.

Except for the Jewish settlers, all of the Strip's residents, natives and refugees, are stateless. They have no passport from the Israeli administration, just as they had none from the Egyptians. West Bank residents are Jordanian citizens and are officially able to travel to and from Jordan and then beyond (although this is subject to the authorisation of Israeli security). Strip residents, on the other hand, are usually unable to enter Egypt, and need a very difficult to obtain *laissez-passer* document from the Israelis to travel abroad.

The Strip has been dubbed 'the Soweto of Israel' due to its unofficial role as a source of cheap labour and for the contrast in the lifestyles of its residents and Israelis. At least half of the region's labour force works in Israel and virtually all of those who stay behind are ultimately dependent on the Israeli economy for their livelihood as well. This dependence will increase as local agriculture declines because of a falling water table that has begun to dry up orchards. Palestinian critics say that with Gaza workers in Israel earning 40% lower wages than Israeli workers, Israel is content to keep the situation as it is. All of these factors serve only to make the residents of the Strip cling even more desperately to the Palestinian identity.

Never a stranger to anti-Israeli violence, the intifada has made the Strip even more of a 'no-go' area for most Israelis. Non-Jews, however, are often made welcome, although women should be prepared for the usual

MEDITERRANEAN SEA

Beach
Jabaliya
GAZA
Nezarim
Nahal Oz
Nuseirat
Bureij
Deir el-Balah
Gush-Katif
Maghazi
Khan Younis
Khan Younis
Rafah
Rafah

Gaza Strip

0   5   10 km

O Palestinian Refugee Camps
.... Demarcation Line

hassles. The tension in the air is very evident, as is the IDF presence with patrols, barbed wire and watchtowers in the towns and the roadblocks in the rural areas.

Note that all the hotels in the Strip are officially (and usually actually) closed to foreigners, and that the IDF may prevent you from entering.

Ask around to find out the current situation – both Israeli and Arab viewpoints are essential. The UNRWA used to organise tours – at the moment they may have their hands full with other matters, but do check (see the Gaza section).

GAZA
(Population: 125,000)

Although there is little left to show for it, Gaza is one of the world's oldest towns. Well established by 2000 BC, it stands on what was in ancient times the Way of the Sea, the main route between Egypt and Assyria. Of great economic and strategic importance, Gaza was one of the Philistines' five great cities. It was then called Aza, probably derived from the Hebrew word *az* (strong) and was called Gaza (Treasure), by the Arabs after the Islamic conquest of Palestine in the 7th century. They renamed the town Gaza of

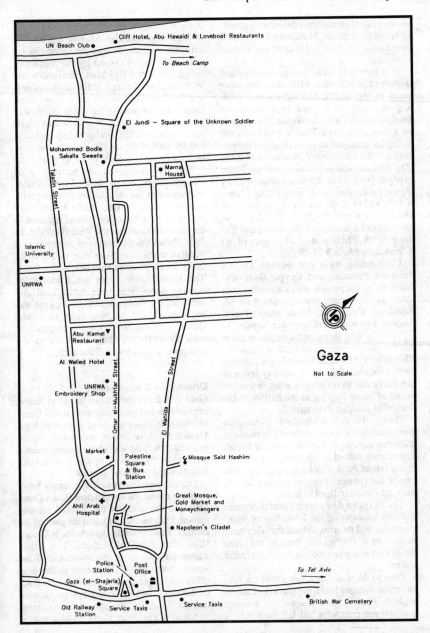

UN Beach Club ●

Cliff Hotel, Abu Hawaidi & Loveboat Restaurants

To Beach Camp

● El Jundi – Square of the Unknown Soldier

Mohammed Bodie
Sakalla Sweets ●

Marna
House

Talatin Street

Islamic
University ●

UNRWA ●

Abu Kamel ▼
Restaurant

Al Walied Hotel

UNRWA
Embroidery Shop

Omar el-Mukhtar Street

El Wahida Street

Gaza

Not to Scale

Market ●

Palestine
Square
& Bus
Station

⚓ Mosque Said Hashim

Great Mosque,
Gold Market and
Moneychangers

Ahli Arab ✚
Hospital

● Napoleon's Citadel

Police
Station

Post
Office

To Tel Aviv

Gaza (el–Shajaria)
Square

Old Railway ● Service Taxis
Station

● Service Taxis

● British War Cemetery

Hashim after Hashim ibn Abd Munaf, grand-father of the prophet Mohammed, who died here on his way back to Hijaz on the Arabian Peninsula.

It is said that Gaza has been taken and destroyed in war more often than any other town in the world. Certainly some well-known events took place here, mostly in biblical times. First mentioned by the Bible as a Canaanite city (Genesis 10:15-19), the Israelites managed to get a foothold only to lose it to the Philistines (Deuteronomy 2:18-23). Samson was imprisoned and died here (Judges 16) and the city was condemned by Amos for its slave trade with Edom (Amos 1:1-7), and by Zephania for its opposition to the Judean kingdom (Zephania 2:1-6). The last biblical reference to Gaza is in connection with Phillip and the spread of Christianity (Acts 8:25-29).

Continuing as a prosperous station between Palestine and Egypt, Gaza was taken by all the powers who succeeded each other in the region: the Greeks, Romans, Muslims, Crusaders, Mamelukes, Turks, British, Egyptians and now the Israelis. In 1779 Napoleon Bonaparte camped here on his Egyptian campaign and called Gaza 'the Guardian of Africa, the Gate of Asia'. During WW I, as one of the main military bases of the Turks and their German allies, it was the scene of heavy fighting as the British forces battled to conquer Palestine.

During the British Mandate, Gaza again prospered as the main centre of the southern Palestine region. At this time a small Jewish community settled in the town, but with the rising tide of Arab nationalism making Gaza one of the centres of opposition to a Jewish state they were obliged to leave.

The Egyptian Army made Gaza their main military base during the 1948 War of Inde-pendence and the area of land that they held at the end of the fighting became the Gaza Strip. This was when today's problems really started.

Prior to the war, Gaza Town and the sur-rounding villages had a population of about 60,000. Now it was flooded with some 150,000 refugees who had left their homes in the north and were unable either to return or to go anywhere else. Making this terrible situation even worse was the sudden isola-tion of the region caused by the politics of being under the Egyptian administration. With Israel bordering it to the north and east and the barren and mostly uninhabited Sinai Desert to the south, the Gaza Strip was forced to adapt itself to a new and harsh reality of the sudden tripling of its population and the loss of most of its revenue sources, as links to the new State of Israel were cut.

The UN sponsored the setting up of refugee camps, but the lack of employment and access to the outside world, along with many related factors, made it virtually impossible for the region to develop even to the limited extent that the West Bank did. In 1956, Israel briefly occupied the Strip as a result of the Sinai or Suez War, took it again in the Six Day War and has held it ever since. The Israeli authorities are blamed for running down what little agricultural and industrial life there was in Gaza by prohibit-ing exports and limiting sales in Israel. During your visit to the town, conversations with the locals are likely to centre on the politics and economics of the area.

Orientation & Information

Gaza is a fairly easy town to get to know, centred as it is on one long main street. Omar el-Mukhtar St runs about four km from Gaza/el-Shajaria Square westwards to the seafront. It is lined with shops and businesses and passes by or near to the town's main facilities and places of interest.

Gaza/el-Shajaria Square is a messy junc-tion that marks the start of downtown Gaza. Down to the south is the disused railway station, built by the British at the start of the century. East, towards Beersheba, is Gaza's 'East End slum', el-Shajaria. The police station (☎ 100) is on the north side of the square, and around the corner is the post office – it is open Saturday to Thursday 8 am to 2.30 pm, and is closed Friday. Service taxis for Tel Aviv-Jaffa operate from nearby.

About a km west, Omar el-Mukhtar St

crosses busy Palestine Square. The bus station and the rank for service taxis running to and from Jerusalem and the West Bank are here.

There are few reminders of Gaza's colourful ancient history to be seen. Sadly, a visit to the town is dominated instead by the harsh effects of more recent political developments.

Your attention will be focused on the refugee camps that surround Gaza Town and dominate the Strip and on the slums and the general aura of neglect, decay and hopelessness. You can find much worse scenes of hardship in the world, but it is the stark contrast between the conditions in Gaza and those you have come to see in Israel that makes such an impact.

As in most Muslim Arab communities, the biggest social event in Gaza is the wedding. With the lack of most other possible diversions here, it takes on an even greater importance as one of the rare occasions for celebration. Especially in view of the economic situation in the Strip, they are lavish affairs with scores of guests, plenty of food, and singing and dancing through the night.

Many Gaza residents have relatives who work in the Gulf countries to provide for the folks back home. These 'expat' Palestinians tend to return for summer and this is the busy wedding season. Every night along the seafront and on Omar el-Mukhtar St you will see processions of cars bedecked with ribbons, loaded with bewildered couples and happy guests and accompanied by the shrill sound of screaming that is a sort of verbal confetti in the Middle East. Out of season, Friday night is wedding night.

Also to be seen are bicycles, brightly decorated with stickers, transfers, lights and, in competition with the many cars, a fancy electric horn.

UNRWA

The organisation's field office is the pastel blue building on Talatin St (this runs parallel with Omar el-Mukhtar St). It is worth finding out if they can arrange a visit to one of the refugee camps in the Strip. At least one

weeks' notice is normally required. Contact the public information office in Jerusalem (see the Jerusalem chapter) or call the Gaza office direct (☎ 861195/8).

Islamic University

Across from the UNRWA complex is Gaza's university, the largest in the Occupied Territories. Funded mostly by Saudi Arabia, the study of Islamic fundamentalism is mandatory here. The students can be a lot less open to foreigners than those on the West Bank, but it may still be worth a visit.

Beach

A combination of the security situation and the local males' lack of self-control at the sight of a woman's knee, makes beach life in Gaza not what it could be. The wreck of a ship just offshore and the oil from tankers near Ashkelon also detract from the stretch of sand. If you fancy a swim, go to the UN Beach Club, just south of where Omar el-Mukhtar St meets the seafront. Although the facilities are only for UN staff and soldiers, you can use the well-kept private beach.

El Jundi (Square of the Unknown Soldier)

This unkempt common on Omar el-Mukhtar St was dedicated by the Egyptian Army who buried one of their dead here and erected the monument in his honour. Shelled by the Israelis in 1956, it has remained in disrepair.

UNRWA Embroidery Shop

East of the Al Walied Hotel on Omar el-Mukhtar St, this shop sells traditional Palestinian embroidery pieces with profits going towards the refugees' welfare.

It is open Saturday to Thursday 6.30 to 11.45 am and 1.30 to 3.45 pm, and is closed Friday.

Markets & Shops

The town's main food market is on the southwest side of Palestine Square, under the corrugated iron roof. There are more stalls across the square to the north-east, on the back street that runs parallel with Omar el-

Mukhtar St and behind the Great Mosque. 'Goldsmiths' Alley' (dating from Herodian times, it is said) runs alongside the mosque.

At the eastern end of the alley a crowd of moneychangers stand around with fists full of dollars and other local currencies.

You can watch cane furniture being made in the workshops at various places in town. Carpets are traditionally made in el-Shajaria, just past Gaza/el-Shajaria Square, and if you ask around you may be led to see an artisan at work.

Mosque Said Hashim

This mosque was erected on the grave of the prophet Mohammed's grandfather. He was a merchant who travelled a great deal between the Arabian Peninsula and Damascus, and he died in Gaza on one of those journeys.

To reach the mosque, head north from Palestine Square to reach El Wahida St, which runs parallel with Omar el-Mukhtar St. Head west (left, towards the sea) and the mosque is down the second turning to the north (right).

Greek Orthodox Church

East of Palestine Square (away from the sea) is the town's Christian Quarter. Follow Rassel Talia St south and you come to this church on the right. With its dome and Arabic signs it resembles a mosque, but a church it is. It was built on the ruins of a 4th-century Byzantine church, but there is little to see. Someone may be available to show you around.

Great Mosque

The Jammal al-Ikbeer, commonly called the Great Mosque, is probably the town's most distinguished building, with its tower dominating the market skyline. Built on the remains of a 13th-century Crusader church dedicated to John the Baptist, it contains a pillar from a 3rd-century synagogue which bears a carving of a menorah with a Hebrew and Greek inscription. Some say that the Crusader church was itself built on the site of a 4th-century church erected by Queen Helena. An underground tunnel that leads

from the mosque to the beach was supposedly dug as an escape route in times of siege. Muslims argue that before the Crusaders arrived it was a mosque during the time of Omar ibn el Khattab, second Kalef of Islam.

Non-Muslims are usually allowed to enter the mosque in between the daily prayers.

Napoleon's Citadel

During his Egyptian campaign, Napoleon Bonaparte camped in Gaza in 1799 to replenish supplies. He commandeered this building as his headquarters. It stands on El Wahida St, east of the Mosque Said Hashim, and has some attractive ornamental stonework from the Mameluke period. It's now a girl's school and to get a close look you normally need to be persistent and ask the caretaker to let you into the school compound after 4 pm when the lessons are over.

Samson's Monument

Continue eastwards along El Wahida St and you come to this arched monument about 200 metres on the north side (left). Called Abu el Azim (Father of Strength), it commemorates Samson. One tradition has it that he lies buried under the Great Mosque.

British War Cemetery

Both world wars saw heavy fighting in the region. In 1917 British and Commonwealth forces, mainly Australian, attacked and took Gaza. During WW II the British base hospital in Gaza received many of the wounded from the desert campaign. The British War Cemetery is about three km from town on the north-bound road that leads from Gaza/el-Shajaria Square towards Tel Aviv-Jaffa, on the east side (right) across from the 7-Up factory.

Places to Stay

Gaza's hotels have been officially closed to foreigners since the intifada began. The prices listed here are a couple of years old, but the lack of business has probably kept prices down anyway.

Across from the municipal gardens on Omar el-Mukhtar St, the *El Walied Hotel*

(☎ 861230) was the cheapest option in town. Although the management are a bit straight-faced and serious, it is a neat, clean and quiet place to stay. A bed in a twin room costs US$6 and you will not normally see many, if any, other guests. There is a 10 pm curfew and checkout time is 9 am. As there is little to do after dark in Gaza this is not much of a problem.

On the seafront, to the left from where Omar el-Mukhtar St intersects, the *Cliff Hotel* (☎ 861353) has singles/doubles for US$15/25, with breakfast included.

Marna House (☎ 86225) is a comfortable private establishment, in a quiet residential street. With a large front garden, terrace and lounge, it is a faded reminder of pre-1948 Gaza; singles/doubles are US$25/45, with breakfast. It's off the main drag, so use the cheap taxi service to find it. Otherwise, head towards the sea along Omar el-Mukhtar St, take the second right past the cultural centre, then take the first right and it's about 50 metres along the street on your left. Most locals know it, so don't hesitate to ask the way.

Places to Eat
Cheap prices abound for fruit and vegetables in the markets, especially if you bargain hard. Felafel is sold on the street and in cafés at prices considerably lower than in Israel, although travellers with sensitive stomachs may not feel that it is really such a bargain. Some of the best hummus is served at *El Khuzinder* (no English sign). It's east of the El Walied Hotel on Omar el-Mukhtar St; look for the orange table-tops and chairs outside. Nearer the hotel and towards the sea, on the corner before the prison, the *Abu Kamel* restaurant serves tasty salads and kebabs.

Despite the spelling, *Borgerland*, north of the Square of the Unknown Soldier, is a surprisingly clean and pleasant place, serving decent fruit shakes, shwarma and salads.

Gaza disputes Nablus' status as the best place for sweets, and there are a number of bakeries producing honey-soaked delicacies to keep the many dentists in business. Arguably the town's best bakery is *Mohammed Bodie Sakalla* (no English sign – look for the white on green Arabic script) on the south side (left) of Omar el-Mukhtar St just before the Square of the Unknown Soldier. A particular specialty here is gataieff, a type of pancake filled with either cheese or nuts, and soaked in honey. Other favourites to ask for are kanafe Arabia and kanafe beljibna.

Fish is another local speciality and restaurants on the seafront compete to attract the bigger spenders. The *Loveboat* and *Abu Hawaidi* restaurants, owned by the Cliff Hotel, are typical with a meal costing up to about US$10 or US$15 per person.

Getting There & Away
The bus links between Gaza and Israel are limited, irregular and unreliable, but fortunately there is an efficient service taxi system that makes the trip comfortable, quick and inexpensive.

Service taxis operate from two different places in Gaza: just north of Gaza/el-Shajaria Square for Jaffa via Tel Aviv (one hour); Palestine Square for Jerusalem (1¾ hours) and West Bank destinations (Bethlehem, Hebron, Ramallah, Nablus, etc).

The Arab bus station is also on Palestine Square, with services to Ashkelon (No 20 – three times daily) and Beersheba (No 40 – twice daily). Local services operate to and from Rafah, Khan Younis, as well as other destinations on the Strip.

Getting Around
With Gaza having a four-km-long main street, the unofficial local taxi setup is great. Instead of walking, stand by the roadside and, by pointing your index finger, hail a taxi. It seems like half of the cars in town act as pirate taxis and everyone uses them. Wherever you go along Omar el-Mukhtar St you only pay about US$0.50. If you want to go off the main road, to UNRWA headquarters for example, you normally need to pay double.

AROUND GAZA

Along with the refugee camps, the Strip's
other towns are worth a visit on days when
the colourful Bedouin market sets up shop.
This means Wednesday and Thursday in
Khan Younis and Saturday and Sunday in
Rafah. Apart from the hectic trading there is
little to see, unfortunately, except more overcrowded slum conditions. Get there on Arab
buses from Palestine Square in Gaza Town.

Rafah's is a particularly sad situation
because the town was divided by the border
drawn up under the Camp David Agreement.
When the Sinai was returned to Egypt in
1979, part of the town went with it. This
resulted in a local version of the Berlin Wall
separating families and friends.

Unable to visit each other, they can be seen
sadly shouting across the fenced-off no-
man's land.

GUSH-KATIF

Gush-Katif, meaning 'bloc picking', is the
collective name for Gaza's group of Jewish
settlements, mainly moshavim, located on
the coast between Deir el-Balah and Rafah.
You really need your own transportation to

get around here, with little or no traffic for
hitching.

Neve Dekalim, Gaza's largest Jewish settlement, features a shopping centre. Near
Moshav Ganei-Tal (Gardens of Dew), the
pleasant Temarim Beach (Palm Beach) has a
resort hotel and nearby is a decent restaurant,
Dekel HaCholot (dune-palm). There is a
horse farm next door and a pleasant natural
lake. South of Neve Dekalim is the better
maintained Ashalion Beach.

Long-term plans of the settlers include a
vision of the Gaza Strip as a beach resort – a
Mediterranean Eilat? The coastal road
running between these beaches highlights
the natural beauty of the area that political
tensions, watchtowers and barbed wire tend
to overshadow.

Parts of the Gaza Strip do have something
of a lush, tropical feel, due to the sand dunes,
palm trees and abundant ground water that
allows vegetables to thrive in the fields.
Especially towards the end of the day, as the
sunlight softens, the sand dunes glow and the
greens of the palm trees and the crops in the
fields make this place of so much hostility
seem almost exotic.

Glossary

HEBREW

Aliya – immigration of Jews to Palestine: First Aliya 1882-1903; Second Aliya 1904-1918; Third Aliya 1919-1923

Asimmon – (*pl* **asimmonim**) public telephone tokens

Atzmaut – independence

Beit – house

Beit Knesset – synagogue

Diaspora – Jewish dispersion or exile from the Land of Israel; the exiled Jewish community worldwide

Eretz Israel – the Land of Israel, commonly used today by Israel's right wing to refer to their preserved borders for the modern Jewish State which includes the Occupied Territories, and sometimes Jordan and/or the Sinai, too

Gush – bloc commonly used for political parties eg Gush Emunim (Bloc of Believers) and Gush Etzion (Etzion Bloc)

Haganah – the Jewish underground army, formed during the British Mandate; the forerunner of today's Israel Defence Force (IDF)

Hasid – (*pl* **Hasidim**) member of an ultra-orthodox Jewish sect

HeHalutz – the Socialist-Zionist pioneer youth movement

Histradrut – Zionist labour federation, or trade union congress

Hof – beach

Hurva – ruin

Kabbalah – Jewish mysticism

Kosher – food prepared according to Jewish dietary law

Kefar – village

Kibbutz – (*pl* **kibbutzim**) communal settlement, originally farms, but now involved in additional industries

Kibbutznik – member of a kibbutz

Kikkar – city, town or village square

Knesset – Israeli Parliament

Likud – major Israeli right-wing political party

Magen David Adom – Red Star of David – Israel's Red Cross

Menorah – seven-pronged candelabra; an ancient Jewish symbol associated with the Hanukkah Festival

Mikveh – Jewish ritual bath

Mishnah – the legal codification of basic Jewish law – the Halakha

Moshav – cooperative settlement with a mix of private and collective housing and industry

Nahal – river; agricultural-military settlement

Sherut – shared taxi (fixed route)

Shuq – market

Talmud – part of the backbone of the Jewish faith: rabbinical interpretations of the scriptures, including the Mishnah

Tel – an ancient mound built up over centuries of urban rebuilding

Torah – the five books of Moses (the first five Old Testament books)

Ulpan – Hebrew school

Yad – memorial

Ya'ar – forest

Yarmulka – skullcap

Yeshiva – Jewish religious seminary

ARABIC

Ain/Ein – water spring or source

Fellah – (*pl* **fellahin**) farm workers

Haj – annual Muslim pilgrimage to Mecca

Hamma – hot spring

Hamman – hot baths

Haram – holy sanctuary

Intifada – the Palestinian uprising against Israeli authorities in the Occupied Territories and Jerusalem

Khan – caravanserai or inn along ancient trading routes

Khatib – low, railed wooden platform where the khatib (reader) sits to recite from the Koran

Kfur – village

Majdal – tower

Mihrab – prayer niche in a mosque, facing Mecca

Minbar – pulpit used for sermons in a mosque

Muezzin – the Muslim man whose job it is to call the faithful to prayer from the mosque's minaret

Ramadan – Muslim month of fasting

Service – shared taxi (fixed route)

Souq – market

Wadi – river bed

Index

MAPS

TEXT

Map references are in **bold** type:

468 Index

Where Can You Find Out.........

HOW to get a Laotian visa in Bangkok?

WHERE to go birdwatching in PNG?

WHAT to expect from the police if you're robbed in Peru?

WHEN you can go to see cow races in Australia?

In the Lonely Planet Newsletter!

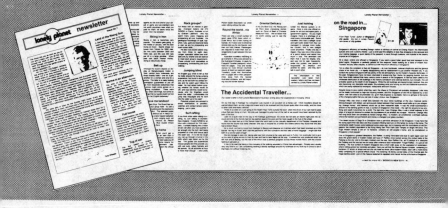

Every issue includes:

- *a letter from Lonely Planet founders Tony and Maureen Wheeler*
- *a letter from an author 'on the road'*
- *the most entertaining or informative reader's letter we've received*
- *the latest news on new and forthcoming releases from Lonely Planet*
- *and all the latest travel news from all over the world*

To receive the FREE quarterly Lonely Planet Newsletter, write to:
Lonely Planet Publications Pty Ltd
PO Box 617, Hawthorn, Vic 3122, Australia
Lonely Planet Publications, Inc
PO Box 2001A, Berkeley, CA 94702, USA

Guides to the Middle East

Egypt & the Sudan - a travel survival kit
This guide takes you into and beyond the spectacular pyramids, temples, tombs, monasteries and mosques, and the bustling main streets of these fascinating countries to discover their incredible beauty, unusual sights and friendly people.

Iran - a travel survival kit
The first English-language guide to this enigmatic and surprisingly hospitable country written since the Islamic Revolution. As well as practical travel details the author provides background information that will fascinate adventurers and armchair travellers alike.

Jordan & Syria - a travel survival kit
Two countries away from the usual travel routes, but with a wealth of natural and historical attractions for the adventurous traveller...12th century Crusader castles, ruined cities, the ancient Nabatean capital of Petra and haunting desert landscapes.

Turkey - a travel survival kit
This acclaimed guide takes you from Istanbul bazaars to Mediterranean beaches, from historic battlegrounds to the stamping grounds of St Paul, Alexander the Great, the Emperor Constantine, King Croesus and Omar Khayyam.

Trekking in Turkey
Explore beyond Turkey's coastline and you will be surprised to discover that Turkey has mountains with walks to rival those found in Nepal.

Yemen - a travel survival kit
The Yemen is one of the oldest inhabited regions in the world. This practical guide gives full details on a genuinely different travel experience.

West Asia on a shoestring
Want to cruise to Asia for 15 cents? Drink a great cup of tea while you view Mt Everest? Find the Garden of Eden? This guide has the complete story on the Asian overland trail from Bangladesh to Turkey, including Bhutan, India, Iran, the Maldives, Nepal, Pakistan, Sri Lanka and the Middle East.

Also available:
Egyptian Arabic phrasebook and Turkish phrasebook.

Lonely Planet Guidebooks

Lonely Planet guidebooks cover every accessible part of Asia as well as Australia, the Pacific, South America, Africa, the Middle East and parts of North America and Europe. There are five series: *travel survival kits*, covering a country for a range of budgets; *shoestring guides* with compact information for low-budget travel in a major region; *walking guides*; *city guides* and *phrasebooks*.

Australia & the Pacific
Australia
Bushwalking in Australia
Islands of Australia's Great Barrier Reef
Fiji
Micronesia
New Caledonia
New Zealand
Tramping in New Zealand
Papua New Guinea
Papua New Guinea phrasebook
Rarotonga & the Cook Islands
Samoa
Solomon Islands
Sydney
Tahiti & French Polynesia
Tonga
Vanuatu

South-East Asia
Bali & Lombok
Bangkok
Burma
Burmese phrasebook
Cambodia
Indonesia
Indonesia phrasebook
Malaysia, Singapore & Brunei
Philippines
Pilipino phrasebook
Singapore
South-East Asia on a shoestring
Thailand
Thai phrasebook
Vietnam, Laos & Cambodia

North-East Asia
China
Mandarin Chinese phrasebook
Hong Kong, Macau & Canton
Japan
Japanese phrasebook
Korea
Korean phrasebook
North-East Asia on a shoestring
Taiwan
Tibet
Tibet phrasebook

West Asia
Trekking in Turkey
Turkey
Turkish phrasebook
West Asia on a shoestring

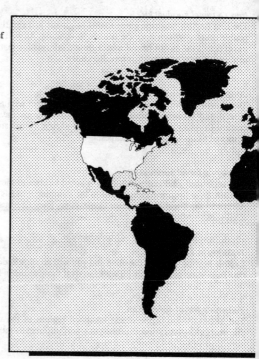

Middle East
Egypt & the Sudan
Egyptian Arabic phrasebook
Iran
Israel
Jordan & Syria
Yemen

Indian Ocean
Madagascar & Comoros
Maldives & Islands of the East Indian Ocean
Mauritius, Réunion & Seychelles

Mail Order

Lonely Planet guidebooks are distributed worldwide. They are also available by mail order from Lonely Planet, so if you have difficulty finding a title please write to us. US and Canadian residents should write to Embarcadero West, 155 Filbert St, Suite 251, Oakland CA 94607, USA, European residents should write to Devonshire House, 12 Barley Mow Passage, Chiswick, London W4 4PH and residents of other countries to PO Box 617, Hawthorn, Victoria 3122, Australia.

Indian Subcontinent
Bangladesh
India
Hindi/Urdu phrasebook
Trekking in the Indian Himalaya
Karakoram Highway
Kashmir, Ladakh & Zanskar
Nepal
Trekking in the Nepal Himalaya
Nepal phrasebook
Pakistan
Sri Lanka
Sri Lanka phrasebook

Africa
Africa on a shoestring
Central Africa
East Africa
Kenya
Swahili phrasebook
Morocco, Algeria & Tunisia
Moroccan Arabic phrasebook
Zimbabwe, Botswana & Namibia
West Africa

Mexico
Baja California
Mexico

Central America
Central America on a shoestring
Costa Rica
La Ruta Maya

North America
Alaska
Canada
Hawaii

Europe
Eastern Europe on a shoestring
Eastern Europe phrasebook
Finland
Iceland, Greeland & the Faroe Islands
Mediterranean Europe on a shoestring
Mediterranean Europe phrasebook
Scandinavian & Baltic Europe on a shoestring
Scandinavian Europe phrasebook
Trekking in Spain
USSR
Russian phrasebook
Western Europe on a shoestring
Western Europe phrasebook

South America
Argentina, Uruguay & Paraguay
Bolivia
Brazil
Brazilian phrasebook
Chile & Easter Island
Colombia
Ecuador & the Galápagos Islands
Latin American Spanish phrasebook
Peru
Quechua phrasebook
South America on a shoestring
Trekking in the Patagonian Andes

The Lonely Planet Story

Lonely Planet published its first book in 1973 in response to the numerous 'How did you do it?' questions Maureen and Tony Wheeler were asked after driving, bussing, hitching, sailing and railing their way from England to Australia.

Written at a kitchen table and hand collated, trimmed and stapled, *Across Asia on the Cheap* became an instant local bestseller, inspiring thoughts of another book.

Eighteen months in South-East Asia resulted in their second guide, *South-East Asia on a shoestring*, which they put together in a backstreet Chinese hotel in Singapore in 1975. The 'yellow bible' as it quickly became known to backpackers around the world, soon became *the* guide to the region. It has sold well over half a million copies and is now in its 7th edition, still retaining its familiar yellow cover.

Today there are over 100 Lonely Planet titles – books that have that same adventurous approach to travel as those early guides; books that 'assume you know how to get your luggage off the carousel' as one reviewer put it.

Although Lonely Planet initially specialised in guides to Asia, they now cover most regions of the world, including the Pacific, South America, Africa, the Middle East and Europe. The list of *walking guides* and *phrasebooks* (for 'unusual' languages such as Quechua, Swahili, Nepalese and Egyptian Arabic) is also growing rapidly.

The emphasis continues to be on travel for independent travellers. Tony and Maureen still travel for several months of each year and play an active part in the writing, updating and quality control of Lonely Planet's guides.

They have been joined by over 50 authors, 48 staff – mainly editors, cartographers, & designers – at our office in Melbourne, Australia and another 10 at our US office in Oakland, California. In 1991 Lonely Planet opened a London office to handle sales for Britain, Europe and Africa. Travellers themselves also make a valuable contribution to the guides through the feedback we receive in thousands of letters each year.

The people at Lonely Planet strongly believe that travellers can make a positive contribution to the countries they visit, both through their appreciation of the countries' culture, wildlife and natural features, and through the money they spend. In addition, the company makes a direct contribution to the countries and regions it covers. Since 1986 a percentage of the income from each book has been donated to ventures such as famine relief in Africa; aid projects in India; agricultural projects in Central America; Greenpeace's efforts to halt French nuclear testing in the Pacific and Amnesty International. In 1991 $68,000 was donated to these causes.

Lonely Planet's basic travel philosophy is summed up in Tony Wheeler's comment, 'Don't worry about whether your trip will work out. Just go!'